JOHN BUTT

A Talib's Tale

The Life and Times
of a **Pashtoon Englishman**

KUBE
PUBLISHING

A Talib's Tale: The Life and Times of a Pashtoon Englishman

First published in England by Kube Publishing Ltd
Markfield Conference Centre
Ratby Lane, Markfield
Leicestershire, LE67 9SY
United Kingdom
Tel: +44 (0) 1530 249230
Website: www.kubepublishing.com
Email: info@kubepublishing.com

Cataloguing in-Publication Data is available from the British Library

ISBN Paperback 978-1-84774-156-1
ISBN Ebook 978-1-84774-157-8

Cover Design: Adilah Joossab
Typesetting: LiteBook Prepress Services
Maps: Maryam Khan
Cover image: Dreamstime
Printed by: Elma Basim, Turkey

CONTENTS

ACKNOWLEDGEMENTS

It has been a little over a year since *A Talib's Tale* was first published, by Penguin India. In fact, its publication coincided with the first week of what turned out to be pretty much a universal lockdown, in March 2020.

Prior to publication of *A Talib's Tale* in India, Yahya Birt at Kube Publishing had expressed an interest in publishing this account of my Life and Times in the UK. Since the Penguin India version had not been available worldwide, I was happy to take him up on his offer.

Yahya Birt also kindly suggested a chapter on my English origins. The book had been quite top heavy with my Pashtoon connections, so I was happy to add that chapter, for the benefit of the UK publication. I am also grateful to Safia Haleem, my former colleague at the BBC Pashto service, for going through the original, Indian version of *A Talib's Tale*. She also suggested one or two additions, some of which I have been able to incorporate into the new edition.

Since the Penguin publication of *A Talib's Tale*, two of its main protagonists, Abdus Samad and Sinjan—another Pashtoon Englishman who also went by the English name of Sean Jones—have left this world. Abdus Samad already had a chapter to himself, but I am happy that I have been able to do more justice to Sinjan and his elder brother Paddy in this new publication, in particular the role they played in my going East, and then have the wherewithal to stay there.

It is inevitable that this account of my life and times will be looked at as a memoir, but I don't really see it like that. I see it more as a look at the lives of some key characters in Pashtoon history, over the last couple of hundred years, the impact they had on Pashtoon history and of course the influence they had on me. I would like to think the book is more about them than me.

As the Pashtoon national poet Rahman Baba, who also gets a look into this book wrote:

خدایه څه شول هغه ښکلي ښکلي خلک
په ظاهر په باطن سپین سپیڅلي خلک

My Lord, what happened to those beautiful souls?
Shining lights they were, inwardly and outwardly.

John Butt
June 2021

PROLOGUE

Those who have been driven out of their homes unjustly, only because they said 'Our Lord is Allah'.

(*Al-Hajj* 22:40)

It was the early hours of Thursday, 20 October 2016. Men were keeping watch on the road between Lower and Upper Pachir. Situated on the lower slopes of Spin Ghar, the White Mountain that dominates the scenery in southern Nangarhar province, in the east of Afghanistan, Lower and Upper Pachir had long been in the sights of Daesh.[1] The militant group had already been lodged for some years in the eastern border districts of Achin, Dur Baba, Spinghar and Deh Bala—districts where the Shinwari tribe live, on the border with Pakistan.[2]

The watchmen were alerted by the sound of some men with donkeys. 'Who goes there?' they called out. '*Mung khro waley yoo*,' came the reply. The men were taking their donkeys up the mountains to collect wood. It is usual for the people of Pachir to set out in the early hours so they can collect wood from Spin Ghar and

[1] Daesh is the name whereby the Islamic State group is known in Afghanistan.

[2] Shinwaris are one of the few Pashtoon tribes who live on both sides of the Pakistan–Afghanistan border. While few Shinwaris would call themselves Daesh supporters, Afghans have learned to adapt to whomsoever is in control of their territory.

bring it back before sundown. However, the men soon returned. 'Daesh have arrived!' they warned the watchmen.

By the time people had said their early morning prayers in Lower Pachir, families were already getting ready to flee. Who knew how long it would be before Daesh were upon them? In fact, they would probably have swooped on Lower Pachir had it not been for the warning given by the donkey drivers. Armed men from Lower Pachir came out of their houses to defend their territory against the encroaching Daesh forces. Daesh were immeasurably better armed than the local Pachir people. They were also battle ready and hardened. In fact, they were equipped with sniper rifles fitted with telescopes. Their marksmen were strategically positioned in the hills above Lower Pachir. Those mounting the resistance in Lower Pachir suffered twelve wounded, six dead.

Men, women and children from both Upper and Lower Pachir were fleeing for their lives. They had every reason to fear Daesh. The people of Pachir were considered to be at the forefront of the resistance to Daesh. While Daesh follow the Salafi, or Wahabi, model of Islam, brooking no customs that to their mind contravene the practice or Sunna of the Holy Prophet, the people of Pachir are more traditional Hanafi, also Sunni Muslims, allowing visits to shrines and including more Pashtoon customs in their marriages, funerals and other functions.

While some districts in Nangarhar are considered more sympathetic to Daesh—Chaprahar, for example, or the neighbouring province of Kunar—Pachir is considered staunchly anti-Daesh, unsympathetic to Salafi doctrines.

The most important thing for a Pashtoon is his honour. And that honour is inextricably tied to her honour: the honour of Pashtoon womenfolk. Stories coming out of Achin, Deh Bala, Dur Baba—districts already to a certain degree under the control of Daesh—had suggested that enslavement was commonly practised in areas that had been taken over by Daesh. Women had been taken away, so the stories went. Certainly, the people of Pachir believed the stories. 'Why did you flee?' I asked one person who had fled from Lower Pachir with his whole family. 'What do you mean? They take away our women.' His reply was emphatic. This pointed to an alarming polarization of Pashtoon society, with some taking women by force and others holding this to be the most reprehensible and dishonourable thing possible—something they would guard against with their lives.

Whole families vacated Pachir with nothing more than the clothes on their back. Women could be seen clutching babies, without even a shawl on their heads—an abject state for a Pashtoon woman to be seen in public. The people of Upper Pachir were also able to make their getaway despite the fact that their territory had been taken over by Daesh. They had the advantage of knowing their land. Daesh forces, said to be numbering a thousand, were not from the area. For the most part, according to reports from areas under their control, Daesh were from the Orakzai tribe, in the Pakistan-administered tribal areas. They were strangers to this part of eastern Afghanistan.

Soon, the people in the district centre of Agam found out about the sudden exodus from Upper and Lower Pachir. They sent all their cars and transport to the villages to help the displaced people reach the eastern metropolis of Jalalabad. Many people from Pachir were already residing there. Most of the newcomers stayed with relatives who were already there, some in makeshift tents, all of them becoming another statistic in the aid agencies' lists of hundreds of thousands of Pashtoons displaced from their homes due to sectarian fighting.

Back in Pachir, young men, the cream of their generation, were left to guard in watchtowers in Lower Pachir, to check the Daesh advance. They could not have known that an onslaught would come from the opposite direction. US forces were based in the airport at Jalalabad. Hearing that Daesh had advanced as far as Upper Pachir, they thought it would be a good idea to bomb them. I do not know how many of their missiles hit the Upper Pachir strongholds of Daesh, but at 11:30 on Saturday morning, a missile fired from a drone hit a tower where five young men of Lower Pachir had been stationed—the front line against Daesh. All five perished. 'You would have been proud of them, had you set eyes on them,' one Pachir person said to me. 'Very little damage was done to the actual watchtower,' one of the men who dug the graves of the young men told me. 'But our sons had been positioned on the third floor of the tower. Their bodies were recovered from the ground floor.'[3]

While I had first arrived in Swat in 1970, I made the valley my home in 1985, after I returned from my studies in a madrasa in India. If Kashmir is heaven on earth, Swat, a valley running due north-south to the north of Peshawar, is known as the Switzerland of the East. In the 1970s, Swat had been a favourite hippie destination; in particular, Madyan. It was in Madyan that I made my home in 1985. In the 1970s, one whole quarter of Madyan, near the tributary river that flows down to the Swat River from Bishigram, was called Da Angrezano Kali— the European quarter—by the local people. In 2009, there were no foreigners left, only me, still living in my home next to the river in Madyan. I was on my way from Madyan to the Swat capital of Mingora one day when I caught sight of men, women and children from a village across the river, milling around, disoriented, most of the womenfolk sitting, their backs to the road, overlooking the dazzling Swat River below them. It was a bright, late spring day. The army was bombarding the village of Upper Mamdheri, purported to be a stronghold of Radio Mulla Fazlullah; in fact, it was right next to the Radio Mulla's own village of Lower Mamdheri.

The strength of the Radio Mulla had been building since 2006, when he was famous for travelling around the area on a white horse. In 2008, he turned from a mulla exhorting people to follow his own puritan version of Islam through his FM radio broadcasts, to one who was taking over Swat territory by force, killing and bombing people and government installations as he went. His demand was the full implementation of *Shariah*—Islamic law. The momentum of this *Shariah* movement had been building since 1994. Then, it had been Fazlullah's father-in-law Sufi Mohammad

[3] Details of the attack on Pachir were gleaned from an inhabitant who fled the district to put up in a tent perched against his father-in-law's house in the provincial capital of Jalalabad. Another Pachir resident confirmed the details provided.

who briefly took over most of the Swat valley, as part of his Movement for Implementation of the *Shariah*. In 1994, it had been the local Frontier militias—fellow Pashtoons—who had defused the situation. In 2008, the same Frontier militias found themselves unable to do so. The Pakistan Army was called in. At the time of the exodus from Upper Mamdheri, the Army was still engaged in battle with the militants.

The women and children from across the river looked dazed. I interviewed quite a few of them. They had received no advance notice of the army operation in their village, which included mortar shelling and house-to-house searching—things that no Pashtoon family could willingly expose itself to. The residents had very little time to flee. Most of them left by the cable car that was the only means of transport across the river. Ironically, the cable car used to be operated by Mulla Fazlullah himself, before he found fame as the Radio Mulla. The interviews I conducted were aired on my own PACT radio station, based in Mingora, the same day.

I had set up PACT Radio in Peshawar in 2005, with a grant from Internews. Internews had set up scores of radio stations in Afghanistan, in the wake of the NATO invasion of 2001. PACT Radio initially referred to the Pakistan–Afghanistan Cross-border Radio Training project. Starting off as a radio production and training operation, it turned into the Pakistan–Afghanistan Cross-border Radio Transmission project, with its establishment of a radio station in Mingora in 2008. PACT Radio had been based in Peshawar for the previous three years. Swat was our first practical, live radio enterprise. Our aim was not to counter or confront anyone—that would have been asking for trouble—but to present the traditional face of Islam and Pashtoon practice in the Swat valley—peaceful, inherently moderate, tolerant, generous, hospitable—the picture that had been presented to us hippies in 1970, and which had attracted many of us, myself included, to Islam.

You could put it another way. The face of traditional Pashtoonwali and Islam that we were seeking to present in our radio broadcasts was the one that came to the rescue of the displaced people after they had been forced out of their homes. Whether it was the local displacements, or the general displacement that took place in May 2009, the people were welcomed with open doors and open hearts of their fellow Pashtoons. It had been in May 2009 that the army had ordered all the residents of Swat to vacate the Valley, to enable them to launch a concentrated operation against the militants. The same feeling of fellowship was in evidence with the Pachir displacement of October 2016, when people from the neighbouring district rushed their vehicles to Pachir to assist the fleeing families. Similarly, when the Swat valley was evacuated, the people of Swabi and Mardan—the districts bordering Swat in the plains—looked upon it as a privilege to make their homes available to the people who had been rendered homeless in Swat. Our Swat radio station was also displaced at this time. We continued to broadcast from our base in Peshawar. We decided to focus on the assistance and refuge being offered to the people of Swat by fellow Pashtoons in the plains.[4] Hospitality amongst the Pashtoons is generous and open-hearted, but it is only for a certain period.

The temporary refuge afforded by one Pashtoon to another creates an impetus for the settlement of the crisis and the return of the displaced people. Indeed, this is what happened, with the displaced Swati people returning to Swat four months later, in September 2019. On the other hand, assistance that comes from relief organizations tends to perpetuate the refugee crisis. We ignored the latter and focused on the former. Not only did it make good sense, it also reflected the essence of Pashtoons life, the spirit that had first attracted me to Islam and to a life amongst the Pashtoon. It was also in line with the PACT Radio motto of 'Traditional Solutions for Modern Problems'. The stories that follow are not only about what life was like amongst the Pashtoons. They are about what still is, in spite of the veneer of conflict, their traditional way of life.

John Butt
Jalalabad, October 2019

---

[4] Along with the PACT Radio station, its manager Adnan Rashid was also displaced from the Swat valley at this time. He now works with the Voice of America's Pashto service in Washington. He and his family were initially accommodated with a family in Mardan, so I have his first-hand account of the hospitality extended to displaced persons from Swat.

I

LOST AND FOUND

I do remember well the hour which burst
My spirit's sleep. A fresh May-dawn it was,
When I walked forth upon the glittering grass,
And wept, I knew not why; until there rose
From the near school-room voices that, alas!
Were but one echo from a world of woes –
The harsh and grating strife of tyrants and of foes.

(Shelley to Mary, from *The Revolt of Islam*)

Looking back, the day that I headed East was the day I left Trinidad. I was nine years' old. I was sitting in the back of the car. My father was driving me to the Port-of-Spain docks, for the first part of our journey to England. I can't remember anything else about my departure from Trinidad. All I remember is letting out a shriek. It was an expression of total misery, a leaving behind of everything I knew and loved.

Mum and I left Trinidad together, just the two of us. My elder brother and sister were already at school in England. Dad stayed behind in Trinidad to look after some business related to our departure from the island where I had been born. My Dad was also born there. Our roots in Trinidad ran deep. My maternal grandmother, Anne-Marie Cipriani, was a cousin of Captain Cipriani. The Ciprianis were a Corsican family, one of the first European families to settle in Trinidad. My grandfather had met her while based in Trinidad with Barclays Bank.

Later on, when Shahnaz and I went to Trinidad on our honeymoon in 1992, I stood before a statue of my collateral ancestor, Captain Cipriani, in Independence Square in Port-of-Spain. 'Soldier, Statesman, Patriot', the inscription read. By then, I had moved on from being a pure Trinidadian patriot. I had been away for much too long. Still, I understood better the feelings of that uprooted nine-year-old. I understood what Trinidad had meant to me. My life made more sense.

My Dad never did take me to see that statue in downtown Port-of-Spain. I do not remember hearing much about family, or our Trinidad heritage as a boy. But he always took me to see the annual carnival on the Savannah. Along with my Dad, I attended every Hindu festival that took place. He loved those festivals. And once, crucially, we paid a special visit to the Port-of-Spain mosque. I may have been cut off from my West Indian heritage. But it was as if the place where I would regain that heritage had been mapped out before me.

I was always of a religious bent. For me, that was one of the best things about Catholic boarding school in England—going to the chapel and daily mass. But sometimes, when I donned the altar-boy vestments, I would break out in a cold sweat. Sometimes, I would even faint. I'm not sure why. At night, I would take my rosary and make a cave for myself under my bed sheets. It had a little altar. I just used to pray, late into the night. If it had been a question of heat and suffocation, then I should have fainted there. But I didn't. Only in the chapel, and only when I was altar-boy.

When I wasn't praying at night, I was crying: crying for Trinidad, crying for my Nanny in Trinidad, Grace, who wrote me the most loving, heart-wrenching letters, crying for my Mummy. In our third term at school, another boy and myself decided we would run away. Whenever a car would appear, we used to hide in the long grass, so that the people in the car would not be able to see us.

We reached quite a good distance from our school, near Arundel in Sussex. Suddenly my companion said to me: 'Let's go back.' I had harboured no intention of going back. The idea of going back had never occurred to me. Nor did the idea of carrying on alone appeal to me. We returned to our school. Still, our night escapade had not escaped the attention of the headmaster, a war hero by the name of Michael Jennings. His wife was with him when he summoned us to his study, to reprimand and punish us. 'Why did you come here in the first place,' his wife asked us, 'if you wanted to run away?' I wish I knew. By this time, my elder brother, Richard, had left for public school. He came to visit me with our parents in a few weeks' time. 'Why, Johnny?' were his first words. I think Richard settled into English life better than me.

I'm not sure if our punishment on that occasion including beating, but it usually did. With a cane, with your pants down, bending over the chair: incessant, merciless, remorseless beating. It was enough to draw blood. It did not bother me. It was the emotional pain of being at that place that bothered me.

Once Mr Jennings pursued me to the chapel, to haul me into his study for a beating. 'What are you doing here, Butt?' he shouted from the door. 'Seeking forgiveness for the multitude?' He was referring to the multitude of sins I had committed. The truth was, I liked praying. I liked being in the chapel. It was the only place of comfort for me, in a sea of misery.[1]

I owned a missal. It was a book containing the texts used in the Catholic Mass throughout the year. It was all in Latin. I loved the Latin Mass. I had no problem in learning enough Latin to understand what was being said in the Mass—the Catholic prayer service. This was the time of the Second Vatican Council called by Pope Paul VI. One thing that was decided was that the Mass would no longer be in Latin, it would be in the vernacular, in other words, in English. I have no recollection of ever attending a single English Mass. I must have done, but the lustre had gone from the Mass.

---

[1] You can read a more favourable account of Michael Jennings by his son, see Luke Jennings, *Blood Knots: Of Fathers, Friendship and Fishing*, UK, Atlantic Books, 2010.

My missal, that I loved and treasured so much, was superfluous. I still kept it on a shelf in my room, but it was a relic. It had no practical purpose. Mass had become mundane by being rendered into English.

This led me to another misgiving. Who had given the Pope the right, even after calling a Council, to change the liturgy of the Church? The Pope was the successor of St. Peter, I was told, to whom Jesus had said:

> Thou art Peter, and it is upon this rock that I will build my Church; and the gates of hell shall not prevail against thee; and I will give to thee the keys of the Kingdom of Heaven; and whatever thou shalt bind on earth, shall be bound in heaven; and whatever thou shall loose on earth, shall be loosed in heaven.

The words themselves are moving. Even now, I write them from memory, where they are etched. Still, I was not convinced that this accolade from Jesus Christ qualified popes in every day and age to the crown of infallibility.

By now, I was studying at secondary school, which is strangely called public school in the private education system in England. My schools—Beaumont in Old Windsor and later Stonyhurst College in Lancashire—were run by Jesuit priests. The fact that I was at Beaumont and then Stonyhurst was not due to me being expelled from one, then going to the other, though I must have come close to being expelled on a few occasions. Beaumont was closed down while I was there. It seems the Jesuit priests were having trouble running two big boys' boarding schools. The two schools were merged. Students at Beaumont were shipped off to Stonyhurst in rural Lancashire.

There were real theologians among the Jesuits' number. Not only that, but classicists also. Father Turner and Father Hull could often be heard speaking Latin to each other in the corridors of Stonyhurst. Looking back, seeing the affinity I later developed for Arabic and Persian classical learning, and taking into account my earlier love of the Latin Mass, I should have buried myself in

Greek and Latin classical learning. I could have benefited a lot. It has always been my belef that a classical education is a real education. With a classical education, one is learning everything in its pristine, original form. It gives one a good basis for any livelihood. My heart was just not in it.

From the age of 13, when I was at Beaumont, my heart was into something else. A Donovan–Dylan controversy was raging: who was better, Donovan or Dylan? It seems strange now, really. Donovan is all but forgotten. If you listen to his old stuff, it has somehow aged. At the time, though, he did make some magical music. Now, nearly 60 years later, Dylan is as relevant as ever. Anyway, Donovan–Dylan seemed to be all that my stable weekly magazine, the *New Musical Express*, was talking about. Both Dylan and Donovan had singles out. Donovan's was *Catch the Wind*, cribbed considerably as I was later to discover from Bob's *Chimes of Freedom*. But the Bob Dylan single that CBS had just released was not *Chimes*, it was *Times . . . The Times They Are A-Changin'*.

I was dying to hear both *Catch the Wind* and *Times They Are A-Changin'*. As it turned out, I heard the latter first. It was a brilliant summer's day in the hills of Great Windsor Park. Shafts of sunlight were beaming in through the windows of the corridor leading from Grammar to Syntax classes.[2] The sound of one voice, one guitar and one harmonica was blasting out, maybe from the library on the Syntax corridor. The guitar, the harmonica, the voice were all emanating from one person. It wasn't a poet and a one-man band. The poet was the one-man band. That was Bob Dylan.

Funnily enough, the person whose silhouette was visible against the shafts of sunlight, walking down the corridor, was a Syntax boy called Palliser. Either a few months earlier, or later, I can't remember which, but it was in the same year, 1963, that Palliser gave the Grammar and Syntax boys news of President Kennedy's assassination. The same corridor, only at the other end. We were all on our way down to the refectory for dinner.[3] There, Father Brogan

---

[2] Even the names the Jesuits gave the classes had a classical ring to them: Syntax was the class before Sixth Form; Grammar the class below that.

[3] Refectory is what Jesuits call the dining hall in one of their institutes.

confirmed the news: "I have to tell you all that the President of the United States has been assassinated." This was shattering news. Bob sang about it recently, in 2020, in his song *Murder Most Foul.* But the moment that is etched even more indelibly in my mind is that other Palliser moment—the song that would become the anthem of my life.

It was a time when you were spoiled for choice. You just did not know which Bob Dylan album to buy. He featured in numbers one to five on the *New Musical Express* album charts, unless of course a new Beatles' album superseded him at number one. I bought *Another Side* of Bob Dylan first. It was the album that contained *Chimes of Freedom*. I had struck gold at its most productive vein. No sooner had he released that album, then he was about to release *Bringing It All Back Home*. When you thought that one album was as much as your senses could take, there came another. There was a joke at the time that if you said to Bob Dylan, 'I really like *Chimes of Freedom*', then Bob would chuckle to himself and say, 'Man, you know *nothing!*' Already, songs one or two albums ahead of *Chimes of Freedom* were reverberating in Bob's head. At the time when people were getting to know *Another Side* of Bob Dylan, he would be thinking in terms of *Highway 61*, the album about which he famously remarked, 'Man, there is stuff on there that's so good, even I'd listen to it.'

By now, Bob Dylan was not only my education: he was my religion. I was listening the other day to an early recording of a song called *When The Ship Comes In*. In between a couple of the verses, Bob can be heard to quip, 'I scare myself!' Scared of what? Quite simply: Judgment Day. Let's not mince our words. The song is about the day when everyone will be brought low before God. Okay, Bobby would say the song was just about when the ship comes in. He was hanging out with Joan Baez when he wrote the song. She was well established on the music scene at the time, Bob Dylan not so much so. The couple went to check in at a hotel. Bob was his usual scruffy self. The hotel refused to allow them into the hotel. Joanie persuaded them to let the young couple occupy a room. Bob's indignation at his initial rebuttal was not assuaged.

That night, Bob wrote *When The Ship Comes In*, with all its invocation of divine retribution.

Down the Ribble Valley from Stonyhurst, there was another school run by Jesuits. It is called Preston Catholic College. Two brothers, older than me by eight and six years respectively, went to that school. They were the brothers Paddy and Sean Jones. Paddy was expelled pretty early from the College. He spent some time running rock cafes in Liverpool, before heading down to London where he became involved, among other things, in the Carnaby Street scene. I met Paddy Jones at the Newport Pagnell service station on the M1, on one rainy autumn's evening in 1969. It was one surreal evening, as if a drama was unfolding before me on the soggy exit lane of the service station. Before Paddy stopped for me, another Rolls had pulled up. He was apologetic that he would be leaving the M1 at the next turn-off, but I could hop on if I liked. I politely declined his offer. It was about another ten minutes before Paddy's Rolls arrived. We were both headed up north. Paddy was going all the way.

Paddy and I talked through the night, as the rain lashed the windscreen. I fulfilled my passenger's duty of rolling joints. I played Paddy a cassette recording I had recently made of Bob Dylan's Isle of Wight concert. Paddy liked it. 'I can make a record out of that,' he assured me, immediately jumping onto a business idea. Paddy gave me his address in Finchley in north London, and asked me to bring the cassette to him there. Paddy's Finchley mansion seemed huge. It was also a hive of activity. In one room, someone would be sharing a chillum with some groupies; another would be bent over a spool-to-spool tape recorder, mixing some sounds; another would be doing something dubious with pills. Paddy chose the room with the spool-to-spool recorder. He asked the guy to copy my cassette recording onto it.

Paddy was enthusiastic about my recording of the Dylan concert. By now, I was headed East. My first stop was to be the caves of Matala in Greece. Paddy told me his younger brother Sean was already out East. 'Get in touch with me once you reach Greece,' Paddy had said to me. 'I will be able to send you some money, once I make a bootleg out of this.' In the meantime, he prevailed on the pills' person to give me a stock of orange and purple pills –LSD and synthetic mescaline. 'Sell these along the way. That will keep you going for the time being. Then write back to me. Wherever you are, I will send you money.' I never did write back to Paddy. I don't know, the frame of mind I was in, I just did not think it would be right to write to someone asking for money. Still, the money from the pills got me as far as Kandahar in Afghanistan. There, I sold the tape recorder on which I had made the Dylan recording.

Fifteen years later, I met Paddy's younger brother Sean in the house Sean had built in Madyan in Swat. I was on my way to reclaim the destiny that I had left behind some ten years earlier, the day I left Trinidad.

II

FRIENDSHIP

One of those who will taste the sweetness of faith is one who loves another, for no other reason but for the sake of Allah.

(Sahih al-Bukhari)[1]

The friendship between John Ryan and myself was rooted in our mutual love for Bob Dylan. We didn't talk much at school. We just listened to Dylan. It was this that led John to think there was 'Too Much of Nothing' in our relationship. That was the song he related to most on Bob's 'Basement Tapes'. I preferred the uncomplicated and joyful 'You Ain't Goin' Nowhere'. I was singing the refrain, riding high on the roof of a bus, as I travelled from Jalalabad to Kabul in the summer of 1970. It was as if I had a premonition of seeing John. After one month in the searing and debilitating heat of Peshawar, it was a thrill to breathe the clear and cool mountain air.

You might be wondering what I had been doing in the intense heat of Peshawar in June, particularly when cooler mountain climes beckoned on every side of the Peshawar valley, in particular in Swat, where I had been living for the last few months, and

[1] The Sahih al-Bukhari Hadith collection.

in Kabul, my destination. It was all down to the Afghan consul in Peshawar. Everyone knew that he hated penniless hippies. This was one of the contradictions of Afghan society. The government disliked hippies, especially impoverished vagrants like me. The population at large loved them, since they adopted their lifestyle, smoked their hashish, stayed in their hotels, even though they did not have much money to spend.

The Afghan consul in Peshawar was infamous for never giving hippies a visa, especially when he found out they had nothing to spend. I thought that I had avoided this impediment by showing him some money that had been kindly lent to me by a fellow traveller staying in the Palace Hotel in downtown Peshawar. 'Okay, come back tomorrow and I will give you your visa,' he tersely told me, not looking up from his counter, just showing me his bald pate as he shuffled passports on the desk.

It did not occur to me that the next day he would ask to see the money again. 'No visa for you,' he said, as he summarily gave me back my passport and sent me away. A month in Peshawar was not the ideal way to spend the blazing month of June. Still, it was not a bad way to become initiated to subcontinental heat and Peshawar life. Daily walks to the Company Bagh—named after the East India Company—in Peshawar Cantonment, past a Lutyens-like cricket pavilion and through the leafy streets of the cantonment, gave me a sense of belonging in this part of the world. The landmarks in the subcontinent that remind an Englishman of home make it relatively easy for a person from England to acclimatize there. I would spend my mornings sitting on a park bench in the Company Bagh, reading some annals of Anglo–Indian life that had been borrowed from the British Council library up the road. In the evenings, I would go and see my friend, the Irishman Leo, in the Pakistan Hotel, which overlooked Kabuli Gate—not surprisingly the gate of old Peshawar city that faces towards Kabul—at the end of the historical Qissa Khawani Bazaar of Peshawar.

I had to spend that month in Peshawar in order to meet John on arrival in Kabul. If I had arrived in Kabul a month earlier I would have missed him. The day after my arrival in Kabul, I was checking my post in the General Post Office (GPO), on the banks of the Kabul River. Nowadays, travellers check their Hotmail and Gmail in cyber cafés when they pull into cities. In those days, there was Poste Restante—a general post box in large post offices where mail for travellers would be collected. It seemed the most normal thing in the world that I should bump into John there. That was the way things worked in those days. A guy would just turn up from the other side of the world and there he would be. The hippie trail was quite confined: Morocco, Crete, Afghanistan, Goa, and in each place, hippies like ourselves had their favourite haunts. John gazed down at me, beaming from the top of the flight of stairs that led to the GPO. I had not even known that John would come out East to join me. Certainly, he had no way of finding out where I was. Nevertheless, the meeting seemed entirely expected and normal, even inevitable, as if it was destined, which of course it was.

John and I had travelled to Greece a couple of summers back, as soon as we left school. The summer of '69 was spent in Morocco. We only went back to England to make some money and to see Dylan play on the Isle of Wight. When we went back from Morocco for the Isle of Wight concert, John had promised to take me in his parents' second car—a Mini. I later found out that his dad had said no, but John took it anyway. He could not let me down. That was the measure of our friendship, particularly seeing that John was very close to his dad. John never did tell me that he had taken his parents' car without permission. His younger sister Mary told me many years later. She also told me that John—who, like me, was pushing seventy—was so much like his father it was scary.

'Come,' I said to John. 'Let's go to my new home.' I was referring to the makeshift home I had made for myself in Swat. I was adopting the role of travelling companion to a man I had met in the Khyber Pass as I travelled from Peshawar to Kabul, prior to my meeting with John. This travelling companion had been the first person to teach me about Pashtoon hospitality. Being from the Afridi tribe that inhabits most of the pass, he had grown up in the Khyber Pass. He was coming home after a long time, having been working for his living in distant Karachi. The passion and emotion of his homecoming was expressed in hospitality and warmth towards myself. 'My home, my country,' he was almost in tears as we travelled up the gorge leading to the Khyber Pass. The love he felt towards his home country was rubbing off on me through the moving expression of his emotions.

My own sense of belonging increased when a tribal policeman climbed onto the bus. These tribal policemen are called levies—*khasadars* in Pashto. Seeing me—the only foreigner in the bus—the *khasadar* asked me for the normal tribal tax: 'Give me two rupees.' Ever since Mughal times, Afridis have levied this tax on foreigners passing through the Khyber Pass. My companion did not even let me grope in my pocket. As he held my hand, to prevent me from bringing out even a paisa, he addressed the *khasadar*: 'You cannot take a single rupee from this person. He is my guest.' The two argued for a few moments. My companion prevailed. Hospitality is a basic tenet of Pashtoonwali—the code according to which Pashtoons live their lives. Exacting tax from foreign travellers may be a convention, but hospitality is a basic code: when convention comes up against code, it is code that prevails.

As we reached the Pashto-speaking heartlands of Jalalabad and Peshawar on our way to Swat, John noticed that I was able to communicate more freely with the locals. In truth, I could only recognize Pashto from other regional languages: Urdu in Swat and Peshawar, Farsi in Afghanistan. In Swat, I had begun to keep a notebook. In the left-hand column was an English sentence or word, in the central column the Pashto equivalent and in the right-hand column the same phrase was translated into Urdu. 'What is this in Pashto?' I would ask anyone I met, pointing to a mountain, a tree, a chair—anything I caught sight of. My informal and spontaneous teacher would be only too happy to oblige, giving me the correct Pashto word, which I would then write down in my book, and if he knew it, the Urdu equivalent also. An eagerness to learn their language endears a foreigner to Pashtoons. Even if they are not native Pashto speakers, all Afghans relate instinctively to Pashto as their national language.[2] While they share Farsi with Iran

[2] At least this was the case in the 1970s, when I arrived in Afghanistan. The association of Afghans with Pashto as their national language has been somewhat diluted over the war years.

and Tajikistan, Pashto is the hallmark of their distinctive national identity.

Quite apart from the language, John noted how at home I was amongst the big-hearted, generous, good-natured Pashtoons of the border regions. The impression was capped by my homecoming on the footbridge that led across the Swat River, to the village of Kalam. The first person to greet me was Noor, a lad who hailed from Madyan, lower down the Swat valley, but was a resident in Kalam. 'The soldier returns,' John said as he noted the warmth of my welcome.

Haakim sahib was a visitor to Kalam at the time. He hailed from Gupis, a town in the Gilgit valley. His name, or title rather, haakim, means ruler. The word is not to be confused with hakeem, which means healer. Often the two words haakim and hakeem are written in the same way—as hakim—in English. Even though those northern areas were in the process of being handed over to Pakistani administration, old feudal rulers such as Haakim sahib still wielded a lot of influence. With his woollen *pakool*, made out of the best quality Chitrali wool, and his meticulously trimmed greying beard, he was a quintessential gentleman from the northern areas. Lean and fit, it was clear that he had been making journeys on foot amongst these peaks and valleys all his life. His ability to traverse the passes was unimpaired, despite his age. Along with his considerable entourage, he was about to travel to his native village. He agreed that John and I—along with a French artist by the name of Odile—should accompany him. What could have been more appealing than a mountain trek at the time? In the case of John and I, the consent was not entirely wholehearted, whereas he clearly was somewhat enamoured of Odile.

A year or two later, Odile wrote a letter to John, asking him about me. 'What happened to John, the poet?' she asked. 'I am sure he must still be living in India or Pakistan.' Odile thought I was a poet due to a poem I wrote to her, painting in the afternoon one day in Kalam:

As you touched the canvas with colours that shine
And scotched the joint that keeps me high

And sketched the night that made me long for daytime
And is it something stretched before your eyes?
Or a wonder hidden in the night skies
That you gaze at?
And the river rolled and tumbled
Throughout the afternoon
And from your painting now I know
It tumbled last full moon.

I was only a part-time poet, but this might have been one of my better efforts. In any case, Odile considered it good enough to attach along with her painting. It might still be hanging there, attached to Odile's poem, somewhere in Swat.

Haakim sahib's entourage consisted of half a dozen people: some natives of the Gilgit valley and other Kohistanis from Kalam and us three foreigners. We set out by foot from Kalam, through the cool and thick pine forests that lie between Kalam and Ushu. Beyond Ushu, the road became rougher. It was what is known as a jeep-able road, but no jeep passed during our whole day of trekking through pine forests that reached down as far as the river. We camped at Mahodand for the night. The word mahodand means fish lake. Our travelling companions caught some trout, which abound in that lake. I offered them the brown rice that I kept in my dad's knapsack—a vestige of his years as a soldier in the Second World War. I suggested that they cook that for our evening meal. One genial Kohistani who was doing most of the cooking for the group declined my offer. 'We prefer to cook this rice,' he said, showing me a sack of white Basmati rice that they had brought with them. That was a general trend amongst local Swatis at the time. White rice—even white flour—was generally preferred to the brown, more nutritious equivalent. Later on, I am happy to say, the trend changed. Swatis now swear by *begumay rijhe*, introduced by a lady from the north of Afghanistan who married in Swat, and who introduced the very strain of brown rice that I carried in my knapsack.

The previous day's trek had just been a gentle initiation in to what was to come. We turned right off the main valley after trekking for a couple of hours the next morning. The tributary valley that we turned into could not really be called a valley. It was more like an extended waterfall. The stream that flowed down the side valley into the Swat River was in fact a torrent that came gushing down the almost vertical slopes of the mountainside. Slowly, we spent the day ascending the winding path that followed this cascading stream. It was a laborious trek. None of my boyhood treks had prepared me for those savage, towering and rugged mountains.

Haakim sahib was well known all along the way. It seemed as if he had relatives in every village and hamlet where we stopped. There was a strip of verdant alpine pasture between the steep path that we had ascended and the mass of glacial snow that lay before us. Shepherds had constructed crofts here, which provided some rustic relief from the ardours of life at this high altitude. Though I was not suffering from altitude sickness, I was exhausted from the day's trek. Later in life, whenever I trekked these remote heights, altitude sickness would afflict me. But not this time.

The exhaustion told on me the next day. In later years, when I made treks at high altitude, my guides would explain to me that one should set out before dawn, in order to cross the glacial fields before the ice starts melting in the morning sun. As it turned out, we did not set out as early as we should have; our hosts were too keen to provide tea and early morning refreshments to Haakim sahib and his entourage. By the time we made a start, the sun had nearly risen. The rest of the party was keen to make progress as quickly as possible, before the heat of the sun started melting the ice. The hard ice on the surface of the glacier formed the only protection from falling into the crevasses that lay beneath.

I did not know this. Odile and John managed to keep up with the rest of the travelling party. I did not. No one was going to wait for me. There was snow on the other side of the pass too. The softer the snow became, the more treacherous the trek would become. While Haakim sahib and his companions constantly egged on John and Odile, I was left to my own devices. My inner and outer strength were sapping fast. With every step, the air became more rarefied, the snow softer, the going harder. As the snow softened in the hot daytime sun, the path became less and less distinct. The more I wandered off the beaten path, the more I plunged into several feet of snow. My breathlessness and panting became increasingly desperate, as I clawed my way out of one hole after another of hollow snow of my own making. In the distance, I could see my travelling companions walking up the cliff, seemingly impervious to my desperate plight alone on the glacier.

Eventually, I made it to the cliff that led to the summit of the pass that separates Swat from Gilgit. Fortunately, there was no snow where the steep climb led to the pass, so I was able to make steady if slow progress. It was a winding path up a sheer cliff-face. It was late afternoon by the time I reached the summit. As I looked out over a magnificent landscape of one lonely, snow-clad peak after another, the mountains took the place of the human companions that had left me behind. I sipped the crisp air and savoured the scene before plummeting down the steep snow-clad slopes on the other side of the mountain. As my ascent in the heat of the day had been ill advised, so my sliding down improvised ski slopes on the other side was also foolhardy, but I was a tired boy. At the foot of the mountain, where the snows turned into a mountain stream, I took my rest. Another party passed by. They greeted me warmly enough and must have been fascinated by a lone European wandering seemingly aimlessly at such an altitude. But they were men in a hurry and passed me by. It seemed like they wished to reach the valley that very evening. It would take me two more nights to reach that nirvana.

Those were difficult days, marked by huge horseflies that ate determinedly into one's flesh during the day and equally persistent mosquitoes at night. It was inhospitable territory, in which I did not see another human being that day or the next. Not like Swat, full of lush pastures and fragrant pine forests. Near a lake on the third day, I met some shepherds who gave me a cup of tea and some bread. It was early the same morning that I stumbled into Andarab, the first village in the Gilgit valley. John was sitting by the side of the stream, as if he was waiting for me, like he had been at the Kabul post office a few months earlier. He took me inside to the male quarters reserved for guests (*hujrah*) where he was staying. Our hosts knew that I had been through an ordeal and treated me to a wide range of mountain delicacies; mostly dairy products but also sumptuous wild mountain spinach, served with a fascinating range of breads, some wafer-thin but covering a wide circumference, others thicker and leavened. We hardly saw Haakim sahib, who had taken Odile inside the home and did not emerge. After a few days, he set off towards his native town of Gupis along with Odile, leaving John and me behind. We never met Haakim sahib again. I met Odile again briefly a few months later, when I returned to Kalam.

It was when John and I reached Gupis that we realized why Haakim sahib, though courteous enough, had been somewhat standoffish towards us. His rival for local influence in Gupis, Raja Hussain Ali Makpon, had been a favourite of the British and had been promoted during the British Raj. Haakim sahib felt that Raja sahib's influence with the erstwhile British rulers had enabled the raja to usurp his own power.

When the raja heard that two young Englishmen were in town, he was thrilled and treated us like royalty. He put us up in the local government rest house, which was just across the main road from his own mansion. Though I was keen to hone my cooking skills in the ample rest house kitchen, the raja did not give me much opportunity. Either he would send us food, or when he was hosting a banquet, he would make sure to invite us.

It was a time when the power of feudal rulers such as the raja was on the wane. Political agents appointed by the Pakistan government were slowly making inroads into the traditional power of local rulers. The attention the raja showered upon us attracted the attention of a local agent of the police Special Branch. 'How did you get here?' He accosted me on the road one day, between the raja's house and our rest house. 'We came over yonder mountain,' I replied, pointing in the general direction of Swat. 'You are not supposed to just cross over a mountain,' the officer said to me, crossly. 'You are foreigners and are supposed to come by plane from Rawalpindi. Furthermore, you are supposed to have a special tourist pass before travelling in this area.' Things could have become nasty, but the raja intervened, on which the Special Branch officer relented. 'Okay, then. Make sure you get a permit when you reach Gilgit.'

There were severe rains that year and there had been a lot of landslides. Although some of the roads in the Gilgit valley were still jeep-able, in general John and I walked everywhere— from Gupis to Singal; from Singal to Gilgit, where we picked up our tourist permit and also gained permission to cross the Shandur Pass from Gilgit to Chitral. We wanted to travel to Hunza, but were not able to gain permission to travel to that fabled land, in the extreme north of Pakistan, next to the border with China. We went as far as we could towards it and saw the road to Hunza—and beyond that to China—being blasted out of the mountain. We heard lots of stories about Hunza, how its inhabitants lived to prodigious ages well in excess of one hundred in many cases—the secret being Hunza water: magical spring water from the land that had been the original model for Shangri-La.

The terrain in Gilgit is different from Swat. Swat is green and verdant throughout the entirety of the valley. Gilgit, and indeed Chitral also, is for the most part rocky and arid. One can go ten, fifteen miles sometimes without seeing a single tree. Then one will come to an oasis, a beautiful green open space, where a stream joining the main river has enabled irrigation canals to be fashioned, making the whole area green and fertile. Because of its terrain, there are a lot of languages in the Gilgit valley—twelve, I was told. Several years later, a language expert in Gonville and Caius College at Cambridge University—the college of the renowned physicist Stephen Hawking—told me that the natural radius of a language is about thirty-five miles. It is through interaction with other linguistic groups that languages spread. Since in Gilgit there is very little interaction between one oasis and another—it is often a whole day's trek after all—languages in the valley have to a large extent remained indigenous to their native oasis. The language experts in Caius College say that Gilgit is the classic example of languages remaining within their natural radius. I wonder if it has remained like that, with the increased mobility and interaction amongst the people of the Gilgit valley.

After a long day's trek through arid countryside, John and I would generally hit on a lush, green spot to rest for the night. In some places, as in Singal and Gupis, we stayed in government rest houses free of charge. More often than not, we slept by the side of the road, with no tent, not even a sleeping bag, just our blankets. I used to enjoy making a fire by the side of the road and cooking whatever greens we could lay our hands on. You could just go to a house and explain to the lady of the house that you were a wayfarer and needed to cook something for your evening meal. She would go to her kitchen garden and bring you some seasonal vegetables to cook.

There was no widespread money ownership in Gilgit in those days. Most households were self-sufficient: they did not have to buy much in the shops. The main things they needed to buy were salt, matches and tea. People generally did without sugar. Instead of sugar, they would put salt in their tea. When they needed to buy some of these consumer items, they would take an egg or two from their home to the shop. 'People keep on saying that things have become so expensive,' one guy observed. 'But I have not noticed things becoming expensive at all. In the old days, I used to get one box of matches in exchange for one egg, and now also I get one box of matches for one egg. There has been no change!'

Months of trekking had made us both tired. My feet were a mangled mess. I had sometimes walked barefoot, and sometimes in Kolapuri-type chappals—simple soles with a strap on top and a toe-hole for the big toe. Such chappals are eminently unsuitable for trekking in such a rocky, mountainous terrain. After we had crossed over the Shandur Pass to the Chitral valley, we found an orchard in the town of Buni. It was the grape season. Far from not making us welcome in his orchard, the owner would augment our generous supply of grapes with food from his own house. It seemed to me a bit like heaven. Then out of the blue came something from John that we had not talked about throughout the summer. 'I have to go.' 'Go where?' I asked. 'Back to England.' 'What for?' John had been admitted into the Royal Holloway College at London University.

My mind flashed back to our days as schoolboys, when we used to learn by listening to Bob Dylan, not in the classroom. 'If you are going to learn, then you can learn much more here, doing what we are doing,' I said to John. 'No,' John said. 'I want to be with the people I love,' meaning his family. I guess I was a little hurt, but there was not much I could say to that. John left. I remained in Buni for a few more days, alone. A few days later, I trudged into the city of Chitral. One foreign traveller saw me on the outskirts of town. 'Are you John Butt, who was travelling with John Ryan?' I told him I was. 'John asked me to send you his love.'

III

YIN AND YANG

We created pairs of all things, so that you might reflect;
So hasten to Allah . . .

(*Al-Dhariyat* 51:49-50)

When I joined Allan Kessing in the caves of Matala in Crete, he came bounding down the cliff-face, with his bundling, muscular physique, to greet me. We had first met in Essaouira, a southern Moroccan coastal town, earlier that year. It was the summer of 1969. Allan was an Australian hippie, with a mop of long blonde hair and a healthy tan. It was growing up on the beaches of New South Wales that had given him his physique and glowing complexion. These could not be attributed to his macrobiotic diet. Still, to me it was not the surfing lifestyle that Allan epitomized. It was macrobiotics, the basing of one's diet on a balance between the twin forces of nature—yin and yang—that Allan characterized. And physically at least, he seemed a pretty good advertisement for a macrobiotic diet.

Along with Bob Dylan, macrobiotics has been a constant companion for me, prior to my acceptance of Islam and afterwards. With age, I have only become more aware of the debt that I owe both to Bob and to macrobiotics. Macrobiotics is something that has been reinforced by my Islamic faith and my study of the Qur'an. The Qur'an lays so much emphasis on the twin forces of nature, how they complement each other and how they weave themselves into each other. Furthermore, the Qur'an adds an all-important and fundamental factor to the twin, opposing forces of nature—the yin and the yang as they are known in Zen Macrobiotics. It adds the missing link that over and above the duality of nature, there is one power that controls the duality. Even the declaration of faith, the *kalima*, is based on the duality of creation. There is negation: *la ilaha* 'there is no God'. Then there is affirmation: *illa'Allah* 'except for Allah'. Allah is one. He is over and above the two-pronged forces of creation. He controls those twin forces. But the negation of all else and the affirmation on our part of the oneness and uniqueness of Allah—that is a natural process, part and parcel of duality.

But I am getting ahead of myself. In Essaouira, where I first met Allan, macrobiotics did seem a bit like a hippie fad, not something that would last. For one thing, what attracted us to macrobiotics, even more than the diet and even more than balancing ourselves in conformity with the twin forces of nature, was another typically hippie element. The popular wisdom was that if you went on a strict macrobiotic diet, you would be on a permanent high. 'Are you high the whole time?' a girl in the caves of Matala in Crete asked me, when she discovered I was macrobiotic. I was a bit non-plussed. Even though we were strict on the diet, we were not perfect macrobiotics. For example, Allan justified smoking dope, though for his part he smoked dope neat, without any tobacco. When he scored a cone of kief in Essaouira, it contained tobacco, which was even more expensive than the grass. Allan was adamant that he did not need the tobacco and traded it back for more kif. So, for Allan, kif was okay for a person following a macrobiotic diet. Tobacco was not. I went along with his verdict, but, in fact, in order to feel the elevation and clarity that a strict macrobiotic diet will give you, you should definitely forgo any other form of inebriation—tobacco or grass.

Still, idiosyncrasy is at the core of macrobiotics. It allows everyone to interpret the macrobiotic philosophy and practice it in his or her own way. I talk about macrobiotics as I understand it. Some may dispute my interpretation of the way macrobiotics works: what is yin, what is yang, how yin, how yang? In a way, that does not matter. What matters is being conscious of these twin and opposite forces of nature and consciously seeking to find a balance between them. And there can be no constant, all-applicable way. It depends on the person and his or her own disposition, how oriented towards yin or yang that person is, what other influencing factors he or she is exposed to—yin or yang. Everyone has to find their own balance. The flexibility of macrobiotics is reflected in the gradations of diet that one may follow within the macrobiotic structure, going from a number seven, solely brown rice, diet, down to a relatively liberal number two or three macrobiotic diet. And it is not only what one eats that is important: there are all sorts of other ways of taking in yin and yang. However, seeing that we are what we eat, a fundamental way of achieving this balanced lifestyle is by having a balanced diet.

As Allan explained to me in Essaouira, all foods contain a certain amount of yang and a certain amount of yin. A perfectly balanced diet contains five parts of yin to one part of yang. Yin and yang are synonyms for the two forces of nature: female and male, light and dark, cold and hot, summer and winter, day and night. The secret to ensuring a harmonious blend between the two forces is not to go to extremes. One is more likely to have a balanced lifestyle if one eats intrinsically balanced foods rather than trying to balance one extreme with another. Macrobiotics teaches one to have a balanced lifestyle, not to lurch to extremes. As the Qur'an puts it, 'We have made you into a middle nation' (*al-Baqarah* 2:143)—inherently and essentially moderate. It is macrobiotics that has instilled in me opprobrium of any extreme interpretation—either undue laxity or harshness—of Islam. An Islamic lifestyle, as well as a macrobiotic one, entails following the golden mean. 'Be neither miserly, nor so open- handed that you suffer reproach and become destitute' *(Bani Isra'il* 17:29). In our hippie interpretation of macrobiotics, however, we used to get a kick every now and then, spoiling ourselves with an extreme food. Yogurt, for example, is a very yin food. If you were on a strict macrobiotic diet and tried some yogurt—as a treat—then it really went to your head. We used to think of it as a macrobiotic acid trip.

When one starts off on a macrobiotic diet, one should go on an exclusive diet of brown rice for seven days: a number seven diet lasting seven days. Brown rice contains a perfect balance of yin and yang. It is also a complete food. This is how one establishes oneself as a macrobiotic, while also cleansing one's system of all the impurities that one might have previously introduced into one's body. After one has completed this diet, one can go on to a number six diet: brown rice with some vegetables. After that one can go downwards, on to a number five, four or three diet, all of which entail the introduction of more diverse foods—in terms of yin and yang. One can have any kind of a macrobiotic diet, really, down to a number one diet, which includes tea, salads, spices—just about any vegetarian food—so long as one is conscious of the balance.

In Essaouira, Allan used to take me for breakfast, first thing in the morning, at a roadside stall that sold boiled chickpeas. Then, in the evening—and this was a great treat—we would make our way to a little café that sold a macrobiotic delicacy: millet bread and barley soup. I can still taste that brown, creamy, steaming barley soup, it was so delicious. The millet bread, dark and crusty, was also pretty good and went down perfectly with the soup. On next to nothing, we had a healthy, balanced, sumptuous macrobiotic diet. Millet seems to grow well in arid places like Morocco. The next place I would come across millet bread was in the desert of Rajasthan, in India.

For now, I was eager to undertake a number seven diet for seven days, the cleansing of one's system that marked one's initiation into macrobiotics. Delicious as our Essaouira diet was, the round-grain brown rice that constitutes a number seven diet was not available there. I took my leave of Allan. 'See you in Matala in a month or two.' I could be pretty sure that Allan would be there. Like he was passionate about macrobiotics, he was also passionate about the caves of Matala.

Brown rice being readily available in England, I undertook the number seven diet there. I then progressed to a number six diet. A number six diet consists mainly of brown rice, some wholemeal bread and vegetables mixed with brown rice. I also took advantage of being in England to buy a number of books on macrobiotics by the guru of macrobiotics, George Ohsawa. My favourite was Zen Macrobiotics. I loved his writing because of its simplicity and practicality. Like macrobiotics itself, it was instantly accessible. One did not have to work overtime, or have extraordinary spiritual insight, to practice this path with a certain degree of understanding as to why it was a path worth following. One could see from Ohsawa's writings that a repository of spiritual, scientific and philosophical tradition lay behind the macrobiotic path.

Though Matala had a lot of plus points, it was not ideal from a macrobiotic point of view. There was no brown rice, no brown bread. Everything was white as sugar. Despite being a keen cook, I let Allan cook for me while in Matala. Allan would buy wheat and corn. These were prepared as chicken feed and were not really fit for human consumption. Forget separating the chaff from the grain, here no attempt was made to even separate gravel from grain. Chaff would have been a blessing in comparison. As I learnt later, in the course of my travels in Afghanistan and the Frontier, it is normal for some stones— even gravel, sometimes—to be found in lentils and pulses. These usually found their way into Allan's pot along with the grain. Macrobiotics assiduously use sea salt in their cooking, and that item was present in abundance on the beach of Matala. Allan just cooked the grain in seawater. That was a process of trial and error. The first time, he used pure seawater. Apart from being unpalatably salty, the wheat remained hard, while the corn turned slushy in the overly salty water. You needed only 5 per cent seawater and 95 per cent fresh water. At the best of times, the grain concoction was not particularly palatable, as you can imagine, but we did not mind. There were plenty of other consolations.

Matala consisted of a series of caves burrowed into the cliff-face. Each cave was designed for human habitation. Allan's cave was one of the best. It had shelves built into the rock-face and a lovely expansive couch, filled with small pebbles that made for a soft and pliable surface to rest on. Allan was not used to accommodating anyone in his cave, but he made an exception for me. Being young—I was still a teenager—he wished to have me under his wing. Allan's cave was next to the Hilton, the main cave in the Matala complex. John Fleming and his fellow Americans, complete with their Triumph 650 motorbikes, were putting up in the Hilton. I did not really visit any other caves, except for Nia's. Her cave was one flight of caves below ours, closer to the sea.

Nia's cave could have been made for her. It was small and private, cosy and nicely done up in her own style. It had alcoves in the wall but was not big enough to accommodate a couch. She had made a bed for herself in one of the longer alcoves. Except for me, I can't imagine that she invited anyone else to her cave. I met her early on in my stay in Matala, which extended over the winter of 1969–70. Allan introduced us. The three of us once went over the ridge to the next beach eastwards from Matala beach. I can't exactly remember, but a girlfriend of Allan's named Hillary might have also accompanied us. It's not surprising my memory is not so clear. All I can remember from that day is Nia.

Allan often makes fun of me, I ask about Nia so often: has he ever heard from her, can he remember her surname? 'You asked me that before John. The answer is still the same. No.' Even as I am writing this, I think maybe she will read it. One never forgets one's first love and my first love she was, even though I did not appreciate it at the time. The more time goes by, the more I realize how lucky I was to have known Nia and be loved by her; and the greater my remorse becomes at having mistreated her and failing to appreciate her. What if I had stayed with her and we had travelled together? Maybe we would have accepted Islam together? It was not to be, but it is difficult to escape such thoughts.

Maybe Nia would not have been up for it, in any case. She was far from a down-and-out hippie. She was posh, beautiful, smart, well-to-do. She looked after herself. I think she was probably in her mid-twenties—quite a few years older than me. For her, Matala was more like a holiday, a winter sojourn. I do not imagine her as a long-term hippie like I was. I imagine her having found a guy who was more suitable for her than me when she moved back to the

States, having children, settling down. That would have been her scene, and she would have done it well.

There is a big factor in Pashtoon life called *peghaur*. I suppose the nearest translation would be peer pressure. Nowadays it is called social censorship. That is what happened between Nia and myself. I was happy with her and liked her for what she was, irrespective of her poshness. But the guys in the Hilton—John Fleming in particular—made fun of me for being with such a posh girl. Maybe they were just jealous. I was young and impressionable, and I bowed to their pressure. Without warning or ostensible reason, I dumped Nia. She never complained, never even asked me why. But she never stopped loving me and continued to be kind whenever we met. The last time we met was when I was about to make the move to Asia. 'John is so together,' she said admiringly of me, as I took my leave of a group of cave dwellers, my eyes set determinedly on Asia and the East. I often wonder if Nia would have accompanied me East if we had stayed together, or if we would have had to part in any case, for me to continue my journey.

Frank was known as Cap'n Amerika in Matala. He and some friends had Triumph 650 motorbikes. Frank was a generous and easy-going guy with a big heart. But he could have killed me with his generosity. In Matala, he lent me his motorbike. Then later, when I met him in Bamiyan in Afghanistan, I found that he and his friends had swapped their motorbikes for horses. He was equally generous towards me with one of his horses. The problem was, I had hardly any experience of riding horses, and none of riding a motorbike. Riding a powerful bike at 110 miles per hour on Cretan lanes is not a wise way to hone one's motorbike-riding skills. Neither is haring along Afghan tracks on a wild Afghan steed, with very basic stirrups and hardly any saddle, a wise way to learn horse riding. I ended up clinging to the horse's mane for dear life as I lunged this way and that. But I survived both hair-raising experiences.

More gentle was the ride Frank gave me to Agios Nikolaos, on the north-eastern coast of Crete, from where I took a ferry to Rhodes. This was the first stage of my journey to the East. I stayed in Rhodes for about two weeks, gazing at the mountains of Asia that would turn out to be my home for the rest of my life while waiting for a fishing boat that would take me to Marmaris, Turkey. In those days, the fishing boat was the only way to reach Marmaris from Rhodes. When, finally, the boat was ready to transport me, it turned out that my fellow traveller was the American consul in Istanbul. He was travelling with his wife. Travelling from Rhodes to Marmaris by fishing boat was not just for the down-and-outs. It was the normal form of transport, even for diplomats.

Soon after I arrived, some local fishermen in Marmaris gave me a fish to eat. That was one of the most memorable meals I ever had in my life. It was a huge fish, freshly caught, garnished with herbs and marinated in lemon juice. I can still taste its sharp flavour. It was just as well I had a good meal in Marmaris because, aside from feta cheese and naan bread in Iranian *chai* shops, I did not have much intake in the way of nutrition right through to Afghanistan. Allan and I had not discovered Greek feta cheese when we were in Greece. I discovered it in Iran, when passing through on the way to Afghanistan. To this day, whenever anyone praises Iranian food and says how lavish it is, I say, 'You mean naan bread and feta cheese?' For me, along with black chai in bubble-glasses, that is Iranian food and it is true—it is sumptuous.

To sit in an Iranian chai-khana and partake of this delicacy on a cold winter's day is such a pleasure. The feta is served automatically with a slice of naan. Perfect macrobiotic fare. Afghanistan has the naan, but not the feta. Several years later I discovered an Afghan delicacy that excels even feta. It is called *krut*. It is a cheese made by kochi nomads. Krut is so delicious and such a powerful food that it will set you up for a journey, for whatever work you have to do, for hours. Just a tiny piece of krut, not even a mouthful, is all you need.

It would have been good if I had known about such delicacies when I first arrived in Afghanistan. At the time, I was struggling with staying macrobiotic on the one hand and maintaining a decent level of nutrition on the other. Diarrhoea and even dysentery are a fact of life for travellers who first arrive in Afghanistan. I had this rather naive idea that a runny stomach was a yin condition and just needed a dose of yang to put it right. Part of it being a yin condition was its softness: it needed to be treated with something hard. That is also wrong. You need to eat something soft—soft rice and yogurt is the best—for diarrhoea. Hard food will only make your condition worse, since it is difficult to digest. The best thing is to take some white rice and mix it with the same amount of split and shelled mung beans. Cook the mixture in plenty of water till it's really soft. Once it has cooked to a mush, add yogurt. This is the best cure for a runny stomach that I have come across. Don't eat anything else until you are better.

The story of that summer is told elsewhere, but I would like to mention my two sojourns in Peshawar in the course of the summer, the same summer when I met up with John Ryan in Kabul. It seemed natural to me to acquire an English copy of the Qur'an. After all, I was accustomed to reading any holy scripture I could lay my hands on. I had already read the Bhagavad Gita and the Tao Te Ching of Taoism. Now that I was residing amongst the Pashtoons, I felt an urge to study the book that led them to pray in such an organized, humble, united and devoted manner, five times a day. It was impressive, the way Pashtoons prayed. Once, from the Palace Hotel in Peshawar, I saw a large group of Pashtoons on the roof of a nearby mosque, offering the daily prayer in congregation. Often in Afghanistan our bus would stop to allow all the passengers to alight, place their sheets and shawls on the ground, which they used as prayer mats, and offer the prescribed prayer together. I felt left out to not be able to join in the experience. I wanted to discover the holy book that inspired them to such strong faith and practice. I went to the University Book Agency, located between the Palace Hotel, where I was residing, and the Pakistan Hotel, where I spent a lot of my time. I bought Muhammad Marmaduke Pickthall's translation of the Qur'an from the proprietor, a graduate of Darul Uloom Deoband[1] by the name of Maulana Fazal Manan. As his name was interesting, so the character of Muhammad Marmaduke Pickthall was intriguing. Just as I kept my copy of his Quranic translation with me, so his ghost hovered over me for several years after my conversion to Islam. From aristocratic

---

[1] The pre-eminent Islamic seminary of South Asia, where I later studied.

English stock, Pickthall had converted to Islam at a time—at the dawn of the twentieth century— when this was a very unusual thing to do. He had made the Indian subcontinent his home. In fact, he was commissioned to do this translation of the Qur'an by the Nizam of Hyderabad, the princely ruler of much of the Deccan, or southern India, during the British Raj.

Pickthall did not claim that his work was a translation of the Qur'an. The Qur'an could only be in Arabic, but it was a rendering into English of the 'inimitable symphony' that was the Arabic Qur'an. It is important for Muslims to differentiate between the Qur'an itself—the revealed book that is in Arabic— and translations of the Qur'an. What makes the Qur'an stand out from other scriptures is its authenticity. It is exactly the same now as it was when it was revealed in the seventh century. The key to this authenticity is the differentiation between the original and the translations. A translation cannot be called 'the Qur'an'. The Qur'an is sacrosanct and is in Arabic alone. The first person to translate the Qur'an, into Persian, was Shah Waliullah, a famous scholar of Hadith who lived in Delhi. He did not call his translation the Qur'an. He called it *Triumph of the Almighty* (*Fath'ur-Rahman*). Even so, Shah Waliullah was accosted at the time for having the temerity to translate the Qur'an into Persian: the Qur'an could only be in Arabic. His critics were right: the Qur'an can only be in Arabic, but Shah Waliullah was also right: the holy book had to be translated so that people could understand its meaning. It is through the interplay of such opposing forces—the yin and yang of the Muslim community—that Islam retains its balance and its authenticity. 'The difference of opinion within my community is its strength,' the Prophet said—*ikhtilafu ummati rahmatun*. It is knowing both sides of an argument that enables Muslims to move forward on the right and middle path. It is this interplay of opposite forces that has always helped me to see both sides of an argument.

Although I had bought Pickthall's translation of the Qur'an, I kept the copy with me for the time being. I only studied it later, in the autumn, after John Ryan had returned to England. It was Ramadan when I delved into the holy book of Islam. I was residing in the Palace Hotel, the same hotel, the same bed on the roof, where I had spent a whole month in the debilitating heat of summer, waiting for my visa. Now it was autumn, and the nights were nippy. I was fasting during the day, feasting at night. My diet mirrored the balance of my daily routine: fresh spinach with creamy yogurt and Peshawari roti. I was accompanied and led through the first days of my fasting by a worker in the Palace Hotel by the name of Ibrahim.

Michael was also residing on the top floor of the Palace Hotel at this time. Michael was one freaked out, wild-eyed hippie. He had been close to Steve Winwood and Traffic, so he said. Traffic, of *Forty Thousand Headmen*—headmen being another name for freaks or hippies—fame, were the kings of psychedelic rock in those days. They were a group from the Midlands of the UK, and Michael was also from the Midlands. Michael was pretty freaked out in his fasting routine too. Far from being quick in breaking the fast when sundown came, he would extend the fast. He said he was giving the fast an extra dimension. The time of the breaking of the fast was a magical one. The teeming streets of Peshawar suddenly went silent. Some people went indoors, others could be seen in little huddles on the side of the street, breaking the fast. Not a single rickshaw, tanga or cart could be seen moving on the streets. Everything was static. Traditionally, Muslims lay a lot of emphasis on reading, studying and reciting the Book of Allah during the month of Ramadan. The Qur'an tells us, 'The month of Ramadan is the month when the Qur'an was sent down for mankind . . .' (*al-Baqarah* 2:185). I also used the month of Ramadan to delve into the Qur'an.

I found that the Qur'an takes macrobiotics to another level. The constriction—yang—and expansion—yin—of the fasting- feasting routine instils this in one. Along with diet, the Qur'an applies the principle of moderation to every walk of life. Islam teaches one to be balanced, to be moderate (*al-Baqarah* 2:143), not to lurch either towards extreme harshness (*ifraat*), or extreme laxity (*tafreet*) (*al-Kahf* 18:28). Follow the golden mean in all things, Islam says, for example, in not going to extremes of munificence on the one hand or miserliness on the other (*Bani Isra'il* 17:29). The Qur'an urges us time and time again to seek a middle way in every walk of life (*al-Hijr* 15:110), balancing the twin forces that propel our existence. Then, at the end of the road, if we have managed to stay on that balanced way, we will find union with the One—the Creator of yin and yang:

> And We have created pairs of all things so that you might reflect. Therefore, hasten to Allah . . .
>
> (*al-Dhariyat* 51: 49-50)

Particularly, the Qur'an cites the opposite forces of nature in support of the existence of one guiding force. 'You cause the night to pass into the day, and the day into the night; You bring forth the living from the lifeless and the lifeless from the living. You give without measure to whom You will,' (*al-Imran* 3:27). The way to achieve balance in one's life is by submitting to the One, the Creator of all things. That is the balanced path of nature: 'Do they seek a path other than the path of Allah, when everything in the heavens and the earth has submitted to Him, willingly or unwillingly? To him they shall all return' (*al-Imran* 3:83).

On a belief basis, the transition from macrobiotic to Muslim was a natural one. From a dietary point of view, it was more of a jolt. Soon after I had converted to Islam, the occasion of the Eid of Sacrifice (*Eid-al-Adha*) arrived. I approached this commemoration of the sacrifice of Abraham—when, instead of a son, Abraham sacrificed a goat—with a considerable degree of trepidation. I had been a macrobiotic vegetarian for several years now. How was I going to eat meat? I bit the bullet, so to speak, and downed huge chunks of meat in a plate of *pulao*, thinking in my mind that I was having an extreme dose of yang. The dose was pretty potent and gave me hallucinations, or mixed-up confusion, one might call it. In typical macrobiotic fashion, I set about trying to make up for it with a suitable intake of yin in the coming days. That was the act of extreme macrobiotics that marked my entrance into the fold of Islam.

IV

TALIB FARMER

There is beauty for you in your cattle, when you drive them home in the evening, and as you lead them to pasture in the morning.

(*Al-Nahl* 16:6)

I was wandering in a daze after John Ryan left me in the Chitral valley, early in October 1970. I returned to Kalam alone. It had been three months since I had set out with Odile and John, in the company of Haakim sahib and his entourage. Odile had long since returned to Kalam. Things had changed in Kalam when I returned after my long summer travels. The atmosphere had turned austere, and the onset of dark autumn did not help.

Our homestead in Kalam was inhabited by the same individuals who had been living there when I left. There was Kenneth Honerkamp and his friend Michael Fitzgerald in one room, Odile and Habib in the room next to them. Kenneth was a giant—well over seven feet tall. His exceptional height, added to a somewhat boyish appearance, meant that he was the centre of attention wherever he went. He and Michael had not moved from Kalam throughout the summer. Michael used to cook for himself and Kenneth. The problem was, in Kalam there was not much to cook or eat except for potatoes. Once, Michael was celebrating a collection of mushrooms from the forest. 'Oh my,' he said sarcastically. 'Now we will make some mushroom soup, some mushroom curry, some mushroom omelette. What else can we cook with mushrooms? Anything but potatoes!'

As Habib, whose house it was, and Odile lived together, there were rumours around Kalam concerning their relationship: rumours that Habib and Odile did nothing to dispel. Habib was from Chal, near Madyan. In Kalam, he combined the duties of being a fixer for foreigners—supplying them with their needs such as hashish—with being a weatherman for the government. His duties as a weatherman entailed climbing the hill on the other side of the river twice a day, once in the morning and once in the evening, checking how much rain there had been, what the temperature was, making a record of it, then returning to his place in the Kalam bazaar, where he continued his role of middleman between foreigners and locals.

When I returned to our homestead after my long summer trek, Kenneth came to the door. I was expecting a normal hippie greeting, something like, 'Hi, man, good to see you.' Instead, I was welcomed with the classic Pashto greeting of '*Jor, takra, khushhal*' (Are you well, strong, happy?) along with the mandatory three embraces that constitute the Islamic *mu'aniqa*, followed by a handshake. It seemed very formal. Before I could ask, 'Hey, man, what's going on here?' I realized that Kenneth and Michael had embraced Islam. They had become Abdul Hadi and Abdul Rahman and were exhibiting all the zeal associated with converts.

Odile was having none of this. There was a lot of tension between her on one hand, and Abdul Hadi and Abdul Rahman on the other. Habib was caught in the middle. As a Muslim, he had to defer to the Americans' Islam. As a hippie at heart, or at least one who made money from hippies, Kenneth and Michael's conversion was not good for business. Nor did it please him that Odile was on her way out of Kalam, finding the excessively pious atmosphere in the village not conducive to staying around. I attended the last dinner that Habib gave for her. 'My last invitation to you,' he said fondly to Odile. After she left, I started living in Habib's room, but

I was clearly a poor substitute for Odile. Habib resented my presence. One cannot blame him for being lovesick for Odile.

The situation was the same for me as it had been for Odile. In the new, austerely Islamic set-up, I was the odd man out. By becoming Muslim, Abdul Hadi and Abdul Rahman had changed the environment for Europeans living in Kalam. Local Kalamis had collected a huge amount of money for Abdul Hadi and Abdul Rahman when they accepted Islam. Now they expected other foreigners like Odile and myself to convert as well. The pressure also told on Habib. In the new climate of piety, he was being condemned for cohabitating with a foreign woman who had not become Muslim. The local pressure was not likely to ease if he housed another European non-Muslim like myself. Kohistanis—the mountain men who live in Upper Swat—are hardy folk. They are zealous when it comes to their faith. They have only been Muslim for about two hundred years, maybe less. Islam came to the upper reaches of Kohistan long after it had made its mark on the lower valley.

Through Habib, stories of Europeans accepting Islam in Madyan filtered back to Kalam. Kalam was very different to Madyan. There was none of the debonnaire spirit of Madyan in Kalam. Kalam is a mountain redoubt—austere and dour. There was no vibrant hippie scene in Kalam. There were just three foreigners in Kalam, four including Odile. There was Abdul Hadi, Abdul Rahman and myself. Odile had already escaped the nest. Of the three remaining foreigners, the Kalam Kohistanis were expecting a 100 per cent success rate as far as conversion to Islam was concerned. Abdul Rahman and Abdul Hadi's conversions, the conversions in Madyan—all contributed to making them more and more expectant that I would be the next in line.

The pressure only increased as Ramadan approached. The first snow of winter had already fallen, and it was only October. I cannot remember the sun shining once in Kalam that autumn: the atmosphere was dark, cold, intense. The situation was becoming impossible: local people insisting that I fast, me not being ready to fast. In my own idiosyncratic manner, I agreed to fast, but only after I had taken breakfast. 'That is my fast. I am not Muslim, to fast like you do,' I tried to fend off indignant and offended

Kohistanis, for whom, of course, that was not good enough. One day, I was actually smoking a joint after breakfast when some people came to visit Habib. They were shocked to see me violating the holy month in such a brazen manner. Finally, it was a row with Habib that brought things to a head. It was a small matter: I wanted to give some puppies a home on our terrace, he, as the owner of the house, was within his rights to refuse to have them there. That was the pretext for my departure. He was probably looking for an excuse to get rid of me. About three days into the fast of Ramadan, I was on the bus heading towards Peshawar.

Whenever I am asked who it was that brought me to Islam, I mention one anonymous person on that bus between Kalam and Mingora, the capital of Swat. In fact, to me, he was more like an angel. Far from knowing his name, I never even saw his face. Our bus stopped at Charbagh, near Mingora. It was time to break the Ramadan fast. Others got off the bus to take a cup of tea and have a snack in a roadside teashop. I stayed on the bus, since I had not been fasting. Far from condemning me: 'Look at that good-for-nothing foreigner who is not even fasting,' one person came up to me and put some dates and pakoras into my hand. 'Go on,' he said, 'break your fast' (*rojha mata kra*). He must have thought that the only conceivable reason that I had not got off the bus to break my fast was that I did not have any money. So he took it upon himself to acquire the great reward (*sawab*) from Allah that comes with providing someone with food with which to break the fast. Though I had not been fasting for the two or three days of Ramadan that I had been in Kalam, I was now. That was the offshoot of this act of generosity on the part of my fellow traveller. More than anything else, it was this act of giving that led me seamlessly to Islam.

Soon the bus arrived in Mingora. That night, I stayed in a hotel next to Green Chowk in the centre of Mingora. It was just a simple Pashtoon hotel, with some rooms and beds in the courtyard that one could sleep on in case one did not wish to pay for a whole room. Though I had not been through any initiation into Islam and had not uttered the testimony of faith, I now fully considered myself a Muslim. Those three words on the bus—*rojha mata kra*—had done for me what none of the forceful proselytizing in Kalam could achieve: they had opened my heart to Islam. Relieved of the oppressive pressure of Kalam, it was a pleasure to arise before *prima luce*, the first light of dawn, and partake of *peshmany*. Peshmany is more commonly known as *sehri* or *suhoor* in the Muslim world. It is one of the hallmarks of the Muslim fast. It is designed to make the fast easier. 'Allah wishes to make things easy for you' the Qur'an says (*al Baqarah* 2:185). According to the Quran, Christians had made things too difficult for themselves with the Lent fast. They were required to have only one meal, at night. Not only did this render the fast of Lent unsustainable, it was also harsh and debilitating for people's health. So peshmany became a hallmark of the Muslim fast, a distinguishing feature. Despite the inconvenience of getting up in the middle of the night and the difficulty of having food at that time, it is important for one's health—and for the viability of the fast—that one should do so.

As I mentioned, I studied Marmaduke Pickthall's translation of the Qur'an in the course of that Ramadan. If there was one verse, one Quranic concept that convinced me more than anything else that I was already Muslim, it was the alignment of Islam with the path followed by nature: 'Besides the religion of Allah do they seek another religion, when everything in the heavens and the earth has submitted to Him, willingly or unwillingly, and unto Him they shall all return?' (*al-Imran* 3:83). So, in following the path of Islam, one was only doing what everything in nature had already done: submitting to the will of Allah. After that, whenever lads in Peshawar would ask me, '*Kalima de waylay dah?*' (Have you uttered the declaration of faith?), I told them yes, I was already Muslim, since being Muslim was something inbred in me, being nothing more than an acknowledgement of the fact that I was part of the universal submission to the will of Allah.

But still people felt that some formal initiation into Islam was necessary. This task fell to Mulla Khalid Khan. He was the village imam in Masma, where I formally entered Islam. During Ramadan, every day, morning and evening, I used to break fast and eat the early morning meal in the milk shop of Aga Mohammad. Aga Mohammad was a dear, huge fellow, presiding over equally huge pans of milk (*doodh*) and yogurt (*dahi*). My macrobiotic fare that Ramadan was Peshawari naan bread, accompanied by spinach and yogurt. I bought the cooked spinach elsewhere and came to eat it, along with the yogurt and naan bread, in Aga Mohammad's shop. There, I became acquainted with his brother-in-law, a civil engineer by the name of Majeed Khan. After Ramadan, Majeed Khan invited me to come and stay in his village, Masma. Masma lies right next to Nasirpur, the first railway station one comes to as one heads east from Peshawar, on the line leading to Rawalpindi and Lahore. These were the days when trains used to run in Pakistan. Masma is known as Chota Walayat due to the large number of British civil servants who resided in the village. The farming land around Masma receives abundant irrigation water from the Kabul River. Orchards of plums, pears and peaches abound. It is also an area replete with history. Nearby Akbarpura received its name from the Mughal emperor Akbar, Timurpura from the Uzbek conqueror Timur who stopped off there.

My first meeting with Khalid Khan was not auspicious. Like many mullas leading prayers in the mosques around Peshawar, he hailed from Swat. In Swat itself, mullas were excess to requirements. They could make a living for themselves and offer a much-needed service if they became imams in Peshawar. There, these imams would lead the daily prayers five times a day and teach the children of the village the Qaida Baghdadi— the basic Arabic and Qur'anic reader—leading to recitation of the Qur'an itself. Most of these imams were not eminent or distinguished scholars. They knew how to recite the Qur'an in Arabic but had varying degrees of expertise when it came to translating the holy book and still less when it came to exegesis. They were known as *Khulasa* mullas—mullas who had studied Khulasa—a basic book of Hanafi fiqh or jurisprudence—but not much else. This book gave them the ability to answer basic questions relating to practice of the faith. With this level of knowledge, you can just about get by as a village imam. When I reached Masma, Majeed Khan took me to see Mulla Khalid Khan. Majeed Khan explained to the imam that I had been fasting during Ramadan and now wished to formally accept Islam. Mulla Khalid asked what my name was.

When Majeed told him it was John, he said that it could now be Jan Mohammad.

I have an English friend, Yahya Birt, who changed his name from Jonathan to Yahya on accepting Islam. Yahya is the son of John Birt—almost my namesake—former director-general of the BBC. Yahya's father will crop up again, later in our story. When asked once, why did you change your name to Yahya? Jonathan replied: 'It seemed like a good idea at the time, but in fact Jonathan is also a perfectly good Islamic name.' That is absolutely right. It is natural, what with the zeal of the convert and the wish to establish a Muslim identity, that one should choose on conversion to adopt a Muslim name. But there is no need to do so. As time has passed, and I have become more and more Pashtoon, I have become more comfortable with the name Jan Mohammad, so long as it is pronounced in the Pashtoon manner—John Mohammad. Still, strictly speaking, John, being the English for John the Baptist—Yahya in Arabic—is more Islamic than Jan. As it turned out, the name I took was not particularly Islamic at all. While Jan goes down fine amongst Asian—Ajami as they are known in Arabic—Muslims, Arabs take the word to mean the devil—the plural of *jinn*—Lucifer himself having been of *jinni* origin:

> And He created the *jinns* from a flame of fire
>
> (*Al-Rahman* 55:15)

Just as well that I have spent my Islamic life amongst Ajamis, who have no problem with the name Jan Mohammad.

If Arabs are not comfortable with my name, I am also somewhat perturbed when, meeting Dutch, Scandinavian or Eastern European people, they pronounce my Islamic name as Jaan or worse still Yaan. I have nothing against Jaan or Yaan, but that is not my name! In fact, in Pashto, Jan is pronounced exactly the same as John in English, and that is how I am comfortable with the name. Pashtoons, in particular, love the name Jan Mohammad. In Persian, the word Jan means spirit, but spirit as in soul, as opposed to spirit as in ghost. 'Jan-e- Mohammad,' my sheikh or spiritual master in India later used to reflect over my name, 'just think about your name—the soul of Mohammad. Meditate over the meaning of your name.'

I had learnt the testimony of faith (*shahada*) that Mulla Khalid Khan asked me to recite. I recited it. It was a low-key affair. It was almost certainly the first and the last time that Mulla Khalid Khan would ever accept anyone into the fold of Islam. He did not give the impression that he considered the task of administering the testimony of faith—'giving the *shahada*', as English Muslims quaintly put it—to be very high on his list of duties. I also did not consider the actual utterance of the shahada in the presence of Mulla Khalid Khan as being integral to my acceptance of the faith. I had considered myself a Muslim from the time I had started fasting, several months earlier, in Charbagh, at the instigation of the kind man who had presumed I was fasting and thrust some dates and pakoras into my hand for the breaking of the fast. That was my road-to-Damascus moment, consolidated by reading the Qur'an during the month of fasting in Peshawar. There seemed to be much more enthusiasm for initiating a foreigner into Islam amongst unlettered folk than there was amongst the clergy. Little did I know that beneath Mulla Khalid Khan's lack of enthusiasm lay a layer of downright scepticism.

Majeed stayed behind in the mosque after I had left, to talk to the Mulla Khalid. When he joined me outside, he told me the mulla had suggested that maybe I was an Englishman who wanted to spy on Muslims from the inside and that might be the reason why I had become Muslim. Such conspiracy theories abound amongst the Pashtoons. They are a legacy of the Great Game of the nineteenth century, when British spies used to pretend to be Muslim— sometimes mullas or herbal physicians (*hakeems*)—in order to make forays into Afghanistan and Central Asia. Their job there was to gather information and to counter Russian influence. My own feeling is that some of these stories are probably exaggerated, but we will have ample opportunity to discuss this later on. It is a tag that has dogged me incessantly, ever since I became Muslim. For the time being, my Islamic credentials were to be put to an even sterner and more intimate test.

A grandson of Majeed Khan's father, Mir Ahmad, took me for a walk in the fields that afternoon. We had nearly reached his cowstand (*ghaujal* in Pashto) when he confronted me. 'So you have converted to Islam, have you?' 'Sure have,' I replied. 'And have you been circumcised?' 'I have, as a matter of fact,' I replied, circumcision being a *Sunnah*—a practice of the Holy Prophet considered absolutely integral to the identity of Muslims. Mir Ahmad was not convinced. 'Show me,' he said. I was reluctant. Mir Ahmad was insistent: 'Show me!' 'Okay, there you are!' I condescended, pulling down my pants. The pleasure on Mir Ahmad's face was clear to see. His face melted when he saw my suitably circumcised willy. 'Okay, now I agree that you are a Muslim,' he smiled, as I put my pants back on.

Now there is a story to tell here. As far as I know, I have never been actually, physically circumcised. In fact, at preparatory school in England, we used to have Cavaliers and Roundheads, after the rival armies in the English civil war of the sixteenth century. Cavaliers were those who had not been circumcised; Roundheads had been. We were just little boys and did not know to be shy about such things. I was always a Cavalier. Somehow, over the years, I acquired the physical attributes of a Roundhead. I was lucky, or should I say blessed. Abdul Samad, who had accepted Islam in the same year in Madyan, was not so lucky. After his grand initiation into Islam in Madyan, he was taken in not such grand fashion to Mingora, where he was circumcised in the local hospital. It is painful enough for young children to have to go through circumcision, but for grown men? Abdul Samad told me it was excruciating, but worth it.

But a greater examination than all that, a real test of my true initiation into Islam, came soon after my arrival in Masma, with the Eid of Sacrifice, which I mentioned in the last chapter. It is true what Allah says in the Quran: 'Do people think that they will get by saying "We believe" and that they will not be put to the test?' (*al-Ankabut* 29:2). The poet Iqbal has taken it one step further. He wrote in Farsi:

Cho meguyyam Musalmanam bilarzam
Ki danam mushilate la ila ra

When I say I am Muslim, I tremble, because I know what difficulties come with uttering the testimony of faith.[1]

[1] Allama Iqbal, *Armaghan-e-Hijaz*, Lahore: Iqbal Academy Pakistan, 2002.

I can relate to that. In fact, my whole life since I became Muslim has been one long test, with hardly any let-up. You will see what I mean as you turn the pages of this book. Does it have to be like that? Well, there is a saying of the Holy Prophet, 'The world is a prison for the believer, paradise for the infidel.' One will always be put to the test in life, whether it is through poverty or wealth, in solitude or in the company of others. To be happy is not really the aim of a Muslim lifestyle. Islam gives one a sense of well-being and resignation in whatever situation one finds oneself.

The life of a Pashtoon has two foundations. On the one hand, there is Pashtoonwali—the Pashtoon code of life. On the other hand, there is the Islamic faith. While Pashtoonwali centres around the men's meeting place (*hujrah*), the place where Islam comes into its own is in the mosque. I have always tended towards the mosque.

Years later, an imam in Samarkand, noticing how I used to spend hours in the magical mosques of that Central Asian city, was to pass on to me an Arabic saying: 'A believer in a mosque is like a fish in water; a hypocrite in a mosque is like a bird in a cage.' My love affair with mosques began in Masma. The magic of the mosque in Masma was its utter simplicity. The floor of the mosque was carpeted with a type of dry grass known as *barwezy*. Though stacked quite thickly on the floor of the mosque, the *barwezy* did not decompose but remained dry, exuding a eucalyptus-like aroma. It remained on the floor of the mosque throughout the winter months. In summer, the *barwezy* would be taken out and replaced with mats made of dwarf-palm (*mezary*). Both *barwezy* and *mezary* are plants unique to the Pashtoon areas. While *barwezy* has a warming effect, *mezary* is cooling and therefore perfect for the summer months. The secret to a cool slumber in summer is to put a cot strung with *mezary* rope on the roof, then place a mezary mat on top of the cot. The effect will be as cooling as one might expect in the searing heat of summer.

A mosque is supposed to be a beautiful place—beautiful in its simplicity, but also in its grace. So many of the mosques built nowadays lack this simple beauty. The mosque in Masma was an example of a pristine, pure, unspoiled mosque. It did not even have a loudspeaker. When the imam wished to announce the call to prayer, he would go to the back of the mosque courtyard, where a raised stone platform, with a few steps leading up to a pedestal, had been constructed. He would stand there and deliver the call to prayer (*azan*). It was the equivalent of the tower in a mosque where the *muezzin* traditionally gives *azan* (*minar*). To my mind, the obsession with loudspeakers—usually ones with imperfect sound systems—has taken away much of the simple charm of mosques. The first time I ever heard the call to prayer was when John and I were sleeping on a hill above a village between Katana and Fez, in Morocco. Without the aid of any loudspeaker, the sound echoed in the hills. Nowadays, I pine for the sound of such pure *azans*.

In the mosque, I embarked on what would become a second education, to follow up the school education I had already acquired as a boy in England. First of all, I set about learning Arabic. To do this, I bought a Qur'anic reader. It is a little pamphlet-type booklet called Qaida Baghdadi with no more than twenty-odd pages. I started learning the Arabic letters and how to recite Arabic words from Mulla Khalid. Being a good and eager student, it wasn't long before I had completed reading the first part of the Quran. Upon completing this, I distributed sweets in the *hujrah* of the main khan of the village, Ashraf Khan. 'You are a complete Pashtoon,' Ashraf Khan's son Rauf complimented my observance of local customs. It is interesting that he did not compliment my diligence as a student of Islam. That was for the mulla to do. He was impressed by my distribution of sweets on the occasion: that was his domain, as the lord of the *hujrah*. It is on occasions such as these that the *hujrah* and the mosque merge, complement and even flow into one another.

I was a strange, unconventional student of Islam (*talib*). From the beginning, I learnt things not in a classroom but from anyone I met. That had been my approach to learning how to speak Pashto. It was now the way I learnt how to read the language. The first Pashto book I bought was a Pashto translation of the *Revelations of the Unseen* (*Futuh'al-Ghaib*) by Sheikh Abdul Qadir Gilani. It was my aim to be able to read both Arabic and Pashto. Arabic, because it was the language of the Qur'an; Pashto, since it was the language of the community amongst whom I had accepted Islam.

I was intent on being fully Muslim, but also fully Pashtoon. There is a joke amongst the Pashtoons that Arabic is the language of Paradise, which is obvious since it is the language in which the Qur'an was revealed, and Pashto is the language of hell. It is just the Pashtoons way of poking fun at themselves. They also say that Pashto, as in Pashtoonwali, is half tantamount to infidelity (*neem kufr day*). They say this because some matters, particularly matters relating to honour, are treated in a more extreme fashion than prescribed by Islam. My feeling is that the Pashtoons are being unnecessarily hard on themselves in calling their way of life *neem kufr* and their language the language of hell. In many cases, in fact it is normal, for both Islam and Pashto to come together in single Pashtoon individuals in the most fulsome way. We will come across many such characters in our tale. The latter-day Pashto poet Amir Hamza Shinwari challenges the idea that Pashto-speakers are hell-bound:

> People say that it is the language of hell
> I will go to heaven with my Pashto.

If Sheikh Abdul Qadir Gilani is considered the patron saint of the Pashtoons, Rahman Baba (1650–1711) is their national poet. But there is next to no Pashtoonwali in Rahman Baba's poetry. He is entirely a saintly, Sufi-like figure. In one poem, he highlights the contrast between himself and his more worldly brother, Aziz Khan:

> Malangs and Khans cannot mix
> Aziz Khan and Malang Abdul Rahman are poles apart.

His poems about the love of God, of the fleeting nature of the world and worldly attachments, the lofty station of the saints and of learning, made a deep impression on me. Yet even Rahman Baba, that most saintly, unworldly, apolitical of figures, sometimes delved into the realm of political comment:

> These oppressive rulers
> Have made home, grave and Peshawar all the same.

While such issues were a sideshow for Rahman Baba, Pashtoon discontent with Mughal rule, and particularly the rule of Aurangzeb, looms large in the poetry of the nationalist, patriotic Khushal Khan Khattak (1613–1689), the other great poet of the Pashtoons. For me, it was Rahman Baba who became a spiritual inspiration. After *Futuh'al-Ghayb*, the next book from which I learnt Pashto was Rahman Baba's *Deewan*, his complete works.

How Rahman Baba became a Pashto reader for me was later a source of amazement to a friend of mine, John Sampson, a Pashto-speaker and son of the eminent Rahman Baba scholar and translator Robert Sampson. 'Rahman Baba's Pashto is quite difficult, isn't it? How did you learn Pashto from Rahman Baba?' The answer was simple: the same way that I learnt Pashto itself. Whenever a word came up that I did not understand, I would ask someone, anyone, what it meant. The same applied to letters of the Pashto alphabet. While I had learnt all the twenty-eight letters of the Arabic alphabet from my Baghdadi Qaida, there are a further sixteen letters in the Pashto alphabet. They also had to be learnt. That was easy. As I carried around my copy of *Futuh'al-Ghayb* or *Da Abdul Rahman Baba Dewan*, I would just ask some educated person, usually one of Majeed Khan's brothers, what a certain letter was when a strange Pashto letter turned up in the text.

There is a lot of emphasis on travelling in Islam, both to the mosque and in search of knowledge. One day, I was working in the fields with Faqi, another of Majeed's father's farmhands, when we saw an elderly gentleman stumbling by. He walked gingerly, with the aid of a stick. Faqir told me that the gentleman walked every Friday to Baba Sahib mosque, near Akbarpura, where he offered his Friday prayers. Baba Sahib must have been a good three to four miles from Masma. Such is the importance and virtue that is attached to walking to prayer. In everyday Islamic jargon, this is called taking a lot of steps to the mosque (*kasrat'al-khata ila'al-masajid*). The idea is that the further you walk to the mosque, the greater will be your reward.

One English convert to Islam whom I knew used to take this too literally. He had heard the saying 'taking a lot of steps to the mosque' so when he walked to his mosque in northern England, he would intentionally take tiny steps! Maybe he would walk round the block a few extra times also. Clearly, that is not the idea, as Mohammad Suleiman—that was the convert's name—later realized. It is not even a question of singling out a mosque that is a long way away. That would be making things difficult for oneself: something that Islam discourages. Life is difficult enough as it is. The point is to make an effort to travel to the mosque, even if it is a fair distance.

It is the same with travelling in search of knowledge. One day, soon after the time of the Prophet (peace be upon him), one of the companions of the Prophet, Abu Darda, was sitting in the mosque of Damascus when a traveller came to him, asking him to confirm a Hadith that he had heard from the Holy Prophet: 'I have come from the town, Medina, of the Prophet for no other purpose than to hear this Hadith from you,' he said. The Hadith that Abu Darda related also concerned travelling in search of knowledge: 'If anyone travels on a road in search of knowledge, Allah will cause him to travel on one of the roads of Paradise.' A person who leaves his home in search of knowledge, the Prophet said, 'is in the path of Allah until he returns.' Even the word *talib* implies travelling for the sake of acquiring knowledge. It was Hadith such as this, glorifying the status of the *talib* and singling him out as one who travels in order to seek knowledge, that gave me an affinity with the word.

My first journey in search of knowledge took me to Swat, to the village of Mulla Khalid Khan. The mulla who had administered the shahada to me was not well and would soon succumb to tuberculosis. He had returned to his own home to see out his days with his young family. The name of his village was Garhi Chupriyal. It turned out that Garhi Chupriyal was a village of mullas. There were too many mullas for them all to be able to earn a living in the village. There were two mosques, with two mullas in each mosque. Then there was the Garhi Shaykh—the most eminent scholar in Garhi Chupriyal. It was to the Garhi Shaykh that *talibs* came from far and wide to learn at his feet and to acquire knowledge. My learning was at too basic a stage for me to study with the Garhi Shaykh. Advanced students would come to him.

Mulla Khalid Khan was not an eminent enough Islamic scholar to attract students in the way the Garhi Shaykh did. Mullas like him were forced to ply their trade, for that was what being a mulla was, in the Peshawar plains. Another such mulla was Muallim sahib. He was serving as an imam in the Musazai area of Peshawar. I would sometimes meet him when I went for Friday prayers in Mahabat Khan mosque in Peshawar, where Muallim sahib also came for Friday prayers. One day, Muallim sahib took me for a walk in the hills behind Garhi Chupriyal. He looked down on the villages, the river and the tapestry of fields below: 'You see, Jan Mohammad, when these people finish eating this maize growing in their fields, then there is nothing further they can do here. They have to go to Karachi to earn their living.' For normal people, it was Karachi. For mullas like Muallim sahib, they could go nearer afield to earn their living, to Peshawar, where they became imams in mosques.

Garhi Chupriyal lies on a tributary that flows into the Swat River from the west, at Matta. I liked the *talib* life in Garhi Chupriyal. Going to the mosque every day, studying basic books of Islamic jurisprudence, revising what I had learnt. I spent some time helping Mulla Khalid Khan, as he spluttered and wheezed from his tuberculosis, collect fodder in his fields. I thought about staying in Garhi Chupriyal for a while. 'Don't even think about it,' the elder brother of Mulla Khalid Khan said to me. 'Our side of the river is not a good place to stay. It is deprived and disadvantaged.' All the attention and investment, he told me, was on the other side of the river. That was where the tourism was too.

I remembered his words many decades later, when the area around Garhi Chupriyal became a centre of radicalism and insurgency in the first decade of the new millennium. Economic deprivation had led menfolk to spend long periods in the Gulf, leaving households rudderless. A new generation of radical, hard-line imams set up radio stations and largely targeted women, promising them the rights that had been assured to them in the Qur'an. It may seem strange, but alongside the 'radio mullas' who were at the head of the Swat uprising of 2007–9, women were also at the forefront of this insurgency, even going as far as to sell their jewellery in support of the mulla-led uprising.

Signs of sectarianism were already evident in Garhi Chupriyal when I was there in the early seventies. I noticed that there were two mosques, right next to each other. Some people went to one mosque, some to the other. The Garhi Shaykh frequented the mosque that was higher up the hill. The mosque that Khalid Khan's family went to was below it, on the precipice of a cliff, with an open front overlooking the road to the town of Matta, and beyond it the river. I always wondered why there were two mosques, and if there was a need for two mosques why the two mosques were right next to each other?

I later learnt that in fact there were two strains amongst the mullas of Garhi Chupriyal. The Garhi Shaykh was one of the main ulema of a sect that was gaining strength amongst the Pashtoons, the fascinatingly named Panjpiris. The name is fascinating because Panjpiri literally means five *pirs*. This can give the impression that the sect owes allegiance to five *pirs*, in other words five spiritual mentors. In fact, this is not the case. They are called Panjpiri because they follow an Islamic scholar who is based in the village of Panjpir, close to the banks of the River Indus in the eastern part of the North-West Frontier Province.

Even though Khalid Khan did not belong to the Panjpiri faction of the village, the very fact that he was from Garhi Chupriyal meant that he had a reputation in some circles for being a Panjpiri. One person who suspected Khalid Khan of Panjpiri leanings was one of the leading members of his congregation in Masma, Haji Qayyum Khan. Often, Haji Qayyum Khan would leave the mosque after offering prayers and follow behind Khalid Khan muttering 'Panjpiri, Panjpiri'. One day I asked, 'What is this Panjpiri?' 'If you say God is one,' Khalid Khan replied with a touch of sarcasm—saying God is one is the most basic tenet of Islam, 'then you are Panjpiri.'

This was a somewhat simplistic way of looking at the controversy between Panjpiris and other Pashtoon Muslims, but it did contain a grain of truth. The popular Pashtoon custom was to practice devotion to saints. More often than not, Panjpiris considered that this devotion crossed the line of what was acceptable from an Islamic point of view. They felt that it ran counter to the duty of a Muslim to pray to one God alone. In this way, the fault lines were drawn for a great battle that was to be waged amongst the Pashtoons between Panjpiri fundamentalists and Pashtoon traditionalists. This battle was to play a great part in my life over the next few years. Indeed, this battle was to lead to the upsurge in sectarian violence that took place in Swat in the 1990s and even more catastrophically in the 2000s.

One can roughly call the Panjpiris a Pashtoon version of Wahabis. Amongst the Panjpiris, there is a streak of the Wahabi type of thinking that we are right, everyone else is wrong, we are good Muslims, everyone else is either a bad Muslim or not a Muslim at all. It is common amongst Panjpiris to call Muslims who pray to shrines idolators (*mushriks*). They consider people who go against what they consider to be the Sunna—the path of the Prophet—to be only marginally better, reserving for them the term innovators or *bid'atis*. In fact, this hard-line mentality is represented by Wahabis in Arabia, by Deobandis in India and by Panjpiris amongst Pashtoons. The difference between the three is related to the environments in which the three sects operate. Wahabis originated in the harsh environment of Najd, in the Arabian Peninsula, and are correspondingly harsh and uncompromising themselves. Deobandis operate in India, a country probably more diverse than any other in the world, in which every hue of thought can be found, so they are more mellow and tolerant than Wahabis, fitting in with every hue of contrary opinion. Incidentally, this also explains how Deobandis became more hard-line when they migrated to Pakistan. In India, Deobandis are part of the diverse and multifarious culture that is India. Pakistan being more monolithic, it tends to make people more hardline in their approach. Panjpiris, for their part, are a Pashtoon sect, tending to see things in terms of black and white. So, despite their differences of approach, all three sects have a similar ideology.

To give you an idea of the Wahabi manner of thinking, an example comes to mind from many years later, when I became imam, that we called Muslim chaplain, at Cambridge University in England. At some point I must have mentioned that I had been to Dushanbe, the capital of Tajikistan, and seen there the grave of one Yaqub Charkhi, a famous saint of Tajikistan. Except that he was not from Tajikistan at all, he was from Logar in Afghanistan.

The point I was making was that in those days, 'nation', 'tribe' and 'country' meant nothing to Muslims. An Afghan could easily come to Tajikistan and become a famous saint of that country. What was important was a person's substance, in accordance with what the Qur'an says: 'We have made you into peoples and tribes, so that you may identify yourselves to each other. The noblest of you in Allah's sight is the one who fears Allah most.' (*al-Hujurat* 49:13)

Some Wahabis at Cambridge—this was the late 1990s and there were quite a lot in those days—seized on this to say what sort of imam was I that I had gone all the way to Dushanbe to visit a grave! They cited a Hadith: 'Animals are saddled only for prayer in the three mosques: the Sacred Mosque, the Aqsa Mosque and this mosque of mine.' They were trainee doctors at Addenbroke's Hospital in Cambridge. They actually published a pamphlet on this count, condemning me, irrespective of the fact that I had not gone to Dushanbe to visit the grave of Yaqub Charkhi, I was in Dushanbe in any case, and Hadith is equally explicit on the point that visiting a grave in order to learn some positive lesson, particularly bringing to mind the life of eternity, is permissible.

The thing was, being English, they thought that I must be Sufi, or maybe of a grave-worshipping type of disposition, whereas in fact my training and upbringing as a Muslim was much more akin to their own persuasion, since I had been grounded in the Panjpiri/Deobandi tradition. That is how sectarianism—being sure one is right and everyone else is wrong, seeking division instead of seeking consensus—can seize hold of one's thinking, even in a place like Cambridge. Something along these lines, on a bigger and bloodier level, happened in Swat in the first decade of the new millennium. We will come to that later in our story, when we talk about Malala Yousafzai. All this time, I was not only studying as an apprentice *talib*, I was also farming.

I must tell you, my initiation into farming was even more painful than my initiation into Islam. It was a freezing cold December morning when I first arrived in Masma. I had spent my first night in Ashraf Khan's *hujrah*. A winter rain had set in, one of those Peshawar winter rains that go on for three or four days, depositing snow on the mountains around Peshawar and doing all but snow in Peshawar itself. That did not deter Majeed's father from summoning me first thing in the morning to accompany him to the fields. A summary nod of the head from the yard outside Ashraf Khan's *hujrah* was all that was needed. The fact that he proceeded to stalk off towards the fields meant that I was supposed to follow. He carried two cutlasses, one of which was for me to use.

These were different from the cutlasses we used to see when I was a boy in Trinidad, where I was born. With those cutlasses, the cutter would remain standing and take a swipe at long grass with a relatively long blade. The Peshawari cutlass that was thrust into my hand was much shorter. It was used with quick backward and forward movements of the right hand, while the grass that was being cut would be clasped in the left hand and then deposited with the same hand in a piece of sackcloth (*taat*) which lay alongside. It is a precise, machine-like operation, made more difficult by the fact that the mixture of clover and lucerne that one was cutting was very short during that cold, wintry time of year. There is minimal distance between the quickly moving blade and the hand with which one clasps the cattle fodder.

It is not only novices like me whose left hand gets in the way of the cutting process; it can even happen to experienced farm hands. When it does happen, a layer of skin is quickly and painfully sheared from the left hand, in which case the only available cure is to smudge wet earth on the wound. If the earth is not wet, it will soon become so as the blood oozes out of the cut. Eventually, the bleeding will stop. Later on, I was to learn that there was another even more popular cure for a cut incurred in the course of cutting lucerne. Instead of earth, apply Pashtoon snuff (*naswar*). These are the cures that farmhands in Peshawar employ. I cannot vouch for their medical soundness. Not only did my hand become lacerated by this whole exercise, I also froze stiff. When it is damp and freezing cold and one is holding wet grass, cutting it and inflicting deep wounds on oneself at the same time, one can become quite miserable. Not that Majeed's father seemed perturbed, neither on his own account nor did he spare any sympathy for me. He just carried on cutting lucerne, impervious to my predicament. He clearly had bad asthma, coupled with bronchitis, because he was continually wheezing. Along with the heavy sound of his breathing, he seemed to be reciting some incantation in time with his breathing. During the entire exercise, he never said a single word to me but was communing with his Creator without pause.

I talked to a neighbour of mine who was a serving tenant of Majeed's family about my predicament. His name was Faqir Mohammad. Babji was the name by which Majeed's father was known. '*Babji der zalim saray day,*' was Faqir Mohammad's response. I was still learning Pashto and did not know the meaning of the word *zalim*. Stupidly, I asked Majeed's brother what it meant. 'Who did you hear it from?' he asked. I told him Faqir Mohammad had called Babji a *zalim saray*. 'It means cruel,' Majeed's brother replied, clearly not best pleased with Faqir Mohammad, effectively his family's servant. One can easily trip up while learning a language and get oneself or others into trouble. Faqir's saving grace on this occasion was that the word *zalim* can be used like the word wicked in English—to express admiration. *Zalim saray* can mean he is a hard-working or accomplished man. Pashtoons even use the word for infidel (*kafir*) to express admiration and awe in some contexts. There is a joke amongst Pashtoons that a couple of guys were passing by a brand new, impressively built mosque. '*Kafir jamaat ye jor karay day.*'(What a splendid mosque they have built.) One of them said to the other, using the word kafir to describe the mosque. 'I bet they will soon bring an infidel mulla in to lead the prayers,' the other quipped. I liked this irreverent humour, which was common amongst the Pashtoons.

Farming in Peshawar is hard and gruelling work, but it was a suitable occupation for me, seeing that I had come to Islam in an attempt to harmonize myself with nature. There could be no better way of doing this than by working the earth. And it was not all blood, sweat and tears. There was no better contentment than to recite the evening prayers on the verge of one's field, looking towards the village, where layers of smoke were settling above rooftops—a sign that the evening meals were being prepared. Then slowly, and in time with the cattle, one moves towards the homestead. Really, this scene and this ambience counts amongst the greatest signs of Allah:

He has created cattle for you: from them you derive food and clothing and numerous other benefits; how pleasant they look when you bring them home in the evenings and when you take them out to pasture in the mornings. They carry your loads to places which you could otherwise not reach except with great hardship—surely your Lord is Compassionate and Merciful.

(*Al-Nahl* 16:5-7)

V

SECTARIANISM

Yet they divided themselves into factions, each rejoicing in what they had in their possession.

(*Al-Mu'minun* 23:53)

When Mulla Khalid Khan left Masma to return to his native Swat, a mulla called Bacha took over as imam in the village mosque. He was the son of the local cobbler; we used to call Bacha's dad cobbler uncle (*mochi mama*). Bacha was not yet an Islamic scholar but was studying to become one. One day, I saw him with his books perched on top of his head, as a farm hand would carry fodder for his cattle, or a woman would carry water. I asked him where he was going and why he carried his books on top of his head. 'That is a respectful way to carry one's books,' he explained, as in the highest possible place. He said he was going to nearby Nasirpur, where a great scholar lived.

I went along to check the scholar out. His name was Maulana Daim'al-Haq. You may be wondering why some imams are referred to as mulla, others maulana. Amongst the Pashtoons, there are many imams who are not really religious scholars; they are what are popularly known as mullas who have studied Khulasa (*da khulase mulayan*), the basic book of *fiqh*, as we saw in the last chapter. These mullas most probably do not know the meaning of the Qur'an but are able to recite prayers nicely, for which purpose they learn some chapters of the Qur'an (*Surah*). They are also able to teach basic Arabic text and Qur'an recitation to young children. They perform a useful function at a village level but are not qualified Islamic scholars. Bacha belonged to this category, as did Khalid Khan.

Daim'al-Haq, on the other hand, was a maulana, a fully fledged Islamic scholar, who had followed a theology course extending over eight years. Students typically complete the course in around thirteen years. A typical *talib* would study some subjects in one place, other subjects in another place, travelling to where scholars were famed for their expertise in those particular subjects. Some prefer to address such scholars as *maulvi*, either while they are pursuing their studies or after they qualify from madrasa. Besides teaching students who came to his mosque, Maulana Daim'al-Haq taught Islamic studies at a local government school. He also gave Qur'anic lectures for men in the mosque, and through the loudspeaker, for women in the home. These lectures were a feature of Pashtoon life introduced by the Panjpiris. Before the Panjpiris, there was not much emphasis placed on teaching the meaning of the Quran.

Before long, I was studying Quran, Hadith and Islamic jurisprudence with Maulana Daim'al-Haq. Daily, I would make the trek to Nasirpur, not with my books on top of my head like Bacha but under my arm. Maulana Daim'al-Haq was my first teacher belonging to the Panjpiri school of thought. He was a young man; it could not have been long since he had completed his madrasa studies. He was from the Akakhel sub-tribe of the Afridis. His original name had been Daim Gul. The Panjpiri influence had rubbed off on him even as far as his name was concerned. Daim Gul means a flower that lasts forever, so he had changed his name to Daim'al-Haq, the eternity of Truth (God), since only God could be forever. Such name changes are a typical feature of Panjpiri thinking.

Maulana Daim'al-Haq was a fully fledged Panjpiri, albeit one who had defected to the more political Jamaat-e-Islami. Besides stressing the oneness of God (*Tauhid*) as the Panjpiris did, the Jamaat-e-Islami also laid a lot of emphasis on presenting Islam as a political ideology and even seeking to set up an Islamic state. If Panjpiris were the Pashtoon equivalent of Wahabis, the Jamaat-e-Islami was the equivalent of Ikhwanis, the Muslim Brotherhood of Egypt. Maulana Maududi had set up the Jamaat-e-Islami in united India shortly before Independence and the Partition of India in 1947. His contention was that Pakistan should not just be a state for Muslims: it should be a state for the implementation of Islamic law.

On the Frontier, a number of students of the Panjpir maulana had joined the Jamaat-e-Islami, amongst them Maulana Daim'al-Haq and his elder brother, Zakir'al-Haq. This had led them to fall foul of the Panjpir maulana, who condemned political activity in the name of Islam. 'Rebellion and destruction in order to gain power.' The Panjpir maulana sahib would dismiss Islamic political activity, commonly known as Islamism. According to the Panjpir maulana, the job of an Islamic scholar was to preach the faith, not vie for political power. It was not as an Islamist but in his capacity as a renowned Islamic scholar that I was attracted to Maulana Daim'ul-Haq. Indeed, his Jamaat leanings were never a feature of his preaching and teaching. His Panjpiri streak, however, was often in evidence, for example when he was asked about this verse in a poem of Rahman Baba:

> If the form of Mohammad had not been created; God would not have created this world.

The inference is that the universe was created singly for the sake of the Prophet of Islam. 'That is nonsense,' retorted Maulana Daim'al-Haq bluntly, quoting a verse of the Qur'an (*al-Dhariyat* 51:56) that says that mankind was created not for the sake of any human being, and the Prophet was after all a human being, but in order to worship Allah. It is put another way in a Hadith Qudsi, a saying of the Prophet that quotes the words of Allah:

> *Kuntu kanzan makhfiyan fa aradtu an 'urifa, fa khalaqtu'l-khalq*

> I was a hidden treasure and I wanted to be known, so I created mankind.

This was the kind of controversy that existed between the literalist Panjpiris and the traditionalists who set a lot of store by the likes of Rahman Baba and sometimes gave what the Panjpiris considered to be excessive importance and status to the Holy Prophet and to saints.

Another poem by Rahman Baba attracted a lot of the ire of the Panjpiris. It was about saints:

> There is no bazaar, busy like the bazaar of dervishes
> In one step, they can reach the Throne of God
> I have seen the magical movement of dervishes.

However, despite my association with the Panjpiris, I never lost my affinity to Rahman Baba.

I was fascinated to know more about the Panjpir maulana himself, after whom the Panjpiri movement had been named. I built up a picture of a saintly looking man, with a flowing white silky beard, advanced in years but in robust health. That was the picture that Maulana Daim'al-Haq had painted in my mind, and that was how I found him, when finally I did meet him. I was now a fully fledged *talib* knowledge. However, the road to Panjpir village led through another region, which, as I was to discover, was a centre of Panjpiri activity: the Afridi tribal territory.

In Masma, I had befriended some Afridis, with whom I moved to Afridi territory. In truth, I could have continued my studies very well in Masma, travelling daily to Nasirpur. Daim'al-Haq would have been the perfect teacher for me for a few years. The reason I moved to the tribal territory was not to further my knowledge of Islam. The decision was made under the influence of the Afridi friends I made in Masma. Around my house in Masma lived families belonging to the Malik-Din Khel Afridi tribe. I was particularly friendly with Laiq Khan. He was the younger of two brothers. His elder brother Swat Khan was in one of the Frontier paramilitary forces that police the tribal territories. I first talked to Laiq when I was sick with dysentery. My sickness had lasted over six months, and I had become so incapacitated that I was unable to look after my buffalo and other cattle. I asked Laiq Khan, 'Would you look after my buffalo for me?' 'How much will you pay me?' came his reply. That forged the tenor of our friendship.

Until I was twenty-one, I had been quite poor. In fact, I had nothing to my name. That was a good state of affairs. Once I turned twenty-one, I inherited my share of a trust fund left to me by my maternal grandfather. He, T.P. Evelyn, was a well-to-do Jamaican businessman. I will go into the pros and cons—it is all cons really—of inheritance elsewhere. The facts speak for themselves. It was an unmitigated disaster. It all started as something that became a cliché for my love of the farming life. My parents wrote to me from England, asking me what I would like for my twenty-first birthday. I told them I would like a buffalo. That was the first chip from my inheritance. The buffalo was a disaster in every way and heralded more disaster to come.

First of all, it turned out to be a stingy buffalo. If a cow is not being cooperative when being milked, one can hold it or tie its legs and thus force it to stay still during the milking process. With a buffalo there is no way of forcing it to be compliant. You can only try and bribe it by putting some choice food in front of it while it is being milked. That choice feed is a tantalizing mixture of straw coated with bran and soaked in compressed cottonseed (*kal*). It is the buffalo equivalent of creamy muesli. It is certainly unheard of for buffaloes to refuse to be milked while being fed this choice food. But the level of stinginess, for that is the word that was used for my buffalo, to which this beast descended was such that it would forget about buffalo muesli, on some occasions it even refused to provide milk to its own calf. As for being mated, it ran a mile; we had to collect it from the other side of Nasirpur when we brought a male buffalo along in an attempt to impregnate our buffalo. My buffalo was literally wheezing with rage.

'Put a *pezwan* on it,' someone suggested. A pezwan is when you make a hole in between the buffalo's nostrils and thread a rope through there. The idea is that the buffalo will go where you lead it, but even a *pezwan* did not work with this buffalo: it would just pull with its nostrils. When it became angry, which was most of the time, it foamed and frothed at the mouth. The best thing that happened with this buffalo was when it went dry—it refused to mate so this state was inevitable—and we put the beast out of its misery by selling it to the butcher.

Instead of becoming a picture of health on account of the milk and yogurt that the buffalo provided, what there was of its produce made me sick with dysentery. The dysentery lasted seven months. Sometimes I was so weak I would faint. I became like a skeleton. I tried every sort of cure: herbal remedies, navel readjustment therapy, amulets and spells. I was wearing an amulet when I finally went to Prime Minister Zulfikar Ali Bhutto's private physician in Peshawar, Dr Raza Ali Khan. Dr Raza saw the amulet around my waist: 'When in Rome, do as the Romans do,' he quipped. The three medicines that Dr Raza Prescribed: Guanamycin, Flagyl and Lomotil; and the diet that he recommended cured me overnight. I have always been a believer in herbal medicine, but at times when it fails, it is good to be able to resort to the modern equivalent.

It was during my sickness that I approached Laiq to look after my buffalo. His family being my immediate neighbours— like me, tenants of Majeed's family—Laiq could see that I had come into money. He could also see that it was Majeed's family who were benefiting from my wealth. Systematically, he started doing them down while praising his own country, Tirah, by promoting the cool summers, the warm, hospitable, big-hearted people, the forests, he made it sound like heaven on earth. I was easy prey for his machinations. In their good-natured way, some Panjpiri *talibs* made fun of me. Lahiq and Mulhiq they called Laiq and myself in an Arabic play of words on Laiq's name. The words Lahiq and Mulhiq mean attached to each other. Well, Lahiq and Mulhiq hatched a plan to move to the Afridi territory.

The first place we moved to was Bara, the first town that one comes across as one enters Khyber Agency, the independent tribal territory, some six miles south of Peshawar. There, we set up a shop together. 'You left Masma like a thief,' Majeed's brother wrote to me in a letter. Mir Ahmad's elder brother Fazl'ur-Rahman came to Bara to try and rescue me and take me back to Masma. That was kind and thoughtful of him. Laiq told Fazl'ur-Rahman that I was bethrothed to his younger sister. There was not much Fazl'ur-Rahman could say to that as the matter was done and dusted. Laiq had indeed told me that he had agreed for his 'flower of a sister' to be engaged to me, though I had never popped the question. As the Panjpiri maulvi who coined the phrase Lahiq and Mulhiq said to me later, 'You acted like a couple of boys who go off together, not listening to what anyone says.'

Luckily, my studies were not adversely affected by the rush of blood to my head that triggered my move to Bara. It helped that Maulana Daim'al-Haq's predecessor in Nasirpur, Maulana Zakariya, who hailed from Kunar in eastern Afghanistan, had moved to Bara after leaving Nasirpur. I tracked him down. He was a lean and good-looking man in his late thirties. As yet not a strand of grey had appeared in his long locks and beard. He had a look of gravitas, a craggy visage quite typical of Pashtoons; an appearance somehow reflecting the rugged landscape of their country. The leanness of Maulana Zakariya enabled him to walk very fast. A year or two later, I remember walking with the chief (*amir*) of the Bara Panjpiris, Abdul Majeed, and Maulana Zakariya towards the village of Panjpir. Maulana Zakariya was walking ahead of everyone else. 'He has no weight to carry, that is why he can walk so fast,' commented Abdul Majeed, who himself carried quite a bit of weight. Being lean and not carrying an ounce of extra weight myself, I always think of Maulana Zakariya when striding ahead of others at a brisk pace.

At the head of the six Bara markets, laid out block-by- block, stands the Bara mosque. Now it is a grand mosque, the biggest in the area. Then it was a modest edifice. The Panjpiris of Bara would assemble in that mosque for Qur'an lessons but would avoid the mosque for prayer. They considered the imam of the mosque—a likeable enough mulla from Afghanistan who was a good preacher—to be an innovator (*bid'ati*) and would not pray behind him. I was puzzled by the Panjpiris' refusal to follow imams such as the Bara imam in prayer. After all, the Holy Prophet had said that 'prayer is a necessary duty for you behind any Muslim, pious or impious, even if he commits heinous sins.' When I put this to the Panjpiris and asked them how they could justify not following this imam in prayer in the light of this Hadith, they said that the Hadith referred to a sinner, it did not refer to an innovator. Scriptures, I have found, are like statistics: one can use them to prove or disprove just about anything. One needs to be sincere with regard to the scriptures in order to grasp the correct meaning. They are so easily manipulated and moulded to mean whatever one wants them to.

I had not realized, before I arrived there, what a centre of the Panjpiri sect Bara was. They had their own structure, with a chief of their own. Panjpiris would explain away multiple sayings of the Holy Prophet stressing the importance of sticking to the community by saying that they themselves were the community: people should not separate from them. It was not they who had separated from the community. It was the community that had become separate from them: the true community and the true Muslims. The same is the case with every sect. They always maintain that they are not just a sect: they are THE sect. This tendency to split up into groups, when the Qur'an has encouraged Muslims to stick together: 'Hold fast to the rope of Allah and let nothing divide you.' (*al-Imran* 3:103) is down to a large extent to the Pashtoon habit of *dalla-bazi*: the Pashto equivalent of gang culture, literally forming a group around oneself.

The chief of the Bara Panjpiris was Abdul Majeed, appointed directly by the Panjpir maulana. He was from the Malik-Din Khel tribe—the largest and most powerful of the eight Afridi tribes. He was a nice looking, jovial, amiable man with a tailor's shop in Bara. I will always remember my first Friday in Bara. Abdul Majeed was beaming, he could not contain his joy at my arrival in Bara. He took me to a mosque where Panjpiris prayed in the lower Bara bazaar. Abdul Majeed was a tailor-master, which meant that he did not actually sew clothes, he just cut the cloth for tailoring. He sat on his counter cross-legged, cutting cloth, while his apprentices and assistants sewed busily on their machines. From his counter, he would communicate the Panjpiri message of pure oneness of the Godhead (*Tawhid*) to his customers. He did so in a good-natured, endearing and highly persuasive manner.

He was a good deal more tactful than his assistant, the organizer (*nazim*) of the Panjpiris in Bara, Samar Gul. Samar Gul hailed from the affluent Upper Qambar Khel sub-tribe of the Afridis. A man of considerable charm, intellect and persuasive powers, he also had a caustic tongue and was quite extreme in his Panjpiri views. Of all the Panjpiris, he took to me the most, which was probably not entirely to my advantage. When Maulana Daim-ul-Haq first visited me in Bara, naturally I welcomed and honoured him as my first Qur'an teacher and also as the teacher who had introduced me to the thought of the Panjpir maulana sahib. I introduced my teacher to Samar Gul. Samar Gul looked at him with a frown on his face and half offered his hand in a cold greeting. 'Why were you so unfriendly?' I asked. 'Because he has given up the membership of our party,' Samar Gul replied. He was referring, of course, to Maulana Daim'al-Haq's joining of the Jamaat-e-Islami.

That was how powerful the *dalla-bazi* group mentality was amongst the Panjpiris. This mentality took precedence over verses of the Qur'an that encourage Muslims to harbour no rancour towards other Muslims (*al-Hashr* 59:10). There are a series of verses in the third *Surah* of the Qur'an encouraging unity amongst Muslims. They start with the verse that I have already quoted, 'hold fast to the rope of Allah and let nothing divide you (*al-Imran* 3:103)'. Amazingly, the Panjpiris took these verses to be justification and even guidance for establishing their own sect: *tasees'al-jamaah*, or forming of your own party they called it. One thing I have learnt from my experiences over the years is that if one is working for the upliftment of Muslims and the revival of true faith, one should do this on an individual level. One should never give a name to any group of people that have gathered with a united sense of purpose. When one has given one's group a name and formed one's own party, then one has gone down the road of sectarianism. We are Muslims, nothing more, nothing less: 'He named you Muslims—those who have surrendered themselves to Allah—in this, as in previous Scriptures.' (*al-Hajj* 22:78)

Another thing I have noticed is that once one has made one's own group, then the process of separating oneself from the main Muslim community leads to no end to the quantity of splits that can take place. Like many of his fellow Panjpiris, Samar Gul later went from being Panjpiri to being out-and-out Wahabi (*ghair muqallid*) in other words not following any of the four established schools of thought.[1] As time went on, I saw that when religious people

[1] *Hanafi, Shafi'i, Maliki, Hanbali:* the four schools of Sunni jurisprudence.

amongst the Pashtoons adopted *dalla-bazi*, it became even more extreme. Recently, the same has been the case with other Pashtoon customs, notably revenge and refuge. Such customs, instead of being ameliorated and reformed in the hands of religious people, have only become more extreme. Perhaps this is because, with religious people, these customs are given religious sanction. Islam should be there to temper the extremities of Pashtoonwali, not to make them more extreme!

One day, my old friend from Kalam, Abdul Hadi né Kenneth Honerkamp, visited me in Bara. Like me, he too had become a *talib*. He had also befriended the Panjpiris. Let me say that for serious students of Islam like Abdul Hadi and myself, it was natural to team up with the Panjpiris. They were the ones who were serious about studying the Book of Allah, as they endearingly referred to the Qur'an, and the science of Hadith. Abdul Hadi was a real student, much more scholarly and academically minded than I was. Later on, he became professor of Arabic at the University of Athens in Georgia, USA. Now he came to see me in Bara along with some of his *talib* friends. They were studying with the Sarkai maulvi sahib, a famous scholar from Swat who resided near Sakhakot, in the foothills of Swat. The Sarkai maulvi sahib was in fact from the town of Durushkhela in Swat, where he had been a well-to-do landowner. He felt that he was unable to dedicate himself to the teaching of Islamic sciences if he was always worrying about his land and other such worldly matters in his native village, so he came to Sakhakot. There, he lived for the most part under the patronage of Malik Rahat Khan of Sakhakot.

Later on, I had the privilege of meeting Rahat Khan several times. Amongst all those I have met, he was one person who combined the best of Islamic virtues—piety, humility and service of the *ulema*—with the best of Pashtoonwali—egalitarianism, generosity, patriotism. Malik Rahat Khan was an old Khudai Khidmatgar. The phrase means servant for the sake of God, not servant of God as it is often erroneously translated. The Khudai Khidmatgars were followers of Khan Abdul Ghaffar Khan, also known as the Frontier Gandhi due to his commitment to non- violence in the struggle for the independence of India. Amongst those who benefited from the service of Malik Rahat Khan were Islamic scholars. It was not only the Sarkai maulvi sahib who lived under his patronage and enjoyed his friendship and respect. Maulana Uzair Gul of the Miangano village near Sakhakot, just like Khan Abdul Ghaffar Khan, another central figure in our unfolding story, and Maulana Mohammad Ahmad, principal of the madrasa in Sher Garh, the next town along the road from Sakhakot towards Mardan, were other *ulema* with whom he was close and enjoyed a fruitful, mutually respectful relationship.

Malik Rahat Khan belied the idea that Pashtoon nationalists might somehow be anti-Islamic, or that Pashtoon nationalism might be inimical to Islam. This idea partly comes from the close association of Ghaffar Khan, the leader of Pashtoon nationalists, with Mahatma Gandhi and from Ghaffar Khan's affinity with India. His opponents took this as a sign that he had sold out to Hindus. One only had to take one look at Malik Rahat Khan to see that this was not the case. Rahat Khan was a true egalitarian Pashtoon who sat on the floor to partake of food with his household staff and tenant farmers, just as he stood with them to pray in one line. Both his Pashtoon character and his Islamic faith imbued him with deep humility. From the perspective of religious scholars, the Sarkai maulvi sahib also represented a balance between Pashtoon patriotism and Islamic scholarship. Indeed, amongst this select group of scholars— nationalists as well as scholars of Islam—was the Panjpir maulvi sahib himself. That is the way it should be. To eliminate extremism on both sides of the political and ideological divide amongst Pashtoons there have to be religious scholars who are also Pashtoon patriots, nationalists who are also lovers of the ulema. People like the Sarkai maulvi sahib on one side, Rahat Khan on the other.

It is to the credit of elders such as the Sarkai and Panjpir maulvi sahibs, as religious figures, that they did not lurch towards the extreme of seeing Pashtoon nationalism as anathema. They were balanced personalities, combining both national and religious values. However, some of the next generation did become extremist. On one occasion some Panjpiri students of the Sarkai maulvi sahib burnt down the shrine of Doda Baba, near Sarkai. This act predictably resulted in outrage. In fact, the situation became critical for the Sarkai maulvi sahib. According to Abdul Hadi, the Sarkai maulvi sahib did not know about the attack, nor did he condone it. But it was he who had to shoulder the blame. Equally predictably, it was Malik Rahat Khan who defused the situation by holding a tribal meeting (*jirga*) and arranging for the rebuilding of the shrine. That was something that only he could do, with his unique standing as a Pashtoon leader and as a man of deep faith. It is men like Malik Rahat Khan, one of the closest followers of the Frontier Gandhi Khan Abdul Ghaffar Khan, servant of men for the sake of God, friend of the *ulema*, and Pashtoon patriot par excellence, who are needed amongst the Pashtoons today.

VI

A TALIB'S TRADE

The best provision is that which one has worked for, with the labour of one's own hands.

(Hadith)

1973

I owe a lot to Maulana Khan Afzal, but two things in particular. For one, he instilled in me a love of India. Secondly, he showed me practically that one should always work for one's living.

When I said to Samar Gul in Bara that I was going to the Afridi heartland of Tirah Maidan, he immediately mentioned Khan Afzal. Laiq's family had some land in Tirah, and he and I had decided to move there for the summer. 'That is great,' Samar Gul said, 'you will be able to study with Maulana Khan Afzal.' Like the Sarkai maulvi sahib, Maulana Khan Afzal was an eminent scholar, but at the time he did not have any students residing with him. He was able to devote all his time to tutoring me. I believe it was largely because Tirah was so inaccessible that there were no other students studying with the maulana. Later on, in the late nineties when I visited Maulana Khan Afzal again, he had a good ten to twelve students studying with him. He had become a focal point for *talibs*, as the Sarkai maulvi sahib had been in the 1970s.

Every day, with my books under my arm, I would make the forty-five-minute walk from Saddar Khel, where Laiq lived, to Landi Kas. Tirah Maidan is a huge, expansive plateau, the like of which there are many in Afghanistan; the Gardez and Logar plateaus are two that spring to mind. The difference with Tirah Maidan is that it is surrounded by richly forested hills, while the hills that surround other Afghan plateaus are mostly bare. Two tributaries of the Bara river meet at the centre of Tirah Maidan, the Malik-Din Khel Bagh. It is the natural capital of Tirah Maidan. The land dips towards that point, as do the streams and the people. From the eastern side, live the tribes of Zakha Khel and the Lower Qambar Khels, known as Shalobaris; on the western side is the huge swathe of Malik-Din Khel territory, and beyond that the Upper Qambar Khels. From Saddar Khel, I would walk down towards the Malik-Din Khel Bagh, then fork right towards Landi Kas, tucked in a hillside between Bagh and Dunga, in Sholobar territory.

I had been studying a Sufi type of Hadith collection entitled *The Path of the Righteous* (*Riyadh'as-Saliheen*). I say it was Sufi oriented as it was mostly organized according to the virtues that Sufis strive to attain: repentance, patience, sincerity, trust in Allah and steadfastness. It is very spiritually oriented. I am glad I began my study of Hadith with this book. It has remained my favourite collection of Hadith; it is extremely cleansing and refreshing. However, Khan Afzal switched me to the more mainstream and standard *Mishkat'al-Masabih*. This book is arranged more conventionally, according to the various strands of jurisprudence: prayer, fasting and the other forms of worship or interaction with Allah (*ibadat*) followed by one's dealings with other human beings (*muamilat*). In the entire Islamic canon, there is this distinction between the rights of Allah (*huqooq'Allah*) and the rights of one's fellow beings, indeed of all Allah's creatures (*huqooq'al-ibad*). While in Hadith study Khan Afzal went for the more orthodox *Mishkat*, in jurisprudence, his choice of book for my study was distinctly unorthodox. His preference was *Taaleem'al-Islam*, written in Urdu by his own teacher, Mufti Kefayatullah of Delhi. 'Along with learning Islamic jurisprudence (*fiqh*) you will learn Urdu,' he recommended. For *Taaleem'al-Islam* I went outside with his elder son Abdul Hakeem, then a teenager. I guess Abdul Hakeem felt more comfortable teaching me with his father not immediately on hand. We sat on the verge of the field, had a laugh and chatted a lot, while at the same time also reading *Taaleem'al-Islam*.

In encouraging me to learn Urdu, it was as though the maulana had a premonition or was goading me in the direction of study in India. It had not been that long, maybe twenty or twenty-five years, since he had returned from studying in the Aminiya madrasa in Delhi. India had rubbed off on him to a considerable degree, in a way making him an unusual Afridi. He even continued to wear a skirt-like garment favoured by Muslims of India (*lungi*) at home. Pashtoons generally consider this garment effeminate. Even the maulana would not be seen in that garment outside the home. I have replicated Maulana Khan Afzal in this regard. Even when I am in Afghanistan I wear a *lungi* in my place of residence; when I am in north India, I wear my *lungi* a little further afield, as far as the local shops; when I am in south India, I wear a *lungi* pretty much all the time. At the time when I was studying with the maulana, I used to ask him a lot about India. In a memorable phrase, he once told me that 'even the dogs of India have manly virtues.' 'What's Delhi like, compared to Peshawar?' I once asked. 'What is Hangu like compared to Peshawar?' he asked rhetorically, referring to a town in the Frontier province, where buses set out towards Tirah. I answered that it was just a tiny town by comparison to Peshawar. 'Well, so is Peshawar tiny compared to Delhi.'

Yet at the same time the maulana was the most staunchly Afridi of all the Panjpiris. He absolutely loved his native Tirah. I am getting ahead of myself here, but when he was expelled from Tirah along with other Panjpiris and resided for a while in Peshawar, he pined for his motherland so much that he used to console himself by reciting poems written by those who had emigrated from Mecca to Medina at the time of the Holy Prophet (*muhajirs*) who sought to express their homesickness for Mecca. He was also invariably cordial with his fellow Afridis, irrespective of whether they subscribed to his Panjpiri views or not. I never saw him take issue or argue with anyone about matters of dogma. He would enact his duties as the pre-eminent Islamic scholar in Tirah Maidan, in the course of which he would explain how important it was to believe in the oneness of Allah and to follow the Sunna of the Holy Prophet. These two things—*Tauhid* and *Sunna*—are the twin pillars on which Panjpiri dogma is founded. But he would never become aggressive towards those who did not subscribe to Panjpiri beliefs.

When I arrived in Tirah in 1973, the influence of scholars who had studied in India was still palpable. Maulana Khan Afzal was not the only scholar in Tirah who had graduated from India prior to Partition. Another was Maulana Sifat Shah. 'He is an Islamic scholar of great depth,' Maulana Khan Afzal said of Maulana Sifat Shah. Sifat Shah was heavy in physique also, a striking looking man with a full, flaming hennaed beard. At the same time, Maulana Khan Afzal had a word of criticism for him: 'He is not paying attention to his teaching duties.' To Maulana Khan Afzal, the life of an Islamic scholar was supposed to be one of balance between imparting Islamic knowledge and working for a living. Maulana Sifat Shah had tended towards preoccupation with making a living. He had bought himself a male buffalo (*sanda* in Pashto) and used to bring timber from the forest. It was true that he spent little or no time imparting knowledge, though I am sure he did so to his own family members and to those with whom he came into contact, through his gentle character and sense of gravitas.

Scholars such as Sifat Shah, who were of a Deobandi/ Panjpiri persuasion, laid a lot of emphasis on working for their living as opposed to living on handouts, which is possible for a mulla, but does not constitute a very dignified livelihood. Besides, it means the scholar is obliged to those whom he is supposed to be in a position to admonish. Maulana Khan Afzal was the same: openly insistent on working with the labour of his own hand. He had a flourishing practice in homeopathic medicine. On Fridays, he would set up his stall at the Friday market of Tirah, known as Bagh. Scholars such as Sifat Shah and Khan Afzal believed that for their credibility and authority as well as their self-respect to be intact, they should not be dependent on anyone but should be self-sufficient. The Prophet laid a lot of stress on maintaining this balance between worldly and religious pursuits and not turning one's faith into a source of earning.

Laiq Khan was petrified of two people: in Tirah, Maulana Khan Afzal and in Bara, Samar Gul. These were the two people who were closest to me. He was worried that they would tell it like it was as far as his own intentions were concerned. Once, Samar Gul took me inside his home to meet his womenfolk. It was just a short, perfunctory meeting. They must have been so inquisitive about this Englishman who was studying with their husband. Not only studying, as after a while Laiq and I had left our shop next to the bus stop in Bara and had joined Samar Gul in his watch shop. Laiq Khan got wind of fact that I had been inside Samar Gul's home—it was a rare privilege for an outsider to be introduced to an Afridi's womenfolk. He suspected that Samar Gul was trying to win me over to his inner circle. He became very wary of me becoming too close to my Panjpiri friends. The same applied, even more, to Maulana Khan Afzal. Whenever any disagreement arose between Laiq and myself, he openly said to me that he felt my teacher was egging me on.

In fact, never once did Maulana Khan Afzal speak to me against Laiq and his family. Neither, for that matter, did Samar Gul. It would not have done any good, in any case. As a Panjpiri friend had mentioned, I did not listen to anyone. Even my mother, thousands of miles away in England, said the same thing when someone did eventually pull me to my senses, 'Johnny, I am so glad there was someone you listened to.' Once, when I was on my way to Peshawar for some reason with Laiq, Maulana Khan Afzal took me aside and said to me, 'If you have five rupees to your name, do not trust even me with it.' Of course, he was talking figuratively. He did not wish to speak directly against the Afridi friends I had made in Masma, with whom I had come to Tirah. But he could see they were exploiting me to wrest my inheritance money from me. Later on, when I had wasted all my inheritance and started working for my living, I realized that it would have been much better for me to have foregone my inheritance from the very beginning. But there are some lessons one has to learn the hard way.

Islam is quite clear on this matter: 'A Muslim may not inherit from a non-Muslim, or a non-Muslim from a Muslim.' Islam teaches us that one is much more likely to be grateful for one's wealth if it is earned 'by the labour of one's own hands', as the Holy Prophet put it. One is also more likely to spend one's wealth wisely and not be extravagant—another requirement of an Islamic lifestyle—if one has worked hard for one's money. Is any inheritance then a dangerous thing? To my mind, yes, it is. I sympathize with those tycoons who have worked hard to accumulate their wealth but do not wish to pass it on to their children, preferring them to work hard for a living, as they themselves have done. In my life, I have thrived when I've worked for my living, as Maulana Khan Afzal taught me to do. When I relied on my inheritance, I suffered and scuppered my wealth. When I have worked hard for my money, I have been careful how I spend it.

1978

Maulana Khan Afzal's premonition, of my move to India for my studies, came true five years after I studied with him. Naturally, I often thought of him when I finally made my way to Darul Uloom Deoband in India to pursue my Islamic studies. For several years I supported myself while in India by plying a cross-border trade between India and Pakistan. I could not have done this without assistance from a Muslim convert from New Zealand who was also studying in Deoband. His name was Abdul Hadi.

'He is a noble man and he will help you in every way,' a Fijian *talib* who was studying in Jamia Ashrafia in Lahore told me, as I made my way from Peshawar to Darul Uloom Deoband. Abdul Hadi had become Muslim under the guidance of Maulana Abu'l-Hasan Ali Nadwi. Known as Ali Mian throughout the Muslim world, Maulana Nadwi is the only notable Muslim scholar about whom I have never heard anyone—no person nor sect—say a bad word. Hailing from Nadwat'al-Uloom, that along with Deoband, is the other great centre of Islamic learning in northern India, he was close to the Wahabi Saudis. While the Saudis had a lot of respect for Maulana Ali Mian, so did people who were completely on the other side of the Islamic spectrum from the Saudis.

Soon after Ali Mian's death at the beginning of the new millennium, I had occasion to visit the Mir-e-Arab madrasa in Bukhara, Uzbekistan. Teachers there told me how Ali Mian had visited their madrasa not so long ago. He was a frequent visitor, in fact. 'He passed away a few months ago,' I told them. I felt privileged that in the historic madrasa of Mir-e-Arab, they were hearing this momentous news of Ali Mian's passing from me. The news was rendered even more significant when I explained to them that he had passed away on the very first day of the new millennium, which was equivalent to the 23rd of Ramadan—known as the Night of Power (*Laylat'al-Qadr*) amongst Muslims. This confirmed the belief of the scholars of Bukhara that Maulana Ali Mian had indeed been a *mujaddid.* A *mujaddid* is just one notch down from a prophet. He or she is sent by Allah in the course of every one hundred years to renew and refresh the Islamic faith. The word *mujaddid* means renewer. That was Ali Mian's unique achievement. He was able to appeal both to Saudi Wahabis and orthodox Hanafis such as those in the Mir-e-Arab madrasa.

Once I arrived in Deoband, I sought out Abdul Hadi, as the Fijian *talib* in Lahore had suggested. At the time, Deoband especially, but to a lesser extent other madrasas founded by Deobandi *ulema* in Pakistan—Jamiya Ashrafia in Lahore and New Town madrasa in Karachi—were magnets for foreign students, mainly those of Indian origin coming from South Africa, Zambia and the West Indies. Nowadays, that generation of *ulema* has established madrasas of their own, notably in South Africa, and there is next to no influx of students to South Asia from abroad. At that time, however, there were plenty, though Abdul Hadi and I were the only Anglo-Saxons amongst them. I found Abdul Hadi in room number five in Ehata Bagh, an enclave of private rooms set aside for foreign students. The room was tiny, more like a cell. It had enough room for Abdul Hadi to sleep in and a little burrow where he kept his primus stove. His speciality was to brew Bournvita every night.

'I have become habitual,' he explained. 'If I do not have my night-cap, I cannot sleep well.' Those were the days when one could not find a single item of foreign origin in India. It was all 'be Indian, buy Indian'. One did not have any choice. Items like Bournvita, which were made in India under a foreign licence, were much sought after.

Abdul Hadi was thrilled to have another European student with him in Deoband. He was a forceful personality and immediately introduced me to every teacher in Deoband, right up to the venerated rector (*muhtamim*) Qari Tayyib. 'Qari sahib, this is Jan Mohammad. He is of English origin and has been studying in the Frontier. Now he has come to study in Darul Uloom.' Only he would have the temerity to walk up to Qari sahib and talk to him like that and get away with it. He was so confident that he did not care about his somewhat incoherent Urdu. I had only learnt a bit of bookish Urdu from books such as *Taaleem'al-Islam*. I could not yet converse in the language, so I spoke to all the teachers in Farsi. They loved that. In the not-so-distant past, as long as the Mughal Empire had held sway in Delhi, Farsi had been the court language of northern India. As is detailed above, Shah Waliullah of Delhi had written his translation of the Qur'an in Farsi. The Pashtoon-accented Farsi that I had acquired in Kabul took the teachers of Deoband back to a time, prior to 1947, when they used to speak Farsi to *talibs* from Afghanistan. Every Afghan *talib* aspires to go to Deoband. Prior to Partition, they used to do so. Despite Abdul Hadi introducing me as an Englishman, most of the teachers in Deoband thought I was Pashtoon: my appearance, my speech, seemed to suggest that. They may have been baffled with regard to my nationality, but English or Afghan, they were pleased to have me in Deoband.

Abdul Hadi did not only introduce me to his teachers. Like me, he had to support himself in his studies. He was doing this by conducting cross-border trade between India and Pakistan. I noticed Abdul Hadi going round with a flash, leather attaché case. 'This is left over from one consignment of suitcases and attaché cases that I took to Pakistan,' Abdul Hadi told me. In Pakistan, you could only find foreign suitcases made by companies such as Samsonite.

'Here in India,' Abdul Hadi explained, 'Samsonite make their own suitcases, right up to international standards, but at a fraction of the price of a Samsonite made in Europe or America, so you can sell them in Pakistan at a handsome profit, and still much less than the price of a foreign-made Samsonite in Pakistan.' Suitcases and attaché cases were not the only items that Abdul Hadi took to sell across the border. Natural perfumes (*attar*), Islamic books and prayer mats were some of the other items in his repertoire. Not only did he have the chain of supply worked out in India, he also knew exactly where to sell every item in Pakistan.

If Khan Afzal was my inspiration as far as plying a trade and working for my living was concerned, Abdul Hadi was my hands-on guide. We were like a modern version of Sindbad the sailor, buying goods in one place that would sell well elsewhere. One of our favourite items to sell in Pakistan was betel leaf (*paan*), much loved in Pakistan Punjab, but only available in India. *Paan* was one of the most profitable items we took to Pakistan. We would take our *paan* straight to a *paan*-seller close to Muslim Masjid in Anarkali in Lahore and collect the cash—four or five times the amount I had paid for it in India. The *paan*-seller would be beaming when he saw me approaching from a distance, coming down Anarkali. I was beaming too. And the business was not one-way. We would bring stuff from Pakistan to sell in India. Polyester cloth from Pakistan was a great favourite in those days, in particular the blue and white colours that girls in Deoband would wear for school. Watches and calculators were popular too. Mufflers went down extremely well in winter. I only needed to stand on the streets in Amritsar for about half an hour, with a few mufflers flung over my shoulder and dangling from my arms. Sardarjis would pay a good price for these mufflers. They would be gone in no time. Foreign items were in big demand in India.

My cross-border business benefited from my access to Bara, near Peshawar. Bara was a duty-free bazaar, at that time supplying the whole of northern Pakistan. The Afridis are legendary businessmen. Afghanistan being a landlocked country, all merchandise destined for Afghanistan came via the seaport of Karachi. From there, it was loaded onto the Khyber Mail, destined for Peshawar.

At Peshawar, it was offloaded and put onto trucks, marked for traders in Kabul. In fact, much of it was not meant for those Kabul traders at all. They had done deals with Bara shopkeepers whereby their names and address would be on the cartons but once the cartons reached the Afridi tribal territory, they would be diverted to Bara instead of Kabul. That was how the Afridis exploited the transit trade between Karachi and Kabul. They ensured that it was not transit at all. It got stuck in their independent tribal territory, where they established a posh duty-free bazaar, more resembling Kuwait than a run-down tribal town.

These Bara shopkeepers then employed *ganda-wallas*, literally people who made little bundles by tying knots in handkerchiefs, Dick Whittington style. It was their job to take these little bundles down country, to Pindi and Lahore. I was also like a *ganda-walla*, only I was taking the bundles a little further than Lahore, to Amritsar and Delhi. Both Abdul Hadi and I were lucky to have Commonwealth passports. Abdul Hadi had a New Zealand passport and I of course had a British one. In those days, no visa was required for either India or Pakistan for Commonwealth citizens. 'As far as I am concerned, the Partition of India has not even happened,' I would sometimes boast.[1]

Later on, Abdul Hadi left Deoband and continued his studies at Jamia Ashrafia in Lahore. I continued doing the cross-border business on my own. I once took a whole bundle of *paan* to Lahore. I was carrying the *paan* Pashtoon-style in my *chadar*. A chadar is the sheet that Pashtoons use to cover themselves, keep themselves warm and pray on. Before the days of plastic bags, Pashtoons used to be expert at tying the corners of their sheets to form little bundles, containing separate items of shopping. However, I was not as expert at this as the Pashtoons were. I had just dumped the sack of *paan* into my chadar and slung it over my back, without even tying a knot. I had already caught sight of the shopkeeper near Muslim Masjid when I

---

[1] I must hasten to add that boasting is a really disastrous course of action, according to Islamic tradition. Whenever talking about any boon, with regard to oneself or any near and dear one, one should always say: 'Masha Allah'—that which Allah wishes will come to pass. (*al-Kahf* 18:39)

heard a shout from behind me: 'Jan Mohammad!' There to my surprise was Abdul Hadi. In between Abdul Hadi and myself, along a considerable stretch of Anarkali, was a trail of *paan* that had fallen out of my improvised bundle. I set about picking up one piece of my contraband at a time, as locals looked disapprovingly at me.

Travelling westwards, the main outlet for my merchandise was Peshawar. Once, I took a healthy amount of *attar* and eye-shadow used by both men and women in the Muslim world (*surma*) to a mosque near Peshawar where Shaykh'al-Qur'an was giving a speech. Shaykh'al-Quran, or the great teacher of the Qur'an, was the Panjpir maulana sahib with whom I was later to study. Little did I know that the Hezb-e-Islami leader Gulbuddin Hekmatyar would also be attending the speech. Hekmatyar used to work a lot for Shaykh'al-Qur'an, due to the influence the latter had with mullas in Afghanistan. He wanted to persuade Shaykh'al-Qur'an to prevail upon his followers to support Hekmatyar's party. Though many Panjpiris did throw in their lot with Hekmatyar, Shaykh'al-Qur'an himself had no interest in encouraging this trend. I also had no interest in joining the melee and meetings inside the mosque. I was only interested in making use of the opportunity to sell my merchandise. As Hekmatyar's bodyguards kept watch with their guns on top of the mosque, I sat on my mat next to the door of the mosque, carefully transferring the contents of my decanters of perfumes into tiny bottles, which I could then sell at a healthy profit. Hekmatyar's crowd also showed an interest in my wares. Just as foreign items were in high demand in India, so merchandise from India, in particular items, such as its pure *attar*, went down well in Peshawar, part of the attraction of such items being their rarity.

Teachers at Deoband were pleased when they heard that I was supporting myself in my studies by doing business, trade or just plain smuggling (*tijarat*). Imam Abu Hanifa had also supported himself by doing *tijarat* while he was studying, so I was told. *Tijarat* has always been a favoured occupation of Muslims. As a young man, the Holy Prophet used to accompany his uncle Abu Talib on business trips to Syria. The Holy Prophet's first wife Khadija was a businesswoman. Pashtoons in particular have adopted this tradition. As a tribal Pashtoon once put it to me, Pashtoons will forge a tunnel through a mountain in order to transport their merchandise to the desired place. Indeed, tribal Pashtoons used to call smuggling 'defence'. It was as if this was their means of defending their independence.

The business that Abdul Hadi and I did together was not on a grand scale, but still I accumulated a healthy bank balance and opened an account at the Punjab National Bank in Deoband. I once left my chequebook with Khalid, a South African student who attended to Mufti Mahmud'al-Hasan. Mufti Mahmud was the great Deobandi mufti of his day. He lived in the Chhatta Wali Masjid—the mosque where his namesake Shaykh'al- Hind Mahmud'al-Hasan was taught the first lesson in the history of Deoband. More than anyone, Mufti Mahmud'al- Hasan embodied the Deoband spirit: deep piety and gnosis, allied with an encyclopaedic knowledge of Islamic jurisprudence. He was both a Sufi Shaykh—his gatherings every afternoon concentrated on self-purification and improvement—and the senior-most mufti in Deoband. Khalid had dedicated his time to the service of Mufti sahib, who was now ageing and almost blind. On receiving my chequebook, Khalid, who admittedly was exceptionally ascetic for a foreign student, was aghast at what a big bank balance I had. 'Wow, you have that much money in the bank?' 'I do,' I admitted. It was only a few thousand rupees, and it had been earned from the labour of my own hand, but to Khalid it seemed like a huge amount.

We would have done well to have kept our business on a small scale, just enough to keep us going in our studies. But as is so often the case in these matters, we became greedy and started shipping more merchandise than we really needed to. On one occasion, we heard that a disciple of the rector of Deoband Qari Tayyib was in charge of customs on the Pakistan Wagah border. On this occasion, two or three South African students were travelling with me. I had given each of them a suitcase full of our usual kind of merchandise. Of course, the customs officer on the Pakistan side let us through, since we were students at the famed Darul Uloom, presided over by his *pir*. But he came out of his office and looked suspiciously at our bags. I felt ashamed. I was aware that the incident did not present Darul Uloom in the best light.

Abdul Hadi had by this time moved to Lahore. It seems he became more interested in business than study. Even the senior administrator at the Jamia Ashrafia where he was enrolled wondered out loud why he had forsaken Darul Uloom Deoband for Jamia Ashrafia. 'Jamia Ashrafia is silver, Deoband is gold,' I concurred with the *nazim*, who nodded his head in agreement. In fact, Abdul Hadi had never been of a very academic bent. Talking about gold, I heard down the grapevine that Abdul Hadi had narrowly escaped arrest in Lahore for possession of a considerable amount of the precious metal. Though my business did not extend to that commodity, I also became greedy and on one occasion was caught transporting too much cloth, plus watches, calculators and mufflers from Lahore to India. Indian customs officials at Wagah border stopped me. 'You are trying to make a fool of us,' the Sikh customs officer sternly told me. I was ordered to take the merchandise back to Lahore. I did so and did not make another business trip.

When one door closes, another opens. I am indebted also to Abdul Hadi for the opening of this second door. When I had first arrived in Deoband he had told me that I was eligible to receive a scholarship from the Indian government—the Indian Council of Cultural Relations (ICCR). I went down to ICCR in Delhi along with Abdul Hadi. The officers at ICCR were extremely helpful. I would need a letter from the institution where I was studying, they explained, and I would also have to approach ICCR through the Indian High Commission in Britain, my native country.

That gave me an excuse to visit England and see my parents. I visited the Indian High Commission in the Strand. The educational secretary was thrilled to hear that I was studying in Darul Uloom Deoband. He gave the required authorization for me to receive a scholarship from ICCR. It was one of the most seamless, stress-free official processes that I have ever been through. By the time I returned to Delhi, I was receiving my stipend from ICCR. An English *talib* at a leading Islamic madrasa was receiving a scholarship from the Indian government to pursue his Islamic studies. It is a series of equations that boggles the mind now. Many years later, I introduced myself to the vice president of ICCR, former vice chancellor of Jamia Millia Islamia in Delhi, Syed Shahid Mehdi, as a graduate of Darul Uloom Deoband and a former ICCR scholar. 'You mean you received an ICCR scholarship to study in Darul Uloom?' Mehdi sahib said to me with incredulity. When I was studying in Darul Uloom, some thirty years before this exchange with Mehdi sahib, receiving such a scholarship from the Indian government seemed normal. Not a question was raised. Later, perhaps as the flow of foreign students coming to Deoband was curtailed and public perceptions of Deoband became more iffy, the notion of a government scholarship to study in Deoband became more far-fetched. Not in my day. Then, Deoband was viewed with the utmost regard: a bastion of the freedom struggle, a centre of traditional learning and a symbol of Indian diversity.

The amount that I received, four hundred rupees per month, was initially ample for my needs. After a year or two, however, I found that it was difficult to manage on four hundred rupees. I went to the ICCR office and told them about my difficulties. 'Oh, funny that you should come at this time,' they said. 'We have already decided to increase your scholarship to five hundred rupees.' That summed up the spirit of cooperation between ICCR and myself. They were alive to my needs even before I told them what they were.

With this amount, I was able to pay rent, buy food and books and also make monthly trips to Delhi. I eventually moved out of Ehata Bagh and rented a house near Darul Uloom in Deoband town. I no longer had to make business trips across the border in order to support myself. I should have been able to concentrate on my studies. That there proved to be another distraction—albeit not of my own making—is another story, which I will deal with elsewhere.

Even more than any book-based knowledge that Maulana Khan Afzal had passed on to me in Tirah, his pointing me in the direction of India in my search for Islamic knowledge, and the example he set in placing teaching and studying apart from working for one's living, stood me in good stead.

VII

TALIB PRISONER

This world is a prison for a believer, paradise for the disbeliever.

(Hadith)

As I write these lines, in 2016, shots are being fired in Kabul over the reburial of a king who ruled in Kabul for some months following the fall of Amir Amanullah Khan in 1929. His name was Habibullah Kalakani. He is popularly known as Bacha Saqao (the son of a water-carrier). He has become a figurehead for the Tajik Northern Alliance in Afghanistan. Some are perplexed: 'They are killing the living for the sake of the dead,' one foreign observer said. It does not surprise me in the least. In 1974, I was taken to account and spent considerable time in jail in Kabul, in reprisal for the suggested role of the British in the fall of Amir Amanullah himself.

It is not history that has become the baggage in Afghanistan; it is people's false and fanciful notion of history. For Pashtoons, Amanullah has become the hero. For Tajiks, Habibullah Kalakani is the one they look up to. In fact, there were both Tajiks and Pashtoons who supported Amanullah in his modernizing reforms in the country, just as there were huge and eventually dominant forces of reaction amongst both ethnic groups that either caused, or benefited from, Amanullah Khan's downfall. One only has to look at the edicts issued by Habibullah as king in Kabul. They were remarkably similar to the writ of the Taliban more than six decades later. The only difference was that Habibullah was a Tajik, the Taliban were Pashtoon. The difference is not ideological, but ethnic.

If there is a clash of ideas, one can discuss things, come to some accommodation and take things forward. If differences are interpreted as ethnic, then they become fixed, with no give or take. That is what has happened in Afghanistan. In 1974, amongst the nascent, progressive, left-wing forces that wrested control in the new government of Daud Khan, the prevalent thinking was that Amanullah Khan had been deposed by an unholy alliance of the British and the mullas. Who better to blame than me: English and a mulla rolled into one?

I am indebted to the fast-talking, lean-looking Ghulam Rasool. He was serving at the Ministry of the Interior when I was taken there from Jalalabad, following my arrest in early 1974. He took me aside, into a separate room, during the course of my interrogation. A Pashtoon from Laghman in the east of Afghanistan, he was instinctively sympathetic to me, due in large part to my fluent Pashto. He explained to me the reason for the antipathy amongst Afghan progressives to mullas, in particular why they were especially allergic to English mullas, in other words me. There were many cases during the Great Game when Britishers came and served as mullas in Afghan mosques, he told me. They would remain there for a long time, then when their mission was complete, it would turn out that they were spies. 'That is why you have come under suspicion,' he explained.

Later, others were to give me one famous example, cited again and again, of a so-called English spy who came to serve in the Pul-e Khishti mosque in the centre of Kabul. I was told how he had led the prayers there for eighteen years. His purpose, so I was told, was to topple Amir Amanullah Khan. Once had achieved, in 1929, so the story goes, he returned to Great Britain, famously writing a letter to his congregation that they would have to say their prayers of eighteen years again, since he had been a British spy all along. Hopefully, no one took up his suggestion of repeating what would have been more than 32,000 daily prayers. They did not need to. In the time of the Holy Prophet, when the focal point of prayer (*Qiblah*) was changed from Jerusalem to Mecca, the Muslims worried about their prayers that had been directed towards Jerusalem. Were those prayers sound? The Qur'an made the matter clear: 'Allah will never let your prayers go to waste.' (*al-Baqarah* 2:143)

'By the time truth arrives,' the Pashto saying goes, 'rumour will have destroyed the whole village.' It is also said that if you tell a Pashtoon that a dog has bitten off his ear, he will immediately run after the dog: he will not check to see if his ear is there or not. In Pashtoon society, rumour has more credibility than confirmed truth. Therefore, it is just accepted that Amir Amanullah was unseated by an unholy alliance of the British and mullas—sometimes the two identities moulded into one. That is what people say, so that is what goes.

No matter then, that there are obvious historical flaws in the story. If the imam had remained in Pul-e Khishti mosque for eighteen years and his purpose had been to raise the Muslim masses of Afghanistan up against Amir Amanullah Khan, he would have had to be a clairvoyant. In 1911, when the imam started his 'mission', Amir Amanullah Khan's father Habibullah Khan was on the throne of Afghanistan. Amanullah only became *amir* when his father was assassinated in 1919. Furthermore, all the political dramas that were played out in the time of Amir Amanullah Khan: his wresting of complete independence from the British in the Treaty of Rawalpindi in 1920; his successful playing of the Russian and British empires against each other; and his reforms that attempted to transform Afghanistan into a twentieth century modern secular state—all the events that might conceivably have turned the British against him—had yet to take place.

Amanullah Khan, hailed as a hero by the progressive, nationalist, more secular lobby of Pashtoon society, vilified by the more conservative, religious sections of society, is arguably the most divisive figure in modern Afghan history. Progressive Pashtoon nationalists like Ghulam Rasool in the Ministry of Interior glorified him. On the other hand, I heard one maulvi I was in jail with say, probably too loudly for his own good: 'Screw the wife of whoever calls him a *ghazi* (a holy warrior)!' That is the title, *ghazi*, by which Amanullah Khan is known amongst those who look up to him. It was in the time of Amanullah Khan that the fault lines emerged in Pashtoon society, with progressives on one side, conservatives on the other. Pashtoon society has been grappling unsuccessfully with this division ever since. The fall of Amanullah Khan in 1929 was a watershed moment in Afghan history. Ever since then, the harmony between the forces of Pashtoonwali and Islam has been upset; the balance between progressive and conservative forces of Pashtoon society battered.

Khan Abdul Ghaffar Khan—the Frontier Gandhi as he was known and the leading Pashtoon nationalist of the twentieth century—is one of those who glorifies the role of Amanullah Khan and talks in his wonderful book, *My Life and Struggle* (*Zama Jhwand au Jadd- o-Jahd*), about how the Pashtoons were united in joining their campaign in support of Amanullah Khan. 'There have been many kings of the Afghans,' he writes, 'but they did not hold any of them so dear as they did Amanullah Khan.' That may have been true of the Pashtoons with whom Ghaffar Khan was associated. However, it was also true that a good number of the Pashtoon tribes responded to the cry of their mullas and rose up against Amanullah Khan.

That these tribes rose up against Amanullah Khan was more because of the *amir's* heavy-handed reform programme than anything else. In particular, the tribes were concerned that Amanullah Khan and his queen Soraya wished to 'remove the veil'. In fact, as the English academic Tommy Wide points out, there were exhortations in this regard, but no concrete steps were taken. Nevertheless, exhortations by the king and queen are even more likely to produce rumours in Afghan society than tangible measures. 'In the debates that followed the initial uprisings, Amanullah attempted to persuade the rebels that he had never had any plan to get rid of veiling, and acknowledged that it would never have been enforceable outside of Kabul anyway—but it was too late.'[1] Efforts, or one

[1] Thomas Wide, 'Astrakhan, Borqa', Chadori, Dreshi: The Economy of Dress in Early-Twentieth-Century Afghanistan', in *Anti-Veiling Campaigns in the Muslim World*, edited by Stephanie Cronin, London: Routledge, 2014.

might say encouragement, for women to remove their veils were accompanied by virulent steps to promote girls' education. Busloads of young girls were seen in the east of Afghanistan, supposedly heading off to Turkey for their education. It was then that the Shinwaris rose up and took Jalalabad. The Shinwaris are a Pash toon tribe straddling the border between Afghanistan and British India, as it was then, Afghanistan and Pakistan as it is now. The Shinwaris are neighbours of the Afridis in the Khyber Agency but also occupy a good deal of the eastern part of Nangarhar province in Afghanistan.

While the Shinwaris were able to take Jalalabad, it was a rebel chief from the Shamali plains north of Kabul who took the capital. This was Habibullah Kalokani, better known as Bacha Saqao. While Amanullah Khan fled to Kandahar then on to British India, Habibullah Kalokani ruled in Kabul for nine months with a Taliban-like iron hand. It cannot be denied that—British involvement in the removal of Amanullah Khan or no—there was a lot of indigenous Afghan opposition to the secular reforms that he introduced.

Progressive Afghans—the type that filled the Ministry of the Interior at the time under the Minister of the Interior Faiz Mohammad Khan—found it more convenient to blame an unholy alliance of mullas and Englishmen for the fall of Amanullah Khan rather than putting his fall down to his heavy-handed programme of reform. Amanullah Khan's programme of reform was not only similar to Kamal Ataturk's in Turkey; it was also modelled to a large degree on Ataturk's programme for the secularization of Turkish society. That has been the bane of Afghanistan over the last century. Reforms have been imported from abroad as opposed to being homegrown. The same Khalqis and Parchamis—the two wings of the Afghanistan Communist Party or People's Democratic Party of Afghanistan to which Faiz Mohammad Khan belonged—were to make the same mistakes as Amanullah Khan, introducing reforms too fast and too soon, later in the decade. They retained the baggage of history—that it was the British and the mullas who had caused the fall of their hero Amanullah Khan—yet they themselves failed to learn the lesson of history. They too fell into the trap of defying and riding roughshod over Afghan conservative tradition and seeking to introduce reforms too fast and too soon.

I was returning from Hajj when I was picked up by the governor and chief of police of Nangarhar province while reading the Qur'an after evening prayers in Nasrullah's serai[2] in Jalalabad. Looked at from an Islamic angle and from hindsight, my arrest was my destiny, my *qismat*. It enabled me to learn a lot of lessons about Afghan history and the divisions in Pashtoon society. Indeed, a few years later, when I was reminiscing with my teacher Maulana Khan Afzal about my time in detention, he said that I would not have been able to learn so much if I had been free during that time. In later years, when I took up a career in the media and humanitarian sectors, I even thought about inserting my time in jail in my CV! Well, now that I have written about it, I suppose it is as good as there on my CV.

Malik Nader Khan Afridi was one of several Pashtoon nationalist leaders putting up at the time in Afghanistan. All of them, Ghaffar Khan himself, Ajmal Khan and Nader Khan, soon returned to their homes in and around Peshawar. They had left Pakistan due to the hostile atmosphere there towards Pashtoon nationalists. At the same time, in Afghanistan, Pashtoon nationalism was actively promoted. It was the heyday of the Pashtoonistan movement. I met Nader Khan in the Tribal Affairs Department in Jalalabad. He tried to reassure me. 'The authorities will just check on you and put their minds at rest. You should have nothing to worry about,' he told me, probably somewhat disingenuously, since he must have known that my release would not be such a simple matter. I went peacefully to Kabul and arrived at the Ministry of the Interior, situated near Char-Rahe-Sadarat in Kabul, eerily close to the Noor Hotel that I had stayed at as a hippie, only some three and a half years earlier. Under Faiz Mohammad Khan—a Pashtoon from the Wazir tribe who, in April 1978, was to become one of the leaders of the Communist Saur Revolution—members of the People's Democratic Party of Afghanistan (PDPA) seemed to make up the bulk of the staff of the Ministry of the Interior. He stacked up his ministry

[2] *Serai* is the old word for inn, or hotel.

with PDPA party members like himself, including the future leader of the Saur Revolution of April 1978, Abdul Qadir Dagarwal.

The PDPA had helped Daud Khan take power in July 1973 and were suitably rewarded with several ministries, amongst them the powerful Ministry of the Interior. I was interrogated for five days in the ministry. At first it was a bit hostile: 'Tell us you are a British spy,' type of thing. Then one official who was particularly hostile towards me went to another room and came back with a snarl on his face and a black electric rod in his hands. He kept poking me with the rod, including in my private parts, making clear his contempt for both British imperialists and mullas, the two contemptible breeds that were now combined before him in the form of myself.

At that time I did not speak any Farsi, or Dari as it is more often known nowadays. I was to learn the language in jail. Farsi is the language of the Tajiks of Afghanistan. In fact, Farsi, Tajik and Dari are different dialects of the same Persian language spoken in Iran, Afghanistan and Tajikistan. During my five days of interrogation in the ministry, it was mainly Dari speakers who laid into me with their electric rods and taunts. Never once was a Pashto speaker hostile to me. In fact, Pashto speakers like Ghulam Rasool tried to take me aside and save me from the onslaught as much as possible. Another official who tried to shield me was Nasrullah, an urbane, young, handsome Pashtoon. At every opportunity, Nasrullah—the name itself means succour of Allah and that is what he seemed—would usher me into his office on some pretext or another. Often, this was to receive some pocket money from the funds that had been with me when I was arrested and which the Afghan authorities had taken into their possession. He would prompt me to write a receipt in Pashto, saying that I had received such and such an amount, taking evident glee in the fact that I spoke and wrote in Pashto. There was a clear affinity towards me from the Pashtoons in the ministry. They seemed uncomfortable with my victimization at the hands of their colleagues.

As I became better acquainted with my fellow inmates, I found that I was not the only one working off the legacy of Amir Amanullah Khan. Besides the British, the other group who were held responsible for the fall of Amanullah Khan were the Afghan clergy (*ulema*). They were also amply represented in the jail. In another quirk of history, one of them was from Khost and he was lame. His name was Mulla Abdul Rahman. The funny thing is that another lame mulla from Khost, known as Lang Mulla, had been the leader of one of the early insurrections against Amir Amanullah. Our own Lang Mulla was not the same person, of that, I am sure. He was a young man, barely in his early forties. There was no way he could have been alive in the 1920s. He was not even known as Lang Mulla in the jail. Giving him the same name as that of one of the main ringleaders of the rebellion against Amanullah would have definitely put him in the hot seat. That is how much history, or rather hearsay, repeats itself in Afghanistan. As I was imprisoned for being a British mulla, I would not be surprised if Mulla Abdul Rahman was imprisoned, and eventually executed, for being Lang Mulla.

Due to the number of *ulema* in jail at this time, I was able to forge ahead with my Islamic studies. Mulla Abdul Rahman became my teacher. With him, I began my study of Persian mystical poetry, which remains one of my favourite areas of Islamic learning to this day. I completed a book of Islamic jurisprudence, *Noor'al-Iidhah*, that I had begun with Maulana Daim'al-Haq in Nasirpur. In particular, I concentrated on Arabic grammar. All the books on Arabic grammar that I studied at this time were in Persian. There is a saying in the Muslim world that the Arabic language has been served by Persian speakers, while the Persian language has been served by Turkic-language speakers. I guess that is because Arabic speakers do not need to learn grammar to know Arabic. It is their mother tongue so they know it automatically. The same is the case with Turkic-language speakers and Persian. One day, I caught sight of Mulla Abdul Rahman, his bare belongings draped in a sheet across his shoulder, making his way out of the Tauqeef prison. He was on his way to Demazang, to begin his ten-year sentence. He did not have time to complete his sentence. When Hafizullah Amin became president of Afghanistan in 1978, he was summarily executed in Demazang jail.

Even at the time when I was in jail, the split between those who supported Amanullah, and his opponents was ideological.

Progressives were for Amanullah, conservatives against him. There was no notion of Amanullah being a Pashtoon king, or Habibullah Kalakani being a Tajik ruler. How, then, did the matter become ethnic, so much so that Tajik supporters of Habibullah Kalakani had now taken to the streets of Kabul and succeeded in giving Habibullah a royal reburial, nearly ninety years after his death? His death did indeed play a role in the ethnicization of the question of the toppling of Amir Amanullah Khan. Following the deposing of Amanullah, the Tajik Habibullah Kalakani remained king in Kabul for nine months. Meanwhile, another member of the royal family, the Pashtoon Nader Khan, was gathering forces in the south of the country in order to retake Kabul. Habibullah Kalakani could not resist these forces and retired to his native Kalakan, not far north of Kabul, leaving the throne to Nader Khan.

There was a spiritual leader (*pir*) at this time known as the *pir* of Tagao. He was respected by both the Nader Khan royal aristocracy and the Tajiks of the Shamali plain such as Habibullah Kalakani. One can say that he epitomized the geography of the Tagao valley itself. The valley reaches up from the Pashtoon banks of the Kabul River at Soribi, turning into the Tajik dominated Najrao valley, which in turn merges with the Shamali plains. The pir of Tagao's spiritual authority also reached out in the same manner. He had crowned Habibullah king in January 1929. Now Nader Khan prevailed upon the *pir*, whose name was Hamidullah Akhundzada, to invite Habibullah Kalakani to Kabul, ostensibly for discussions. Habibullah came to Kabul, under assurances from the Akhundzada. There, he was summarily executed along with his followers.

The redoubtable Tajik mujahid commander Ahmad Shah Massoud was later to exploit this event. He often showed people pictures of the execution, as an example of what the Pashtoon royal establishment would do to the Tajiks to prevent them from gaining power. He had a point. Habibullah Kalakani was not the only person to rebel against Amir Amanullah. The Pashtoon Shinwari had also risen up and taken Jalalabad. But Nader Khan did not take any reprisals against the Shinwaris, as he did against Habibullah. And the southern tribes of Paktia and Khost—the very tribes that had supported Nader Khan in regaining the throne—had also mounted rebellions against Amanullah. If it was a matter of complicity in dethroning Amanullah, the Shinwaris and the southern tribes were also guilty. But they were Pashtoon and thus escaped scot-free.

In those days, every prisoner in Afghanistan had to fend for himself. You had to survive on the money brought to you by visitors. If you did not have any visitors, or if they did not provide for you, then you had to cook for someone else, or someone else provided for you out of the goodness of their heart. Before I had my own money, which came to me from my father through the British embassy, I spent several months cooking for others. Like I honed my Islamic learning in jail, so I honed my cooking skills.

All foreigners who were in jail in Kabul were housed in what was known as the Tauqeef prison inside the provincial headquarters (*walayat*). Besides housing foreigners, the Tauqeef was also where remand prisoners—those who had not yet been sentenced—stayed. Normally, as in other countries, when a person is arrested or accused of a crime, they are either eligible for bail or they are put on remand. My case was different. I was like a political prisoner. I had not been accused of any crime— there were just insinuations against me—so I was not eligible for bail. Initially, certain officials in the Ministry of the Interior wished to house me in the main, Demazang prison of Kabul.[3] Maybe they wished to keep me away from foreigners, who in their turn would inform the embassy of my imprisonment. In any case, I did not spend even one night in Demazang. The superintendents of the prison decided—seemingly off their own bat—that since I was a foreigner and had not been convicted of any crime, I should be kept in the Tauqeef prison where all foreigners were housed.

[3] Demazang was the precursor of the now infamous Pul-e-Charkhi prison to the east of Kabul city. At the time of my internment, the Pul-e-Charkhi jail was being built. The site of the former Demazang prison is now home to the Afghan Border Police.

It seems that the Ministry of the Interior did not even know that I had been moved from Demazang to Tauqeef. The first they heard about it was when a delegation from the ministry visited Tauqeef prison about one year later. 'I thought you were in Demazang,' one of the members of the delegation said to me in Dari. He must have been one of the ones who had sent me there in the first place. By then, I knew good Dari, having picked it up in jail. 'Well, they sent me here instead.' If I had stayed in Demazang prison, I could have disappeared without trace.

The delegation had come to the jail to check on prisoners, how long they had been there, how long it was taking for their cases to be settled, that sort of thing. I might have done well to recount to them in my own context the tale of an earlier delegation, that uncovered the existence of a number twenty prisoner in the jail. Fortunately, I had not cracked under the pressure of, relatively speaking, quite gentle torture. If you beat and torture an innocent victim enough, even if he is the unlucky 'number twenty',[4] then sometimes he will crack. According to some, it is better to crack, since then you can tell the judge that your confession was extracted under torture. That is what happened to Fazal Karim and Ghulam Sakhi, two inmates whom I befriended on the first day that I arrived in the Tauqeef prison. Or they befriended me rather. It was a cold, forbidding winter's evening in late February 1974. Considering the mild Kabul winters of the recent, global warming times, people cannot imagine how cold winters were in those days. From the time the first snows fell in November or maybe December, until well into February or even March, everything was frozen. Now, in late February, slushy snow still lay on the ground outside and in the yard of the prison. I was ushered down a freezing corridor and

[4] The 'number twenty' expression comes from a story that was prevalent in Afghan jails in those days. A delegation came to the jail and was asking all the prisoners what they were in jail for. One prisoner told them: 'All I know, sir, is that I was accosted in the street and told that I was number twenty.' It turned out there had been twenty prisoners in the jail, but one went missing, so the authorities went and captured the first available person. There were lots of 'number twenty' prisoners in Afghan jails.

directed by the prison guards to the cell that housed Fazal Karim and Ghulam Sakhi.

It was quite a shock, when I first set eyes on their cell. I say 'their cell'. In fact, there were twenty-three people lodged in their cell. And it was not a very large cell. Length-wise, there was room for two-and-a-half beds; width-wise, two beds. So how on earth did twenty-three people fit in that cell, you might ask? This was done by one bed being stacked on top of another, and then another on top of that. It was a bit like an Indian train, where there is often a three-tier sleeper system. Except in this case, there were people underneath the bottom bunk also. It was a seething beehive of human activity. Cold and suspicious faces met me: 'Oh no, not another one! Where on earth is he supposed to stay?' Understandably, no one was willing to accommodate me in his space. The only ones who immediately warmed to me and extended me their hospitality were Fazal Karim and Ghulam Sakhi. They were from the Shinwari tribe—neighbours of the Afridis. That was why they befriended me, added to the fact that I reminded them of Pashtoonistan—as the Pashto-speaking Frontier was known at that time in Afghanistan. 'It is such a carefree part of the world,' Fazal Karim remarked one day. They invited me to join them under one single bed. At least the close proximity of one human being to another helped ward off the cold, there being no heating in Afghan jails.

Like many prisoners, Fazal Karim and Ghulam Sakhi did not reveal the real nature of the accusations against them to anyone, not even to me who became a person who shared their eating bowl and saucepan (*andiwal*). 'Oh, we just had a car accident,' Ghulam Sakhi explained somewhat unconvincingly. 'There are lots of spies in this jail,' Fazal Karim once told me, so prisoners prefer to keep mum about why they are in jail, just in case the person they are talking to is a spy planted to goad some information out of them. Nonetheless, Fazal Karim and Ghulam Sakhi really were my good friends and taught me a lot about prison life.

They had good reason not to reveal the real cause of their imprisonment to me. Later, I was able to put two-and-two together and surmise—I can say this now because they were exonerated of any wrong-doing by the judge—that in fact, they were accused of providing women from the tribal territory for a prostitution ring in Kabul. Pimpism (*murdagoi*) is a crime that is quite common in Kabul. Indeed, although they were innocent, the police had managed to beat them into giving a confession. Fazal Karim was distraught when prosecutors demanded a sentence of five years imprisonment for them. 'Five years!' he was in tears and could not believe his ears. Imagine then his glee when the judge released the two of them. 'You have been treated in a very cruel fashion,' the judge had said to them, referring to the beating that had extracted a false confession from them. Fazal Karim and Ghulam Sakhi were so quick to pack their things and leave the jail that they did not even say goodbye. I don't blame them for not returning to visit me in the jail.

Come spring in the prison, a lot of inmates moved out of their cells, into the prison yard. Some even erected tent-like shelters to protect them from the rain. As a result of the exodus to the yard, things became less congested in the cells. Spring and summer were a good time in the prison, though the mornings did become extremely long. I joined up with a couple of Pashtoon nomads (*kochis*) of whom my best friend was Naib Gul, from Maidan Wardak. You might think he was a strange jail-mate of mine, seeing that he had been accused of killing an American tourist in Soribi. Soribi lies about halfway between Kabul and Jalalabad. I could picture that poor American tourist, walking innocently around Soribi, just like I had done a few years earlier. 'All he had with him was a bunch of onions,' another prisoner told me. The ringleader of the gang that was convicted of his murder was Sarwar. He was already doing a long jail-term for the murder. Naib was nabbed later on. He seemed a long way from the wanton criminal that he was accused—and later convicted—of being. He missed his young wife terribly. She used to come and visit him in the jail, suitably covered of course, but they would have intimate conversations in the corner of the courtyard. Then he would come back to his patch in the prison yard, his eyes glistening with tears, and sing ballads to his beloved in his tuneful voice.

The prison guards were not professional guards, in that they had not been trained to be prison guards but were conscript soldiers. It was the same with the police constabulary and army—they all came from the same conscripts. Traditionally, the Afghan Army had always been a conscript army. Everyone was required to do two years of military service (*askari*). This military service was a great source of national unity in Afghanistan. A Pashtoon from Kandahar, for example, might do his military service in a Tajik-speaking area such as the northeast province of Badakhshan. An Uzbek Afghan from Jauzjan might just as easily serve in the Pashto-speaking east of the country, the *mashriqi*. This gave Afghans of every ethnic hue a great sense of belonging to the larger Afghanistan, besides being a part of their own ethnic group. Conscripts who served as guards in the prison (*askars*) struck up great friendships with prisoners: after all, they were serving two-year terms—albeit as conscripts not as prisoners—themselves. Often, in order to augment their paltry allowance, the *askars* would sell the loaf of brown bread that they received every day as part of their daily allowance. I used to love that bread—it was called *silo* bread after the big flour mill in Kabul where it was baked—and I would try and buy one every day from one of the *askars*.

The *aksars'* meagre allowance was barely enough to cover their *naswar* costs. *Naswar* is the chewing tobacco that Afghans love to pop, either between their gum and lip—that is more the Pashtoon style—or underneath their tongue as Kabulis do it. *Naswar* is highly addictive and intoxicating. Some of my jail-mates used to challenge one another to take *naswar* when they broke the Ramadan fast in the evening, then try to walk in a straight line from one end of the jail yard to the other. They could not. Later on in my internment, an American in the jail decided to embrace Islam. His name had been James, and he became Jamaluddin. I invited him to dinner. 'I don't think accepting Islam will help you much in getting free,' I quipped. 'I was put in jail because of being a Muslim.'

Jamaluddin wanted to try some *naswar*. I gave him some. I did not expect such a violent reaction—he sat back in his chair stunned, then exploded in a cascade of vomit. That was how strong the seemingly innocuous mixture of ground tobacco and whitewash was—the Pashtoons prefer to mix the ground tobacco with the ash of walnut trees. Pashtoons love their *naswar*. They have special, ornate *naswar* tins, decorated round the edges with beads and with a mirror in the middle. Generally, after popping some *naswar*, a Pashtoon likes to look at himself in the mirror of his *naswar* tin for a while, as his head swims under the influence of the drug.

As I mentioned, I spent a lot of time as a cook in jail. Abdul Salam and Abdul Haq were two brothers whom I cooked for. They were in jail on a murder charge. They were from a well-to-do, landowning family from Laghman. They had a run-in with their cousins, hence the murder charge. They did not need me to contribute money to any food kitty and were quite happy to foot the bill themselves. They appreciated having an English cook, though, particularly one who knew what he was doing. 'He knows the sequence of cooking a good meal,' the elder brother Abdul Salam once complimented my cooking.

Pashtoons will not generally talk about their relationship with their wives. It is secret. In jail, it is different. There, they miss their wives that so much that they are more open in talking about their mutual love. Naib Gul could hardly talk, or sing, about anything else but his young love. As for Abdul Salam, he went into intimate details about how he and his newly wedded wife only got round to performing the statutory bath one is required to have after having sex (*ghusl*) after one week of being in bed together! It was good to hear about this more human side of Pashtoon life, as opposed to the front of propriety they will observe in everyday life.

I was never alone. Along with Abdul Salam and Abdul Haq, I had my patch at one end of the jail yard. It was a perfect place for spring and summer. In Kabul, it hardly ever rains during the summer months. Since this was a remand jail, there was always a quick turnover of prisoners. One group of *andiwals* would quickly make way for another. The only ones who were permanent in this jail were people who had fought with others in the main jail, the Demazang, so could not go back there, or people like myself whose case was slow in coming to court. Naib Gul was shifted to Demazang once his long prison sentence was passed. Abdul Haq and Abdul Salam were shifted back to Laghman. The next to appear after they left were Said Amin and Aurangzeb. They were relatives of Malik Nader Khan, the Afridi chieftain whom I had met in Jalalabad, at the time of my arrest. They said they were in jail for smuggling Russian medicine into Afghanistan. It does not sound like a very likely story, I mean, relatives of the mighty Nader Khan going to jail on such relatively trivial charges? Aurangzeb even said he was Nader Khan's brother. In retrospect, it seems more likely that they had come to spy on me. In any case, we spent some good time together and whatever other account they gave of me, I expect at least they complimented my cooking.

Our jail housed a few hardened gangsters who had been transferred from Demazang because they had fought, or even killed someone, in Demazang. The main prison fights were between Panjshiri and Kandahari gangs. Both Juma Khan and Siddiq were Kandaharis who had killed Panjshiris in Demazang. Juma Khan ran a little tea shop and baker's oven in the remand jail, so he was well set up, though of course he was deprived of his freedom, and no matter how well one is set up in jail, it cannot compensate for one's lack of freedom. Juma Khan did not talk very much, though he was always eminently polite. He was quite surly and you could easily see him being the big gangster that he in fact was.

Juma Khan's shop was situated in the middle of the jail yard, opposite the mosque. The mosque was just a smaller yard in the middle of the larger jail yard. It was not covered. There was a two-brick high wall around the mosque, which was where those who wished to enter took off their shoes. The mosque yard differed from the rest of the jail yard in that it had a cemented floor and had mats made of *mezaray* that were oriented towards the direction of Mecca (*qiblah*), to which Muslims turn at prayer. Those who sat in the mosque—it was really more a prayer area since it did not have a *mihrab*[5]—did not necessarily enter the mosque to pray; they may have wished to have a private chat. That is typical of the way a mosque is used by the Pashtoons. It is called a place of congregation (*jamaat*) as opposed to a place of prostration (*masjid*), which is more common in other parts of the Muslim world.

---

[5] The *mihrab* is the niche in a mosque where the imam stands. Without a *mihrab*, a prayer-area cannot be strictly speaking designated as a mosque.

The Pashtoon mosque is used for assembly: as an expression of Pashtoonwali, as well as for prayer.

You may find it strange that Juma Khan was able to run his own shop inside the jail, but that is the way jails were run in Afghanistan. Prisoners were put inside and left to look after their own affairs as opposed to being accountable to some jail authority. There was a superintendent of the jail, who was a government official, but he stayed in his office and looked after administrative matters. He also had a deputy, who was a prisoner. He was known as the head (*bashi*). To all intents and purposes the *bashi* was indeed the head of the jail. He did not allow fights in the jail, unless of course they were fights in which he was involved, of which more later. He turned a blind eye to Ismat's activities, for example. Ismat sold hash and opium in the jail. There was no searching of prisoners to speak of, after they received visitors. Visitors spoke to prisoners through a grill, which allowed money, food and less innocuous items, such as drugs and knives, to change hands. Wives came to see their husbands and often could be seen in a discreet corner of the visitors' area, where they were able to at least hold hands with their husbands. Others knew better than to look. In fact, the Tauqeef jail, like other jails in Afghanistan, was like a little Afghanistan itself. Life went on inside the jail much as it did in the outside world.

With time, I also became an old-timer in the jail, and my status amongst the inmates was further enhanced by my relative affluence. After the British embassy learnt of my imprisonment, they informed my father, who then arranged for money to reach me through the Foreign Office and the embassy. This enabled me to employ a cook rather than be a cook for others. I even built a two-storey residence in the corner of my cell! Downstairs was my kitchen, upstairs my sitting abode, which I also curtained off so that I could have some privacy when I wished. My cook was Gulzar Khan, who hailed from the Shah Shaheed area of Kabul, near Karte Nau in the east of the city. That was where he was from, but he had lived most of his life in India and Pakistan and was very familiar with Urdu. He could cook both Afghan and Indian food. His spinach was particularly delicious. He was in jail, so he told me, because of a twenty-one-year-old murder case, which had only now come to court. I knew better than to ask any questions.

Tor Bachae Kandi was a notorious do-no-gooder (*badmash*) of Kabul. When he entered the Tauqeef jail, immediately the word went round: 'Tor is here.' His father was a tailor from the Shahre Nau area of Kabui, who was known as Kandi (sweet) so Gulzar told me because of his sweet nature. Tor immediately took a liking to me. He had his sweet side, though he could also be extremely intimidating and threatening. When in the latter mood, it seemed he would stop at nothing. He even went to the extent of teaching me *shifar*, which is a kind of code language used by Afghan criminals. *Shifar* is formed by taking a Farsi word, putting the first syllable of the word at the end of the word, and inserting 'ga' at the beginning. In this way, a simple word like *man* (me) becomes '*ganamay*'. Seasoned criminals can speak *shifar* very quickly. No one else can understand what they are saying.

I fell foul of Tor towards the end of my term in prison. He gate-crashed on a dinner I was hosting for another prisoner by the name of Sayyid Yaqub. Tor was in a drunken state. I did not have much time for him in that state, and cold-shouldered him. This did not go down well with Tor. 'Look at the bloody Englishman,' he said angrily. 'I do not respect the president of Afghanistan, but I respect him and he treats me in this manner!' He started hitting me. I remember that he hit me seventeen times! I don't know how I managed to keep count, since he was hitting me quite hard. I did not have the physical wherewithal to react, but Sayyid Yaqub reacted on my behalf. 'Don't hit him Tor, I told you!' Tor carried on hitting me. It turned into a fight between Tor and Sayyid Yaqub. Soon, Tor's whole gang, including the *bashi* of the jail, Qasim Wardak, appeared with their knives. I don't know how Sayyid Yaqub survived—I had retired to another corner of the cell—but soon he and Tor were being carted off to the Demazang jail, Tor shouting that he would do this and that to the wife of the president of Afghanistan, as they took him away. It so happened that my friend Ghulam Rasool from the Ministry of the Interior had become superintendent in the Demazang jail. 'That goddamn Englishman was insulting the president of Afghanistan, that's why I hit him,'

Tor told Ghulam Rasool. 'Come off it,' the superintendent rebuked him. 'You were the one who was insulting the president. Everyone heard you.' Anyway, Ghulam Rasool tied Sayyid Yaqub and Tor with the same chain in solitary confinement for a couple of weeks and told them to fight as much as they liked now.

Soon, as superintendent of the Demazang prison, Ghulam Rasool came to visit Tauqeef jail. He made a beeline for my cell and asked after my wellbeing. I was used to jail life by then, and as I mentioned earlier, was well set up in jail. Ghulam Rasool was struck by the improvement in my condition, from a disoriented captive to established convict. He was also happy that I had received the order for my release. He was a Pashtoon after all, so was naturally sympathetic towards me. I later heard that he had been killed in a helicopter crash, after the communist coup in Afghanistan in April 1978. As for Tor, later on I asked about him also. 'Wow, you know old-timers like Tor,' the gentleman I asked, an elderly son of Kabul by the name of Asad, now residing in America, replied. 'Tor was killed by Najib.' He was referring to Dr Najib, who after the Soviet invasion of December 1979 became head of the secret service (KHAD) and was eventually promoted to the presidency in 1986. Presumably, Najib did not kill Tor with his own hands—though he would have been one of the few people big and strong enough to actually do that—but I take it Tor died while Najib was the head of KHAD, hence the attribution of his death to Najib.

In the night before my release, Tor became quite menacing towards me. I felt quite uneasy. He was the kind of guy who could do anything and not feel a morsel of remorse: a typical psychopath. It was difficult to keep my distance, while not again giving him the impression I was cold-shouldering him. That had triggered the previous attack. Anyway, morning dawned and I left the jail. I sure was glad to get out of there alive.

VIII

PANJPIRI WARRIOR

So oh my brother
Tell your lover
What guided another
To your lovely place
Where you spend your days
In the lovelyplains
Pure and vast
Of Kajuray . . .
And your cousin brave
Is digging a grave
By the door
And my home is not of this world
Any more
Cos the world was much more cruel
Than I saw

(Fragments of a dream put into poetry
by Pashtoon Englishman)

It was a sunny, summer's afternoon in Tirah Maidan. The year was 1973. I was sitting outside, revising the lesson I had learnt that day from Maulana Khan Afzal. The expansive Hadith collection of *Mishkat'al-Masabih* was opened in front of me. Suddenly a man rushed across the field in front of me, gun in hand. There were shouts of protest from the ravine alongside us, where a man was being captured. The man was shoved inside the very house in front of which I was revising my lesson. The man who was taken captive was Islam Gul. He had been captured by his first cousins, Mohmand and Jabbar. They had some inheritance-related dispute. I was ushered away from the house where Islam Gul was detained, across the defile where the main path runs. From there, I surveyed the scene opposite. I saw Islam Gul jump from the first floor of the house and escape. In a couple of days, Islam Gul's younger brothers, Samand and Kokay, arrived from Peshawar. The stone was broken (*kanray mat sho*) between Islam Gul on the one hand, and Mohmand, Jabbar and all the other cousins—including Laiq, who had conspired in taking Islam Gul captive—on the other. In other words, there was open warfare between these two branches of the same family. None of the cousins were able to leave their houses. Islam Gul and his brothers were bound to be lurking.

One evening, Laiq and I broke the curfew and ventured out of Laiq's house, to go to the house of Mohmand and Jabbar. As Laiq entered the field at the end of which the house was situated, a shot rang out. Laiq fell down, shot in the ankle. He and I crawled back to the house from which we had come. There was no more shooting. Laiq moaned all night from his wound. '*Wa aday, wa aday*,' he cried out. I could not quite catch what he was saying, so I asked his cousin Shinay. 'It means, oh mother, oh mother, because one's mother is the closest person to one, so a person naturally says those words at a time of extreme pain,' Shinay told me.

Within an hour or two of Laiq being shot, Maulana Khan Afzal was on the scene. He had come in the dead of night, walking at least one hour to get from Landi Kas to Saddar Khel, in order to attend to Laiq. Of course, he did so on my accord, he had no reason to go out of his way to nurse Laiq. After suitably bandaging him and giving him medications to soothe his pain, he left, but not before he had offered a long and heartfelt prayer, some of it audible, for peace amongst his people and in particular in this household. Some of it was inaudible, no doubt the inaudible part was that I should find deliverance from the household in which I was waylaid and found myself besieged on all sides.

That was when Zafar Khan, the Panjpiri warrior after whom this chapter is named, came in. Like Maulana Khan Afzal, I am sure he also only went out of his way to bring peace to the Saddar Khan clan due to my presence amongst them. He and I had struck a close relationship since I had arrived in Tirah. He came from the neighbouring village and was a Panjpiri, so he naturally had an affinity towards me. He wanted to extract me from this feuding situation in which I found myself. Such situations can lead to a never-ending and ever-escalating cycle of revenge amongst the Afridis. Islam Gul's brothers shot Laiq because he had been involved in the attempted capture of Islam Gul. Laiq would now shoot any of Islam Gul's brothers, since they had spilled his blood (*ar ye mat wo*) as the Afridis say. Zafar Khan would not let such a situation develop, since he knew that I would suffer as a result. Otherwise, Zafar Khan would not benefit in any way from mediating in the dispute. Zafar Khan was the kingpin of the village next to Saddar Khel, which was where Mohmand, Jabbar, Islam Gul and Laiq lived. First of all, both sides accepted Zafar Khan as a mediator in the dispute. His next step was to arrange a truce, so that both sides could attend a *jirga*. A *jirga* is a Pashtoon tribal court of law, set up to settle disputes. In its ideal form, it is a replica of a verse of the Qur'an:

> If two parties of believers fight against each other, make peace between them; then, if after that, one of them transgresses against the other, fight the party that transgresses until it submits to the command of Allah. Then, if it complies, make peace between them with equity, and act justly. Truly, Allah loves the just. (*al-Hujurat* 49:9)

In this case, while Zafar Khan arranged a truce, he also prevailed upon them to hand over jurisdiction (known as *wak* amongst the Afridis) to him. This meant that he had the authority to negotiate a settlement between the two parties, a settlement that they were duty-bound to accept. This led to a peace agreement between Mohmand and Jabbar on the one hand and their cousin Islam Gul on the other.

Clearly, only a man who wielded power and authority could broker such a settlement. Zafar Khan had both in ample measure. He was one of the lions of the Afridis. A tribal leader of considerable charisma, he commanded devotion and loyalty amongst his relatives and friends, and no little fear amongst his enemies. He was not an old man, maybe in his late thirties, but his hair had grown grey quite prematurely. This only served to increase his standing amongst the Afridi tribes, who respected age and appearance along with conviction, clarity and persuasiveness in a person's speech.

Zafar Khan retained a boyish enthusiasm and sense of mischief and fun. His gait and bearing were those of a young man. He strutted rather than walked, stopping something short of a swagger. He would always be seen with a rifle slung over his shoulder, but such was his demeanour of a natural warrior that he might have been more at home with a sword. Indeed, he walked as if there was a sword swinging alongside him, in time with his passage. Swashbuckling is the word I would use for Zafar Khan. He did not have a lot of men at his command, one or two elderly uncles, a nephew by the name of Fauz Khan and another nephew who was lame but tagged along gamely. The secret of his power and reputation was not the men at his command, nor great wealth. His power came from the unity of his household and from his strong leadership. He was also a leading member, and one of the most feared, of the Panjpiri sect.

Fast forward to the spring of 1976. It was some three years after I had first come to know Zafar Khan in the summer of 1973. A united front of all eight Afridi tribes had come together with the express aim of toppling the Panjpiris. It is difficult to tell where the anti-Panjpiri conflagration began. Some might think it all began on the plains of Kajuray, where I had built a house with the wealth of my inheritance for Laiq and his family. One might say the saga began one morning in the Old Bara mosque when someone started inveighing against the Panjpiris from the balcony of the mosque as the Panjpiris held their daily Qur'an dars. Uttering a few expletives, one particularly burly Panjpiri, Khan Haider from the Sholabar Afridi tribe, who was close to the Panjpiri Qur'an teacher Maulvi Naquib, made his way up to the first floor where he gave the heckler a beating. Things were becoming heated in the confrontation between Panjpiris and their traditionalist opponents.

Some might think that the conflict began when the second-in-command in the Panjpiri hierarchy, Maulana Abdul Salam from Rustam, arrived in Bara to give an address in the mosque. He was refused permission to speak in the main Old Bara mosque, where Panjpiris held their daily dars. He went to another mosque and delivered his talk from there. From the loudspeaker, the theme of his talk filtered into every home and shop in Old Bara bazaar: 'Who is more in the wrong than one who prevents Allah's name from being mentioned in His places of worship.' (*al-Baqarah* 2:114).

Or one could say that it was my return to Kajuray from Kabul jail that enabled the anti-Panjpiri forces to mobilize. I was made into the figurehead. With me in the firing line, the anti-Panjpiri forces were able to make out that the Panjpiri movement was all a British plot to undermine Islam. I was crucial to the anti-Panjpiri propaganda. As we have seen previously, such rumours spread like wildfire amongst Pashtoons. They love rumours. Pashtoons need strong leadership that will urge them to delve to the bottom of matters and not believe every rumour that they hear. 'The biggest lie,' the Holy Prophet said, 'is to pass on everything one hears.' Lies certainly destroyed my village, but as I will point out, I cannot really blame the Afridis for believing those lies.

As the anti-Panjpiri forces began gathering on a plot of land just west of the Bara market, most of their vitriol was directed at me. If the anti-Panjpiri propaganda was to be believed, I was bankrolling Panjpiris and had created the so-called heretical group in order to drive a wedge in the Muslim community. Like most of my other troubles at the time, this problem stemmed from my inheritance. In the forefront of the accusations against me were two brothers of the Bar Piwari, the Upper Piwaris, clan of the Malik-Din Khels. They too had every right to feel aggrieved.

The names of the brothers were Kachgoul and Miramjan. I mentioned earlier that Laiq and I had opened a shop in the Afridi smuggler's bazaar of Bara, close to Peshawar. We left that shop and its contents to a scion of the Upper Piwari clan, close relatives of Kachgoul and Miramjan, by the name of Latif. It was Latif who had gone with me to Masma to take my things from my home. I went stealthily by *tonga* from Peshawar to Masma. I took my things, piled them in the *tonga* and left, without saying a word to anyone. Majeed's brother Hameed was right when he wrote to me that I had left like a thief. The reason for the Upper Piwaris' grudge against me was this: they contended that Laiq had assured Latif that he would have a half share in my wealth. I have no way of knowing whether Laiq did make such an assurance to the Upper Piwaris or not. It was a case of Laiq's word against theirs. In any case, I took Laiq's side. So along with Laiq, I also became a sworn enemy of the Upper Piwaris.

You can imagine—or maybe you can't—the tone of the Bar Piwari brothers' accusations against me as they addressed the gatherings that assembled daily, just up from the Upper Bara bazaar. Kachgoul was a master of colourful language. According to him, I was immoral and was compromising the morality of Afridis. I would not wish to mention some of the things said about me—I will leave that to the imagination of the reader— but I should put on record that everything was absolutely proper between Laiq's family, with whom I was living, and myself. Laiq's sister, who was engaged to me, always covered her face in modesty in my presence. That is the way with Pashtoon girls. They will not show themselves to the person they are going to marry until the marriage itself. And the guy should not go anywhere near her house, either. True, I had broken the latter rule, but I did not break any others. Like the other accusations against me, the accusations of misconduct were nonsense.

It was something of a surprise for me when Ghazi Gul turned up in our Kajuray home one mid-morning. Ghazi Gul was a Malik-Din Khel tribal leader, no friend of the Bar Piwaris, but he had a brother—Baghi Gul—on the anti-Panjpiri tribal committee. Ghazi Gul advised me to accompany him to speak to the assembled anti-Panjpiri hordes, tell them about my acceptance of Islam and that I could not be blamed for having fraternized with the wrong people. I went along with Ghazi Gul. The crowds parted to make way for me as I arrived to address the assembled throng. 'I came amongst you as a convert to Islam,' I addressed the crowd. 'I was studying the Qur'an. If I came into the company of the wrong people, you should have warned me off them.' I looked towards the Bar Piwari Miramjan as I spoke these words. He was looking at me knowingly. He had in fact warned me off the Panjpiris. He had called out to me one day, a year or two earlier, when I was on my way to the daily Qur'an *dars*, which at that time were taking place with Maulana Zakariyah in the New Bara market. 'Do not study with the Panjpiris,' he had said to me. 'Study with the Tablighis instead.' Just as I was loath to mention this exchange, Miramjan also refrained from doing so. In Miramjan's case, his reticence was because, along with the Panjpiris, the Tablighis were also being targeted by the Afridi tribal force (*lashkar*).

It is a formidable force, an Afridi *lashkar*. The story goes that it was the Ottoman Turks who, in the wake of the First World War, bequeathed eight flags to the Afridis—one for each tribe. 'Whenever you raise these flags, we will come to your assistance,' the Ottomans promised the Afridis. It is strange to think how the Ottomans could make such a promise to the Afridis, at a time when their own empire was teetering on the verge of collapse. The bequeathing of the flags to the Afridis coincided with the Khilafat Movement (1919–24), formed in support of the Ottoman Caliphate by Indian Muslims. It was a time of great emotional support for the Turkish Caliphate on the part of Indian Muslims. Just as no one thought how they would be able to save the Ottoman Empire, at a time when it was already doomed, so no one wondered how the Ottomans in their febrile state would be able to save the Afridis—or anyone else for that matter—from the British.

The flags retained great emotional power and significance among the Afridis. Whenever the tribes united and raised these flags, all Afridis tagged along, in the process forming a *lashkar* comprising several thousand men. Once, during the 1930s, the flags had been raised against the British themselves. That lashkar petered out very quickly. I was told by one person who was himself part of that lashkar that he was on his way to Peshawar, to join the lashkar, when he saw others beating a retreat in the opposite direction. He also retired to the safety of the Afridi tribal territory.

The 1950s and 1960s had been a time when Afridi lashkars had been formed to maintain propriety in people's behaviour and to discourage vice. These *lashkars* were mostly led by Mulla Khaista Gul from Nader Khan's Zkha Khel Afridi tribe. One year, the *lashkar* turned their ire on radios, which had just found their way into the land of the Afridis. Radios must have been considered objectionable due to the music they blared out. First of all, the *lashkar* confiscated radios from culprits who were found to be in ownership. Then the radios were lined up on a cliff face and shot! More pertinently, just one year before the anti-Panjpiri *lashkar*, while I had been in jail in Kabul, there had been an Afridi *lashkar* targeting those who had signed up for a road to the hallowed Afridi territory of Tirah. The *lashkar* burnt down a few houses—those of tribal elders who had signed up for the road—and fined a few others who had supported them.

Now the Afridis were preparing to do the same to the Panjpiris. Only that there were many more Panjpiris than there were ones who had signed up to a Tirah road. I was one of the Panjpiris whose house was targeted for torching. It must be said, I was not very sincere when I visited the embryonic tribal lashkar and swore off the Panjpiris. Even after my recantation, I attended the Panjpiri dars on a few occasions. Meanwhile, the Bar Piwaris were busy telling the anti-Panjpiri hordes that I was still in league with the Panjpiris and that I should be targeted by the *lashkar*. But news of this did not filter through to us. We still lived in the hope that my exoneration would be the final word on the matter. As the anti-Panjpiri gathering turned into a lashkar, under the eight black flags of the eight tribes of the Afridis, we found ourselves in a quandary. While other Panjpiris were in no doubt that their houses would be burnt down and had set about emptying them of all their property, and especially of women and children, we dilly-dallied. The *lashkar* would definitely hear if we emptied our house and would take it as an admission of guilt. But if we did not empty our house, we risked having a full house burnt down. This would be almost unprecedented. Houses are often burnt down in the tribal area, both by the government under the Frontier Crimes Regulation, and by lashkars, but this is always done with a warning. Even lashkars do not violate the sanctity of the home by attacking a house where women and children are lodged.

So, as the *lashkar* crept up from the Bara bazaar towards Kajuray in a caravan of some 120 buses along with multiple private cars and Suzuki vans, our hope was that our house would be spared. The heat and haze of the early summer sun on that sunny April morning was intensified by smoke spiralling from houses, angry hordes pummelling the turf. The *lashkar* made its way up the plains and along the canal that ran just below our house.

Most of the *lashkar* had already passed our house, travelling up the ravine that ran between our home and the Kuhay mosque, that stood nearby our home. Then suddenly a group of *lashkar* members, under the leadership of the Upper Piwari brothers, broke off from the main *lashkar* and descended on our home. Women and children were cooking the midday meal as stones started descending on the perimeter walls and gate. Within no time, some *lashkar* members had scaled the walls. Women and children ran in panic towards the next-door home of Abdul Hakim. I braved the storm of stones to venture outside, holding my hand up towards the advancing hordes and pleading with them to stop their onslaught, asking them what I had done wrong. 'We do not wish to harm you,' the crowd was remarkably good-natured. They also stopped pelting stones when I appeared at the gate. 'But there is no way now that your house can be saved.' Already, smoke was rising from the beams of what had been our home. 'Make your way to that nearby home,' one particularly good-natured young man, who was clearly concerned for my safety, told me. 'No one will harm you there.'

Making use of the Pashtoon tradition of refuge (*panah*), I made my way to the nearby home, accompanied by the young man who had expressed concern for my safety. I sat in the *hujrah* of Abdul Hakim, which also served as a shop serving houses in the neighbourhood. There was trepidation and silence, accompanied by some sympathy from Abdul Hakim, as we sat together in the closed *hujrah*, door tightly locked. The sound of the marauding *lashkar* could be heard from afar. Suddenly, in contravention of the custom of *panah*, the sound of Kachgoul's voice could be heard from outside: 'Where are you Englishman?' He used the derogatory term *feringi*, a word that dates from the time of the Crusades when the Christian forces were known as Franks, translated into Farsi, Pashto and other Eastern languages as *feringi*. 'I know you are here, you bastard. I tell you, if you do not come out of this house here and now, I will burn it down as well.'

Such a stand-off had probably taken place several times before. Pashtoons giving refuge to someone—in this case me— and some big power—in this case Kachgoul and his Upper Piwari clique—threatening the asylum giver and seeker with dire consequences if he was not given up. Abdul Hakim never gave the hint of a suggestion to me that I should give myself up, even less that he would even countenance the thought of giving me up. For my part, I could not bear the thought of Abdul Hakim's house being burnt down because of me. Better to give myself up to the *lashkar* and save Abdul Hakim, I thought. I stepped out of Abdul Hakim's *hujrah*. Kachgoul grabbed me by the scruff of the neck and took me to the Kuhay mosque. There, outside the mosque, he tried to initiate my lynching, tearing some of my clothes. I do not wish to claim any miraculous powers, but it is a fact that I heard the sound of my clothes being ripped here and there. Later, when I checked them, they were all intact. Far from anyone following Kachgoul's lead of lynching me, others sought to protect me and led me to the room of the imam of the mosque. Kachgoul went about his job of burning down other houses in the Malik-Din Khel area. In the evening he returned to the mosque. 'I have kept a golden bullet for you,' he told me, pointing his pistol at my head.

Masil Khan, son of Sardar who was my neighbour in Kajuray, came to the mosque. 'My dad has arranged with the committee that you will stay in our house.' He walked me across the ravine. I looked at the smouldering remains of our home as I entered the home of Sardar. I spent a few comfortable days in Sardar's *hujrah*. Some people visited and chatted with me. One told me how the Panjpiris had emigrated en masse to Palosi village, near Peshawar University. Another told me how the lashkar had chased after a bus belonging to my in-laws, but they had managed by a hair's breadth to get the bus out of the tribal territory and into Peshawar district.

The day after I moved into Sardar's home, he took me for a walk to the hill that stands in the middle of the Kajuray plain. On one side is Malik-Din Khel territory, on the other the Upper Qambar Khel tribe have their land. Upper Qambar Khel was a stronghold of well-to-do Panjpiris. Haji Yarmat Shah, Abdul Akbar, Samar Gul, Mir Badshah, along with several others. One by one I saw their houses, places where I had spent nights, had good times, been entertained, go up in smoke. There was an inevitable feeling on my part that I was somehow to blame, but no Panjpiri would ever have cast any blame on me. For Sardar, it was a chance to see the *lashkar* go about its destructive task. For him, it was a form of entertainment. My heart was heavy as we walked across the plains back to Sardar's home—my place of detention. It was the end of an era, the end of the world as I knew it. Who knew where all the Panjpiris—those who had been my only friends since I had arrived in Afridi country—would go now, what would become of them, would I ever see them again? It seemed not. I was at the beginning of one-and-a-half years of captivity by the Afridis. Like Afghanistan, I came to know the Afridi tribal territory from the inside.

The next stop for the Afridi lashkar was Tirah, the centre of the Afridis where, like Kajuray, there were dozens of Panjpiri homes that stood condemned to the torch. But the Afridi lashkar was not able to take the direct route to Tirah, straight up the Bara valley. On that route, right at the strategic confluence of two streams, lived the Kuki Khel tribe. Nawab Zaman Khan, who belonged to the Kuki Khel tribe, had built a huge fort in the hills near Dwa Toi. Dwa Toi literally means the confluence of two streams. Here, one stream comes from Tirah Maidan, the other from Spin Ghar: the White Mountain that dominates the skyline of the eastern Afghanistan city of Jalalabad. Indeed, Spin Ghar, or Murga as the Afridis know it, is a focal point for Pashtoon tribes from Khost to Tirah, Kurram to Nangarhar. The fort of the nawab was the pride of the Kuki Khels, indeed of all the Afridis. You could call it the castle of Tirah, it was that famous.

For some reason, the *lashkar* were intent on demolishing this castle. It was not clear on what pretext the fort had been slated for demolition, but the Kuki Khels were having none of it. 'If you have noticed anything wayward in us, come and burn down our fort yourselves,' the nawab's son Khalifa addressed their tribe, along with his nephew Enayat. 'But if you do not consider us worthy of punishment, then do you wish the Afridi *lashkar* to come here and wreak destruction on us, and on others in our tribe?' The Kuki Khel tribe supported their chieftains and refused to let the *lashkar* set foot on their land. They even brought the old cannons from the time of Nawab Zaman Khan out and placed them on the border of their territory. 'Come here at your peril,' they were telling the *lashkar*. The *lashkar* thought better of it.

Along with learning of the resistance of the Kuki Khels, I also learnt, piece by piece, about the less successful resistance of the Panjpiris in general. As the *lashkar* could not take the direct route to Tirah, they took a more circuitous one and eventually arrived at Zkha Khel Bagh in Tirah Maidan, the first Afridi tribal centre that lay on their route. There are three centres of the Afridis in Tirah Maidan. One is the Zkha Khel Bagh, and there is also a bagh in the territory of the Upper Qambar Khel tribe, at the far end of the Tirah Maidan. But the main bazaar (*bagh*) of the Afridis is the Malik-Din Khel Bagh in the centre of Tirah, at the confluence of streams flowing from the territory of the Lower and Upper Qambar Khel tribes. At the approach of the *lashkar*, Panjpiri leaders—Khan Afzal, Haji Khan Mohammad, Zafar Khan and others—held their counsel under the leadership of Mulla Mir Rahman. They wanted to devise a strategy to save their homesteads in Tirah. Besides their actual houses, 'built up with enormous labour, and after several years of work, for in Tirah, forts are not built by contract',[1] there were their assets: in the case of Mulla Mir Rahman, an orchard of some three score fruit trees; in the case of Zafar Khan, a pine forest on the hill above his village. Afridi *lashkars* do not observe the humanitarian law laid down in the Qur'an, according to which,

[1] Robert Warburton, *Eighteen Years In The Khyber, 1879–1898*, John Murray: London, 1900.

even in battle, one is not allowed to wilfully destroy crops or trees.[2] The Panjpiri leaders would have to find a way to stop the lashkar.

The Panjpiris discussed their strategy. Zkha Khel Bagh, where the lashkar had gathered, was close to the homestead of Mulla Mir Rahman. It was here, Mulla Mir Rahman, Zafar Khan and the other Panjpiris decided, they would meet the lashkar. In typical Pashtoon fashion, they decided that first of all they would try and reason with the lashkar. The Pashtoons call reason *lar*, literally, road: to follow reason is to follow a road. If lar did not work, it would have to be war.

It was decided that Mulla Mir Rahman would lead the party of Panjpiris conducting the discussions. He would talk to the leader of the lashkar committee, Abdul Karim, in the Zkha Khel Bagh. Zafar Khan would lead the men at arms—scores of Panjpiris who would be hidden in ravines around the *bagh*. If there was no sign from Mulla Mir Rahman and their comrades in the *bagh*, they would hold their fire. If things turned nasty in the meeting, the shots would rain down on the committee members from Panjpiri marksmen.

Now that they had arrived in Tirah, *lashkar* foot soldiers were given time off to go and see their families. Most Afridis have one house in Tirah, another in the plains. The *lashkar* had endured weeks of hot marching, from the plains of Kajuray up the Bara valley to Tirah, the heat of the early summer only exacerbated by the heat of the blazing Panjpiri houses that they burnt along the way. Only a hard core of committee members and *lashkar* stalwarts remained as they held counsel in the Zkha Khel Bagh.

'You say that the Panjpiris were exposed as heretics in a debate,' began Mulla Mir Rahman, flanked only by a few of his own relatives. Mulla Mir Rahman was addressing directly the lashkar leader Abdul Karim. Mulla Mir Rahman's reference was to a debate that had been held in the Khyber political agent's office, before the conflagration in Kajuray started. The lashkar had spread the word that the Panjpiris had been defeated in the debate. The Panjpiris, for their

[2] *al-Baqarah* 2:205

part, also claimed victory. As is usually the case with such debates, there was no clear outcome, giving both sides the chance to claim victory. It had been a pretty pointless exercise.

Abdul Karim knew nothing of the debate and cared even less. He was only interested in burning down the houses of Panjpiris. 'You are like a shepherd who has been with his sheep and goats all day,' he roughly addressed Mulla Mir Rahman. 'Then when you come home in the evening, you ask what has been going on in the jirga. I cannot explain everything to everyone.' More words may have been exchanged, but it was this exchange that proved too much for Mulla Mir Rahman.

The venerable looking maulana, his handsome and dignified face framed by an off-white beard and a snow-white turban, usually wrapped his white chadar around his shoulders, or draped it over one shoulder. On this occasion, his chadar was hanging over his arm. As he walked towards Abdul Karim, it did not seem as if he posed any threat. What Abdul Karim and the other committee members flanking him did not know was that he had concealed a pistol under the chadar. 'You are talking to men now,' Mulla Mir Rahman hissed at Abdul Karim. 'You had better talk like a man.' It was a strange thing to say, since Mulla Mir Rahman did not give Abdul Karim a chance to change his manner of speaking. He shot him in the mouth.

This was a cue for a volley of bullets to pour down from Zafar Khan and the other Panjpiris positioned around Zkha Khel Bagh. One of the Upper Piwari brothers, Miramjan, was hit, and his dead body lay alongside that of Abdul Karim. Having finished off as many of the committee members as they could, the Panjpiris beat their retreat. Meanwhile, the remnants of the lashkar were already reassembling. One Panjpiri, a neighbour of Maulana Khan Afzal by the name of Maulvi Raza Khan, was stopped and shot dead as he fled to his home.

The Panjpiri thinking was that if they eliminated the lashkar leaders, the *lashkar* would disperse. In fact, the opposite happened. Instead of becoming demoralized, the *lashkar* was energized. 'They have killed the leaders of Islam!' the cry went up. When it became clear that their attack on the *lashkar* leaders had not produced the desired result, the Panjpiris emptied their houses and made their way out of Tirah. Now, besides their houses being doomed, their lives were in danger. The case of Maulvi Raza had shown that. In any event, it was now a case of a life for a life.

It was at this time that the *lashkar* committee summoned me to Tirah. 'Jan Mohammad does not stand a chance now. They will certainly exact revenge by killing him,' the Panjpiri Mulla Katchgoul, not to be confused with my nemesis, the Bar Piwari Katchgoul, said to Zafar Khan as they made their way out of Tirah and left their homes to be burnt down by the lashkar. As we will see in the next chapter, the opposite was the case. While the shooting of the lashkar leaders might not have worked as far as the Panjpiris in Tirah were concerned, it worked in my case. New *lashkar* leaders were put in place, sympathetic to myself. That is a separate story, of which more later.

For now, Zafar Khan and the other Panjpiris were exiled from Tirah. Zafar Khan, for one, was busy plotting his revenge. He initiated the process with a bang. That very winter, barely six months after the Panjpiris' houses in Tirah had been burnt down, I was still a captive, living with Ziarat Shah in Dunga. It was Shalobar Qambar Khel territory. Ziarat Shah's son Surup Shah had gone to the Malik-Din Khel Bagh to collect weekly supplies. I was looking up from my reading of the Quran, gazing out across the plateau of Tirah Maidan towards the old village of Saddar Khel where I had lived in the summer of 1973, when I had been studying with Maulana Khan Afzal. This being such a brilliant winter's morning, my gaze towards my old haunts was particularly acute. I could make out individual houses of Saddar Khel village and Zafar Khan's village above it—now largely razed to the ground since the ravages of the *lashkar*. Above it was Kas and the path leading to the small Adam Khel enclave in Tirah, which we will look at more closely in the next chapter. The stillness of the scene was strangely shimmering in the sun, as if it was the calm before the storm.

Suddenly, as if on cue, the still of the winter morning was broken by the surreal sight of smoke billowing from a house in Kas. I did not know whose house it was, but Surup Shah told me when he returned from his day's shopping that it had been the house of *lashkar* committee member Wali Mohammad. Word had also reached Malik-Din Khel Bagh of who had burnt down Wali Mohammad's house. It had been the redoubtable Panjpiri warrior Zafar Khan.

Since the Panjpiris' expulsion from Tirah Maidan the previous summer, Zafar Khan had been living in the Afridi enclave of Mirobak village on the outskirts of Hangu, below the Samana Heights. Mirobek was a delightful place, tucked between two hills, with greenery and lush plains stretching out towards the Indus valley to the east. As they were together in Tirah, so the household of Zafar Khan was together in Mirobek. All the cousins were living there.

From Mirobek, Zafar Khan only needed to catch a bus to the Dabori bazaar, where the road from Hangu towards Tirah came to an end. From Dabori, there was no end of passes over which he could cross over into Tirah Maidan. There was no reason why anyone should get wind of his arrival in Tirah. In any case, the committee were nowhere to be found in Tirah during those winter months. They had made their way to the warmer climes of Kajuray and Peshawar, like most Afridis. Wali Mohammad was also in the plains of Peshawar. Zafar Khan knew the area well. It was his home turf. He had decided to start his process of revenge by targeting the house of his close neighbour Wali Mohammad.

The male members of Wali Mohammad's household who had remained in Tirah Maidan were all out in the Malik-Din Khel Bagh, buying their supplies for the week. Zafar Khan knew this would be the case. That is why he chose Friday for his attack. As he burst into Wali Mohammad's house with his nephews, armed with spray-cans of petrol, Zafar Khan ordered the womenfolk to leave the house. They initially refused. 'I would not like to have to burn down this home with you all inside,' Zafar Khan warned them. They tried to take some of their most valued possessions, but Zafar Khan did not allow them the time. His nephews were already inside the house, spraying petrol onto the pinewood beams of Wali Mohammad's fortress.

This was the first, symbolic act of revenge by the Panjpiris. Zafar Khan had laid down his marker. There were to be many more similar acts. One year later, the Panjpiris had been rehabilitated. It was just before I left the Frontier to pursue my studies at Darul Uloom Deoband in India. I was living an itinerant existence and sometimes used to visit Zafar Khan in Mirobek, sometimes in Tirah Maidan. One late afternoon, I was on my way to visit him in Tirah Maidan. As I neared his homestead, I saw his nephews busy working in the fields, digging up the earth as people do in the mountain areas in order to make the fields more fertile. 'Oh, come here, Jan Mohammad. Sit to one side, would you?' they called out to me as I approached. They gave me no inkling of what was about to unfold.

Then down in a small ravine, where the path ran alongside the field, a man appeared. He was following a donkey carrying a sack of flour that he had just brought from the mill. Suddenly, out of nowhere, two or three men pounced on him. He was taken protesting into a nearby house, where Zafar Khan was awaiting him. Sternly, he said to him, 'Awal Khan! I will be taking you to account for all the saplings you took from my nursery.' Zafar Khan was referring to a nursery of small saplings that he had nurtured; he owned part of the forest on the hill above his village. The nursery, like the rest of Zafar Khan's property, had been destroyed by the Afridi lashkar. Apparently, according to the information that had reached Zafar Khan, Awal Khan had helped himself to a large number of saplings.

In fact, this was just bravado on the part of Zafar Khan. According to the unwritten law of the Afridis, he would not be able to claim damage done by the *lashkar* from Awal Khan or anyone else since this damage was not the responsibility of any individual but had been inflicted by the whole Afridi tribe. So Zafar Khan devised a ploy to circumnavigate this difficulty. He made a fictitious case against Awal Khan, stating that he had sold him opium and hashish, but Awal Khan had never paid him. Awal Khan was released once he had supplied suitable assurances that he would repay the money due to Zafar Khan for the 'hashish and opium' he had sold him.

After these two symbolic acts of revenge—the burning down of Wali Mohammad's house and the arrest of Awal Khan—Zafar

Khan did not have to do much more. He just had to sit and hold court in Malik-Din Khel Bagh. People would come to him, often people who had heard that he knew about their participation in the lashkar, to seek an out of court settlement. Later, along with a leading Panjpiri from the Shalobar Qambar Khel tribe by the name of Haji Ghafoor Khan, Zafar Khan led a series of lashkars, seeking to keep the upper hand over the committee faction that had burnt down the Panjpiri houses in the lashkar of 1976. In fact, with new players, the same drama was being enacted until recently in Tirah and Kajuray, with the Lashkar-e-Islam representing the Panjpiri faction, the Ansar'al-Islam being the new incarnation of the more traditional-minded committee.

For Zafar Khan, it was a game that he enjoyed playing: 'We are involved in a tussle, Jan Mohammad,' he once told me, with his mischievous grin and the swank that was his trademark, to indicate that he had everything in perspective and was not taking things too seriously. 'Sometimes they come out on top, sometimes us.'

Photo courtesy: The Begums of Bhopal

A dynasty of Pashtoon women in central India.
Begum Shahjehan, Begum of Bhopal 1868–1901

Photo courtesy: Brian Anderson

Pashtoon Englishman had unhindered access to the Constitutional Loya Jirga, held in Kabul in December 2002. Here, the current Afghan President Ashraf Ghani can be seen in the background waiting to take the stage of the Loya Jirga.

Photo courtesy: *Life* magazine

Badshah Sahib, ruler of Swat from 1926–1949, when he abdicated in favour of his son.

Photo courtesy: John Butt

Darul Uloom Deoband, where Pashtoon Englishman spent five years as a student.

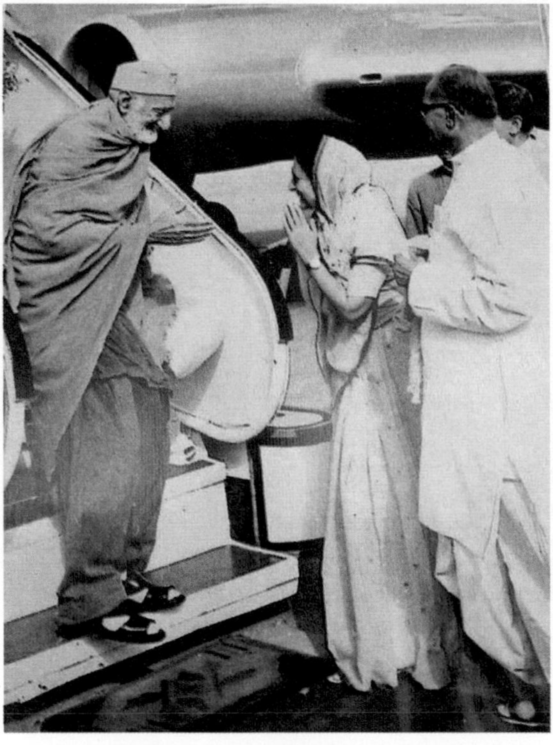

Photo courtesy: The Times of India Group

Frontier Gandhi—Bacha Khan—being received by Prime Minister Indira Gandhi in Delhi.

Photo courtesy: Abdul Samad

In his element—Pashtoon Englishman in Peshawar city, mid-eighties

Photo courtesy: Amanullah

Mahodand Lake in Upper Swat, where the two Johns spent
the first night of their trek.

Photo courtesy: Rajat Malhotra

Modern mulla—Maulana Wahiduddin Khan receives the Rajiv Sadbhavana Award—peace award—from Sonia Gandhi, 2010. In the background is Dr Karan Singh, head of ICCR.

Photo courtesy: Abdul Samad

Mohammad Suleiman, who joined Pashtoon Englishman in Deoband for a short while, and Pashtoon Englishman's lifelong friend Abdul Samad—the Shaykh who got away.

Photo courtesy: Shah Jehan mosque

Pashtoon English mosque—Shah Jehan mosque in Woking in the U.K. The first mosque to be built in the U.K, it was financed by Begum Shah Jehan, ruler of Bhopal.

Photo courtesy: Abdul Samad

Pashtoon Englishmen—Abdul Samad and Jan Mohammad—in Kalam in the 1980s.

Photo courtesy: John Butt

The khanqah—spiritual training centre—of Maulana Ashraf Ali Thanvi in Thana Bhawan, India.

IX

CAPTIVE ENGLISHMAN

If I am going to die, then I have a long journey ahead of me and must eat well.

(Pashtoon Englishman, when under sentence of death from an Afridi *lashkar*, summer of 1976)

I had been told, when I first arrived in Tirah in the spring of 1973, that I was the first Englishman to set foot there since the Tirah Expedition of 1897. This was not strictly true.[1] In 1923, seventeen-year-old Molly Ellis, daughter of the Kohat deputy commissioner, was kidnapped from her home in Kohat by Ajab Khan Afridi and spirited away to one of the furthest recesses of Tirah, the Khanki valley. In the process of kidnapping Molly, they murdered her mother. Fifty-odd years later, in the early summer of 1976, I retraced the route taken by Molly, also as a captive of the Afridis. Indeed, I found myself in the same place where Molly Ellis had been detained. We were both held in Chamkani village, in the Bara

[1] An Afridi elder by the name of Bahadar Khan, whom I talked to in 1973, remembered the British expedition of 1897 as if it was yesterday. He was the one who suggested I might be the first Englishman to set foot in Tirah since then.

River valley, leading to Tirah. While Molly was brought over the pass from Dara AdamKhel, my journey to Chamkani took me over the Shin Qamar Pass, which leads from Bara and the Bara hinterland of Kajuray. Both routes meet at the village of Chamkani, overlooking the cascading, red-coloured Bara River. The Tirah hills are composed of red sandstone, which washes off into the Bara River. Prior to being taken to Chamkani, I had been staying in the wild, scenic spot of Red Mountain, known as Sur Ghar. I had gone to Sur Ghar from Sardar's place, near the Kuhay mosque. The committee seemed to wish to move me around, from place to place, in case anyone got wind of where I was being held. The place where I stayed in Sur Ghar belonged to one of the Malik-Din Khel tribe, Khan Mohammad.

Sur Ghar was virgin territory. Until recently, it had been jungle. When Khan Mohammad arrived in Sur Ghar, he cleared an area for his house. Then he scoured the neighbouring territory for suitable places to fashion fields. I helped him with one of the fields, digging, removing rocks, loosening earth and bringing it to the front of the newly formed terraced field in order to fashion a level field. This was hard, hard work. Sometimes, huge boulders would have to be extracted from the earth—an exhausting task. This is done with what Pashtoons call a *jabal.* A jabal is a thick long iron rod that one can use to reach the base of rocks embedded in the mountain. Slowly and painstakingly, one was able to extract them. Then we needed a pickaxe to break the rocks into more manageable pieces. The relatively gentle work was done with a *kashay*, a utilitarian type of hoe with which one moves the earth to the front of the soon-to-be terraced fields. My kind captors left this easy part to me.

I was totally in my element in Sur Ghar. Khan Mohammad had dug a small irrigation canal, diverting water that came down from the Red Mountain heights through a jungle that was the nearest thing I had ever seen to the Trinidadian rainforest of my childhood. It was such an enchanting spot that I decided to make a little prayer and meditation spot next to a small stream where huge lizards, partridges and snakes kept me company. I put a *mihrab* there, which caused my hosts some concern. A *mihrab* is the niche in a mosque that marks the place of prayer. They said that once there was a *mihrab*, it would have to be maintained, and they did not know whether they would be up to the task. I went ahead and fashioned a *mihrab* anyway. I wonder if my hosts have kept that spot as a mosque, in memory of the Pashtoon Englishman who built it.

One day I was working with Khan Mohammad, carving a terraced field out of the mountain that lay on the other side of the stream where I had made my prayer place. Khan Mohammad's father, who lived in another part of Sur Ghar, came to visit us. 'You really get a feel of the spirit of Islam when you talk to Jan Mohammad,' Khan Mohammad told his father, who nodded in agreement, with some degree of surprise, since the propaganda about the Pashtoon Englishman must have been contrary to what his son said. This was the impression of everyone with whom I stayed during my captivity. Furthermore, my captivity was a learning experience for me that passed in unceasingly excellent company.

One could easily forget, living in Sur Ghar, that there was a *lashkar* in the Afridi country, wreaking havoc and destruction wherever it went, and that I was their prisoner. I was jolted back to reality when an emissary arrived from the lashkar committee. They were asking for my parents' address. It seemed that they were trying to demand a ransom for me. I wrote back to the committee in Pashto. 'Since there are certain specific allegations against me, I should have the opportunity to answer them according to Islamic law. I see no reason to contact my parents, or to provide my parents' address.'

The emissary returned after a day or two. 'You have been summoned by the Afridi *lashkar*.' Khan Mohammad explained to the emissary that I had twisted my ankle and would only be able to meet up with the committee if a mule was sent to transport me. Khan Mohammad's request was an example of the unremitting kindness with which I was treated—not always by the *lashkar* committee itself but by the families to whom my care had been delegated. In one-and-a-half years of captivity with the Afridis, I never had occasion to be offended with my captors. I was always treated like a family member, with utmost consideration.

It was true that I had twisted my ankle in the course of my exertions in Sur Ghar. But the committee did not believe me. They thought it was a ploy to prevent me having to present myself before the committee. If it had been a ploy, it did not work. A mule was duly sent. I made my way on the mule over two passes—one that separates Sur Ghar from Kajuray and the Shin Qamar Pass that separates Kajuray from the Bara River valley. It took most of one day to reach Chamkani village. Here the Bara River is a mountain torrent cascading down from the mountains of Tirah. When it comes to the plains of Kajuray and flows on to Peshawar, it is a gentler, meandering set of streams. I was taken immediately to the large *hujrah* of one Hakim Khan. His house was slated for being given the torch the next day. It was part of the punishment meted out to those who were on the blacklist of the *lashkar* that they should accommodate and feed the *lashkar* for at least a day prior to the actual torching of their house. I joined the hordes that were enjoying the enforced hospitality of the doomed Hakim Khan.

There were a couple of anomalies about the punishment to be meted out to Hakim Khan. For one, Hakim Khan was not an Afridi. He belonged to the Story Khel sub-tribe of the Orakzais. Orakzais were neighbours of the Afridis in Tirah. The Story Khel had become de facto Afridis due to their location in the Bara valley and their proximity there to other Afridi tribes. Being de facto, though not actual Afridis, they even had a representative on the lashkar committee. And members of their tribe, such as Hakim Khan, were also liable to be punished by the laskhkar.

This brings us to the second point regarding Hakim Khan. He was definitely not a Panjpiri, so why was he being targeted by the anti-Panjpiri tribal lashkar? It was for his famed oppressive and cruel practices that he was to be punished. There was a story that once Hakim Khan had been having his hair cut. In those days, the barber did this with a *paki*—a blade that as teenagers in England we had callously called a 'cut-throat'. As the barber went on to shave Hakim Khan's face, he foolishly quipped, while brandishing his naked blade, 'You would be very easy for me to pick off now, wouldn't you, Khan?' He meant it as a joke, of course. Unfortunately, Hakim Khan took it seriously and wishing to eliminate a potential threat, pulled out his revolver and put paid to the poor barber. That was the reputation of ruthlessness and cruelty that

Hakim Khan had. The *lashkar* took it upon itself to cut him down to size.

As I arrived at Hakim Khan's mosque and *hujrah* complex, people were performing ablution for the late afternoon prayer. Katchgoul was also there: 'You fox,' he addressed me aggressively, probably referring to my twisted ankle, as I prepared for the prayer along with others. Amongst all the committee members, Katchgoul's hostility towards me was unmatched. He was a good-looking man, with fair skin, well built with a shining white beard. His clothes were generally white and he carried a holster slung over his shoulder. He walked with a swagger and used to shoot his mouth off a lot, particularly when I was in range. A close relative of the Upper Piwari Latif, he must have been particularly angry that I had thrown in my lot with his Saddar Khel rivals. Besides the personal grudge, I provided lethal propaganda for the commitee against the Panjpiris. According to him, I was their English agent, who had paid off all the Panjpiris and created this so-called heretical sect. But Katchgoul realized that eventually he would have to produce some proof to back up the allegations.

Katchgoul was strangely silent the next morning when the committee sat me down on the banks of the Bara River. 'We want you to admit that you have been funding the Panjpiris, that you are the brains behind them; we want you to write a list of the Panjpiris and how much salary you were giving each of them,' the head of the committee, Abdul Karim, addressed me sternly. I was sitting opposite him. He was squatting, while I was sitting cross-legged on the sand. On either side of us sat members of the committee. The Upper Piwari brothers, Katchgoul and Miramjan, were silent. They had cleverly co- opted Abdul Karim to do their work for them.

He was doing a good job this morning. 'We will give you till this evening,' he continued. 'If you do not admit by then that you have been funding the Panjpiris, we will kill you at four o'clock this afternoon.' 'Allah has given me life, only He can kill me,' I replied, echoing the words of Abraham when he was threatened with death by his nemesis Nimrod (*al-Baqarah* 2:258). Abdul Karim's reply echoed the reply of Nimrod himself: 'You will see if I can kill you or not.' *'Ana uhyi we umeet'* ('I give life and death'). I thought of the words of Nimrod when Abdul Karim said this. His deputy Aziz-ur-Rahman, better known as Alizri, spent the whole day trying to persuade me to write the false confession that the committee wished to extract from me. The committee had reason to be concerned. They had already made these allegations against me. Now they were on their way to the Afridi centre of Tirah. The tribes there were bound to look into whether there was any substance to the allegations they had been making against the Pashtoon Englishman, known as *feringi*. They were trying to fabricate the evidence that they claimed already existed. I had no intention of being party to their plot.

Alizri and I formed a good bond during the day. He kept trying to impress on me that the committee meant what they said. They would kill me if I did not admit to the crimes they had accused me of. During our conversations, a couple of things I said made a special impression on him, which he used to recount to others. The *lashkar* was carrying on up the Bara valley, on its way to burn the house of a Panjpiri from the Story Khel tribe. En-route, we stopped to have a meal in a *hujrah*. It was a delicious meal of free-range eggs and thick, leavened roti—a typical Tirah brunch. I ate a hearty meal, having worked up an appetite following the committee tribunal and a long morning's walking. 'There is no point in you eating at all,' Alizri said in jest. 'You are going to die in any case, so what is the point of eating?'

I must stress that nothing Alizri said during the day came across as unkind or hurtful. Even this comment was meant and taken in good humour. 'If I am going to die,' I replied, 'then I have a long journey ahead of me and must eat even more.' Alizri thought that was very funny and often used to tell others about the exchange. 'So where would you like to be buried?' Alizri asked me as we proceeded towards the Panjpiri's house. 'I would like to be buried in any graveyard of the Muslims.' That was also a meaningful statement for Alizri. If he had not been convinced beforehand of the falseness of the charges against me, then he was now. And he was to show it.

The Panjpiri's house was burnt down. Smoke rose amidst the trees that surrounded the homestead. The crackling of the fire mixed with the rustling of the leaves on the trees, disturbed by the unexpected furnace. It was a shrill sound, as if nature was itself rebelling against the extreme heat caused by the burning edifice. Seemingly impervious to his fate as well as to the possibility of receiving further reprimands from the *lashkar* for fraternizing with the *feringi*, the Panjpiri whose house was being destroyed came to me. His face was kindly, his words sympathetic. He had no thought of his own predicament and was thinking only of me.

Following the torching of the house, the *lashkar* assembled in the field. 'You are about to be killed, admit to what the committee are accusing you of,' some young guys came and pleaded with me, clearly concerned on my behalf. I told them I was innocent and the committee was more likely to kill me if I caved in to their demands than if I remained firm. From afar, I saw Abdul Karim addressing the assembled throng. 'We have this *feringi* with us. He is not admitting to his crimes. What shall we do with him? Shall we kill him?' Then I saw Moosa Khan, another committee delegate, like Alizri and Abdul Karim from the Shalobar Qambar Khel tribe, getting up and answering Abdul Karim. I could pick out a few words of what he was saying. 'We are on our way to the centre of the Afridis. The tribes are waiting for us there in Tirah. Can you imagine what they will think if the feringi they had heard about is no longer with us, if he has been killed? They will conclude that it was all a pack of lies on our part. What answer will we give the tribes? Wait till we reach Tirah Maidan then we will decide what to do with him, in consultation with the tribes there. That is the centre of the Afridi tribes, it is there that his fate should be decided. If we do anything to him here, we will appear as thieves.'

Moosa Khan's argument won the day. And there was another argument that held sway on that day. It was that of Daulat Shah, the Story Khel representative on the lashkar committee. 'You bring him from Afridi territory and now you want to kill him in our Story Khel territory?' he contested, playing on the fact that Story Khel were an Orakzai tribe, not an Afridi one. 'If anyone as much as throws sand at him, I will shoot a bullet at that person.' 'Okay,' the committee told him, 'if you are so concerned about him, you look after him.' Daulat Shah recounted the tale to me as we took the forty-five-minute walk to his own Chamkani village, across the Bara River from the house of Hakim Khan, where we had spent the previous night.

With his tall frame and strutting carriage, Daulat Shah appeared self-assured, but he must have been a worried man. As the *lashkar* representative, he had just been complicit in burning down the house of Hakim Khan. Hakim Khan was powerless now—at present all temporal power lay with the committee and the lashkar—but in the fullness of time, when the dust settled, Hakim Khan would return to being the formidable powerhouse that he previously was. How would Daulat Shah and his family contend with him then? Daulat Shah had another reason to be nervous, stemming from his own committee. The committee had handed me over to Daulat Shah, for safekeeping. And there was a price on my head.

The Afridi *lashkar* had read the riot act to Daulat Shah and his Story Khel tribe when they complained about the prospect of me being killed on their territory. 'If he gets away from you,' the committee had told them, 'nine of your houses will be burnt down, and you will have to pay nine hundred thousand rupees, one house and one hundred thousand for each tribe of the Afridis.' In those nine tribes, they also included Story Khel, which was a bit of a cheek, considering that Story Khel were the ones who stood to be penalized were I to escape. In fact, in all my months of captivity, it never occurred to me to escape. What would people think of me then, were I to make a getaway? They would think that all the allegations against me were true.

My Story Khel hosts were understandably wary. They had heard about a *feringi* who might be some early version of Spiderman, climbing up and down walls. Flying away into the night would be nothing for the fabled *feringi*. So, when I reached the house of Daulat Shah in Chamkani village, I was kept on the top floor of their four-storey house. For the most part, I was kept in fetters. These consist of two iron bars. The base of each iron bar is clamped around each ankle. The iron bars join together at the top, which one can hold in one's hand or even attach to the cord of one's trousers. It is amazing, how an Afridi house comes equipped with fetters, as if they are expecting prisoners at any time. Daulat Shah's elderly uncle seemed contrite when he saw me offering prayer in fetters—something of an art. 'The last English person to be held prisoner by the Afridis, Molly Ellis, also stayed a few nights in this village of ours,' he told me with a tinge of pride.

It was against this backdrop that, escorted by Daulat Shah and his band of men, I arrived in Tirah Maidan. The committee had sent for me. Daulat Shah came to collect me. They kept silent about what had transpired in the meantime. I remember looking up the Bara valley one evening, seeing dark clouds and having a sense of foreboding that something calamitous had happened. The *lashkar* must have also felt the same. Abdul Kareem and Miramjan were both by this time dead men, having been attacked by the Panjpiris under the leadership of Maulana Mir Rahman. The rest of the committee had been able to mobilize tribal opinion against the Panjpiris who had killed the self-styled 'leaders of Islam'. The Panjpiris had fled for their lives. It was expected that the committee would wreak their revenge on me.

Contrary to expectation, the slaying of certain *lashkar* leaders served to ease the pressure on me. With his brother Miramjan dead, Katchgoul seemed demoralized. He never again tormented me, or even said a word to me. The committee summoned me to a house above the Malik-Din Khel Bagh. The mood was hostile towards me, but the new leader of the *lashkar* was Alizri. The bond that he had formed with me on that day in the Bara valley, when death had stalked at my door, now came to the fore. Of course, he could not show his sympathy for me in public. Indeed, when he marched me down to where the *lashkar* was assembled in the Malik-Din Khel Bagh, it could have been for any purpose. He stood me up on the destroyed wall of the *sarai* of Haji Bahadari, a Panjpiri stalwart of Tirah. 'This is the *feringi* that we have been holding,' he told the assembled hordes. 'We will continue to hold him and will consult with you about his fate.' 'I would also like to say a few words,' I began. Some people at the front of the crowd were keen to hear me say a few words. 'You will not speak.' Alizri stifled my words and the crowd's enthusiasm to hear me.

One cannot blame him. He could not afford to let me address the *lashkar* masses, with thousands in attendance in the main centre of the Afridis. That might have scuppered the committee's plans. But the crowd's enthusiasm to hear me speak, and Alizri's determination not to let me say a word sowed seeds of doubt in the minds of the masses. What was the committee trying to hide? Alizri led me away and handed me over to another committee member from his own Shalobar Qambar Khel tribe, Akhtar Gul. Alizri accompanied me some way from the Malik-Din Khel Bagh towards the Shalobar Qambar Khel border. 'Do not worry,' he whispered in my ear. 'I promise you, there is no danger to your life.' Except for Abdul Karim and the two Bar Piwari brothers, the statement was typical of the unremitting kindness I received from my Afridi captors over one-and-a-half years. Far from harming me physically, they also went to extreme lengths to ensure that my feelings were never hurt.

By taking me away from the Malik-Din Khel tribe and putting me in the custody of his own Shalobari Qambar Khels, Alizri showed that he meant what he had said, that there would be no danger to my life. For the rest of the one year of my detention, I remained with the Shalobar Qambar Khel tribe. First, I stayed in the Tanday village in an area of Shalobar Qambar Khel called Dunga. Akhtar Gul was my host there. He was one of three brothers. He had an elder brother by the name of Sarwan and a younger brother by the name of Mina Gul. Mina Gul is now Haji Mina Gul and quite a leader of the Shalobari Qambar Khels, so I hear. My life became pretty normal in Tanday village. I was living in the *hujrah* of Akhtar Gul, praying in the mosque five times a day. Sometimes, I would take a walk around the village with Sarwan. A distinguished, pious-looking gentleman, he also liked chatting and cracking jokes, basically flirting, with the Sikh ladies in the village as they returned from fetching water.

'What can I bring you from Peshawar?' Mina Gul asked me on one occasion, when he was leaving for the provincial metropolis. I told him I could really do with a copy of the Persian translation of the holy Qur'an—the first translation to be completed in South Asia—by the venerated muhaddith of Delhi, Shah Waliullah. Mina Gul brought me back the version published by Taj Company, with the translation written under the original Arabic text. I will always remember the look of glee and satisfaction on his face as he approached our *hujrah*, gripping the copy of the Qur'an in his hand. Nothing that he had brought from Peshawar for his family could compare with this gift that he had brought for the Pashtoon Englishman who was captive of the Afridis—his honoured guest.

Perhaps the committee did not want to leave me in one place too long, and the *hujrah* where I stayed in Tanday village was quite exposed to outside visitors. Anyone could come and see me. The committee clearly wanted me to be somewhere more secluded. So one day some people came from the nearby mountain recess of Landaur and took me over the pass that leads from Dunga to Landaur. Landaur is an interesting name. The name is shared with a place above the mountain town of Mussoorie, in the Garhwal hills of northern India. The name Landaur—so plaques in Mussoorie proclaim—is derived from the name of a town in Wales[2]. It comes as no surprise that the British were able to give the name of a Welsh town to a Mussoorie mountain station that was a Christian and missionary centre, but that they were able to give the same name to a far-off recess in the Tirah valley is more surprising.

Landaur is a mountain enclave tucked away above Tirah Maidan. It has two parts, one of which is attached to Shalobar Qambar Khel and one of which belongs to the Malik-Din Khels. Further up in the mountains from Landaur is a place called Landaki, inhabited by the Qamar Khel tribe, the smallest of the eight Afridi tribes. In Landaur, I was to stay with a family that included two brothers by the names of Dur Akbar and Sayyed Akbar. For a while, I put up with their elder brother at the top of Landaur. When I arrived from Dunga, immediately his son went to work massaging my feet and legs, even though it had not been a particularly long journey, to make sure that no stiffness ensued from my exertions. It was just an act of kindness and consideration towards me. My host had an expansive *hujrah*. Whenever the menfolk were out, his wife would put in a discreet appearance at the door, telling me how honoured they were to be looking after me, how they just wanted me to be happy and that if I needed anything in particular, I should let her know.

---

[2] The Welsh spelling of the name Landaur is Llanddowror.

It was during these autumn days, in the run-up to Ramadan, that I started fasting every day, not only during Ramadan—that is obligatory for every Muslim—but outside Ramadan also. It was due to the affinity between Qur'an recitation and fasting that I took this step. It seemed more appropriate that I should take in the spiritual food of the Qur'an, while at the same time depriving myself of physical food. During the day, once the autumn sun became warm, I would take myself to the roof of the *hujrah* and recite the Quran, along with the Persian translation of Shah Waliullah that Mina Gul had bought for me. More than any other time, this was the time that I became familiar with the Book of Allah. Typically, it took me about ten days to complete the Qur'an once—in original Arabic and in Persian translation. I did not take any notes, but I reflected on the contents as I went along and took strength from the words of the holy book in my predicament. I would conduct my recitation of the Qur'an during the morning, come down to the mosque for the afternoon prayers then spend some time on the *hujrah's* verandah in the company of other villagers.

One afternoon, something happened that summed up the kindness of the Afridis—my captors—towards me. I was sitting in the midst of a group of men in the *hujrah* when I accidentally let off a fart. One thing that had been ingrained in me from an early time by the Afridis was that if you let off wind noisily in public then it is a matter of such shame that one might even have to leave one's native land. That option was not open to me. I was abashed and ashamed at having let off wind so loudly and so publicly. I could not face the other men in the *hujrah* and escaped to the darkness of the room adjoining the verandah. I just lay there on my own, staring into the darkness, wondering how I was going to face these people, whom I saw day in and day out, in the future.

Later on, some of the villagers quietly joined me and sat around the room, on the beds along the walls of the room. They made casual conversation amongst themselves. They did not show any signs of having noticed any embarrassment on my part. Then, in the course of their own conversation, one of them said to the other: 'Wasn't it funny how Sarfaraz farted in the *hujrah* this afternoon!'

Immediately, my shame was relieved. They had all thought it was Sarfaraz! In fact, they had known very well it was me, but had only put the blame on Sarfaraz, a village youth, in order to relieve my embarrassment. Only total empathy with a person can enable one to be so considerate of his feelings and to act in a manner designed to make him feel better. I wonder if that empathy came naturally to them or if they had discussed amongst themselves what they could do to make me feel better. I get the impression that while sitting on the verandah, they had probably given each other the eye, let's go inside and cheer poor Jan Mohammad up.

Sometimes, we would go to the family *hujrah* higher up the mountainside during the day. We were spending the day at the higher *hujrah* one day when I saw an elderly gentleman in the verandah of the lower *hujrah* examining the bedclothes. What had he been doing, I asked Sayyed Akbar later. 'It was a funny thing,' Sayyed Akbar replied. 'He came to the *hujrah* and said that he can tell what sort of a person a guy is from the smell of the bedclothes he sleeps in: "Since I have heard so much about this *feringi*, I would like to examine his bedclothes. I want to ascertain if he is like people say he is, or if it is a load of lies and propaganda."' So they gave him my bedclothes to examine. He sniffed the bedclothes all over. 'And what was his verdict?' I wondered. 'He said there was nothing wrong with you and that you were a good person and a pious Muslim,' Sayyed Akbar replied.

Autumn is also the time of the passing of the cranes from their summer abode in Kazakhstan to the places in India where they spend the winter. I had often heard the cranes passing this way and that during the time I had spent in Tirah. They tend to travel at night and chatter during their flight. Quite often one catches sight of them at dusk. It being autumn, these cranes (*zanay*) were on their way to India. As I gazed at them flying overhead, I had a clear premonition that one day I would be free of my detention and would follow them to India. That trail of cranes in the sky that I saw in the evening in Landaur was leading me, beckoning me, to the land of my dreams. Later on, when I was studying in India and had also begun reading Rumi, I penned this verse:

Wild cranes
From Turkestan way
Bless you
For showing the way
To a lone prisoner
Stranded midst foes
To a freedom visioner
Lost in the woes
Of worldly contention.

Wild cranes
You showed me the way
Now I linger with parrots
Down in Hindustan plains
They may be the ones who showed others the way
Captives in cages
Back in Rumi's day[3]

While the wild cranes
Have gone back
Turkestan way.

Ramadan passed, autumn turned to winter and once again I returned to Dunga. This time, it was to the house of Ziarat Shah. A man wizened before his years, he was the perfect guard for a captive. He himself was a captive, not having left his home for the last twenty-five years. The reason was an ongoing feud with the people who lived across the way. Strangely, Ziarat Shah's son Surup Shah used to leave the home at will and seemed to be under no threat. In some Afridi feuds, the son—indeed any male family member—would be pursued in the same way as the father. But not

[3] The reference is to a parable in Rumi's Mathnavi, where a trader on his way to Hindustan asks his pet parrot what he would like from India. The parrot asks him to convey his salams to his fellow parrots in India. The parrots in India feign death. When the pet parrot does the same, his owner releases him from the cage. It is an allusion to the Sufi adage: 'Die before you die.' Then you will attain freedom.

in this case. Ziarat Shah made the best of his time at home. He could fashion almost anything out of dwarf palm, surely one of the most versatile raw materials in the world. As its name suggests, unlike other palms, dwarf palm grows not as a tree but in clumps. The most common thing that is made from it is rope. The rope is woven into beds that adorn every Pashtoon *hujrah*. But beds were child's play for Ziarat Shah.

Almost anyone could fashion beds from dwarf palm. Ziarat Shah's speciality was sandals made of dwarf palm. These sandals became my staple footwear. In the old days, these sandals (known to Afridis as *saplai*) were the standard footwear of most Afridis. In winter, they would have goatskins up to their knees and saplai on their feet. The soles of *saplai* had a firm grip in the snow. When you wore *saplai* in Peshawar, people tended to take fright, imagining that the wild Afridis from the days of Haji Multan had returned to maraud Peshawar. Haji Multan was a famous robber from the Zkha Khel Afridi tribe, who in the 1930s used to specialize in robbing the Andarshahr area of Peshawar city, near Mahabat Khan mosque where many jewellers have their shops.

It was not only saplai but anything that was needed around the house—prayer mats, bread baskets, items of that nature— that would be quickly put together by Ziarat Shah. But that was not how he made his living. For a living, he made felt rugs. The wool for the felt rug would be spun in the *hujrah* where I was staying. After spinning, it would be arranged into a thick pad, resembling a mattress, then soaked in soapy water. It was then tied tightly inside a mat made of dwarf palm—what else? After which the wool would stick together and congeal into a slim rug. The coloured pattern was added later on. Ziarat Shah's son and brother-in-law would join him in their home-based rug-making business. It did not cost a lot to live in Tirah, and they seemed to be managing well.

The six hundred rupees that they received per month from the *lashkar* committee to look after me also came in useful. In fact, they used some of the money to buy a cow, after which we had a constant supply of milk for our tea. So much did the cow become associated with me that she was moved into the same room as me! That was the warmest place in the house. Perhaps this was one reason for the respect shown to me by the people who looked after me, because of the extra income that came into the family. This tallied with the traditional Islamic opinion of a guest, that he is a blessing since he brings his own provision with him. So I was a particularly blessed guest, since the provision was particularly evident.

The salary given to those who looked after me was from the whole Afridi tribe. Now I was also the guest of the Shalobar Qambar Khel sub-tribe of the Afridis. They also wished to bestow some particular favour on their honoured guest. They decided that since it was winter, and I should be kept warm during the winter, Ziarat Shah should cut down one oak tree on my behalf from their forest, the firewood of which would last through the winter. It was a great act of generosity on the part of the Shalobar Qambar Khel tribe. Small matter that the firewood did not have time to dry before the winter. It burnt our eyes as we tried to make it burn. Afridis do not use chimneys. They just lie low in the room while the smoke rises towards the ceiling. But wet oak makes so much smoke that there was no refuge even on the floor. The smoke must have been even worse for the cow, staying in the same room as us, who had no choice but to suffer in silence.

As winter set in, Ziarat Shah and his family took on another house for the winter months. This is customary amongst the Afridis, who like to go to the warmer climes of Peshawar and Kajuray during the winter, leaving their houses in Tirah empty. Ziarat Shah's family took on one of these empty houses. There tends to be a lot of snowfall in Tirah. If a house is empty, the snowfall can be very damaging, especially for the flat roofs, from which snow has to be shovelled off as soon as it falls. So Ziarat Shah was paid by the owner to take on an expansive four-storey house, so he could look after it and keep it free from snow. The house had a lovely verandah on the top floor. There I spent my days, reciting the Qur'an and usually fasting. My daily fasts had now been replaced by fasting every other day. One Panjpiri friend, his name was Aslam, came to visit me. He was a particularly saintly looking, pious but also an affable young man. He had been a tailor in Abdul Majeed's shop in Bara. He was soft-spoken, always smiling, a picture of gentility. 'Do not fast every day,' he said. 'Fast every other day, fasting on alternate days is known as the fast of the Prophet David (*saum-e-Daud alaihi's-salam*) and is considered the most excellent of fasts.'

I noticed that on the days when I was fasting, my concentration on Qur'an recitation was more total. It was as if the more one divested oneself of worldly food, the more receptive one became to the spiritual food of the Qur'an. In addition to the Qur'an I also started studying Hadith, the traditions and sayings of the Holy Prophet. An elder of the Shalobar Qambar Khel tribe, Qazi Hamid, visited me and asked me if there was anything he could bring for me. Since he was an an Islamic scholar (*alim*), I asked him if he could lend me a copy of *Mishkat'al-Masabih*, the collection of Hadith that I had been studying with Maulana Khan Afzal. Qazi Hamid was happy to oblige. Continual study of the most essential Islamic scriptures—the Book of Allah and the sayings of His Prophet—helped embed these holy books in my mind and make-up. In later years, I have always been able to hone in on an appropriate verse of the Qur'an, or a suitable saying of the Holy Prophet, to apply to a certain situation. This is a legacy of my days in captivity, my fasting and my constant recital of the holy books during that time.

Life did have its light side. Since Tirah is a cold, mountainous area, no crops grow there in winter. The fields are empty, which means a field day for the boys, who use the fields for play. The game of choice of the boys in the neighbourhood was a crude version of the rounders we used to play as kids called *ghundaska*. *Ghundaska* actually means a ball. The ball was a work of art, fashioned by women in the household. It was made from scraps of cloth, sewn together as tightly as possible into a ball. *Tirahwal ghundaska* was a cross between cricket and baseball. The field was designed like a cricket pitch, but the bat was more like a baseball bat than a cricket bat. When a batsman hit the ball and ran, he would be out if the fielder threw the ball and struck him before he made it 'home' in one of the two wickets. It was just as well that the boys' mums made the balls tight, but relatively soft, to lessen the pain of the impact.

By now, the committee had outlived their purpose. Having burnt down all the Panjpiris' houses, there was nothing else for them to do. The only thing left was to decide what to do with me.

My own case became something of a cause célèbre in the tribes. The tribes would gather every Friday, after the Friday prayers in the mosque in the Malik-Din Khel Bagh. Ziarat Shah's son Surup Shah used to bring back regular reports from the gathering. My continued detention was the main topic of conversation amongst the tribes. A joker called Mir Afzal aside, the mood was in favour of settling the matter of my detention. Mir Afzal was a law unto himself. His main argument was that I was the grandson of Molly Ellis. He maintained that I had come to take revenge for the murder of Molly's mother. The story amongst the Pashtoons is that Ajab Khan and his gang treated Molly Ellis honourably, and that is so. But it is also a fact that, in kidnapping her, Ajab Khan had killed Molly Ellis' mother. So according to Pashtoonwali, Molly Ellis' grandson would have had legitimate cause for revenge.

Later on, I was lucky enough to meet Molly Ellis, on two occasions, in fact, in the early nineties. Molly, whose married name was Wade by then, was living in an old folks' home in Woodbridge in Suffolk. Prior to visiting her, I also met the son of Ajab Khan Afridi, Nek Mohammad Ghazizoi. He wished to send a shawl to Molly. When I offered this to Mrs Wade, she was shocked. 'Nek Mohammad, of all people,' she almost scoffed. It was as if the fact that Molly's mother had been murdered by Ajab Khan had been forgotten. She took the shawl, but somewhat unwillingly.

People laughed at Mir Afzal, as so did I when I heard his stories from Surup Shah. Later on, when I met Mir Afzal in the Malik-Din Khel Bagh, we had a very cordial and good-natured conversation. It is good to have people like him around, for entertainment value.

A Shalobar Qambar Khel tribal leader by the name of Gulab Khan had caught the public mood regarding my predicament. Gulab Khan was the elder brother of Haji Ghafoor Khan, who was later to become a leader of the Afridi lashkar in his own right. But Haji Ghafoor Khan was too tainted with the Panjpiri brush to be able to speak up himself, for now at any rate.

Every Friday, in the gathering of the Afridis that took place after congregational prayers in the Malik-Din Khel Bagh, Gulab Khan would address the assembled tribes. It being winter, the committee and their henchmen were in the low-lying plains of Kajuray. 'What is the point of keeping this feringi as a prisoner?' Gulab Khan would ask without fail, every Friday. 'Let's bring him out into the open. If he has done something wrong, we can decide what to do with him. But if he is innocent of all the accusations that have been levelled against him, there is no reason why he should remain prisoner.'

The tribes responded positively to Gulab Khan's reasoning. My release soon became a matter of time. When it came, I was brought before a tribunal of scholars and elders. I presume it was representative of all the Afridis, but the people I recognized on the tribunal were Shalobar Qambar Khels. The hearing took place in the *hujrah* of their famous the elder teacher (*masharay ostaz*). The elder teacher himself had passed away. One of his sons, Abdul Hadi, lived and worked in Afghanistan. He was a public prosecutor (*saranwal*) in Afghanistan. At this time—remember it was the mid-seventies and the height of the Pashtoonistan movement—for an Afridi to live and work in Afghanistan was a sure sign that he was a true Pashtoonistani who looked to Afghanistan as the mother country.

Abdul Hadi's elder brother had inherited the mantle of his father. He was sitting at the head of an arc of eminent-looking Islamic scholars, resplendent in their turbans, robes and long grey, white and hennaed beards. The only one who spoke to me was Maulana Sifat Shah. He was a Panjpiri—as we have seen he was a graduate of Darul Uloom Deoband—but had escaped punishment from the committee by recanting. Though Panjpiri in his beliefs, he had never signed up to the Panjpiri party as such. He had not become sectarian, nor had he side-lined himself from the mainstream of Tirah society. That is how he managed to save his livelihood and home. 'Are you a Muslim?' he asked. 'Of course I am, praise be to God,' I replied. 'Kindly recite to me the testimony of faith.' I recited the kalima (*La ilaha illa'llahu Mohammad-ur-rasool'ullah*). They announced my freedom. I was no longer a prisoner. I was taken to the Dabori bazaar and put on a bus to Peshawar. My sojourn in Tirah had come to an end.

It came as no surprise, considering the disturbances in Tirah that had centred on my person, that I became a centre of attention for authorities in Peshawar after my release. I had lost my passport in Tirah. Katchgoul had brandished it in front of my face when I was first taken captive. I went to the British High Commission in Islamabad and applied for a new passport. I told the consular officer how I had lost my passport in the tribal territory while being taken captive and there had been no police station where I could lodge a complaint. 'If there had been, I would have drawn their attention to my own plight!' 'That sounds like a very unlikely story.' With these words, the consular officer dismissed my request. My quest for a new passport took me to the deputy commissioner's office in Peshawar. His scribe kept me waiting in an adjoining room and I did not even meet the deputy commissioner. When an inspector of police turned up, along with some of his constables, the scribe signalled in my direction: 'He is the one. Seize him.'

The inspector arrested me and took me to the eastern cantonment police station. From the onset, the officers in the police station made clear their wish to release me as soon as possible. I think it was just the fact that I was a foreigner who had accepted Islam which led them to be keen to release me, being almost embarrassed by my arrest. Forget the fact that it was the deputy commissioner who had arrested me. As the senior-most law enforcement officer of the Frontier province, the deputy commissioner's word should have been the final one. Forget also the fact that I had been arrested under the 14th Foreign Act: for being without a visa, or in my case passport. The only legal outcome of my arrest was deportation from the country. The officers in the police station had other ideas. 'It is Thursday afternoon,' they pointed out to me. At this time, the government of Zulfikar Ali Bhutto had made Friday a day off in Pakistan. If I were not released on Thursday, I would have to wait until the courts reconvened after the weekend. Those manning the police station clearly did not want that. They wanted to see me free. Quickly, they took my statement. It is difficult to know what to say in a statement when there is no specific crime. In any case, I mentioned the loss of my passport, my efforts to report the unusual circumstances of its loss and my request for a new passport. Buckets of rain started pouring down. The elements only increased the urgency of the situation.

My friend Malik Azeem Khan came to the police station, along with a lawyer he had commandeered. Small in stature and light in build, Azeem Khan was possessed of a ferocity that belied his slender stature. He occupied with equal energy and confidence the roles of village chieftain and court operator, for often village disputes would end up in the city courts (*kacharis*). That is how he looked at my case, as a personal matter that had come to the courts. Malik Azeem Khan was one of a small group of Panjpiris who were committed active members of the Pakistan People's Party of Zulfikar Ali Bhutto. His politics were secular. At the same time, he was a devoted man of faith, committed to the Panjpiri cause. 'Do not worry,' he assured the officers in the police station. 'We are working on it. We will get him out of here in a short time.'

Before long, I was summoned before the on-duty magistrate, who happened to be Esa Khan from the Afridi Kuki Khel tribe. He was a grandson of Nawab Zaman Khan, who fifty years earlier had played a role in the release of Molly Ellis. In the wake of my release from Tirah, I had come to know Esa Khan quite well. I often visited their home in the Kakshal area of Peshawar. Esa Khan had no idea that I had been arrested. As I entered his court he greeted me warmly: 'Jan Mohammad, welcome to my court!' He sprang to his feet and came forward to embrace me. Never had a defendant enjoyed a warmer reception on entering the court where his case was about to be judged. Noticing the police constable accompanying me, he became somewhat uneasy. 'I hope everything is okay,' he asked, looking to one side of me, then the other. Azeem Khan explained to him the situation and told him that the deputy commissioner had put me behind bars. 'Oh well,' Esa Khan put on a serious tone, 'I guess I will have no option but to remand him in custody.' As Azeem Khan and his lawyer friend began to protest, Esa Khan laughed. 'I am only joking, silly. I hope you did not charge him any fees,' he added, turning to the lawyer. 'Of course not,' Azeem Khan answered on behalf of the lawyer. 'He spent last night in my home in the village!'

Esa Khan had utilized his power as a magistrate to release me, but the question of my passport remained. I needed the cooperation of the deputy commissioner in order to procure a new one. I visited Faridullah Shah, one of the senior-most former administrators of the Frontier Province. He was a friend of Sardar Abdul Rashid, who will be occurring further, later in our story. Faridullah Shah rang the deputy commissioner. 'Jan Mohammad wants to leave Pakistan. He says that he regrets living in Pakistan. He wants to go and live in India. But to do this, he needs a passport!' Faridullah Shah was intentionally putting the deputy commissioner to shame by telling him I wanted to leave Pakistan and go to India. Still, it did not seem to entirely do the trick. When Faridullah Shah put down the phone, he warned me to be careful since the deputy commissioner might arrest me again if I went back to see him. The deputy commissioner was even more incensed now that I had managed to escape his grasp thanks to the intervention of Esa Khan.

I was living like a fugitive now, knowing that the authorities would arrest me if they were able to track me down. Sometimes, I would spend my nights in the tribal territory, where two Malik-Din Khel tribesmen, Akbar Khan and Haji Nawab, were committed to helping me. Of course, they were both Panjpiris. As far as their commitment to the Panjpiri cause and to helping me were concerned, Akbar Khan and Haji Nawab were one. Otherwise, they were deadly enemies, saddled with an age-old vendetta that no one could resolve.

With the encouragement and support of Akbar Khan, I decided to turn my attention to the political agent, under whose jurisdiction my passport had been lost, and who knew the whole story of my extended stay amongst the Afridis. That did not prevent the political agent from also putting me behind bars. Another stay in jail followed, this time longer than before. Under the Frontier Crimes Regulation, a law introduced by the British under which the tribal regions are governed, the political agent rules as a type of dictator in the tribal agency over which he presides. As the Afridis are accustomed to saying, the political agent is the police, the judge and the jury. Eventually Akbar Khan offered surety on my behalf. I also received the documentation I had been looking for. I went to the British High Commission to receive my passport.

'I spent two weeks in jail since you refused to give me a passport when I came previously,' I told the consul. 'Oh, you were in jail for a couple of weeks?' the consul did not seem overly disturbed. He seemed more concerned about the whereabouts of another English Muslim. 'Did you come across another Englishman, with a Muslim name, Abdul this or that? We are trying to trace him.' It seemed I was not the only English convert who had become lost in the Frontier. I told him I had not come across any such person, gratefully took my passport and started packing my bags for India.

It was a sacred journey for me, from Peshawar to Deoband. The path that I took was one that had been taken by many Pashtoon *talibs* in the past. Ever since the establishment of Darul Uloom Deoband in the nineteenth century, Pashtoons had been making their way down the Grand Trunk Road from Peshawar to Deoband. Since 1947, these journeys had been cut short due to the difficulties Pashtoon *talibs* had in obtaining a visa to study in Deoband. It was a tradition that I, as a Pashtoon Englishman with the freedom of a British passport, was now able to revive.

X

THE BOOK OF ALLAH

And that I should recite the Qur'an (Wa an atluw'al-Qur'an)

(*Al-Naml* 27:92)

Ever since I started studying with Maulana Daim'al-Haq in 1971, and continued studying with Maulana Zakariya and Maulana Khan Afzal in 1973, it was my dream to go and study with the teacher of my teachers: Shaykh'al-Qur'an Maulana Mohammad Tahir Panjpiri. In the month of Ramadan, 1973, I realized that dream. I went to Panjpir village for the annual study tour (*daura*) of the Holy Qur'an.

When you have heard much about a person you tend to build an angelic image in your mind. Often, when you see that person in real life, you might be disappointed that his appearance does not live up to one's expectations. Not so Shaykh'al-Qur'an. He looked like a saint. He dressed simply. He wore a simple white cap, such as would normally be worn by any Pashtoon from the mountain valleys of Swat or Dir. No turban or anything ostentatious. His beard was like pure white silk. Not only was his appearance striking, his command of his native Pashto was total. He spoke the pure Pashto that people in the plains learn from their mothers. Pashto is a strange language. Generally, the more one becomes educated the worse one's Pashto becomes since it becomes adulterated with English and Urdu words. This was not the case if one received one's education at the feet of Maulana Mohammad Tahir. One's Pashto became more colourful, richer, purer in the company of the Shaykh. Added to his colourful vocabulary was the fact that he spoke with the attractive lilt of his native Swabi—the district where the village of Panjpir is situated, on the banks of the River Indus.

People are often amazed at what they generously call the pure Pashto that I speak. 'Where did you learn such Pashto?' they ask me. They are even more amazed at my answer: 'In madrasa.' Generally, Pashtoon nationalists look at mullas and madrasas as the antithesis of Pashtoonwali. Be that as it may, it certainly was not the case with Shaykh'al-Quran. Quite apart from learning the Qur'an—of course Panjpir was the place where one could really explore the Book of Allah—by attending the madrasa in Panjpir one came to appreciate the Pashto language even more. The Panjpir maulana sahib was not only Shaykh'al-Quran. In the same way as Maulana Mahmud'al- Hasan was known as Shaykh'al-Hind—the shaykh of Indian nationalism—Maulana Mohammad Tahir also deserved to be called Shaykh'al-Pashto—the Master of Pashto.

So great was Maulana Mohammad Tahir's belief in the Pashto language that he did one extraordinary thing. He recited the Qur'an in Pashto. While his students kept their eyes fixed on the holy book and its Arabic text, he would be running through the Pashto translation without any reference to the original Arabic. Read the holy book in Arabic, but understand it and preach it in Pashto, he seemed to be telling his students; as the Qur'an says, in the language of one's people (*bilasani qaumihi*). (*Ibrahim* 14:4)

So much for the Pashto and the person of the maulana, now we come to the Panjpiri part. As you will have gathered, rank- and-file Pashtoons frowned on the name Panjpiri. 'Panjpir' means five *pirs*, a *pir* being a spiritual guide. That is what seemed suspicious to Pashtoons. It sounded as if the Panjpiris had five imams, instead of the four imams of Sunni Islam. 'Where does the fifth *pir* come from?' would be a typical comment against the Panjpiris. But in fact, Panjpir is the name of the village from where the Panjpir maulana hails. It is said in Panjpir village that the village got its name from five holy men—in other words *pirs*—who had lived in a cave on the mountain that dominates Panjpir village. It is strange how the name Panjpir crops up in different places. There are five *pirs*—known in Pashto as *pinzuh peeran*—buried in the village of Hazarkhanay, on the outskirts of Peshawar, regarding whom a famous song has been sung:

Da khar puh khwa, khwa, khwa ke Pinzuh peeran dee yera

Right next to the city, you know There are five *pirs*, my friend.

So in fact there was nothing sinister about being a Panjpiri. All it meant was that one was associated with that particular village, either because one was from the village or because one had studied in the Panjpir madrasa. At that time, however, it was tantamount to abuse to call someone a Panjpiri. The Panjpiris, for their part, far from shying away from a label that they realized irked others, revelled in it. Take the beginning of the chapter of the Qur'an entitled The Believers (*al-Mu'minun*) which gives the qualities of true believers: they are humble in their prayer; they eschew frivolity; they give charity; they safeguard their chastity; and they keep their promises (*al-Mu'minun* 23:1-9). Five qualities? Panj pir! Shaykh'al-Qur'an would emphasize the point jokingly and point out that one had to be Panjpiri—one endowed with these five qualities—in order to be a good Muslim.

It was much the same with Abdul Ghaffar Khan's Red Shirts, as the Khudai Khidmatgars were called by the British. The British pounced on the fact that they wore red shirts. In fact, the shirts that the Khudai Khidmatgars used to don were red because of the natural colour—derived from the root of the dwarf palm—in which their homespun cotton clothes were dyed. 'The natural white colour of the homespun cotton used to become dirty very quickly, so we dyed them red,' Ghaffar Khan's son-in-law Yahya Jan explained to me. When it became clear to the Khudai Khidmatgars that the British government was seeking to malign them by dubbing them Red Shirts, then they also called themselves by the same name, *sur posh*, with pride and a good deal of relish. They took perverse pleasure in the fact that by using this name they were annoying the British. The moral of the story? Do not pick on faults of the Pashtoons that you object to: they will only accentuate those faults in order to annoy you.

A mountain and a river: that sums up the village of Panjpir. The village is nestled on the mountainside, but the madrasa of Panjpir lies on the banks of the river. Normally, the river is no more than a stream. In those days, in the early seventies, one had to cross the river by foot, there being no bridge across it. During the rainy season, when the floodwaters came down from the mountains to the north of Panjpir, the river turned into a torrent. Even the madrasa was prone to flooding at that time. At such times, one had to approach Panjpir from a roundabout route, through the neighbouring Zeda village.

I do not know the exact numbers, but there were a good 1,500 to 2,000 students in attendance when Shaykh'al-Qur'an gave his annual series of Qur'an lectures during Ramadan. Of these, 80 to 90 per cent would have been from Afghanistan. Most of the others were from Frontier districts bordering Afghanistan— Bajaur, some maybe from Dir, adjacent to the Swat valley. As the years unfolded, I was to realize that this preference, amongst Afghan Pashtoons in particular, for madrasa education had a lot to do with the manner in which secular education had been introduced in Afghanistan. Particularly during the time of Amir Amanullah Khan (1919–29), school education was introduced along very secular lines in Afghanistan, with girls who went to school being forced to take off their veils. Such acts of enforced secularization created a perception amongst sections of the rural population that school education corrupted the values of the youth, that it took them away from their traditions and made them less worthy Muslims and Pashtoons.

While madrasa students distrust the school system of education, the opposite is also true. Amongst those educated in schools there is also a perception that madrasas are antiquated institutions that practice rote learning and produce mullas who are only good for the mosque or the madrasa and cannot make any meaningful contribution in mainstream life. This is not the case. In fact, a madrasa education is akin to a classical education in the West. Old-fashioned it may be, in need of reform, definitely, but meaningful nonetheless. It was a great regret of mine that despite studying with the Jesuits in England I had not concentrated on a classical education. The Jesuits are masters of the classics. At Stonyhurst, where I went to school, some of the Jesuit priests would even talk to each other in Latin! I guess by immersing myself in a madrasa education, I compensated for my failing to pursue a classical education as a boy in England.

To my mind, a classical education is a good education. It is real education. It enlightens you in every walk of life. Philosophy, logic, science, drama, grammar, history, theology, sociology, literature, medicine, political theory—there is not a single field of learning that is untouched by a classical education. In the West, after receiving a classical education, you are able to advance in whichever walk of life you wish since you have become well versed in the basics. A legitimate criticism of a madrasa education might be that it is too tilted towards theology. It does not deal with other areas that classical works of Islam have covered. Madrasa students may graduate from madrasa without, for example, knowing anything about the ground-breaking work of Ibn Khaldun on the lessons of history, the causes of the rise and fall of empires. Eminent figures such as Ibn Khaldun are more appreciated by Western orientalists than they are by the Islamic scholars who teach in madrasas. It is not as if the work of Ibn Khaldun is in any way profane. It can be seen as an elaboration and explanation of a verse of the Quran, 'Say, "Lord, Sovereign of all sovereignty. You bestow sovereignty on whom You will and take it away from whom you please."' (*al-Imran* 3:26)

Still, this does not make madrasa education any less worthwhile as classical education. A madrasa student can easily branch off into other areas of study, on the basis of his or her classical madrasa education. I cannot recall Shaykh'al-Qur'an delving into the works of Ibn Khaldun, but he did explore works that lie beyond the normal ambit of a madrasa curriculum. For example, the *Life of Animals* (*Hayat'al-Haywan'al-Kubra*) by Al-Damiri, a classical work on zoology. Its starting point is the verse of the Qur'an that points out that all animals and birds have their own communities, like human beings.[1] One of Shaykh'al-Quran's favourite books was the masterful work of Ibn Battuta, on the 'marvel of travelling', documenting his travels from his Morocco to India and China, from which Shaykh'al-Qur'an used to quote extensively. What Ibn Battuta did was nothing more than put into practice the stress that the Qur'an lays, in several places, on learning lessons from travelling in the land (*al-sayr fi'l-ard*).

There was a lot of emphasis on teaching the Qur'an to women in Panjpir and on the rights of women in the holy book. When introducing the Women *Surah* in the Qur'an (*Surah an-Nisa*), Shaykh'al-Qur'an used to narrate a novel interpretation of a saying of the Holy Prophet:

> I am fond of two things in this world, the Holy Prophet said: women and perfume. And my refreshment—the coolness of my eye—comes from prayer.

What this Hadith meant, Shaykh'al-Qur'an used to explain, is that the Holy Prophet was devoted to promoting women's rights. Shaykh'al-Qur'an dedicated many hours of his lectures to extolling the elevated role of women as guardians of the home. Madrasa students practice more repetition (*takrar*) than silent revision as is the practice in the West. This system of *takrar* in Panjpir was based on interaction. One student, who excelled in his studies, would repeat the lesson of the day to two or three other students who were in his revision group. In these revision groups, there was more discussion of the content of classes than during the lecture itself, when students did not ask questions. Madrasa students liken the process of preparation for classes to a farmer tilling his field prior to planting a crop. This part of the process is done by the teacher, who prepares in advance for each class that he gives. It is the teacher also who then sows the crop. The teacher, after all, is the farmer. The next stage, of ensuring that the lesson sinks in, like the farmer

---

[1] Al-Anfal 8:38

levelling the ground after planting his crop, is *takrar*—the repetition of what one has learnt.

In the early 1970s, Maulvi Tayyib, the son of the Panjpir maulana, was too young to preside over these revision groups, but when I attended the Panjpir maulana's Daurat'al-Qur'an in thc late seventies, he was the one who was presiding over the main revision group. Maulvi Tayyib had by now inherited his father's mantle and presided over the Panjpir madrasa. Just as he was the spitting image of his father physically and sounded like him when he spoke, so his lectures were almost complete reproductions of what his father used to say and that Tayyib used to repeat in his revision sessions at the end of each day. One area in which Tayyib fell short of his father is in his recitation of the Qur'an. Whereas Shaykh'al-Qur'an's recitation, both in Arabic and Pashto, was extremely tuneful, Tayyib's delivery of the Qur'an recitation and its Pashto translation was somewhat monotone by comparison.

For me, much of the beauty of Islam comes from practice of the Sunnah. A Sunnah is basically a practice of the Holy Prophet that we emulate in our lives, little things such as putting extra water in one's soup in the evening so that there is enough to give to one's neighbour. Visiting the sick is another Sunnah. 'Inshallah, you are being purified by the virtue of your sickness.' Muslims are encouraged to say to the sick person, or words to that effect: words of upliftment and encouragement. I have had many occasions to visit the sick and have witnessed with my own eyes the improvement in a person's condition due to such a visit. Part of the etiquette (*adab*) of visiting the sick is that one should not stay for a long time, lest the sick person becomes tired. There are countless Sunnahs of this nature, covering the way one sleeps, the way one eats, the way one walks, the way one talks—every area of one's life and dealings with others. By practising these Sunnahs, one's bearing becomes imbued with Islamic beauty.

As Islam has become more politicized before my eyes over the last fifty years, the emphasis has been more and more on *Shariah*—Islamic law—as opposed to the Sunnah—the practice of the Prophet. This is nothing short of a tragedy. The Sunnah is a personal thing and can be practised by everyone individually. *Shariah* is the responsibility of society or the state: who is going to implement it? Who is going to practise it? Society and the state are nothing but a conglomeration of individuals. Unless everyone implements Sunnah on an individual level, how will *shariah* come into society? It can't, hasn't and never will, unless every individual works on him or herself.

With respect to political Islam, I would just like to quote one sentence uttered to me by a South African contemporary of mine in Deoband, Maulana Mohammad Afzal Afriqui. It was the most succinct critique of Islamism that I have ever heard. 'Our politics should be Islamic,' he said, 'but our Islam should not be political.' Political Islam is the ruination of Islam. It leads one to seek power in the name of Islam. It is the root cause of all the conflict that has raged in the Pashtoon areas over recent decades. Sadly, those who call themselves followers of Shaykh'al-Qur'an have played a major role in that conflict, even though the Shaykh himself was a dire opponent of political Islam. The political interpretation of Islam can be so beguiling. Perhaps Shaykh'al-Qur'an should have done more to dissect this political interpretation, as Maulana Wahiduddin Khan did in India. Had he done, his own students and followers would not have adopted this political philosophy in droves.

But this politicization of the Panjpiri movement happened later. In the early 1970s, when we were students in Panjpir, we were just thinking of becoming better versed in the Book of God, adhering better to the Sunnah of His Prophet and living in thoughts of Allah and His ways. Concepts such as establishing an Islamic state were complete anathema. 'Destruction and rebellion all for the sake of gaining power,' ('*At-takhreebu wa'l-baghawatu li tahseel'il-qudrati*') was Shaykh'al-Qur'an's damning definition of political Islam.

One thing happened to me in Panjpir that reinforced that Ramadan showed how much we were living in God's world. The Qur'an lecture would finish at the time of early afternoon prayer. Then, having offered the afternoon prayer, most students would have an afternoon nap. It was Ramadan. It was also summer and the nights were short. One needed to catch up on one's sleep. An afternoon nap was also an apt way to truncate the day, when the long hours of daytime fasting began to drag and the heat began to sap one's energy.

One afternoon, I had a particularly deep sleep. I woke up, thinking it was morning, as one often does when one has slept deeply during the day. Drowsily I went outside and relieved myself. Dawdling back to my quarters, I looked up towards the sun. Seeing that the sun was in the west—it was late afternoon by then—and still being under the impression that it was morning, I thought that the Hour had come: the sun had risen from the west! This had been mentioned by the Holy Prophet as being one of the final signs of the Last Day. I am pleased to say that the realization that it was the end of the world was not a cue for panic on my part. I was completely calm about the prospect. For several minutes, I remained convinced that the Last Day (*Qiyamah*) had arrived. I might even have been a little disappointed when it dawned on me that it was in fact afternoon, not morning, and that the advent of the Hour had been a false alarm.

I had already studied the third *Surah* of the Holy Qur'an (*Surah al-Imran*) with Maulana Khan Afzal in Tirah and knew how it dealt with Christian dogma and Muslim–Christian relations. I asked Shaykh'al-Qur'an to go into special detail in that *Surah* so that I could deeply imbibe the concepts it imparted. Shaykh'al-Qur'an obliged. He explained in the light of *Surah Al 'Imran* how the word 'son', if indeed it did appear in the New Testament, did not literally mean 'son', but it meant one who was dear to God, as a son was dear to a father; how Jesus worked extraordinary miracles but this was not because of any intrinsic power on his part but because of miraculous powers that were bestowed on him by God. Right up to Shaykh'al-Quran's passing in 1986, he recounted the story of how a young Muslim convert from England had asked him to go into great detail regarding *Surah al-Imran*.

One thing really struck me about *Surah al-Imran*. It had been revealed when a delegation came to Medina from Najran. The aim of the delegation, which included eminent theologians, had been to preach Christianity to the Muslims. They might well have heard about Islam from their brethren across the Red Sea, in Abyssinia. They knew the Muslims well. A group of Muslims had migrated to Abyssinia from Mecca, prior to the emigration or *hijrah* to Medina. There was a lot of mutual respect between the two groups. When the Holy Prophet received news of the death of the Negus, the king of Abyssinia, he offered funeral prayers in absentia on behalf of the king. And when the delegation came from Abyssinia to try and win the Muslims over to Christianity, the Prophet even allowed them inside the mosque of the Prophet in Medina. That is what happens when the Muslims feel confident in themselves and in their faith. Any attempt to win them over, far from being seen as a threat, is seen as an opportunity to put across their own faith and beliefs.

When I returned from Deoband to study the Qur'an one last time with Shaykh'al-Qur'an, in 1978, I was a pre-eminent student of his. I would be seated on the Shaykh's right-hand side during his lectures. His son Tayyib would be seated on his left-hand side. Seated alongside the Shaykh, we would face the rows of students, thousands of them who had come from the furthest reaches of the Frontier and Afghanistan for the Shaykh's lectures. The fact that I had come from the hallowed Darul Uloom in Deoband enhanced the respect that was accorded me, not only by other students, but by the Shaykh himself. One day, after his Qur'an lecture, Shaykh'al-Qur'an turned to me from his floor-level lectern. 'It is so good that you have gone to Deoband for your studies,' he was clearly envious of my ability to pop effortlessly across the Indo–Pak border, as he had done in pre-Partition India when there was no border. I was able to do this, of course, by virtue of my British passport. At this time, indeed until 1984, British citizens did not need a visa to visit, or even to reside and study as I was in, either India or Pakistan. 'Could you not try,' Shaykh'al-Qur'an continued, 'to acquire a visa for Tayyib, so that he can also study in Deoband?'

While I was able to travel between Deoband and the Frontier at will at this time, it was clearly beyond me to make arrangements for a Pakistan citizen such as Tayyib. One wonders how things might have panned out over ensuing decades if Tayyib had studied in multicultural, tolerant and cosmopolitan India, instead of in the relatively harsh and monolithic environment of the Frontier. Very differently, most probably.

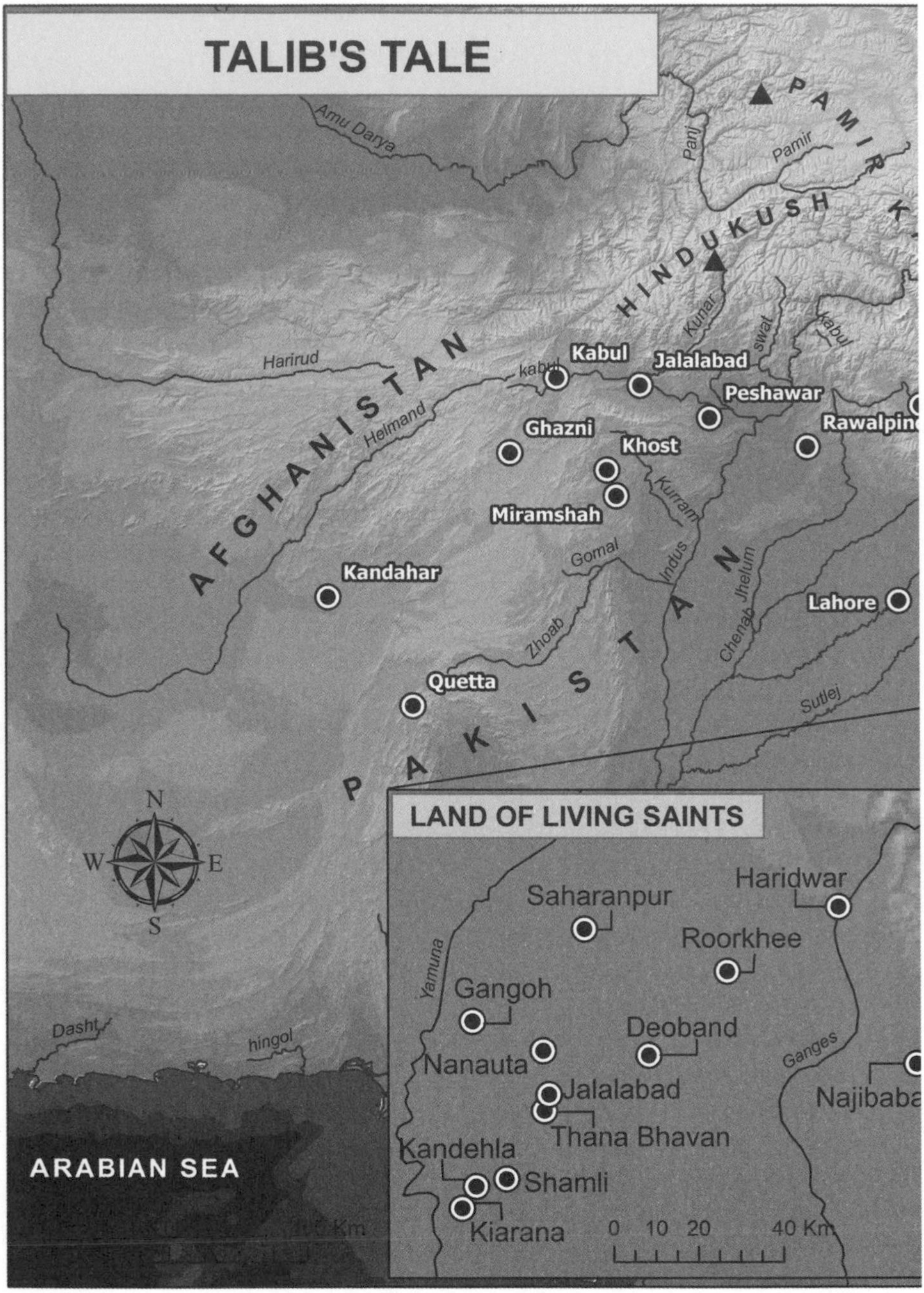
TALIB'S TALE
PAMIR
Amu Darya
Panj
Pamir
HINDUKUSH
Kunar
swat
Kabul
AFGHANISTAN
Harirud
kabul
Kabul
Jalalabad
Peshawar
Rawalpin
Helmand
Ghazni
Khost
Kurram
Miramshah
Gomal
Indus
Jhelum
Kandahar
Lahore
Zhoab
Chenab
Quetta
PAKISTAN
Sutlej
N
W
E
S
Dasht
hingol
ARABIAN SEA
LAND OF LIVING SAINTS
Haridwar
Saharanpur
Roorkhee
Yamuna
Gangoh
Deoband
Nanauta
Ganges
Jalalabad
Najibaba
Thana Bhavan
Kandehla
Shamli
Kiarana
0 10 20 40 Km

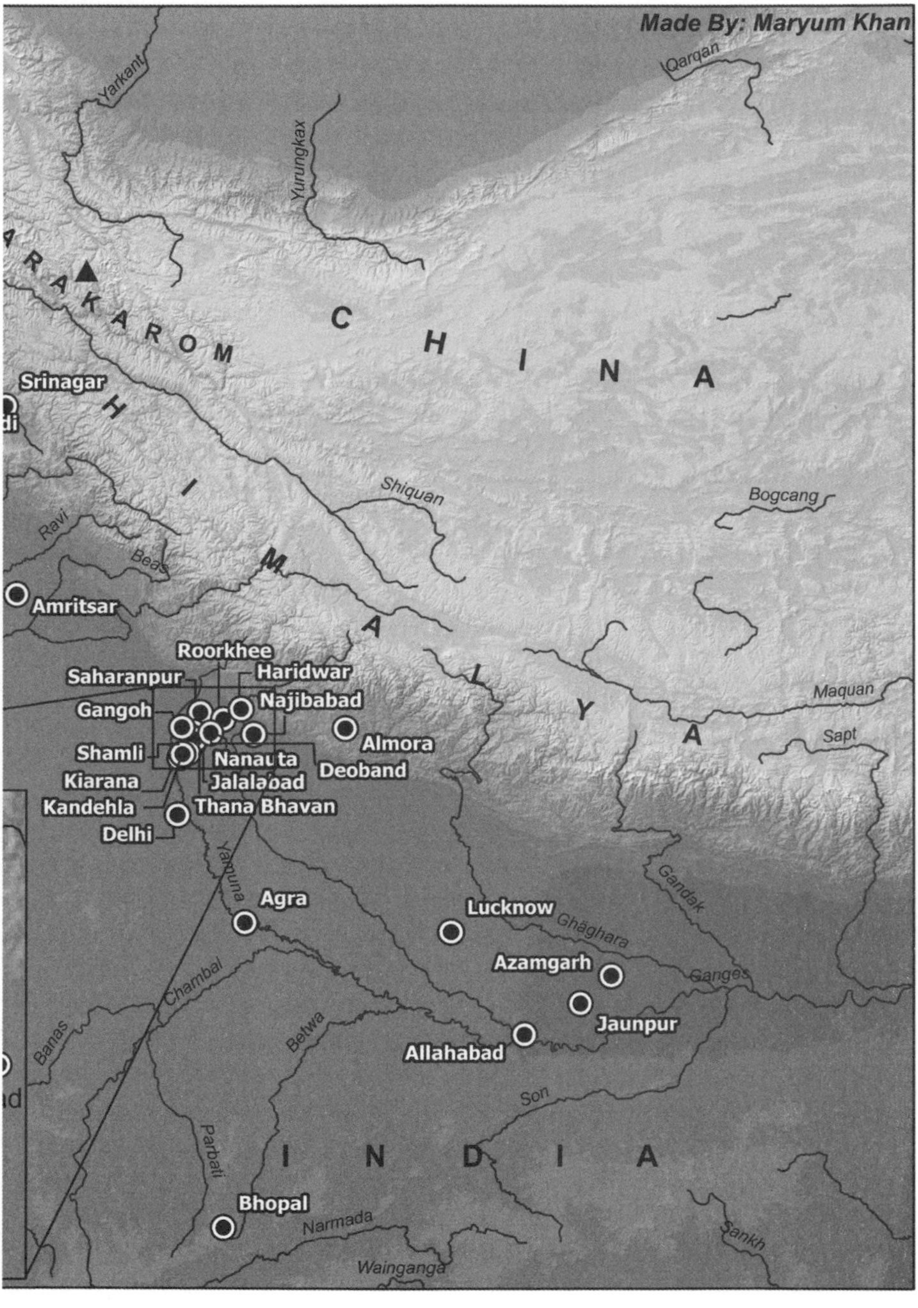
Made By: Maryum Khan
Yarkant
Qarqan
Yurungkax
KARAKORAM
CHINA
Srinagar
HIMALAYA
Shiquan
Bogcang
Ravi
Beas
Amritsar
Roorkhee
Saharanpur
Haridwar
Najibabad
Gangoh
Almora
Shamli
Nanauta
Deoband
Kiarana
Jalalabad
Kandehla
Thana Bhavan
Delhi
Maquan
Sapt
Yamuna
Gandak
Agra
Lucknow
Ghāghara
Azamgarh
Ganges
Chambal
Jaunpur
Betwa
Allahabad
Banas
Son
Parbati
INDIA
Bhopal
Narmada
Sankh
Wainganga

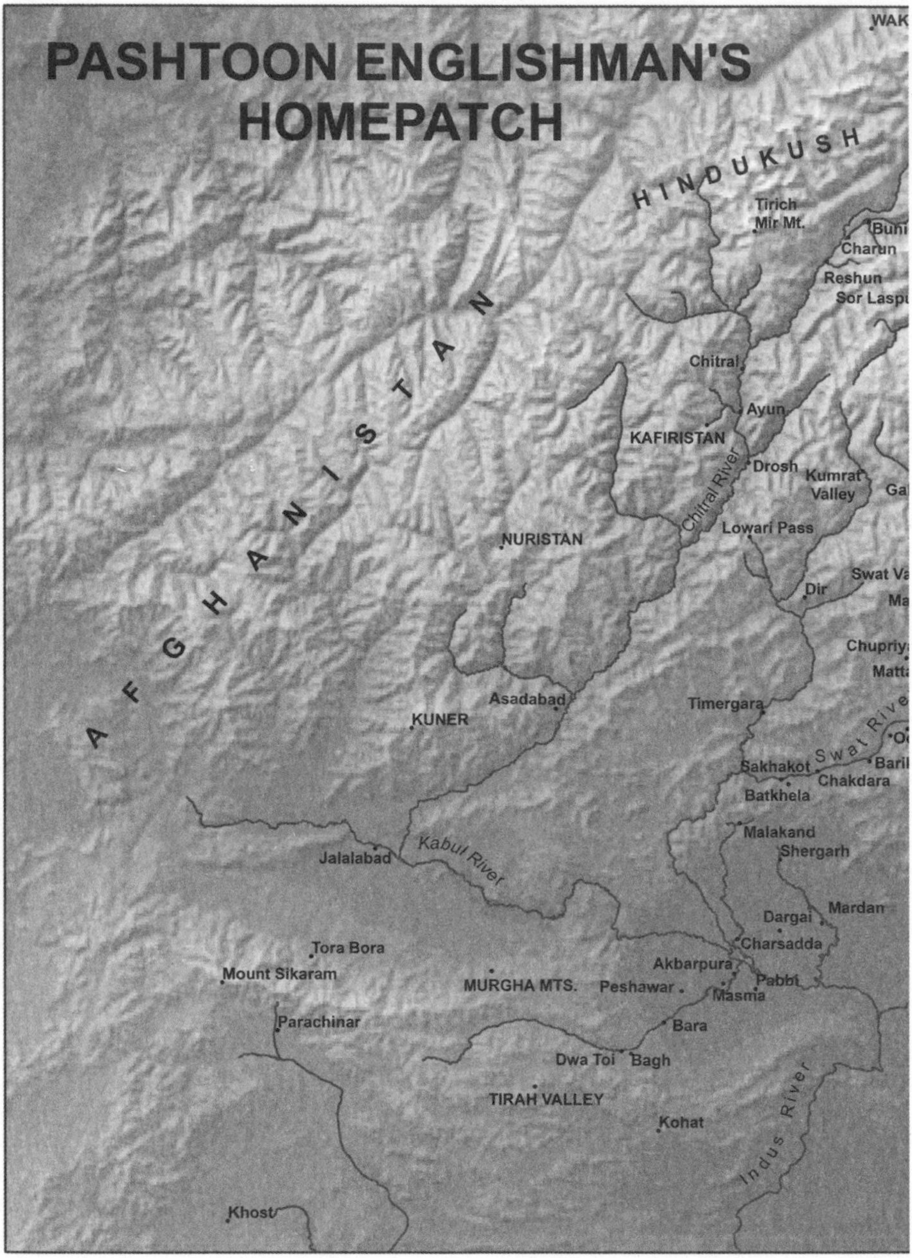
PASHTOON ENGLISHMAN'S HOMEPATCH
HINDUKUSH
AFGHANISTAN
Tirich Mir Mt.
Charun
Reshun
Chitral
Ayun
KAFIRISTAN
Chitral River
Drosh
Kumrat Valley
Lowari Pass
NURISTAN
Dir
Timergara
Asadabad
KUNER
Swat River
Sakhakot
Chakdara
Batkhela
Malakand
Shergarh
Jalalabad
Kabul River
Mardan
Dargai
Charsadda
Tora Bora
Akbarpura
Mount Sikaram
MURGHA MTS.
Peshawar
Pabbi
Masma
Parachinar
Bara
Dwa Toi
Bagh
TIRAH VALLEY
Kohat
Indus River
Khost

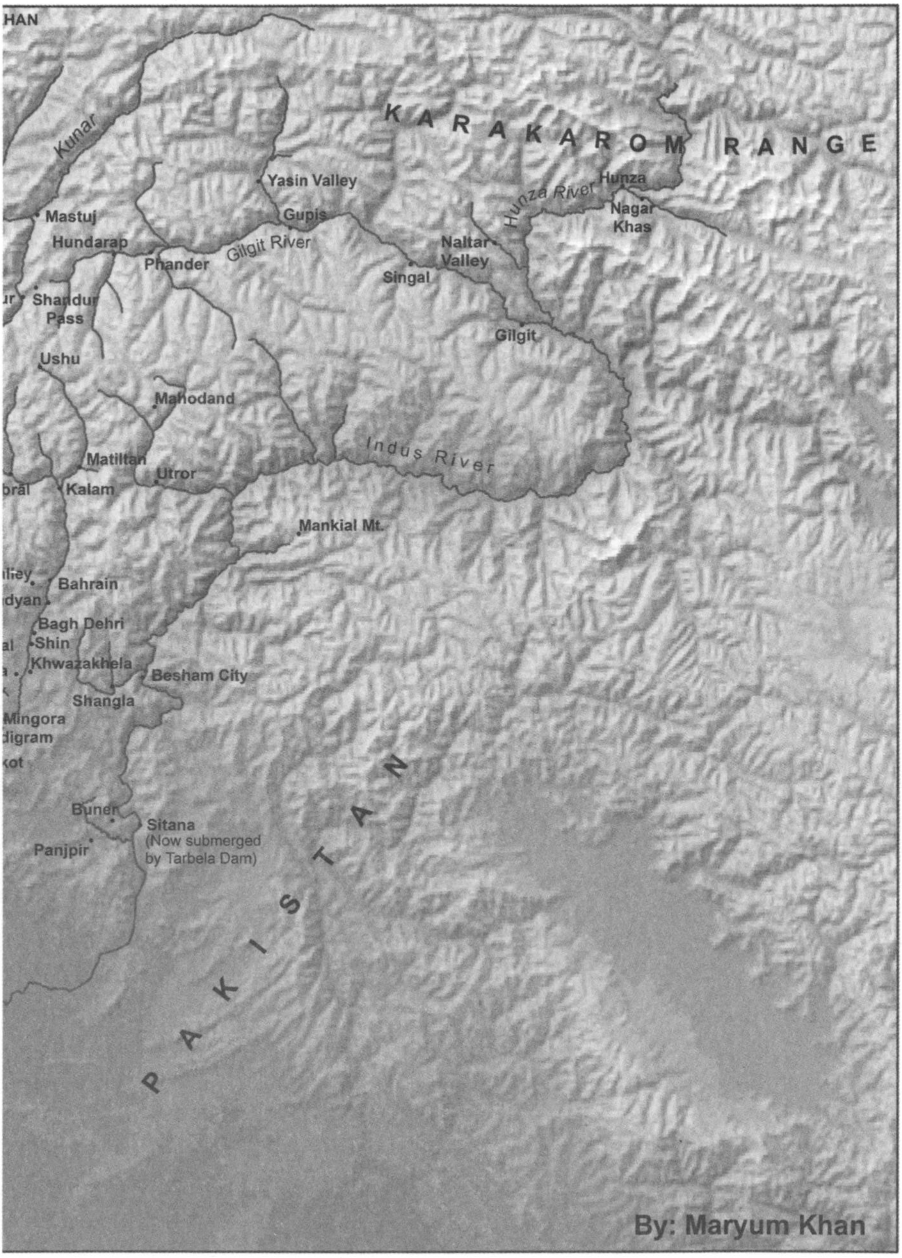

HAN
KARAKAROM RANGE
Kunar
Yasin Valley
Hunza
Hunza River
Nagar
Khas
Mastuj
Gupis
Hundarap
Gilgit River
Naltar
Valley
Phander
Singal
Shandur
Pass
Gilgit
Ushu
Mahodand
Indus River
Matiltan
Utror
Kalam
Mankial Mt.
Bahrain
Bagh Dehri
Shin
Khwazakhela
Besham City
Shangla
Mingora
Buner
Sitana
(Now submerged
by Tarbela Dam)
Panjpir
PAKISTAN
By: Maryum Khan

XI

THE MILITANT TENDENCY

Did our revered teacher Maulana Nanutvi found this madrasa only for educational purposes? It was founded in my presence and as far as I know one of its main purposes was to compensate for the losses incurred in 1857. Those interested only in education are free to do as they like, l do not want to be an obstacle in their way, but I stand for those objectives which the founder of this Darul Uloom had in view and for whose achievement he worked hard.

(Shaykh'al-Hind Mahmud'al-Hasan[1])

The romantic affiliation that exists between Deoband and the Frontier preceded the establishment of Darul Uloom Deoband in 1865. It goes back even further, but for our purposes that affiliation can be traced to 1823, when a young firebrand preacher from the United Provinces betook himself to the Frontier hills. His name and the name of his band of followers, who remained in the Frontier hills for generations after his passing, turned into the stuff of legend. His name was Sayyed Ahmad Barelvi. His followers, who

[1] Quoted by Faruqi, Ziya-ul-Hasan, *The Deoband School and the Demand for Pakistan*, Asia Publishing House, Bombay, 1963.

lived for several generations in the caves of Frontier districts such as Bunir and Dir, were known as the mujahideen. In many ways, these mujahideen were the precursors of various militant and resistance groups that have sprung up among the Pashtoons since the 1980s. We can call the latter the neo-mujahideen, so similar are they to their 19th century progenitors.

Sayyed Ahmad Barelvi was certainly a hero of the Panjpir Maulana Sahib and his followers. To them, he was the first major figure who inveighed against what they saw as un-Islamic practices that existed among the Pashtoons. The things that the Panjpiris rounded on were the very things that had also incurred the wrath of Sayyed Sahib: contraventions of *Tauhid*—praying to saints in shrines, for instance—ways of conducting functions such as births, marriages and funerals that resembled Hindu practice more than the Sunnah of the Holy Prophet. One thing that Sayyed Ahmad and his followers came down particularly hard on was a reluctance among Pashtoons to allow remarriage of widows. In the Hindu religion, remarriage of widows is taboo. This Hindu practice had rubbed off on Muslims. In all these things, the agenda of Sayyed Ahmad and his Hindustani mujahideen was pretty well identical to that of the Panjpiris, who followed them more than a century later. The two movements were also strikingly similar in their geography: the location where they both grew was in the eastern part of the Frontier, bordering the Indus.

In two particular ways, however, Sayyed Ahmad's movement was ahead of its time. For one, Sayyed Ahmad inveighed against the practice of giving refuge to criminals (*panah*). It is strange really, since this was a practice that Sayyed Ahmad's followers were to benefit from in coming decades. In their case, it was the redoubtable and intensely loyal Sayyed Akbar Shah of Sitana who granted the Hindustani mujahideen *panah*. Of course, neither party looked at the mujahideen as criminals. To both Sayyed Akbar Shah and the followers of Sayyed Ahmad, the latter were mujahideen, fleeing persecution from the British. As we have seen in recent decades, at the end of the 20th century and beginning of the new millennium, when the question of *panah* has become a *cause célèbre*, it is a matter of perception: one man's mujahid is another man's terrorist.

The other matter in which Sayyed Ahmad was ahead of his time was in his prohibition of bride price. He drew a line between bride price (known among Pashtoons as *walwar*) and dowry (*mahr*). *Mahr* is an Islamic practice, Sayyed pointed out. It is the amount paid by a husband directly to his bride. On the contrary, *walwar* consists of the parents of the bride selling her off, the money not going to the bride, but to her parents. Sayyed Ahmad and his followers came down hard on bride price. Allied with his insistence on marriage of girls once they reached a marriageable age, this was depicted in some quarters to be motivated by self-interest—an attempt to win young brides for his band of mujahideen. This factor, an apparent affront to the honour of their womenfolk, enabled mullas to turn at least some of their congregation against Sayyed Ahmad and his band of mujahideen.

Sayyed Ahmad must have been a man of enormous charisma. Just look at the people who followed him. His right-hand man in the Frontier was Shah Ismail, a direct grandson of Shah Wali-Ullah, the fabled Muhaddith-e-Delhavi and the pre-eminent Islamic scholar of his time. One would have expected Sayyed Ahmad to swear allegiance to one of Shah Wali-Ullah's family. But no, it was Shah Ismail, along with his cousin Abdul Hayy, who swore allegiance to Sayyed Ahmad, rather than the other way round. If the mind boggles at how the rising stars of the Shah Wali-Ullah family in Delhi swore allegiance to a newcomer on the spiritual scene like Sayyed Ahmad, this astonishment is nothing compared to the extraordinary scenario of Sayyed Akbar Shah, undisputed leader of the Yusufzais and a direct descendant of the Holy Prophet, swearing allegiance to an outsider like Sayyed Ahmad Barelvi. Yet this is exactly what happened. Sayyed Akbar Shah took Sayyed Ahmad as his spiritual leader. Over the course of three or four years, inspired by the support of Sayyed Akbar Shah, the Yusufzai and Khattak tribes of the plains between Buner and Peshawar, united around the person of Sayyed Ahmad Barelvi. For some time, Sayyed Ahmad was even able to hold sway in the Frontier metropolis of Peshawar. There, he minted a coin in his own honour, in the name of Ahmad the Just, Sword-Glitterer, Defender of the

Faith, much as in our own time similar figures leading similar movements have called themselves Commander of the Faithful.[2]

Ostensibly, Sayyed Ahmad and his followers came to the Frontier to do battle with the Sikhs who, under Ranjit Singh, had taken and ransacked Peshawar in 1823. But it was the religious establishment of the Pashtoons, the mullas, who baulked at this firebrand who preached a strict interpretation of Islam that undermined their authority. Like many leaders among the Pashtoons, Sayyed Ahmad went too far, too soon—at least for his own good. In late 1830, he was forced to leave Peshawar to its Durrani Sardar governors. Along with Shah Ismail and a group of his followers, he crossed the Indus, to do battle with the Sikhs in the Hazara hills. He left behind him lieutenants in all the Yusufzai and Khattak villages of the *sama* plains, west of the Indus.

Every year, in his Qur'an dars in Panjpir, Shaykh'al-Qur'an Sahib would gesture towards the Mahaban hill, to the east of Panjpir. 'On that hill,' he narrated, with not a little bitterness, 'one night a beacon was lit. It was a signal to put to death every single one of Sayyed Sahib's lieutenants.' There was no doubt in the mind of Shaykh'al-Qur'an where the blame for this slaughter lay: with the conservative clergy, with whom he himself had been at odds all his life.

The slaughter of Sayyed Ahmad's lieutenants, the death of Sayyed Ahmad himself, must have rankled with Sayyed Akbar Shah, who had put his honour on the line to protect Sayyed Ahmad and his band of mujahideen. The remnants of the mujahideen now found a home at Sayyed Akbar Shah's fastness of Sitana. Sitana had almost impregnable defences. Ranjit Singh tried to breach them, as did his general Hari Singh. They failed. On one side was the River Indus, easy enough for a force to reach the east side of the river, but how to cross the river? On the other side were the mountains of Buner, which were not penetrated by any invading force until the Ambela

[2] The information on Sayyed Ahmad minting a coin in his own honour is taken from Sir Olaf Caroe's The Pathans. The claim is disputed according to new research, still to be published, conducted by former BBC Pashto service head Safia Haleem www.safiahaleem.com

campaign of the British—against the mujahideen and their protector—in 1863. Even then, the British did not reach anywhere near Sitana. The raid was a punitive one against the Indian mujahideen, in retribution for some raids they had launched on the border of British India. It was only after the formation of Pakistan, and the building of the Tarbela Dam that the descendants of Sayyed Akbar Shah were dislodged from Sitana. Sitana was submerged in the waters of the Indus and Sayyed Akbar Shah's family settled in other parts of the Frontier. Like Sitana itself, they disappeared without trace.

Around 1912, one student came from the Frontier to Deoband who would become part of a new attempt to stir up the Frontier tribes against the British. His name was Uzair Gul. He was from the Kaka Khel Miangan.[3] While most of the Kaka Khels inhabited the area around Kaka Sahib's grave near Nowshera, there is also an enclave of Kaka Khel Mians in the Sakhakot area, on the way from Peshawar to Swat. Even in later years, Uzair Gul was a striking looking man. I met Uzair Gul in the 1980s, along with his co-villager, the Khan of Sakhakot and famous Khudai Khidmatgar Rahat Khan. We have already come across Rahat Khan, great friend of the learned, and servant of his people, in connection with his support for the Sarkai Maulvi Sahib, the teacher of Abdul Hadi. Uzair Gul was nearing 100 years old when I met him. Still, he cut a lean figure, with a red, hennaed beard. He was resting on his bed, but sat up on seeing Rahat Khan, his acquaintance of a lifetime. Who knew if they would be meeting each other again in this life? As a fresh-faced youngster from the Frontier, Uzair Gul immediately became a favourite of the senior teacher at Deoband, Mahmud'al-Hasan, known as Shaykh'al-Hind. Shaykh'al-Hind was

[3] Miangan, or Mians, are the second highest caste among Muslims. Sayyeds like Sayyed Akbar Shah and Sayyed Ahmad Bareilly are direct descendants of the Prophet. They occupy top spot. Then come Miangan like Uzair Gul, who are descendants of saints.

amongst those, in the tradition of Sayyed Ahmad Barelvi, who had grand visions about how the Frontier could become a cradle of insurrection, an inspiration for other parts of India to free themselves from British rule.

The first of Shaykh'al-Hind's proteges in the Frontier was Haji Sahib Turangzai. An Islamic scholar from the village of Turangzai near Peshawar, Haji Sahib Turangzai had remained in close consultation with Shaykh'al-Hind from the time he first travelled to Deoband in 1878. In 1914, Shaykh'al-Hind encouraged Haji Turangzai to move from his native village of Turangzai to the nearby tribal territory. From there he was supposed to launch jihad on the British government. Up till then, Haji Turangzai had taken an educational approach to internal reform, weeding out bad customs so that the Pashtoons could flourish. Under the influence of Shaykh'al-Hind, Haji Turangzai changed tack, and adopted the path of violent jihad.

The village of Turangzai lies on the road between Charsadda and Tangi. The villages dotted along the road to Tangi, Utmanzai, Turangzai, Umarzai and Sherpao, are like a roll-call of modern Pashtoon history. Before Utmanzai is the village of Rajar, where later Ghaffar Khan and his Khudai Khidmatgars set up cotton mills, part of the continuing efforts of Ghaffar Khan, the Frontier Gandhi, to give the Pashtoons an indigenous, independent economy. The efforts of Haji Sahib Turangzai and Ghaffar Khan followed one from the other, in the same way as their villages, Utmanzai and Turangzai, respectively, follow on from each other.

We can also see the reform activities of Haji Turangzai—and after him Ghaffar Khan took up the gauntlet—in the same context of those of Sayyed Ahmad. They concentrated on ridding society of things like extravagant expenditure on weddings. This expenditure only burdened people with debt. In all these efforts, the emphasis was always on following the Sunnah of the Holy Prophet, as opposed to custom. Furthermore, as we saw with the movement of Sayyed Ahmad, there was emphasis on giving dowry to the bride, not paying the father for the hand of a bride. The practice of bride price led to selling off of young women, irrespective of the Islamic factor of compatibility between spouses (*kufu*). Haji Turangzai also projected the role of Pashtoon jirgas, the traditional Pashtoon mechanism for settling disputes. In practice, Haji Sahib Turangzai was establishing a parallel society for the Pashtoons, based on their own traditions. No surprise, then, that the British frowned on his activities.

In all their activities, Haji Turangzai and Ghaffar Khan were in close contact with their counterparts in Deoband. On their visits to Deoband, they went to great lengths to avoid the government intelligence that was inevitably following their movements at the time. This scrutiny forms the backdrop to the next part of our story. One of their favourite meeting places and stop-off points was the Fatehpuri Mosque in Delhi. The Imam in Fatehpuri at this time was one Maulana Saif-ur-Rahman from Doaway village in Hashtnagar, the home district of Ghaffar Khan. He was an intermediary between Deoband: Shaykh'al-Hind, in particular, on the one hand, and Haji Turangzai and Ghaffar Khan on the other. Sometimes, meetings were held in the mosque. Almost always, the Pashtoon pair would stay in Fatehpuri, en route between Deoband and the Frontier.

According to Ghaffar Khan's account, it was a message from Shaykh'al-Hind, brought to Haji Turangzai by Maulana Saif-ur-Rahman, which gave the signal for Haji Turangzai to set up a base in the tribal territory.

Haji Sahib Turangzai's departure for the tribal territory was just one part of a grandiose scheme that had been formed in the mind of Shaykh'al-Hind. Another part was for another of his lieutenants, Maulana Ubaid-Ullah Sindhi, to move to Kabul. Meanwhile, he himself would go to Hijaz, where he would speak with the Turkish representatives in Mecca. The idea was that the Central Powers, as the German–Ottoman alliance in the First World War was known, would attack India through Afghanistan. There, Afghan forces, to be raised by Maulana Ubaid-Ullah Sindhi in Kabul, would reinforce them. They would be further reinforced on their way to India by a tribal army, which would have been gathered around Haji Turangzai. Then they would release India from the clutches of the British. This scheme germinated in the mind of Shaykh'al-Hind. Quite apart from all the pieces of the jigsaw that had to fall into place, it was surprising that it did not occur to the Shaykh that if the Turks, Germans and Afghans were to deliver India from the British, then would they leave India to the Indians? Hardly likely. They would have been more likely to carve India up among themselves.

In fact, not a single piece of the jigsaw fell into place. We will look at the difficulties Haji Sahib Turangzai encountered in the tribal area in our chapter on Ghaffar Khan. Maulana Ubaid-Ullah Sindhi admitted later on that his 'conscience was not ready for this migration' to Kabul, but it was the wish of Shaykh'al-Hind that he could not contravene. Later, however, the point of his self-inflicted exile became clear, and he said that he claimed to be proud to be part of Shaykh'al-Hind's plans. He became part of an ineffectual government in exile in Kabul, along with other Indian revolutionaries. When he arrived in Kabul, the government was headed by the sympathetic Amir Habibullah Khan, but, after Habibullah's assassination in 1919, his son Amanullah had no wish to incur the wrath of the British by launching a war of independence on behalf of Indian revolutionaries, particularly one doomed to obvious failure.

Well before this, in October 1915, Shaykh'al-Hind arrived with a few followers in Arabia. It was there that his scheme really became unhinged. He was soon able to meet up with the Turkish governor, Ghalib Pasha. He explained to him his plan to open up a new front against the British, in Afghanistan and India. Of course, he would need the Germans and the Turks to assist by attacking British India via Afghanistan and the Pashtoon tribal areas, where Haji Sahib Turangzai would have raised a lashkar in their support. There was a question of how these disparate and different groups of freedom fighters could communicate with each other, considering the tight surveillance of their movements by British intelligence. Ghalib Pasha duly gave Shaykh'al-Hind a letter assuring Indians of support in their quest for independence. Shaykh'al-Hind sent that letter safely enough, between the false boards of a wooden box. Eventually its contents reached the ears of the pervasive British CID. Of even more interest to their intelligence department was a letter written by Maulana Sindhi in Kabul. In order to conceal the letter, Maulana wrote the letter on a piece of silken cloth. The message was given to one Shaykh Abdul Haq, who in turn was supposed to deliver it to Shaykh Abdul Rahim Sindhi. It was the latter's job to deliver the letter to Shaykh'al-Hind in Hijaz. Unfortunately, Shaykh Abdul Haq gave the letter instead to one Khan Bahadur Rab Nawaz Khan, who was a close collaborator with the Punjab CID department.

A number of Shaykh'al-Hind's collaborators were arrested due to the contents of this silken letter. While the Turks were in control in the Hijaz, Shaykh'al-Hind was safe there. That changed with the success of the Arab Uprising, well known in the Western world due to the collaboration of Colonel Lawrence, known as Lawrence of Arabia, with the Arab tribes under Sharif Hussain. Along with Ghalib Pasha himself, Shaykh'al-Hind was besieged in Taif, near Mecca. Soon, he and his companions found themselves the guests of Sharif Hussain's son Abdullah. In a gesture of typical Arabian hospitality, Sharif's son put on a dinner for the Indian delegation, as yet unaware that this group of Indian scholars had been organizing an uprising against the British, in collaboration with the erstwhile Turkish authorities. Still, Shaykh'al-Hind saw the writing on the wall. He was trying to leave Jeddah when Sharif Hussain had him arrested.

Shaykh'al-Hind was handed over to the British authorities, along with his companions. These included Shaykh'al-Hind's eventual successor at Deoband, Hussain Ahmad Madani, and the Pashtoon Uzair Gul. The British sent them to Malta, a kind of prototype Guantanamo, where they spent three years before being released in 1919. Shaykh'al-Hind made good use of his time in Malta by completing his translation into Urdu of the Holy Qur'an. The translation was later combined with the exegesis of Deoband's senior Qur'anic teacher, Shabbir Ahmad Usmani, to form the Qur'anic exegesis and translation known throughout South Asia as *Tafsir Usmani*, which is also respected in Afghanistan. During the time of King Zahir Shah, it was translated into Dari and Pashto and distributed by the Ministry of Education in Afghanistan. Even nowadays, Urdu versions of the Tafsir bear tiny inscriptions, showing the day when Shaykh'al-Hind reached this point in his translation, in the prison of Malta.

Shaykh'al-Hind passed away in the same year as he was released from the Malta jail, in 1920. His release was a major event for the fledgling freedom movement. Mahatma Gandhi travelled from Ahmadabad to Bombay—a ten-hour train journey—to meet Shaykh'al-Hind, and brief him on developments with the freedom movement. Shaykh'al-Hind had time to accomplish two land-breaking tasks before his death. The first was to lay the foundation stone of Jamia Millia, a university along the lines of Aligarh, but independent of the British. The second was to issue a fatwa, urging Muslims to join up with people of other faiths in non-violent resistance and non-cooperation against the British. Force was not the way to dislodge the British from India. Shaykh'al-Hind was right. Darul Uloom had been founded to redress the reverses of 1857. However, he left behind in the Frontier another of the lessons of 1857 and indeed of Sayyed Ahmad and the Indian mujahideen: that this would not be done by force of arms. It would be done by force of character, in other words, through non-violent resistance.

XII

PASHTOONS IN DEOBAND

Seek knowledge, even if it lies in a faraway place such as China.

(An Arabic saying)

My arrival in Deoband, in April of 1978, mirrored that of the arrival of another Pashtoon *talib*, Abdul Rauf Ghaznavi, some two years later. Abdul Rauf was in fact the name that he acquired after he came to Deoband. He was born Kifayatullah in the Afghan province of Ghazni. At an early age, he came with his family as an Afghan refugee and settled in the city of Quetta. He and his younger brother Rahmatullah dedicated themselves to acquiring Islamic learning. The young Kifayatullah had already completed the study tour (*daura*) of the six authentic collections of Hadith in Quetta when he set his sights on travelling to Deoband. He wished to study the Hadith from the *mashaikh* of Deoband. Ever since the inception of Deoband in the mid-nineteenth century, the aspiration of Pashtoon talibs had been to study in Deoband. However, after the Partition of India in 1947, fewer and fewer students were able to make the journey to Deoband, what with visa requirements and progressively worsening relations between India and Pakistan making cross-border travel between the two countries all the more problematic.

Instead, Pashtoon *talibs* turned to madrasas established by Deoband scholars who had opted to move to Pakistan in 1947. There was a madrasa in Lahore, made famous by Maulana Idrees Kandhelvi, a scion of a famous family of Islamic scholars belonging to Kandhela, now situated in the Muzaffarnagar district of Uttar Pradesh. The madrasa had been named Jamia Ashrafia, after the peerless Deobandi Sufi scholar Ashraf Ali Thanvi. Prior to moving to Pakistan, Maulana Idrees had been Shaykh'at-Tafseer, the senior teacher of Quranic exegesis, at Darul Uloom Deoband. In the mid 1950s, he took over as Shaykh'al-Hadith in Jamiya Ashrafiya.

There was the Darul Uloom at Korangi in Karachi, established by an anointed disciple of Maulana Ashraf Ali Thanvi, Mufti Mohammad Shafi. Of all the madrasas modelled on Deoband and established in Pakistan in the wake of Partition, the most popular amongst the Pashtoons was the New Town madrasa of Maulana Yusuf Binori—himself hailing from Peshawar. All these madrasas, as well as several others, had impeccable pedigree and wide appeal. Still, like I had said to the New Zealander Abdul Hadi, they were silver compared to the gold of Deoband. None of them could match the lure and reputation of Darul Uloom Deoband itself. This aura and magnetism only increased with the distance created by Partition, when actually studying in Deoband became a more and more distant dream. By the late 1970s, when I reached Deoband, and the early 1980s, when Maulana Abdul Rauf managed to make his way to the dreamy minarets of this madrasa town, the days when Pashtoons mingled in their scores amidst students from all over India in the expansive lecture halls of Deoband were a distant memory of days long gone.

The affection that Pashtoons have always had for Deoband was mutual. Deoband has always considered the Frontier hills and Pashtoon lands to be its true catchment area. Pashtoon students excelled in piety, zeal, hardwork and in their Islamic character. They were quick to endear themselves to their teachers. I saw this nostalgia, this longing for Pashtoons to once again be studying in Deoband, when I myself arrived in Deoband.

The eight years that I had spent amongst the Pashtoons had seen me adopt not only the language of the Pashtoons but their dress and habits also. Not able as yet to speak Urdu, on arrival in Deoband I conversed with my teachers in Farsi, the language that I had learnt in jail in Kabul. Of course, my teachers did not suspect that this chaste Farsi was learnt in such disreputable surroundings! They looked upon the Farsi that I spoke as the cultivated tongue that had been the lingua franca of north India prior to the occupation of the British in the early nineteenth century. It had been normal practice for Pashtoon students who used to come to Deoband prior to Partition to speak to their teachers in Farsi. Pashtoons, particularly those Pashtoons who hail from Afghanistan, are generally able to converse in Farsi and this fluency only increases with the Farsi books that they study.

In Deoband, I never introduced myself as a Pashtoon, I always told the truth to the ulema, that I was an English convert to Islam who had been living and studying for some time in Afghanistan and the Frontier. Maybe some teachers half believed me. If they were sceptical, for the most part they kept their scepticism to themselves. They may have harboured a secret belief that this particular Pashtoon was so ingenious that he was pretending to be English in order to ensure that he could stay in India and study in Deoband! If they did think this, this would only have increased their admiration of the Pashtoons. Look at the lengths to which these Pashtoons will go, they would have thought, even to the extent of pretending to be English, to fulfil their dream and gain admission in Deoband!

This admiration can only have increased with the arrival, a couple of years later, of a true Pashtoon: Abdul Rauf Ghaznavi. Abdul Rauf embodied the piety, the saintly demeanour, the strict adherence to Sunna, the timeless aura, the medieval bearing of one of the saints of his native Ghazni. It is said that there are ninety-nine saints buried in Ghazni. Indeed, the place is replete with history and spirituality. Being the seat of power of the famed medieval conqueror Mahmud Ghaznavi, its claims to statehood precede those of modern Afghanistan. Mahmud Ghaznavi was not Pashtoon, he was from Uzbek, Turkic stock, closer in blood ties to the father figure of current-day Uzbekistan Amir Timur, Tamberlane, than to the Pashtoon conqueror and founder of modern-day Afghanistan

Ahmad Shah Durrani. But Mahmud Ghaznavi was not unlike Pashtoons in that he made his way to Hindustan to partake in the riches of India. There were some like Mahmud Ghaznavi, and indeed Ahmad Shah Durrani, who went to India for adventure, plunder and ambition. There were many, like Abdul Rauf, who went in search of knowledge. While some Pashtoons returned to their Frontier hills, many stayed in India.

One who stayed, in the wake of Partition, was Hakeem Misbah'ad-Din. The title hakeem is like doctor, in this case a doctor of herbal medicine. Hakeem sahib originally hailed from Mardan, the second town of the North-West Frontier Province. He was studying in Deoband when the Partition of India happened in 1947. He kept a house in Deoband, but his main base was in Delhi, where he had set up a publishing business. His sons still run the publishing business from Old Delhi. Hakeem sahib was a man of fair complexion, befitting his Pashtoon genealogy. He stood out and was a fine example of Pashtoon stock in the plains of northern India. We often would take the train from Deoband to Delhi together. Once, when we were standing on the station platform in Deoband, he pointed out to me the vast sugar mill. 'You know, the sugar mill in Deoband and the one in Mardan [the Mardan sugar mill is the biggest in the Frontier] have the same ownership.' To both Hakeem sahib and myself, this was another example of the close ties that had always existed between Deoband and the Frontier, ties loosened by the separation and indeed estrangement of the two countries.

When Hakeem sahib was at Deoband, one of his best friends in the madrasa was Abdul Razzaq, a Pashtoon from the central Indian princely state of Bhopal. Abdul Razzaq was destined to become the mufti of the city of Bhopal. When the young Misbah'ad-Din visited Bhopal along with Abdul Razzaq, the town's Pashtoon character made a big impression on him. He looked at Bhopal as a home away from his Mardan home. Here, over several centuries, the Pashtoons had carved a state for themselves. The Pashtoon state of Bhopal dated from Mughal times. It was consolidated, formalized and recognized as the nawabate of Bhopal during the days of British rule. The founder of the Bhopal Pashtoon dynasty was Dost Mohammad

Khan. Dost Mohammad Khan was from Tirah. He hailed from the Orakzai tribe. Like many of his generation, during the reign of Emperor Aurangzeb he came to the plains of Hindustan seeking riches and adventure. Originally sent to Bhopal to quell a rebellion there, he soon set up the foundations of a modern state.

From the beginning of his rule over Bhopal, Dost Mohammad found that he was able to boost and consolidate his power with Pashtoons—mostly Orakzais like himself—coming from the Frontier. It was upon their loyalty that he could completely depend. Until they became established and were able to make houses for themselves, these Pashtoons for the most part lived in huts made of a local reed used for mats. They became known, after the reed from which they constructed these huts, as the *baro-kat* Pashtoons: the Pashtoons who cut reeds (*baro*) in order to make dwellings for themselves. Amongst these *baro-kat* Pashtoons were the forefathers of Mufti Abdul Razzaq. His forefathers were not Orakzais but hailed from the Gadoon Amazai area in the hills near the Indus River, above the towns of Swabi and Panjpir.

Mufti Abdul Razzaq had never been to the Frontier but had zealously preserved his Pashtoon identity. He conversed in Pashto fluently. I had the honour, during my stay in Deoband, to accompany Mufti sahib on the first trip he ever made to the North-West Frontier Province. The trip took place shortly before Hakeem Misbah'ad-Din's son Salahuddin married the daughter of Mufti Abdul Razzaq. Mufti sahib wished to make the acquaintance of Hakeem sahib's family in Mardan since the two families were about to become related. I sat next to Mufti sahib all night in the Government Transport Service bus that was taking us to our destination. His emotion, on returning for this first time, as a sixty-year-old man, to the land of his forefathers was palpable. The respect with which Hakeem Misbah'ad-Din's elder brother, Hakeem Zia'al-Islam, received him in Mardan was deferential. 'I cannot put into words my feelings on returning to the Pashtoon heartland,' explained a visibly moved Mufti sahib as he sat opposite me in the *hujrah* of Hakeem Zia'al-Islam in Mardan.

Bhopal is considered to be a *nawabate*, but it would be more accurate to call it a *begumate*, which means a dynasty of Muslim

Pashtoon women ruling over a predominantly Hindu population in central India.[1] In the late 1940s, when the young Misbah'ad-Din visited Bhopal along with his friend from Deoband Abdul Razzaq, the *nawabate/begumate* was coming to an end. The last nawab, Hamidullah Khan, was in the process of ceding his princely state to the Government of India. The final *begum*, Abida Sultan, had emigrated to Pakistan. But vestiges of the princely state remained.

Bhopal remained a magnet for Pashtoons from the Frontier. None epitomized this more than one Hakeem Abdul Hamid. Originally hailing from the Swat valley, he had married into the family of a previous mufti of Bhopal, Mufti Abdul Hadi. Abdul Razzaq, himself destined to inherit the mantle of the mufti of Bhopal, introduced his young friend Misbah'ad-Din to Hakeem Abdul Hamid. There was already a close affinity between the two. Hakeem Abdul Hamid was also a lone Pashtoon from the Frontier, who had settled in Bhopal. And he was also a practitioner of traditional herbal medicine (*hakeem*). The young Misbah'ad-Din was doing his traditional medicine—also known as prophetic medicine (*Tibb-e-Nabawi*)—course at the College of Ayurvedic and Unani Medicine, set up by Hakeem Ajmal Khan (1863–1927) in Karol Bagh in the west of Delhi. Hakeem Abdul Hamid, it turned out, had qualified as a hakeem from Lahore Tibbiya College. 'But that is where my father studied,' exclaimed Misbah'ad-Din. 'What was his name?' 'Ahmad Noor,' came the reply. The two were overjoyed. Hakeem Abdul Hamid from Swat had come upon the son of one of his best friends. Both came from the Yusufzai tribe, who inhabit both Swat and Mardan. The son of his friend had turned up on his doorstep in central India! Like Abdul Hamid, Misbah'ad-Din had left all his relatives behind in the Frontier. The budding hakeem Misbah'ad-Din was already like a son to the senior Abdul Hamid. It was not long before Hakeem Misbah'ad-Din became engaged to Hakeem Abdul Hamid's daughter.

Hakeem Misbah'ad-Din in his turn became a fatherly figure to me. Hakeem sahib kept a house in Deoband. The first thing he would do when he arrived there would be to notify me. I would

[1] The Begums of Bhopal, by Shaharyar Khan, published by I. B. Tauris

go to their house and enjoy Pashto conversation, good food and healthy company. I taught one of his daughters, Nazima, Pashto. When his elder son donned the Hindustani *kurta-pyjama* instead of the more typical Pashtoon *shalwar- kamees*, his father held me up as an example: 'Look at Jan Mohammad. He has travelled the whole world, but he has chosen Pashtoon clothes.' Once, I took another English student at Deoband, Mohammad Sulaiman, to see Hakeem sahib. Like me, Mohammad Sulaiman was a Muslim convert. He possessed a brilliant mind and skill for learning languages, but he tended to act in a whimsical manner. Once, he had collected money from Gujarati Muslims in his native Preston and nearby Blackburn to support his journey to Deoband for Islamic studies. However, when his plane landed in Baghdad on the way to India, he decided that he would like to explore the holy places of Baghdad and not make his way to Deoband on that particular occasion after all. Such behaviour was typical of Mohammad Sulaiman. It was not that he had wished to deceive his Gujarati benefactors: that was just the way he was, unpredictable. It was on one of the occasions that he did make it to Deoband for a short spell of study, that I took him to see Hakeem sahib. As he had done with his own son, Hakeem sahib held me out as an example. Quoting a Pashto poem, '*laka wana mustaqeem puh khpal maqam day,*' he pointedly told Mohammad Sulaiman how Jan Mohammad was 'like a tree, fastened in its own position.'

'Go to China in search of knowledge,' goes an ancient Arabic saying (*utlubu'l-ilma wa lau kana fi's-seen*). For Pashtoons, in place of China you may substitute India and particularly Deoband. Following in this tradition, the young Kifayatullah arrived in Deoband from his native Afghanistan determined to complete his studies in Darul Uloom; such was the allure, the status of Deoband in the eyes of Pashtoons. He went on to become one of the great Deobandi scholars of his day. When he graduated from Darul Uloom, he was quickly inducted there as a teacher. His younger brother Rahmatullah also joined him in Deoband. Along with completing the degree of excellence (*aalim-fazil*) course, Rahmatullah also became a mufti in Deoband. After I left Deoband, Abdul Rauf and his brother Rahmatullah kept the Pashtoon flag flying at Darul

Uloom. Maulana Abdul Rauf was more austere than his younger brother. It was common for students in Deoband to play volleyball, football or badminton in the late afternoon. Maulana Abdul Rauf would sometimes watch the badminton, but would never play, even admonishing others, in his usual smiling and good-natured manner, for 'playing all the time'.

One of those who in the words of Abdul Rauf was 'playing all the time' was his younger brother, Rahmatullah. Rahmatullah was a great lover of volleyball. One day he fell on top of his own hand while playing. His hand sustained a fracture and was in plaster. The Shaykh'al-Hadith of the day in Deoband, Maulana Naseer Ahmad Khan, was himself a Pashtoon. He hailed from Bulandshahr, close to Delhi. One day, Rahmatullah was sitting in the lecture hall of Hadith study attending Maulana Naseer Ahmad Khan's *Bukhari* lecture. From his lofty perch, from which the Shaykh was able to survey students, Maulana Naseer spotted the plaster on Rahmatullah's arm. 'What sort of a Pashtoon are you,' asked the maulana in a good-natured, jovial manner, 'that even your arm gets broken?' 'A Pashtoon fell on that arm,' Rahmatullah replied, referring, of course, to himself. 'That is why the arm broke.' The whole lecture hall broke into laughter. Rahmatullah was that quick on the uptake.

I was three years into my studies in Deoband when arrangements began for the centenary celebrations of Darul Uloom. In fact, the celebrations were about fifteen years late, since Darul Uloom's centenary had been in 1965—one hundred years on from the landmark teaching under the pomegranate tree of Maulana Nanotvi to Mahmud'al-Hasan. It was during the preparations for the centenary celebrations that a historical rift within the Deobandi movement came out into the open.

The rector of Darul Uloom, Qari Mohammad Tayyeb, was from one strand of Deobandi thinking. His nemesis, Maulana Asad Madani, was from another strand. Qari Mohammad Tayyeb had been a disciple (*murid*) and was a leading successor or *khalifah* of Maulana Ashraf Ali Thanvi. Maulana Ashraf Ali Thanvi had himself been a khalifah of Haji Imdadullah. Following the failure of the 1857 armed uprising against British rule, Haji Imdadullah migrated to Mecca and became known as the émigré to Mecca (*muhajir-e-Makkavi*). It was as if this act of emigration—removing himself from the arena of conflict and dedicating himself to worship—marked out those who followed the Imdadullah/Ashraf Ali Thanvi Sufi order. They would remain aloof, looking to improve themselves rather than being bitter at the excesses of the world around them.

We will be looking in more detail at the Thanvi school of Sufism later. My sympathies lay with this school, while Maulana Abdul Rauf was firmly in the Madani camp. Unlike the Thanvi wing of Deobandi thought, the Madanis believed in political activism. More than anyone, they looked for their inspiration to Shaykh'al-Hind Maulana Mahmud'al-Hasan (1851–1920). He will be appearing later in our story, in the chapter on the Frontier Gandhi. When he died in 1920, his mantle was taken up by Hussain Ahmad Madani, later Shaykh'al-Hadith of Darul Uloom Deoband. This was how Darul Uloom had existed since its very inception. While the administration was against any involvement in politics, Maulana Madani and before him Shaykh'al-Hind were actively involved in politics. Up till now, the two groups had co-existed, the Madanis as teachers, the Thanvis in the administration. Now, in the wake of the centenary celebrations at Darul Uloom Deoband in 1981, the Madani group launched its bid for power.

My predilection being for the Thanvi school of thought, I used to regularly attend the Sufi teach-ins (*majalis*) of both Qari Tayyeb and Maulana Maseehullah Khan, the latter also a successor of Maulana Ashraf Ali Thanvi. Maulana Maseehullah was based in Jalalabad, not to be confused with the more famous Jalalabad in Afghanistan, but a small village near Maulana Thanvi's own home village of Thana Bhavan[2]. Fundamental to the teaching of all Maulana Thanvi's successors was that students should not get involved

[2] As Shaharyar Khan has explained in his book the Begums of Bhopal, Jalalabad near Thana Bhavan, had since Mughal times been a stopping-off point for Pashtoons, when they arrived in India from the Frontier.

in politics. It is for students to strive for Islamic learning and wisdom, to come closer to Allah through prayer, meditation, self-improvement and remembrance of Allah, as well as study. Maulana Maseehullah Khan was particularly insistent on this matter. 'One dimensional and focused study,' and 'empty your mind of everything else and study,' were phrases that he would often repeat. Students did not yet have rounded knowledge, the teachers and *mashaikh* of the Thanvi school used to say. Now was not the time for them to become involved in political activity. Political leaders could easily use students' half-baked knowledge and raw emotions to create a rabble in support of their own aims.

The Madani bid for power, added to my loyalty to the Thanvi school, left me disillusioned. By now, I was regularly visiting Maulana Wahiduddin Khan in Delhi, who had taken over as my guide and *murshid*. I would have liked to have been more regular in my studies in Darul Uloom and to have benefited more from the study of Hadith that is concentrated in the final two years—the small and the great study tours of Hadith. But I was going through the motions. My heart was not in it. I had been put off by the *ulema* infighting. Nor did Wahiduddin Khan particularly encourage me to be regular in my studies in Darul Uloom. 'All you have to do now in Darul Uloom is receive a certificate,' he stressed. 'For you, there is no substitute to a certificate from Darul Uloom Deoband.' I took my exam, passed in second division and received my certificate.

How I could have benefited from conscientious study in my last two years at Darul Uloom! In the penultimate year, one studies Mishkat'al-Masabih. Right from the time I had accepted Islam, I had an affinity for this collection of Hadith. I had bought an English translation of Mishkat and went through it thoroughly, in the process acquainting myself, as least with the meaning of Hadith. Then I had continued study of Mishkat with Maulana Khan Afzal. Now, in Darul Uloom, Mishkat was allocated to my favourite teacher of all those teaching in Darul Uloom, Maulana Zubair. But my Mishkat year was ruined by continual strikes in support of the Madani party. Along with putting a stop to studies inside Darul Uloom, the Madanis set up an alternative Darul Uloom—known simply as 'camp'—near to Darul Uloom. It would have been best for my education to have studied there. Abdul Rauf was doing so and did his best to persuade me also to study in the camp, but I was dogged in my loyalty to Qari Tayyeb. I could not bring myself to be affiliated with the rebel Madanis, by studying in their camp. Not wishing to join the rebel camp and with no studies to pursue inside Darul Uloom, where strikes and non-cooperation had curtailed all classes, I spent more and more time away from Deoband. I was away from Deoband when the students from the camp stormed Darul Uloom by night and took it over. One of the first acts of the invading army of students was to break into my room and ransack it. This was the second time—the first time had been when my house was burnt down in Kajuray some seven years earlier—that my possessions, including all my Islamic books, had been ransacked, looted and destroyed by an invading Muslim force.

That same night, the son of Hussain Ahmad Madani, Maulana Asad Madani and his supporters established their authority in Darul Uloom. One Maulana Marghub-ur- Rahman, a Madani loyalist, was appointed as rector. Qari Tayyeb's son Maulana Salim set up a rival, parallel Darul Uloom, which they called Darul Uloom Waqf. I had no wish to study in a rival Darul Uloom. To me, that would have been the same as studying in the camp Darul Uloom. I stayed in the original Darul Uloom for my final year of study of Hadith, irrespective of the change of administration. This is my reading of the Qur'an[3] and literally scores of Hadith: one is to be loyal to the leader at all times, but if the leader changes, be loyal to the new leader.

I think some teachers at Deoband were secretly ashamed of my room having been ransacked and all my belongings, including Islamic books, being stolen or destroyed. They could see the disaffection of this previously dedicated student. On one of the occasions that I did attend a Hadith lecture, Maulana Saeed Palanpuri made a point of praising me in front of all the students. 'I was extremely impressed by the exam paper of Jan Mohammad,' he said, referring to the mock exams. 'His written Urdu was so

[3] 'Believers, obey Allah and obey the Messenger and those who have been entrusted with authority among you.' (Al-Quran, 4:59)

good that I thought, "How can a foreigner write such good Urdu? Did he copy off someone or something?" Then I saw that he had written some English words in parentheses, and I realized that Jan Mohammad had indeed written this paper himself.' In those days, Maulana Palanpuri was teaching *Tirmidhi*, one of the main collections of Hadith. His lectures were always a highlight, worth attending for his deep understanding and original thought. Maulana Palanpuri is now Shaykh'al-Hadith in Deoband[4], a position he thoroughly deserves. Even when I was studying at Darul Uloom, he was the outstanding teacher of Hadith. He was not loath to speak his mind. 'One will only be promoted in this madrasa system, until one is too old to be up to the job.' It is true. It is difficult to supersede seniority, not only in madrasas, almost anywhere. As for Mufti Rahmatullah, he returned to the Pashtoon parts, doing spells of teaching in Kandahar in the nineties, and later in Quetta. However, Pashtoon students were not long able to benefit from the considerable knowledge and status he had acquired in Deoband. He too became prey to the conflict in Afghanistan, being gunned down by unknown assailants—even if they are known they always do remain 'unknown'—in 2013 on the streets of Quetta. Even more than his elder brother Abdul Rauf, who remained in Karachi, he was well known as one of the outstanding scholars of his day in southwestern Afghanistan and Balochistan. It is a sad fact that Pashtoon *ulema* who have spent time in Deoband, more than having a calming effect on Afghanistan turmoil, tend to get sucked into it.

[4] Maulana Saeed Palanpuri passed away in 2020.

XIII

SUFI SAINT

Lo, those who are friends of Allah, they will have no reason to fear, nor will they grieve. Those who believe, and refrain from wrongdoing.

(*Yunus* 10: 62-63)

There were many in Deoband who eschewed the political involvement of Shaykh'al-Hind. Foremost amongst these were the administrators of Darul Uloom itself. In 1913, they had prevailed on Shaykh'al-Hind's collaborator, Maulana Ubaid-Ullah Sindhi, to move from Deoband to Delhi. They had also tried to persuade Shaykh'al-Hind to desist from his political activities. From their point of view, Darul Uloom had been established solely to enable Muslims to advance in traditional Islamic learning and to strengthen themselves spiritually. To their mind, it had never been envisaged as a base for political activity. It was this estrangement between the two strands of Deobandi thought—the purely scholastic and the more political—that led to the Deoband upheavals of the early eighties.

In the history of Deoband, two people particularly embodied this purely educational and spiritual approach. One was Maulana Ashraf Ali Thanvi, 'the pre-eminent Sufi of modern India'. The second was the disciple, one of the many anointed khalifas, of Maulana Thanvi: Qari Mohammad Tayyeb, rector of Darul Uloom for fifty years from the early thirties until my time in Deoband in the early eighties. To say that Ashraf Ali Thanvi was the greatest Sufi scholar Deoband has produced is like saying that Bob Dylan is the greatest singer-songwriter of the modern age. The volume of their work testifies to it. There can be no doubt about it. Thanvi did not delve into Hadith scholarship that much. He left that department to other eminent contemporaries such as Maulana Anwar Shah Kashmiri (1875–1933), but his Qur'an exegesis, *Bayan'al-Qur'an*, has no parallel, even if it is dense and somewhat difficult to read. One contemporary of mine in Deoband, a brilliant student with a penetrating mind, Maulvi Talha, had this witty off-the-cuff reply to my observation that *Bayan'al-Qur'an* should be translated into English: 'It should be translated into Urdu first!' It is, of course, in Urdu anyway, but Talha's point was taken.

For me, it was the scholastic and spiritual side of Deoband that held special appeal: the large lecture halls in which students and teachers sat on the floor, with low desks on which to place their books; the ancient buildings that spoke of dedication to learning; the afternoon *majalis* with the great Sufi mashaikh of Deoband. These *majalis* were the perfect foil to the academic learning of the day. By day, you became imbued with *Shariah*. In the late afternoon, you advanced in the path towards Allah (*tareeqat*). At the time when I was in Deoband, there were two great Sufi mashaikh who received their followers and disciples every afternoon. One was Mufti Mahmud'al-Hasan, not to be confused with Shaykh'al-Hind, whose name was also Mahmud'al-Hasan. In fact, as his title indicated, Mufti Mahmud'al-Hasan was more a jurist who was also a Sufi. He was a balanced Islamic scholar, adept at both *Shariah* and *tareeqat*, but heavier on the *Shariah* than on the *tareeqat* side. He hailed from the village of Gangoh, near Deoband, that was also the birthplace of Rashid Ahmad Gangohi, one of the founding fathers of Darul Uloom Deoband. I would say that Rashid Ahmad was also more a jurist who was also a Sufi, rather than the other way round. The gatherings of Mufti Mahmud'al- Hasan were held in a room in the Chattarwali Masjid. This was the mosque where

Darul Uloom was born in 1865. Under a pomegranate tree in this mosque, the founder of Darul Uloom, Qasim Nanutvi, imparted some lessons to Shaykh'al-Hind. Darul Uloom grew from there.

As I made clear in the last chapter, my own affinity (*munasibat*), as one would say in Sufi terminology, was towards the Thanvi line embodied in Qari Mohammad Tayyeb. I soon heard about another anointed successor of Maulana Thanvi who lived near the maulana's own village of Thana Bhavan, about fifteen miles from Deoband. His name was Maulana Maseeh-Ullah Khan. His *khanqah* was in a village called Jalalabad. A *khanqah* is the equivalent of an ashram, in Hindi, monastery in English. It is a place where a Sheikh receives and trains his disciples. Of course, the Pashtoon origins of Maulana Maseeh-Ullah Khan appealed to me. So did the name Jalalabad, with its resonance of one of the main cities in the Pashtoon parts, in the east of Afghanistan. In fact, the association of Jalalabad with Pashtoons went beyond its name: it was indeed an outpost of the Pashtoons in north India, a place where Frontier Pashtoons would stop off on their way to Delhi and the other cities of northern India. It was in Jalalabad that the founder of the state of Bhopal, Dost Mohammad Khan of the Orakzai tribe, had found repose before he moved to the Mughal court and from there to Bhopal.[1]

However strong the connections of Jalalabad with the Pashtoon parts, that was not what attracted me to the village. It was more the proximity of Jalalabad to Thana Bhavan, the native village of Maulana Thanvi and the place where this master Sufi scholar made his khanqah. It was also the configuration of Jalalabad in a chain of villages that lay in this section of northern India, close to the Himalayan Garhwal foothills. This is a tract of country, Doab, lying between the courses of the two great rivers of northern India: the Ganga and the Jamuna. The area is famous for centres of Hindu pilgrimage: Rishikesh, where the Ganga issues from the mountains into the Gangetic plains, and Haridwar a little further downstream. Little known is a series of villages that begin from the

[1] Details of the importance of Jalalabad to Pashtoons are discussed at length in Shaharyar Khan's book, *The Begums of Bhopal.*

town of Deoband, some thirty-five miles southwest of Haridwar. Due west from Deoband lie the villages of Nanuta and Gangoh. Nanuta spawned the founder of Darul Uloom Deoband, Maulana Qasim Nanutvi Gangoh and his successor Rashid Ahmad Gangohi. In Thana Bhavan, south of Nanuta, are memories of Maulana Thanvi himself, along with his own *pir*, Haji Imdadullah. South of Thana Bhavan lies Kairana. It was from Kairana that Maulana Rahmatullah Kairanvi hailed. Maulana Rahmatullah Kairanvi had singlehandedly stood up to the Christian missionaries who made a concerted effort to waylay Muslims in the nineteenth century. Both Maulana Kairanvi and Haji Imdadullah died in Mecca. Both had to leave British India, Haji Imdadullah due to the association of his disciples with the anti-British uprising of 1857, Maulana Kairanvi due to the famous debates he held with the stalwart of the Church Missionary Society, one C.G. Pfander.[2]

Another village south of Thana Bhavan, Kandhela, has provided the main leaders of the Tablighi movement over the last hundred years. *Ulema* were concerned at the success of the Arya Samaj Hinduization programme directed at Muslims. Prominent amongst these ulema was Ilyas Kandhelvi, who went on to found the Tablighi movement. Ashraf Ali and Ilyas Kandhelvi were two of a group of ulema who travelled to Mewat, where apostasy was mostly taking place. First of all, they held meetings with Mewat elders, explaining some fundamental tenets of Islam and their responsibilities as Muslims. They felt that it was only ignorance of Islam that led to the people of Mewat turning to Hinduism in droves. This was the practice that later became known in Tablighi parlance as *gasht* (walking around and imparting Islamic teachings to people). The *ulema* consulted with each other in the course of their travels and in their assessment of the situation. They decided that a knowledge

---

[2] When Christian missionaries arrived from England in the 19th century, they set about undermining Islamic beliefs and seeking to convert Muslims to Christianity. No one was more active in this regard than C.G Pfander. He wrote a book entitled *Mezan-ul-Haq*. The first generation of Deoband scholars rose to the challenge. Here, the outstanding figure was Maulana Rahmatullah Kairanvi. He authored a riposte to *Mezan-ul-Haq*, entitled *Izhar-al-Haq*. It is still considered the standard work, from an Islamic standpoint, in Muslim-Christian polemic.

of the duties of the Mewati tribes as Muslims could not be inculcated through meetings alone. The first plan that they hit on was to establish little learning centres in Mewat where people could come and learn about Islam. The learning centres were well enough attended. But an evaluation of their impact showed that they had one drawback. People were coming to the learning centres and taking in some of the teachings. However, once they returned to their own village environment, they once again followed the Hindu practices they had learnt from the Arya Samaj.

It was then that Ilyas Kandhelvi developed a plan that was to be incorporated into the Tablighi movement. Maulana Ilyas and his colleagues decided it would be better to take the tribes out of their own environment. That is how the Tablighi practice of *tashkeel* began. Tashkeel involves leaving one's environment in groups of seven or eight people, with a chief at one's head. These groups are deputed to a certain area for a period of one week, forty days, four months, one year. There, they travel from mosque to mosque talking to people about the six principles of Tabligh.[3]

The Tablighi movement is now a worldwide movement. Admirable though its work has been, and still is to a certain degree, the guardians of the movement would do well to recall the example of their founders in being flexible and responding to needs in different ways. If they were to conduct an assessment of the impact of their work, for instance if they were to track the extent to which those who venture out in Tabligh continue their good habits after they have completed their time in Tabligh, they may find that the same thing is sometimes happening now as happened in Mewat following the establishment of the original learning centres. In other words, some people are going back to their old habits once they finish their forays into Tabligh.

---

[3] These six principles are:

1. faith in Allah, the meaning of la ilaha ill'Allahu;
2. prayer;
3. remembering Allah;
4. manners;
5. purity of intention; and
6. preaching and teaching the word of Allah.

Another disadvantage of the inflexibility of the Tablighi approach has been that it has emerged as a kind of parallel Islam alongside real Islam. The six principles of Tabligh have become like a rival to the five pillars—faith, prayer, charity, fasting and pilgrimage—of Islam. The word *tabligh* means communication, in this case communication of the word of Allah. It can loosely be translated as preaching. Obviously, there are multiple ways that people can conduct this activity. It is not solely performed by travelling from mosque to mosque and preaching the word of Allah in mosques, as the Tablighis do. Quite often, that is tantamount to preaching to the converted. Any other form of *tabligh* is generally not even accepted as *tabligh* by the Tablighi movement. By casting the six principles and practices of *tabligh* in stone, the Tablighi movement is itself in danger of becoming an innovation (*bidaat*) against which the founders of the Tablighi movement inveighed.

One day in the mid-eighties, I was sitting with the Khudai Khidmatgar Malik Rahat Khan in his *hujrah* in Sakhakot in the North-West Frontier Province. Alongside him was a veteran Muslim Leaguer, Mohammad Ali Khan from Mardan. The two were old friends and on the best of terms, despite being political rivals, Rahat Khan being from the Khudai Khidmatgar wing of the Congress party and Mohammad Ali from their opponents the Muslim League. 'This is the type of guy who should be doing Tabligh,' Mohammad Ali Khan gestured towards me. Mohammad Ali's point was that Tabligh should be conducted amongst non-Muslims, and I, being originally English, would know the mentality of Europeans and how to couch the teachings of Islam for a European audience.

Malik Rahat Khan went on to relate what had happened to him when he was on his way to hajj. 'I told some Tablighis in Karachi that I was on my way to hajj. "Oh, our hajj is in Raiwand," they told me,' Raiwand being the Pakistan centre of the Tabligh movement. Perhaps that was an extreme example, and the words were most probably uttered by some over-zealous, under-educated Tablighi, but the case points to a Tablighi malaise that sees their way as the way along with Islam itself, the *Tablighi Nisab*[4] as the holy book

[4] Written by another scion of the Kandhela Tablighi clan, Maulana Zakariya

along with the Qur'an, and their six principles as the basis of their faith along with the five pillars of Islam.

So captivated did I become with the network of villages that lie north and south of Thana Bhavan that I took to walking the twenty miles or so that lay between Deoband and Jalalabad, where I regularly went on the weekends to attend the majalis of Maseeh-Ullah Khan. It had been Maulana Khan Afzal's elder son, Abdul Hakeem, the one who first taught me Urdu in Tirah, who first mentioned to me the propensity I have towards *mujahidah*. 'You know, Jan Mohammad,' he said to me one day. 'You have conducted a lot of *mujahidah*.' I took what he said with a pinch of salt and belittled my efforts in this regard. 'No, Jan Mohammad,' he insisted. 'We are in a good position to judge this. You have certainly conducted a lot of *mujahidah*.'

In Islamic terminology, *mujahidah* is the struggle, the deeds one performs to defeat one's inner enemy—one's own self. It involves pushing your body to the limit in order to suppress the inner self that is desirous of this and that. The word *mujahidah* comes from jihad, a general word for struggle. It shows that the real jihad is the struggle one conducts to control one's own self. Abdul Hakeem was referring to the long months—years even—of fasting that I undertook during my years in Tirah, which he had been witness to. I sometimes used to fast while walking the twenty miles to Jalalabad, even during the searing summer months.

Along with his khanqah, Maseeh-Ullah Khan kept a madrasa named Miftah'al-Uloom. It was popular with South African and English students in particular. I became friendly with two lads from Blackburn, Farooq and Inayat-Ullah. I even stayed with their families on my visits to England, becoming particularly close to Farooq's family. Inayat-Ullah was a model student and also a dedicated disciple of Maseeh-Ullah Khan. For Maseeh-Ullah, the greatest attribute that a student or a spiritual adept could have, was to be focused. He was pleased to see that I was friendly with Inayat-Ullah. '*Buhut aik suu larka hai*,' our shaykh praised Inayat-Ullah for how he focused on his studies as well as his spiritual development, to the exclusion of all else. It was a lack of this level of focus that precluded my initiation into the Thanvi school of Sufism, as was initially my intention. I was too eclectic to be able to cut out everything else and focus solely on my academic studies and spiritual initiation. Inayat-Ullah was the opposite. He went on to be one of the main khalifas of Maseeh-Ullah, a fact reflected by him being chosen to lead the funeral prayers of his shaykh when Maseeh-Ullah passed away in 1992.

Ramadan was a particularly magical time in Jalalabad, with Maseeh-Ullah Khan's *majalis* taking up the whole of the long summer mornings. In the evening, there would be the extended *tarawih* prayers, which lasted late into the night. Before that, another session with the shaykh would be held in the late afternoon. These were specialist sessions, for spiritual adepts. The basic text would be Maulana Thanvi's *malfuzat*, collections of what Thanvi said in his *majalis*. These have been collected into many volumes by the disciples and followers of Maulana Thanvi. Maseeh-Ullah always used to say that the next best thing after actually sitting in the company of one's shaykh and hearing what he said was to read his *malfuzat*. The *majalis* are off-the-cuff affairs. The shaykh just says what comes into his head. The aim of the shaykh—certainly according to the Thanvi school of Sufism—is to eradicate any of the vices that he is able to detect in his disciples. It might be pride, avarice, anger, jealousy; whatever. Sometimes, Maulana Maseeh-Ullah would tell us, it was not possible to eradicate a vice. In that case, when the vice could not be eradicated completely (*izala*), then one would have to make do with redirecting that vice in a positive direction through the process known as *imala*.

The example that is often given of how one can redirect a certain negative trait in a positive direction is that of Umar bin al-Khattab, the second successor or khalifah of the Holy Prophet. His anger was legendary. Indeed, prior to his acceptance of Islam, he took up his sword in a fit of anger and decided to do away with the Holy Prophet. On his way, he met a clansman of his, who, noticing Umar's determined and furious expression, asked him where he was off to. 'I am going to kill Mohammad, who has sown division amongst our people,' Umar answered him. His clansman derided him. 'You would do well to worry first about your own family members, your own sister and brother-in-law, who have accepted Islam.' The news shocked Umar, who was immediately diverted towards his sister's house. 'I had better kill them instead!' These were the days when the Meccan Qur'anic *Surah* named *Ta Ha* had just been revealed. It was being recited in the house of Umar's sister Fatima when Umar descended upon the household. He grappled with Fatima's husband and drew blood from Fatima when she went to defend her husband. Seeing blood on the body of his sister, Umar's resolve weakened and he asked to see the verses they had been reciting. Fatima showed them to Umar, who was won over by the beauty of the verses that he read: '*Ta Ha*. We have not sent the Qur'an down to you to distress you.' This dramatic incident signified the redirection—the *imala*—of Umar's anger from the negative aim of killing the Holy Prophet to becoming equally fierce in his defence of Islam.

During my time in Jalalabad, I visited the *khanqah* of Maulana Thanvi in Thana Bhavan. It was as if the shaykh were still living there. The word *khanqah*—the Arabic is *zawiyya*—is sometimes translated as monastery and the Thanvi khanqah did look like a mini monastery. Thanvi's disciples used to live in tiny cells where they would recite the remembrance of Allah that their shaykh would prescribe for them: pray, eat, study and sleep (*dhikr*). Food came from a central *langar*.[5] The cells were still there when I visited Thana Bhavan in the early eighties, the khanqah itself not only intact but spick and span. The poems of Khwajah Aziz'al-Hasan Majzub were prominent. They were inscribed in beautiful handwriting in key places such as next to the room of Maulana Thanvi. No one enshrines the life and mission of Ashraf Ali Thanvi more than Majzub. Not only did he write beautiful poetry about his time with Maulana Thanvi, he also provided proof that a free spirit could flourish in the highly disciplined and austere environment of the Thanvi khanqah. One of his famous poems was written when he had been expelled from the khanqah for some contravention of the khanqah rules:

> He is not going to open the door, I am not going to leave it Everyone is in charge of their own affairs, sometimes he holds sway, sometimes me

[5] A *langar* is a place where food is cooked and distributed free, mainly for devotees or spiritual adepts.

Like his *Malfuzat*, a number of Maulana Thanvi's books were written in fact by other people on the basis of the words of the shaykh himself. This was true of his magnum opus, *Behishti Zewar*. *Behishti Zewar* is a compendium of both Islamic theology and Islamic lifestyle. It is a painstaking, methodical, thorough and comprehensive work. What is especially unique about it is that it was written especially, though not exclusively, for women; hence the title, *Heavenly Jewellery (Behishti Zewar)*. Not only does the book tell people about a simple, unadulterated Islamic lifestyle, it motivates women in South Asia to become literate, explaining to them letter-writing and giving advice on rearing children. It also provides recipes for cooking dishes, gives instructions for home cures, includes inspirational biographies of women saints of Islam. It shows women the way to learning in a uniquely feminine manner.

Next to the Qur'an, *Behishti Zewar* is the most ubiquitous book in mosques as well as in homes in South Asia. Like the Qur'an itself, it is a sacred book to be found on the shelves in the homes of Pashtoon womenfolk. It needs to become more of a manual, something that people live by, a great resource to have in the activity and learning centres—places where women meet, take literacy classes and learn about health and hygiene— that have been established from place to place for Pashtoon womenfolk. I believe that to do justice to *Behishti Zewar*, it should be taught in the original Urdu, with translation into Pashto, like Arabic books are generally taught in Pashtoon madrasas using the original text with translation into the vernacular. But there are good translations, and we have put one in our mosque in my current workplace in Afghanistan. It is where ladies congregate when they are waiting for their turn at drama recording. I will be explaining later, in the chapters concerning the nineties until the present day, how I turned to radio drama as a modern form of storytelling, entertaining as well as enlightening listeners on key issues of the day.

The same applies more generally to the Sufi/scholastic school represented by Maulana Thanvi. The Pashtoons could do with a big injection of this school. It is true, there were several anointed successors of Maulana Thanvi who hailed from the Frontier. Foremost amongst them was Maulana Faqir Mohammad from Landi

Arbab, on the outskirts of Peshawar. He counted amongst his disciples many influential Frontier figures, including Shaykh Hasan Jan, the Shaykh'al-Hadith of the Imdad'al-Uloom madrasa in Saddar Bazaar in Peshawar. A student of another khalifa of Maulana Thanvi, Maulana Mohammad Idrees, who settled in Lahore and taught at the Jamia Ashrafia, was Shaykh Hasan Jan of Peshawar, who adhered religiously to the Thanvi way. I knew Shaykh Hasan Jan quite well. His madrasa was close to our PACT Radio[6] office in Peshawar in the latter part of the noughties. To my mind, he was an embodiment of Thanvi thinking.

Once at PACT Radio we produced a programme on student involvement in politics: should they be involved or not? Amongst others, we interviewed Shaykh Hasan Jan for the programme. 'We discourage students from being involved in politics,' he enunciated the Thanvi position very clearly. 'The reason for this is that students tend to be emotional, and their emotions can be misused by political leaders.' Maulana Thanvi or Maulana Maseeh-Ullah Khan could have uttered the words themselves.

One would not have envisaged the ending for Shaykh Hasan Jan. In Ramadan of 2007, the very year when we produced the programme on student involvement in politics, some local people came to the Darwesh Mosque in Saddar Bazaar, where Shaykh Hasan Jan was based. 'Our sister is getting married,' they told Shaykh Hasan Jan. 'We would like you to solemnize the *nikah*,' in other words, perform the marriage ceremony. Shaykh Hasan Jan accompanied the men without question. When they reached Wazir Bagh, on the outskirts of Peshawar, they shot Shaykh Hasan Jan dead. As with all such murders of prominent *ulema* in Pakistan, no one has ever got to the bottom of who murdered the shaykh and why. However, there is consensus that his enunciation of views on a number of issues in line with the peaceable nature of Thanvi thought did not fit in with the agenda of some elements. It is sad to say that this is how far politics amongst the Pashtoons has strayed from the thought of the great shaykh.

---

[6] PACT Radio was the radio production company I set up in Peshawar in the mid-noughties.

XIV
MODERN MULLA

The secret of being human is to be adjustable
(Insaan naam hai adjustability ka)

(Maulana Wahiduddin Khan)

'People think I am a master type,' Maulana Wahiduddin said as he was addressing some guests in the early eighties in his old office in the Jamiya building in Galli Qasim Jan in the middle of teeming Old Delhi. 'But, in fact, I am a pure mulla.' It must be said that this Maulana is a mulla with a difference, educated in a madrasa with a difference. Wahiduddin's madrasa education came not in the conservative, fiqh-oriented Darul Uloom Deoband, but in the comparatively progressive, Qur'an-oriented Islahi madrasa in his native Azamgarh.

It is common for Muslim families in north India to send one of their sons to a religious madrasa while the other siblings go through the normal school system. Generally, it is the dullest of their sons who are sent to a madrasa. In the case of Wahiduddin, it turned out that it was the son with the most precocious intellect of all who went to a madrasa. His searching intellect did not rest at examining the classical works of Islam. He wanted to learn also about modern sciences. He took to delving into libraries around Azamgarh. Almost inevitably, this intellectual search, into science, philosophy and all branches of modern learning, took him away from orthodox Islamic practice for a few years. He rediscovered Islam, with the basis of a classical Islamic education, from the point of view of a modern, scientific-minded seeker.

When I met Wahiduddin Khan, I was going through a similar phase. The upheavals at Deoband had been a chastening experience. Not only had they disturbed my studies, they had exposed to me what seemed to be the greedy, power-chasing nature of some of the *ulema*. This seemed to me the very mentality that gave birth to Islamism—grabbing power in the name of Islam. In every way, it was Wahiduddin Khan who guided me in a new direction at the time, encouraging me to stick with my studies at Deoband while giving me an alternative path, within Islam, to explore. That path, charted out in Wahiduddin Khan's writings, made refreshing sense. It was all so new and original yet firmly based in Islamic thought. 'Everything falls into place,' I told Wahiduddin, referring to his writings and his thought in one of the many and frequent private discussions we used to have. 'There is a great affinity between the two of us,' he concurred, referring to the kind of—affinity (*munasibat*) that exists between a shaykh and his disciple.

It is an affinity that has lasted till the present day, though I have moved on in terms of being a member of Maulana's inner circle—his 'team' as they refer to themselves. But on the rare occasions when I visit him in Delhi, he receives me warmly. 'You are a peaceful mujahid,' he is kind enough to accord me the greatest accolade I could imagine. 'When you come, it is as if the whole world has come.' For my part, I cannot imagine doing the work I am doing amongst the Pashtoons without having been steeped in Maulana's thinking.

It was Talha, my contemporary in Darul Uloom Deoband, who first introduced me to the writings of Maulana Wahiduddin Khan. Talha drew my attention to Maulana's *Mistaken Interpretation* (*Tabeer ki Ghalati*) a critique of political Islam. In this book, Maulana deals with the political interpretation of Islam, particularly as expounded by Maulana Maududi.[1] Deobandi scholars have written dozens of books criticizing the writings of Maulana Maududi. These books tend to concentrate on secondary points, not fundamental ones in terms of Maulana Maududi's ideology. None of them get to grips with the political interpretation of Islam, the idea that the aim of Islam is to establish an Islamic state, of which Maulana Maududi has been one of the leading exponents in modern times. The failure of Deobandi scholars to dissect the political ideology of Islam has meant that many of them, particularly in Pakistan and Afghanistan, have by default adopted this ideology. We saw this in the power struggle at Deoband. The only Islamic thinker that I know of in the modern age to unravel the political ideology that has come to be known as Islamism is Wahiduddin Khan.

Well, there might be others who have unravelled Islamism, but I have not come across them. Though one thing Maulana said to me was along the lines of what I heard from Hamza Yusuf, head of the Zaytuna Institute in California and a leading light of Western Islam. Hamza Yusuf is on record saying words to this effect: 'There are a lot of things that humanity is in need of and that Islam can provide, but a political system is not one of them.' If one were to say to a Westerner, for example, that Islam has a very good political system, one that is to be emulated, then they are likely to say that their political system is much better. Where is the model political system in the Muslim world? The West has democractic, transparent and accountable government. What has the Muslim world got to show, except for corruption and dictatorship? Western government's democracy may not be perfect, but would seem to be an improvement on the political model in most Muslim countries. Political Islam is a non-starter.

In Afghanistan nowadays, political Islamic thinking is pretty well established across the board. It is difficult to find an Islamic scholar in Afghanistan who is not an Islamist—a believer in the so-called Islamic political system. I put this point to one teacher

[1] Originally from Aurangabad in India, Maulana Syed Abu'l-Aala Maududi was the progenitor of political Islam in South Asia. With the formation of Pakistan, he emigrated to Pakistan. He passed away in Lahore in 1979.

of mine, Maulvi Naquib of Kunar. It was Maulvi Naquib who had been teaching the Qur'an in Bara, immediately prior to the upheavals there in 1976. 'You know, Jan Mohammad,' he said to me, at what was probably our last meeting before he passed away a few days before Ramadan in 2017, 'along with preaching the word of Allah, one has to have power (*hakimiyat*) for one's preaching to be effective.' 'Well,' I said, 'all these people who have had a government in Afghanistan over the last few decades, they have not made a very good job of enforcing the will of Allah, have they?' 'The job has been entrusted to the wrong people,' he replied. It always seems to be entrusted to the wrong people.

In a phrase that has always remained with me as far as political Islam is concerned, Sayed Lal, the son of Haji Bahadar Khan from Tirah, once said to me that Islamic government is good government. It is not the enactment of certain laws and certain punishments: it is the establishment of the rule of law, to whatever legal system that law may conform. I have already mentioned the words of a fellow student of mine in Deoband, Maulvi Afzal Afriqai, 'Our politics should be Islamic, but our Islam should not be political.' To me, the tragedy of political Islam—giving precedence to *Shariah*—is that it has put personal Islam—following the Sunna—into the background. The Sunna pertains to the character and actions of the individual. Incorporate Sunna into the individual, from the governed to those who form the government, and you have an Islamic society, an Islamic state. Maulana Wahiduddin Khan's thinking, surprisingly enough, would seem to tally with that of Margaret Thatcher, who coined the famous phrase: 'There is no such thing as society. There are individual men and women, and there are families.' Political Islam aims Islam at society, or, even more impersonally, at the state. That is why it cannot catch on. Sunna concentrates on the individual and the family, where it is relatively easy to implement.

In later life, I have often found Jamaat-e-Islami members—Jamaat-e-Islami being the political party formed by Maulana Maududi—quite cooperative in initiatives I have started to enable madrasa graduates to make a meaningful contribution in the mainstream of modern life. This cooperative and positive attitude has given me the impression that in forming a political ideology based on Islam, the Jamaat-e-Islami were seeking to make their faith into a relevant force in the modern age. But, by choosing the political path, they were opting for a short route to modernity and one fraught with dangers. For if one sees Islam as a political ideology and makes it one's aim to establish an Islamic state, then one is inviting politicians to use Islam to gain political power. In the process, one is devaluing one's faith, making it into an avenue for worldly advancement as opposed to eternal salvation. Islam becomes a tool in the hands of politicians instead of a model according to which one should live one's life. I find this debasement of Islam the most disillusioning factor in so-called Muslim countries such as Pakistan and Afghanistan. I have found societies considered secular—England, Uzbekistan and especially India—much more conducive to the practice of Islam as a potent spiritual force in one's life. There, nothing could be gained from the politicization and subsequent devaluation of the faith.

One cannot just conduct outreach or communication of the message of Islam (*dawah*) in a vacuum. One needs an entry point. Islamists have taken the wrong, but most convenient, entry point: politics. For Wahiduddin Khan, the entry point is science. The opening lines of his book *The Emergence of Islam* (*Zuhoor-e-Islam*) align three major events in the history of mankind: the emergence of Islam, the Big Bang that led to the creation of the universe and the knowledge explosion—one could call it the scientific revolution—that followed the establishment of Islam on earth. The Big Bang that led to the creation of the universe is mentioned in *Surah al-Anbiya*:

> Do not those who deny the truth see that the heavens and the earth were joined together and that We then split them asunder? And that We have made every living thing out of water. Will they still not believe? (*al-Anbiya* 21:30)

The emergence and subsequent dominance of Islam (*al-Fath* 48:28) paved the way, in Maulana's sweeping view, for the scientific revolution of recent centuries. The seeds of this knowledge explosion were sown in the Muslim world, but the tree bore fruit in the Western world:

> We shall show them Our signs in the universe and within themselves, until it becomes clear to them that this is the Truth. Is it not enough that your Lord is the witness of all things? (*Ha Mim al-Sajdah* 41:53)

How was it that meaningful scientific advances and discoveries were all made in the Muslim world? In a telling and convincing narrative, Maulana traces the original development of modern scientific thought to the Qur'an itself. The dominance of Islam established belief in one God: everything else—the sun, the moon, the stars, the universe—were objects of creation. As such, they could become objects of research also. The world of Christianity reacted with horror when Copernicus and Galileo put forward the heliocentric view that the sun, not the earth as had previously been thought, was at the centre of the universe. Such views were considered heresy in the Christian world. It seemed that Christian teachings themselves precluded such a theory: the son of God—according to Christian beliefs—had come to earth, so the earth had to be the centre of the universe. Though the Qur'an deals with the orbits of the sun, the moon and the stars in some detail, nothing in the Qur'an precludes the idea that it is the earth that revolves around the sun, not vice versa. This is an example of how the Qur'an paved the way for the scientific revolution. If this revolution was first facilitated and found expression in the Muslim world, it was the West that soon took up the baton of scientific advancement. The Qur'an had predicted this: 'We shall show them Our signs in the universe and within themselves,' here, 'them' meaning non-Muslims.

First of all, it was Muslim thinkers who took knowledge of astronomy, chemistry, mathematics, geography, zoology, botany and other sciences forward. In fact, it was Islam, with its strong emphasis on *Tauhid*—the oneness of almighty Allah—that freed the human mind. No area was off limits as far as human research was concerned. This enabled Muslims to leap ahead in scientific research and discovery. With the Crusades, Europeans, who were still caught in the clutches of the Dark Ages, saw that the only way they could catch up with the Muslim world would be by emulating the Muslims with regard to scientific learning. This was how the Renaissance came about in Europe. Now Maulana urged the Muslim world to repay the compliment, to acquire modern scientific thinking from the Western world and to take it forward, as the West did in the Middle Ages.

There are other, more constructive examples of interaction between the Muslim world and Europe than the Crusades. One that Maulana was particularly fond of citing was the relationship between the Muslim geographer Al-Idrisi and Roger II (1095–1154), founder of the Norman dynasty in Sicily who 'made Sicily a meeting place of European and Arabic scholars'. Of these Arab scholars, Al-Idrisi was the most eminent. Maulana wrote about how he became a close friend and adviser to Roger II, at whose court he served as official geographer. Roger II originally invited Al-Idrisi to Sicily to make a map of the world for him.

> Here we can see the cause of the esteem in which Muslims were held in times past. They made Islam a dominant force on the world scene, not through protests and demands, nor from spreading conflict and terror, but through being useful to the world. By virtue of hard struggle, they established themselves as intellectual leaders of the world. They had something that others did not have, so people flocked to their sides. That was how Muslims raised their standing in the world in times past. It is by the same method that they can improve their position today, and build for a better future.[2]

Make a contribution, be useful to the world, make yourself wanted, that is what Wahiduddin urges Muslims to do. I cannot think of any passage that has so moulded my own thinking in later decades. To me, living Islam is all about making a positive contribution to

---

[2] Maulana Wahiduddin Khan, *Zahoor-e-Islam*.

human endeavour. Be a giver, not a taker. One can only make this contribution if one is at peace with humanity. The Holy Prophet was keen to have interaction, to mingle with the people of Arabia, so that they could taste the joy of Islamic spiritual edification. That is why he unilaterally made peace with his enemies at Hudaybiyya. The background to the Peace Treaty of Hudaybiyya goes like this. In the year 6AH, the Holy Prophet saw a dream that he was performing the ritual circumambulation (*tawwaf*) round the holy Kaaba in Mecca. He set out with 1,500 of his followers with the intention of making his dream come true. When the band of believers reached Hudaybiyya, the Quraysh blocked their way, preventing the Muslims from proceeding towards the holy mosque. Negotiations between the two sides followed. Eventually, peace was made. Under the peace treaty, the Muslims would be allowed to visit the holy city the next year—not in that particular year.

Not only this, other conditions under which peace was made seemed entirely favourable to the Quraysh. If any member of the Quraysh sought refuge with the Muslims, he would be returned, but the Quraysh would not have to return any Muslim who sought refuge with them. In the course of writing the peace agreement, the Holy Prophet first of all dictated the words 'These are the terms of the truce between Mohammad the Messenger of Allah and Suhayl the son of Amr [Suhayl being the envoy of the Quraysh].' Suhayl protested: 'If we knew you to be the Messenger of Allah, we would not have barred you from the House, neither would we have fought you; but write Mohammad, the son of Abdullah.' Ali had already written the words 'Messenger of Allah'. The Prophet told him to delete the words. Ali found himself unable to do so. The Prophet asked Ali to show him the words on the scroll. He then deleted them himself.

Umar found the terms of the truce so humiliating that he could not contain himself. As we have seen, Umar was quite prone to anger. Rising to his feet, he went to the Prophet and said: 'Are you not the Prophet of Allah?' 'I am,' the Prophet answered. 'Are we not in the right and our enemies in the wrong?' he said. Again, the Prophet told Umar he was right in his assertion. 'Then why yield in such lowly wise and against the honour of our faith?' said

Umar, whereupon the Prophet replied: 'I am the Messenger of Allah and I will not disobey Him. He will give me victory.' The fact of the matter was that the Holy Prophet was willing to accede to any of the demands in order to achieve one thing: peace, and with it, free access to the people of Arabia. That is what happened after the Peace Treaty of Hudaybiyya. 'People were at peace and mixed freely with each other,' wrote the Qur'an commentator Ibn Kathir. This exposed people to Islamic thought. By virtue of the pulling power of Islamic thought, what seemed at the time like a defeat turned out to be a 'manifest victory.' (*al-Fath* 48:1)

So, in other words, the Muslims made unilateral peace so that the real power of Islam—the *dawah* power—could come into play. The great example in Islamic history of *dawah* power being utilized and standing the Muslims in good stead, as cited in the writings of Wahiduddin Khan, was following the invasion of the Muslim world and the sacking of many of the great cities of Islam by the Mongols. In military terms, the Muslims were defenceless in the face of the mighty Mongols. However, they had another resource at their disposal, which the Mongols were not able to resist. That was *dawah* power—the power of their faith. Within two generations of the Mongols laying waste to vast tracts of the world of Islam, the Mongols had themselves been converted to Islam. Such was the power of Islamic thought.

Maulana urges Muslims to go on the front foot, like the Muslims at the time of the Holy Prophet who unilaterally made peace so that they could enrich humankind with Islamic thought. We saw this previously, with the example of the theologians of Najran who visited Medina at the time of the Holy Prophet, ostensibly to win the Muslims over to Christianity. The Holy Prophet welcomed them. They might have been wishing to convert the Muslims but their coming would give Muslims a chance to put across their vision of Tauhid—the pure unity of the Godhead. As related by Ibn Kathir, the companions of the Prophet were somewhat hesitant. 'Should we allow them into the mosque?' they asked the Holy Prophet. 'Let them in,' he replied. The Prophet craved any peaceful interaction between his followers and those of other faiths. It gave the Muslims a chance to enrich humanity with their thought and wisdom.

This is the motivation behind Mahad'ad-Dawa, the higher learning institute for madrasa graduates that I have been running in Jalalabad and Kandahar since 2008.[3] To my mind, we are providing a blueprint of Maulana's thought in action. We are seeking to give Muslim scholars the opportunity to contribute to humanity in a host of fields. It is not just about training madrasa graduates to become journalists, businessmen, hakeems, humanitarian workers, lawyers, politicians even— whatever career they wish to take up. By teaching all these subjects within the framework and in the light of Qur'an and Hadith, we are seeking to enrich all these fields of study with Islamic thought. The aim is for the Pashtoon madrasa fraternity to feel motivated and emboldened that yes, we really do have something that could benefit mankind. Let us make peace with the whole world so we can contribute to the cause of human endeavour with the wisdom we have at our disposal.

'Which of my books do you like best?' Maulana once asked me. I replied without hesitation, '*Zuhoor-e-Islam*.' Maulana smiled: 'It's a very controversial book,' he remarked. The cause of the controversy is a chapter it contains on imams Hasan and Hussain, the two grandsons of the Holy Prophet. Imam Hussain took the path of active, armed resistance to authority that appeared to him without sanction and oppressive. This authority was embodied in the person of the Ummayad ruler, Yazid. As the whole world knows, Imam Hussain was martyred along with seventy of his followers on the field of Karbela. It was one of the epochal events of Muslim history and eventually led to the Sunni-Shia schism in Islam. That was the Hussainian model, well known and much emulated. However, very few know about the model established by Imam Hasan, Hussain's elder brother.

Imam Hasan was a contemporary of the father of Yazid, Amir Muawiya. When Amir Muawiya established the Ummayad kingdom in Damascus, Imam Hasan had a commensurate force at his disposal, in Medina, the city of the Holy Prophet. Being the grandson of the Holy Prophet, he had every reason to consider himself

---

[3] Mahad'ad-Dawa (MDI) is now an entirely online institute: www.dawmahad.org and www.facebook.com/dawamahad

the rightful ruler, particularly in view of the fact that he was the son of the final caliph, Ali. However, for the sake of Muslim unity, Imam Hasan decided against contesting Amir Muawiya's rule. 'If the Caliphate was rightfully Muawiya's,' Imam Hasan asserted, 'then he has acceded to what is rightfully his. If it was rightfully mine,' he continued, 'then I have ceded my own right to Muawiya.' Hardly anyone knows about the sacrifice of Imam Hasan for the cause of Muslim unity. Yet, in a Hadith related by Bukhari, Abu Bakr paints the touching scene of the Holy Prophet on the pulpit in his mosque with his grandson Hasan next to him. The Holy Prophet was looking one moment at his congregation, the next moment towards Hasan. 'This son of mine is a *sayyed*,' the Holy Prophet said—*sayyed* being a descendant of the Prophet. 'He may well turn out to play a conciliatory role between two great armies of the Muslims.'[4]

Despite this clear prophesy of the role Imam Hasan would play, it is amazing how sensitive people are to any mention of Imam Hasan in the same bracket as Imam Hussain. Maulana told me how one person had come to him following the publication of *Zuhoor-e-Islam*. 'You have even got the nerve to raise your pen against the grandson of the Prophet,' the gentleman challenged Wahiduddin, referring, of course, to Imam Hussain. 'All I did,' Maulana countered, 'was to highlight the role of Imam Hasan and he also, after all, was a grandson of the Holy Prophet.' In a meeting with Shahid Mehdi, former vice chancellor of Jamiya Milliya Islamiya, where Maulana's daughter Farida was a professor of Islamic studies, Mr Mehdi told me how he could not forgive Wahiduddin Khan for what he saw as the maulana's criticism of Imam Hussain. I myself have first-hand experience of the extreme sensitivity that exists to any highlighting of the role of Imam Hasan. I was once pen-pals—that's the old term for Facebook friends—with a person named Safoora Ahmad Khan, a brilliant artist and photographer from Lahore, a person with a love for Islamic history and a flair for bringing Islamic heritage to life in the most vibrant imaginable

[4] The Hadith is in Bukhari and also in Dr. James Robson's translation of *Mishkat'al-Masabih,* Volume II, page 1351

forms. Once she told me that she was going to Iran to join in the Ashura commemorations of the martyrdom of Imam Hussain. I was foolish enough to mention that I hoped the sacrifice of Imam Hasan would one day be celebrated with the same fervour as Imam Hussain's martyrdom was celebrated every year. That was the last I heard from Safoora, who immediately 'unfriended' me, clearly offended that I should mention Imam Hasan in the same breath as Imam Hussain.

Not only Shias, my fellow Deobandis also don't like Wahiduddin Khan much. When I ask them the reason, they generally say that in one book, he said now was the time to follow Jesus' Sunnah. I have not found the place in any of maulana's books where he said this, but I would not discount it. In saying follow the Sunnah of Jesus, maulana would not be discounting or belittling the *Sunnah* of the Prophet Mohammad, which Muslims naturally adhere to. He would just have been saying that Jesus was also a prophet, and the example that he left to the world of 'turning the other cheek' is most applicable to Muslims nowadays. Not that it is in any way inimical to the Sunna of Mohammad Mustafa either. *'Requite evil with what is better,' the Qur'an says, 'then you will see that one who was your enemy has become your dearest friend.'* (*Ha Mim al-Sajdah* 41:34) So, in order to accentuate and emphasize the current applicability and suitability of that pacifistic model, maulana might also have mentioned the model of the prophet Jesus. It is the same with the model of Hudaibiyya. Focusing on this model does not mean that at some times, Muslims might not be called in to fight in defence of their faith and to avoid persecution for the sake of their faith (*al-anfal* 8:39). There may be times when that model is more applicable. Now, however, it is high time for Muslims to make unilateral peace, as the Prophet and his companions did at Hudaibiyya. The conflicts in which Muslims engaged in the modern age, far from removing persecution of Muslims (*fitna*) and being the only justifiable casus belli that is mentioned in the Qur'an, have actually brought about and become the cause of their persecution. The same also with the Hasanian model. To emphasize its suitability to the situation in which Muslims find themselves is not to belittle or discount the Hussainian model.

From 1982 until 1988, I buried myself in translating Maulana's articles one by one. At this time, I was living a pretty hippie existence, or should we say that I had graduated to being a Muslim *malang*.[5] Sometimes I was in the deserts of Rajasthan, sometimes in the mountains of Himachal or Nepal, sometimes in the hippy enclave of Pahar Ganj in Delhi, sometimes in a *barsati* apartment I took in the western Delhi borough of Karol Bagh. Later, I moved back to Swat. With the help of my translations, Maulana's daughter Farida was able to bring out an English version of his monthly journal *Al-Risala*. Though I did not know it at the time, this was my initiation into journalism. What was of overriding importance to Maulana in his journalism was not the 'who did what, when, where, why and how' of a story. It was more what we could learn from the story, how it could help us to live our lives. Even more than the details of the story, it was the moral of the story that mattered.

It did not matter if the story came from the human world or from the divine world. An example from the divine world that Maulana was fond of recounting was the tale of a man who wanted to see a big, verdant tree growing in his garden. He took a fully-grown tree and transplanted it in his garden. After a few days, he was shocked to see that instead of the branches of the tree expanding, they withered and died. This was because he had taken the short route to seeing a tree standing tall in his garden. The only way to see a verdant tree growing in his garden would be to take a young sapling, plant it and nurture it over several years. Then, in time it would grow into a proud, tall tree. So it is in life. If one wishes to achieve some great aim, then one has to pursue a long drawn-out and laborious process. There are no shortcuts. Maulana's focus on the moral of a story was the foundation on which I was later to build traditional journalism that concentrated on what we could learn from a story rather than on the details of the story itself. The details were only important in so far as they carried the moral of the story.

I was living happily in India, not expecting ever to leave, when a bolt came from the blue. It was 1 June 1984. I was living in my

---

[5] A *malang* is a Muslim version of what Hindu's would call a sadhu—an ascetic or in Pashtoon Englishman's case, more a hermit.

barsati flat in Karol Bagh at the time, working as usual on my translations of Wahiduddin Khan's articles. I learnt that from that day, Commonwealth citizens would have to apply for an Indian visa to live in India. Until that time, British passport-holders like myself were exempt from having to hold a visa to stay in India. I applied for a visa and stayed for another few months, but after a while I thought, why not move back to the Frontier? Pakistan had still not introduced the visa rule for foreign citizens. It had been six years since I had come to India as a Pashtoon/English *talib*.

'My family originally came from Swat,' Maulana once told me. Like so many other Pashtoons, his forefathers had settled in one of the Pashtoon nawabates of north India; in Maulana's case, in the sultanate of Jaunpur, near Maulana's native Azamgarh. It was appropriate then that the bulk of my work with Maulana's mission should be conducted in the valley of Swat, my original Islamic home and the valley from which Maulana's ancestors had hailed.

XV
FRONTIER GANDHI

The more the Pashtoons advance as a nation,
the more we Pashtoons will advance as individuals

(Bacha Khan, *My Life and Struggle*)

Just imagine if Nehru had not become prime minister after the freedom of India in 1947 but had been imprisoned for another few decades by the new regime that took over in India. Unimaginable, isn't it? Well, that is exactly what happened to Khan Abdul Ghaffar Khan, the greatest 'peaceful mujahid' anyone can imagine. He was the one who had struggled for independence from the British, and he was the one who was imprisoned and persecuted by the government that took over in Pakistan after independence. The reason? He had been against the Partition of India. Having said that, he declared his loyalty to Pakistan once the breakaway State was created. That was not good enough for the Pakistan establishment, who continued to brand him a traitor, a Congressite and worse.

The character assassination aimed at Khan post-1947 was even more unrelenting than his imprisonment. Ghaffar Khan's daughter Mehr Taj, the longest surviving of all his children, once pointed out to me that her father was not so badly treated by the British as he was by the Pakistan authorities. 'The British respected Bacha Khan [as Ghaffar Khan was also popularly known] but his treatment at the hands of the Pakistan authorities was even more harsh than that meted out to him by the British.' The comparative respect Khan received from the British was due in part to the respect he accorded them, where respect was due.

It was unusual for Indian freedom fighters to accord the British such respect, but Khan Abdul Ghaffar was a big-hearted freedom fighter. So, I should add, was Maulana Wahiduddin Khan. In his book *Hind-Pak Diary*, Maulana—himself a Gandhian figure amongst Pashtoons of South Asia—recounts the tale of an Englishman by the name of Mr Larry who lived near their village in the Azamgarh district of Uttar Pradesh. He ran a farm in the hamlet of Baseenpur. The nearest railway station to Baseenpur was Shah Ganj. In order to reach this railway station, Mr Larry used to pass by Maulana's house on horseback. Maulana's family being freedom fighters and anti- British, they disliked the fact that an Englishman was passing by their homestead. They asked him to take another route to the railway station. Mr Larry did not pay any attention. One day, as Mr Larry was on his way to the railway station, Maulana's family stopped him and forced him off his horse. In contravention of Gandhian principles of non-violence, they gave Mr Larry a good beating. Presumably, Mr Larry could have lodged a complaint with the government, but he did not do so. Instead of taking any retaliatory measures, Mr Larry just changed his route to the railway station, opting for a longer route. He did this to avoid any confrontation and pre-empt any untoward incident. At the time, Maulana was a young man. He admits that he felt a sense of pride that his family appeared to have got the better of an Englishman. Now, with the benefit of hindsight, Maulana wonders why, instead of confronting Mr Larry, they had not sought to benefit from him, from the advanced agricultural methods that he practised, not to mention from his self-effacing, even Gandhian, reaction to the violent attack.

Hatred of the British, Maulana suggests, prevented people from benefiting from them. 'Unfortunately,' he writes, 'just about every major movement launched in the sub-continent over the last 100 years has been based on hatred.' In fact, Maulana could have made an exception in the case of the great Pashtoon leader Khan Abdul Ghaffar Khan's Khudai Khidmatgars. In terms of Pashtoon leadership in the twentieth century, Ghaffar Khan was a colossus. The Khudai Khidmatgars that he founded were attached to the Indian National Congress. They were as intent on Indian independence, and I suppose one could say anti-British, as anyone. Yet surprisingly enough, by his own admission, it was an Englishman who inspired Khan Abdul Ghaffar Khan to dedicate his life to the service of the Pashtoon people. Anti-Britishness did not prevent Khan from taking the good and leaving the bad as far as the British were concerned. The inspirational figure in Khan's life was Mr Wigram, his teacher at the Mission School, Peshawar. The young Ghaffar Khan was extremely impressed by Mr Wigram and his brother Dr Wigram. Both of them had dedicated their lives to the service of the Pashtoon people. The fact that the Wigram brothers were of English origin made Ghaffar Khan look up to them even more. Look at how they have come from another country, another nation, another religion, the young Abdul Ghaffar thought, yet they have devoted their lives to the service of Pashtoon children. Abdul Ghaffar Khan was particularly impressed by how Wigram sahib donated his salary for the upkeep of poor Pashtoon children, who otherwise would not have been able to study at Mission School. 'It was he who moved me to serve my people,' Khan recalled in his book *My Life and Struggle* (*Zama Jhwand au Jadd-o-Jahd*).

If one is surprised at the source of Ghaffar Khan's inspiration being an Englishman, the source of my becoming familiar with the life, sacrifice and struggle of Khan Abdul Ghaffar Khan is no less surprising. Sardar Abdul Rashid had been a member of the Pakistan Muslim League, responsible for the formation of Pakistan and direly opposed to Bacha Khan's Khudai Khidmatgars. As head of the Khudai Khidmatgar party, dedicated to 'serving others for the sake of God', Ghaffar Khan had been loyally attached to the Congress party of Mahatma Gandhi and Jawaharlal Nehru. One factor that softened Sardar sahib's attitude to Bacha Khan was the friendship between Sardar sahib and Bacha Khan's son-in-law, Yahya Jan. The latter had served as education minister in the government of the North-West Frontier Province prior to Partition in 1947. Also, as a key member of the Muslim League, Sardar sahib had been witness to the excesses of the Muslim League against Bacha Khan. He had seen how Bacha Khan had campaigned all his life and rendered sacrifices more than any other person in order to raise awareness amongst the Pashtoon people, making them in the process fit for independence from the British. Then, when Pakistan was formed, instead of his struggle and sacrifices being acknowledged, he was made to suffer even more.

Sardar sahib was fond of telling a tale. On the formation of Pakistan, many erstwhile members of the Khudai Khidmatgars joined the Pakistan Muslim League. Mian Jafar Shah Kaka Khel is one name that springs to mind in this regard. When they were challenged on this, one of them, Arbab Abdul Rahman of Nagoman, near Charsadda, said they were like watermelons, 'green on the outside and red on the inside', green being the colour of the Muslim League, red the colour of the Khudai Khidmatgars. Amongst this ilk, Sardar sahib could also have counted himself.

Nowadays, the Bollywood star Shah Rukh Khan is known as King Khan. In his day, Ghaffar Khan was the King Khan— Bacha Khan—of his age. He received the name Bacha Khan after he began his life's mission. He always stressed that his was a social movement, not a political one. Early on in his career, at a meeting he held aimed at rooting out social ills in his native village of Utmanzai, he pointed out that there should be a chairman of the meeting. The villagers suggested that he himself should be chairman. When Khan acquiesced, the simple and uninitiated villagers gave him the name Bacha Khan—King Khan—not seeing the difference between the chairman of a meeting and a king. Khan Abdul Ghaffar Khan, they thought, must have been crowned king since he had become chairman of a meeting.

'Let's do a translation of Bacha Khan's autobiography,' Sardar sahib suggested to me. It was the mid-eighties and the time of the Afghan jihad. The gulf between the two forces— the progressive nationalists and the religious conservatives—in Pashtoon society seemed more evident than ever. The progressive, nationalist, secular Pashtoon forces had no time for jihad. In fact, they were sympathetic to the socialist government in Afghanistan and even had a soft spot for their Soviet backers, against whom jihad was being conducted. On the other hand, there was the religious, conservative lobby that sympathized with the jihad and was allied to various jihadi groups. Bacha Khan was the hero of the nationalist, progressive wing of Pashtoon society, vilified by the leaders of jihad. The mid-eighties were also the heyday of General Zia-ul-Haq's military rule. There was a tight ban on the original Pashto version of Bacha Khan's autobiography. The only place where the book was available was with Haji Ghulam Ahmad Bilour, a man of stock from Peshawar City. The Bilour family had been loyal Khudai Khidmatgars and were still in the vanguard—not to mention being bankrollers—of the Pashtoon nationalist movement. Yahya Jan was deputed to purchase a copy of this supposedly seditious book. He brought it back to Sardar sahib, a paperback edition published by the Afghan government, the cover a suitably blazing red. There was something gloriously conspiratorial about Sardar sahib, a former chief minister of the Frontier and inspector-general of the Frontier police, purchasing and translating along with me a book that was banned in Pakistan, the author of which was considered an anti-state personality.

Sardar Abdul Rashid had also served as Interior Minister of Pakistan from 1969 to 1971—under the martial law regime of Yahya Khan. His most famed achievement during that time was to issue a Pakistani passport to Khan Abdul Ghaffar Khan. At that time, Ghaffar Khan was living in exile in the eastern Afghan city of Jalalabad, near the Torkham border, with Pakistan. Sardar Sahib was so unassuming. He never told me about this. I had been introduced to Sardar Sahib through my father, who was worried about me being in the tribal territory in the early seventies. With good reason, I must say. My father contacted the last British governor of NWFP, Sir Olaf Caroe, who contacted Sardar Sahib. In his discreetly flamboyant manner, Sardar Sahib sent a servant of his—Shinkay was his name—to the Malik-Din Khel Bagh in Tirah. 'When you are next in Peshawar, do go and see Sardar Sahib,' and he gave me his address. It was the beginning of a long friendship. Besides being unassuming, he was politically astute. 'John, what is your opinion of the Partition of India?' Sardar Sahib asked me in the eighties. I told him I was against dividing a nation on the basis of religion. 'You are right,' he said, 'If there had been no Partition of India, there would have been no Soviet invasion of Afghanistan, either.'

The first impression Bacha Khan's book made on me was what a graphic account it was of Pashtoon life and of the struggle for independence.[1] His Pashto writing style was the epitome of what good writing should be, as Wahiduddin Khan had described good writing to me. 'It should be simple enough for a small child to read, and a highly literate, educated person should also not consider it below his level.' One of the first things I learnt from Bacha Khan's book was that the secular, nationalist, progressive forces in Pashtoon society had not always been at loggerheads with their conservative, religious counterparts. Indeed, when Bacha Khan launched his political career in the early twentieth century, his closest associates were religious scholars, adherents of the Deoband school, followers of Shaykh'al-Hind Mahmud'al-Hasan. Bacha Khan had taken the Sufi oath of allegiance (*bayat*) with Shaykh'al-Hind. Shaykh'al-Hind, as his title suggests, was the supreme nationalist, along with being one of the leading Islamic scholars of his day. Personally having an affinity to both Pashtoon nationalists and to Deoband, the story of how this unity of approach turned into mutual antipathy and stand-off was to me the most intriguing aspect of Bacha Khan's life. It also presented the greatest challenge: how to bring these erstwhile united forces that had grown so far apart together again?

Turangzai and Utmanzai are two neighbouring villages in Hashtnagar district. The area is the political, cultural and historical powerhouse of the Pashtoon plains. The word Hashtnagar means eight cities. The 'hasht' is Persian, the 'nagar' Hindi. The area fuses Afghanistan with Hindustan. In the early twentieth century it was also a place of fusion of religious and political forces as the most renowned religious scholar of the time, Haji Fazal Mahmood Turangzai, joined forces with Khan Abdul Ghaffar Khan of Utmanzai village to raise the awareness of their people. The basis of their

---

[1] Khan Abdul Ghaffar Khan, *Zama jhwand au jadd-o-jahd.*

unity was the Deoband madrasa and in particular their attachment to Shaykh'al-Hind Maulana Mahmud'al-Hasan. The focus of their work was the establishment of independent schools. These schools were unique in several ways. For one, they combined religious and contemporary education. And they were completely independent of the British government and education system.

Bacha Khan became connected with Deoband through these independent madrasas. He established them along with a group of like-minded, nationalistic persons. Most of them, including the patron of the schools, Haji Turangzai, were *ulema*. The *ulema* who joined hands with Bacha Khan in setting up these schools were progressive-minded individuals. One general impression I have gained over the years is that the more thorough an Islamic scholar's education has been, the more he is open to contemporary sciences and contemporary education. The *ulema* who joined Bacha Khan in his promotion of independent schools were solid, well-qualified scholars. Other rank-and-file mullas bitterly opposed the schools.

Khan recalls a meeting he had in Mufti Abad, near Utmanzai. The people of Mufti Abad had asked for a school to be set up in their village. A meeting was held regarding the launching of a school. One mulla came to the meeting fully armed, with books in one hand and a gun in the other. He was known as Chitrali Mulla. In the middle of the meeting, he stood up and declared, 'I do not agree with this education that Abdul Ghaffar Khan has started. Nor is it proper education.' To illustrate his point, the mulla opened one of the books he had brought with him. 'Look at some of the things that are written in the textbooks. For example, "one dog barks [*Ek kutta bhonkta hai in Urdu*]."' Warming to his task and adjusting the rifle on his shoulder as he shuffled his books, Chitrali Mulla cited a sentence in another book. 'And look what is written here, "A big fig." What is that supposed to be? Is that supposed to be knowledge?'

Now Chitrali Mulla turned his attention to his gun. 'I have come here,' he announced, 'to settle the matter once and for all, either by the book or by the gun.' Bacha Khan answered him with his usual mixture of sarcasm, wit and logic. 'You know full well that I have nothing to do with guns, Mulla sahib. But if you go from here to

Utmanzai and talk to a cousin of mine, his name is Mohammad Khan, about guns, then you will come to your senses.' Mohammad Khan was a notorious gunslinger and sharpshooter from Utmanzai. Thinking of his redoubtable figure and looking at the mulla clasping books in one hand and a gun in the other, the gathered individuals could not resist a sneer at the mulla's expense. 'Look, Mulla sahib,' Bacha Khan reasoned with him, 'it is obligatory for every Muslim to acquire knowledge. You do not let children study in the schools set up by the British. So you should have made alternative arrangements for them to acquire knowledge. But you have not done so, nor do you allow us to do so. So what will be the fate of our people?'

Mullas cited Urdu and the English language as a reason for them opposing the independent schools, conveniently ignoring the huge dose of religious education that the schools imparted. The emphasis on religious education in these schools was largely on account of the fact that the majority of those responsible for establishing them were ulema. Bacha Khan was convinced that it was not the nature of the knowledge they were imparting that mullas were opposed to: it was knowledge itself. The mullas felt that if the Pashtoons became educated, they would not listen to their mullas. 'Their business would be left stone-cold dead,' was Bacha Khan's way of putting it. Seeing that opposition from mullas to the independent schools was entrenched, Bacha Khan and his friends approached Haji Sahib Turangzai to become patron of the madrasas. Haji Sahib Turangzai was someone the mullas could not challenge. He was the pre-eminent religious leader of the day amongst the Pashtoons. But as it turned out it was not the mullas or the British who proved the undoing of the independent schools.

Ironically enough, it was the Deoband leadership itself, seemingly out of touch with the needs of the Pashtoons, who undermined this effort. Under the guidance of Shaykh'al-Hind, the focus of Bacha Khan and his associates' efforts switched from educational to insurgent activity. That insurgent activity, as it was to turn out, was to prove fatal for the madrasas that Bacha Khan and his friends had established. Prior to Shaykh'al-Hind seeking to form a grand alliance including the Ottoman Turks and the

Afghanistan government for the deliverance of India from British rule, the Deoband shaykh had been seeking to establish a base in the tribal territory. Shaykh'al-Hind had an idea about the tribal territory that it was independent of the British, and from there it would be relatively easy to conduct jihad. In fact, Shaykh'al-Hind's ideas were even more grandiose. As mentioned elsewhere, he had an extraordinary vision of the Turks and the Germans attacking British India through Afghanistan and the tribal areas. 'You go to the tribal territory, find a suitable place as a base for jihad, then Maulana Ubaidullah Sindhi will come to check the place out,' Shaykh'al-Hind had told Bacha Khan on one of the latter's trips to Deoband.

It was not an easy matter for Bacha Khan to scour the tribal territories for a suitable base. He was also faced with divided loyalties. He was twenty-five now and a married man with children, but, as is normal in a Pashtoon household, he could not contravene his mother's wishes. He knew that she would never allow him to embark on such an expedition to the tribal areas. But he could not go against his shaykh's wishes either. So he told his mother a white lie, that he was going to Ajmer Sharif to visit the grave of Moeen'ud-Din Chishti. Meanwhile, he set out for Malakand and then Dir. During the course of his reconnaissance mission Bacha Khan had to traverse huge distances by foot. People from the Pashtoon plains, like Bacha Khan, find it notoriously difficult to trek in the mountains and Bacha Khan was no exception. His heavy build only made mountain walking even more difficult. The first place he wanted to check out was Chamarkand, in Upper Dir. It had already been established as a jihadi centre by Najmuddin Akhundzada, the famous mulla of Hadda, near Jalalabad in Afghanistan. Fearing the influence of this uncompromising and plain-speaking saintly figure, the king of Afghanistan at the time, Amir Abdul Rahman, had temporarily expelled the Hadda Mulla from Afghanistan, upon which he had taken up residence in Chamarkand, close to the Afghanistan border. Due to its jihadi heritage, this would have been an easy place to sell to Shaykh'al-Hind. But Bacha Khan was not satisfied with Chamarkand as a centre.

The place itself seemed idyllic. Chamarkand was a small plateau on top of a mountain, 'a spring of fresh water, hot in summer, but cold in winter, a tall poplar tree was growing next to the spring. Next to it was the Hadda Mulla Sahib's mosque and next to that a communal kitchen (*langar-khana*) a few vacant rooms alongside it.' On the other side was a little homestead, surrounded by fruit trees, a flower bed and a little field. A *murid* of the Hadda Mulla lived there. He told Bacha Khan about the days of the great saint, how people had flocked there from all over the Pashtoon parts. The place had tradition. It was also remote, and it seemed, protected. I must say, if it had been me looking for a secluded place to establish a centre, I would have settled on Chamarkand. But Bacha Khan felt otherwise. He thought that Chamarkand was too small to accommodate the centre that Shaykh'al-Hind had in mind. Instead, Bacha Khan settled on the Mamound territory of Bajaur as a suitable place for Shaykh'al-Hind's base. The agreement was that Bacha Khan would find a base, then wait for Maulana Sindhi to come to check the place out. Bacha Khan whiled away the time waiting for Makhfi sahib and Maulana Sindhi by going on retreat in a mosque in Mamound territory.

Pashtoons like to attribute all sorts of extraordinary miracles to their saintly figures. When Bacha Khan went on retreat, local people took to thinking of him also as a saintly figure. They came to him, asking him to offer prayers, write amulets and cast spells on their behalf. One woman came to him and told him about her son. 'He is three years old,' she said, 'but I am unable to wean him off my breast.' 'I'll tell you what to do,' Bacha said to her. 'Get some red chilli paste and rub it on your nipple. Inshallah, your child will give up breast milk.' The next day, she came back very happy. She gave a big jar of honey to Bacha Khan and thanked him profusely. 'Allah accepted your prayer,' she told Bacha Khan. 'Now my son does not come anywhere near my breast. Even if I offer my breast to him, he is not interested.' Pashtoons tend to be very quick to attribute a supernatural cause to something, when in fact it is a simple matter of cause and effect. 'How could the boy have accepted his mother's breast? Red chilli paste had been applied to it!' Bacha Khan recalled with a chuckle.

Bacha Khan waited and waited, but there was no sign of Maulana Sindhi. Eventually, he returned to Utmanzai. In fact, Shaykh'al-Hind's plans had changed. He had despatched Maulana Sindhi to Kabul instead. There, Maulana Sindhi spent eight years, waiting for deliverance from the Turks and the Germans, who by this time had been defeated in the First World War, the Ottoman Empire and Caliphate in tatters. Though Bacha Khan does not admit it, the whole episode must have been disillusioning for him. It made him realize that if he was to achieve tangible improvements in the life of his people, he would have to act independently of Shaykh'al-Hind, and Deoband. He became more committed to a peaceful approach. Bacha Khan now distanced himself from Deoband, and became more and more close to Congress.

The distance between himself and the ulema only increased with the downfall of Amir Amanullah in Afghanistan in 1929. Bacha Khan put the blame for Amanullah's downfall squarely on the shoulders of the Mullas. In the late eighties, I used to regularly visit Bacha Khan's eldest son, the poet Ghani Khan in his family home in Mohammad Naray, near Utmanzai. Ghani Khan himself epitomized the estrangement of his father from the world of religious scholars. 'To start off with, my father put me in madrasa,' he told me. 'His thinking was that if his son was a religious scholar, he would be an unstoppable political force. Then, when the mullas unseated Amanullah Khan, he immediately took me out of madrasa, saying that he would never let his son study with the mullas again.'

The other name that has been accorded to Bacha Khan—the Frontier Gandhi—goes down well in India, where the Mahatma is almost universally revered. There, the name constitutes the highest praise. It is an acknowledgement of the fact that Bacha Khan was as committed to a peaceful approach as Gandhi was. Amongst his own Pashtoon people, it is not such a popular name, used in fact by those who wish to revile Bacha Khan, and make out that he sold out to Hindus. In Pakistan, where just about everyone is a Muslim, people tend to see things in such black and white terms. Those who wish to malign Bacha Khan have pounced on this name, making out that he was somehow estranged from Islam. Nothing could be further from the truth. There were various reasons for the distance that developed between him and the Pashtoon religious establishment, but these did not mean that he was in any way estranged from Islam. There were a number of Islamic scholars in India—Maulana Abul Kalam Azad is one outstanding example—who were close to Mahatma Gandhi and to Congress. Far from frowning on them for this, other Muslims saw it as a feather in their cap. The Frontier Gandhi title became a problem for Bacha Khan, in Pakistan, only after the Partition of India. This perception only served to widen the gulf between the Pashtoon nationalist, progressive wing—epitomized by Bacha Khan—on the one hand, the religious establishment on the other. It is a separation that continues to this day. It is because of this separation that the Pashtoons are tearing themselves apart.

XVI

FROM FLOWER-POWER TO *DAWAH*-POWER

If you turn away, He will bring another nation in your place. Then they will not be like you.

(*Muhammad* 47:38)

It is something of an anomaly that Islam, despite its broad appeal, has yet to produce a figurehead who can really promote the religion in the West. Most notably, Hinduism has been able to bridge the gap between its own culture and Western culture. Look at Swami Vivekananda (1863–1902). In his short life, ever since he descended on the World Parliament of Religions in Chicago in 1893 and stunned those in attendance with the words: 'Sisters and brothers of America!' he held magnetic appeal for Westerners. One of the first to flock to his banner was a New York socialite by the name of Josephine Macleod (1858–1949). She was one of those who accompanied the Swami on his first-ever trip to Almora, in the Kumaon hills in north India, in 1898. She was not the only Westerner to accompany the Swami on that trip. Margaret Noble—better known as Sister Nivedita—was another.

It was then that Swami Vivekananda meditated at the Kasar Devi shrine, on the ridge above the town. That was the spark that turned Kasar Devi into a magnet for Europeans, right up to the present day. Richard Alpert, Allen Ginsberg, Timothy Leary, Ernst Hoffmann, Hermann Hesse: the list goes on. Which luminary of the Western counter-culture has not been to Almora? Richard Alpert and Ernst Hoffmann are better known locally by their Hindu and Buddhist names, Ramdass and Lama Govinda respectively. Perhaps the most famous of all the Westerners to flock to Almora over the last century was Sanyata Baba. His name is inscribed on the Kasar Devi shrine. There is a memorial to him nearby. It is almost forgotten that his real name was Alfred Sorensen. He started off as a Danish horticulturalist. But the magnet of Kasar Devi is down to one man: Swami Vivekananda. Without him, there would be no modern myth of Kasar Devi. Everything he touched turned to gold. It was Sister Nivedita (1869–1911) to whom the Swami looked to become a standard-bearer for Indian women. Like the Swami himself, Sister Nivedita died relatively young. Even before her death, she became somewhat disaffected with the Ramakrishna Order due to her involvement in Indian nationalistic politics. After her death, Josephine Macleod—until her dying day unflinchingly loyal to Swami Vivekanand and his Ramakrishna Order—singled out one Beatrice Cooke (1889–1966) as the right person to continue the work for the upliftment of Indian women that Sister Nivedita had started before she became distracted by nationalist politics. Beatrice had come to the Ramakrishna Order as the young mother of two children and the wife of a senior official in the Indian Railways. She was not happy with the role of a memsahib. She gravitated towards the Belur Math, the headquarters of the Ramakrishna Order.

Josephine Macleod had it in mind that Beatrice Cooke would start the Women's Movement at a place called Shyamlatal, not far from Mayawati, where there was already an ashram of the Ramakrishna Order. Mrs Cooke meanwhile had set up her own ashram in Roorkee. There, her commitment to the Vivekananda cause was beginning to waver. Like Sister Nivedita before her, she was becoming involved in nationalist politics. The crisis came in the mid-1930s. The civil disobedience protests had reached a peak at this time. There were ruthless reprisals against the protesters. Beatrice Cooke felt duty-bound to leave her ashram in Roorkee and help those wounded in the protests. The Ramakrishna Order gave Beatrice a stark choice: desist from involvement in the civil disobedience movement or leave the ashram. Beatrice felt shunned by the order. She left her ashram. In Roorkee, there was a sister religious institution, a madrasa of the Deoband school by the name of Madrasa Rahmania. Beatrice was in touch with that madrasa and knew one of its teachers, a Pashtoon by the name of Uzair Gul. Not only was Uzair an exceptionally handsome man: 'you could just look at him,' according to one contemporary, he was also from the Shaykh'al-Hind wing of the Deobandi school of thought. In other words, he and his Deobandi associates had no problem with involvement in nationalistic politics. Uzair Gul had a particularly long track record of active involvement in Indian nationalism.

Beatrice Cooke married Uzair Gul and embraced Islam at the hand of her new husband. This news was a shock for her old friend Josephine Macleod. When Beatrice wrote to her, telling her of her remarriage, Josephine replied: 'So your husband is going with you on your vacation to save your reputation. Good. Reputation is important. But character is more important.' Whatever resentment Josephine Macleod may have felt towards her old friend, it did not stop her from visiting Beatrice Cooke later in that year, 1938.[1]

In 1945, Uzair Gul returned with Beatrice to his native village of Sakhakot in the Swat foothills. She died in 1966. Maybe due to the restrictions on women having a public role in Pashtoon life, she hardly ventured from her home, only occasionally visiting Sardar Abdul Rashid in Peshawar. It was he who introduced me, posthumously of course, to Mother, as she became known amongst the Pashtoon Kakakhel clan to which her husband belonged. Beatrice Cooke was a mother figure to me also in the eighties when I lived a hermit's life in Swat, seeking to remove myself as far as possible from the prominent obsession with the Afghan jihad and

[1] Pravrajika Prabuddhaprana, *Tantine: the life of Josephine Macleod*, Calcutta: Sri Saradha Math, 2008.

rediscover the eclectic, unconventional hippie road that had led me to Islam. I had a picture of Mother in my room in Madyan. She was quite the prototype hippie, with beads round her neck, a good-looking, beaming lady, seemingly content with the life of a mulla's wife. As Sardar Abdul Rashid said to me, 'She never complained'.

I never really was one of the Madyan crowd. If I had been, I would probably have felt greater affinity to another progenitor of Islam in Europe, Shah Shahidullah Faridi (1915–1978). Shah Shahidullah may not be a household name in his native Britain, but he went one better. He became a well-known shaykh in his adopted land of Pakistan. Born John Gilbert Lennard in London, he and his elder brother were inspired by the great Sufi classical work, the *Kashf'al-Mahjub* of Al- Hujwiri, to travel to India in search of spiritual enlightenment. Both of them accepted Islam (took *shahada*), with the younger brother becoming Shahidullah and the elder, Farooq Ahmad. This search led to Shahidullah being initiated into the Chishti Sufi order by Sayed Mohammad Zauqi Shah, from Hyderabad in South India.

Sayed Mohammad Zauqi Shah took time before he accepted Shahidullah into the Sufi order. He was made to earn the trust of his shaykh before he was accepted as a disciple. He showed his sincerity and patience. Later on, his deep-rooted holiness and sincerity in the divine path was to reap two benefits: besides being accepted as the trusted disciple and successor of Sayed Mohammad Zauqi Shah, he also married the shaykh's daughter. The trust shown in him by his shaykh also rubbed off on his disciples. It is a long haul and a difficult task for a European convert to Islam to earn the trust and respect of born Muslims. It is probably something that I have not managed, despite living for fifty years now amongst the Pashtoons. Perhaps this came easier to Shahidullah, who had done the hard part by earning the trust of his shaykh. Almost all his tutelage and later on his ministry as an active shaykh were conducted in Urdu.

Early in the 1980s, a group of English Muslims took up residence in Pakpattan. Their leader was my lifelong friend Abdul Samad. One of Abdul Samad's entourage in Pakpattan was a German Muslim by the name of Haroon. He was a disciple of Shahidullah. After

Shahidullah's death, Haroon took up the mantle of being shaykh of the Chishti order. However, it was not Haroon but Abdul Samad who was earmarked by his own shaykh, Abd'al-Qadir As-Sufi, to be the successor of the Shah Shahidullah mantle. In the early eighties, Abdul Samad was asked by the shaykh to go to Pakpattan in Punjab and establish a centre there for British Muslims. It had been in Pakpattan that Baba Farid had established his branch of the Chishti order in the twelfth century. Haroon later took over the house where Abdul Samad set up his khanqah in Pakpattan. So the house continued to be a centre of devotions and remembrance of Allah (*dhikr*) of the Baba Farid/Sayed Mohammad Zauqi Shah/ Shah Shahidullah branch of the Chishti order.

If there is one person who has the charisma, the pulling power, the freewheeling spirit, the talent and the imagination to become a centre of attraction for Westerners seeking to learn about Islam, it is Abdul Samad[2]. Indeed, for a while, in the late seventies and early eighties, he was known as Shaykh Zamzami and had a good number of followers. At that time, he was based in Norwich, England, with a group of European Sufis who still inhabit the area around the Ihsan Mosque in Chapelfield in the centre of the city. One person who visited him at that time was a young Timothy Winter, later to become an English shaykh—Shaykh Murad—in his own right. He noted how Abdul Samad was a calm, serene, in Timothy Winter's words 'Central Asian type of presence' in the Norwich community.

I have never seen him like that, since Abdul Samad has always been a friend: one of the lads, rather than one to put on a pedestal. Indeed, I think that is the reason why he—rather than Haroon—did not step into the Shaykh's shoes in Pakpattan. As Abdul Samad himself said to me, he had no interest in the Shaykh thing. It was thrust on him. Abdul Samad had been one of the class of Madyan Muslims of 1970. Our paths crossed again when I returned from Deoband and Delhi to the 'native country'—to the Frontier. Except, for the time being, I had no village of my own to go to. I was staying with old friends in Bara when one day, there was an

[2] Abdul Samad passed away after these lines were written, in June 2020.

unexpected visitor at Abdul Hakim's (the son of my teacher Khan Afzal) shop in Bara. It was Abdul Samad. Abdul Samad's life had been in parallel to my own ever since Habib told me in Kalam in 1970 about him and Rebecca—later to become Fatima—accepting Islam in Madyan in 1970.

Rebecca had been in the caves of Matala the previous winter. Some of the caves were quite posh. But none of them were posh enough for Rebecca. She preferred to stay in a rented house in the village of Matala on the other side of the beach from the caves. The fact that she did not commune too much with the hippy crowd gave her a kind of mystique. But like other travellers who had spent the winter in Matala, she moved on to the next stage of the hippie trail—in her case Madyan. When I heard from Habib that Rebecca was living with an English person named David in Madyan, I would ask Habib about them regularly.

Rebecca had turned up her nose at a cave in Matala, preferring conventional rented accommodation. Now David had brought her down to earth, so much so that she had no compunctions about living in a barn in Chal. Chal lies about five miles up the Bishigram tributary, which flows into the Swat river at Chal. It was in Chal that they both accepted Islam. David had been given an English translation of the Holy Quran—the Glorious Qur'an by Mohammad Marmaduke Pickthall. It was the same translation that I read when I was in the process of coming to Islam. Both he and Rebecca read it. In fact, from the very first day when he was given this translation David did not put it down until he had finished it. Of course, lots of children visited their barn from the local village of Chal. 'What is this you are reading?' they were naturally inquisitive. David told them he was reading the Qur'an in English. That encouraged the children. One boy taught David how to recite *Al-Fatihah*—the opening chapter of the Qur'an—and *Ayat'al-Kursi*—the famous verse of the Qur'an that describes the throne of Allah 'encompassing the heavens and the earth'. Stories filtered back to Chal about how this European couple was close to accepting Islam. In fact, David was English and Rebecca American Jewish. Maybe a gentle push would be helpful? So a guy from Chal called Abdul Aziz with a red, hennaed beard came and told them to become Muslims. They uttered the kalima and the locals were very happy. The local mulla in Chal said they should be married so the couple had a nikah.

The fact of the matter was that in that summer of 1970, the people of Swat had a surge of *dawah* spirit, *dawah* being the process of attracting and calling people to Islam. They added their own dose of *dawah* power to the flower power that had arrived on their doorstep. This is what happens when Muslims feel they have something to give to mankind. Swatis were full of confidence in themselves, their way of life, their religion. The hippie influx was a God-given gift to them, an opportunity to enrich others with the wealth that they felt had been bestowed on them: the wealth of Islam. It had been just one year since the princely state of Swat had been absorbed into Pakistan. You would be hard-pressed to find another enlightened welfare state in the Muslim world—indeed anywhere in the world—the like of that forged by Badshah Sahib and his son Wali Sahib, the ruling dynasty of Swat.

Nothing much had changed since the absorption of Swat into Pakistan, not yet at any rate. When one crossed the border of the Swat state at Landakay, one still felt like one was entering another country. The Swat militia that manned the checkpoint was always cheerful and welcoming. There was a formality of showing one's passport and writing one's name in a book. Poplar trees lined avenues leading up the valley—tunnels of love marked with cheerfulness and healthy spirit. Though not everyone embraced the spirit, those who embraced it did so as if by accident, like a philosopher or scientist who has a eureka moment. They had to be ready to embrace that moment. When David and Rebecca became Muslim, it seemed to be by accident, but everything had been leading up to that accident—that twist of fate.

Whenever a foreigner accepted Islam, as David and Rebecca had done, there was a celebration in the town. It might not have been everyone's cup of tea—it certainly would not have been mine and fortunately I was spared any such show—but often the person who had become Muslim would be paraded through the bazaar and given money by all and sundry. The money was an outward symbol of the inner wealth the person had inherited in accepting

Islam. When David became Muslim, they took him to Madyan bazaar, carting him all around the bazaar, which was a long road of shops about three hundred yards long. Besides money, shopkeepers gave him tea, sugar and foodstuffs. Along with inviting him to Islam, Abdul Aziz had also given David a piece of paper on which his Muslim name—Abdul Samad—was written. Although he had no idea what being a Muslim entailed, he was very impressed with the locals as they were so poor and lived such difficult lives, yet they were very generous, unlike so many people he had seen and met on his travels. The same day, they left him in the bazaar in a teashop. There, he was approached by a guy wearing a long black shirt with a lot of beads around his neck and a begging bowl made of wood. The man stood out with his long hair and a beard. He gave Abdul Samad ten rupees, a good amount of money in those days. He said it was from the Kaana pir sahib who lived in another valley. The pir sahib was this man's spiritual guide. He said the pir sahib had heard about Abdul Samad's Islam and was pleased. That was why he had sent the ten rupees.

Pashtoons tend to be insistent that those who accept Islam in their midst should get themselves circumcised. Though the real word for circumcision is *khatna*, it is known amongst Pashtoons as *sunnat*. It is as if circumcision encompasses all the *sunnah*—the path of the Holy Prophet—in their eyes. Being circumcised is seen as key to a person's identity as a Muslim man. We have already seen, in the course of my own acceptance of Islam, how Mir Ahmad demanded visual proof of the fact that I was circumcised. While Abdul Samad was staying in Shagram, he became friends with a Yugoslavian by the name of Abdul Rahman. He also had become Muslim. A friend of theirs in Shagram—Mir Noor Hakim—was not far short of Mir Ahmad. That was one of the first things he asked Abdul Samad: have you been circumcised? Abdul Samad had to admit he had not been through the rigmarole of having the skin of his dick truncated. 'Well, I think you should,' Mir Noor Hakim advised him with a smile. 'I mean, if you go on pilgrimage to Mecca and someone sees your uncircumcised dick then they won't believe you're a Muslim. They will think you must be some Western spy trying to gain access to the holy places.'

So off the two went to Mingora. Two men in their early twenties going to be circumcised courtesy of the Wali Sahib's national health system in Saidu Hospital. The operation went well. The next day, they both managed to hobble to the hash shop in Mingora. They thought that getting high would relieve the pain. Certainly, it helped. Abdul Samad recovered fairly quickly but Abdul Rahman's wound developed an infection and he acquired a big boil on his backside. Back in the village everyone would tell him, 'Congratulations Abdul Rahman, why not take a seat!' knowing that the poor guy could not even sit down due to the boil on his bottom! When Abdul Rahman left Shagram, he became a malang and went to live in Pir Baba. He had a *pir sahib* from Peshawar—one Pir Durrani—who had a house near the grave of Pir Baba's wife Pir Abai. Abdul Rahman lived there for a number of years.

Later on, Abdul Samad returned to England and joined a group of Sufis who had made a community under Shaykh Abd'al-Qadir As-Sufi in Norwich. Abdul Samad had not had any formal Islamic education, he had not studied in a madrasa, but he had spent extended periods in the Tablighi Jamaat and had picked up considerable knowledge along the way, enough to be invited to be imam in the Ihsan Mosque, formerly a Congregationalist chapel from which Chapelfield acquired its name. Abdul Samad's likeable personality, perennial cheerfulness, good humour and affinity with Sufism soon propelled him to number two in the hierarchy of Shaykh Abd'al-Qadir as-Sufi's Muslim community in Norwich. Abdul Samad has a refreshing and unfailing capacity to see good in people. I visited Norwich in 1979 while I was in England to apply from the Indian High Commission for a scholarship to continue my studies in Deoband. It was amazing to think that I had never met Abdul Samad until then. I had followed his progress so keenly from afar that I felt as if I knew him. There were a number of Sufi-looking Europeans knocking around the Chapelfield area. 'Can you tell me where Abdul Samad hangs out?' I asked one of them, an American. 'He is Shaykh Zamzami now,' the American Sufi replied somewhat snootily, as if I had no business calling him Abdul Samad!

In any case, he showed me Abdul Samad's house. There was always a group of Sufis hanging around with him. They were seated on the carpeted floor, him on a mattress. His back was facing a bay window. The summer light shone in generously. It was every bit the Moroccan *minza*, the Pashtoon *hujrah*, the *pir sahib's* seat (*gaddi*). I saw Rebecca—now Fatima—once in Abdul Samad's house in Norwich. Some repairs were going on. Fatima was directing operations in an authoritative and good-humoured manner. From the dainty hippie girl of Matala she had filled out, having mothered three children, and had grown in confidence also, being the wife of the shaykh. She was also extremely personable, unlike the impression she had given in Matala. Still, I was shy and did not introduce myself to her. Partly, there was the residual mystique from the Matala era. Then there was the fact that she was the wife of Shaykh Zamzami, so the factor of not being too forward with Muslim women also came into play, I guess. So I never did meet Fatima, at least not to talk to. She remained this fleeting, ethereal presence, in Matala, in Madyan and in Norwich.

Later, I got to know Abdul Samad's third wife, the charming, pious, beautiful, wise, good-natured Sakina from Morocco, very well. She has always been a supportive rock in my life, someone I can talk to and who understands. 'I am so lucky to be married to Sakina,' Abdul Samad once told me. But why did he leave Fatima? I think he was unable to hit it off with her posh east coast, Jewish American family. 'They made me feel like I was this small,' he once said, gesturing towards the ground. For my part, I was a strong advocate—for the time being at least—of monogamy and sticking to one partner, through thick and thin. My Catholic upbringing may have contributed to this outlook. Marriage is a difficult area for hippies who become Muslim.

As a Muslim, one is not allowed to sleep around. At the same time, hippies who become Muslim find it difficult to stick to one partner. This clash of priorities often leads to a quick turnaround of marriage partners amongst European Muslims. They have wives like hippies have girlfriends. Maybe now converts to Islam have settled down, stopped having fantasies about two or three wives and stuck to one partner. Abdul Samad mirrors this transformation, from marrying several times to settling down and sticking to a partner. For a while, after his separation from Fatima, he was married to Rahma. A couple of years later, he married Sakina, mother of six of his children. As for me, I jumped on the bandwagon late, both as far as marriage and remarriage were concerned. I was not married until well into my forties. When I remarried, Abdul Samad joked, 'What a good idea!' His wife Sakina was present. 'You,' she laughingly addressed her husband. 'You have had your turn!'

XVII
JOURNALISM NURSERY

Ya watan ya kafan—Our country or a shroud

(Slogan of Dr Najib at the time of the battle for Jalalabad)

I had been a recluse in Madyan for the better part of four years when, in 1988, some lads came to the top of the cliff above Qamar Landi. They called me up, perhaps not wishing to negotiate our dogs. 'Rahmat Shah asked you to come to Peshawar to join his newspaper.' That is all I remember them saying. Then they left. I was ready for a new chapter in my life. The time was right for me to come out of my hermitage and to assume a more public role.

The newspaper in question was the *Frontier Post*. I had never known Rahmat Shah personally, but I had known his father, Ghalji Haji Sahib, and cousins from my time in Bara, and he had of course known of me. Rahmat Shah Afridi and a Shinwari associate of his, Mumin Khan, had set up the *Frontier Post* a few years earlier. Mumin Khan kept a low profile. His role in the setting up of the paper was always a secret, either unintentionally or because Mumin Khan wanted it that way. The *Frontier Post* is known as Rahmat Shah's baby. Mumin Khan is more famous for the mosque that bears his name in the village of Pawaka, bordering Peshawar.

Much of Pawaka has now been taken over by the posh neighbourhood of University Town. Old school Peshawarites know the area around Mumin Khan's mosque as Pawaka. Those who arrived more recently on the block call it University Town. Mumin Khan is old school. He still lives in Pawaka.

Until now, despite my long years of residence in the Frontier and my work in the *Frontier Post*, I have never met Mumin Khan, though I have a picture in my mind of a person not particularly distinguishable from a normal Pashtoon, moustachioed—by now he must be a greybeard—not of a very hefty build and donning a Chitrali *pakol* (woollen cap). I have no idea: did I catch a glimpse of Mumin Khan somewhere or is this the picture that has developed in my imagination of this semi-mythical, ethereal figure. Still, I will stick to my description since that is the type of person Mumin Khan is: difficult to pin down.

Mumin Khan hails from the Shinwari tribe, Rahmat Shah from the Afridis. The Afridis and Shinwaris are natural trading partners. Both tribes dominate the mighty Khyber Pass linking Peshawar with Afghanistan. Rahmat Shah Afridi was completely different from Mumin Khan. Young, dashing, handsome, outgoing, with more than a streak of rashness—he was everything that Mumin Khan was not. He was too upwardly mobile for his own good. In the middle of the 1980s, at the height of military rule and martial law in Pakistan, Rahmat Shah established a left wing—one might say revolutionary— newspaper: a national daily from Peshawar. I was not to know this at the time, but there had been something of a purge at the *Frontier Post* before I joined the newspaper. The editor, Aziz Siddiqui, and the managing editor Farhatullah, Babar, had been ousted. A far less competent team, Rahmat Shah's younger brother, Muzaffar Shah, and a fulsome Kashmiri by the name of Qaiser Butt, had replaced them. I guess the loss of personnel was one reason for Rahmat Shah calling for me. Be that as it may, I jumped at the opportunity.

When I arrived in Peshawar from Madyan, I went to see Rahmat Shah. It was evening. He was reading a newspaper in the editor's office. The impression was that he was skimming through the newspaper, perhaps pretending to take in more than what he was actually able to fathom. He immediately gave me a room in the grounds of the *Frontier Post* office, which he had reserved for himself but did not use. Rahmat Shah was not highly educated, but he had a love of learning. He was a patron of the arts and literature, if not artistic or literary himself. He had gathered together at the paper some of the great literary and journalistic figures of the Frontier, and some from Punjab also. The *Frontier Post* was everything it should not have been in the ultra-conservative, mulla-oriented and jihad-supporting regime of General Zia-ul-Haq. It was irreverent, secular, left-wing and Pashtoon nationalist. It stood for peace and warned of the dire consequences of what it called the Kalashnikov and heroin culture that had been introduced to the Frontier with the Afghan jihad. Looking back, all the predictions that the *Frontier Post* made seem to have been borne out. It had been wishful thinking to entertain notions of Peshawar remaining immune from the fighting in Afghanistan when for so long it had been a base for all the factions caught up in that conflict.

When I arrived at the *Frontier Post*, two changes had taken place on the bigger scene. For one, the martial law of General Zia-ul-Haq had ended abruptly when the plane in which he was travelling crashed near Bahawalpur. From nowhere, Benazir Bhutto was propelled to power. Benazir and her father had dominated the Pakistan political scene ever since I arrived in the country in 1970. I have no idea what Zulfikar Ali Bhutto was like as a politician. I do know that the Madyan crowd were happy while he was prime minister. Once he came to Madyan as prime minister. He heard about one English woman. Khayrunnisa, who was staying in Madyan and had married locally. He asked her to come and see him. When she came, he asked her if there was anything he could do for her. I would like a Pakistan passport, she told him. He told her it would be done, and was as good as his word. She still visits Madyan periodically, with what she calls 'Bhutto's passport'.

Z.A. Bhutto was executed early on in Zia's presidency. His daughter Benazir had mostly been under house arrest over the last ten years. Her ascent to power in 1988 was a time of immense excitement in Pakistan. I came down from Madyan to see her inauguration on TV at a friend's house in Peshawar. It is no exaggeration or embarrassment for me to say, as a Swat hippie-hermit at the time, that when I heard President Ghulam Ishaq Khan announce on the radio that Benazir would be the prime minster, I came out of my Swat cottage late at night and danced to the moonlight in my garden. It was amazing to see this young, beautiful, confident lady being feted by the very generals who until then had been persecuting her. Everyone seemed to be welcoming the coming to power of Benazir Bhutto. The election that brought her to power had not handed an overall majority to any party. Benazir's Pakistan People's Party was the largest party. No one made a move to cobble an alliance against her. Even Wali Khan, the son of Bacha Khan and an age-old foe of the Bhutto family, could be seen beaming when he announced that Benazir had the right to form a government. The truth was that Benazir came to power on a wave of goodwill. No one could stand against her. To me, it seemed like a bloodless revolution, organized from on high.

At the same time, another bloodless coup had taken place inside the *Frontier Post*. Journalists willing to tow the authorities' line had replaced journalists of integrity. Key here was Qaiser Butt. He came in as chief reporter, but, in effect, you could say he was managing editor. He ran the *Frontier Post*. He was known in the newspaper as a functionary of the powerful military intelligence unit, the Inter-Services Intelligence or ISI, but I was never able to confirm this. One day, some reporters accosted him. Maybe they had had a drink or two. Journalism and boozing—as I was to discover—go together in Pakistan. Anyway, the reporters said to Qaiser Butt, 'Hey, Qaiser Butt, people say you work for the ISI. Tell us, would you, what is your rank? Are you a general, a colonel, a major or what?' It was all good-natured fun and they had a good laugh over it. ISI influence is indeed rife in Pakistani journalism, but it does not work exactly like the irreverent reporters had suggested in jest to Qaiser Butt. A journalist who works for the ISI will not normally be a member of that organization, still less an army officer of rank. One journalist at the *Frontier Post*, Ikram-Ullah from Mardan, told me that most journalists in Pakistan worked part-time for the ISI. The way it worked was that sometimes the ISI would bring pressure to bear on this or that journalist to publish certain news or write a certain column. Other items would be written with integrity, in the process bolstering the writer's reputation and acting as a front for the more pernicious news that would be inserted here and there. 'Everyone does that,' Ikram-Ullah Hoti asserted, perhaps exaggerating somewhat. Christina Lamb was at this time working as Pakistan correspondent for the *Financial Times*.[1] She was more charitable and estimated that half of Pakistani journalists were at least to a certain degree tools of the ISI.

Alongside Qaiser Butt, Rahmat Shah's younger brother Muzaffar Shah was installed as the editor of the *Frontier Post*. Not having one iota of experience in journalism, this was a ridiculous move on the part of the newspaper. It was definitely done under pressure. Generally, the way the government brings pressure to bear on newspapers is by denying them government advertisements. Though newspapers may earn some revenue from advertisements from private companies, the bulk of revenue accrues from government advertisements—tender notices and suchlike. The *Frontier Post* cost a huge amount of money to run. Even the combined wealth of Rahmat Shah and Mumin Khan could not keep the paper going forever, nor would that have been sustainable. There had to be some money coming in apart from the paltry sum accrued from selling newspapers. Without government advertisements, it would be difficult for even the *Frontier Post* to survive. The Muzaffar Shah-Qaiser Butt combination was brought in to bring government advertisements—denied due to the paper's recalcitrant and rebellious policy—back to the newspaper.

I spent my first few days at the *Frontier Post* on the news-desk, learning my trade as a journalist. Kamil Bangash was my great buddy. Kamil was good *Frontier Post* stock. He was the son of Afzal Bangash, who had founded the Mazdoor Kisan Party—literally the party of the labourers and farmers. As you might guess, the Mazdoor Kisan Party was on the left of the political spectrum compared to the mainstream Pashtoon nationalist party of Bacha Khan's son Wali Khan, the National Awami Party. Later on, the words Awami and National changed places when the party

[1] Christina Lamb, OBE was later to become foreign editor of the *Sunday Times*.

re-formed, having been banned during Z.A. Bhutto's premiership. Predictably, Afzal Bangash fell foul of Wali Khan when he started inciting the tenant farmers of Hashtnagar to take over the land of the land-owning Khans—amongst whom was Wali Khan himself. It is said that Wali Khan's nephew Faridoon Khan, the son of the poet Ghani Khan, openly supported Afzal Bangash and displayed the Mazdoor Kisan flag—bright red with a white star in the middle—in his *hujrah*. Such was the stock from which the *Frontier Post* drew its staff.

Kamil would have graced the newspaper as editor. Tall, charismatic, handsome, with a commanding and confident presence and with a perfect command of English, he was a real friend, someone you could depend upon. It made one feel good to be around him. He might have been the same age as me—I was in my late thirties by this time—or a bit younger. His hair had some strands of grey but his face was young. I became a family friend, not only visiting the house Kamil had inherited from his father on Kohat Road in Peshawar, but also becoming friendly with his brother-in-law, Dr Nawaz Bangash, and his wife, Kamil's sister Zoya, in Birmingham, England. It is so often the case in Pashtoon families that real Pashtoon values are enshrined in the womenfolk. This was the case with Zoya. When, a couple of years later, I accompanied a load of Pashtoons from England to some Pashto conference near Bonn in Germany, Zoya would be walking up and down the aisle of the bus for most of the journey, chatting with all the passengers, engaging them in lengthy conversation, enquiring after their welfare, catching up with them. It was as if she knew everyone, which she did, had not seen everyone in a very long time—that was also the case—and really wanted to be updated on everyone's news.

Kamil was the same when I came to the *Frontier Post*. He took me under his wing. Any fledgling journalist around whom he put his arm, as he did with me, would have thrived and grown in confidence. I did also. I spent just one week on the sub-editing desk. The Friday magazine did not have an editor. It was Thursday when I was told to prepare a magazine to go with the morning edition. I got going immediately, Kamil by my side. He took me through the whole rigmarole: choosing an article, picking pictures to go with it and then taking it to the computer section to have the article composed. I would generally bypass the proofreading section and take my copy straight to the computer section. There were three female computer operators, Bushra, Bilquees and Dur-e-Shahwar alongside a host of males. Being a native English speaker, they appreciated the chance to learn from me and improve their spelling. For my part, it was good to get the work done quickly, especially now that I was producing a whole weekend magazine in one night. It was also a pleasant change for me to have a tiny bit of innocuous female company after years living in Pashtoon segregated society, in madrasa and then as a reclusive hermit in Swat.

At the end of the night, so that I could see the fruits of our efforts, Kamil took me to the printing press at the rear end of the Frontier Post building. Almost immediately, the magazine we had produced could be seen in fresh print. You could smell the newsprint, glistening on the pages of the paper, which we leafed through before the bundles were piled into the backs of pickup trucks to be taken far and wide, throughout the Frontier and down into Punjab. It is an exciting and stimulating activity, newspaper journalism. There is a down-to-earth, desperado side to it, a feeling of living close to the edge, with deadlines always looming. Every day is a new day, with the tensions and angst of the previous day forgotten. Given the tense excitement of the journalist's life, emotions boil to the edge on almost a daily basis only to cool down the next day. There is a day-to-day cycle, as if the life of a newspaper journalist is one day at a time or in the case of the editor of a weekend magazine, one week at a time. At the age of forty, I had found my vocation in life. I took to the profession like a lamb takes to the lush pastures. Everything I learnt stuck, and quickly became second nature.

Due to the tense nature of a journalist's life, drinking usually becomes an important part of the lifestyle, not least in Pakistan. Some end up doing it in excess. Kamil was one of these excessive drinkers. Though blessed with a strong physique to go with his handsome features, I worry about what this drinking might have done to his health. I have not seen Kamil since the early nineties. These were the days of cheap Soviet imports to the Frontier. Everywhere on the streets of Peshawar you could find Soviet goods.

Even a wide variety of Soviet literature was available at news stalls. Amongst the Soviet imports was cheap vodka. It was to Russian vodka that Kamil had recourse when his favourite staple, Scotch, was not available. Pashtoon drinkers do not just have a bottle of Scotch on the shelf and enjoy a tipple or two in the evening, as my dad used to do. They devour a bottle of Scotch in one sitting; in the case of vodka, maybe two or three bottles. To my mind, it was this drinking habit that prevented Kamil from realizing his true worth and potential in both the political and journalistic fields.

I was given pretty free rein at the *Frontier Post*, particularly during my stewardship of the Friday magazine. I used my time there to glorify things Pashtoon. As often as not, I would write the cover story of the magazine. My standout piece was an article on Ghani Khan, the elder son of Bacha Khan and the pre-eminent contemporary poet of the Pashtoons. Ghani Khan had led an unconventional life, even for a staunch Pashtoon like himself. He lost his mother at an early age. It was the end of the First World War and an influenza epidemic[2] gripped large parts of north India, including the Frontier. In the Frontier, this epidemic was known as a *waba* (a plague). It was like that, since it was almost always fatal in those who fell victim to it. Ghani Khan caught the virus and was near death. In his autobiography, Bacha Khan tells how his wife circled the bed when Ghani lay stricken with fever. 'Oh my God,' she prayed to Allah. 'Take the sickness away from my boy and give it to me instead.' And that is what happened. Ghani recovered, but his mother died a youthful death.[3]

When Ghani was a young boy, Bacha Khan decided to put him in a madrasa. Looking back, Ghani thinks it was a political move on his father's part. 'He thought that if my elder son becomes a big mulla, then no one will be able to compete with me in the political arena.' To my mind, it was more than just a cynical political move on Bacha Khan's part. In the early part of his political career, his closest associates were for the most part ulema—religious scholars of the Deobandi school. It was natural that he would want his

---

[2] This was the Spanish Flu Pandemic.

[3] Khan Abdul Ghaffar Khan, Zama Jhwand au Jadd-o-Jahd

eldest son to become a religious scholar. Whatever the motives, everything changed in 1929 with the toppling of Amir Amanullah Khan in Afghanistan, largely at the behest of the ulema. 'My father immediately took me out of madrasa. I was left neither here nor there.' After this, Bacha Khan was to have no more truck with the mullas, being particularly offended by Afghan and Pashtoon ones, though he continued to be friendly with ulema from India. Neither did Ghani Khan harbour any lingering affection for the mullas, despite having nearly become one.

As he grew into a young man, Ghani Khan spent more and more time in India with his father. Bacha Khan's Khudai Khidmatgars were closely aligned to the Congress party and the Quit India movement. Along with Mahatma Gandhi, the Khan family became close to the Nehrus also. Ghani Khan recounted to me how there had even been rumours of some romance between himself and the young Indira Gandhi. Indira had herself dismissed the rumours, Ghani Khan told me: 'From the time that I first entered their home, she called me Ghanibhai—my brother Ghani. How could she be carrying on with someone whom she had called her brother?' In fact, Ghani was in love with another girl. She was from a Parsi family of Bombay. Her name was Roshan. The Parsis are Zoroastrians, remnants from pre-Muslim Iran who settled in India, mainly in Bombay. 'It took six years for her family to agree to us getting married.' When they did finally get married, Roshan moved with Ghani to his home village of Utmanzai, in the Hashtnagar countryside. It was a purely Pashtoon, rural setting, which could not have been further removed from the sophisticated Parsi environment of Bombay. Roshan settled there happily, never making heavy weather of the simple, spartan conditions.

While I was keen on promoting Frontier culture, the owner of the newspaper, Rahmat Shah Afridi, was inclining towards the Punjab nerve centre of Lahore. He was now spending most of his time in Lahore, where he had groomed a number of journalists. He brought them over to Peshawar now and then. On one occasion, an entire crew of young ladies came over. The idea was that I would run a Peshawar branch of the magazine section while Rahmat Shah handed over the running of the magazine section of the

Frontier Post to these young ladies, and indeed he did so. Amongst the ladies who would run the magazine from Lahore were Cassandra Balchin and Beena Sarwar, who became distinguished journalists later on. At this time, they were at the beginning of their careers.

Rather than running a magazine section from Peshawar, I took over editing the leader pages of the newspaper. It was a promotion from magazine editing. I moved to the former managing editor's office across the yard. I still had Rahmat Shah's room as my residence. I had some close friends at the *Frontier Post*, amongst them an illustrator on the magazine section by the name of Zuhoor. He was worried about the magazine moving to Lahore. What work would he have? You can be a cartoonist for the newspaper, I suggested. The transformation was seamless. Zuhoor went on to become one of the foremost cartoonists in the country, and still is. Another of my friends at the paper was Zahid, from Mardan. Later on, when I was running a BBC office in Peshawar, Zahid was shortlisted for a position with the BBC Pashto service in London and moved there. Some people thought, Zahid was an English-speaking journalist, not a specialist in Pashto. When he moved to London, it took him some time to become fluent in writing and broadcasting in Pashto, but he worked on it and with his lucid Mardan accent, became an accomplished Pashto broadcaster. It was the same with me. My Pashto was honed later, at the BBC. As leader-page editor of the *Frontier Post,* I pretty well had free rein to print what I liked and to nurture the columnists I took a fancy to. My best columnist was a young man from Peshawar city who wrote brilliantly and was sitting his civil service exams. He wrote a column about the Pakistan Army. 'It is such a powerful army,' he wrote with considerable wit and irony: 'it has conquered its own country four times!' He was referring to the army coups against elected governments that have been mounted in Pakistan. 'In Bismarck's Germany,' he wrote, 'the army was a State within a State. Pakistan is a State within an army.' That has become even truer nowadays, when the army no longer has to mount coups in order to keep the state to heel. They call the shots anyway. I have not checked the rule book, but in Pakistan there are two entities that you are not allowed to criticize: one is

Mohammad Ali Jinnah, the founder of the country; the other is the army. It is said—again I have not looked at the penal code to find out if this is true or not—that you can get eight years in jail for both offences. So no surprise then that some ISI guys turned up at the office to ask how the article found its way into the paper and who wrote it. Qaiser Butt told me about their visit. The sleuths got no further than his office, and I heard no more of it. I do hope the young gentleman did well in his civil service exams. He certainly had the brains.

But one does have to be careful about what goes in to print. Muzaffar Shah must have been nervous with me at the helm, hoping that I would not go too far. In the early days of the newspaper, one Mahir Ali was editor of the *Frontier Post* magazine section. He too is now a distinguished journalist in his own right. His father Mazhar Ali Khan ran a fantastic weekly Magazine called *Viewpoint* from Lahore. I was a subscriber. In my house in Swat I had a pile of *Viewpoints* alongside my pile of old Soviet *Sputniks*—the Soviet version of *Readers' Digest*. *Viewpoint* was the most purely socialist, revolutionary magazine I have ever read. Mazhar Ali Khan's wife Tahira Ali was also a lifelong struggler for human and women's rights. Besides Mahir, they had an elder son Tariq, well known in the UK as a revolutionary student leader in the late sixties and the author of many books, including *Street Fighting Years*, inspired by the similarly titled Rolling Stones' song. I mention Mahir Ali's background to show the calibre of personnel that Rahmat Shah had initially assembled at the *Frontier Post*.

One week, Mahir Ali printed a picture of Adam and Eve in the Friday magazine. Mullas and *talibs* in madrasas got wind of it. Adam is mentioned as a prophet in the Quran, and Sunni Muslims hold that one should never make an image of a prophet. The thinking behind this ruling, though it has scarcely been articulated, would seem to be that once one has made an image of a prophet, it would be a short step before they became objects of worship. So images of prophets are particularly discouraged. After Friday prayers the following week, *talibs* from madrasas and mosques from all over Peshawar descended on the *Frontier Post* offices. The word was that many of the attackers came from the nearby Imdad'al-Uloom madrasa, named after Haji Imdad-Ullah and purportedly following the Thanvi school of thought. Maulana Thanvi would certainly not have condoned such direct action. A reporter working at the *Frontier Post* at the time saw a truckload of bricks being delivered to the newspaper offices shortly before the attack. The attackers set fire to the printing press and smashed computers and fax machines.[4] The management called the police, but no one come to their rescue. This was the type of mob rule and direct action—circumventing the course of law—that was to become common in Pakistan.

One ISI officer who was a regular visitor to Qaiser Butt's office was Major Aamir. He was the son of Shaykh'al-Qur'an, my own teacher, the Panjpir maulana sahib. He seemed embarrassed for me to see him and never acknowledged my presence, though he knew I was his father's student. He became notorious later on for his alleged role in Operation Midnight Jackal—a plot against Benazir's government. The plot failed and Major Aamir was sent home without his uniform, though he denies this and says that he was not part of the operation and was cleared by the army.[5] There were persistent rumours over the next decade that he had a role in the Swat insurgency, when religious hardliners sought to take control of the Swat valley. This insurgency reared its head on two occasions, once in 1994 and then again—more menacingly and much more catastrophically—in 2008–09. The ringleaders of these insurgencies, Sufi Mohammad and, later, his son-in-law, Mulla Fazlullah, were certainly close to and had spent considerable time in the Panjpir madrasa. More about that in the final chapter of this book, on 'The Battleground of Education'.

The *Frontier Post* was leftist and Pashtoon nationalist. The staff at the paper had no sympathy with the Afghan jihad. The popularity of the newspaper lay in its anti-establishment, almost revolutionary nature. The Muzaffar Shah-Qaiser Butt combination wished to maintain that popularity and character while at the same

---

[4] Details of the attack came from Mohammad Zahid, a reporter at the *Frontier Post* at the time who was later to become a BBC journalist.

[5] *Dawn* profile of Major Aamir, 6 April 2014, http://www.dawn.com/news/1098065

time not alienating the establishment to too great an extent, in the process pulling in government advertising. It was a difficult tightrope to negotiate. Another of Qaiser Butt's visitors was a publicist on behalf of the Hezb-e-Islami of Gulbuddin Hekmatyar, one Nawab Saleem. I doubt if that was his real name since it is not a very Afghan name, but he is well-known by it so we will go with it. He used to bring not-very-well-written articles for printing. He would give them to Qaiser Butt, who would hand them to me. I suppose I should have printed them in order to keep a balance in the newspaper, but I could not bring myself to do so. To my mind, they were just not up to standard, either from a language point of view or with respect to the arguments that they contained. Nor did they fit in with the tenor of the paper.

But then, a lot of the letters to the editor that came to my desk were not well-written, but I would do considerable work on them, improving the language, polishing them and putting them to print. Like most broadsheets, the *Frontier Post* had two editorial pages. My ambition was to have one of those pages composed entirely of letters to the editor. On a few occasions, I did achieve this target—unprecedented for any broadsheet I know of anywhere in the world. The letters that were sent to us were just so interesting and painted such a multifaceted tapestry of Frontier life. The vast majority of the letters to the editor did not contain political views, comment or reaction: they just brought attention to problems being faced at the grass-roots by ordinary people in various far-flung corners of the province. Some of them focused on a matter of particular interest—an archaeological find, a person of unusual talent—in their area that would otherwise have missed the spotlight.

But no paper can remain exempt from politics, and the *Frontier Post* was of course deeply political. As I mentioned, the late eighties were a time of immense hope for myself and like-minded people amongst the Pashtoons. There was young leadership, not only Benazir in Pakistan, but Rajiv Gandhi in India. The two young premiers met early on in Benazir's premiership. In fact, the meeting happened around the time I joined the *Frontier Post*. I reflected the hope that surrounded this meeting in the Friday magazine with a picture of Rajiv and Benazir alongside a picture of their parents—Indira Gandhi and Z.A. Bhutto—meeting at Shimla in 1973. Muzaffar Shah mentioned to me that he liked that correlation. But for young Pashtoons at the *Frontier Post* it was not Benazir or Rajiv Gandhi who caught their imagination. It was the president of Afghanistan, Dr Najib, who embodied their aspirations. His imposing physique, his statesmanship, his natural leadership qualities, his strikingly handsome persona—everything marked him out as a leader of the Pashtoons, indeed as a national Afghan leader.

Dr Najib became president of Afghanistan in 1986 and had deep roots in the Frontier, which increased his appeal for Frontier Pashtoons. At the time Sardar Daud was president of Afghanistan, in the early 1970s, Najib's father Akhtar Mohammad Khan was posted to Peshawar as Afghan commercial attaché. He had an office in the Afghan Building in the Qissa Khwani Bazaar in the centre of Peshawar City, the very building from which, as hippie travellers, we used to take the Afghan Post bus from Peshawar to Kabul. His home was in Chinar Lane, in the posh university town suburb of Peshawar. As luck would have it, or maybe by design, this was the very lane where the daughter of Bacha Khan—Mehr Taj—resided along with her husband Yahya Jan and the rest of her family.

The female connection was important, since the main task of Akhtar Mohammad Khan was to strengthen contacts with prospective Pashtoonistan leaders—Pashtoon nationalists—in and around Peshawar. In this connection, the services of his young daughter Kokay were indispensable. Women are able to act with a lot more impunity than men in Pashtoon society. While Pakistani authorities would closely scrutinize the movements of Akhtar Mohammad Khan himself, his daughter Kokay could enter and leave the house on Chinar Lane without attracting much attention from the Special Branch officers parked outside their house. The contacts that Akhtar Mohammad forged with Pashtoon nationalist leaders in the Frontier at this time, with the help of Kokay, remained intact in coming decades. These ties ensured that Kokay's elder brother Najib, then a medical student at Kabul University, was bolstered by considerable good will from Pashtoon nationalist leaders in the Frontier as he pursued his upward political trajectory in Afghanistan, first to socialist revolution in 1978, then to leadership of the Afghan intelligence agency KHAD in the early eighties, and finally to the pinnacle of power in Afghanistan in 1986. No national leader in Afghanistan since King Zahir Shah was able to span the cleavages in Afghan society like Dr Najib. He was rural Pashtoon by descent, but an urban Kabuli by birth; a commoner, he married into royalty—his wife Fattanah was a descendant of Amir Amanullah Khan, king of Afghanistan between 1919 and 1929; and, crucially for his reputation, standing and broad-based appeal, Najib was an Afghan politician who, due to the efforts of his father and aided by his sister Kokay was able to reach across the Durand Line—the border between Afghanistan and Pakistan—to Pashtoonistan.[6]

By the time I was at the *Frontier Post*, the word Pashtoonistan had been dropped from the lexicon of both Afghan leaders and leaders of the Pashtoon nationalist movement in the Frontier and Balochistan, who had taken to using the less politically sensitive term 'Pakhtunkhwa'. Indeed, the word 'Pakhtunkhwa' was later to be adopted as part of the name of the Frontier province, which is now known as Khyber Pakhtunkhwa. However, in the 1970s, when Akhtar Mohammad Khan was based in Peshawar, at the time I was in jail in Kabul, Pashtoonistan was the buzzword. At that time, Radio Kabul was running a daily Pashtoonistan programme full of Pashto songs and Pashtoonistan propaganda. Especially popular was the Hujrah Majlis on Thursday evenings, graced with live music from some of the best Pashto masters.

Pashtoonistan was the name given by the Afghan government to the Pashto-speaking parts of Pakistan—the Frontier province and part of Balochistan. Indeed, the government of Sardar Mohammad Daud Khan had made the Pashtoonistan issue—Afghanistan's claim to the Pashto- speaking parts of Pakistan—its flagship issue. The Pashtoon nationalist exiles residing in Kabul—prominent

---

[6] I spent considerable time in the late nineties and early noughties in Tashkent, where Kokay and her family were residing as refugees, and picked up these nuggets from several conversations I had with Kokay over the years.

amongst them being Ajmal Khattak—were considered Pashtoonistanis. The figure most associated with Pashtoonistan, the great Pashtoon nationalist leader Khan Abdul Ghaffar Khan, had finished his self-imposed exile in Kabul and Jalalabad and had returned to Peshawar a year before Daud came to power and the Pashtoonistan issue came to prominence. Still reviled by the Pakistan establishment, Ghaffar Khan had been issued with a Pakistani passport, paving the way for his return to Pakistan, by none other than my friend Sardar Abdul Rashid when the latter was serving as minister of the interior in Islamabad.

I should give some background on Pashtoonistan. The Pashtoon nation is split in about half, between Afghanistan and Pakistan. This is a result of an agreement made in 1893 between the foreign secretary of the British Indian government, Mortimer Durand, and the king of Afghanistan, Amir Abdul Rahman Khan. Mortimer Durand had an otherwise undistinguished career. However, his name has lived on in posterity. This is because of the border that he delineated, along with the *amir* of Afghanistan, between Afghanistan and British India. This later became the border between Afghanistan and Pakistan. Effectively, it split the Pashtoon nation in two. It is known to this day as the Durand Line. Pashtoon nationalists do not refer to the border between Afghanistan and Pakistan as a border. They call it instead the Durand *Karkha* (the Durand Line), almost forgetting that the Durrani Afghan king, Abdul Rahman, was just as complicit in drawing it as the British civil servant by the name of Durand. The border should more correctly be called the Durrani–Durand Line.

In the run-up to independence, when it became clear that a referendum would be held in Muslim-majority provinces to see whether those provinces wished to join an independent India or Pakistan, Ghaffar Khan argued for a third option—an autonomous province for Pashtoons—to be on the table in the predominantly Pashto-speaking North–West Frontier Province. The British dismissed the request. The Khudai Khidmatgars, for their part, boycotted the referendum. The Pakistan option gained a huge majority in the referendum and the North–West Frontier Province joined Pakistan. The Pashtoonistan issue has remained a gripe on the part of the Afghan government ever since. Though it is now officially off the agenda, it remains the basic bone of contention between the governments of Pakistan and Afghanistan. Pakistan's main concern is to prevent a leader who would be in a position to promote Pashtoonistan from remaining in power in Afghanistan. One might say that this has been the overriding priority of the Pakistan government, ever since the creation of the country, with regard to its policy towards Afghanistan.

Through its proxy mujahideen groups and their Arab friends, Pakistan tried hard enough to dislodge Najib during the time I was at the *Frontier Post*. When Soviet forces withdrew from Afghanistan in 1989, most observers gave the Afghan president a few weeks in power. Without Soviet support, his government would soon be dislodged, they said. In fact, Dr Najib's stature grew and grew. The key battle in this regard was the battle for Jalalabad. No sooner had the Soviet forces completed their withdrawal from Afghanistan, in the spring of 1989, than the mujahideen groups, with support from the Pakistan ISI, attacked the eastern Afghan province of Nangarhar. Their intention was to take Jalalabad, the capital of Nangarhar, and use it as a springboard to mount an attack on Kabul itself.

Entering Afghanistan through Shinwari territory, it was easy enough for the mujahideen to take the districts of Kot and Naziyan, in the east of Nangarhar. The mujahideen quickly advanced as far as Samar Khel, about fifteen miles to the east of Jalalabad. At one point they took Jalalabad airport, also situated to the east of the city. But the Afghan forces quickly galvanized, retook the airport and reopened the road to the border town of Torkham. The battle-hardy Uzbek forces of the warlord General Dostum, during the time of Dr Najib the de-factor ruler of the north of Afghanistan, came down from the north to bolster the beleaguered divisions based in Jalalabad. Food was in short supply in the Nangarhar capital, but the sense of resistance and solidarity amongst the residents was rock solid. Pashtoons in the Frontier also shared the solidarity with their kinsfolk across the border. The victory was sealed with the arrival of Dr Najib himself at Jalalabad airport, where he sounded a theme that would echo for several decades: 'Our neighbour will not allow us to live in peace.' His slogan *ya watan ya kafan* (country or shroud) is still the stuff of graffiti in Kabul and Jalalabad.

The dreams that were vested in Dr Najib lived on for a few more years. As for the hopes that Benazir would build a new future for Pakistan, those were dashed quickly as she fell prey to the greed of her own party-wallas and the interference of the military, who were determined at all costs to keep power in their hands.

And what of Rahmat Shah? In the late nineties, he was arrested in Lahore. Apparently, he was caught with some twenty kilos of hash in his Mercedes. Enquiries led the authorities to a truck loaded with 650 kilos in nearby Faisalabad. Rahmat Shah was in jail for a long time—nearly ten years. For a time, he was on death row in Kot Lakhpat jail. He was released in 2008, his death sentence having been commuted to a life sentence when he was hospitalized due to ill health.[7] According to his family, he continues to be in a poor state of health. Still, the legacy that he left by investing money in the future of Frontier and Pashto journalism continues to be felt in newspapers, radio stations and TV channels around the world.

---

[7] *Dawn* report on Rahmat Shah's release, 25 May 2008, http://www.dawn.com/news/304324/rehmat-shah-afridi-freed-on-parole

XVIII

BBC

Your husband is a broadcaster.

(Bashir Harji to Shahnaz, his elder sister)

I left the *Frontier Post* in 1991 and returned to England. There were a lot of reasons for my leaving. For one, Qaiser Butt was angling for my room. The writing was on the wall. My time was up at the paper. More importantly, journalistically, I had to move elsewhere. It was the perfect time to try my hand in England.

Back in England, before long I was trying my hand at other things besides journalism, in particular socializing with women. It was time for me to make an attempt, after a number of false starts, at the age-old *Sunnah* of marriage. My friend Sean Jones would take me to parties. Sean was one of the most famous members of the Madyan crowd. Since 1985, I had been living in his house in Madyan. He, meanwhile, had moved to England. The parties that Sean took me to at 118 Haverstock Hill were particularly enjoyable. There would be a campfire and some live music from Margo Sagov. Margo was an accomplished musician from the area. She had a band and did gigs in her spare time, for the love of it. Her day job was being an architect. Her preference was for jazz, but I used to pester her for Dylan numbers, especially *Knocking on Heaven's Door*. She would kindly oblige. One day, Margo was not there. I made up for her absence by playing a new cassette by the Travelling Wilburys. I played it again and again. And there were other consolations. It was on that occasion that I met Shahnaz. Homely, friendly, sociable, good-looking, loving—I looked into her eyes; we felt the mutual affinity. I walked her to the gate. 'Can I walk you home?' I asked. 'It's okay, I have a car,' she told me, pointing over to a black, shining VW Golf, which flashed as she clicked the doors open with her key. I liked her even more.

We began going out together. The only problem was, I was already going out with a Pashtoon lady named Noori. Before I moved to London, I was living near my parents, in Farnham. Some people told me about Denis Richardson. He speaks good Pashto,' I was told. Denis Richardson lived in Godalming, quite near Farnham. I gave Denis a ring and he came over to collect me. He was living with his wife, Honi Gul, in a flat in Godalming. He did indeed speak excellent Pashto. In fact, he spoke Pashto at home with Honi Gul. She was from Mardan. 'When I first saw her, she was climbing a tree outside her home. I thought, "This is the most beautiful girl I have ever set my eyes on,"' Denis told me. When she had grown up a little more, Denis married her. He was known as Badshah Gul in Peshawar. He was an out-and-out missionary, but well-respected. As I have already said, Muslims should be strong enough in their own faith to be able to resist missionary activity without banning it. If Muslims have the right to preach their faith in Christian countries, then what right do they have to prevent Christians from preaching their faith in Muslim lands? None whatsoever, and if Muslims are aware of their faith, they can use the preaching of Christians to their own advantage and as an opportunity for them to put their own faith across.

It was at Denis Richardson and Honi Gul's place that I met Noori. She was Honi Gul's niece. Denis' description of when he first set eyes on Honi Gul would not have been out of place with respect to Noori. She was a lady of outstanding beauty. For sheer beauty, I think she rivalled, or even excelled, Rekha, the Bollywood actress, in her prime. And she had the height to go with her looks.

Honi Gul was encouraging her to get married. 'Silly girl! You are growing older,' she reminded her niece—in fact Noori could not have been more than thirty-five. 'You are going to be left all alone if you do not marry. John would be a good choice, wouldn't he?' To this Noori quipped, 'John does not have any money.' Noori did live in high society. She told me she had lost a good deal of money in the Bank of Credit and Commerce International scandal that had rocked Pakistan as well as the rest of the world. BCCI had been accused of laundering a huge amount of drug money in the USA, most notoriously on behalf of General Noriega. The bank was closed down, causing untold loss to investors, amongst them Noori.

So I was going out with Noori when I met Shahnaz. A couple of things about Shahnaz won me over. For one, she was so big-hearted with regard to Noori. She would send me to her hairdresser and dress me up for my dates with Noori. On one occasion, she even gave me a T-shirt—one of her favourites and a particularly posh one—for me to wear for Sunday lunch with Noori! Noori and I took lunch next to the Thames that day, but I was thinking about Shahnaz. My mind was made up. Only once did Shahnaz show some jealousy towards Noori. That was when I told her of Noori's beauty. 'You are saying that as if I am ugly or something.' Shahnaz was a bit offended. I had not meant it that way. Shahnaz is also beautiful. Another thing about Shahnaz was that she seemed more likely to give me the constant companionship and support that I craved. Noori was quite busy and had to be booked in advance. Shahnaz did her day job, then she was free to go to the movies, to have dinner, to just hang out.

It was probably because I was so preoccupied elsewhere that I never pursued a third option that might have presented itself to me, namely Safia Haleem. Let me first make clear that Safia and I have never been romantically involved. But Shahnaz often used to say to me: 'You and Safia would have made a good couple.' I never thought about it that way. Still, I will never forget the impact when I first set eyes on Safia. I was dazzled. If I had not been so occupied elsewhere, it could have been love at first sight. It must have been a Sunday since there was only her and one other person working in the BBC Pashto section, on the sixth floor of the old Bush House, where BBC World Service was based in those days. I entered the large, sunlit room. Safia was going about her work. She was dressed in dark, emerald green, with chequered patterns intricately woven on her chemise in silver thread. It was a typically Afghan outfit. Her poise, her confidence in her work, her manner, everything about her impressed me deeply. We went down to the canteen and had lunch together. We did go out in the evening together, once or twice. Once we met up with Sean as well. Remembering me as a hermit in Swat, he made fun of me: 'You cannot see Shahnaz because you are seeing Noori, but at the moment you are with Safia,' he joked. The *malang* had gone mad.

I did not have the generosity of spirit to admit it, but just as Shahnaz thought Safia and I would have made a good couple, Shahnaz and Shiraz would also have made a good couple. Shiraz and her were distant cousins. They were both originally from East Africa. Shahnaz's family had come to England at the time of the Idi Amin expulsion of Asians from Uganda. Shiraz's family was based in Kenya. The two of them had just about grown up together. If arranged marriages had still been customary amongst families such as Shiraz and Shahnaz's, the two would almost certainly have been paired off together. Even their names—Shiraz and Shahnaz—fitted in with each other! Shiraz is a joker, sometimes to outrageous proportions. He is a dentist. Along with having his private clinic in Wimpole Street, he used to work in South London, at St George's Hospital in Tooting. One day, I visited him there. He was joking with the nurses. He pointed to the badge pinned to one of their breast pockets. 'Oh, that one is called so-and-so,' he said pointing to the lady's name on the badge. 'What is the other one called?' The nurse just laughed. It was an outrageous and sexist joke. I certainly would not have been able to get away with making a remark like that. Safia once said to me that I was a serious guy and should not make jokes—they did not come off. She would definitely have been right in this case. But Shiraz could pull it off.

The time when I first met Safia was, in fact, about my first visit to the BBC Pashto section. My association with the BBC started with an advertisement in the *Guardian* newspaper inviting applications for a producer on *South Asia Survey*, an excellent English programme on South Asian affairs. There was a great team working on *South Asia Survey*, including Jaswinder Singh, Tinku Ray and Frances Harrison, whom I got to know well. Later, Frances helped me a lot with radio production, of which I had no previous experience. Anyway, I applied for the job. The head of *South Asia Survey*, Nick Nugent, wrote back to me: 'You do not have the radio experience needed for this post,' he pointed out, 'but you have unique experience of South Asia. Call in sometime so we can see how you might contribute to our programmes.'

Contribute I did, on a range of topics in Urdu, English and even Hindi. In the early days, I did not do anything in Pashto. The head of the Pashto service, Gordon Adam, was away on secondment with the BBC Asian Network in Leicester. When he returned, I walked into his office, attached to the office where I had first met Safia. I introduced myself, and so began an association with the Pashto service that was to last through the nineties. The highlights were my trips to Afghanistan, Balochistan and the Frontier. Gordon Adam had novel ideas for the Pashto service. The service had been set up due to the Afghan War of the 1980s. Since the Foreign Office funded the World Service in those days, they must have thought that a Pashto service for Afghanistan made sense. That was the way the World Service worked. The BBC could not set up a new language service without word coming through from the Foreign Office. As for what went into that service, there the BBC was editorially independent. Predictably, there were more listeners amongst Afghans than amongst Pashto speakers from Pakistan. Gordon set in motion a Pashto service caravan that would tour the Pashto-speaking provinces of the Frontier and Balochistan. I was also slated to be part of the caravan.

We travelled in a minibus with a loudspeaker fixed to its roof. We would stop off at every main town and talk to the assembled masses. In Thana, at the foot of the Malakand Pass leading to Swat, young men told us how the West was hypocritical: they supported annulment of elections in Algeria because those elections had brought an Islamist party to power. 'They only believe in democracy that brings their own friends to power.' Young Afghan refugees in Timurgarha in Dir revoked the idea of the return of Zahir Shah to Afghanistan. 'We will welcome his return in a hail of bullets,' one said. My own feeling is that this hostility to the former king of Afghanistan came from Islamist elements who were disaffected due to his philandering reputation. Others pined for him, and admired him for keeping the country together and united. On the Pashto service caravan, we wanted to talk about and promote our Pashto programmes. Naturally enough, with the BBC in town, young men in particular wished to talk about politics.

With me on the Pashto service caravan were Safia—she is from Peshawar—and Gauhar Rahman Gauhar, an experienced and unique Pashto broadcaster who hails from Zeda in Swabi district, near Panjpir. I say Gauhar is unique because he broadcasts in pure, almost antiquated Pashto. I am usually not of the school of broadcasters that feel their job is to purify the language in which they broadcast. My thinking is that we should broadcast in the language that is most understandable and familiar to the people we broadcast to: the common man and woman on the street. However, if anyone can pull off broadcasting in an uncommon tongue, it would be Gauhar sahib. The thing is, his brand of Pashto may have been unusual—unique, as I said—but it was not elitist. There was a logic and a familiar ring to it that any Pashto-speaker could understand. For Gauhar sahib, a mundane sentence like: 'Firing has stopped.' Would be made colourful: '*Daz-duz puh tap-tup walar day.*' Almost, you can tell what he means just from the sound of the words in the sentence. Pashto is a very onomatopoeic language. Gauhar sahib used this aspect of the language to full effect.

When our bus entered a town, the loudspeaker on the roof of the bus would announce our arrival—that the BBC Pashto service had arrived and anyone who was interested in meeting up with them should 'Come to the centre of town!' Hordes would arrive. First of all, Gauhar would emerge, then Safia and myself. Safia thought it was very funny, the way the crowd would shout 'John Butta', adjusting my name to its Pashto, vocative form.

On the tenth anniversary of the Pashto service, I put together a report to commemorate the occasion. That was my debut in broadcasting for the Pashto service. We had taken a launch out on the Thames to mark the occasion. Gordon was full of such ideas. Amongst the guests were some Pashtoons from the Khattak tribe, living in the renowned Khattak outpost of Aylesbury. I had talked to everyone on the launch about what the Pashto service meant to them. It became quite an important report, marking as I said the first ten years of the Pashto service. My producer on this occasion was Ismail Niaz. I was planning to introduce myself by my Muslim name, Jan Mohammad. Ismail Niaz said that would not be a good idea. People would say, 'If his name is Jan Mohammad, then why does he speak Pashto in a strange kind of accent?' Ismail felt it would be better to introduce myself as a Pashtoon Englishman and use my English name, John Butt. I thought it was wise and practical advice on the part of Ismail. So as far as the BBC was concerned, I reverted to the name John Butt. Some Afridis and others who knew me from before and heard my reports made a big thing of this: 'Look, he is using his old English name. He must have reverted to his old faith!' Some Pashtoons tend to make a lot of such minor matters. One of the Afridis who made a big deal of this was Haji Hanan, managing director of Toyota Frontier Motors. 'So what is wrong with the name John Butt?' I asked him when he accosted me on this point. 'Don't you have lots of Janbat Khans and Gulbat Khans in Tirah? So, if I am John Butt, have I committed a crime?'

My job now was to make daily reports—packages, to use the technical radio term—for the evening current affairs programme. At this time, just about everyone in Afghanistan was listening to the BBC Pashto service. There was nothing else to listen to or watch except for Radio and TV of Afghanistan (RTA) and people wanted another opinion besides the official government line. In the morning, I would check with Rahimullah Yousafzai, the BBC reporter in Peshawar, what topic would be good to concentrate on, then I would call up the concerned people and finally, I would put the package together in time for the evening show. Radio packages are pretty formulaic: one person puts forward one view, another presents the opposite view and there is a neutral observer who does not really have a view. That is how the BBC achieves its balance. The balance ensures that the report maintains the status quo. Later, at PACT Radio, I changed this approach, covering topics that were more related to people's needs and orientating the reports towards making a difference for the better, while at the same time talking to a good number of people, so there would be more likely to be a diverse range of views.

I made several trips as a producer of the BBC Pashto service to Afghanistan, the Frontier and Balochistan. The first one was at the time of the fall of Dr Najib's government in April 1992. After the victory of Dr Najib's forces in the battle for Jalalabad in the spring of 1989, the Afghan president consolidated his grip on power for a good two years. This started unravelling with the mujahideen conquest of Khost in the spring of 1991. The mujahideen were composed of the disparate forces that had been fighting the Soviet Union in the 1980s. Besides the seven parties of mujahideen that had been cobbled together in Pakistan, there were some Shiite groups that had been formed in Iran. One mujahideen group was predominant in one area, another elsewhere. It was a recipe for civil strife that ensued in Afghanistan until the rise of the Taliban in 1994.

Khost was pretty easy for the mujahideen to take, being cut off from the rest of Afghanistan but very accessible from the stronghold of Jalaluddin Haqqani in Miramshah, across the border in the tribal area of North Waziristan. Haqqani was one of the few mujahideen leaders who was actually an Islamic scholar, having graduated from the Haqqani madrasa in the North–West Frontier Province. He had been one of the earliest of the mujahideen to launch resistance to the Communist People's Democratic Party of Afghanistan (PDPA) government[1] in Kabul that held sway from 1978–9, and then the Soviet troops that came to bolster the PDPA government at the end of 1979. The mood in the BBC Pashto service was quite different to that in the *Frontier Post*. While the BBC

[1] The People's Democratic Party of Afghanistan, the communist government that ruled in Afghanistan from 1978 and through the eighties. When Dr Najib became president in 1987, he relabelled the PDPA as the Watan—Country—party, hence the slogan by which he is most remembered, *Ya Watan ya Kafan*—Country or shroud.

was supposed to keep a balance, the Pashto service had been set up by the Foreign and Commonwealth Office in order to bolster the anti-Soviet resistance in the country, so naturally that was the way it leaned. Gordon Adam himself seemed to be sympathetic towards the mujahideen. One could see his celebratory mood whenever the mujahideen conquered some new territory. I think his deputy Nabi Misdaq was a closet Khalqi—sympathizer of Dr Najib's People's Democratic Party of Afghanistan. Certainly, when Khost fell to the mujahideen he made a lot of reports that the mujahideen were ripping doors off shops and taking them to Pakistan to sell. Between Nabi Misdaq's Khalqi sympathies, and Gordon Adam's sympathies for the other side, somehow a Pashto service balance was achieved.

I tried to reflect the facts, which when I went to Kabul in April 1992, after Dr Najib's government had fallen, were pretty damning with respect to the mujahideen. The support of General Dostum was crucial to Dr Najib. His battle-hardy and ruthless fighters even came in useful for Dr Najib during the battle for Jalalabad, as we have seen. After the fall of Khost, it was General Dostum's turning on Dr Najib that proved the next nail of Najib's coffin. General Dostum had been the undisputed king of the north of Afghanistan. He ruled like a kind of viceroy, on behalf of Dr Najib. When General Dostum turned against Dr Najib, there was no way the Afghan president could survive. Only when he realized that the capital was slipping out of his hands did he try to make his way to the Kabul airport to join his young family in Delhi. There also it was members of General Dostum's militia that did not allow him to travel. President Najib was detained in the United Nations building in Kabul.

I do not know why General Dostum rebelled against Dr Najib, and if he regretted having done so, causing his downfall; indeed, if he regretted stopping Dr Najib travelling to Delhi, resulting eventually in his death.[2] I had the opportunity to ask General Dostum in an interview I did with him, in the course of the Constitutional Loya Jirga, held at the end of 2003. This was the second of two Loya Jirgas held in 2002–3. Attached to the Loya Jirga secretariats, I had

[2] Dr Najib was hauled out of the United Nations building in Kabul and killed by the Taliban, when the Taliban took Kabul in September 1996.

unique access, in the course of both these Loya Jirgas, to delegates. The aim of the Loya Jirgas was to chart a course for the country, in the wake of the fall of the Taliban. It was a time of great hope for Afghanistan. I made dozens of reports at the time, reflecting that hope. I did not make a habit of interviewing high level politicians, but I made an exception in the case of General Dostum. He was a good interviewee. The interview was held in the Loya Jirga tent. When I looked round, there were a good seventy to eighty people standing in a circle, listening to the interview. General Dostum is a likeable and affable man. I had just accosted him and started interviewing him—no niceties or introductions. He did not baulk for a second but answered each of my questions frankly, standing up for democracy and freedom of speech. After that, whenever I saw him in the Loya Jirga, he would look at me with a twinkle in his eye and say, '*Shumoro khuub interview dodam ne*?' (I gave you a damn good interview, didn't I?) 'Everyone makes mistakes,' he said in the course of the interview, 'I have made mistakes.' Until today, I regret not having interjected at that point to ask him, 'What do you think General sahib, was your betrayal of Dr Najib a mistake?' I wonder what he would have said. One really has to be on the ball in the course of interviews to ask the right questions at the right time. Otherwise, it was a good interview, one of the best political interviews of my journalistic career, but it had that one flaw.

Gordon Adam and David Page sent me to Afghanistan to cover the mujahideen takeover in April 1992. David Page was assistant head of the Eastern Service. The Eastern Service included the Pashto, Urdu, Farsi, Hindi, Nepalese and Burmese sections. There may even have been a Sinhala section thrown in there too. David was very much the eminence grise of the Eastern Service. He loved the BBC. Later in the nineties, when some restructuring took place at the BBC World Service and the old Eastern Service was changed to the South Asia region, David found himself out in the cold, which was a tragedy for the BBC and must have been hard to take for David also. Along with Gordon Adam and Nick Nugent, he had also helped me 'get a foot in the door' of BBC, as he himself put it. Anyway, Gordon and David felt I would be a good person to cover the takeover of Afghanistan by the mujahideen.

Those were pretty gung-ho days in the BBC. There was not the obsession with security or even legality that there is nowadays. The more dangerous the place, the more likely it was that the BBC would send you there, or at least leave it to your discretion as we shall see in the course of my next trip to Afghanistan. Anyway, there I was, on my way to Kandahar from Quetta, with no Afghan visa—we did not do visas in those days: we preferred to take one of the many smuggling routes available to cross the border. The plan was that I would take the road from Kandahar to Kabul, and then cover the capital also. There had been a lot of rain that spring. The *lalma zmaka* (unirrigated land) was lush with green wheat. As for Kandahar, it was a den of anarchy, confusion and lawlessness. It was the time of transition, from the Watan Party[3] operatives of Dr Najib, to the mujahideen hordes that had swamped the city. Gul Agha Sherzai was from one of the mujahideen factions, known as the Mahaz-e-Milli or National Front. He had managed to wrest control of the Governor's House in the centre of town. He was strong in Kandahar mainly due to the reputation of his father, Haji Latif, better known as the Lion of Kandahar. Haji Latif had earned his spurs, and been killed, fighting the Soviets. Maulvi Naquibullah was from what became the ruling party on a national level, the Jamaat-e-Islami (Islamic Party) of Burhanuddin Rabbani. He had to make do with the army garrison. One commander belonging to Sibghatullah Mujaddidi's Najat (Salvation) party had taken over the airport. Another commander, Abdul Ali, was holding sway at the radio station. He was from Sayyaf's party that had been formed in order to unite all the seven groups. It ended up being an eighth group in its own right. The main commander of Gulbuddin Hekmatyar's Hezb-e-Islami, known as Sar Katib, set up his stronghold at Bagh-e-Pul, on the road to Herat. There were representatives of each one of the seven parties that had been formed in Peshawar, armed to the teeth, in various parts of the city. And those were the Sunni parties. There were also a lot of Shias in Kandahar. Appropriately, their two main parties had been set up in Iran. Strong in

[3] Dr Najib changed the name of the PDPA to Watan Party after he became president, to give it less of a communistic, and more of a patriotic hue.

Kandahar was the Harakat-e-Islami (Islamic Movement) of Ayatullah Mohsini, himself from Kandahar, while the biggest Shiite party on a national level, Hezb-e-Wahdat, was more prominent in Kabul.

Kandahar was like a tinderbox. It could explode at any time. I was advised by a BBC fixer to go and see Pasanay Mulla, the pre-eminent Islamic scholar in Kandahar. He would be able to give you a good perspective on all the parties vying for power in Kandahar, my fixer Ibrahim, told me. Maybe he knew something that I didn't, since in fact Mulla Pasanay was one of the leading ulema associated with the nascent Taliban. I made my way to the base of Pasanay mulla sahib in Panjwai. It so happened that on the day I went to Panjwai, the ulema of Kandahar were holding deliberations as to what they should do under the current situation. Pasanay mulla sahib spoke to me. Alongside him was a venerable white-bearded Islamic scholar. My notes from this meeting were washed away in the floods in Swat in 2010, but I believe his name was Maulana Ishaq sahib. He was much more polite than Pasanay mulla sahib, who was always quite tetchy whenever I met him. Amongst those who were present on that day was the young Mohammad Hasan Akhund, later to become governor of Kandahar at the time of the Taliban. When I met him during his governorate, he told me that at the time of those deliberations they, the Taliban, were in a position to take over power. That was what they were discussing that day in April 1992 in Panjwai. 'But we decided to give the gunslingers [the name by which the Taliban referred to the mujahideen commanders who held sway in Kandahar] a chance to get their act together.' According to Mohammad Hasan, they made their move when the situation became hopeless, late in 1994.

It is worthwhile to say a word or two about who the Taliban originally were. They were groups of *talibs* loosely associated with two of the mujahideen parties. These two parties were breakaway groups of the Hezb-e-Islami of Maulvi Khalis and the Harkat-e-Inquilab-e-Islamic of Mohammad Nabi Mohammadi. The *talibs* liked these two parties because their leaders considered themselves Deobandis. Maulvi Khalis had by all accounts actually studied in Darul Uloom Deoband. The make-up of these two parties was considered more scholarly than that of the three parties that were out-and-out Islamist: the Jamiyat-e-Islami of Burhanuddin Rabbani, the Ittehad party of Professor Sayyaf and the Hezb-e-Islami of Engineer Gulbuddin Hekmatyar. The names of all the party leaders testify to another differentiation between these two groups: the Islamist parties were led by people who had studied in the conventional education system, while the parties favoured by the taliban were led by people who had studied in traditional Islamic madrasas, following the Deoband curriculum.

The Islamic students or taliban—we will not start using the capital T until the time when they actually took power in late 1994—were affiliated with these parties but also had their own organization. They were like societies—*talibs* call them *anjumans*—that exist in almost every educational institute anywhere in the world. These societies were organized on a regional basis. For example, madrasa students from Kandahar had their own society. Mulla Omar Akhund, later to become the leader of the Taliban with a capital T, and Mohammad Hasan Akhund were prominent in this society. So was Abdul Salam Zaeef, author of the book *My Life with the Taliban*. The society of taliban from Paktia and Khost was organized under Abdul Hakeem and Abdul Kabir. The name of the society was Jamiyat-at-Tulaba-e-Paktya wa Khost. Later, in the Taliban government in the 1990s, Abdul Hakeem became governor of Zabul, while Maulvi Kabir was governor of Nangarhar until taking over as deputy head of the Kabul Governing Council. There were similar societies of madrasa students from other parts of the country. The Badakhshan madrasa students' society was one particularly prominent one. There was a separate society composed of Wardak students. The group that was meeting that day, in April 1992, was the society of Kandahar students. They decided to stay their hand and let the gunslingers take a swing at things for the time being.

One good English-speaker by the name of Engineer Khalid Pashtoon was the right-hand man of Gul Agha Sherzai. Engineer Pashtoon and Gul Agha were waiting for Dr Najib's governor, Mohammad Akram, to vacate the governor's office so that Gul Agha could move in. Gul Agha was in the room next door to Mohammad Akram's. I spent a lot of time with Mohammad Akram. It was a sad time for him and he was concerned for the future. On a subsequent trip to Kandahar, he and his family were under house arrest in the garrison. I visited the whole family there. They were still apprehensive but were being patient and seemed to be making the best of things. Muneer Mangal was the commander of the Kandahar garrison. He was often in evidence in Mohammad Akram's office. 'Oh, you are going to Kabul. I wonder if you could be so kind as to give this letter to my family in Kabul and let them know I am alright. I am just waiting to grow a beard—that is one's visa nowadays,' he joked, 'then I will be on my way to join them in Kabul.' I searched out Muneer Mangal's home in the Karte Char area of Kabul and gave them the message. Muneer Mangal rose to be deputy minister of the interior in Karzai's government. I went to the ministry a couple of times in the hope of seeing him, just for old time's sake, but was unable to do so.

There are so many stories to be told from these days, stories that did not find their way into the reports that I sent back to London. Sending reports—that was a story in itself. There was no phone in Kandahar, as evidenced by Muneer Mangal having to ask me to take a message with me to Kabul. In order to send reports from Kandahar to London, I had to travel to the Pakistan border town of Chaman. One day, as I was sitting on the roof of a bus on my way to Chaman, a familiar voice called out to me from the roof of the same bus. 'Nice to see you, Jan Mohammad!' The voice was familiar, so was the accent. It was not a Kandahari accent, though the young man had donned a Kandahari *topi* (cap) in order to fit in better in the Kandahari milieu. It was an Afridi accent. The young gentleman concerned was a close business associate of the family of Rahmat Shah, my former boss at the *Frontier Post*. I knew better than to ask him what had brought him to Kandahar. Neither did I have to. 'Come and spend the night with us,' he invited me to the house of his business colleague in Chaman. There we spent the night in conversation and enjoyment, and I also managed to send a report or two to London.

Once I had finished my work in Kabul, I took a shared taxi from Kandahar to Kabul. Amongst the other passengers was a guy who eventually alighted in Kalat, the capital of Zabul province. Next to him was a prisoner of his. '*Da zama bandi day*,' he explained to the other passengers, telling them 'This is my prisoner.' Yes, of course, I mean everyone should have a prisoner, shouldn't they? It goes without saying. In Wardak, which is pretty evenly populated by Hazaras and Pashtoons, Hazaras were checking ID cards and so were Pashtoons. Hazaras are one of the four main ethnic groups that make up Afghanistan—Pashtoons, Tajiks, Hazaras and Uzbeks. The Hazaras are unique in that they are all Shias. The others are Sunni. Which *tanzeem* (political party) do you belong to? Everyone was being asked. I belong to BBC *tanzeem*, I answered. They did not ask for any ID. I can't remember if I even had one, but I had a visiting card. The only person I saw being taken out of our shared taxi as a result of these enquiries was a young Hazara lad. He might have been a conscript in Dr Najib's army. I hope he got home okay.

I sent a standout ten-minute Pashto report from Kabul on the chaos that reigned in the capital city. All the *tanzeems* were marking out their territories in preparation for the civil war that was to ensue and would last until the Taliban took over Kabul in September 1996. The groups that had been supported by the West as well as by Pakistan and Iran over the last decade laid waste to the capital. The report that I sent from Kabul gave expression to the voices, in particular the fears, of rank-and-file citizens of the city. Safia Haleem back in London was kind enough to say that it was the best report she had heard. That was quite a compliment, coming from her. No doubt it added to my already burgeoning reputation. Having an English name and clearly being a Pashtoon Englishman broadcasting in accented Pashto made me quickly into a household name. I cannot confirm that any parents named their children John Butt, but certainly it was given as a nickname to people who spoke like me. A Radio 4 crew came to the Frontier at this time. They were doing a programme on the *hawala* banking system, whereby Pashtoons sent money all over the world. The *hawala* banking system has largely been outlawed in the age of what has become known as the war on terror. The presenter of the programme was Tim Sebastian. His producer told me that when they went to the border town of Torkham, they were surprised to hear people call out to them. 'John Birt, John Birt,' they thought people were saying. 'Gosh,' they said in surprise, 'these people are pretty well-informed about the latest appointments in the BBC.' It was shortly after John Birt had become director-general of the corporation. Only later did they realize that the people were saying, 'John Butt, John Butt.' 'You're popular in this part of the world, aren't you?' Tim Sebastian's producer said to me admiringly. It's true. I was.

One day, David Page and Gordon Adam were sitting together in Bush House. They gave me a ring. 'John, you are doing a damn good job. We would like you to stay for the time being.' I should have stayed. The only problem was, Shahnaz was expecting Surriya, our first and, as it turned out, only child. It was a bit of a shock for Shahnaz, though it should not have been. After all, that is what people live together and get married for, isn't it? Shahnaz was keen for me to return to London and be with her. I could have explained to her that the BBC like the job I am doing and would like me to stay. One day, soon after she discovered that she was expecting her first child, she was caught driving at 90 mph in her Golf on the A14, from Bury St Edmunds to London. 'Why are you breaking the speed limit?' the cops asked her. 'I am pregnant,' she said, as if that had anything to do with it. Logic was never Shahnaz's strong point, as Shiraz fondly pointed out. He was good at picking up on such things. 'Only Shahnaz could say: "Is Friday the twenty-second a Friday?"' he once wryly observed. Anyway, Shahnaz being pregnant did not really have anything to do with me staying on in Kabul, either. So for me to say to David and Gordon, when they asked me to stay on in Kabul, that Shahnaz was pregnant was also illogical. But there was nothing David and Gordon could say to that really. Reluctantly, they agreed for me to return to England.

On my next duty trip to the Frontier, Balochistan and Afghanistan, I brought Shahnaz with me, pretty heavily pregnant by then, but just able to fly. Frances Harrison from the programme *South Asia Survey* was by now a good family friend. She also came with us. She and her husband, Kasra Naji from the BBC Persian service, were about to start a freelancing stint in Pakistan. There is no need for me to talk about the programmes I made on that occasion. They were on the aspirations of Afghan youth. What happened between the programmes, so to speak, was much more interesting. Shahnaz came with me to Quetta. She saw me off at the bus station, where I took a Datsun—that is what we called converted pick-ups in those days—to Chaman. Meanwhile, Shahnaz returned to Islamabad to spend time with Frances.

By now, the Chaman residence of Rahmat Shah's business associate was my regular office and stop-off point in Chaman. All BBC offices and correspondents with whom I was likely to be in touch had the telephone number of that delightful and hospitable gentleman's house. To paraphrase Bob: 'No, I ain't gonna say his name.' That night, I received a call from Lyse Doucet. Lyse was at that time Islamabad correspondent for the BBC. 'John, I must tell you, today Hekmatyar issued a statement saying that he will kill any BBC person who sets foot in his territory. I just wanted to warn you. It is entirely up to you if you wish to proceed to Kandahar or not.' I rang Shahnaz in Islamabad. 'There is this death threat against BBC personnel. Shall I go or not?' 'Go!' she replied. When I told that story to Shahnaz's sister Shemin, she found it very funny. I went, and stopped off with some party-wallas of Gulbuddin Hekmatyar on the Afghan side of the border at Spin Boldak. They were pleased to see me and invited me to join them for a cup of tea.

To make the series on Pashtoon youth that I had been sent by the BBC to make, I went to Khost via Miramshah and the border crossing of Ghulamkhan, both in the North Waziristan tribal agency. In Miramshah, I was the guest of Haji Pazeer, a senior journalist in North Waziristan. 'I have found a very good person to take you to Khost,' he said to me. 'Great,' I replied. I had not really needed anyone to escort me across borders before, but North Waziristan being tribal territory, I thought it may be wise to have a local person familiar with everyone along the way to accompany me. Only when I was near my escort's place did Haji Pazeer tell me who the gentleman was. 'He is a very kind gentleman by the name of Said Amin. He is the representative of Gulbuddin Hekmatyar's Hezb-e-Islami here in Miramshah.' I must say, my heart did sink somewhat and as I got out of the car, I took Haji Pazeer aside. 'Haji sahib,' I said, 'I will go with this person, it is not a problem, but perhaps you should know that the other day Gulbuddin Hekmatyar issued this death threat against BBC personnel.' 'Just don't worry about it,' Haji Pazeer reassured me.

Said Amin was a good escort and host. In Khost he took me to the Hezb-e-Islami office, where I spent an enjoyable night in the office of Engineer Mahmud, commander of all Gulbuddin's forces in Greater Paktya—Khost, Paktika and Paktya itself. They were even kind enough to arrange an escort to take me to Gardez the next day. But the funniest thing happened when I was leaving Khost. We were saying our late afternoon prayers by the banks of a ravine. A relative of Haji Pazeer turned up out of the blue, from Miramshah. 'Oh, John Butt, I am so glad to see you and that you are having a good time, and I am so glad to see that this young gentleman is escorting you and that you are in such good company. We are all looking forward to seeing you back in Miramshah very soon!'

This was his way of saying to the person accompanying me—on behalf of the mighty Wazir tribe—that I was a guest of the Wazirs and they had entrusted me to my hosts in Khost. And as everyone knows, Pashtoons will go to war on behalf of a guest. The relative of Haji Pazeer had come all the way from Miramshah to deliver this message to my escorts in Khost.

Not only did I brush up on my Pashto a lot while working for the BBC, I also learnt a good deal about the Pashtoons.

XIX

STORYTELLER

New Home, New Life *taught us a lot. It told us our history, culture, our existing values.*

(Nazir Ahmad, a *New Home, New Life* listener in Kandahar City, 2014)

I have no idea why Gordon Adam thought I would be a good guy to head a *The Archers* clone for Afghanistan. *The Archers* is a radio soap opera that has been running on the BBC Home Service—now known as Radio 4—since the Second World War. Gordon had this bright idea that there should be an *Archers* for Afghanistan: a radio soap opera dedicated to Afghan reconstruction, as *The Archers* had been envisaged as a tool for reconstruction in the post-war years.

Yes, it was very optimistic, in the early nineties, to think that Afghanistan would be entering an era of post-war reconstruction. It was also optimistic to think that I would be any good at running a soap opera for Afghanistan. I mean, I had no drama experience, not even any management experience. But the post was advertised and I was encouraged to apply—a clear sign that I was a leading candidate. I got the job.

The first thing I did was to arrange an appointment with Liz Rigbey. Liz had been editor of *The Archers* for some time. She was now script consultant for what seemed to me the sinisterly named *Marshall Plan for the Mind*. The original Marshall Plan happened in the post-war years. It was an American-financed plan for European reconstruction after World War II. The Marshall Plan for the Mind was a plan to assist the former Soviet Union in embracing capitalism. The BBC, no doubt with encouragement from the Foreign Office, thought that radio drama would be a good tool with which to explain how a market economy works.

Later in the nineties, the then prime minister Tony Blair made a cameo appearance on a Russian soap opera—I believe its name was *Dom Sem* (Neighbours)—produced by the *Marshall Plan for the Mind*. Liz Rigbey was a consultant with this soap opera. I remember one of his lines was 'in Britain, we have a saying: education, education, education'. Damn cheek, he pinched that saying from Lenin! I am sure lots of *Dom Sem*'s Soviet listeners picked up on that. As I was later to discover, the West even took the concept of storytelling based on keeping the listener on the edge of his/her seat from a well-known Islamic classic, *The Thousand and One Nights*. However, for the time being, I was more concerned with learning the basics of storytelling.

I had come to the right person. Liz was a darting, dashing, enthusiastic, painstaking, articulate mentor. 'Do Afghans have a tradition of storytelling?' she asked me. 'Of course they do,' I replied, not at that time knowing much about Afghan storytelling, but I did know that children in Swat used to sit riveted every night listening to the tales that their grandfather or grandmother would tell them. Prior to radio and television coming on the scene, an elderly grandmother or grandfather used to provide the entertainment in Afghan households. Some of these stories originated in Pashto and Farsi folklore: the stories of Mumin Khan and Shireen, of Yusuf Khan and Sherbano, of Farhad and Shireen. Shireen, as you can see—the word means sweet—is a popular name for the heroine in these regional variations of *Romeo and Juliet*. You can also surmise that while people everywhere love a story, they particularly like a love story.

Liz told me how *The Archers* had initially been carried along on the back of a blossoming romance between Phil and Grace Archer. Phil loved Grace, but he had no money. In order to marry her, he had to become a successful pig farmer. 'The nation,' Liz explained, 'was hooked on the romance. But in the process, they became expert pig farmers!' That is certainly one way that educational radio soap opera can work, but as I discovered, in Afghanistan one has to be careful with the romance part. In the early days of our Afghan *The Archers*, we had a romance, but we modelled it too closely on what a romance is like in Europe. We arranged clandestine meetings between the young couple. I quickly put a stop to this approach after some pretesting of the episodes that we did in Afghan refugee camps in Peshawar. 'What have you learnt from the soap opera?' Was one of the questions we asked in the pretesting. 'I have learnt never to let my daughter out of the house,' one lady answered, rather surprisingly. Why was that? 'Because if she leaves the house, she might meet a boy, they might have a romance, then my daughter will never be able to get married,' she replied, giving the example of the couple in our soap opera. Our romance was not Pashtoon enough. It was having the opposite effect. So we confined it within the bounds of Pashtoon propriety.

With Liz's encouragement and guidance, I took to the task at hand with enthusiasm. By the time I went on a management course at the BBC, I had a plan in mind for setting up the soap machine, as Liz called it. 'Wow, you've got it worked out, haven't you?' one of my fellow participants observed. At the time, Behrouz Afagh, hitherto from the BBC Persian service, was deputy head of training. 'He's got the best job in Bush House,' he observed about me. And when it came to setting up the office in Peshawar, I was able to function for about a month without any money! No funds had yet come in for BBC AED—the Afghan Education Drama—as I christened it. Everything was done on credit, through a friend of mine in Tehkal, on the outskirts of Peshawar, Ghafoor Khan.

At the time, a famous Pashtoon singer, Qamar Gula, was living in Peshawar. I had been a fan of Qamar Gula's for twenty years, since my prison days in Kabul in the early seventies. Her husband, the inimitable Zakhel, had been a stalwart of the specialist *Hujrah*

Majlis programme in the 1970s. The *Hujrah Majlis* was a music lovers' treat. It was placed in the iconic Pashtoonistan programme. The Pashtoonistan programme aired every day of the week in Daud Khan's time. On Thursday evenings, in the *Hujrah Majlis*, the programme was devoted to live music as was typically played in Pashtoon hujrahs. The tone of the music was mainly eastern Afghan. That was the typical character of the *Hujrah Majlis*. Otherwise, there are so many genres of Pashto music. While Zakhel was in the classical mould, his wife Qamar Gula was more part of popular culture. She put mainly contemporary poetry to compelling, tuneful songs. Her voice sounded as if it was ringing around the mountains of the Pashtoon lands.

So what better way could there be to inaugurate our office than by inviting Qamar Gula to play for us? She came to our new office, in Gul Mohar Lane in Peshawar's University Town, along with her sons and nephews. It is typical for a Pashtoon ensemble to contain members of the same family. She sang all the classics that I had been listening to for two decades: *I Flew Like a Pigeon* (*Laka Kontara Alwatama*) an ode to her beloved as she pretended to be a pigeon, hovering above his homestead, and the entrancing *Let's Make a Hut in the Jungle* (*Raza Chi Yaua Jora Kroo Jungara Puh Zangal Ke*), written by the Shinwari poet Amir Hamza. Haji Ghafoor Khan came out in front of Qamar Gula and performed an ecstatic dance. She saluted him, acknowledging his deep appreciation of the music. It was a thrill for everyone to have a chance to see Qamar Gula live. It was my first live music recording—later I was to record most prominent Pashto singers. I still have a copy of the recording. The evening cost twelve thousand rupees—that would have been about two hundred dollars in those days. I thought it was a good deal but Gordon questioned the propriety of such a 'stand-out' expense. I reckoned it was important, to instil the right spirit in our office.

The beginning of BBC AED was on a wing and a prayer. There was the factor of there not really being any money, only verbal commitments to Gordon Adam from the likes of UNICEF and ICRC. It took a month or two for these to materialize. And then the run-up to setting up the soap was surreal. On one of my previous

BBC duty trips, I had occasion to interview Zia-ul-Qamar, a senior teacher at Edwardes College in Peshawar. The interview was about the influence of satellite TV on Peshawar, in particular Indian shows. 'And look at the Indian soap opera *Gul Mohar Lane*,' he pointed out. 'The situations that develop in that drama are similar to those we face in our own lives.'

I scoured through the satellite TV schedules looking for *Gul Mohar Lane* but could not find any drama by that name. But when BBC AED established its office in Gul Mohar Lane, it struck a bell. 'Maybe this is the soap opera that Zia-ul-Qamar was referring to, reflecting real-life situations,' I thought. In any case, it was a strange and surreal coincidence. Later, we held a meeting with all the development actors and humanitarian agencies in Peshawar. We wanted to apprise them of our plans and explain to them that we would need their input to ensure that all the storylines of the soap opera would be on message, so to speak. I told the participants I was still looking for a name for the soap opera. Afterwards, a guy came up to me and said to me simply, '*Staso da dramey num Naway Kor, Naway Jhwand day*.' (The name of your soap opera is New Home, New Life.) Just like that. No introduction. No suggestion, it was more a statement of fact. The name stuck.

After twenty-five years in the radio drama business, I now know that you can do things on a shoestring and with a streamlined budget. Liz is right: soap opera is a machine. But it does not have to be a big machine. It can be a small, economical, well-oiled machine. Not being aware of this, initially we set about putting in place a big machine, with as many as twelve writers, several proofreaders, scores of actors and actresses, computer operators to write the scripts, and a synopsis coordinator to translate the drama synopses into English. In soap operas, a synopsis of each scene and episode is all-important. That is because each plot is so involved as it unfolds over several months that without a synopsis—in other words a structure—the writers will become entangled in the plot. To paraphrase Liz, 'writers hate writing them, editors hate reading them, but without a synopsis, there can be no soap.' She likened a synopsis to a skull. 'Even the most beautiful face does not have a beautiful skull, but no skull, no face.'

The problem was finding the staff for such a huge machine. We needed people with drama experience and people who could write in simple but eloquent Pashto and Dari. The soap opera was going to be in both these main languages of Afghanistan. In Peshawar, there were no eminent Dari writers, Peshawar being a centre of Pashtoon culture. Though Peshawar has great drama writers of its own, we needed to recruit Afghan Pashto writers, not ones from the Frontier. Our soap was aimed at Afghanistan, so the writers also had to be Afghan. Where to find such writers? It was then that something happened that solved our predicament. I don't know the intricacies and realities of the military situation on the ground in Kabul at the time, but what was bandied around was that Hekmatyar had launched a bombardment of Kabul on 1 January 1994. The civil war that ensued—it had been brewing ever since the mujahideen took over the capital in April 1992—led to an exodus of Kabul inhabitants from the city. Amongst them were the intelligentsia, the cream of Kabul's literary community. Many of them descended on our BBC AED office.

Amongst those who arrived at the *New Home, New Life* office a bit later than everyone else was Shirazuddin Siddiqui. Good-looking, speaking excellent English, completely bilingual in Pashto and Dari, he stood out from the other arrivals. His qualifications also appeared to be good. He had taught drama at Kabul University. By the time Shirazuddin applied for a position with BBC AED, most of the scriptwriters had already been appointed. Khaliq Rashid had taken his place as a proofreader. I knew him from a previous visit to Kabul with the BBC. He was able to confirm the professionalism of Shirazuddin, who joined Khaliq as the second proofreader, with Khaliq working on the Pashto scripts and Shirazuddin looking after the Dari scripts. Another person to turn up at BBC AED was Shireen Sultan. She was from Peshawar. Enthusiastic, energetic, bubbling with personality and good humour, I quickly appointed her to be in charge of audience research. Some of the initial dramas had already been recorded. Shireen took them to the Afghan refugee camps near Peshawar. There she set up listening panels to find out what people thought about the storylines of *New Home, New Life*.

It was during the course of this pretesting that we found out about the hidden message in our romantic storyline and quickly put an end to it, or at least confined it within the parameters of Pashtoon propriety. We were able to catch the popular mood more accurately with the first episode of *New Home, New Life*. Fittingly enough, it told the story of one of the families of Upper Village, where the radio drama was based, returning home from their time as refugees in Peshawar. On the way back to Upper Village, they were looted at one of the check-posts that at the time were ubiquitous all over Afghanistan. Besides communicating educational messages, it was always the aim of *New Home, New Life* to reflect the situation in the country. The time when the soap was set up, in the early 1990s, was a time of commander power in Afghanistan. All over the countryside, gunslingers had set up *pataks* (check-posts) at which they would loot and fleece the public. It was very difficult to travel in the countryside in Afghanistan in those days.

The power of radio drama is that no one feels targeted. People can see a reflection of themselves in the characters, but since these are fictional characters, they do not feel threatened. Rather, they have a chance to laugh at themselves and mend their ways before it is too late. We used this unique capacity of radio drama to lay into the commanders. We even showed one commander—Commander Shakoor—being boycotted by the local community because they were fed up with his cruelty and extortion. No one would provide him with men to carry out his nefarious activities. He mended his ways. No sooner had he mended his ways than another commander, the aptly named Haibat—which means terrifying—appeared on the scene. He made a pact with Jabbar Khan, the local khan in Upper Village. Part of the deal was that Jabbar Khan would give Haibat the hand of his daughter Shaperay in marriage.

Shaperay was having none of this. Why should she marry a man more than twice her age who already had a couple of wives and was a toothless, cruel brute? Together with the scriptwriters, we deliberated long and hard regarding what action Shaperay would take to avoid this cruel travesty of a match. We decided it would be best for her to attempt suicide but for the attempt to fail. We did not want to start a trend in Afghanistan of young women, married off to older men for the sake of money, committing suicide. I remembered a case that had been related by Bacha Khan. When he was passing by the Sardaryab bridge across the Kabul River one day, he saw a young lady jump off the bridge. Despite the attempts of local residents to rescue her, she drowned. Bacha Khan looked into the background to the case. It turned out that she had killed herself rather than be married off to an old, previously married man, as her father had agreed in exchange for a handsome amount of money. It is because of cases such as these that Pashtoon women have composed countless couplets:

> Stand up for my honour, my dear friend!
>
> My father is a profiteer and wants to give me away to the highest bidder.

So we decided that Shaperay would eat a lump of opium from her father's stash but would not die. It worked. Jabbar Khan decided that he could not let his daughter kill herself just to fulfil his promise to Haibat Khan. His daughter's life was more precious than his pledge. Of course, this led to a long vendetta with Haibat Khan in which Shakoor played a big role in combatting his former rival commander. Soap opera is both a huge responsibility as well as a challenge. One is literally holding the lives of one's listeners in one's hands. Give them the right message and they gain a life. Give them the wrong message, and they can easily lose their life. This was especially true of *New Home, New Life*. I do not know of any soap opera that had greater power than this radio drama. At the time, there was next to no entertainment—in fact I think I can safely say there was no entertainment—for the people of Afghanistan apart from this soap opera. Our audience research regularly showed above 70 per cent of the population tuning in. We had unprecedented listenership and wielded commensurate power. We had a huge duty to use that power for good.

Along with the Taliban, who started taking over the country at the end of 1994, *New Home, New Life* can take some credit for the demise of the commanders—the gunslingers—in Afghanistan. As the Taliban spread across the country, the first thing they did was to eliminate the commanders and clear the country of check-posts and robbers. *New Home, New Life* had certainly reflected the public disgust with the gunslingers. I remember, early in 1996, meeting a former commander who was now toeing the Taliban line in Ghazni, which at that time had already fallen under the control of the Taliban. 'You people at *New Home, New Life*,' he told me laughingly. 'You were the bane of us commanders!' Now there were new priorities. We held off—against my better judgment, it has to be said—running a storyline that would have seen Jabbar Khan's daughter-in-law Gulalai beaten up by Haibat in revenge for Jabbar Khan calling off the commander's engagement to Shaperay. Since our audience research team had witnessed a woman being beaten in Kabul, apparently for not adhering to the strict dress code of the Taliban, I felt that it would be suitable to run a short storyline showing Gulalai being dealt with by Haibat in this way and universal opprobrium of such cruel treatment of women ensuing in the radio drama. That is the wonderful thing about radio drama. One can broach such sensitive issues head on; instead of seeking to justify themselves, people who are doing such things themselves feel they had better mend their ways before they are found out, not realizing that they have already been found out.

Another storyline focusing on Gulalai showed how effective this approach can be. Gulalai was also a health worker in the local clinic. However, Jabbar Khan felt it would not be suitable for his daughter-in-law to be working outside the home. 'What will people say?' he said. 'That Jabbar Khan is depending on his daughter-in-law for a living?' So he forced her to stay at home instead of going to work in the health clinic. It just so happened that in those days the ladies of Upper Village were doing some carpet weaving. Amongst them was Jabbar Khan's wife Taj Bibi. One day, they all came down with food poisoning and had to be taken to the hospital. Jabbar Khan would not let his wife go to the hospital as there was no lady doctor to treat her. The punch line was easy. 'You are the one who has stopped Gulalai from working in the clinic!'

It just so happened that in those days I made a fact-finding trip to Kandahar, the headquarters of the Taliban, who at the time were at the zenith of their power in Afghanistan. I went in April 1997. I thought it would be a good idea to try and meet Mulla Omar, so I went along to his house, wrote a note in Pashto telling the Taliban leader who I was and sent the note inside. Meanwhile, I waited at the gate, chatting with some of his guards. 'Hey, John Butta,' they said to me. 'We do not hear your voice on the BBC nowadays. What happened to you, man?' I told them I was head of *New Home, New Life* so did not get a chance to do much actual broadcasting. 'Oh, you are in charge of *New Home, New Life*, are you? You have a Taliban representative on *New Home, New Life*, don't you?' I said no, there was no particular Taliban representative. 'Yes, there is,' they laughed, 'it is Jabbar Khan!' 'How on earth can he be your representative?' I said to them. 'He is an old, chillum-smoking, opium-growing good-for-nothing. He is nothing whatsoever like you!' 'Yes, he is,' the young *talibs* corrected me. 'He does not let his daughter-in-law go to work!'

Around this time, Shireen Sultan and her audience research team were visiting Jalalabad. As they passed by the Public Hospital, Sihat-e-Aama, in Jalalabad, the Taliban authorities in the hospital accosted them. 'So you guys are from *New Home, New Life* are you? Why are you running storylines suggesting that we do not allow women to go to work? Would you like to come inside and see how many women are working in our hospital?' At that time, I also visited the Indira Gandhi Hospital in Wazir Akbar Khan in Kabul. There also plenty of women were working as doctors and nurses. I cannot say that our storyline was solely responsible for women returning to work in health facilities during the Taliban time, but, as with our earlier storyline on the gunslinging commanders, it certainly helped capture the public mood, not to mention need, and gave impetus to this change of policy.

I never did get to meet Mulla Omar, but I did meet the person who was considered to be number two in the Taliban movement, the governor of Kandahar, Mohammad Hasan Akhund. We had a long and engaging conversation. 'What messages would you like us to communicate in *New Home, New Life*?' I asked him. He told me that a lot of people who returned from Pakistan to Afghanistan did not realize how strong the currents were in Afghan rivers. Children thought they could just swim in Afghan rivers, like they did in Pakistan. They tended to get washed away in the currents, he told me. The other point he mentioned was the value of time. 'Do not waste time,' he stressed. 'A person who wastes time is a big thief.' I found Mohammad Hasan Akhund to be a thoughtful, friendly person. He certainly was so to me. He remembered my visit to Panjwai, as a BBC reporter, in 1992. However, he was not so polite towards everyone. I heard that in one meeting with UN officials in Kandahar, he threw a thermos full of tea at one of them.

The thing is, the Taliban related to our storytelling approach and responded positively to it. I visited several Taliban departments while I was in Kandahar. In the *shahrwali*—the city municipality—the deputy head told me that *New Home, New Life* was '*tadbeer'al-manzil* '. The use of this term pleased me very much since I had first heard it from Shaykh'al-Quran in Panjpir. The phrase '*tadbeer'al-manzil*' refers to education on how one should act in the home sphere: mother and child health, relations between various members of the household, things like that. Several *Surah's* of the Quran, particularly *Surah an-Nisa* (women), *Surah an-Noor* (light), *Surah al- Hujurat* (apartments) are devoted to tadbeer'al-manzil. It was a great compliment, I felt, on the part of the deputy *shahrwal* to refer to *New Home, New Life* in this manner. I suppose it was also a backhanded compliment on the part of some hardliners in the Taliban ruling council when they brought up the subject of *New Home, New Life* in one of their meetings in Kandahar. '*New Home, New Life* is education,' they contended. 'It should be our job to impart education to the Afghan people, not the job of the BBC.' 'That is true,' others in the ruling council responded, 'but until and unless we have the expertise and wherewithal to impart this education, we should be happy that the BBC is doing so.' It goes without saying that the latter argument won the day.

Those who are aware of the situation in Afghanistan under the Taliban may wonder how our audience research team, under Shireen Sultan, managed to work under their regime. Wasn't it forbidden for women to work outside the home? It was, but not for us. Once, Taliban authorities in Kunar challenged Shireen and her team. 'Oh, you are from *New Home, New Life*, Nazir's drama,[1] are you? That's okay then. You are free to work wherever you wish.' I

---

[1] Nazir was a very popular character of *New Home, New Life*: A comic character, the servant of a generally villainous character, Jabbar Khan.

have thought long and hard about why it was that *New Home, New Life* was so influential with them. I believe this was because it tapped the tradition of storytelling that is so deeply embedded in Islam. As Shaykh'al-Qur'an used to put it, the Qur'an puts forward three types of argument, three types of proof of the power of God. On the one hand, there are the proofs provided by nature—scientific and empirical evidence—one may call these proofs. Then there are the proofs of revelation, the miracle of the Qur'an, for example—its inimitable style, its enduring appeal and relevance. Then there are stories, for the most part stories about the prophets. These stories are based on the elemental principle of drama: negative characters—those who do not believe; positive characters—the prophets and their companions; and transitional characters—those who believe on the basis of the preaching and actions of the prophets and their companions. So characterization, one of the key principles of radio soap opera, is familiar to people of faith-based learning, as the leaders of the Taliban such as Mohammad Hasan Akhund were.

The other key element in radio soap opera is suspense, keeping listeners wondering what is going to happen next. The origin of suspense is also familiar in the Islamic world, from the inimitable and ground-breaking *The Thousand and One Nights* (*Alfu Laylah wa Laylatun*, as the original is known in Arabic) the stories of which are laden with suspense. These tales from the Abbasid era—the glory days of Baghdad—constitute the invention of modern soap opera. They are the perfection of both suspense and storytelling that I still aspire to in both storytelling and soap opera. Then, besides the elements of characterization and suspense, there was the fact that any criticism, any helpful suggestions as to how people might wish to change their behaviour, are couched in oblique terms in radio drama. No one takes offence. We have seen how this was helpful with the case of the commanders and the women's employment storyline that at least helped the Taliban to allow women to return to work in health facilities.

There was a lot more that we could have done to influence Taliban policy and which I should have insisted on as the head of BBC AED. To this day, I feel great remorse that we did not highlight the big issues of the day. We had already shown that our storylines could be helpful in pushing the Taliban in a more positive direction.

In my own defence, by this time I had handed over the running of the drama to Shirazuddin, who had risen to be deputy head of BBC AED. I did indeed draft two storylines on hot issues of the day, but they did not see the light of day. I was Shirazuddin's boss, I should have ensured that the storylines ran. In the case of the beating of women storyline that I mentioned above, I had a long, heated discussion with Shirazuddin over my dinner table in Peshawar, in the presence of Gordon Adam and my boss at BBC World Service, David Morton. Shirazuddin's contention was that running this storyline would put our audience research team at risk in Afghanistan. To me, that showed a lack of understanding of the power of drama. None of my seniors took my side. Shirazuddin was by this time the blue-eyed boy of the BBC. My star was on the wane.

No one says such things openly, but to this day I feel that the predominant desire amongst secular Afghans, and in the West, is to wish groups like the Taliban away, rather than to seek any kind of constructive dialogue—even less a rapprochement—with them. There is an aversion to seeking common ground, working together or even trying to bring groups like the Taliban within the fold, so to speak. To my mind, this attitude has contributed to the ever-deepening conflict that has dominated world politics over the last decade and a half. The Talib ban on opium production in Afghanistan is a case in point and shows the situation clearly in microcosm. In 2000, the Taliban issued a decree banning opium cultivation and production in Afghanistan. The story in Afghanistan was that Mulla Omar had seen a dream suggesting that the drought in Afghanistan—the country had suffered about eight years of drought—was due to their cultivation of opium. It is believable that Mulla Omar might have taken this step on the basis of a dream. That is the kind of people the Taliban are, or at least were. One should note that a Talib ban meant a ban: such was their authority in Afghanistan. After the ban, no one in Afghanistan would have the temerity to grow the crop. However, instead of reacting positively, the reaction of the international community was almost universally negative: oh, they have only banned opium cultivation and production in order to push up the price of the stockpiles they already have! It was as if the international community was frustrated with the Taliban for doing something so civilized. How dare they rob us of a reason to attack them!

This reaction of the international community caused the Taliban considerable annoyance. They did not reverse their decision, but it was at this time that they started thinking: what can we do that will really annoy these damned Westerners? We have done something that they should welcome, but they are using it as an excuse to attack us even more. It was then that they hit on the idea of blowing up the Buddhas of Bamiyan, something they enacted in March 2001. When I visited Kandahar in April 1997, the Taliban had no intention of blowing up the Buddhas. They castigated the Western media for spreading rumours suggesting that this was their intention. At that time, AFP had interviewed a commander in Ghorband, near Bamiyan. His name was Abdul Wahid. 'What are you going to do with these Buddhas in Bamiyan when you take Bamiyan?' the AFP reporter had somewhat mischievously asked. Predictably enough, Abdul Wahid said he was going to blow them up. 'What the hell are you guys in the media doing interviewing commanders about policy matters?' senior Taliban officials in Kandahar said to Alan Johnston and myself. 'We are the policymakers. Such matters concern us.' Alan at that time was BBC correspondent in Kabul. Some of you may remember that later on he gained worldwide fame when he was abducted in Palestine. He still works on the Middle East for the BBC. Alan accompanied me on my trip to Kandahar. 'Do you not intend to blow them up?' we asked Mutawwakil,[2] amongst others. No, he told us, since the Buddhas were not being worshipped, there was no reason to blow them up. One other senior official of the Taliban—Bashir Agha, deputy head of foreign relations likened the Western media's scaremongering about the Buddhas of Bamiyan to a Persian proverb:

Ab na raseeda, moza az pa mekashee

You have not yet reached the water, but are already taking off your shoes

[2] Abdul Wakil Mutawakkil, a senior Taliban leader and at this time foreign affairs spokesman of the Taliban.

This situation had not changed by March 2001—still, no one was worshipping the Buddhas of Bamiyan. By this time, I had taken over as Muslim chaplain—imam—at Cambridge University. I took it upon myself to write to Mulla Omar, in Pashto, on my chaplaincy letterhead, giving reasons from the Qur'an why in my opinion the Buddhas should not be blown up. First of all, I rang the head of the information and culture department in Kandahar, Abdul Hayy Mutmain. 'I want to write to your head requesting him not to blow up the Buddhas,' I told him. 'Could you please give me a fax number?' He gave me the number and added that this fax machine was in Mulla Omar's own room. One reason that the Taliban were giving for their intention to blow up the Buddhas was that it was possible, if the Buddhas remained intact, that they would be worshipped once again. How, I pointed out in my letter, could Muslims give up worship of God on High and start worshipping mud and stone? Was this not an underestimation of Islam, not to mention of Afghans? I also cited the example of Pharoah's mummy,[3] which is still preserved in the Cairo Museum and which the Qur'an has mentioned is 'a sign for coming generations' (*Yunus* 10:92), in other words a sign that the power of Allah exceeded even that of a great ruler like Pharoah. These Buddhas were also a sign of how great a civilization preceded Islam for Islam to have superseded it, I pointed out. But it was too late, as everyone knows. The hardliners had gained the initiative within the Taliban. Their mind was made up. The Buddhas were going to be destroyed.

[3] That is the Pharoah who was ruling Egypt at the time of the Prophet Moses, and who was drowned in the Red Sea, as Moses and the Children of Israel escaped to Palestine.

XX

BATTLEGROUND OF EDUCATION

Recite in the name of your Lord—the Creator. He created mankind from a clot. Recite, and your Lord is the Most Munificient. He taught use of the pen, and He taught man what he knew not.

(*Al-Alaq* 96:1-5, the first verses of the Qur'an that were revealed to the Prophet)

It was early 2008 when a friend of mine from Madyan, Ahmad Hussain, said to me, 'John, you have to do something to fix the situation in Swat. You can do it, no one else can.' Ahmad Hussain was Khayr'an-Nisa's second husband, after she was divorced from the pir sahib of Madyan. Ahmad Hussain and Khayr'an-Nisa had married in Abdul Samad and my house in Peshawar, in 1985. They then moved to England. Later, Ahmad Hussain married Saima, from the Mian clan of Madyan. It was when Ahmad Hussain suggested it, that I determined to set up a radio station in Swat, one reflecting the traditions and wishes of the people of the Swat valley.

I was in a good position to do this. Ever since 2004, when I set up PACT Radio in Peshawar, I had been building up *Da Pulay Poray* (Across the Border), the PACT Radio brand. Like my involvement in the constitutional process in Afghanistan from 2002 to 2004, the story of PACT Radio started with a call to my chaplaincy in Cambridge. This time the call came from Ivan Sigal, regional director of the Internews Network in Bangkok. He wondered if I would be interested in heading a Pakistan–Afghanistan cross-border radio project for Internews. I had already worked with Internews in Afghanistan. They had set up dozens of local radio stations up and down the country. I jumped at the idea. I was interviewed for the job on the phone, pretty much then and there. As far as I know, I was the only candidate. It was my job. It was meant for me.

The name PACT came from different sources. First of all, it came from the origin of the word pact, in other words pax, which means peace. Our programmes would be aimed at the establishment of peace. The programmes would promote and extol peace. Secondly, the funding for PACT came to Internews through another organization called Pact, so our project was quickly labelled the Pact project. Thirdly, and probably most prominently, it was the Pak–Afghan Cross-border Radio Training project (PACT Radio). There was also a loose association with Pashto, pronounced as Pakhto in the northern part of the Pashto-speaking parts. Our programmes would have a Pashto character. There were some objections from Internews. But the name fitted. It still does, more than fifteen years on from our foundation. Funding through Pact and Internews quickly petered out. But PACT pressed on as an independent production company. So did the Da Pulay Poray brand. In 2011, it relocated lock, stock and barrel to Afghanistan, where all its operations are now based[1], in the predominantly Pashto-speaking east and south of the country. But between 2007 and 2009, Swat became the focal point of its activities.

Swat has been a recurring theme throughout this book. As a hippie then a *talib* in the 1970s, as a hermit then as one of the editors of the *Frontier Post* in the 1980s, as head of BBC AED in the 1990s, then while heading PACT Radio in the noughties, I was always returning—most weekends—to my home in Swat. It was my adopted *watan* (home country), my *kali* (village). Even more than that, it represented my spiritual identity. It was the supreme

[1] PACT Radio folded in 2020, with the retirement of Pashtoon Englishman.

hippie home of the 1970s; I came to being a Pashtoon, being a Muslim, being a *talib* in Swat. Dozens of my fellow hippie wayfarers, Aisha and Suleiman, Abdul Samad and Fatima, Mustafa and Saleema, also came to Islam in Swat. It was hardly believable that it had become a centre of conflagration. It was certainly not acceptable. I took up Ahmad Hussain's suggestion and made it my mission to do what I could to restore Swat to its peaceful, harmonious nature: the nature that had first captivated me when I walked over the Malakand Pass in early 1970 in the company of Boris and Cheryl and looked down on the tapestry of tiny and terraced fields that made up the Swat valley.

The first time Swat blew up was in 1994. It was the exact time, in November 1994, that the Taliban reared their head in Kandahar. Strange really, two movements, almost exactly the same in their aims and constitution, making themselves manifest at the same time in the extreme southwest and the extreme northeast—at opposite ends—of the Pashto-speaking world. At the head of the Swat movement of 1994 was Sufi Mohammad. In a flash, his movement for the enforcement of Islamic law, Tehreek-e-Nafaz-e-Shariat-e-Mohammadi (TNSM), had taken over large swathes of the Swat valley, including the airport at Kanju, across the river from the Swat capital of Mingora. The occupation of the TNSM extended into the Dir valley, adjacent to Swat, and to the Indus valley, running parallel to the east of the Swat valley. The movement was particularly strong in Matta, across the river from Khwazakhela and at the mouth of a Swat River tributary that runs down through Garhi Chupriyal, where I studied for a short while in the early 1970s. There, in Matta, TNSM rounded up a large number of lawyers and judges and kept them hostage in the district courts. There was supposed to have been a battle for the airport, which was also in the hands of TNSM zealots, but the word was that the Pashtoon Frontier Constabulary and Frontier Corps militiamen were firing in the air, not wishing to kill their Pashtoon brothers, especially ones who had risen in support of *Shariah*.

There are a couple of clues here as to the origins and causes of the *Shariah* movement in Swat. The first factor is the emphasis on law and order. The demand for *Shariah* was in fact a demand for law and order. Ever since Swat had become part of Pakistan in 1970, miscarriages of justice were commonplace. People were paying bribes and getting off scot-free for the most terrible crimes. It was just such an incident, of a man going free when he had killed his own child at the instigation of his second wife, that led to the anger in Matta, so people said. The Swat insurgencies of the nineties and noughties were thus essentially movements for law and order. From 1920 until 1970, Swat had been ruled by a father-son dynasty. The father was known as Badshah Sahib, the son, as Wali Sahib. Their full names were Miangul Abdul Wadood and Miangul Jehanzeb. The title *mian* means that a person is descended from a saint. The people of Madyan—people like Ahmad Hussain—were *mians* by descent from Akhund Darweza. The rulers of Swat were *mians* by virtue of descent from Saidu Baba of Swat. Being direct descendants of the Saidu Baba naturally added to the legitimacy of this father-son team, particularly in view of the fact that Saidu Baba's shrine is located in the middle of Saidu Sharif, the seat of government of Swat.

During the time of the Swat dynasty, law and order was exemplary in Swat. It really was a model, modern Muslim welfare state. Badshah Sahib had concentrated on law and order. During his reign, in the early decades of the twentieth century, he confiscated weapons from the general public and settled all vendettas. He established peace and the rule of law in Swat. Badshah Sahib abdicated in favour of his son, Wali Sahib, in 1949. Wali Sahib focused on building a welfare state in which everyone was assured of free healthcare and free education, not to mention access to justice. It was only twenty-four years after the end of Wali Sahib's rule that the clamour for *Shariah* reared its head. In fact, this movement was more a longing for the rule of law of Wali Sahib's time than a demand for *Shariah* in itself. In the time of Wali Sahib and Badshah Sahib, there was indeed *Shariah* in Swat. Yet it was the type of enlightened *Shariah* that welcomed Queen Elizabeth to Swat in 1961, at the height of Wali Sahib's rule. People in Swat were restless, frustrated at the turmoil that had ensued in their valley following the accession of Swat to Pakistan. They gave vent to their frustration in a demand for *Shariah*.

We mentioned Matta as one of the centres of Sufi Mohammad's *Shariah* movement. Matta lies on the western side of the Swat River. Not only Matta, but all towns on the western side of the Swat River were prone to radicalization at this time and even more so later when Sufi Mohammad's son-in-law Fazlullah launched a far harsher, uncompromising and radical movement in 2007–08. Towns on the other, eastern side of the river were largely untouched by these movements. Noticing this, my mind went back to when I returned to Swat from Deoband in 1984. I was looking for a place to live and thought of Garhi Chapriyal, just up the tributary river from Matta, on the western side of the river. 'This is not a good place to live,' Mulla Khalid Khan's brother told me. 'Our side of the river is no good.'

On the eastern, more developed side of the river, the main road runs from Batkhela to Mingora, then on to Madyan at the beginning of Upper Swat. All investment, all tourism, is on the eastern side of the river. The menfolk on the western side of the river have no choice but to work in Karachi and the Gulf, leaving families to fend for themselves back in Swat. With the restrictions on the movement of women in Swat, it is difficult for mothers and elder sisters to keep an eye on male children outside the home. They become easy prey for radicals. I had experience of such extremist Matta mullas on the way to Peshawar one day. It was around 2006. There were a couple of radical mullas sitting in the bus. I happened to be reading

D.H. Lawrence's *The Rainbow* that day, to while away the time while I was making the five-hour or so journey to Peshawar. I must say the two mullas seemed like latter-day Panjpiris. I could recognize this from the tone in which they accosted some students sitting near them in the bus, whom for some reason they accused of being members of Maulana Maududi's Jamaat-e-Islami.

The driver turned the music on. 'Turn that bloody music off,' they said to him, or words to that effect. 'It's my bus and I can do what I like,' the driver was not in a mood to be intimidated by these rampant mullas. The two mullas turned to me, buried in *The*

Rainbow. 'Can't you see this grey-bearded man?' they said, trying to press their point home. 'Can't you see he is reading the Quran?' I considered caution the better part of valour and refrained from saying that on this occasion I was not reading the Holy Book but in fact was reading a book by the author of *Lady Chatterley's Lover*. The bus drove on to Mardan, where the pair of mullas decided to alight. They had already paid as far as Peshawar and wanted a refund. 'Go on your way,' the bus conductor told them. He refused to give them back a paisa. 'It's the same price to Mardan as it is to Peshawar.' Everyone heaved a sigh of relief. 'These are Swat's version of Mulla Omar,' one of the passengers remarked to me. I nodded. 'A good deal worse than Mulla Omar,' I thought. That is indeed how it turned out.

In 1994, the head of the Frontier Corps was a major general by the name of Fazal Ghafoor. A thorough Pashtoon gentleman, he preferred not to use force to solve the crisis. This was in evidence in the 'battle' for the airport, when his men fired in the air rather than kill their fellow Pashtoons. Major General Fazal Ghafoor made it his business to find Maulana Sufi Mohammad. He persuaded the maulana to prevail upon his men to vacate the places they had occupied. The TNSM activists had taken over key locations not only throughout the Swat valley but also some in the Indus valley. Starting from the Matta courts, along with the lawyers and judges who had been taken captive, the pair of Pashtoon elders, Fazal Ghafoor and Sufi Mohammad, went from place to place. Sufi Mohammad would say to people that he had not enjoined on them to use force and take hostages. He would use his authority to ensure that they released all the hostages and vacated the government buildings they had occupied. Some vague assurances were also given regarding the implementation of *Shariah*, which of course were never carried out.

As with the Taliban that TNSM spawned, Maulana Sufi Mohammad and his followers were very strict about not allowing photography. This, alongside music, was the type of superficial measure they attached a lot of importance to in their version of *Shariah*. As he was leaving Matta with Major General Fazal Ghafoor and their repertoire, Sufi Mohammad said a few words to the assembled people from the press. Then he held up his hand to tell them not to take photographs. Zubair Mir, a photographer with the *Frontier Post*, mischievous as ever, clicked him just as he was holding up his hand. Below the photo was a caption 'Maulana Sufi Mohammad asking press people not to take his picture'. It was a good photo. Part of the deal with Sufi Mohammad was that *Shariah* would be introduced in Swat. The provincial government called it *Nizam-e-Adl* (the System of Justice). Of course, they were not sincere in their promise, nor was it practical. How can one introduce a system in one part of a province, in one part of a country, which does not pertain in the rest of the country? And anyway, what did they mean by *Shariah*? A few punishments? Banning of music and films? Surely there should be more to *Shariah* than that. Why did they not say: we want you to impose the rule of law—whichever law—while at the same time enforcing it?

The next impractical and implausible step taken by Sufi Mohammad was in 2001. The American bombardment of the Taliban government was about to go into full swing in Afghanistan when Sufi Mohammad decided to take a lashkar of people from Swat and Dir to Afghanistan. He was able to rouse public emotions to such a pitch that a huge number of people took part in his lashkar. Some of them were even carrying spades as weapons: perhaps they took the name of the Americans' favourite weapon, the Daisy Cutter, a bit too literally. Even the Taliban authorities in Afghanistan implored the Swat lashkar not to come, telling them that there was nothing they could do to help and that they themselves would become a target for American bombs and the Taliban would have difficulty accommodating them, but Sufi Mohammad was not preoccupied with practicalities. His job was rabble-rousing. When Sufi Mohammad returned to Pakistan with a depleted lashkar he was promptly sent to Dera Ismail Khan jail—the most feared and austere jail in the Frontier. The government of General Musharraf was after all an ally of the Americans in the war on terror. Sufi Mohammad remained in jail until the government hauled him out in 2008 in an attempt to pacify the now more radical and extreme Swat *Shariah* hordes—followers of his son-in-law, the infamous Radio Mulla Fazlullah. I guess they were hoping that the same trick that had worked with Fazal Ghafoor and Sufi Mohammad in 1994 would work again in 2008. But things had moved on from then. The *amir* now was Fazlullah. No one was ready to listen to the elder Sufi, least of all his own son-in-law.

Others who had joined in the *lashkar* to Afghanistan had been released, so people said in Swat. Sufi Mohammad, they said, had preferred to remain in jail since the people who had lost loved ones in the doomed *lashkar* wanted to ask him why he had taken them to Afghanistan. Almost every village seemed to have lost some men in the *lashkar*. In my own adopted village Madyan, for instance, one Taalimand joined the *lashkar* and never came back. Malala Yousafzai also mentions one such person in her graphic account of the rise of militancy in Swat, *I am Malala.*[2] I am not sure how true it was that the government was keeping Sufi Mohammad in jail at his own request to protect him from the angry people of Swat, but it shows the resentment that he aroused in Swat following his futile trip to Afghanistan.

The cry of these zealots—from Sufi Mohammad to Fazlullah—was *Shariah* or Martrydom (*Shariat ya Shahadat*). Both Sufi Mohammad and Fazlullah are said to have studied at some stage in the Panjpir madrasa, Sufi Mohammad under Shaykh'al-Qur'an himself. They would have done well to remember the shaykh's focus on the *Sunnah*—something that every individual is able to adopt—as opposed to *Shariah*, which is a society matter, out of the control of any individual. Or maybe I am doing Fazlullah a disservice. I never met him or Sufi Mohammad, but when I used to pass through Fazlullah's village on my way to Madyan on the weekends, people would tell me that he was so attached to the *Sunnah* that he preferred to ride on a horse, like the Holy Prophet, as opposed to using a car. That would seem to be an example of getting the wrong end of the stick as far as the *Sunnah* is concerned. If only he had considered the use of bombs and suicide bombers as also against the *Sunnah* and had stuck to using a sword instead. That

[2] Malala Yousafzai and Christina Lamb, *I Am Malala: The Story of the Girl Who Stood Up for Education and Was Shot by the Taliban*, Little, Brown and Company, 2013.

would have been a favour to all concerned. When he started taking over large swathes of Swat territory and blowing up people, our caretaker in Swat, Ghani-ur-Rahman, commented to me that the Pakistan Army was bound to enter into the conflict to take back the territory. That is what happened. This time, it was not possible for the Frontier Corps and Frontier Constabulary to contain the situation. As if to press the point home, there was a big bomb attack on their headquarters near the river, on the route to Kanju in Mingora. Whether by accident, design or invitation, the Pakistan Army was quickly on the scene. The only lasting outcome of the Swat *Shariah* movement has been that while in the past Swat was a backwater, the valley has now become a base for the Pakistan Army.

A couple of events contributed to the strengthening of Radio Mulla Fazlullah. One was the earthquake of October 2005. It just so happened that the earthquake was strongest in those areas of Hazara and Pakistan-held Kashmir where militant camps had been established. The inmates of these camps who survived the earthquake had to be moved elsewhere. A number of them were moved to Swat, where they bolstered the cadres of Mulla Fazlullah. I personally know the case of one Haji sahib in Tehkal, on the outskirts of Peshawar. The case is typical of how young, impressionable madrasa students ended up in these camps. His son was learning the Qur'an in the Namak Mandi madrasa in Peshawar. He had memorized more than half the Qur'an when, all of a sudden, there was no sign of the boy. After asking several people about his son over a period of about two weeks, Haji sahib was led to a camp in the Icherrian area of Mansehra. There, he found his son being given jihad training. Haji sahib is a big and fearless guy. He is a pious Tablighi type also. He grabbed the guy in charge of the camp by the scruff of the neck. 'Did I send my son to learn the Qur'an, or did I send him to learn how to shoot a gun?' He took his son back home. Another factor that contributed to the intensity of Fazlullah's movement was the storming of Lal Masjid in Islamabad in July 2007. The two brothers who ran Lal Masjid, Abdul Aziz and Abdul Rashid Ghazi, were close to Fazlullah. They had started introducing the same type of Taliban writ in Islamabad, the national capital, that Fazlullah had introduced in Swat! In particular, their wrath was focused on music, DVD and CD shops, as if all un-Islamic activities were contained in listening to music and watching films. The thing that was unique about Lal Masjid was that its main cadres were made up of women. Alongside the boys' madrasa in Lal Masjid was a flourishing women's madrasa in which the wives and daughters of the brothers Abdul Aziz and Abdul Rashid were active. The government of General Pervaiz Musharraf moved in, killing well over a hundred people in a determined operation to flush militants out of Lal Masjid. Abdul Rashid Ghazi was amongst those killed in the operation. Some of the militants were able to escape to Swat. There was a marked hardening of the tone of Fazlullah in Swat following the Lal Masjid operation.

Before Malala Yousafzai was asked by Abdul Hai Kakar of the BBC World Service to write a diary of a school-going girl out of school, PACT Radio started making moves to set up our own live radio station in Swat. A former colleague of mine at the *Frontier Post*, Gul Kareem, was now working with the press and information department of North-West Frontier Province. He was in touch with a colonel of the Signals Unit based in the Malakand Pass, Colonel Muzaffar, about setting up a radio station by the name of *Hamara Swat* (Our Swat). One of the journalists and trainees at the PACT Radio office in Peshawar was Adnan Rashid. He was a native of Saidu Sharif, just upriver from Gulkada, where Malala's family lived. He and I entered into discussions with Colonel Muzaffar, who seemed happy that professional journalists should take on the task of setting up the radio station as opposed to the army putting out propaganda. As with PACT Radio programmes in general, our approach in Swat was non-confrontational. We did not pick a fight with anyone. We could not afford to do so, with our office in the middle of Mingora known to all and sundry and our broadcasts going out morning and evening. In particular, we sought to temper the divide between school education and madrasa education. In her graphic and vivid autobiography, *I Am Malala*, Malala tends to make out that school education is the only worthwhile education. In fact, she ridicules madrasa education.

> In Pakistan, madrassahs are a kind of welfare system as they give free food and lodging, but their teaching does not follow a normal curriculum. The boys learn the Qur'an by heart, rocking back and forth as they recite. They learn that there is no such thing as science or literature, that dinosaurs never existed and that man never went to the moon. *I Am Malala*, Malala

Such inaccurate ridicule of the madrasa system is only likely to increase the divide between those who favour madrasa education and those who favour school education. Our approach in Swat was to lessen this divide, not exacerbate it. In our morning transmission, we included a Qur'an lesson with an explanation of the holy book as well as recitation. It is important for people to get into the habit from a young age of reflecting on the verses of the Qur'an, not just reciting them parrot-like. We also had a programme called *Question and Answer*, in which people could ask questions on major themes related to the practice of their religion. On one occasion, a listener did comment to Adnan, 'You've got a lot of religious programmes, haven't you?' but generally, our religious programmes went down well. Once, Da Pulay Poray Radio in Swat was off-air for a few days—I can't remember for what reason. A lady phoned into PACT Radio and told us that every day boys and girls would come to her house to learn the Qur'an from our programme. 'They are just sitting here doing nothing now,' she complained, 'because your programme is off-air.' She was happy when we assured her that Da Pulay Poray Radio would be on-air again soon.

I was reminded of the danger of playing to the Western gallery on the issue of education when Malala gave a speech to the Nobel Committee in Oslo, accepting her Nobel Peace Prize. Malala's oratory on this occasion was outstanding. As far as the content of the speech was concerned, she plied her usual line of the Taliban being against education and education being so important, especially for girls. It sometimes sounds as if the main battle between the Taliban and their opponents is being waged in the field of education. Does it really have to be so? The word *talib* does after all mean seeker of knowledge. There is no question of any *talib* or any Muslim being against education. The question, in a Pashtoon context, is which education. The Taliban would contend that a madrasa education is more important for women than a modern school education. There are flaws in this argument—both school and madrasa are important. There are also deficiencies in the modern madrasa curriculum, which some are seeking to address. By the same coin, it also might be true that the normal school curriculum does not seem very relevant to a Pashtoon girl, who is likely to get married while still in her teens and subsequently bring up her children. Maybe both school and madrasa curriculums should be looked at to make them more oriented towards the needs of women in traditional Muslim societies. In any case, no useful purpose is served by denigrating madrasa or school education. They need to coexist.

It may come as a surprise to some, considering that the two groups are considered poles apart, but to my mind the people who have been marginalized more than anyone else in Pashtoon society are *talibs*—madrasa students—on the one hand and women on the other. We made a special effort to involve both these groups in our work. In 2008, PACT Radio started setting up media training centres in madrasas on both sides of the border. These training centres have produced some of our best reporters. One Swat *talib* who followed our radio journalism training course in Darul Uloom Sarhad in Peshawar became one of our most active Swat reporters. In those days, anyone who looked like a *talib* in Peshawar was liable to be picked up by the police. That is what happened to our Swat reporter when he was on his way to our training. When he, along with another *talib* friend of his, did not turn up to the training one day, we looked into why they were absent, found out about their arrest and were able to persuade the authorities to release them, upon which they resumed their training with us in Darul Uloom Sarhad.

We did quite a few training courses in the run-up to the launch of PACT Live Radio Swat.

The most satisfying, by far, was one that I conducted along with one of our senior producers from Peshawar, Freshta Shaykhani. Freshta was originally from Panjshir in the Tajik heartland of

Afghanistan, but she had become acclimatized to life in Peshawar and spoke good Pashto. She even had a role in our Da Pulay Poray radio drama. Over one week, we trained about eighteen female reporters from the length and breadth of the Swat valley. Militancy was at its height in Swat when we conducted this training in the Wali Sahib's old guesthouse, now the White Palace Hotel in Marghuzar, above the Swat capital of Mingora. I must say the ladies concerned were brave to venture out during that time. Many of the ladies who were trained did contribute to our programmes, but some of them also faced problems later on, for example, peers would make fun of their fiancés: look at the girl you are going to marry, she is reporting on the radio! Another outgoing girl from Mangalore, where there are a lot of Buddhist remains from the old Gandhara civilization that once flourished in Swat, faced problems with her uncles, who did not let her go to work. Her own parents obviously had no problem with her working since they had let her go to the workshop in the first place. All our work, involving both conservatives and progressives, madrasa- educated and school-educated, *talibs* and women, was aimed at healing the big rift in Pashtoon society, a rift that stems to a large degree from where a person was educated.

EPILOGUE
THE CONFLUENCE

I will not give up, until I reach the confluence of two streams.

Al-Kahf 18:60

If one thing is clear from the preceding pages, it is that there is cleavage, a rift in Pashtoon society. This is the rift between the two wings of Pashtoon society, the religious, conservative elements on the one hand, and those who associate with the more secular side of Pashtoon life on the other. Looking at my own life, wedged in between these two bodies of Pashtoon opinion, one thing that stands out is that I have imbibed influences from both strands: I have drunk from both streams of Pashtoon society—the religious and the secular. I can, and do, see both sides of the picture. Of that I am grateful.

One can put a date on the rift. It was 1929, when Amir Amanullah Khan abdicated as king of Afghanistan. Amanullah Khan has become a hero for the secular progressive forces amongst the Pashtoons. But clearly the Pashtoons were far from united in support of Amanullah Khan. Before finally abdicating and ceding power to the Tajik leader Bacha Saqao, Amanullah Khan had faced two uprisings from Pashtoon tribes. Firstly, there was the uprising of

Gud Mulla—the lame mulla from the southern tribes of Khost. If that uprising had been repelled, the next uprising, by the western Shinwari tribe, was key in deposing Amir Amanullah. As the Shinwaris took Jalalabad, Bacha Saqao descended on Kabul, triggering the amir's abdication.

If there is one person who embodied the rift, it was Khan Abdul Ghaffar Khan, known amongst the Pashtoons as Bacha Khan. Until 1929, Bacha Khan had been arm-in-arm with the *ulema*. He had taken his lead from Deoband. Almost all those who joined him in setting up independent schools in and around his home village of Utmanzai were *ulema*. The patron of the schools was Haji Sahib Turangzai, the outstanding spiritual leader in the Hashtnagar area. Ghaffar Khan's eldest son Ghani was a student in madrasa. But with the abdication of Amir Amanullah in Afghanistan, all that changed. Ghaffar Khan blamed an alliance of the British and the Muslim clergy for opposing Amanullah's reforms. In future, he set himself apart from the *ulema*. Ghani was taken out of madrasa. The battle lines were drawn for an ongoing tussle between Pashtoon nationalists and Pashtoon clergy, between the secular and the religious. The Pashtoons are still living with this confrontation. There is another lesson to be learnt from the Amanullah Khan saga. It is that in order to achieve anything worthwhile amongst the Pashtoons, one has to take the *ulema* with one. Any initiative that does not have the clergy's blessing is doomed to failure as far as the Pashtoons are concerned. It is a lesson that the next great leader of the Pashtoons, the president of Afghanistan from 1986 till 1992, Dr Najib, learnt over the course of his years in power. From this point of view, Dr Najib's career trajectory can be seen as the reverse of that of Khan Abdul Ghaffar Khan. Whereas Ghaffar Khan went from being a close associate of the *ulema* to distancing himself from them, Dr Najib went from being a firebrand revolutionary to one who courted the *ulema*. In the latter years of his time in power, Dr Najib pursued a policy of National Reconciliation. His main aim was to bring those who had been in the forefront of the counter-revolution—particularly the *ulema*—into the national fold and create a national government. But attitudes on both sides were too entrenched, outside interference too obstructive. Dr Najib's

National Reconciliation made little headway. If there is one lesson I have learnt from the lifetime I have spent amongst the Pashtoons, it is that the key to Pashtoons living at peace with themselves is to heal this rift between progressives and conservatives—the secular and religious elements of Pashtoon society—that bedevils their public life.

Might it be possible to escape from this cycle of violence, with each side becoming progressively more uncompromising, and to engage with the other side in a proactive manner on the basis of the principles of one's own faith? Why not try to escape from this destructive spiral? Would there be any chance of reversing this trend by tapping the rich veins of Islamic thought and seeking to contribute thereby to the advancement of human endeavour? This is the task that I, in my own field, have taken upon myself. Being both a media professional and a scholar of Islam, I felt it might be useful to train madrasa graduates for a career in the media. On all sides there was resistance to this idea and not only from Pashtoons.

Even at Cambridge, when I suggested to the Cambridge Muslim College, that maybe a media studies course could be introduced in the college, there was coolness to the idea, on the grounds that madrasa graduates had little interest in a career in the media. The reaction in Afghanistan has been much the same. In 2009, I held a meeting of Islamic *ulema* in the eastern Afghan city of Jalalabad. One of the aims of the meeting was to galvanize support for my organization, PACT Radio, in setting up media training centres in madrasas. It has to be said that ten years on, I am still grappling with this challenge. The paradox was not lost on some media people who came to cover the event. They were perplexed. Some of them asked me, 'What on earth have madrasa graduates got to do with the media?'

I gave them my own example. I came to a career in the media through a madrasa education. As we have seen, the culmination of the madrasa course, extending over the better part of a decade, is the study of Hadith. Hadith is generally translated as traditions from the Holy Prophet's life. It would be more accurate to call them news stories. The word *hadith* literally means news. A Hadith is in fact a news story from the Prophet's life. These stories have been collected and collated by the *muhadditheen*—the compilers of the collections of Hadith. The *muhadditheen* can be seen as expert journalists, painstakingly checking each news story to establish its authenticity, cross-checking their sources to find out which version of the story fits best with all the available accounts. That was the first stage in my journalistic education: the study of Hadith—establishing the veracity of the news story.

The second stage was what to learn from the news story. Here, my traineeship with Wahiduddin Khan stood me in good stead. Over six years—from 1982 to 1988—I churned out news story after news story on behalf of Maulana's *Al-Risala*, not just for the sake of recounting what happened—that was only an incidental part of the telling of the story—but to learn from it. What was the moral of the story? In our journalism, that was the crucial factor, as it was for the *muhadditheen*—the original journalists—as well. Besides reproducing each Hadith, they also wrote books explaining the meaning and the moral of these stories, how we could apply the stories to our own lives. Wahiduddin Khan was doing the same thing, only in a contemporary context.

I later moved from this field of factual journalism to fictional storytelling, another area in which there was a rich well of Islamic tradition from which to pick. One could say that one is more able to reflect reality in a fictional format since one is escaping various limitations—censorship, litigation, reprisals, offence, wall of silence—that may curtail one's ability to reveal all the details of a news story. Imagine if Sheherazade—the lady who told the tales of *The Thousand and One Nights*—had confined herself to true stories when addressing her husband, the demented king Shahryar. He would have lost patience and put her to death in no time. There are many instances where fiction reflecting fact is more powerful, more practical and more representative of the true situation than fact itself.

Considering that every stage in my journalistic evolution stemmed from my education in a madrasa and my tapping veins of Islamic thought and tradition, it was natural that I should seek to impart the media skills I have developed and honed over several decades to madrasa students like myself. They would be the ones best suited to this alternative type of approach, oriented towards finding solutions to problems as opposed to highlighting and giving publicity to them, only to see those problems fester and multiply.

From the media, I moved on to other fields of study in which it was possible to enhance the understanding of modern concepts by placing them in the context of the Qur'an and Hadith. The contribution to be made by Islamic scholarship to fields such as human rights, humanitarian principles and international humanitarian law is immense. Yet it is in the field of environmental studies that the vision of Islam is particularly clear, penetrating and edifying.

Early in 2010, the Prince of Wales paid a visit to Kabul. Amongst a few other Islamic scholars in Kabul, I was invited to meet the prince. I think we struck a chord. In any case, his private secretary invited me to come along to a lecture the prince was going to give later in the year at Oxford University. The lecture was on Islam and the environment. It seemed strange to some that the heir to the British throne should give a talk on this subject. For me, it was a welcome acknowledgement of the strong position that Islam takes on harmony with nature and care for the environment, starting of course with the standout verse on environmental protection, 'Man has wrought corruption with his own hand, on land and sea.' (*al Rum* 30:41)

In a way, the lecture that the prince gave was extraordinary. I was left wishing that Pashtoon Islamic scholars could talk in those terms, casting light on the big issues of the day from an Islamic perspective. My mind went back to my days in the khanqah of Maulana Maseeh-Ullah, near Thana Bhavan. Time and again, the maulana would comment on how we had become estranged from our own concepts (*ajnabiyat hogayee*). I thought also of a poem of Shaykh Saadi of Shiraz:

> *Khushtar an bashad ki zikr-e-dilbaran Gufta ayad dar hadith-e-digaran*

> How sweet it is when your beloved is mentioned In the conversation of others

The thing is, 'others'—in this case Prince Charles—have landed upon the efficacy of Islamic teachings and the part they have to play in making a better world and bringing human beings together mostly by accident. Muslims have played a minimal part—if any part at all—in communicating these teachings to the rest of the world. There was a lot in the prince's speech that was worthy of reflection, but I would like to focus on one point he made about water, chemical fertilizers and organic farming. He started by quoting the final verse of *Surah al-Mulk (the Sovereignty)*: 'Have you not seen that if I suck your water into the earth, then is there anyone who can give you flowing water?' (*al-Mulk* 67:30) 'This is the divine hospitality,' he explained, 'that offers us our provision and our dwelling places, our clothing, tools and transport.'[1] My mind flicked to another verse of the Qur'an, 'He has provided you with everything you have required. If you were to count the blessings of Allah, you would not be able to count them all.' (*al-Nahl* 16:18)

My experience is that it is easier to get Westerners like Prince Charles to acknowledge the contribution of Islam to visionary thinking on big issues of the day such as the environment, than it is to bring the secular Pashtoon intelligentsia to acknowledge this contribution. To my mind, it is Islamic scholars who have to make the first move. If only Muslim scholars could forget about their political differences—could forget about power politics altogether—and concentrate on formulating and expressing Islamic teachings in consonance with and in the context of the day. For example, the *ulema* could start by taking a pacifist stand. If only they could say with one voice to their nationalist, progressive and secular counterparts: Islam does not brook or tolerate any atrocities against non-combatant civilians. With modern weaponry, if there is war, atrocities are bound to be committed against civilians, so let us move together to outlaw war altogether. Let us move beyond the international humanitarian law of the Geneva Convention, which establishes 'rules of engagement', and say categorically

[1] The Prince of Wales' speech on Islam and the Enviroment can be read here: https://www.princeofwales.gov.uk/speech/speech-hrh-prince-wales-titled-islam-and-environment-sheldonian-theatre-oxford

that there can be no lawful war. Let us do this fairly and squarely on the basis of Islamic teachings. In the process, maybe the Pashtoon intelligentsia and the Pashtoon *ulema* could come together. Then, maybe, just maybe, there could be peace in their lands and they could present a picture of Islam to the world similar to the one they presented to me and dozens of other hippies half a century ago. A picture of a peaceful, down-to-earth, simple faith, full of humility and hospitality, in which people seek harmony with nature and with their fellow humans, and, in the process, learn to live in peace with their Creator.

GLOSSARY

Afridis: a Pashtoon tribe, inhabiting the Khyber Pass and neighbouring hills and plains, the Afridis are made up of eight sub-tribes.

Ajamis: name given to Muslims who hail from Asia, who look to Persian as their classical Islamic language as opposed to Arabic.

Azan: the Muslim call to prayer. It used to be delivered from a raised portion of the mosque—that is what minarets were originally for—but is now delivered through loudspeaker, spoiling its simple and pure appeal.

Bayat: the act of a disciple swearing allegiance to a Sufi master or pir.

Bid'at: innovation, things which are added to Islam after the time of the Prophet.

Deobandis: those who adhere to the school of thought affiliated with the Deoband madrasa.

Durand Line: de facto border between Afghanistan and British India. Agreed by British civil servant Mortimer Durand and King Abdul Rahman Khan of Afghanistan, it split the Pashtoon nation in two, as many nations of South and Central Asia, from Kashmir to Kazakhstan, have been split in two or even three parts by British and Russian carving up of the region.

Feringi: Persianization of Frank, as the Europeans were known at the time of the Crusades. So when a European is referred to as a Feringi, it is usually in a pejorative sense, as one who is antagonistic towards Islam.

Ghundaska: Afridi form of rounders.

Hadith: plural Ahadith, literally news from the life of the Prophet, the word is more generally translated as traditions from the Prophet's life. That is also a correct interpretation, since it is on the basis of Ahadith that Muslim traditions emerge.

Hakim: pronounced Haakim, a ruler. In Talib's Tale spelt Hakim.

Hakim: a traditional herbal physician, practioner of the Greek system of medicine. Pronounced Hakeem but usually written Hakim. In Talib's Tale, written as Hakeem to differentiate it from Hakim, meaning a local ruler.

Hanafi: followers of one of the four schools of Sunni jurisprudence, that was founded by Imam Abu Hanifa.

Imam: literally a leader, but commonly used for one who leads prayers in a mosque.

Ikhwanis: those affiliated to the Ikhwan'al-Muslimeen, an Egyptian political party opposing secularism and promoting the foundation of an Islamic state.

Jamaat-e-Islami: religious political party set up by Maulana Maududi, dedicated in Pakistan to foundation of an Islamic state; more aligned to social work in countries where setting up an Islamic state is not a practical possibility. Closely aligned ideologically with the Egyptian Ikhwan'al-Muslimeen.

Khanqah: a Muslim monastery. Where Muslims—Sufis in particular—go to purify themselves from blemishes in their character, embellishing themselves instead in characteristics that will endear them to Allah.

Khulasa: a rudimentary book of Hanafi jurisprudence that enabled a mulla to lead prayers in the mosque, without having qualified from a madrasa.

Langar: a location for free distribution of food, usually focused on a religious institute.

Lar: literally a road, among the Afridis and other Pashtoon tribes, the word refers to trying to avert confrontation by talking: 'jaw-jaw is better than war-war'.

Lashkar: a tribal force, particularly of Afridis.

Madrasa: an Islamic school. Typically, the curriculum of a madrasa will include memorisation of the Holy Quran and an eight year Islamic theology curriculum, culminating in study of Hadith. This is what makes a student into an aalim—a master of Islamic sciences.

Malang: a Muslim ascetic. Commonly known as a dervish in Persian, a malang generally lives off alms and is supposed to devote himself to Allah instead of being involved in worldly matters.

Mezaray: along with cannabis, mezaray has a claim to be the national plant of the Pashtoons, known as dwarf palm, one can fashion a range of products from dwarf palm: mats, prayer-mats, coasters, baskets, flip-flops—it is a really versatile plant.

Miangan: Pashto plural of Mian, a descendant of a holy person.

Mu'aniqa: embrace that Muslim men give each other three times—left, right then left again—when they meet. It is followed by musahifa, the customary handshake.

Mufti: one who is qualified to give verdicts—fatwas—related to Islamic jurisprudence. A Mufti is more senior than a maulvi—one who has received a degree of excellence in Islamic theology.

Mujaddid: A mujaddid is one notch down from a prophet. A mujaddid is sent by Allah in the course of every century or so to renew and refresh the Islamic faith. The word mujaddid means renewer.

Mujahidah: from the same root as the more famous jihad—mistakenly interpreted as holy war—mujahidah has been described as the greatest jihad—the battle one conducts against one's own self to curb one's base instincts and desires.

Naswar: Pashtoon cross between snuff and chewing tobacco. Lethal combination.

Panah: the Pashtoon custom of giving refuge to those fleeing, from justice or injustice. The custom is probably meant for giving refuge to those fleeing from injustice, but it has come to be more and more for those fleeing from justice. This has caused Pashtoons untold problems in recent decades.

Pashtoonwali: the unwritten Pashtoon code. There are various opinions on what constitutes Pashoonwali, but one can say that upholding the honour of women comes top of the list. Then there is hospitality. Closely linked to that is the custom of giving refuge to one who seeks it; and taking revenge, particularly for murder of one's kith and kin.

Peghaur: social censorship, peer pressure. One may be indifferent to taking some action, but be pushed into it by someone's rebuke, particularly aspersions on one's honour. That is peghaur.

People's Democratic Party of Afghanistan, known as PDPA and in Pashto simply as Khalk—People—those affiliated with the party as Khalkis: the Communist party of Afghanistan that seized power in Afghanistan in April 1978, but wielded considerable power in Daud's time, also. Later renamed Watan—Country—Party.

Peshmany: the early morning meal during the month of fasting, peshmany or sehri (suhoor) as it is more commonly known in the Muslim world, is one of the hallmarks of an Islamic lifestyle.

Pir: a Sufi master.

Qaylula: the afternoon siesta, much loved by Muslims around the world, particularly those living in hot climates. One advantage of the qaylula is that it enables one to spend a substantial period of the night in prayer and study.

Serai: an old style inn or hotel, where there would be facilities for horses' and camels' as well as humans' refreshment and rest.

Shahada: the declaration of faith that makes someone a Muslim. Shahada differs from the kalima in that kalima is the actual testimony of faith; shahada is to declare it, to make it one's own and to make oneself a Muslim.

Shifar: literally code, but commonly used in the Kabul underworld as the code language for the Kabul underworld.

Sunnah: a practice of the Holy Prophet. A little thing—like removing some obstacle from people's path, observing the early morning meal in Ramadan—that encapsulate an Islamic lifestyle. Among Pashtoons, the practice of male circumcision is known as sunnah.

Tablighis: a Muslim revivalist movement, formed to counter the influence of several Hindu—Arya Samaj—revivalist movements set up at the beginning of the 20th century.

Talib: a student of Islam, one who travels in search of knowledge. This is one of the most excellent activities of an Islamic lifestyle. According to the Prophetic tradition, one who goes out in search of knowledge is in the path of Allah until he returns.

Thawab (pronounced sawab by Pashtoons): the reward you receive from Allah for doing a good deed.

Ulema: religious scholars. Plural of aalim.

Wahabis: an uncompromising hardline sect formed in the Arabian peninsula in the 18th century by Mohammad Ibn Abdul Wahab. Adhering to a strictly puritan form of Islam, Wahabis tend to consider anyone not with them, against them. They condemn anything that does not accord to their interpretation of Tauhid—Oneness of Allah in his Being and His Attributes—and Sunna—the practice of the Prophet.

Walayat: literally seat of government. Those who knew united India before Partition would refer to London as walayat.

INDEX

Q

T

An Aesthetic Underground

A LITERARY MEMOIR

JOHN METCALF

BIBLIOASIS

Library and Archives Canada Cataloguing in Publication

Metcalf, John, 1938–, author
An aesthetic underground / John Metcalf.

Includes bibliographical references.
Issued in print and electronic formats.
ISBN 978-1-927428-95-5 (pbk.). — ISBN 978-1-927428-96-2 (epub)

1. Metcalf, John, 1938–. 2. Canadian literature (English)—Publishing—Ontario—Erin. 3. Canadian literature (English)—20th century—History and criticism. 4. Porcupine's Quill, Inc. 5. Editors—Canada—Biography. 6. Authors, Canadian (English)—20th century—Biography. I. Title.

Z483.M48A3 2014 070.5092 C2014-904560-3
C2014-904561-1

Edited by Dan Wells
Copy-edited by Jennifer Franssen
Cover and text design by Gordon Robertson

Canada Council for the Arts / Conseil des Arts du Canada
Canadian Heritage / Patrimoine canadien
Ontario Arts Council / Conseil des Arts de l'Ontario
50 years of Ontario government support of the arts
50 ans de soutien du gouvernement de l'Ontario aux arts

Biblioasis acknowledges the ongoing financial support of the Government of Canada through the Canada Council for the Arts, Canadian Heritage, the Canada Book Fund; and the Government of Ontario through the Ontario Arts Council.

PRINTED AND BOUND IN CANADA

FSC www.fsc.org
MIX
Paper from responsible sources
FSC® C004071

This book is for

Ron and Kate
Elizabeth and Ethan
Dan and Chantal

Every teaching institution will have its department of cultural studies, an ox not to be gored, and an aesthetic underground will flourish, restoring something of the romance of reading.

— HAROLD BLOOM, *The Western Canon*

It seemed unto [Don Quixote] very requisite and behooveful . . . that he himself should become a knight-errant, and go throughout the world, with his horse and armour, to seek adventures, and practise in person all that he had read was used by knights of yore; revenging of all kinds of injuries, and offering himself to occasions and dangers, which, being once happily achieved, might gain him eternal renown.

— CERVANTES, *Don Quixote (Shelton's translation, 1612)*

Did I not tell your worship they were windmills? and who could have thought otherwise, except such as had windmills in their head?

— SANCHO PANZA to DON QUIXOTE

CONTENTS

A VIGNETTE

WHEN I WAS FOURTEEN and attending Beckenham Grammar School for Boys I began spending my Saturdays hanging around in the yard of the High Street auctioneer. Viewing took place from ten until noon and the auctions started at one and went on until four o'clock when the vans started backing in. Porters in green aprons manhandled sideboards and wardrobes and held aloft at the auctioneer's "What am I bid?" the silver-plated coffee sets, the brass fire irons, the baize-lined canteens of cutlery with one fish knife missing.

What attracted me was not the auction but the two coffin-sized boxes on trestles in the yard. These were crammed with the books, spines up, which accumulated from estate sales. They were priced at sixpence each. I stood by the boxes and tidied up the rows after people had rummaged. Customers soon assumed that I was employed to stand there and started giving me their sixpences. These I took into the office.

The clerk in the office with his catalogues and lists of the lots was obviously suspicious of my motives and I'd often glance up to see him standing in his doorway, cigarette smoke curling into one eye, staring.

Touching the books gave me profound pleasure. I became so familiar with them, with their bindings, decorations, and typefaces, that I played a game Saturday after Saturday, guessing at a glance a book's probable date of publication. Mostly they were novels by the likes of William Harrison Ainsworth, Dornford Yates, Henry Rider Haggard, Sheila Kaye-Smith, Warwick Deeping, A. J. Cronin, Enid Bagnold, Ngaio Marsh, Mrs. Humphry Ward, Rafael Sabatini, Anthony Hope, Margery Allingham, and Hilaire Belloc—literary detritus specific to that time and place. But occasionally there were older books in pictorial boards or decorated cloth, my favourite among them the endless novels of G. A. Henty. I was also attracted to the short stories of W. W. Jacobs who was much admired, I later discovered, by P. G. Wodehouse. I was drawn to the work initially by the brilliance of Jacobs' illustrator, his friend Will Owen. For years I reread *Many Cargoes*, *Odd Craft*, *Sailors' Knots*, *Captains All*, and *Short Cruises*.

After a couple of months the clerk grew tired of my constant interruptions to deposit coins in the old Player's Navy Cut tin and told me to keep the tin outside and give him the money at the end of the afternoon.

Some while later came the day when he suggested that I keep half a crown for myself. I somehow knew that accepting the money would change the relationship in a way I didn't want, so, fighting my shyness, I wondered if instead I might have a couple of books every week. This request seemed to confirm him in his mild contempt of me and reassure him of my harmlessness.

I wanted those Henty books. I didn't necessarily want to read them, though I did read some. What I wanted was to *own* them. Not just three or four or ten. I wanted to own *all* of them. A few minutes at the public library told me there were more than eighty. And so the collection began to grow. *Under Drake's Flag*, *The Lion of the North*, *With the Allies in Pekin*, *With Clive in India*, *With Wolfe in Canada*, *True to the Old Flag* . . .

This vignette suggests four motifs which seem to have played themselves out all through my life. The first is books themselves. The second is collecting things. The third is a certain independence of mind and judgement illustrated in my indifference to the clerk's contempt. The fourth is the almost magical inability to acquire money.

THE CURATOR

MANY AUTOBIOGRAPHIES of writers present a picture of a shy and lonely child delivered from solitude and unsympathetic surroundings by the power of the Word, the child's mind captured, for example, by the illustrations in Foxe's *Book of Martyrs* or struggling with the text of the only book in the house, *Pilgrim's Progress*. Good examples of this typical experience are recorded in James Laver's *Museum Piece* and in Jocelyn Brooke's *The Military Orchid*.

My own childhood was nothing like this. I cannot remember a time when I was not surrounded by books. My father, a Methodist minister, had a fairly large library, most of the volumes, to be sure, theological, but he also had most of the standard poets and first editions of the novels of Conrad and Hardy. Among the more "modern" poets, he owned Masefield, Housman, Chesterton, Belloc, Yeats, and Blunden.

After he died and I was looking through what books my mother had not promptly donated to Oxfam, I was amazed to find Wilde's *De Profundis*. I'd probably seen it when younger but thought it to be a work of theology.

My mother read all the time. Her reading wasn't literary. Her favourite material was historical novels and detective stories. These came from the Public Library, from Boots Library, and Timothy White's Lending Library. The historical novels were of the Georgette Heyer variety, bodice rippers but "nice" bodice rippers, the detective stories by Dorothy L. Sayers, Agatha Christie, Margery Allingham, and Ngaio Marsh. I associate all these writers, whom I loathe, with the smell of bath salts and talc, doubtless an early memory of trips to Boots Chemists.

These detective story writers seem to me, now, to mirror and perpetuate the nastiness of British class preoccupations. The superintendent or the well-bred amateur sleuth was always assisted by the comically lower-class and utterly thick but throbbingly loyal sergeant or manservant. So it was in the 1930s, the Golden Age of detective fiction, with Margery Allingham's Albert Campion and his "gent's 'elp," Magersfontein Lugg, and it *still* is seventy years later with Colin Dexter's rather highbrow Inspector Morse and funny old Sergeant Lewis, dim but devoted as a Labrador.

When I was a child I read quickly, usually taking about two hours to finish a book. On wet days I read my ration of library books in one gulp and often returned in the evening for three more. On the other hand, I was eleven before I could tell time. I can still see the tears of exasperation and rage starting in my mother's eyes as she moved the cardboard hands on the cardboard face and asked me what time it was if the little hand was on one and the big hand was on nine. She might as well have been talking to me in a foreign language.

Oddly enough, all this reading did not mean that I was "bookish"; quite the reverse was true. School always baffled me. I'd like to pretend that I was so brilliant I was bored by school. But that isn't true. I was baffled. The only subjects in which I did well were English and history. English because I did it automatically. When it came to grammar and parsing, I had no idea of what people were talking about. It took lessons in

Latin years later to drive home what was meant by "adjective" and "adverb." History fascinated me because I felt lapped in it. Lord Macaulay said that history must be "burnt into the imagination before it can be received by the reason," and it was certainly seared into mine. Long barrows, dolmens, hill forts, standing stones—all sang to me of where I had come from and who I was.

I passed what was called the eleven-plus exam—an instrument for sorting out grammar school hopefuls from secondary modern fodder—only because my mother drilled me in sums and suchlike.

It quickly became apparent that if I were ever to do anything at all in life it would be on the "arts" side of affairs, though any prospects whatsoever seemed more than doubtful. At thirteen I was declared ineducable in math and I stopped taking the subject altogether. The fact that my math teacher that year was abnormally small and looked like a Japanese sniper as drawn in American comics and drove home his points with the rung of a chair may have had *something* to do with it. But not much. The truth is that numbers cause a pain in my forehead.

It's interesting that if I'd been educated in Canada I'd never have reached university because I'd never have passed the requirements in math. In England it was permissible to replace math by a science. Physics and chemistry were as incomprehensible to me as math. Math, I could see, did somehow relate to life; there were all those problems about how much wallpaper you'd need to paper a room eighty-three feet long with eight dormer windows. But physics! As far as I could see all it involved was lowering weights on bits of string into calibrated tubes of water to see how much overflowed. I couldn't understand why anyone would *wish* to know that. Chemistry was a touch more entertaining because of the fire and smoke but I never seemed able to grasp the *motives* for these activities.

Physics and chemistry, then, being incomprehensible, left only biology. I spent most of my free time—alone but not lonely—watching animals, hunting for snakes, searching for fossils, and fishing in the Avon and Stour. I could have taken the biology teacher to the one locality in Hampshire where smooth snakes were to be found, where bee orchids grew, where the lampreys gathered, where there were the sets, earths and holts of badgers, foxes, and otters, but all this, I quickly realized, was nothing to do with biology. Biology was copying diagrams.

School ground on towards my fourteenth year. I did badly in everything except English and history. Even my toast-rack in woodwork took two years and about three hundred feet of lumber.

The English teaching I received between the ages of twelve and fourteen was, I realize now, superb. Our only activities were précis, paraphrase, exercises in comprehension, and essay writing. In other words, we were drilled in logic, in the steel structure of the language. Literature was dealt with in the following way: each term we were given a list of twelve novels to read at home. This meant that in a school year we read a minimum of thirty-six novels. At the end of each term we were given a test cunningly designed to reveal if we had in fact read them.

"With whom did Jim Davis shelter after the fight with the revenue officers?"

The following books were on those lists and suggest the general flavour of the reading: *Jim Davis, Treasure Island, Kidnapped, King Solomon's Mines, The History of Mr. Polly, A Tale of Two Cities, Tarka the Otter, Oliver Twist, Allan Quartermain, Kim, David Copperfield, Three Men in a Boat, Prester John, The Thirty-nine Steps, Rodney Stone, The White Company, The Cloister and the Hearth, Rookwood*, etc.

All good stuff for boys and entertaining. The idea of discussing such things as plot and characterization would never have occurred to my teachers.

And a damn good thing too.

(I suspect that nowadays these books would be considered far too difficult in syntax and vocabulary and entirely lacking in *relevance*. I prefer them, however, to the books with titles like *Jennifer's First Period* tailored to the supposed interests of adolescents.)

This, then, was my "official" life until I was fourteen.

But I have another set of memories covering the same years which I realize now, groping back, are the *really* important ones.

They are disjointed.

Very early, being with my father in Foyle's. He is searching along the bottom rows of second-hand tomes in theology. We are in a basement, in a canyon of books. Our hands are glazed black with that peculiar kind of muck that grows on old books. My father has bought me a book to keep me quiet as he roots and rummages. It is *Struwwelpeter* with the horrifying illustration of the leaping man cutting off the child's thumb. Afterwards, we have tea in a Lyon's Corner House.

Another memory of my father, a man I wish I'd known. He was a distant figure, not given to conversation, eccentric. He silenced quarrels between my brother and me by a prim clearing of his throat. As he was a Methodist minister, he was relatively impoverished. Money was never thrown around. It was, in fact, pinched. On a rare summer holiday in Swanage we were walking past a junk shop. In the window hung a blown-up, varnished blowfish, a prickly globe of wonder. In we went. The fish was two shillings and sixpence. My father bought it for me. He also bought me some bound folio volumes of an illustrated magazine which formed a history of the First World War. And, as we were about to leave, he pointed out the sword of a swordfish and suggested that it was, if not rare, then at least unusual, and precisely the sort of thing that, if passed up, would remain a source of regret forever after.

This was not condescension on his part nor, I suspect, a desire to please a small boy. He was never "nice" in that way. It was a seriously held opinion.

Later, a collection of *Superman* and *Combat* comics, real American ones with glossy covers, not the dowdy British reproductions. These desirables were the stakes in games of marbles and nearest-to-the-wall with cigarette cards.

Later, still, *Boy's Own Paper*, all kept in severe order by volume and number.

Collecting, then. My father collected obscure books on theological matters. My brother collected coins—a harmless hobby which led eventually to his becoming Keeper of the Heberden Coin Room at the Ashmolean Museum. His bibliography lists over two hundred publications and his reputation is international.

When he was eleven and I was six my parents gave him an unused room for a museum. It had been a pantry. He filled it with coins, fossils, mineral specimens, pottery shards, a hair from an elephant's tail, a clay oil lamp from Palestine, medals, a Prussian dragoon's sword, an embroidered Chinese slipper. He charged ½d admission. He also put out a weekly newspaper printed in purple on a gelatine pad. This too cost ½d. One copy of one issue remains. The newspaper was called *The Curator*.

When he retired from the Ashmolean in 1998 he gave a speech at a farewell lunch and said in part: "We try to share our knowledge and our enthusiasm generously and freely, with undergraduates, with graduates, with our museum colleagues in this country and elsewhere, with amateur collectors, with the public at large, with children . . .

"In a clamant world, we need to know what we stand for, we need to be always ready to share our values, while insisting on the disciplines of exact learning and rigorous argument, and serenity of judgement."

The word *clamant* suggests him exquisitely.

All sorts of antiques and curios were cheaper when I was a boy and far more readily available than now. I had small collections of swords and pistols. At about the age of ten I had acquired, by swapping, a "horse pistol"—a battered percussion cap job—and a bullet mould. I began an obsessive manufacture of lead bullets in the kitchen using one of my mother's saucepans. I have scars on my hands to this day from molten lead. I cycled all the way from Southbourne to Ringwood to buy a tin of percussion caps from a compliant gunsmith. But the powder defeated me; I couldn't get the mixture right.

My passion for bullet making led me into crime. I was apprehended removing lengths of lead plumbing that were still attached to houses.

My brother grew copper sulphate crystals in pie dishes and mineral gardens under waterglass in casseroles.

My father steeped his vile home-grown tobacco in other kitchen utensils and "cooked" it in the oven.

My mother bewailed the state of her pots and pans and, I suspect, suffered something close to a breakdown as the house filled with coins, books, snakes, nature specimens, hedgehogs, ammonites, belemnites, trilobites, caterpillars, butterflies, setting-boards, nets, killing jars, stone-age hand axes, slow worms, green-throated sand lizards, *Observer Books* of Trees, Wild Flowers, Birds, Reptiles . . . volume after volume in the *British Naturalist* series, owl pellets, fishing tackle, seething tins of gentles, hypodermic syringes, and cloudy jars of formaldehyde containing newts, leeches, ticks, internal organs.

My mother claims that she came home from shopping one day to find me and two friends about to open up a squirrel we'd shot. Her horror was not that we'd dispatched the poor creature but that we had it pinned down for dissection *on the bread board.*

Setting-boards for butterflies and moths, the rustproof black pins, the cork-lined exhibition cases—all came by mail from an emporium in South London. The store's catalogue featured treasures beyond the dreams of avarice—fossils, arrowheads, scrapers, neolithic hand axes (the *polished* ones), Roman terracotta lamps, sundry wondrous antiquities. The very *name* of this store, which I've never visited, had the same effect on me as Chimborazo and Cotopaxi had on the boy in Walter J. Turner's poem "Romance"; it was called Watkins and Doncaster.

(On my first return from Canada to visit my mother she confided one afternoon that she was very worried about some shotgun shells that the tide of collecting and slaughter had deposited in a cupboard some twelve years earlier. She was worried that they would explode. She said they often made her feel low and that she wept thinking about them. Amazed, I asked her why she hadn't thrown them out. She said that she hadn't wanted "the blood of the dustbin men on her conscience." And if that isn't a detail from a Thurber story, I don't know what is. For some obscure reason it reminds me of the black Thurber maid who always referred to the fridge as "that doom-shaped thing in the kitchen.")

Collecting is intimately connected with writing. With mine, certainly. There is an affinity between the two activities. The *kind* of knowledge that comes out of collecting differs from purely formal knowledge. It is informed by love and lust. Collecting sharpens and trains the eye. It forces contact with the particular. Collecting is conservative, historical, archival. Collecting is evaluative. It demands judgement. It leads inevitably to ever-expanding interests. Collecting, then, is not mere accumulation. The creation of a collection and its tending is an intricate aesthetic affair. The knowledge gained can be gained in no other way.

The collector is usually seen by the non-collector as obsessive and harmlessly loony but I hold that whether he collects Regency furniture or hand-painted chamber pots, the collector's real is more real than yours. Simply, he *sees* more.

MR. WHITE AND BERNARD HALLIDAY

THE NEXT TWO PHASES of my adolescent reading were dominated by the external examinations: the Ordinary Level exams and the Advanced Level exams. The Ordinary Level exams were equivalent to Canadian high school matriculation and were usually sat at the age of sixteen. Advanced Levels were sat two years later and were used to regulate entry to universities.

At sixteen I was still mutedly unhappy and unsuccessful at school. I was used to being told I was dim and thick and had come to believe it. My brother, Cambridge now behind him, had been and continued to be unbelievably brilliant. My school career was compared at all points with his and was found wanting. My body was flooded by naughty hormones and the air was heavy with rebellion.

I claimed I wanted to be a professional boxer.

Under the guidance of an ex-sergeant from one of the more thuggish branches of the British Army—"Partial to 'im, are you? Don't *'ug* 'im, *'it* 'im"—I learned, as Henry Cooper put it, to "work downstairs."

My mother's anguish and pressure increased as the exams drew nearer. The forecasts for my future were grim—on good days I might, if lucky, aspire to become a plumber's mate, on bad days the gallows beckoned. My father grew more grimly silent. And so, perhaps to please my parents, perhaps simply infected by the prevailing hysteria, I started to work. Everyone was impolitely amazed when the letter arrived from the Ministry of Education. I had passed the Ordinary Level examinations in every subject I had sat. My mother, typically, wondered aloud if they'd got my name confused with some other Metcalf.

I had had no patience with school or schoolwork up to the time of the Ordinary Level examinations simply because my interests were passionately engaged elsewhere. I was in a constant and what felt like holy connection to the natural world. My time was spent with the intensity of dream fishing for roach and perch, chub, dace, rudd, bream, and tench, names which are a poetry still. School was an abstraction to me many levels removed from the thrill of the red-and-black caterpillars of the cinnabar moth feasting on goldenrod, or the tense but fluid coiling of an adder about to strike.

But I was beginning to waken from that dream; it was becoming less intense, less consuming as the sexual current pulled me more towards the social world. I began to realize that I had arrived at a crossroads. My mother nagged and urged, wanting me to stay on at school. I countered with odd schemes which drove her to the very verge. One proposal I remember making was that she stake me the passage money to Georgetown, British Guiana, where I would become a pork-knocker high up the Orinoco River working illicit diamonds. My father, while these battles raged—for that is what they were—sucked on his pipe and did his sage-nodding-in-silence thing.

I *said* I wanted to become a club fighter because this caused maximum annoyance and distress but even I knew that I was indulging in fantasy. I didn't have the weight, the height, or the reach. I'd seen the life, seen the pugs in the gyms. And I wasn't hungry for it. For me it was a kind of playing. When I sparred with Dell Latter in a Croydon club I was on the receiving end of a controlled violence I knew I couldn't muster.

But there were things going on in my mind I *wouldn't* talk about. I was reading confusedly and with odd motivations. I read a lot of books about art and art history. I had a strange conviction I might become a painter, strange because I was utterly incapable of drawing. In the odd state I was in this did not seem to matter. I also read books about religious subjects, hoping to discover compelling arguments for becoming an atheist because painting and atheism and drinking the turpentine from your paintbox like Utrillo seemed to fit together inevitably.

I read Jessie L. Weston's *From Ritual to Romance* and Frazer's *The Golden Bough* because of the footnotes in *The Waste Land* and this was the first time that the idea of footnotes and bibliographies dawned on me. Before I had resolutely ignored them. But then I was unable to grasp the idea of telling time until I was eleven. So perhaps this was simply another instance of weird wiring. My reading began that meandering course it's followed ever since.

From D. H. Lawrence to Katherine Mansfield to John Middleton Murry, to Frieda's ex-husband Ernest Weekley, to Gurdjieff, Ouspensky, Mme Blavatsky, and Annie Besant's *Wisdom of the Upanishads*, to Roger Fry and Clive Bell and Vincent's letters to Theo. From the gibberish of "significant form" forward to the gibberish of Herbert Read and back to Ruskin and Pater and then forward once again to Whistler's *Gentle Art*—on and on unendingly and, in large part, uncomprehendingly.

I was sullen and rude at home. I felt myself too refined, too sensitive to endure the narrow rectitude of the manse. These comic pretensions were doubtless fostered and "swollen"—and "swollen" is very much the word—by my discovery of Oscar Wilde and Huysmans's *A Rebours*.

Not very deeply hidden in the preposterous stew of adolescent rebellion and desire and aspiration was the desire to escape the pietism of my mother and live a life more generally louche and rowdy.

I wrote about this time in my life in a mock memoir called "Private Parts" in the book *Girl in Gingham*.

Irving Layton wrote for Michael Macklem, Oberon Press's publisher, a lavish blurb.

"Many thanks to you and Metcalf for the pleasure 'Private Parts' has given me. It's almost as great as that given to me by my own."

Well, the novella isn't *that* good but here's an extract:

> I haunted the local library in my quest for knowledge. Not only was it a very good library but I lusted after one of the younger librarians who had a nice smile and breasts which gave the impression of great solidity. I spent hours wondering how much they weighed, what one would feel like hot and unconfined.
>
> It was in the library that I found one day a book called *The March of the Moderns* by the art historian William Gaunt. I have never seen or read the book since. It struck me with the radiance and power of revelation. The mundane world fell away; I was oblivious to the smell of floor polish and damp raincoats, the click of the date-stamp, the passage of other browsers along the shelves. I read standing up until closing-time and then took the book home and finished it in bed.
>
> The book revealed to me a world where brilliant but persecuted people drank champagne for breakfast and were pissed by lunch, took lobsters for walks on leashes, shaved off half their moustache, sliced off their ears and gave them to prostitutes, possessed women by the score, consorted with syphilitic dwarves, *lived* in brothels, and were allowed to go mad.

Somewhere in the sun, D. H. Lawrence was at it.

Hemingway was giving them both barrels.

Ezra was suffering for the faith in an American bin.

All painters were everywhere possessing their exotic Javanese models.

I, meanwhile, was in Croydon.

But Art was obviously the answer; it was just a question of finding my medium. The problem with the novel was that writing took a long time and nothing interesting had happened to me. I tried poetry for a time being particularly drawn to the Imagists because they were very short and seemed easiest to imitate. H.D. was one of my favourites. Painting, because of the models, attracted me most but I couldn't draw anything that looked like anything; abstraction was the answer, of course, but secretly I thought abstraction not quite honest. I had a go at a few lino-cuts but gouged my hand rather badly. Drama was soured for me by memories of endless pageants and nativity plays where kids tripped over the frayed carpet and I had to say:

"I bring you tidings of Great Joy."

But I was not depressed.

I settled down to wait. I lived in the manse, ate scones, and went to school, but I was charged with a strange certainty that I was somehow different, chosen, special; my Muse, in her own good time, would descend and translate me from Croydon to the richer world where women and applause were waiting.

My career crossroads was solved not by a choice but by a command. After the results of the Ordinary Level exams were known I was summoned by the headmaster. All previous visits had involved a cane. The headmaster's name was Mr. White. I have no idea of his Christian name; everyone was so in awe of him that I suppose we thought he hadn't got one. We were in such terror of his besuited bulk, his jowls, his massive *presence* that if he appeared in a corridor boys moved to the walls and froze like cars getting out of the way of a blaring ambulance. Though the terror was in his silence.

I tapped on the door.

"You wished to see me, sir."

"Ah, *Metcalf*. The boy pugilist. Sit."

Flowers in the cut-glass vase in the window behind him, sun dazzling on the glass-fronted bookcases, two white marble busts on columns of men in wigs.

"Our first encounter, Metcalf, was concerned with your putting pieces of carbide in inkwells. Producing a stench—methane, was it?—which forced classrooms to be vacated. Highly amusing. Highly amusing."

He hooked his thumbs into his gown.

"Your career subsequently has been marked by obstinacy and obduracy."

He shook his head slowly and as if in sorrow.

"The Bunsen burner? Hmmm?"

"Yes, sir."

"The machete-thing?"

"Bowie knife, sir."

"I am not interested in the *detail* of your armaments."

"No, sir."

"That playground altercation. An ugly exchange of blows for which I had the honest pleasure of thrashing you. Hmmm? Hmmm?"

"Yes, sir."

"What are we to do with you, Metcalf?"

"I don't know, sir."

"Annealing, wasn't it? When you attempted to burn down the metalwork shop."

"It was an accident, sir."

"One might observe that a disproportionate number of accidents seem to happen in your vicinity. Hmmm? Hmmm?"

"Yes, sir."

"And nagging at the edge of my mind is something to do with a pipette. A pipette and another boy's blazer pocket. Also you?"

"Yes, sir."

"You seem to have an antipathy towards science, Metcalf, but I have been looking at your Ordinary Level results and your marks in English were extraordinarily high. I have spoken to Mr. Rule who rashly used of you the word 'brilliant.'"

He stared at me.

"I sense in you, Metcalf, abilities untapped. But tapped they will be. I will myself tap them. And I will tap them very hard. We'll see how 'brilliant' you are. I have decided that you will win a State Scholarship and go to a decent university where you will take an Honours degree in English. All schools of English require Latin at the Ordinary Level as a prerequisite. You have no Latin as your appalling behaviour and lack of effort precluded entry into the Latin stream. It is therefore my intention to teach you Latin in one year. I shall take you from your present state of numb ignorance to an ability to sight translate the set books—Caesar and Ovid—next year."

He regarded me.

"This will require of you a great deal of hard work."

"Yes, sir."

"No time for games with carbide or machetes."

"No, sir."

"That then is settled. You'll need . . . Blue and yellow, the cover."

"Pardon, sir?"

"The primer, boy. The primer you'll need. *Teach Yourself Latin*. That's it. Now away out of my sight and buy one."

I entered upon my final two years of secondary education known in England then as the sixth form. I was studying only two subjects, English and history. I had only two classes a day and spent the rest of the time reading. I could come and go as I wished and no longer was required to wear school uniform.

On the first lordly day of the new term I rolled into school late, wearing a deadly elegant pair of suede shoes.

"Good God, Metcalf!" exclaimed my history teacher. "Those are the shoes of a Nigerian pimp!"

Why, I wondered, Nigerian?

Every lunchtime I reported to Mr. White's study where he corrected my exercises in grammar and translation. I learned enough Latin to develop a keen regret that I hadn't been taught Greek and Latin from my elementary school years. I came to love the discussions about the connotations of words, the propriety of diction. I also came to understand that Mr. White was infinitely kind and his verbal *harrumphing* an act to amuse himself.

There were only seven students in the English class, all of them very bright and intense, and we were fortunate in our English teacher, a newly minted double first from Cambridge. He had been a student of F. R. Leavis's and so taught us the close reading typical of what was then called New Criticism. When I did go to Bristol University my tutor was L. C. Knights, the founder of *Scrutiny*, which was edited largely by Leavis; so the man had, indirectly, a considerable influence on my life. So closely did we read in that sixth-form class that we came to look on William Empson's *Seven Types of Ambiguity* as light entertainment.

The set books for the Advanced Level exam were works by Chaucer and Shakespeare and a representative clutch of writers from the Romantic period—Wordsworth, Blake, Keats, Byron, and Jane Austen. But these were merely the skeleton of what we studied. I read more in those two years than I'd ever read before. It is impossible to convey the intellectual excitement of those two years. The cliché of being in a pressure cooker is exactly right. Nearly everything that has come afterwards has been an anticlimax.

We read the texts minutely. The placing of the texts in a larger framework was left entirely to us. It was simply *assumed* that we would read literary histories, other books by the set authors, their contemporaries, literary criticism, and period history. I read unceasingly, all day and far into the night; the weekly essays on subjects of our own choosing provided an opportunity to marshal new information and ideas.

I'll try to suggest the breathless, careering quality of the reading. Starting *Northanger Abbey*, the teacher suggested the obvious point that one couldn't really approach it without knowing what was being parodied—which led to *The Castle of Otranto*, *The Monk*, Lewis's *Tales of Terror*, *Vathek*, *Rasselas*, *The Mysteries of Udolpho*, *The Italian*, Charles Maturin's *Melmoth the Wanderer*, and *The Fatal Revenge, or the Family of Montorio*, dire tomes such as Praz's *The Romantic Agony*. Which led to Byron. To Quennell. To revolutions: to Garibaldi, Bolivar, Marx, Proudhon, Bakunin, and Kropotkin. Background books like Watt's *The Rise of the Novel* led, in turn, back to previously unread novels—lesser Defoe, tedious Samuel Richardson, the minor Fielding, Smollett, the *other* Sterne. And somehow forward to the diaries of the Austen period—marvellous gobs of gossip—to Captain Jesse's *Life of Brummel*, the mystic doings of Lady Hester Stanhope, to T. H. White's *The Age of Scandal* and then, of course, like a homing pigeon to White himself who led back to Malory who led to the *Mabinogion* which somehow led to Robert Graves who in turn led back to the Greek myths and *The White Goddess* and to archaeology—Mortimer Wheeler, Sir Arthur Evans, Michael Ventris and Minoan Linear B which led to Jean-François Champollion, Cycladic figures, the Rosetta Stone, Napoleon, fast detour through the French Revolution with side trips to Sade and a glance at *Venus in Furs*, back to Arthur Bryant's popular history of the Peninsular War Campaign and on and on and on.

The same sort of thing with Blake. Off to Swedenborg. To engraving. Back to Hogarth. Forward to Samuel Palmer and Stanley Spencer. Back to British Israelites, to Sir Joshua

Reynolds's *Discourses*, to the 1831 *Life* of Henry Fuseli, to Gilchrist's *Life* of Blake himself, to Fuseli's *Reflections on the Painting and Sculpture of the Greeks*. Side trips to John Wilkes—what *was* the connection?—to Fox and Pitt. Stubbornly back to the texts themselves. Baffled.

What a relief it was when an eminent professor at university said in a seminar group, "What would you say was the *key* to approaching Blake?"

My God! I thought. Is there a key? Something vital I *haven't* read?

Into the thick silence, he said, "Well, the key thing about Blake was that he was a bit potty."

I've often thought of those two sixth-form years and wondered where the energy came from. I can only suppose it was repressed sexuality. There were heated rivalries amongst the boys and we were all devoted to our teacher and I think he too felt for us a kind of love. I'm not implying that this was homosexual but there was certainly some kind of sexual current. I think there always is in good teaching.

But current or no current and current of whatever nature, I would have traded away all this intellectual passion, the pleasure of a perfectly landed right hook, the ooziness of thick paint on canvas, the astonished joy on first reading "though moles see fine tonight in the snouting velvet dingles," I would have traded away all this and any imagined future for the possibility of touching the breasts of the girl who lived next door but one away. Her name was Mary.

My real initiation into the world of books happened just before I went to university. My father had been transferred from Beckenham to Leicester, an unlovely city. Although it had been an important Roman administrative centre little of any antiquity had been spared. The factories were brutal, the streets and housing mean. Guidebooks describe the city as: "Noted for its bulk manufacture of boots and shoes."

I fell into the habit of walking every day to the museum. They had on display a small collection of oils and watercolours by Edward Ardizzone whose work as an illustrator I'd been drawn to some years earlier when I'd seen his cramped and spiky drawings in H. E. Bates's two story collections, *My Uncle Silas* and *Sugar for the Horse*.

Strolling back home one afternoon along New Walk, trees and shrubbery on one side, small houses on the other, I saw a sign in a window: Books. I opened the front door and found myself in a small hallway which was stacked with books on either side. Books almost blocked the staircase to the second floor. I edged along the hall until it opened onto what must once have been a sitting room. It was now a cave of books. Shelved floor to ceiling but most of the floor stacked perilously with thousands more books. Most of them were leather bound.

Sitting at a desk in the middle of the room was a Dickensian figure in rumpled cardigan, *muffler*, pipe ash and dottle. Behind thick glasses his eyes were swimmy as raw oysters. He wore woollen gloves with the fingers cut off. There was a strong suggestion about him of a Peter Sellers character. I asked if I might look round. Although it was full summer the gas fire burbled and popped in the room's silence. On the desk top were a packet of Chocolate Wholewheat Digestives and a large magnifying glass.

Most of the books were eighteenth and early nineteenth century, bound in full calf, but here and there standing out because of their lighter colour were earlier books bound in vellum. I had not had the opportunity before to handle so many old books. On the bottom shelves massive leather-bound folios. I was mesmerized. I felt excited and in some way upset. I was unable to take it all in. *Flustered* is perhaps the word. Titles appeared out of the blur of leather and cloth. Dugdale's *Antiquities of Warwickshire*, William Camden's *Britannia*, Layard's *Nineveh and Its Remains*, Surtees's *Jorrocks's Jaunts and Jollities*, Thomas Love Peacock's *Headlong Hall*.

It felt to me like uncovering a treasure trove, a Sutton Hoo of books, one glittering marvel after another. The room was very hot and the smell of leather heavy. I felt almost as if I were sinking into the books, swooning. I found a three-volume leather-bound edition of *The History of Tom Jones, a Foundling* and asked how much it was. He opened the first volume and peered through the magnifying glass at the title page.

"Are you a local boy?"

"No, we've just moved here."

"I don't get many boys in here local *or* otherwise."

"The books are beautiful."

He looked up at me with swimmy eyes.

"Beautiful," he repeated. "Hmm. Well, well. You're a rum one and no mistake."

"Why rum?"

"And what will you do with our Mr. Jones?"

"Well, I like the story," I said and then, shy and blushing but somehow compelled, rushed on, "but I'd like to own a book that someone held and read in the eighteenth century."

He twisted his head round and up and opened his mouth and made a caricature of astonishment.

"'Pon my soul!" he said. "*Upon my soul!* Ten bob."

I was soon going to see Bernard Halliday nearly every day. It was a fortunate conjunction for both of us as I was eager to learn and he was lonely and longing to teach. He instructed me to buy John Carter's *ABC for Book Collectors* and his *Taste and Technique in Book Collecting*. Then I was to read Lowndes's *Bibliographer's Manual of English Literature*. Later he guided me through the gruelling terrain of Ronald McKerrow's *An Introduction to Bibliography for Literary Students*. He taught me to read catalogues and gave me old catalogues from Maggs and Quaritch.

"Always read catalogues," he'd say. "Catalogues are where all the knowledge sifts down to."

If I made mistakes he would say sternly, "It behooves you to know what's o'clock." The tea I brewed for us he dismissed as "maiden's water." Modern first editions were anathema. "No different from gambling." And then with shaking shoulders he forced out, "Some bloody pillocks collect . . . *detective stories!*"

I soaked up Mr. Halliday's outpouring of information. How to clean dust-soiled vellum bindings. Better than any gum or rubber eraser was white sliced bread. How to straighten bowed boards. Leather soap. Neat's-foot oil. The uses of lighter fluid.

I wallowed in bindings and leathers and fonts, in all the lovely jargon of the trade, half-titles, colophons, blind stamping, foxing, black letter, washed leaves, cancels . . . I came to believe that there were few things in the world more beautiful than the deep burning black of Baskerville type on crisp rag paper.

The best part of this education, however, was simply handling the books in their hundreds, coming to an understanding of the meaning of condition. I would take volumes to him excavated from the filthy piles and he would say, "So *that's* where that went. Well! Well! Interesting old book that. Russian. St. John Chrysostom. Know what that means? 'Golden Mouth.' Homilies, these are. Parchment and written in a nice hand. How much? Oh, I don't know. I could let you have it for nine thousand . . ."

He would then break down in rheumy mirth and mop at his eyes with his grubby handkerchief.

He did give me what are called "reading" or "working" copies of various of the well-known eighteenth-century novels. Both terms mean "damaged" or "in non-collectible condition." I remember taking to Canada Mackenzie's *The Man of Feeling*, Graves's *The Spiritual Quixote* (much appreciated because it is a satire on Methodism), and Smollett's *Roderick Random*. He also gave me "reading" copies of anonymous eighteenth-century novels typically written "By a Lady."

Anonymous novels are catalogued, incompletely, in a work by Halkett and Laing entitled *A Dictionary of the Anonymous and Pseudonymous Literature of Great Britain*. I've never read any kind of survey which talks about them *as literature*. During those visits to that filthy house with the musty smell of old leather and old paper in my nostrils, I imagined reading those novels in Halkett and Laing and writing about them as the matrix, as it were, from which rose the peaks of Richardson, Fielding, Smollett, Sterne . . .

That germ of an idea never left me and many years later in Canada, after various false starts, and with some guidance from the Vancouver book dealer William Hoffer and with the almost fatherly advice and encouragement of the Ottawa dealer Richard Simmins, I did form a collection of over five thousand volumes which documented the short story in Canada in the twentieth century. I also built collections of Contact Press and the House of Anansi Press, both of which were bought by the National Library of Canada.

ALMA MATER

DISSOLUTE would perhaps be the best word to describe my university years. I left home at eighteen to go to Bristol and never went home again. Set free for the first time in my life and entirely lacking any form of supervision I began to lead a life of excess. I was celebrating my escape from my mother and her cheerless and puritanical background which firmly equated sex with sin. I was also celebrating my escape from a suffocating and numbing middle-class existence.

In the story "Single Gents Only" I wrote:

> But he found it easier to approach what he would become by defining what he was leaving behind. What he most definitely *wasn't*—hideous images came to mind: sachets of dried lavender, Post Office Savings Books, hyacinth bulbs in bowls, the *Radio Times* in a padded leather cover embossed with the words *Radio Times*, Sunday-best silver tongs for removing sugar-cubes from sugar-bowls, plump armchairs.

My years at Bristol seem to me now sunlit and lazy and always expanding and deepening in new pleasures. The intellectual aspect of the university did not weigh on me. It was all something of an anti-climax after the intensity of those sixth-form years. There were gaps to be plugged, of course, and I plugged them; I endured the tedium of Chaucer's supposed translation of *The Romaunt of the Rose*, Malory's *Morte d'Arthur* and Burton's *The Anatomy of Melancholy* and suchlike—the sort of works that Philip Larkin would have dismissed as "ape's bumfodder."

The main chore at Bristol was having to attend weekly seminars for three years in Anglo-Saxon. After having ground through the vocabulary and grammar I was able to translate such gripping fragments as remain: *The Battle of Maldon*, the poems of Cynewulf, the voyages of the intrepid Ohthere and Wulfstan, and *The Battle of Brunanburh*, a poem of 73 lines about a battle between an army of Norsemen and Scots and an army of West Saxons and Mercians. The location of Brunanburh is unknown but it was apparently near the sea.

Oh, wens and thorns!

It was not enough to keep the mind alive.

The only other constraints on a carefree life were a Shakespeare seminar with L. C. Knights and occasional meetings with my Moral Tutor, the poet Charles Tomlinson. He was myopic and morose and kept the blinds and curtains in his office permanently closed so that meetings with him were like sitting in a gloomy tent. It surprised me that this frail little man rode a motorcycle. He kept it in the office beside his desk because he claimed his landlady's dog had once bitten it. I was supposed to write essays for him but he hadn't sufficient energy to invent titles and I really couldn't spare the time. After a few visits I stopped going regularly and just popped in occasionally to see that he was all right.

Insofar as I could, I let the university fall away from me. I was supposed to wear a gown at all times, not only in the university but in the streets. I did so for the first couple of weeks, then stopped as I looked and felt daft. On colder nights I wore it in bed.

Pubs became my second home. Rough pubs sold Somerset "scrumpy," a still cider, somewhat sour and of ferocious potency. Really rough pubs sold a truly disgusting Bristol speciality, a half-and-half mixture of draught bitter and draught port. I became so accepted in my local that I was asked to join the darts team, a great honour in a pub where students were barely tolerated. Many of the clientele were Bristol-born Jamaicans, street-fighting men who lived by breaking and entering and extortion and, in one case, because of the girth of his appendage, by starring in extremely rude movies.

The landlord's wife produced such typical pub fayre as cheddar cheese cobs, Scotch eggs, Cornish pasties, pork pies, and pickled eggs in a jar of cloudy liquid. Someone had printed on the jar's label: No Farting. She it was, rather than her husband, who waded into altercations; even the Jamaicans were frightened of her. It was the sort of pub where on the evening opening hour of six, old men with the shakes would say, "Just pick that up and hold it to my lips, boy." Others would wag a fatherly finger and say, "You take after me, lad. Never more than thirteen pints a night."

My other consuming interest was, of course, girls. I went from the famine of a single-sex school to feast. It seemed I was never without female companionship, none of it serious on either side in a long-term kind of way but always generous and affectionate and often torrid. The most extraordinary of these liaisons happened in Jersey where I was by accident working on a farm and sleeping in a barn with peasants brought in from Normandy as casual labour. Among them were identical twin sisters, largish girls, and I ended up in bed with both of them at the same time. There had been nothing Casanova-ish on my part. They just came and got me.

I had deliberately delayed applying for a room in a Hall of Residence in the hope that by the time I did they'd all be taken. A Hall of Residence sounded institutional to me and unlikely to tolerate what I vaguely had in mind. I was more interested in what the university called Alternative Accommodation and alternative accommodation I certainly got. My story "Single Gents Only" has more than a tinge of autobiography in it. "The Lady Who Sold Furniture" also has a basis in fact. In the first weeks of that first term I moved four times. I stayed in a succession of peculiar places. One was actually a boarding house with long-term non-student residents who addressed each other as Mr. and Miss. They were variously weird—a walleye, a toupee, tics—and all behaved with a creaking formality. Dinners were eaten in mincing, lip-dabbing silence. The owners of this mausoleum exhibited a ghastly gentility, the husband, cavalry twill trousers, Viyella shirts, and lemon silk cravats, his having been a pooh-bah of some sort in Uttar Pradesh. I thought of him as "The Major." Mrs. Major draped herself in ankle-length Paisley-pattern material. At night she left out in the dining room festive thermos flasks of cocoa and biscuits on doilies for the inmates.

In the hall suspended from a mahogany frame hung a huge Benares brass gong chased and enamelled in red and green. On the frame's mahogany ledge lay a padded striker, a long mahogany handle and a fleece-covered head the size of a baseball. Arrived back from the pub on my fifth night of residence and standing in the silent hall I could no longer resist the golden invitation. I gave the gong a two-handed BONG. The sound was astounding. The sound waves shimmered on for ever. In a panic I put the striker back on its ledge but it fell and as I stooped to pick it up my head hit the edge of the gong again. The inmates began to come down the staircase in their dressing gowns and leather slippers and stood whispering and sibilant. Mrs. Major appeared horribly without makeup and wearing a hairnet. I started up the stairs towards my room.

Someone said, "One can't just . . ."

I could feel all their eyes on my back.

I got the boot in the morning from The Major.

I found a room in a house of students the next day through an advertisement in the Students' Union building. Settled in, I fell into the habit of reading into the small hours and getting up at about 11:30 in the morning. Breakfast was usually scrumpy and Madras beef curry.

At a party one night I met a first-year student called David Hirschmann. He was taking an honours degree in philosophy. Standing in the kitchen, David pouring wine for revellers, we started chatting in an idle sort of way. After a couple of hours the conversation had become deeply personal. We left the party and walked and talked, sat in a park on a bench and talked. Talked until dawn surprised us. By breakfast time we had agreed that we had to move in together as soon as this could be arranged. It was a relationship that lasted for many years. I was very shaken last year when other Bristol friends, Charles and Penny Denton, wrote to tell me that David had cancer of the brain. He had been given, they said, about three months. I was making preparations to go to see him when Penny Denton wrote again to tell me he had died.

David was gentle, kind, quick-witted, but at the same time rather clumsy and goofy. One Sunday evening four of us decided that we wanted to go to a restaurant in Clifton but we had no cash. David was the most respectable-looking of us, so we decided that he should put on his suit and see if the owner would accept a cheque. The restaurant had about eight tables and the owner cooked on an open grill at the far end of the room. David opened the door, did something Tati-like with his umbrella, and quite literally *fell* into the restaurant, landing heavily on his back. Guido, the owner, hurried between the tables and stood looking down. David, bright red in the face and still supine, said, "May we pay by cheque?"

David's father was a doctor in Hampstead. His mother had been a matron in a large London hospital. Perhaps because of this background he was fastidiously clean and when we were living together he would actually dust things and put books into piles and hold wineglasses up to the light to check them for cleanliness. He used to nag me.

"Surely you don't expect her to sleep in *those* sheets, do you?" We were in a way like the Odd Couple. David would listen to Pablo Casals playing the unaccompanied cello suites; I would then claim the record player to listen to the majestic misery of Ma Rainey singing "Deep Moanin' Blues" and "Daddy, Goodbye" along with jugs booming and kazoos blatting.

David's girlfriends continued to be hopelessly neurotic. We suffered through a girl who appeared far too frequently in the middle of the night weeping and accusing David of base infidelities, a girl who swallowed pills and had to be pumped out, a kleptomaniac on probation, a girl who was quite enthusiastic about sexual intercourse but who refused to remove her bra, saying only that she "couldn't," and a girl who cut herself. I think he was attracted to the idea of helping them.

Eventually a small group of us, David, Charles Denton, Penny Player, and Walter Smith lived together in various combinations. Wally had two great enthusiasms—wine and bullfighting. Hemingway's *Death in the Afternoon* was a Bible in whatever rooms we were occupying. Harvey's, the famous Bristol wine merchants and purveyor of Harvey's Bristol Cream, held an annual sale of half bottles of discontinued wines; Wally spurred us on to buy dozens of these. We were, he said, to taste them and make notes about each in an attempt to educate our palates. To Wally's distress we drank the entire "cellar" over a two-day period, in a fug of cigarette smoke, and shot pigeons from the window with my Belgian .410 shotgun.

One of David's great enthusiasms was films and we went every week to the university film society. I watched all the classic material, not realizing at the time that I was getting an education in writing. We watched Sergei Eisenstein's *The*

Battleship Potemkin, *Alexander Nevsky*, and *Ivan the Terrible*, Erich von Stroheim, Luis Buñuel, Vittorio de Sica, Robert Bresson's harrowing *Diary of a Country Priest*, all the early Bergman—*Summer with Monika*, *Smiles of a Summer Night*, *The Seventh Seal*, *Wild Strawberries*, *The Magician*.

I was particularly attracted to the silent comedies, to Buster Keaton, Harold Lloyd, Harry Langdon, and Charlie Chaplin. I loved the timing and grace of these performances. But perhaps my favourite films were Jacques Tati's *Jour de fête*, *Les Vacances de Monsieur Hulot*, and *Mon Oncle*. There are scenes in all three films which I've treasured for most of my life. Who could be unaffected by the postman in *Jour de fête* diverging from the Tour de France to cycle full-tilt into a lake? What could be funnier than Monsieur Hulot being catapulted into the sea by the sudden tightening of a tow-rope he is stepping over? It is the *delicacy* of Tati that enraptures me. I believe profoundly in the Hulot world.

The best was yet to come in the sixties and early seventies. In Montreal I used to go regularly to the Elysée theatre, which showed Bertolucci, Fassbinder, Fellini, Antonioni, and Satyajit Ray. Then suddenly I lost interest in films. The world had changed. Films shrank towards cartoons. The last film I had any relish for was Fellini's *Amarcord* in 1973.

David's death brought me back into contact with Charles and Penny Denton. After university Charles went to work as a freelance television producer. He then became ATV controller of programs. He was head of BBC TV Drama for three years. Governor of the British Film Institute. He is a member of the Arts Council of England and a Fellow of the Royal Society of Arts.

I have a memory of coming home one afternoon to hear Charles playing his saxophone. The sound seemed to be coming from the bathroom. He was sitting in a tub of hot water, sax over the side.

I said, "Why have you got your jeans on?"

He said, "It's solid, man. It's concrete."

Who can foresee the future?

One enthusiasm I didn't share with David or any of the others was rock climbing. I had joined the university club in my first week. I have no idea why. Experienced climbers taught beginners the mysteries of belaying, of feeding rope to the leader of the pitch, and the uses of slings, pitons, and carabiners. We climbed in the Avon Gorge on a cliff face very close to the Clifton Suspension Bridge. The club had a handbook of the various climbs and graded them for difficulty. One nightmare was called Dawn Walk, a traverse pitch which was completely unprotected. A tiny fault perhaps an eighth of an inch wide led upwards across the rock face. The only holds were flakes, cracks, and crimps. It was essential to keep moving as there was nowhere to rest.

After a few months I started going to Wales with some of the other club members. We went to the Llanberis Pass and climbed the gloom of the Idwal slabs. I wonder sometimes why I suffered the terrors of Idwal. The pitches were cruel, the bruising from the ropes after coming off the face was Technicolor. Nowadays, the prospect of mounting a stepladder induces mild hysteria and nausea. Changes with age, someone told me, to the inner ear.

In 1958 Wally Smith was agitating for a visit to Spain. He performed veronicas and naturels with sheets and raincoats; he begged us to charge him; he accepted ears. He practised that arms-wide, defiant thrusting out of chest and loins towards the bull known as an *adorno* until we reminded him that Hemingway had considered it vulgar. We decided that as true believers in Hemingway we'd go to the fiesta of San Fermín in Pamplona. We planned to hitchhike down through France and cross into Spain at St. Jean de Luz, take a bus to San Sebastian, and a train from there to Pamplona. We planned not to hitchhike in Spain because the word was that the Guardia Civil were erratic.

David and I hitchhiked together and made good time towards Bordeaux. We were dropped off one lunchtime on the outskirts of Angoulême. I was ravenous and we found a small café with outside tables alongside a chicken run. The owner came out and we ordered omelettes and salads.

"It's not very clean, is it?" said David.

Who'd been tiresome for two days about toilets.

Clean it wasn't and it stank of chicken shit but it turned out to be the site of a miraculous event.

The omelette was runny inside. The salad was slices of tomato in a vinaigrette dressing with fresh-ground black pepper. This was the first omelette I'd ever eaten. It was superb. I was astonished. I had eaten things before that my mother *called* omelettes but compared with *this* delicacy they were like shoe soles.

Food in England in the fifties was as bad as food is now in the Balkans. My mother's cooking was good but it was narrowly traditional. To this day she cannot envision rice or pasta; they are too deeply foreign. The British are capable of almost any culinary perversion: curry on chips, spaghetti on chips (or toast!), Chip butties. English awfulness about food can undermine the strongest ethnic traditions; in a Chinese restaurant in Soho I was once served sweet-and-sour Brussels sprouts.

My wife, Myrna, remembers the childlike wonder with which the British greeted eggplants. The Sunday colour supplements carried photographs of them, articles explained what they were, recipes suggested what might be done with them. This was in 1965.

Unless one were wealthy or had travelled widely I don't think many young people in the fifties in England had much idea of what food might be. The war years had been grim. Compulsory cod-liver oil and concentrated orange juice for children, the residue of the tablespoon of oil reacting with the sweetness of the juice to produce daily and instant nausea before school. School dinners. Powdered milk. Powdered eggs. Strawberry jam made of turnips.

The B.C. novelist John Mills grew up in London. He told me that they used to have a version of spotted dick for school dinners. It was made from flour and water and steamed in a cylinder which opened in half lengthways. The resultant grey-white tube of pudding was then cut into rounds. The children called this dessert "dead man's leg."

This simple meal in Angoulême was momentous for me; it was the first time I grasped the *idea* of food.

When I think now of Spain I think always of being in the *plaza de toros* after the *paseo* but before the first bull has erupted from the *toril.* In my mind's eye I see the first matador's *cuadrilla* flaring out the yellow-and-magenta fighting capes and sprinkling them with water to weight them against even a flip of evening breeze.

Workmen preparing to work.

The fiesta in Pamplona is rather frightening if one is sober. The entire town is drunk for days on end. It vibrates with crazed energy. From early morning when the signal rockets go up to announce that the bulls have been released, are coming *now,* six Miura bulls jostling along the streets with four steers to calm them, the mob of runners glancing back to see the horns swaying behind them, until 5 p.m. when the *corrida* starts, the entire town drinks.

Sometimes a bull gets separated from the herd and the police yell and scream warnings as a solo bull is dangerous and will kill. Many of the young *aficionados* are still drunk from the night before when they pile into the *plaza de toros* ahead of the running bulls. After the bulls are herded into the *toril* a young heifer with padded horns is loosed into the ring. The *aficionados* perform self-absorbed, exaggerated passes with jackets, shirts, or sheets of newspaper.

A very tall boy from California takes the heifer by the horns and dumps it on its side rodeo-style. The Spanish boys are outraged at this insult to taurine dignity and mob him and beat him rather badly.

Many of the peasants in their traditional white clothes with red neckerchiefs and red cummerbunds and nearly all the hundreds of American and British students carry the traditional wineskins from which they drink all day. The skins are coated inside with pitch which renders the wine even more vile than it naturally is. In the restaurants, the waiters, unasked, put on every table three opened bottles of wine—red, white, rosé. The stacks of saucers rise on the outdoor café tables which are haunted by sellers of lottery tickets and beggars hawking postcard photographs of Franco. Shoeshine boys crawl under tables grabbing at feet until they are heaved away.

In this alcoholic haze things happen. A brass band appears playing a *paso doble*, a procession of giant puppets meanders past, figures representing Kings and Queens and Moors. Groups of peasants spring suddenly into one of the local dances. A statue of the Virgin Mary is borne about the town seated on a throne; the throne is carried on the shoulders of young men all wearing blue blouses. A large open car drives up and down the streets. In the back sit three young women in white ruffled dresses who throw the heads of fresh flowers into the crowds. No one knows who they are. In the middle of the square a priest in a black soutane, gravely drunk, is conducting a series of *verónicas* with an American flag.

None of this seems peculiar.

We were lucky that year to see graceful and heart-stopping fighting by Paco Camino. The choreography and rhythm of the passes was thrilling; he was fighting so close to the bulls that their withers bumped him pass after pass smearing him with blood. He was taking his *alternativa*. We saw fights on the way home in the hills in Huesca, the buildings still pocked with Civil War bullet holes, in Bilbao, in San Sebastian, and then over the border in Pau and Dax, all getting progressively worse.

I went to Pamplona again in 1959 with a girlfriend. It was the year Hemingway was writing *The Dangerous Summer* for *Life* magazine. He was following the mano-a-mano fights by Antonio Ordóñez and Luis Miguel Dominguin. On one of the days of the fiesta Hemingway was seated at the *barrera* with his entourage of about seven people. The first matador spread a fighting cape over the *barrera* in front of Hemingway and dedicated to him the Miura horror that had just trotted out into the sunshine.

Walking back into town from the *plaza de toros* after the fights were over I saw Hemingway and his group. Two of these were young, beautiful American girls and there was a girl even younger, dark-haired and sounding Irish. I was callow enough to speak to him. I told him I loved his writing. For a famous man accosted in the street by a kid he was civil enough.

Back in Bristol these sunlit days came to an end. We had graduated and David set off to Cambridge to begin a Ph.D. in philosophy. I've always remembered his answer attempting to explain to me what philosophy was all about if it *wasn't* about what constitutes living a good life. "Well," he said, with a certain exasperation, "it's about what we *mean* when we say 'I posted a letter.'"

Christ!

Charles and Penny got married and Charles moved into the world of documentary films. He directed one that involved endless travel in the United States and endless nights in isolated motels. I asked him if this wasn't tedious. "Oh, no," he said. "I always travel with Trollope's *Chronicles of Barsetshire*." Wally disappeared into the mysteries of the wine trade. I felt lonely and abandoned. I could think of nothing I wanted to do. I was reluctant to give up idleness, curry for breakfast, darts, and beer, and so, adrift, I signed up for the buffooneries of a year in the Bristol University Education Department to acquire a teaching certificate.

University departments of education seem to be universally staffed by dimwits and ninnies. I could barely endure the indignities of that year and attended lectures as rarely as possible. It was intellectually repugnant. One woman lecturer advocated the choral speaking of verse as a way of leading children towards the light. A tall bearded Quaker in Quaker sandals considered Tolkien's *The Hobbit* an excellent vehicle of moral instruction; part of his course involved drawing dragons, Orcs, Gandalf, and Bilbo Baggins with coloured pencils *on parchment*. Others favoured recorder playing and the singing of roundelays. Origami. Aquariums. Calligraphy. Hamsters. The year was like being incarcerated in a twee loony bin.

My first year of teaching was even worse. I disliked the incipient violence which brooded over what I will call Bluebell Secondary Modern School. The headmaster was obsessed with Control and gave a strong impression of being insane. I sketched a portrait of him in my novella "The Lady Who Sold Furniture."

The bus lumbered down from my flat towards Bristol city centre, through all the commerce, on through the drab streets of terraced houses and small shops—newsagents, fish and chips, turf accountants—towards the decaying prefabs and the rawness of the housing estate served by Bluebell School. The invisible dividing line between the city I lived in and the city I worked in was marked for me each morning by a butcher's shop whose windows announced in whitewash capitals:

UDDER 9D PER POUND

I pretended an enthusiasm for teaching but could never persuade myself that each day wasn't futile. Teaching remedial reading and spelling to twelve-year-olds bored me. Reading the adventures of Nigel with a little West Indian girl leaking tears and snuffling.

"They always on at we."

"Who is?"

"Calling us nigger."

Staring blankly at her until it dawned that we were dealing here with the word "Nigel."

Added to such daily jollities as this were the supervision and consumption of school dinners and the recounting by some of the dullest men I've ever met of the nature of the previous evening's television programmes.

I'm what I'd call a Selective Viewer but honesty compels me to admit that last night's documentary on edible fungus . . .

At the end of this year I got a job in a reform school. In one of my stories I called this degrading establishment the Eastmill Reception Centre. The centre took in convicted boys from London, the Midlands, the West Country, and Wales and evaluated them for permanent placement in Borstals. In this dolorous dump I taught English. I think I reasoned to myself that if I didn't like teaching at the secondary modern level I'd move much lower academically and become something more akin to a social worker saving souls. I was infected at this time with mildly leftish sentiments and actually voted once for Harold Wilson, an act which now shames me profoundly.

I find that I often catch in fiction the essence of a place better than I do in exposition, probably because exposition is closer to reportage and fiction is a distillation.

What follows is from "The Eastmill Reception Centre," though it also captures something of Bluebell Secondary Modern.

> I soon lost my nervousness of these boys under my charge. As the days passed, I stopped seeing them as exponents of theft, rape, breaking and entering, arson, vandalism, grievous bodily harm, and extortion, and saw them for what they were—working-class boys who were all, without exception, of low average intelligence or mildly retarded.

We laboured on with phonics, handwriting, spelling, reading.

Of all the boys, I was most drawn to Dennis. He was much like all the rest but unfailingly cheerful and co-operative. Dennis could chant the alphabet from A to Z without faltering but he had to start at A. His mind was active, but the connections it made were singular.

If I wrote CAT, he would stare at the word with a troubled frown. When I sounded out C-A-T, he would say indignantly: Well, it's *cat*, isn't it? We had a cat, old tom-cat. Furry knackers, he had, and if you stroked 'em . . .

F-I-S-H brought to mind the chip shop up his street and his mum who wouldn't never touch rock salmon because it wasn't nothing but a fancy name for conger-eel.

C-O-W evoked his Auntie Fran—right old scrubber *she* was, having it away for the price of a pint . . .

Such remarks would spill over into general debate on the ethics of white women having it off with spades and pakis, they was heathen, wasn't they? Said their prayers to gods and that, didn't they? *Didn't* they? Well, there you are then. *And* their houses stank of curry and that. You couldn't deny it. Not if you knew what you was talking about.

These lunatic discussions were often resolved by Paul, Dennis's friend, who commanded the respect of all the boys because he was serving a second term and had a tattoo of a dagger on his left wrist and a red and green humming-bird on his right shoulder. He would make pronouncement:

I'm not saying that they are and I'm not saying that they're not but what I *am* saying is . . .

Then would follow some statement so bizarre or so richly irrelevant that it imposed stunned silence.

He would then re-comb his hair.

Into the silence, I would say,

"Right. Let's get back to work, then. Who can tell me what a vowel is?"

Dennis's hand.

It's what me dad 'ad."

"What!"

"It's your insides."

"What is?"

"Cancer of the vowel."

The *only* good thing about Eastmill was that I met there the school's psychologist, James Gaite. Jim was my age, not long out of the University of Hull. His job was to interview the intake, administer standardized voodoo tests, and then assign the boys to particular reform schools, all meaningless, of course, since boys were always sent where there happened to be room.

Jim was very clever, funny, cynical, and stylish. He had been educated at a minor public school before university and affected a manner languid and rather snotty. He worked ambitiously to secure the most prestigious academic jobs and having secured them despised them. It became a pattern in Canada, the USA, and Australia. It added up in the long run to a peculiarly hollow life. The essence of the matter was, I think, that he believed in nothing and was bored. He died of cancer in Adelaide in 1999.

But in 1962 Jim was a lifeline in Eastmill. We were the only two men in the establishment with any education. We were the only two men who could not have been described as brutal. We amused and entertained each other. We could talk of books, music, film, and painting as an antidote to Eastmill's daily grind.

Again, from "The Eastmill Reception Centre."

Every afternoon was given over to Sports and Activities.

Cricket alternated, by Houses, with gardening. Gardening was worse than cricket. The garden extended for roughly two acres. On one day, forty boys attacked the earth with hoes. The next day forty boys smoothed the work of the hoes with rakes. On the day following, the hoes attacked again. Nothing was actually planted.

The evening meals in the Staff Dining Room, served from huge aluminum utensils, were exactly like the school dinners of my childhood: unsavoury stews with glutinous dumplings, salads with wafers of cold roast beef with bits of string in them, jam tarts and Spotted Dick accompanied by an aluminum jug of lukewarm custard topped by a thickening skin.

Uncle Arthur always ate in his apartment with the wife referred to as "Mrs. Arthur" but always appeared in time for coffee to inquire if we'd enjoyed what he always called our "comestibles."

Mr. Austyn, referred to by the boys as "Browner Austyn," always said:

May I trouble you for the condiments?

Between the main course and dessert, Mr. Brotherton, often boisterously drunk, beat time with his spoon, singing, much to the distress of Mr. Austyn:

Auntie Mary
Had a canary
Up the leg of her drawers.

Mr. Grendle drizzled on about recidivists and the inevitability of his being dispatched in the metalwork shop. Mr. Hemmings, who drove a sports car, explained the internal-combustion engine. Mr. Austyn praised the give and take of sporting activity, the lessons of co-operation and joint endeavour, the Duke of Edinburgh's Awards, Outward Bound, the beneficial moral results of pushing oneself to the limits of physical endurance.

But conversation always reverted to pay scales, overtime rates, the necessity of making an example of this boy or that, of sorting out, gingering up, knocking the stuffing out of etc. this or that young lout who was trying it on, pushing his luck, just begging for it etc.

When the Protestant School Board of Montreal recruiters placed advertisements in the local papers and conducted interviews in a Bristol hotel, Jim and I decided to sign on. We were both appalled by Eastmill, bored, restless. Montreal, we decided, could not be worse than being locked up with 160 dim, sad, smelly boys. And the pay compared with what we were getting at Eastmill seemed princely.

The formalities were simple. We merely had to furnish evidence of sobriety and moral probity attested to by a minister of religion and the results of a Wassermann test proving that we were not riddled with pox or clap. I promptly wrote a sickening letter and signed it as the Vicar of St. Michael and All Hallows and some days later took my place in a long line of subdued Jamaicans at the Bristol Royal Infirmary's VD Clinic. Two men in white lab coats were indulging in unseemly badinage with the clientele.

When my turn came, the technician said, "Well, then, where have you been sticking it?"

"I haven't recently," I said with some asperity, "been 'sticking it' anywhere. I'm not here for medical reasons. I only need a test because I'm emigrating."

He stared at me.

Then he shouted, "Hey, George. Come over here and listen to this one."

During these years I'd been living in rooms rented from Robert Giddings, a university friend. He had found a small house secluded at the end of a laneway and had rented it immediately. He called this house Quagmire Lodge. Bob had had the misfortune of contracting polio at the age of eleven and was confined to a wheelchair but such was his vitality and enthusiasm that one tended to forget entirely that he was crippled.

We shared a non-Leavisite passion for Dickens, Smollett, and Fielding, and Bob later in life went on to publish books on all three. This passion for the eighteenth and early nineteenth centuries meant that the house was festooned with late-state pulls of Hogarth's *Harlot's Progress*, *Rake's Progress*, and *Marriage à la Mode*. These and the caricatures of Thomas Rowlandson were then fairly cheaply available. Bob's other, slightly eccentric, passion was for German military marches. I would sometimes come home to find Bob wearing a German infantry helmet and rows of Wehrmacht medals, red in the face with the exertion of conducting records of the Berlin Military Police Band.

I chose not to probe into this enthusiasm.

We lost touch when I came to Canada but Bob phoned me last year around the time of David's death and we caught up with each other's doings. He had just retired from Bournemouth University which he claims has the distinction of being absolutely the worst university in the United Kingdom. He mentioned that he'd published an autobiography which was concerned with his life in schools and academe as a disabled person. He sent me a copy of *You Should See Me in Pyjamas* and I read with fascination of his childhood years in residential hospitals. And then I came to his years as an undergraduate at Bristol and was very surprised to read the following:

> One of the most entertaining characters I met at Bristol was my friend John Metcalf. He was a vicar's son, but none the worse for that. Going around with John was a laugh and a nightmare at the same time as you never knew what was going to happen next. In those days there was a great working-class thing on the go, Richard Hoggart had only recently published *The Uses of Literacy* and among the vogue books were *Room at the Top*, *A Kind of Loving*, and *Saturday Night and Sunday Morning*. We went about

completely Sillitoed most of the time. It was all donkey jackets, football, Anger and Centre 42 (with exhibitions of workers' tools arranged in backgrounds by Feliks Topolski). John had a flat cap he called his Sou'Wesker. When we were not actually out banning bombs, or compelling the government to resign, or bringing the South African economy to its knees by refusing to eat their rotten old pineapple chunks, we were in pubs swilling the plebeian natural cider. One Friday, having achieved some sort of physical parity by encouraging friends to get paralytic, we left for home. John didn't make it back to his flat. His flat-mate assumed that he had picked up some bird, and went to bed. He'd be home the next day. But he wasn't. Nor the next day. No one saw him for two weeks. Then he suddenly reappeared. He'd fallen off the docks, landed in an open boat and finished up—penniless—in the Channel Islands where he'd had to get a job packing tomatoes to earn his fare back.

One of his relatives gave him a pocket-sized radio as a birthday present. It never worked properly but by turning the volume up suddenly you could get a sound like a burst of applause in radio programmes. John always carried it with him to provide instant approbation for wit and repartee. He eventually became literary editor of *Nonesuch* and soon we were in hot water, which resulted in our being brought before one of the university's most senior administrators.

We wanted to publish John's review of *Lady Chatterley* (just published unexpurgatedly by Penguin) in the university newspaper. The authorities had hit the ceiling. We were threatened with rustication, suspension and all the terrors of the earth. John stuck it out. The interview was, as they say, a stormy one. The authorities insisted that nothing should appear which might bring a blush to the cheek of a young person. Some of the short words used had, it seems, caused offence. We were interviewed by a man called Landless. In the course of this scene, without batting an eyelid, John called him Landslide, Landscape, Landgrave, Landlord, Landwehr, Landlubber and Landmine. The result was a compromise. The review appeared but contained such gems as "Lawrence overworks his vocabulary, especially the words ___ and ___."

But his finest hour was on teaching practice. Taking a class for the Napoleonic wars he was interrupted by a boy who said: "We got one of they cannon things at home. Our dad's in the Navy and they use them for warnings an' that. I'll bring it in tomorrow." The next day the boy duly appeared, staggering under a weighty load. "I got it, sir! And all the gubbins that go with it. Okay if we fire it out the window?" To his everlasting credit, John decided to go and ask the headmaster first.

The school was a vast modish glasshouse and after several long corridors and staircases John reached the headmaster's office. He knocked on the door. "Come in!" As he entered there was a dull boom in the distance. "My God!" exclaimed the startled headmaster. "What on earth was that?"

"That's just what I came to see you about," said John calmly.

They rushed to the scene. In the classroom they found a large black circle on the wall, surrounded by an irregular pigmented mosaic of all the colours of the rainbow. The young cannoneer explained that they had decided it would be too dangerous to fire it out the window and to fire shells, so they had filled it with a box of coloured chalks and fired it at the classroom wall. Several windows had shattered. The whole episode caused quite a stir in our university department, but then great emphasis had been placed on the value of visual aids in those days. John went on to become a very successful teacher. Abroad.

A TERRIFYING LEGACY

JIM HAD CHARGED ME with securing us an apartment. He had flown from England to visit some friends in the States where he was busy philandering. I was limp and exhausted when the Cunard liner *Carinthia* docked in Montreal. I'd been throwing up for days; my stomach had first contracted in Liverpool when they'd switched on the engines.

I walked from the docks to the YMCA. Montreal was a throb and an exotic blur. I was bemused by size, speed, noise. An English eye could hardly make sense of it. Skyscrapers, huge cars, signs in French, police with sunglasses, paunches, and unthinkable *guns*, not a chemist's in sight but drugstores as in Raymond Chandler, crazed drivers, on Ste Catherine Street crushes of people seemingly from all over the world, neon signs, air conditioning, a sense everywhere of unimaginable affluence, shimmering heat, abominable beer . . .

I soon found us an apartment on Lincoln at Guy and thought it palatial compared with student digs in Bristol. I was later to realize it was verging on slummy but couldn't see that then.

Jim bowled into town driving a vast and vulgar red car with white upholstery.

August rolled into September and school started.

I was teaching English at Rosemount High School in the city's east end. I found out on the first day that I was also teaching Canadian history which was unfortunate for the students as I didn't know any. After Bluebell and Eastmill, Rosemount was like a rest home. The students were polite, tolerant of the idea of learning, and mostly able to read. No one threatened me with a knife. It was refreshing.

The England I'd just left was a homogeneous society and one simply didn't come across many non-English people even at university. My most exotic racial experience at Bristol was sharing a room for a few weeks with Mrs. Bandaranaike's nephew. So I was fascinated with classes of such disparate backgrounds—Italian, Greek, Lebanese, Latvian, Chinese . . . I suddenly had a great deal to learn.

The students were pleasant and co-operative. The staff in the English department, however, were in the main gruesome. I wrote about them in an essay in my 1992 anthology *The New Story Writers*.

> The head of the English department was a faded lady of ghastly, dentured gentility who wrote poems and had published a volume of them at her own expense. I can see that little book in my mind's eye even now; it was bound in nasty blue fabrikoid. One of the poems was called "Modern Menace" and warned the reader about the dangers of alcohol. My favourite lines ran:
>
> *For ways we have against this Brute,*
> *If offered sherry, say, "Make mine Fruit!"*
>
> Once a term she would correct a set of essays from each of my classes to discipline me and to show me how a seasoned professional did the job. All her corrections were neatly written in the margins in red ink. She once ringed in red in a student's essay the sentence "My father just

grunted" and wrote in the margin: "Only *piggies* grunt!!!"

Even now, some thirty years later, I still remember the mind-numbing meetings of the department. One of the compulsory textbooks contained Hemingway's story "After the Storm" and it baffled them. How could one teach it? What, Miss Perkins wanted to know, constituted a correct answer about it on the exam? Why couldn't he *say* what he wanted to say? *Exactly!* Quite right. *Get his point across.* Whatever the point might *be.* What in God's name, demanded Mr. Lumley, was it *about.* It was like watching frowning chimps trying to extract a peanut from a medicine bottle.

Jim adjusted to life in Canada far more quickly than I did. The one area where I found it impossible to adjust was language. When people spoke of "a bunch of the guys" I had to repress chidings about flowers and bananas. The spelling *gray* for *grey* distressed me for years. It was decades before I could substitute *aluminum* for *aluminium*. But when I did submit to Canadian or American usage I felt like a ham actor.

In my first Canadian spring one of the teachers said to me, "A bunch of the guys are going sugaring off. Want to come?" I gave him a *very* old-fashioned look.

The problem with these people as teachers was that they were not very well educated, remained incurious, didn't read, had no love of what they taught. They were simply doing a job. They were plonkingly *ordinary* and they inevitably turned out ordinary students who inevitably went on to swell Canada's dullness.

In 1972 I published a novel called *Going Down Slow* which drew on my experience of Rosemount High School. The novel's protagonist, David, is having an affair with a student, Susan. The following lavatorial scene which declines and deflates into one-line paragraphs and silences suggests, I hope, the emotional and intellectual desolation of that school.

> He looked out over the white-painted glass on the bottom part of the high window. It was snowing again, light flakes drifting. The air was yellow with the gloom of a storm. Goal-posts stuck black out of the snow-covered playing field. Just below in the yard, three men in overcoats were standing around Mr. Cherton's new Sting Ray. Mr. Davidson. Mr. Monpetit. The flow of water gurgled back into silence.
>
> David mounted the stand and stood in the middle of the three stalls. He unzipped his trousers. Rubber footsteps squelched in the cloakroom. The swing-door banged open and Hubnichuk came in. They nodded. Hubnichuk was wearing a shabby blue track-suit.
>
> He mounted the stand to David's left. Standing back, he pulled down the elastic front of his trousers. He cradled his organ in the palm of his hand; it was like a three-pound eye-roast. Suddenly, he emitted a tight high-pitched fart, a sound surprising in so large a man.
>
> Footsteps.
>
> Mr. Weinbaum came in.
>
> "So this is where the nobs hang out!" he said.
>
> "Some of them STICK OUT from time to time!" said Hubnichuk.
>
> Their voices echoed.
>
> Mr. Weinbaum mounted the stand and stood in front of the stall to David's right.
>
> "If you shake it more than twice," he said, "you're playing with it."
>
> Water from the copper nozzle rilled down the porcelain.
>
> There was a silence.

David studied the manufacturer's ornate cartouche.

The Victory and Sanitary Porcelain Company.

Inside the curlicued scroll, a wreathed allegorical figure.

Victory?

Sanitation?

Mr. Weinbaum shifted, sighed.

"I got the best battery in Canada for $18.00," he said.

If "David" was having an affair in *Going Down Slow* with "Susan," John was having an affair with a student called Gale Courey. Gale was not in any of my classes but I'd noticed her in the halls not only because of her lushness but because she was always carrying jazz records. We talked together about jazz.

I had been a jazz fan since the age of twelve and during my Beckenham years had gone regularly to the London club at 100 Oxford Street where Britain's top traditional bands played—Humphrey Lyttleton, Chris Barber, and Alex Welsh. I had a large record collection of the classic material—King Oliver, Louis Armstrong, Jelly Roll Morton, and Johnny Dodds. I had a particular liking for Morton's trumpet players, Bubber Miley and Ward Pinkett. Tommy Ladnier, too. I also owned all the usual blues singers—Ma Rainey, Bessie Smith, Ida Cox, Bertha Chippie Hill—but came early to the heterodox judgement that it was hard to better Morton singing "I'm the Win'ing Boy" or Jack Teagarden shlurping and mushmouthing his way through "Stars Fell on Alabama."

England and Europe were far more receptive to the traditional jazz revival than were the States and we enthusiastically bought all the recordings. Someone—was it Lomax?—found Bunk Johnson in the parish of New Iberia and bought him teeth and in New Orleans Sharkey Bonano, Papa Celestin, George Lewis, Paul Barbarin, and Percy Humphrey recreated bands to play the old music. Much of this music came out on a label called Good Time Jazz and a good time it certainly was. I saw the last of it in 1963 in New Orleans. I wrote about that visit in my novella "Private Parts."

> I drove to New Orleans through the increasing depression of the southern States, illusions, delusions lost each day with every human contact, until I reached the fabled Quarter, and sat close to tears listening to the Preservation Hall Jazz Band—a group of octogenarians which as I entered was trying to play "Oh, Didn't He Ramble"; the solos ran out of breath, the drummer was palsied, the bass player rheumy and vacant. The audience of young Germans and Frenchmen was hushed and respectful. Between tunes, a man with a wooden leg tap-danced. I knew that if they tackled "High Society" and the clarinetist attempted Alphonse Picou's solo, he'd drop dead in cardiac arrest; the butcher had cut them down and something shining in me with them.

Gale told me one day about a Montreal club she frequented called Tête de l'Art where she was going that evening. She suggested I join her.

As I walked into the club that night the compère was at the microphone introducing the band. "*Messieurs, Mesdames,*" he said and then turned and gestured at the pianist. "*Orace Silvair!*"

And Horace Silver it was, a blistering quintet with Blue Mitchell on trumpet and Junior Cook on tenor sax. It was the first time I'd heard hard bop. I was transfixed.

I ought to say something here about music in the sixties in Montreal because it was both burden and delight to me. It was, of course, a Golden Age, though I didn't quite realize that at the time. There were three currents of music flowing through the city's clubs at once. The first current was the blues/folk current or blues-packaged-as-folk.

This played at a tiny club on Victoria Avenue called the Finjan which was owned by an Israeli named Shimon Asch. Later, the same people would play at the Seven Steps on Stanley Street. There one could hear such performers as Sonny Terry and Brownie McGee. I remember one night shortly before Christmas being in the Finjan with perhaps six other people in the audience listening to John Lee Hooker. I remember the evening vividly because he sang a song entitled "Black Snake Sucking on My Woman's Tongue" and in the intermission had a screaming match on the phone with a woman in the States.

The second current flowed through the Esquire Show Bar. The Esquire featured weird rock bands like the Blue Men who all had their hair dyed blue but it also featured quite regularly the Chess label bands from Chicago. So it was nothing special to drop into the Esquire to hear Bo Diddley, Muddy Waters, and Howlin' Wolf. Bo Diddley was always a delight because he was consciously a *show* with the two maracas girls in skin-tight gold lamé jumpsuits displaying lots of jolly cleavage.

Muddy Waters and Little Walter singing "Long Distance Call," "Honey Bee," and "Standing Around Crying" were already a transcendent experience.

Howlin' Wolf was not as subtle as Muddy Waters but I think in the end he was a better bluesman. There was a *ferocity* about his band that left the listener seared. He had an almost sullen, glowering presence on stage, visibly impatient while others soloed, prowling with his harmonica, tense to be back in the fray. He never, ever gave the impression that this was just one more gig in a dirty, pissy-smelling bar. When he played, he played balls out.

His usual crew in Montreal was Willie Dixon on double bass, Jimmy Rogers and Hubert Sumlin on guitars, Otis Spann on piano, and usually Fred Below on drums. To have heard the band play "Little Red Rooster" and "Spoonful" is to have had the bar set very high for this kind of music.

I once took Alice Munro to hear Howlin' Wolf and asked her afterwards what she'd thought. She said rather faintly, "I couldn't have imagined it."

The third current of music flowing through the city was jazz. First at the Tête de l'Art and later at the Casa Loma. At these clubs through the sixties I heard most of the jazz giants—Horace Silver, McCoy Tyner, Hank Jones, Sonny Rollins, Stitt, Monk, Dizzy, the Modern Jazz Quartet, Zoot Sims, Pepper Adams, Stan Getz, Cannonball Adderley, Art Blakey, the Basie band playing the Neal Hefti charts . . .

The list was endless.

All this was delightful but it was also nearly killing me as I had to be in school at 8 a.m.

When I came to draw on the experiences of that first year in Canada in my novel *Going Down Slow* I used as the book's epigraph a line from a Howlin' Wolf song: "The men don't know what the little girls understand." Gale certainly understood more than most; she was the *oldest* student I've ever encountered.

We had not been particularly discreet that year. Rather, we had been publicly frolicsome, frequenting restaurants, jazz clubs, and movies. My insouciance suddenly started to feel dangerous. What was that sound? Could that be the Presbyterian posse not far behind? I resigned from the School Board at the end of the year and got a job in another jurisdiction.

Sometime during that second year one of my students brought into class a flyer advertising a CBC short story writing competition designed to find and encourage New Canadian Writers. She must have left it on my desk and I must have inadvertently gathered it up along with a stack of exercise books I was taking home to correct over the weekend.

Something, probably everything cumulatively thus far in my life, prompted me to enter the competition. I spent the weekend writing my first short story. It was called "Early Morning Rabbits."

It was a special *kind* of story that many writers write at the start of their careers. These stories are always about childhood and place. For some children some places are experienced as holy. For some writers, sights and sounds, these profound surfaces, survive pristine in memory into adulthood.

"Early Morning Rabbits" was about my young self on my uncle's farm in Cumberland. It was to me a magical place. I knew every inch of Low Bracken Hall, the run of its drystone walls, its warrens, its woods, the stream that dropped pool by pool down from the tarn on the fells to join the beck in the valley bottom. Even the barn and my uncle's workbench with its Gold Flake tins of wire, solder, washers, spark plugs, and split pins burned in memory. The grease gun for the tractor with chaff stuck to it . . .

Alice Munro has a couple of stories, "Images" and "Walker Brothers Cowboy" in *Dance of the Happy Shades*, which are precisely of this type. Mary Borsky's shimmering evocation of Salt Prairie in *Influence of the Moon* contains such examples of the type as "Ice" and "World Fair." In Clark Blaise's *Southern Stories* "Broward Dowdy" is another gem. Their stories are achingly beautiful and sophisticated while "Early Morning Rabbits" was, I'm afraid, rather florid. I chose to include it in my first book, *The Lady Who Sold Furniture*, in 1970 but I had by then recognized this fruity quality and toned it down. I'd probably derived it in part from "The Peaches," a story in Dylan Thomas's *Portrait of the Artist as a Young Dog*.

I sent this effort in to the CBC and was astonished when it won a prize. Two hundred dollars, as I recall. A base part of my mind calculated that I'd only need to write three a month to live like a lord. And indeed I began to scribble away.

I realized, however, that I knew very little about the genre. I had read Katherine Mansfield and Ernest Hemingway and Dylan Thomas and obviously Chekhov and Guy de Maupassant but the short story had not been taught as a form at school, and literature much past the end of the nineteenth century had not been encouraged at Bristol University. The attitude there, and a reasonable one, was that contemporary and recent writing was what one read for entertainment and as part of being a civilized person. The short story was perceived as being basically an *American* enthusiasm and therefore really beyond the purview of Britons.

I launched myself into an intensity of self-education. I read Ring Lardner's *You Know Me Al*, lapping up that vernacular. Followed by *The Love Nest* and *How to Write Short Stories (With Samples)*. I read Sherwood Anderson's *Winesburg, Ohio*, which was brilliant, followed by several of his dreadful novels. I read, and was ravished by, Flannery O'Connor. Was overwhelmed by Eudora Welty and read and reread her. Tried to read Faulkner but couldn't. Read in rapid succession Katherine Anne Porter, Caroline Gordon, John Updike, Grace Paley's *The Little Disturbances of Man*. Returned to *Dubliners*. Meandered off into Saroyan, Joseph Mitchell, Nathanael West, Irwin Shaw, Peter Taylor . . .

What I was after, beyond the aesthetic experience itself, was to gain some idea of what possible shapes stories could take. I was also feeling out the shape of the tradition.

At the same time I was trying to acquaint myself with Canadian contributions to the form. This turned out to be simple. The only story writers at the time with published collections were Hugh Garner and Morley Callaghan. Both were touted within Canada as giants and both were unreadable, Garner because of his sentimentality and crudeness, Callaghan because his writing was flatly ludicrous.

(Unknown to me then there were two further collections of Canadian stories just published, Hugh Hood's *Flying a Red Kite* and Ethel Wilson's *Mrs. Golightly and Other Stories*.)

Robert Weaver and William Toye wrote of Callaghan in *The Oxford Anthology of Canadian Literature*: "Today he is admired by most younger writers of fiction in Canada as their only true predecessor in this country . . ."

This judgement is hilariously wide of the mark. Most "younger writers of fiction" would tend to fall about laughing at a writer capable of perpetrating: "She stood on the corner of Bloor and Yonge, an impressive build of a woman, tall, stout, good-looking for 42, and watched the traffic signal."

Although everything I was reading was new to me I had at the same time a sense that I was engaging with the past. Wonderful as Eudora Welty's *A Curtain of Green and Other Stories* was, it had been published in 1941. I had a sense of John Updike as a near-contemporary and read with great pleasure and attention *The Same Door* and *Pigeon Feathers and Other Stories* but Updike was associated with the fabled *New Yorker* and moved in a world which was not the world of *The Canadian Forum* and *Fiddlehead*.

I had no sense of there being a great literary presence in Montreal, Toronto, or Vancouver; there was no Canadian tradition or body of work I could hope to join. The country lacked what would be called today an "infrastructure"—the literary equivalent of roads, sewers, electric power, railroad tracks—and I've spent nearly all my life in Canada editing, writing, anthologizing, publishing, exhorting, teaching, and collecting in a probably vain attempt to help put the necessary infrastructure into place.

The smart writers did exactly the reverse; they positioned their work in England and the United States.

I had by now piles of stories and mounting piles of rejection slips. It is usual to submit stories to magazines singly; in desperation, I sent a bundle of sixteen to *Prism International*. I was astonished when they wrote back accepting eight. And they made a fuss about them, too, saying how the stories stood out from the general ruck of submissions. They were published in the Summer and Autumn issues of *Prism International* in 1964. The person instrumental in all this was Earle Birney.

When his *Collected Poems* came out years later he inscribed a copy for me and wrote: "To John Metcalf whose fiction I've admired and continued to read ever since he sent Jake Zilber and me a stack of his short stories which we were happy to publish in *Prism International* back in the sixties when that journal was still international."

I reread those stories before writing this and found them, not surprisingly, to be no better than most juvenilia, though the themes that were to occupy me for so many years were already there. I reworked "Early Morning Rabbits" and I took some material from "Just Two Old Men" and used it in the novella "The Lady Who Sold Furniture." The rest of the stories I'm happy are forgotten. I winced at the ghastly pretentiousness of the title I'd given to the group of stories: *The Geography of Time*. I can only beg that I was young. But I was pleased to note that George Johnston had a poem in that Summer issue; he is one of Canada's finest poets and in *The Cruising Auk* wrote one of Canada's most elegant books. Years later at the Porcupine's Quill I had the honour of bringing out his collected poems, *Endeared by Dark*, which George, until I dissuaded him, had wanted to call *From a Rhyming Brain*.

Gale and I were still going out together but we seemed to be quarrelling rather pointlessly. I think looking back that we were both unsure of what we wanted next. Gale was also under pressure from her parents. They were Lebanese Canadian and seemed to my WASP stolidity excitable and volatile. I had been to their apartment for meals on various occasions and the evenings passed in uproar and cacophony which seemed friendly in intent. But her parents blew hot and cold. Her father would from time to time work himself up into tirades about the nasty anatomical things he was going to do to me with his bare hands while her mother would leave block-lettered notices in the fridge reading: NONE OF THIS GOOD FOOD FOR GALE.

At the end of term I was having a beer at a neighbourhood bar and fell into conversation with a man at the next stool. His name was Meunier, from Alberta, visiting family. He, too, was a teacher, principal of a high school. While in Montreal he was going to run some ads to secure a teacher of English. Several glasses of beer later, seduced by the high salary, I signed on the dotted line. I think that I was unconsciously simply putting some distance between me and a situation about which I wasn't decided.

This impulsive and rash act landed me the following September in Cold Lake, Alberta, honorary second lieutenant at the Cold Lake RCAF base. The base itself was featureless, a bland suburb set down in the wilderness. The nearest patch of civilian civilization—the *only* patch—was about three miles away. It was called Grand Centre. Grand Centre comprised three or four houses, a trading post that exchanged little wooden kegs of nails and the like for pelts, a laundromat, an RCMP lock-up, and a tiny Chinese restaurant that offered Canadian-Chinese food in red gooey sauce.

The contiguous Indian reserve with its abandoned cars and tumbledown hovels patched with sheet tin was a persuasive argument for assimilation.

The long winter began. Teachers drove to school from the barracks, plugged their cars into block heaters, and left the engines running all day. The cold was beyond description or belief.

I spent most of the year playing billiards and darts and going slowly stir-crazy. One was not supposed to win at darts or billiards if playing against an officer senior in rank; it was not done; it was considered bad form; I became unpopular.

The Wing Commander suggested I get my hair cut. My hair was, apparently, setting a bad example.

To whom and of what?

Did I not respect the feelings of the mess?

Not so's you'd notice.

Had I no respect for his rank?

Not a jot. Not a tittle.

Midmorning every day a Thunderbird fighter flew to the base in Comox, British Columbia, to pick up salmon for lunch.

Every day at lunchtime the Americans landed to refuel; they were flying the H-bomb around the world.

For lunch they ate the four-bean salad and the salmon.

Some people used to drive to Grand Centre to wave at the train.

Others watched the clothes tumbling in the laundromat.

Some drove to Grand Centre to eat toast at the Canadian-Chinese restaurant.

I was writing to Gale almost daily and phoning her as I could. Her letters became increasingly important to me. I was still worried about the amount of dope she smoked; she was still impatient with my "square" disapproval. I was irritated by her vocabulary, the *shit* she *scored*, the *smoke* she *toked*. Little did I know that it was soon to become a lingua franca. I remained irritated by her contempt for a university education; she was concerned that I might become an academic. She wanted me always to be "free." Never, she begged me, become *boring*. The gathering of rosebuds while she might was her general plan of action.

When the snow and ice reluctantly disappeared to be replaced by mud and mosquitoes and my servitude ended, I returned to Montreal, and Gale and I, despite the tensions between us, were married in a rather hugger-mugger fashion by a United Church cleric who obviously regarded the union with reservations but needed the money.

After a few days we left for England where we intended to stay. For a year at least we were going to live on the money I'd saved at Cold Lake. I was going to write. We went to Bristol and stayed for a while with David Hirschmann and his wife, Jill, while looking for a flat. Gale seemed to have difficulties distinguishing between pounds and dollars and kept coming home with dismaying "bargains." I was also improvident, buying at an auction one day a Victorian chaise longue and a Regency mirror six feet high with gilded columns and capitals and gadroon beading. The end of the money was in sight.

I got a job teaching English in a Catholic comprehensive school which served a nearby housing estate. It was a grim employment. The school was staffed by teachers whose main qualification was their faith, rural Irishwomen who as they sipped their orange-coloured tea in the common room would say into the silence, apropos of God knows what, "And a blessing it is, a blessing it is."

The principal was saintly and ineffectual. When it was reported to him that the children had *again* poured their free milk into the grand piano, he murmured, "We live in an imperfect world."

The school was openly violent. Classes were searched for knives. Mr. Murphy, the deputy head, kept a cane down the leg of his trousers and would draw it like a sword, cutting at the legs and hunched backs of troublemakers. A boy in one of my "slow learner" classes set fire in his desk to a Bible and Lamb's *Tales from Shakespeare* which my predecessor had used as a remedial text. The female school-leaving class flatly refused to work, claiming that they attended only "for the cooking." After lunch, police cars and a Black Maria returned the apprehended shoplifters.

My decision to go to Canada for the first time in 1962 had been made without much thought. Neither Jim nor I at the time had any idea of leaving England permanently. We were simply bored and looking for new experience. My life was split between a decaying past which exercised a great power over me and a present which was unbearable and stretched ahead like a life sentence. Even then, I suspected that it was dangerous to live for the past and I knew I had to get out of England and escape from its dream. Joyce Cary's novel *To Be a Pilgrim*, a volume in *The Horse's Mouth* trilogy, brilliantly portrays a man in thrall to that dream of Englishness.

Had my job been interesting and comfortable, I'd doubtless have succumbed to the dream and lived out the rest of my life clad in tweed with vacations spent taking brass rubbings in medieval churches. But life at Bluebell Secondary Modern and the Eastmill Reception Centre was neither interesting nor comfortable. The staff were caricatures, the headmasters clinically insane. The pupils ranged from the merely drooling to the psychopathically loutish.

Bluebell Secondary Modern was the sort of school where homework was never assigned because the pupils returned with notes written on torn brown bag paper which said:

> Dear teacher,
> He have not done his sums because
> its bad for his "nerves"
> Thanking you, I Remain
> Signed Mary Brown *(Mrs)*.

The remedial mornings were divided by school dinner from the remedial afternoons.

From a utensil of medieval aspect and proportions, greasy stew studded with emerald processed peas was ladled by the grubby monitor. The stew was followed by steamed pudding and aluminum jugs of custard topped by a thickening skin.

Leaving was no difficulty.

Return to Canada was a relief. Canada, after England, seemed filled with rising hope. Expo 67 in Montreal marked some kind of high point. My writing career was soon to get under way. My daughter was born in 1969. Looking back now, I would say that the euphoria everyone seemed to be feeling began to fall apart in about 1975.

I suffered from the delusion that Canada could be improved. Since then, I feel that year by year Canada has been in continuous cultural decline. Our schools are a disaster. Our public life is a grim farce; the present minister of defence was unaware of Dieppe and confuses Vimy with Vichy.

The leaching away of knowledge, taste, and sophistication might be well suggested in this June 1989 *Ottawa Citizen* column by Marjorie Nichol.

> Pierre Juneau, the retiring president of the CBC, has had an eventful public career. It is doubtful, though, that Juneau will ever forget the events of the afternoon of May 24, 1989.
>
> On that day Juneau appeared, probably for the last time, before the Commons committee on communications and culture, which examines CBC policy and spending.
>
> The main topic of discussion, not surprisingly, was the draconian cuts to the CBC budget meted out in the new federal budget. Over the next four years $140 million will be lopped off the corporation's budget.
>
> Juneau painted an extremely bleak picture of the CBC's future, predicting that "a slaughter" will be required to keep the broadcasting behemoth afloat.
>
> Committee members badgered the president to say how he would deal with the corporation's fiscal crises. He demurred, stating repeatedly that salvaging the CBC will be a task for its next president to be appointed next month by Brian Mulroney.
>
> The newly appointed chairman of this prestigious Commons committee is Felix Holtmann, a two-term Conservative MP from the Manitoba riding of Portage-Interlake.
>
> What follows is a verbatim excerpt from that committee meeting.
>
>> Chairman Holtmann: ". . . I have listened to CBC radio, CBC television back home and you have programming that sometimes goes on for hours without any advertising in it at all. Either there are no

listeners or you are afraid to advertise. I do not know what the darn reason is.

"But I think if you advertised even a little you would wake some people up who were listening to some of these long, drawn-out musicians from some other country . . ."

John Harvard (Lib-Winnipeg/St. James): "You are talking radio?"

Ian Waddell (NDP-Port Moody/Coquitlam): "What is it, Bach or something like that?"

Chairman Holtmann: "Something like that. Why should they get to listen to that for nothing?"

Harvard: "Nothing?"

Chairman Holtmann: "Why are you afraid to advertise and recover, well, the money. Of course the taxpayers are paying for it, if you are not advertising. Why are you not throwing an advertisement in every once in a while to pay for that programming?"

Harvard: "My God."

Pierre Juneau: "Mr. Chairman, since I said CBC management would present to the CBC board a list of every possibility, no doubt that one will be included. I would not call it an option, because I personally would be against it."

Chairman Holtmann: "You personally would be against it?"

Juneau: "Yes, I would."

Chairman Holtmann: "I do not understand that."

Juneau: "I will explain why, but never mind. As I said, I will not be there when the decision is made . . . There is a condition of licence, and if you read the Broadcasting Act, a condition of licence is like law. There is a condition of licence that prohibits advertising on CBC radio except in very, very few cases . . ."

> Chairman Holtmann: ". . . You said you are against it; I suppose your board is against it too, or something like that."
>
> Juneau: "I would say the majority of the board are."
>
> Chairman Holtmann: "What is the rationale for being against something like that? What is cultural to Canada's culture to listen to Beethoven? Is it because you are interfering with our culture? You guys have lost me on that one."
>
> At the close of the committee hearing Chairman Holtmann confessed that culture and communications are not his first area of expertise or interest.
>
> As he put it, "Hogs and cows are things I have been associated with more." He then wished Juneau "good luck in any retirement that you get involved with."

But it is not simply living in cultural desolation which is turning my thoughts again towards England. It is the pain, more heartfelt every year, of not living in history.

The English past still grips me. The parish church, Norman, with its yew trees and lichened tombstones, the pub, the village green or square, behind the high stone walls the manor house . . . I am still a captive of the dream.

Momentous as getting married and moving to England and then returning to Canada had been, something equally momentous had occurred in my artistic life. In 1964 I had happened upon a book which exploded upon me. It overwhelmed me. I was *consumed* by this book. It was so big, so perfect, so merciless that I could live inside it. The book was Richard Yates's story collection *Eleven Kinds of Loneliness.* Years later *Esquire* wrote of him, "Richard Yates is one of America's least famous great writers."

The book had been published in 1962. It was a first book of stories. The author was older than me but not by much. The stories were dazzling. It wasn't the writing itself which excited me so much. Yates had a simple and unadorned style. What excited me was that someone had produced a work of art which was within striking distance of perfection and they'd done it not in 1941 but *now, today*. The book opened up the possibility that someone else could attain the same distinction. It gave me a mark to aim at. It also validated the entire genre for me, made me feel intensely that a lifetime spent in achieving just one such book was more than justified. With at this point just a handful of juvenile scribbling to my name, I consciously dedicated the rest of my life to achieving that book and to the service of literature in general in my time and place.

This zeal may sound priggish but I was in a state of exhilaration. Yates made me feel what Philip Larkin felt on hearing Sidney Bechet:

> On me your voice falls as they say love should,
> Like an enormous yes.

By the end of 1999 all of Richard Yates's novels and story collections were out of print. Writing of him in the *Boston Review*, the novelist Stewart O'Nan said:

> Across his career he was consistently well-reviewed in all the major places, and four of his novels were selections of the Book-of-the-Month Club, yet he never sold more that 12,000 copies of any one book in hardback.
>
> If his work was neglected during his lifetime, after his death it has practically disappeared. Of the tens of thousands of titles crammed into the superstores, not one is his . . .
>
> To write so well and then to be forgotten is a terrifying legacy. I always think that if I write well enough, the people in my books—the world of those books—will

somehow survive. In time the shoddy and trendy work will fall away and the good books will rise to the top. It's not reputation that matters, since reputations are regularly pumped up by self-serving agents and publicists and booksellers, by the star machinery of Random House and the *New Yorker*, what matters is what the author has achieved in the work, on the page. Once it's between the covers, they can't take it away from you; they have to acknowledge its worth. As a writer, I have to believe that.

This is the mystery of Richard Yates: how did a writer so well-respected—even loved—by his peers, a writer capable of moving his readers so deeply, fall to all intents out of print, and so quickly? How is it possible that an author whose work defined the lostness of the Age of Anxiety as deftly as Fitzgerald's did that of the Jazz Age, an author who influenced American literary icons like Raymond Carver and André Dubus, among others, an author so forthright and plainspoken in his prose and choice of characters, can now be found only by special order or in the dusty, floor-level end of the fiction section in secondhand stores? And how come no one knows this? How come no one does anything about it?

THE YEARS WITH ROSS

IN 1966 I WAS CONTACTED by Earle Toppings, then senior editor at the Ryerson Press. He was working on an anthology entitled *Modern Canadian Stories* selected and edited by Giose Rimanelli and Roberto Ruberto. Earle Birney contributed a foreword and had been influential behind the scenes. They wished to include two of my stories previously published in *Prism International*. This was an important publication for me for a variety of reasons. The book represented only the fourth time since Raymond Knister's *Canadian Short Stories* in 1928 that Canadian story writers had been anthologized. I had been placed in the company of people whose work interested me—Mordecai Richler, Alice Munro, Hugh Hood, Ethel Wilson, and Irving Layton. It also introduced me to Earle Toppings, who became a friend. Lastly, it had given me an entrée to the Ryerson Press.

I used to send Earle stories which he read and discussed with me but wisely refused to publish. He thought I needed a book from a smaller press first. He took it upon himself to take a group of my stories to Stan Bevington at Coach House. Stan accepted the book and I was set to become the first collection of fiction that Coach House published. I knew nothing much about Coach House or Stan Bevington other than that he was a honcho in the Toronto counterculture. After a couple of months had gone by I phoned Stan to inquire about progress. Everything, apparently, was fine, just fine, but there hadn't been any, well, you know, man, actual *physical* progress, though . . .

About three anxious months later, still no news, I phoned again. My tentative questions were followed by a silence as of profound thought.

"Hello?" I said.

"Look, man," said Stan, "if you're going to hassle me I'm not doing the book."

And he didn't.

My writing life was absorbing me to the point that I realized I could no longer afford to work full-time. I resigned from Northmount High School and looked about for part-time work. Just before the term ended I was visited by the board's consultant in English, Charles Rittenhouse. Charles had been very active in amateur theatre—always a bad thing—and was given to gesture and noisy recitation. He was related by marriage to the Holgate family and had several of Edwin Holgate's prosaic canvases in his apartment. He sat on the edge of my desk and said that he considered me the most interesting young teacher in the system and asked me to work with him on five textbooks for which he had a contract with J. M. Dent and Sons.

The series was called *Wordcraft* and books 1 to 3 were written by Charles, me, and Juliette Dowling. *Wordcraft Junior* and *Senior* were written by Charles and me alone. Actually, largely by me with Charles acting as taskmaster. The purpose of the books was to interest children in the history of words, to build vocabulary, and to provide exercises in precise usage.

We wrote *Wordcraft* 2 and 3 in 1968 and they and other textbooks I compiled were to prove very important in my writing life. They sold astonishingly well and brought in just enough in royalties each year to persuade me that I had enough "base" money to risk one more year without full-time employment.

I had also been earning money by editing school text editions with notes, questions, and exercises for Bellhaven House. I prepared editions of *The Razor's Edge*, *The Daughter of Time*, and *Flight of the Phoenix*. These appeared in 1967 and 1968. Also in 1968, I put together with Gordon Callaghan, a fellow teacher, a textbook called *Rhyme and Reason* to teach children how to read poetry. *Wordcraft 1* appeared in 1969. In 1970 Gordon and I compiled a poetry anthology for high school use called *Salutation*. Also in 1970 Rittenhouse and I put out *Wordcraft Senior*. Again in 1970 I published *Sixteen by Twelve*. The idea behind this old warhorse was simple. I chose twelve writers and asked them to write a piece about writing to accompany their story or stories in the book. I wrote brief biographies and included an informal photo of the writer. These devices seemed to give the book a certain intimacy and personality. The writers I chose were Morley Callaghan, Hugh Garner, Margaret Laurence, Hugh Hood, Mordecai Richler, Alice Munro, Shirley Faessler, Alden Nowlan, George Bowering, David Helwig, myself, and Ray Smith.

The book is still in print and still selling well after more than thirty years. It ought to have been scrapped and updated years ago. When I did attempt to present different writers in a similar collection called *New Worlds* in 1980—such writers as Merna Summers, Alden Nowlan, W. P. Kinsella, Jack Hodgins, C. D. Minni, Norman Levine, and Terrence Heath—the book didn't sell well and the reports from the McGraw-Hill Ryerson salesmen were that the teachers hadn't heard of any of these writers.

Year after year *Sixteen by Twelve* has underwritten my fiction and criticism. It typically produces four thousand dollars a year. The Dent *Wordcraft* books used to bring in fifteen hundred to two thousand a year but sales are more or less finished; I suspect the books are now too challenging for the students' dwindling abilities.

It is for me rather saddening to look at *Sixteen by Twelve* today. Seven of those twelve writers are now dead, four of the seven from drink. Given Canada, perhaps not surprising. Frederick Philip Grove wrote: "There is no greater curse that can befall a man than to be afflicted with artistic leanings, in Canada."

That comma might be the best thing he ever wrote.

The royalties rolled in as a delightful extra. The motivation for compiling these and later books was less financial than educational. I was at that time interested in teaching and I believed that Canadian children ought to be in contact with Canadian art. *Sixteen by Twelve* was, apparently, the first Canadian textbook of Canadian stories ever. Gordon Callaghan and I put together *Rhyme and Reason* and *Salutation* simply so we'd have intelligent material to teach. Very little infrastructure had been put into place by the early sixties and we both felt a need to shape and civilize. Only years later did we realize that it was like throwing stones into a bog.

In 1963 W. H. Auden wrote: "The dominions . . . are for me *tiefste Provinz*, places which have produced no art and are inhabited by the kind of person with whom I have least in common."

Difficult not to concur.

I have often thought about this surge of publishing at the beginning of my career and of the textbooks that came later—*Kaleidoscope: Canadian Stories* (1972), *The Narrative Voice* (1972), *The Speaking Earth: Canadian Poetry* (1973), *Here and Now: Best Canadian Stories* (1977), *Stories Plus* (1979), *New Worlds* (1980), *Making It New* (1982), *The New Story Writers* (1982) and *Canadian Classics* (1993).

Had I remained in England a similar surge of publishing would not have occurred because I could not have imagined it. Textbooks in England were written by heads of department in famous public schools or by lecturers in departments of education and certainly not by lowly toilers at Bluebell Secondary Modern. There was besides a resource pool of thousands of educated minds on which publishers could draw. Also to the point, there was no *need* of new textbooks.

Canada offered me the freedom to do anything I could imagine. The negative side of this freedom was that it was a freedom which arose from ignorance and indifference. There was certainly little competition. In the sixties Canada was an intellectual and creative wasteland with a large percentage of its population functionally illiterate.

Royalties fluctuated and it wasn't possible to rely on them and so a part-time job was necessary. Irving Layton suggested to me that I try Ross High School. At that time it occupied the upper floor of a takeout Bar BQ chicken joint on Decarie near Vezina. It was a private institution that catered to students who had failed in the state schools or who were disaffected, stoned, or simply idle. Classes were small as were the four rooms into which they were crammed.

Mr. Ross also had a sideline of rich immigrant students mainly from Taiwan and India.

"What I am not understanding, sir, is the whereabouts of your motorcar."

Preceding me as heads of the English department had been the proletarian layabout poet Bryan McCarthy, author of *Smoking the City*, layabout novelist John Mills, and Irving Layton. Whenever I asked Harry Ross for a raise he always replied, "Who do you think *you* are? Irving Layton?"

Myrna once told me that years before I knew her, McCarthy, a boozehound and notorious wastrel, had taught her dancing "by the binary method." I've never had the moral courage to press her on what "the binary method" actually entailed.

I sketched this curious school in a story called "The Years in Exile" and again fiction feels more accurate than fact.

Rosen College Preparatory High School occupied five rooms on the floor about the Chateau Bar BQ Restaurant and Takeout Service. There were three classrooms, the Library, the supplies locker, and the Office. The staff was all part-time and so in my five years I came to know only the morning shift—Geography, Mathematics, and Science. At recess, the four of us would huddle in the supplies locker and make coffee.

Mr. Kapoor was a reserved and melancholy hypochondriac from New Delhi who habitually wore black suits and shoes, a white shirt, and striped college tie. His only concession to summer was that he wore the gleaming shoes without socks. I remember his telling me one day that peahens became fertilized by raising their tail feathers during a rain storm; he held earnestly to this, telling me that it was indeed so because his grandmother had told him, she having seen it with her own eyes in Delhi. He taught science in all grades.

Mr. Gingley was a retired accountant who taught Mathematics and wore a curiously pink hearing aid which was shaped like a fat human ear.

Mr. Helwig Syllm, the Geography teacher, was an ex-masseur.

Mrs. Rosen, who drew salaries as secretary, teacher, and School Nurse, would sometimes grip one by the arm in the hall and hiss: "Don't foment. My husband can fire anyone. *Anyone.*"

Mr. Ross was actually a genial man but with marked eccentricities. He lived to do battle with the education department bureaucrats in Quebec City who were continually finding him in violation of codes and attempting to close him down. They claimed he had no gymnasium; he countered that he had an arrangement with the Y. They announced an inspection of the library; he gave me taxi money to transport suitcases of my own books into the library cupboard for the duration. They claimed the school afforded no toilets for the students; he countered that the school had a toilet arrangement with the Bar BQ management. On and on it went, Mr. Ross in wheezing chuckles as he recounted his latest coup against the faceless ones.

The years with Ross were the happiest years of my teaching career. I remember going to him on the first day I worked at Ross High School and asking him for chalk. He took two sticks from a box and wrapped them in a twist of paper. Next week I asked for more. He looked astonished and said, "You've *had* your chalk for this year!" But he wasn't always penny-pinching and if I was late in the morning and had had to skip breakfast he would go to a nearby restaurant and bring me coffee and hot buttered toast in waxed paper which I'd eat while teaching Chaucer.

I taught in the mornings and walked home at midday. I usually then corrected essays for an hour or so. I was correcting class sets for the Protestant School Board of Greater Montreal for fifty cents an essay. I liaised with the English department head at Northmount High School, a charming Englishman who wore silk suits and who used to say to his students, "If you don't be quiet, I shall go *quite rigid*." We liked each other. In the late afternoons and early evenings I worked on fiction.

My writing was going well. I was getting stories published in the literary magazines and there were signs and portents everywhere. I was awarded a Canada Council grant in 1968. I remember taking that cheque to a branch of the Banque Nationale near our apartment. The teller examined it and said, "We don't cash cheques from foreign countries." A hint of things to come.

I was awarded the President's Medal of the University of Western Ontario in 1969 for the best short story of the year. That was "The Estuary." Mordecai Richler selected "Keys and Watercress" for his Penguin anthology *Canadian Writing*

Today. During these years Professor Alec Lucas at McGill was working on an anthology for the American paperback company Dell. The book was called *Great Canadian Stories* and it finally appeared in 1971. I had met Alec Lucas at a launching party for a young protégé of Louis Dudek's. Drink was flowing abundantly and Alec endeared himself to me eternally when Louis Dudek rose and quieted the uproar, saying, "And now I think the time has come to listen to our young poet." Alec said loudly into the silence, and in a *petulant* tone, "They always have to *spoil* these occasions."

Alec had fallen into the habit of summoning Ray Smith and me to the McGill Faculty Club at lunchtime to pick our brains for his anthology. He was going to include both of us but wanted our opinions of our contemporaries. These lunches were nearly always purely liquid as the food in the faculty club was disgusting. One day someone wrote in chalk on the club wall: *The poor hate you*. I picked up the nub of chalk and wrote underneath: *They wouldn't if they'd eaten here*.

Most excitingly, I was selected for *New Canadian Writing 1969*, the second volume of a series published by Clarke Irwin. The year before, they had published *New Canadian Writing 1968* with stories by David Lewis Stein, Clark Blaise, and Dave Godfrey.

In the publisher's foreword to the 1968 book Bill Clarke wrote:

> The stories in this collection are representative of the current trends, of the move away from the old established patterns towards new methods of conveying impressions. They are not necessarily the *best* stories that will appear in this decade but they are important in that they are indicative of the work being done by young Canadian writers today. It is the publisher's intention to continue this programme with the publication of other volumes of a similar nature.

New Canadian Writing 1969 was the final volume in the series.

Clark's stories were "The Fabulous Eddie Brewster," "How I Became a Jew," "The Examination," and "Notes Beyond a History." Bill Clarke was exquisitely mannered and perhaps excessively genteel. He felt that "How I Became a Jew" had in its blunt usage of the word *Jew* the potential to offend. Clark and I were vastly amused when he proposed that Clark change the title to, "How I Became a Jewish Person."

New Canadian Writing 1969 also contained stories by D. O. Spettigue and C. J. Newman. I had five stories in the book: "The Children Green and Golden," "Walking Round the City," "Robert, Standing," "Our Mr. Benson," and "The Estuary." These stories caused quite a stir and were singled out in reviews. As a result Clarke Irwin proposed that I publish a collection with them. This appeared in 1970 and was entitled *The Lady Who Sold Furniture*.

But many other changes were accompanying these little literary triumphs and trophies. The most momentous event in these years was the birth of our daughter, Elizabeth, in 1969. I went with Gale to the hospital, of course, but the usual happened. I cannot stand other people's pain and I usually faint or vomit. Receiving pain while falling off cliffs or in the boxing ring is somehow different; one is to a degree immune, perhaps because charged with adrenalin. Gale was in labour and extremely vocal. I was distressed and lurched out into the corridor, my vision a migraine-like blizzard of white mesh. I bumbled along the wall and fell through a pair of swing doors and then fell down a flight of stone stairs. After I had come to and after my vision returned to normal I ignominiously got a taxi and went home to bed.

Elizabeth was a great joy to me and especially so when she was learning to talk, which she did early. She used to deliver long, excited monologues with many repetitions attempting to describe or explain such things as thunder. She sounded oddly like Lucky's speeches in *Waiting for Godot*.

There was something irresistibly delicious about a two-year-old standing staring at a large toy lion and saying admiringly, "My word!" Though usually sunny, she had cross days and on one of these I'd taken her to a zoo. I said to her with forced parental enthusiasm, "Oh, look, Elizabeth! A llama!"

She glowered at the beast.

Then said plonkingly, "What's it for?"

There were changes, too, on the job front. I stopped marking exercise books partly because I was busy writing texts and partly because I couldn't stand any longer changing *their* and *there* and *its* and *it's*. The increasing frequency of the publication of my stories meant that I was building a small reputation and that reputation was opening up new employment possibilities. I was beginning to review for the *Montreal Star*. By strange chance, I was to review Eudora Welty's lovely last novel, *Losing Battles*. Mr. Ross remained intransigent about wages, so with considerable regret I left the old bugger to his comic machinations. By 1970 I had acquired two part-time jobs, one teaching writing at McGill for Bharati Mukherjee, the other teaching literature at the Loyola CEGEP.

There is for a writer nothing quite like the experience of a first book. No subsequent book means quite as much. To hold that first book in one's hands is to hold proof that one indeed is what one has for years dared and hoped to be. I was so elated by *The Lady Who Sold Furniture* that I put copies in every room in the apartment so that I could see it and stroke it wherever I was.

The book contains five short stories and a 102-page novella. Although I still quite like the stories the meat of the book is the novella. In the novella I managed to deploy what I'd been struggling to teach myself in the preceding years. I'd wanted to get away from plot and towards a story that moved forward in a different way. What I was after, though I couldn't quite articulate it, was a story that was powered through images that generated strong emotion. I wanted a story propelled by a series of emotional jolts. This, in turn, implied a close observation of surface and detail. In acutely observed surfaces are depths. To deliver the emotion the language had to be utterly clean and sharp, cuttingly precise. Dialogue, too, had to make demands on the reader. It had to be fast, full of implied tone, utterly lacking in "stage directions"; in brief, the dialogue had to be a performance in which the reader took part.

It was here perhaps that everything collecting had taught me was brought into play. Everything that paintings had taught me. Everything I'd learned from the Imagist poets. Everything I'd thrilled to in the theatre.

My short stories had been tending in the right direction—"Keys and Watercress" and "Dandelions" move forward in intense images—but I could not then have expressed as a theory what I was grappling with. I was listening to CBC *Anthology* one evening when an actor started reading a story called "Images" by a writer named Alice Munro. I think this was in 1968 but it might have been 1967. It certainly preceded publication of *Dance of the Happy Shades*. I was galvanized by this story. I recognized immediately what she was doing. She had succeeded brilliantly at the very thing that I was still messing with and by using the title "Images" she'd pointed out the method of her fiction. She allowed my own thinking about these technical problems to expand. I wrote to her in great excitement and we entered into a correspondence which lasted for years.

In 1985 *The Malahat Review* (Number 70) put out under the editorship of Constance Rooke "A Special Issue on John Metcalf." I was immensely flattered by Alice Munro's contribution and immodestly quote it here. It refers back to the sixties and the story "Images."

On John Metcalf: Taking Writing Seriously

I think John wrote to me for the first time after a story of mine was read on the radio, before I had published any books. Or maybe it was just after the first book came out. I was living in Victoria then. I had absolutely no status as a writer. A creative writing teacher at the University of Victoria had told me that I wrote the kind of things he used to write when he was 15. So I was quite surprised by this letter of appreciation. I was stunned by it, really—it was a bouquet, a burst of handsome praise. He had taken the trouble to do this—to write so generously and thoughtfully, to a writer he didn't know, a writer of no importance, no connections. He didn't do that out of kindness alone, though it seemed to me so wonderfully kind. He did it because he believes writing is important.

I didn't meet him until three or four years later. We wrote letters. We wrote about what we were working on and what a hard time we were having with it and what we thought about each other's writing, and other people's, too. We developed then what I hate to describe as a literary friendship—that sounds to me too pretentious and genteel for the letters we wrote—but I suppose that's the kind of friendship it was, and is. He was bracing and encouraging and not always uncritical. I was learning that remarkable respect for his opinion that many of his writer friends have. I've never lost it. Praise from him, you feel, is real gold. Once he is your friend he will back you up and make allowances for your quirks and problems and refrain from blabbing your confidences, he will be kind and loyal and affectionate, but he won't tell you he likes your writing if he doesn't. I have the feeling—and I'm sure there are other writers who have it—that he is one person who can tell where the soft spots are, where the words are pasted over the cracks, can tell what's fake, what's shoddy, what's an evasion, maybe even mark the place where a loss of faith hit you, not momentously like an avalanche but drearily like a dry trickle of clods and stones. It won't matter what compliments you've been getting from other quarters.

This makes him sound like one of those mentors people idealize from the past—a wise ironical fellow, incorruptible, never fooled. It's absurd to make him into anything like that. He never set himself up to be anybody's literary conscience—that's a rickety business you have to develop for yourself—and he has a blind spot or two, like the rest of us. If I do think of him this way, as somebody sitting out there *not being fooled*, I probably should apologize for it. But it is very useful, and our friends all have their uses.

And it's exactly how I do think of him. I'm grateful to him, and so I should be.

He does take writing seriously, that's all it is. He has a consistent, natural respect for it, which is something a lot rarer than you'd think.

By the time I came to write "The Lady Who Sold Furniture" I knew exactly what I was doing and why. The novella still stands up for me after all these years. It hasn't lost its flavour. These are the first two paragraphs:

> Purple. Purpleness with a zigzag line of black. A zigzag line of black stitching. Peter pushed the bedspread down from his face and moved his head on the pillow. He expected for a second to see above his head the raftered darkness of the barn and to hear the clatter of sabots on the cobbles, the everymorning shout of *Monsieur Anglais!* But the only sounds were sparrows on the window sill and the distant rattle of the milkman's van.
>
> Sunlight lay over the floorboards and the worn carpet. His boots and rucksack lay where he'd dropped them the night before. The sole of one boot was grey with caked mud except where the tips of the steel cleats glinted in the sunshine.

The Lady Who Sold Furniture was published in 1970. Clarke Irwin printed 1,500 copies but bound up only 750 copies. These were bound in black cloth. Some years later they bound the rest in grey cloth. Copies of this second binding are still available from ECW Press. This means that the book has sold fewer than 1,500 copies in thirty-nine years.

The novella is also available along with two others—"Girl in Gingham" and "Private Parts: A Memoir"—in *Shooting the Stars*, published in 1993 by the Porcupine's Quill; a glance at my royalty statements shows that *Shooting the Stars* sold in 1999 0 (zero) copies with a wild surge in 2000 to 4 (four) copies, slumping in 2001 to 0 (zero) again.

Reviews in 1970 were very favourable and the book is routinely mentioned as a landmark volume in histories of literature and guides to culture. In *The Oxford Companion to Twentieth Century Literature in English*, edited by Jenny Stringer, the entry on me reads in part: "His abiding reputation as one of the finest prose stylists in contemporary Canada was established with the vividly observed and imaginatively disquieting stories collected in *The Lady Who Sold Furniture* (1970)."

Surely this critical encomium and my book's virtual disappearance require some kind of explanation?

In 2001 I wrote an essay for the *National Post* which attempted to explore the reasons for the similar neglect of Blaise and Levine; the conclusion I arrived at was that Canadians merely parroted American estimations and as a society were incapable of informed, independent judgement. This provoked a vicious, personal letter to the *Post* from Douglas Gibson of McClelland and Stewart.

My piece was called "Canadian Classics" and I'd like to quote from it:

> Let us probe a little deeper into my contention that Canada cannot elect "classics" by considering the careers of

two other writers, Clark Blaise and Norman Levine. If I had to pick the best six story writers in Canada I would certainly select Alice Munro and Mavis Gallant and I would with equal certainty select Clark Blaise and Norman Levine.

I would have to admit that Blaise and Levine are lesser writers than Munro and Gallant. They have written fewer and less complex stories and both have a narrower range both of subject matter and emotion. Yet they remain so obviously in the same league as Munro and Gallant. Both men have written stories which are at the centre of Canadian achievement in the short story form. Both voices are wonderfully individual and alive. I cannot imagine Canadian literature without thinking of such Levine stories as "A Small Piece of Blue," "Something Happened Here," "By the Richelieu," and "Champagne Barn." Nor can I imagine Canadian literature without thinking of such Blaise stories as "A North American Education," "The Salesman's Son Grows Older," "Eyes," "How I Became a Jew," and "Meditations on Starch."

Despite the bizarre inclusions and the even more bizarre exclusions we must put *some* weight on the fact that both Clark Blaise and Norman Levine are given entries in *The Cambridge Guide to Literature in English* and *The Oxford Companion to Twentieth Century Literature in English.*

The Oxford Companion says: "Levine's spare, understated prose style is seen at its best in his short stories. Predominantly first-person narratives, they exhibit a keen eye for external details, but their prime concern is with the subjective experience of the outsider."

Of Blaise's work *The Oxford Companion* says: "The autobiographical dimension in much of his highly regarded fiction is integral to his treatments of the impermanence and relativity of personal identity . . . His short stories in *A North American Education* (1973), *Tribal Justice* (1974), and *Resident Alien* (1986) are widely considered to represent his central achievement."

All this is to say, then, that thus far Blaise and Levine have survived the process of literary winnowing and were picked to represent Canada in two international compilations that survey world writing in English. As were Alice Munro and Mavis Gallant.

Why is it, then, that Clark Blaise and Norman Levine are largely unknown or ignored in Canada? Why is it that Norman Levine's stories have so long been out of print? Why is it that Norman Levine's work is not taught in any Canadian university? Why is it that Blaise's *A North American Education* and *Tribal Justice* languish in the respectable ghetto of New Press Canadian Classics *still in the first issue of the first printing sixteen years after publication?*

"Place him with Alice Munro and Mavis Gallant," declares *Maclean's Magazine* of Blaise.

What happened?

Because Blaise's career did not flourish in the USA there was no pressure on Canada to recognize a compelling writer in our midst. *A North American Education* and *Tribal Justice* remain two of the most glowing and obviously important volumes of stories ever published in Canada. And this is to make no mention of the delights of *Resident Alien*, *Days and Nights in Calcutta* and *Man and His World*.

Although Blaise was well reviewed, the *New York Times Review of Books* describing the stories as "glittering," *The New Yorker* did not adopt him and his publisher, Doubleday, did little to promote him. Canada remained deaf to his prose, and to the prose of his wife, Bharati Mukherjee.

Norman Levine's obscurity in Canada is even more curious than Blaise's. Ron Corbett, an *Ottawa Citizen* columnist, wrote a profile of Norman Levine recently and said: "Today, how Mr. Levine will be remembered in Canada is a question not only unknown, it is one largely unasked. None of his books or stories are taught at a Canadian university . . . Viking-Penguin, the last company to publish a new Levine book, says it has no plans to publish another one."

Corbett then goes on to quote Penguin Books Canada publisher Cynthia Good. She had published *Champagne Barn* and, later, *Something Happened Here.*

Corbett quotes her as saying: "At the time, we considered Norman to be on a par with Alice Munro or Mavis Gallant. We weren't alone. That's how many people viewed him at the time."

Norman Levine remains the writer he always was, a writer of central importance, one of Canada's best.

Here is a suggestion of the way Levine's work has been received elsewhere: ". . . passionate and brilliantly rendered" (*New Statesman*), ". . . masterly . . ." (*Times Literary Supplement*), "Impressive and fascinating . . ." (*Frankfurter Allgemeine Zeitung*), "Timeless elegance . . ." (*The Times*). "Norman Levine is one of the most outstanding short story writers working in English today" (*Encounter*).

Levine has been only nominally published in the USA.

Clark Blaise *has* been published in the USA but by a low-key publisher which treated him as a "mid-list" writer; he was not, in other words, heavily promoted.

It is curious that European and British praise for Levine has not been echoed in Canada. Such praise seems no longer to carry as much authority for Canadians as American praise. When one considers the careers of all four writers it is difficult to avoid the conclusion that the success of two of them and the relative obscurity of the other two centre upon publication in the USA and more particularly in *The New Yorker*. Further, it is difficult to avoid the conclusion that, were it not for American endorsement, Alice Munro and Mavis Gallant would languish in exactly the same Canadian obscurity.

Norman Levine and Clark Blaise are nearing the end of careers; they have behind them achieved bodies of work. What is there to say to brilliant writers nearer to the beginnings of careers? What is there to say to Caroline Adderson, to Terry Griggs, to Annabel Lyon, to Michael Winter? And to all the other writers who are part of our current flowering in the Canadian short story?

The fame you are so properly seeking cannot be conferred in Canada or by Canada. Canada cannot hear you. Canada cannot recognize you. Canada will not read you unless you are validated elsewhere.

THE MONTREAL STORY TELLERS

I CALLED HUGH HOOD at the end of 1970 and proposed to him that we put together a group of writers to give readings in high schools and colleges. The group came to consist of Hugh, Ray Smith, Ray Fraser, Clark Blaise, and me. I won't go into great detail about the Story Tellers because there is a book edited by J. R. (Tim) Struthers called *The Montreal Story Tellers: Memoirs, Photographs, Critical Essays*. The book appeared in 1985 and was published by Montreal's Véhicule Press.

I would, however, like to reminisce about Hugh Hood. Noreen Mallory, Hugh's wife, phoned us on Tuesday, August first, 2000, to tell us that Hugh had died. He had for some years been suffering from Parkinson's disease. The funeral service was held on August third. Myrna and I drove to Montreal. The congregation was sparse. Only two other writers were present. Joel Yanofsky was there to report for the *Gazette* and W. J. Keith and his wife, Hiroko, had come down from Toronto. The Montreal writing community was conspicuously absent.

The *Globe and Mail* asked me to write an obituary. An excerpt follows:

Hugh Hood, who died on Tuesday in Montreal, was a man of vibrant and engaging eccentricity. He was a cornucopia of information which he imparted relentlessly. The range of his knowledge was astonishing: history, literature, theology, Haydn, Canadian politics, hockey, baseball trivia, the names of the sidemen in every obscure band Bing Crosby sang with, the names of the scriptwriters on every *Carry On* film.

He had something like a photographic memory and when we were driving to readings in Montreal during the 1970s, he would unreel for us long quotations from P. G. Wodehouse, Anthony Powell, Evelyn Waugh and Raymond Chandler. Our task was to guess the title and date.

Hugh was eccentric variously. His dress was usually casual. He sometimes invested in new sneakers. He organized his writing life under strange numerical schemes which made vital sense to him but which were incomprehensible to his listeners. He boasted that his car was the cheapest new car that it was possible to own in North America. At that point, this was a Russian Lada with holes in the dashboard where the instrumentation would have been had he taken those options.

My wife and I were once driving with Hugh to Toronto to read at Harbourfront. As we pulled out of the drive, my wife asked Hugh why he had not put on his seat belt. Taking in a comprehensive survey through the ages of the doctrines of Free Will, Salvation, Law, and the nature of the Social Contract, the answer lasted until we were approaching Oshawa.

I recall, too, with great affection, a cross-country reading tour that Hugh and I did with Leon Rooke when the three of us were published by ECW Press. Leon and I used to trade our Air Canada chicken for his wine. He loved the chicken and would talk at length about the cleverness of its packaging, the beauty of plastic, form and content, Marshall McLuhan, *Japanese* packaging . . . a typical Hoodian arabesque.

Hugh ate vegetables only from tins. His soup of choice was Campbell's. He described most cuisines as "foreign muck." He insisted his coffee be instant.

I shall miss him.

Ray Smith wrote an obituary for the *Gazette*, opening with the following anecdote:

> It was 1971 and the five Montreal Story Tellers were taking Canadian literature to a West Island high school, one of a series of school readings we did over two years. I think Raymond Fraser was on stage when in the wings John Metcalf told the rest of us that his marriage had collapsed.
>
> We sympathized, offered beds, names of lawyers, shrinks. Hugh Hood privately slipped John a piece of paper.
>
> "You'll need this," Hugh murmured.
>
> When he looked at it later, Metcalf found it was a cheque for $400.
>
> That would be about $1,800 today. John was amazed, but only briefly. Of course Hugh would do that, not because he was rich, for he wasn't, but because he was Hugh.

All of the Story Tellers wrote memoir pieces for the book Tim Struthers compiled and I'd like to quote excerpts from Ray Smith's. It gives an affectionate portrait of Hugh and suggests something of the hilarity of the Montreal Story Tellers expeditions.

> The five of us are in Hugh's car driving to a reading. Probably along some ghastly six-laner like the Decarie Expressway. Known as "The Big Ditch," it has concrete

walls fifty feet high. A dangerous and depressing place. Hugh gleefully extols freeways, concrete, and the Decarie.

"Yessir," he exults, "they ought to pave the island from end to end. Concrete is civilization."

He goes on in this vein. I never know if he is being serious or trying to get a rise out of someone. John plunges in. "You are being deliberately perverse, Hugh." John's ideal landscape is perhaps filled with the barren hills and green valleys of Yorkshire or Cumberland; he looks upon a life which includes the Decarie Expressway as something from Hieronymus Bosch, and his life here as a punishment for an adolescence spent in furtive wanking.

"Perverse?" Hugh cries. "Shit no. Do you realize that if the Romans . . ."

Given half a chance, Hugh will talk on the history of concrete all the way to the reading, be it in Rosemere or be it in Vancouver. Long before that, John will have thrown himself screaming from the car; or will be in paroxysms of hysterical laughter. But neither is given a chance: Clark interrupts with an apt quotation from Rilke, Schiller, or Pushkin; someone whose work I have never read. Clark quotes in the original language.

In the back seat, I murmur to Fraser: "Bring out the Argentine brandy."

"Bulgarian this week," says Fraser as he digs the mickey from the inevitable Air Canada bag. "Bulgarian was only 19.6 cents an ounce."

Fraser uses a housewife's calculator to buy his booze. We each take a pull and Ray offers it around but all refuse. Fraser and I are, of course, the only Maritimers in the group.

Hugh and Clark are now fully into the discussion about concrete.

"Those nineteenth-century romantics are ontological arseholes," Hugh is saying.

In rebuttal Clark summarizes Bergson.

Another car comes close to ours. Hugh rolls down his window and yells, "Watch out, you stupid fucker, the future of Canadian literature is in this car."

Metcalf says, "Quebec drivers are all either suicidal or drunk. Probably both."

Clark quotes Alberto Moravia on Italian drivers. In Italian.

I remark that I once skimmed a Moravia novel. The cover had promised steamy sex, but the text was a philosophical working out of exquisitely attenuated ennui.

Clark quotes Anouilh on ennui.

Fraser's nerve breaks and we get another pull at the Bulgarian.

"Moravia is a teleological arsehole," says Hugh. In illustration he quotes two pages of a Moravia novel he read in 1947. He quotes in English.

Now John reaches for the bottle. "I saw a great line yesterday in *The High Window* by Raymond Chandler: 'large moist eyes with the sympathetic expression of wet stones.' Superb."

Hugh quotes the next two pages of the novel.

I interrupt to point out a girl standing at a stop light and wearing a see-through top and no bra. Hugh sings a song he has written about lingerie. I never did learn the words, but something like:

Your girdle is a hurdle
I never want to jump
But your garter belts send me
And bikini panties rend me
And black stockings bend me
Into a hump-hump-hump!

On the last line Hugh bounces vigorously in his seat.

> A good thing we are no longer on the expressway, for the car swerves into the next lane and heads for a lamp post. As Hugh nonchalantly regains control, John remarks in tightly controlled hysteria: "Hugh, if I might make a small suggestion . . ."
>
> Hugh ignores him; he has noticed a fellow in jeans and jean jacket staring in amazement from the sidewalk. Hugh rolls down the window.
>
> "Hump-hump-hump!" he bellows. "Culture!" He guns the car around the corner. "And why don't you get a haircut, you long-haired hippie freak." He rolls up the window. "That's telling him."
>
> Clark quotes Yukio Mishima on lingerie. This time he quotes in English.
>
> Fraser flourishes the bottle. Metcalf grabs it in desperation.
>
> I reflect that whatever Hugh's estimable qualities—and they are many—if he wore a hat it would inevitably bear a card reading: "In this style, 10/6."

Ray is referring here, of course, to the Tenniel illustration.

We are probably too close to Hugh's novel sequence *The New Age* to form a judgement yet. I feel that some of the novels are more successful than others but I have not yet been able to absorb all twelve books and see them as one. Many readers have problems with Hugh's meanderings down byways of information, his asides, his digressions, feeling that these are blemishes on the books' artistry and destructive of the suspension of disbelief. Other readers feel that Hugh's disquisitions are an essential part of his charm. The novella *Five New Facts About Giorgione* would be a good starting point for coming to some decision about this argument. I found the book maddening.

I feel much clearer about Hugh's early work perhaps because I have lived with it for so many years. In any literature there are certain works which seem obviously to stand in the national canon. I am convinced that Hugh's *Around the Mountain* is one such book. It is my favourite among his short fiction. It was conceived and written as a cycle of twelve stories which together capture Montreal as it was in 1967. Exhibiting an endearing innocence Hugh thought it would sell to American tourists wanting a souvenir of Montreal and Expo 67.

Since Hugh's death I have put together for the New Canadian Library a selection of his stories with an Afterword. The selection is entitled *Light Shining Out of Darkness*, that title being the title of one of the selections. I like to think the title expresses the essence of Hugh's life and writing.

CONDUCT UNBECOMING

Aunts Aren't Gentlemen is P. G. Wodehouse's last complete novel. It was published in 1974 when he was ninety-three. He died in 1975 leaving behind a first draft of *Sunset at Blandings*. During the sunset years of the late sixties and seventies it seemed to me that many women stopped behaving like gentlemen.

Sisterhood was relentless. Bastions were stormed, institutions toppled with maenadic energy. Women were joining consciousness-raising groups and, once raised, were everywhere forsaking their husbands for electric toothbrushes. Men, meanwhile, were wagging around like bewildered golden retrievers unable to figure out their transgression and dispirited by the mistresses' permanent scowls.

I once saw a Margaret Atwood novel on offer in a dealer's catalogue which was described as being inscribed: "To ___ in feminist frenzy." "Frenzy" aptly describes those heady days. By coincidence, it was Margaret Atwood who gave me my first personal encounter with the feminist schtick. We had been reading together one evening for David Helwig at Queen's University and a group was going on to Toronto the next day by train for some other literary event. I asked people in the group who wanted coffee or soft drinks and went to the serving hatch. On return, I handed a coffee to Margaret Atwood who asked me how much it had cost. I did my gentlemanly mumble saying it was of no import. She *demanded* to know what it had cost. I had no idea as I'd paid for various drinks with a twenty-dollar bill. Why, Margaret Atwood demanded to know, should I pay for her coffee? What was my motivation? Was I really unaware that I was patronizing her? Demeaning her? Belittling her? Was I unaware that I was showing contempt for women . . . I received the full nine yards.

What I'd *thought* I'd been doing was getting her a cup of coffee.

Ah, well.

Loyola, along with every other campus in the country, throbbed with radical energy. Gale was often on campus, often in the faculty club. Aggressive feminism was central to the Zeitgeist. It wasn't an intellectual or practical feminism—equal pay for equal work, say—but rather an implacable emotionalism directed against the opposite sex. I am not meek by nature and during 1970 and 1971 our relationship became increasingly testy.

Gale was pregnant with our second child and demanded an abortion. I was strongly opposed but felt rather helplessly that it wasn't my decision to make. She found a doctor willing to claim that the pregnancy was detrimental to her mental health and the operation was performed at a local hospital. Shortly after this she started spending time with a Loyola student called Elizabeth Bateman.

Elizabeth Bateman was tall with lank and malodorous hair. She was probably mucky for ideological reasons. She called herself Bitsy. She wore boots and suspenders. She claimed to be a photographer. Gale declared herself passionately in love with this unappetizing creature. The lesbian life, she announced, was the life for her. And she intended it, she said, for our daughter, Elizabeth, too. I objected to the situation and left the house, moving into what amounted to a commune of Loyola faculty members whose marriages had gone awry. Gale referred to this house as Heartbreak Hotel.

I sued for divorce. Gale did not even attend the hearing and I was granted the divorce and custody of Elizabeth. I was preparing to move to Fredericton where I had been offered a year's work as writer-in-residence. Elizabeth was still living with Gale and Bitsy as I hadn't wanted to move her into temporary accommodation. In Fredericton I was going to share a house with my friend Douglas Rollins, a fellow teacher who was studying for a Ph.D.

Gale came to see me one afternoon and said that she had changed her mind about the divorce and wished to go to Fredericton with me. The decree was not yet absolute and she asked me to cancel the action as a demonstration of my general faith and devotion. This I did because I still loved her and was distressed about Elizabeth's emotional state. We went to the Palais de Justice and I filled in the paperwork.

My friends were incredulous.

My lawyer was apoplectic.

A few days later while I was picking Elizabeth up to take her out to play Gale told me that she had no intention of going to Fredericton, that she had had no change of heart, that she had deceived me just to have another chance at custody. She also allowed that she thought I was simple.

I again sued for divorce, this time being granted the divorce but denied custody. Gale's parents committed breathtaking perjury. It was a sour day. The judge, too, seemed to think that I'd acted rather irresponsibly in cancelling the first divorce.

Various people have asked me how I could have been so stupid. It *was* stupid, I suppose, in the terms of the workaday world. But what had been at stake was very important. It was the right *sort* of mistake to make, and I'm not sure I wouldn't make a similar sort of mistake again.

What does this sad catalogue leave me feeling thirty years later? My position is close to the sage words of P. J. O'Rourke, who in *Age and Guile Beat Youth, Innocence and a Bad Haircut* wrote:

> Miniskirts caused feminism. Women wore miniskirts. Construction workers made ape noises. Women got pissed off. Once the women were pissed off about this they started thinking about all the other things they had to be pissed off about. That led to feminism. Not that I'm criticizing. Look, Babe . . . I mean, Ms . . . I mean, yes, sir I *do* support feminism. I really do. But that doesn't mean I want to go through it twice.

WRITER-IN-RESIDENCE

MY FIRST STINT as a writer-in-residence was at the University of New Brunswick in 1972–73. I was offered the appointment through the good offices of Kent Thompson, a fellow writer and a professor in the UNB English department, who argued that the university should assist younger writers instead of automatically piling honours on those already laden.

I had first met Kent when he was editor of *The Fiddlehead*, the literary magazine which has been associated with UNB for so many years and which has done so much to encourage young poets and fiction writers. In 1970 Kent organized under the umbrella of *The Fiddlehead* a conference of writers and critics to discuss the current state of fiction in Canada. It was Kent's conviction that the critics were years behind the writers and he hoped the conference might stimulate some of them to grapple with the sudden sophistication that Canadian fiction was exhibiting. Nothing of the sort happened, of course, but it was interesting and instructive to spend time with Hugh Hood, Dave Godfrey, Rudy Wiebe, and David Helwig.

Dave Godfrey was then a bright star in the firmament of Canadian letters, having helped found the House of Anansi and having written a bulky and ultimately incomprehensible book called *The New Ancestors*. He now designs computer software. He was at the time rabid with nationalism and my accent and antecedents seemed to rub him up very much the wrong way; at breakfast in the Lord Beaverbrook Hotel he read the stock market reports in a marked manner. I was relieved to discover, however, that his rage was general; during a dull but unexceptionable paper by Professor Hallvard Dahlie entitled "Self-Conscious Nationalism in the Novels of Hugh MacLennan," Godfrey suggested that Professor Dahlie would benefit from "a good bum-fuck" administered by Scott Symons. This was a form of ideological re-education which had not previously occurred to me.

If the academic offerings were tedious, the discussions among the writers were of great interest. I can recall my enthusiasm at the time for the ideas of the Imagists and how those ideas could be worked out in the story form. I began in the discussions at that conference what has turned into the lifelong task of attempting to teach academics the necessity of an aesthetic approach to literature. I'm now convinced it's a task that's largely hopeless.

Canadian literary studies and "scholarship" have always been lax and undemanding. It is a field which attracts second- and third-rate minds. Such widely published critics as John Moss, who was a Ph.D. student at Fredericton when I was writer-in-residence, can to this day write gibberish such as the following and still retain the regard of his colleagues: "This novel, as much as any, shows why Callaghan is a significant writer in the Canadian tradition without necessarily being an accomplished artist. [WHAT?] The prose is awkwardly simplistic, but forceful and direct . . . [WHAT?] He is probably the best example we have of the serious artist as entertainer." (WHAT?)

The author of these moronic sentences is considered one of the chief adornments of the University of Ottawa's English department.

The lax and slapdash are everywhere. Three tiny examples suggestive of the whole. *Going Down Slow* concerns a teacher's affair with a student. The entire plot centres on the affair's illegality. *The Oxford Companion to Canadian Literature* describes the student, Susan, *as a fellow teacher*. Again, the new dictionary, *The Canadian Oxford Dictionary* (1998) has an encyclopedic element and carries hundreds of biographical entries. I am listed, correctly, under Metcalf but in company with Charles Theophilus Metcalf, governor general of British North America (1843–45) whose name is not Metcalf but Metcalfe.

The entry for Ethel Wilson reads: "South-African-born Canadian novelist and essayist. Her many collections of stories include *Love and Salt Water* (1956) and *Mrs. Golightly and Other Stories* (1961)."

Ethel Wilson published only six books in her career. Four of the six were novels. One was a book containing two novellas. *One* was a book of short stories. One is not "many." *Love and Salt Water*, identified by Oxford as a story collection, is, in fact, a novel.

But does any of this petty detail *really* matter?

Yes.

William Hoffer, the fabled Vancouver antiquarian book dealer, once wrote about Canadian writing: "The complicated pocket watch of literature has been replaced by a rude drawing of a watch with no moving parts."

"In Canada," he used to say, "*approximations* are good enough."

My office in Fredericton was in the old Arts Building between the offices of Robert Gibbs and Fred Cogswell. Robert Gibbs often held long discussions with students about Pre- and Post-Confederation poets, none of whom I'd read. He also had briefer and more interesting chats with his bookcase, briefcase, and filing cabinet.

Fred Cogswell used his office as warehouse and editorial centre for Fiddlehead Poetry Books, an enterprise distinct from *The Fiddlehead*. He was always extremely affable and kept me abreast of the doings of all his poetesses. These conversations were baffling because his starting point was always an outcropping of some buried lode.

An entirely typical exchange would run as follows:

"She's feeling a lot better now."

"Oh, hello, Fred. Pardon?"

"Much closer to a decision."

"Oh. Good."

"We went for a long walk on the beach on Sunday."

"I see."

Silent puffing on his pipe.

"His big mistake, you see, was to offer marriage."

"Mistake?"

"It offended her deeply."

"Oh."

I had no idea to whom these daily bulletins referred and so they all combined in my mind into a composite, into an Identikit portrait of a Fiddlehead Poetry Books poetess—youngish, good-looking, sexually unhappy or inverted, offended at elemental levels by the world's *coarseness*, terribly sincere, terribly sensitive, terribly intense—in sum, not unlike the Madeline Basset to whom Bertie Wooster often refers with a shudder.

These chapbooks were unspeakable. During the years of his editorship he published 307 of them. At first I thought his motivation must be the desire for contiguity with young female flesh but came to understand that, worse, he actually believed in all this jejune inadequacy. I held the position that such an outpouring of drivel was an example of bad coin driving out good, that his wretched pamphlets took away attention from the three or four good poets we should have been reading.

I had, of course, got it all wrong. Fred's contribution was of the kind Canada understood and wanted. It was a kind of "outreach," the literary equivalent of helium balloons on strings and painting the faces of children at "cultural" events. Cogswell was made a member of the Order of Canada in 1981.

A recent Canada Council jury award prompted David Solway into velvety rage and a comic tour of the stunning banality of a new book by a Fiddlehead Poetry Books veteran. I quote from his essay "Getting on the Gravy Boat."

> In 1999 Sharon H. Nelson, the author of ten little-known and largely unreviewed chapbooks dating back to 1972, received a $20,000 Canada Council Arts Grant to write a book of poems. Two and a half years later an eleven page collection appeared, entitled *How the Soup Gets Made*. Not counting a 12th page of Notes in which we are given a definition of *parmentier* and a detailed recipe for its preparation, this averages out to approximately $2000 per page, a sum whose literary amortization may in this case prove highly problematic.
>
> To get some sense of what this modest work entails, let us embark on a quick tour of its pages. The book begins with its title poem where we are initially apprised that
>
> Today I made leek and cauliflower soup
> because Brenda had dental surgery this morning . . .
>
> —which is surely a direct if unexpected way of whetting the reader's appetite. While the soup is on the boil, we discover that the poet, speculating over the destiny of her restorative bouillon, is also thinking of
>
> Rahel and Bella and Maureen
> all of whom can't eat anything made with *allium* . . .
>
> And of Maxiane who "no longer eats potatoes." Once we have digested these disturbing facts, however, we

learn to our immediate relief that Brenda is recovering well, and soon the steamy kitchen of Nelson's culinary imagination begins to fill with ever more Goddesses of the Soup, a numinous sorority which proceeds to

> cook soup against the chill,
> and welcome the companionship of friends
> whose presences pervade the air
> with the rising scent of braising vegetables . . .

Solway's comic performance here can only *suggest* the contagion Cogswell spread for so many years.

Long after my stint at UNB was over I was chatting to Kent Thompson about the general *looniness* of Fredericton and the astonishing marital frolics of the English department; he corrected me sharply, pointing out that the loony one had been me. And I suppose there's truth in that too; I was distraught about my wife and daughter and Fredericton offered few distractions from grief.

In fact, as far as I was concerned, Fredericton had little to offer at all. Its pizza parlours featured pizzas studded with turd-like mounds of hamburger and signs proudly claimed: Topped with Genuine (Mild) Canadian Cheddar. All Chinese restaurants served things in red sauce. I loathed the pretentiousness and *awfulness* of the vast Salvador Dalí painting in the Beaverbrook Art Gallery, so I rarely went there. I was banned for life from the River Room of the Lord Beaverbrook Hotel for unplugging two amplified Spanish singers from Saint John. I felt isolated, aware always of the oppressive miles of forests black and dripping.

Years later when we were living on a farm in Ontario, Myrna and I were part of a group sponsoring some young refugee men from Vietnam. One of them, Cuong, said one day, "In Hong Kong . . . lights! . . . music! . . . women! In Canada . . . tree, tree, tree." How deeply I empathized with his boredom!

One of Fredericton's few solaces was the presence of Alden Nowlan. He held court in a small house on the edge of campus and along with the painters Bruno and Molly Bobak and several talented musicians was one of UNB's permanent artists-in-residence.

Alden's house was a mecca for visiting writers and for troops of young poets who dropped in for encouragement, words of wisdom, beer, and the ever-present gin. Evenings with Alden always began with great affability but the emotional direction of the evening could veer as the level in the gin bottle dropped. Or on some evenings, bottles.

Alden was a very large man. Operations on his throat for cancer had left his voice growly and his face puffy and this, combined with his bulk and beardedness, suggested an obese bear as he sat in his armchair sweating and rumbling and roaring about the monarchy (he supported the Stuart Pretender) or about the paucity of scientific evidence of the world's being round (he was a founding member of the Canadian Flat Earth Society).

Alden was brought up in a small village in Nova Scotia in conditions of dire poverty. He was an autodidact and proud of the fact. But it also made him prickly. He was likely to attack and bait visitors for the relative ease and comfort of their circumstances, demanding to know how with their obvious gentility and education they could hope to understand "life."

To hear Alden's account, he never saw paper or pencil until the age of twenty-five. Some professorial visitors seemed to feel shame at their lack of humble origins and at their ordinary fathers who hadn't gnawed at the bark of trees to sustain life. Alden derived a great deal of entertainment from these exercises.

I was rather bored by the romanticism of the idea that the life of New Brunswick peasants was somehow more "real" than the life of, say, Toronto stockbrokers and I used to tell him to stop talking balls. It was at about this point that the evenings degenerated into slurred and rumbling abuse.

Patrick Toner has written a biography of Nowlan entitled *If I Could Turn and Meet Myself: The Life of Alden Nowlan*. In it he recreates the first time I went to Nowlan's house in 1970 during Kent Thompson's conference.

> Kent Thompson was not a frequent visitor to the Nowlan household. The man he brought that night, John Metcalf, was a first-time visitor. He had made a good impression among the UNB faculty, so good that it was generally understood that he might soon become a familiar face. Nowlan was holding forth in the den about a topic central to his mythos: the poverty of his youth. He catalogued his various deprivations like a mantra. "We had no indoor plumbing, no running water. I didn't even learn how to use a telephone until I had moved away at the age of 19 . . ."
>
> "Yes, I know how that is," Kent Thompson said from the corner where he had been listening. "I, too, had a pretty impoverished childhood."
>
> The guests could not listen to Thompson; they were too focussed on Nowlan, who fixed the professor in his stare while Thompson spoke. People started looking away. There was a void of silence before Nowlan responded.
>
> "Oh, yes, Kent," he said, his voice steady. "I know that you knew just what it was like. Take your family for instance. They were so poor they could only afford to trade the car in every second year . . ."
>
> "Oh, come off it, Alden," Thompson protested.
>
> But Nowlan was relentless. "You were so poor that you could only afford a party line for your telephone, so poor that you sometimes had only beans and bacon to go with your potatoes . . ." And on and on, every word twisting the knife deeper.

Thompson had not had an easy week, either, what with the stress of organizing the conference. He put down his glass in disgust and walked towards the door. "That's right, Kent," Nowlan persisted. "Go back to where you are wanted, because it's not here."

Metcalf had had enough, too. "Alden, you've obviously had way too much to drink, and have no right to subject Kent or anyone else to your blatherings."

But Thompson had already grabbed his coat, nearly in tears, muttering on his way out, "I know one thing: I'm sick and tired of taking all this shit." Metcalf followed . . .

The next day Nowlan remembered enough about the night before to know that he owed Thompson a huge apology. There were a few people brave enough to remind him. "You were wrong and I'd be a shit to myself and to Kent if I didn't say so," Metcalf wrote on Monday, after cooling down. "Which, being said, I hope we can proceed as before and that you'll reply to this. You must know that I admire your work this side idolatry."

So what had this jolly evening been about? The bellicosity of gin, anti-Americanism, and Alden's insecurity in educated company.

He was kind and attentive to the young poets who hung about the house but he rarely criticized their work or put to them the necessary steel. And not one of them has emerged as a writer of any significance. Part of this acceptance was, I'm sure, kindness and camaraderie. Part of it may also have been a lack of knowledge about the traditional forms and techniques.

The camaraderie had a special Maritime tinge and was destructive to certain of these aspiring poets. When Charlie Parker was dying in the apartment of the Baroness Pannonica de Koenigswarter from the combined effects of heroin, ulcers, and cirrhosis of the liver the attending doctor asked him if he drank. Parker is alleged to have replied: "The occasional glass of sherry." I've been known to sip the occasional sherry myself and don't object at all to taking off the edge of day at about 4 p.m., but Alden drank violently and pathologically. When I once suggested that fifty-two ounces of undiluted gin was going at it rather hard, he countered by saying that where *he* came from he was not accounted a drinker. And that remark is revealing. Nova Scotia and New Brunswick are drunken and violent societies. Drinking is equated with manliness. Alden endorsed this suicidal drinking as part of being both man and poet. The legacy he left to some of those impressionable boys caused years of suffering.

I had, of course, known his poetry before going to Fredericton. When I wrote to him after that unpleasant evening in 1970 and criticized his behaviour I rather smarmily used Ben Jonson's phrase about Shakespeare to describe my liking for his work . . . *this side idolatry*. (It is taken from Jonson's 1641 tribute to Shakespeare in *Timber or Discoveries* and I assumed Alden would recognize it.)

I must confess that these days I'm very far this side idolatry. That holds true of many other writers whose work I've liked. I think I had a longing for the work to be better than it was.

"With the passing of time," Bill Hoffer used to say, "we stand the more clearly revealed."

The poem "Palomino Stallion," though it dates from 1974, can reasonably represent what Alden was writing in the early books.

Though the barn is so warm
that the oats in his manger,
the straw in his bed
seem to give off smoke—

though the wind is so cold,
the snow in the pasture

so deep he'd fall down
and freeze in an hour—

the eleven-month-old
palomino stallion
has gone almost crazy
fighting and pleading
to be let out.

The early poems seemed at the time to possess a spontaneity which was refreshing. The volumes I'm referring to are *The Rose and the Puritan*, *A Darkness in the Earth*, *The Things Which Are*, *Under the Ice*, and *Wind in a Rocky Country*. But what seemed spontaneous then strikes me now as lax, lacking tension, insufficiently wrought.

The simplicity and charm would later coarsen into folksiness and sentimentality. In fact, this decline began with *Bread, Wine, and Salt* which was awarded the Governor General's Award in 1967. The later poetry became far too prosy and he gave in to the desire to be warm, wise, and "philosophical." Cracker-barrel philosophy, I'm afraid, and at the end of *that* road lies the *Reader's Digest*.

The early poems remind me strongly of certain poems by D. H. Lawrence and Raymond Knister, brief arpeggios which, as Kingsley Amis might have said, do not resonate *enough*. Nowadays I'd trade reams of Nowlan for just one stanza by the ineffable Eric Ormsby.

Alden once wrote to me: "*If* there comes a time when truck drivers read poetry, mine will be the poetry they'll read."

And I'm afraid that might well be his work's epitaph.

The term ground on. Eager students with manuscripts did not appear. In the endless hours, I wrote some short stories, "The Strange Aberration of Mr. Ken Smythe," "The Practice of the Craft," "The Years in Exile"—collected with others, and published in 1975 in a volume called *The Teeth of My Father*.

During that year I also helped to found the Writers' Union of Canada. I chaired a committee made up of Margaret Laurence, Alice Munro, Fred Bodsworth, and Timothy Findley which was responsible for drawing up the criteria for membership. There was a deep split from the very beginning between those who wanted a union and those who wanted something close to the idea of an academy. Everyone, however, feared that the proposed union might become merely another cozy, mushy version of the Canadian Authors' Association and any accommodation seemed worth avoiding *that* fate; the chasm between those who were frankly elitist and those who were unionist was papered over. We compromised eventually by making membership dependent on having published a trade book (i.e., a non-textbook) with a non-vanity press. Acceptance or rejection of an application for membership, however, lay with the Membership Committee.

I loved the euphoria of the first meetings, the sense of community, but the Union grew larger and its ranks filled with people who had published genuine trade books but *what* books: cookbooks, bizarre litcrit, kiddylit, how-to, Saskatchewan on $5 a day. The union soon bulged with people I'd never heard of and didn't want to know. Pierre Berton even tried to bully the membership into closed-shop politics.

I served on the national executive of the Union for its first three years but quit in umbrage over Graeme Gibson's proposal that the Union supervise the putting together of a series of anthologies for school use. I had nothing against missionary work, but I argued that if this were done the contents of the anthologies would seem to have Union imprimatur, that it would seem as if the Union were saying, "This is Canadian literature." My other strong objection was that the anthologies were thematic in structure. Producing a book called, say, *The Immigrant Experience* reduced the stories and poems in it to mere illustrations of sociology and history. In other words, I felt that the thematic approach to literature was anti-literary.

Irving Layton once wrote to me in a letter about the publication of some of his poems, ". . . there's lotsa love in you John, and that puts us roaring and clattering on the twin rails of glory." And, indeed, glory has always been my desired destination.

Poor Irving! He himself has been effaced by Alzheimer's, he's been abandoned by his publishers, largely forgotten by the public, his books entirely out of print except for the Porcupine's Quill version of *Dance with Desire*. Not much glory there, Irving, old love.

Accomplishment and glory need their rewards and in the arguments leading up to the founding of the Union, Kent Thompson and I had a vision of the institution's headquarters, a large stone mansion in Ottawa or Toronto, a somnolent library—literature, history, reference, with a sprinkling of *erotica*—log fires, deep leather chairs. A silver handbell which, when rung, brought forth Scrotum, the wrinkled old retainer, with his silver salver. Thinly sliced caraway cake and fino sherry in the mornings. Or oloroso if you *must*. Hot canapés in the afternoon. Savouries in the evening featuring the Gentlemen's Relish, Patum Peperium.

I found my favourite clubland story in A. D. Peters's autobiography. He was Evelyn Waugh's literary agent. Peters's club was closing for refurbishment and its members were farmed out to other clubs for the duration. When the club re-opened, A. D. Peters and another man were standing at the urinal having a pee and gazing round at all the glittering brass, the gleaming porcelain, the roseate copper tubing. Peters's companion said to him: "Makes the old cock look a bit shabby, doesn't it?"

Memo to Kent: *We'll have to get Scrotum a green baize apron to wear while polishing the silver and I also feel quite strongly that we ought to force the shifty old sod to iron the daily newspapers as well. Would white gloves be going too far?*

Our visions of elitist pleasures soon paled into the boring realities of rules of procedure, contract clauses, royalty rates, kill fees. "Glory" didn't get a look-in. And then, year after year descending into the bile of "gender," "race," "appropriation of voice," "women of colour." Most good writers left this snakepit or simply did not attend. It was not an appropriate context for the women who'd written "Labour Day Dinner" and "Speck's Idea" or for the men who'd written "A Small Piece of Blue" and "A North American Education."

In more recent years the Union has generated the moral fervour of a revival meeting. Their righteous antics delight. The Union news-letter presented this unintentionally hilarious account of the activities of one of their earnest and doleful Committees.

> On February 1, Ontario writers and the National Council wined and dined with members of the Racial Minority Writers' Committee, at 21 McGill Street. Jill Humphries, TWUC's Ontario Co-ordinator, and Jillian Dagg, the Ontario Rep, had arranged for a very nice dinner, good wine (a bit expensive), and had managed to attract a record number of people (76) to the event. It was a good evening.
>
> But can you imagine? A women's club, a club of well-to-do women, preserves, in two corners of the auditorium/banquet hall, gilded plaster sculptures of children carrying baskets of fruit on their heads. Not just any children, no, little black children, little slaves.
>
> Neither Jill nor Jillian had inspected the hall prior to the dinner, nor could they have suspected the presence of imperialist or colonialist works of art there. I must admit that I myself perceived the statues only after the salad . . .
>
> After the meal, I gathered my courage, went to their table and asked them how they felt about these objectionable objects. They were angry, of course, outraged. No,

> they said, such things cannot even be sold to an antique store or some place like it, "they must be destroyed!" A copy of this letter will go to the McGill Club and I hope its Board of Directors will do away with all mementos of shameful times. I did not inspect the place from top to bottom, but who knows, there may be more such things in other nooks and crannies.

How marvellously *relaxing* it must be to have a mind so basic!

The choice of Union over Academy was an inevitably Canadian choice. Leftish rather than rightish, fair and aboveboard rather than snooty, no nasty or disturbing judgements needing to be made. The Union reflected the politics of Graeme Gibson and Margaret Atwood and their set; they've always believed in organizing and melding literature and institutions and directing them towards nationalist ends.

One of that year's few pleasures in Fredericton was meeting John Newlove. He came to UNB to give a public reading and I was keenly interested to attend. I knew the poetry he'd already published and was reading his current work as we were both appearing in the same magazines. He loomed large on my horizon. I loved the *tone* of his writing.

I produced a version of our meeting as the opening paragraphs of a story called "The Teeth of My Father."

> Adrift one afternoon on a tide of beer and nostalgia in the River Room of the Lord Beaverbrook Hotel in Fredericton, my friend and I traded stories of our dead fathers. We drank until the bar began to fill for Happy Hour. He told me how his father had employed him every Saturday and how every Saturday evening before being allowed out his father had forced him into a game of poker to recover the day's wages. We drank until the free cheese, olives, and melba toast were wheeled away

at six. I told him of my father's teeth; he, of his father's three-and-a-half-year disappearance for a drink. I, of my father and the loose box; he, of his father's contempt of court charge. I, of my father and the consequences of the VD pamphlet. We drank until shortly before his evening flight to Halifax was due.

It was Cyril Connolly, I believe, who said that drinking is a low form of creativity. A perceptive remark. Drinking also prompts my memory. Walking home on wilful legs in the cold night air, my drunkenness unlocked the smells and textures of the receding past, recalling incident and anecdote I had not thought to tell in the bar's warm comfort. Lurching up Forest Hill, I remembered my father's tobacco growing, and worse, its curing, our cinema outing; the afternoon he felled the kitchen; the tubular steel incident. And it was on Forest Hill, although I'd often told the story of his teeth, that I realized for the first time how genuinely and entirely eccentric my father had been.

(I have decided to tell the truth. My stories in the River Room were not purely nostalgic; they were calculated to be funny and entertain my friend. My friend was more an acquaintance, a man I admired and wanted to impress. And "wilful legs" was plagiarized from Dylan Thomas.)

I dedicated this story to Alice Munro. She dedicated one to me called "Home" which appeared in *New Canadian Stories 1974*. This was because we'd been talking to each other about what "autobiography" in fiction meant. Alice felt it nearly impossible emotionally to write about her mother. I think she felt also that to write about an experience was in some way to betray it. We were both experimenting with the idea of commenting *on* the story *within* the story—as I do in the bracketed paragraph above. We were attempting to make the stories more "real" or "truthful" by "confessing" to their artificiality.

In later years I came to believe that there is no such thing as autobiography. There are arrangements of words on a page. There is rhetoric. We are not recording; we are creating. I was charmed by a statement I read recently by Quebec abstractionist Claude Tousignant. He wrote: "What I advocate is the notion of paintings as beings, not representations." It immediately struck me that the finest stories are also "beings" rather than "representations," magical worlds wrought by language.

But to return to John Newlove.

In centuries past itinerant craftsmen travelled from mill to mill seeking work recutting the blunted patterns of grooves on the faces of the millstones. Over the years tiny slivers of metal worked their way into the men's hands, causing blue and black ridges and worms beneath the skin. Millers wanted experienced men and so used to say to the masons, "Hold out your hands and show me your metal." If one wanted to see John Newlove's metal one would need an MRI machine.

One ankle is held together by a metal pin, the ankle broken during a drunken fight in the kitchen of Al Purdy's house in Ameliasburg. Newlove claims that Purdy dropped on him, or threw at him, a water cooler. His thigh is held together by a large pin which was put in after a severe fall off a bar stool in Regina. One knee contains metal acquired after he fell down over a small drain in Peter Milroy's front garden after having been thrown out of the house for attempting to kick down the door of Peter's wine cellar. The scars are multiple. It seems that all John's life has been an effort to outrun sorrow and melancholy, the darkness everywhere in human life that weighs upon him. Many of his early poems are about hitchhiking; he's always been on the road escaping from and travelling to.

> Every muddy road I walk along
> I am the man who knows all about Jesus

but doesn't believe. My fat ass
trudges on. I am so weary. Lord;
beer is my muse, my music.

John's drunken exploits are legion. Everyone, it seems, has Newlove stories. Newlove biting strangers at parties; Newlove putting his false teeth in a stranger's beer glass; Newlove awaking in an abandoned lot in the back of a taxi, his body heaped with empty cans of Newcastle Brown Ale. Newlove flying back to Nelson and getting off the plane drunk in Castlereagh instead of Castlegar and summoning a taxi to drive him 175 miles through the midnight Kootenay mountains. Newlove ordering vodka after vodka with the stern command: "No fruit or vegetable matter."

My most preposterous Newlove story concerns a bookstore in Toronto which was called About Books. It was on Queen Street West and was run by the antiquarian dealer Larry Wallrich. John and I had stopped in there one morning and Larry and I soon got deeply involved in some Robert Graves limited editions. Larry also brought out some prized Graves manuscript written in fountain pen on flimsy blue sheets of what looked like airmail paper. The poems were from *Fairies and Fusiliers* and probably dated from 1916 or 1917. Larry described to me the difficult research to identify the poems, difficult because Graves had suppressed the volume.

Newlove, bored with all this antiquarian chit-chat, wandered off and returned half an hour or so later with a bottle of vodka, a carton of orange juice, and three Styrofoam cups. He seemed slightly unsteady. He pulled up a chair and asked us if we wanted a drink. Both Larry and I said that it seemed a little early. The inevitable occurred. Wrestling to open the carton, he knocked over the vodka. It gouted onto the manuscript sheets and instantly the ink began to blur and fuzz. Larry and I were so shocked neither of us said anything. We just stared.

John started looking shifty, then cowed, gazing up at us like a dog expecting a smack. Then, as we stared at him, he reached out and peeled off two or three sodden pages and in an act of expiation stuffed them into his mouth, chewing and painfully swallowing.

And that was in the morning.

In the afternoon, I got him back to the Royal York Hotel where I was staying. This involved John on his hands and knees in taxis, his mistakenly urinating into the clothes closet, his lying on my bed to sleep, my attempting to remove some of his clothes so he'd be more comfortable, his accusations that I was molesting him homosexually, his attempts to hit me. In the end I got so cross I gave him a good clout in the head and he went to sleep.

But—obviously—there was another John. Those who loved him and his poetry knew that the pain that enveloped and consumed him was real. We knew him as a soft-spoken gentleman, a technician in sophisticated verse, a voracious reader of history, a curator of anecdotes, a collector of Victorian travel books, a hoarder of ancient Syrian pottery and Athenian silver tetradrachmas.

Concerning Stars, Flowers, Love, Etc.

Make it easier, they say, make it easier. Tell
me something I already know, about stars or flowers or,
or happiness. I am happy sometimes, though
not right now, specially. Things are not going
too good right now. But you should try
to cheer people up, they say. There is
a good side to life, though
not right now, specially. Though the stars
continue to shine in some places and the flowers
continue to bloom in some places
and people do not starve in some places

and people are not killed in some places
and there are no wars in some places
and there are no slaves in some places
and in some places people love each other,
they say. Though I don't know where. They say,
I don't *want* to be sad. Help me not to know.

For John's fiftieth birthday I gathered together and printed up poems people had written in tribute. Using a line from one of his poems I called the pamphlet "Everyone Leans, Each on Each Other: Words for John Newlove on the Occasion of His Fiftieth Birthday." George Johnston, now lost to Alzheimer's, one of the most important poets Canada has ever produced though almost entirely unknown, wrote one of his renowned occasional poems which gorgeously captures his feelings for John and speaks for all John's friends.

A Palimpsest for John Newlove's Fiftieth Birthday Party

Everyone is wise. John Newlove is
a master in his versifying and he
knows things he cannot explain to the others,
though he tries as hard as he can anyways.

God only knows what he is up to tonight
making his way to eternity, through destiny
manufacturing chaos into rhythms
and all the while observing himself
wrapped for fifty years in the cold dark cloak
of fate, and making poetry of his doubts.
How splendid, how pregnant, all his poetry,
and not composed of vegetable peels, either.

How important it makes him in our eyes.
Though we are in a land of loonies, we can feel

that he has done us all good in his fifty years
and we hope he will have many more to do us good.

It has been a long, dear association
making the alien recognizable
in ourselves—and why should it ever end?
Think of that, John, if you can bear it, tonight.

When John got wind of the publication and the proposed party he said that he would leave town on the proposed date and berated me bitterly when I gave him a copy of the tribute, complaining that I had lumbered him with the unwanted task of having to write thank-you letters to all the contributors.

Over the years after Fredericton our paths crossed continually. John wrote a book called *The Green Plain* which he dedicated to me. Together we published a book called *Dreams Surround Us*. He moved back to Toronto and then after some years moved back west to Nelson, B.C., where he taught at a community college. Letters were sporadic. Then I heard that the college had closed and that he was without work. Soon after this I heard that he was in a hospital there.

Late one night the phone rang and the ghost of John's voice whispered, "You've got to get me out of here. You've got to get me a job." He'd been hospitalized because of his drinking, apparently, and the doctors had given him six months to live if he continued.

At the time Myrna was working for the Commissioner of Official Languages doing mystic things with computers. Her immediate boss was Pierre de Blois, a *bon vivant* and *bon viveur*. She persuaded Pierre that the Commissioner really needed an English-language editor for the department's unspeakably dreary magazine, *Language and Society*. We looked up and copied out reams of quotations about John from literary guides and encyclopedias and Myrna wrote up a magisterial CV.

We felt forced to say to Pierre that there *was* a tiny problem, that John had been known from time to time to, well, tipple. Pierre made a Gallic gesture and uttered a French equivalent of *Pshaw!* An interview was arranged. I went out to the airport at midday to meet the plane. John was, inevitably, inebriated. I got him home and into the shower. Made him eat scrambled eggs and toast, phoned Pierre and got the interview delayed for two and a half hours. I walked him down to Pierre's office. By this time he was running with sweat and was so nervous he was scarcely able to speak. The difficulty of the interview, I understand, was compounded by the fact that the interviewer was a weird Englishman so shy and withdrawn he could scarcely speak in public. Pierre, typically, solved this problem by asking the questions *and then answering them*.

John emerged from this strange non-interview with the job secured and at a considerable salary and dined with us every night for a month until Myrna found him an apartment which he later complained about because he said the garage it faced was ugly.

Myrna kept her eye on him and if he arrived squiffy in the morning she and a friend would take his arms and march him back into the elevator again and send him home in a cab.

Soon he burst forth in beautifully cut Harry Rosen suits and was obnoxious. He would phone me at odd hours and say, "Let's go out and cause some *serious* trouble!" Walking home from the post office one day with my mail I saw him on the street and holding up the letter said, "Hey, John, I'm in *Who's Who*." He said, "Who isn't?" John checking his stride and glancing back at the panhandler sitting with his kerchiefed dog with its one eye a spooky milk-blue and saying, "No, but I *would* be willing to assist you financially by killing your dog." Asking him on another occasion for the loan of twenty dollars which he begrudgingly withdrew from his fat wallet saying, as if in moral disapproval, "Why don't you find a fucking job, Metcalf."

In 1993 I had the honour of helping John put together a new Selected Poems. Porcupine's Quill published this volume as *Apology for Absence: Selected Poems 1962–1992*. We launched the book at a reading series I was running at Magnum Book Store. It was a delight to hear John reading with tight passion such classic poems as "Samuel Hearne in Wintertime," "The Pride," "Doukhobor," and "Ride Off Any Horizon."

I concluded my introduction of him to the Magnum audience by quoting from a review written by Robin Skelton ten years or more earlier of John's preceding selected poems, *The Fat Man*.

Skelton wrote:

> The poetry itself is enormously well crafted, subtly controlled in tone, and richly various in style, even while remaining consistent to what emerges as an overall purpose to portray the human tragedy with an economy and elegance that succeed in making the whole book a tribute to courage and a statement of the awesome spiritual strength of man.
>
> This *Selected Poems*, omitting as it does many of the poems of pure reportage and of whimsy which lessened the impact of some of the separate collections, is one of the most impressive to have been published in the English-speaking world in the last twenty years.

"What," I asked rhetorically, "would Skelton say of this even more splendid selection?"

Newlove rose, walked to the lectern, nodded acknowledgement to me, and said in his habitual sardonic manner: "The last time I saw Skelton was at a party in Victoria and he was wearing a colander on his head with feathers taped to it. However . . ."

Recently, after sporadic illness and a long period of sobriety and quiescence, John erupted again. His wife, Susan, was in Vancouver visiting their daughter and he phoned asking me to buy him a bottle of vodka and bring it to his house. He said he was too sick to go out. I debated about this for a while but decided I'd go and urge him to sober up before Susan returned. When he opened the door I could see he was shaking, sweating. I gave him the vodka and urged him to drink just enough to straighten himself out and then go to sleep. He asked me to unscrew the top of the bottle. Then he asked me to pour a shot into a glass. Then he asked me to hold the glass to his lips. The shaking became less violent, and after a few more sips, stopped. I delivered my speech sternly and turned to leave.

He smiled at me.

He said, "I can feel it singing in my blood."

"Go to bed," I said, "you horrible old bugger."

In the summer of 2001 Susan phoned us to say that John was in hospital. He had suffered a major stroke. Myrna immediately sent white orchids to his hospital room. When I walked in he was strapped into a wheelchair. All of his right side was dead. He could not speak. He looked at the orchids, then at me, and nudged with his left hand as if to say: *you, you*. I talked to him for a while, not really knowing what I was saying, until sorrow silenced me and I sat holding his hand and stroking his hair, taking liberties with his dignity for which in earlier years he'd have tried to knock me down.

RESURRECTION

WHEN THE TERM ended in Fredericton I went back to Montreal to look for work. In Fredericton I'd had the daily company and friendship of Doug Rollins. In Montreal I was alone and my depression fed on itself in the silent apartment and grew more intense and convoluted. Gale had renounced the lesbian life and, taking Elizabeth with her, had decamped to New York where she lived, serially, with members of Dave Liebman's jazz band.

I managed to get two part-time jobs teaching at Loyola and Vanier CEGEPs. It took all my energy to work and to hold myself together sufficiently to see Elizabeth and look after her in the holidays. During these two years I spent a lot of time with Ray Smith and I doubt I would have survived without his wonderful kindness and concern.

I knew that I was becoming seriously ill but couldn't see beyond where I was. I suffered suffocating dreams. I woke some mornings to find tears running down my face. I felt incessant grief. I *leaked* tears. I could feel myself becoming more and more emotionally frail. My weight had dropped to under 120 pounds.

I decided that I had to get help and I was sufficiently deranged that I sought the services of a psychiatrist. I drew on these experiences in my novella "Girl in Gingham." Again fiction is more vivid that fact. My protagonist in the novella is an antiques appraiser called Peter who is divorced and is persuaded by a friend to avail himself of the services of a dating service called CompuMate.

> The woman situation had started at the same time he'd stopped seeing Dr. Trevore, when he'd realized that he was boring himself; when he'd realized that his erstwhile wife, his son, and he had been reduced to characters in a soap opera which was broadcast every two weeks from Trevore's sound-proofed studio.
>
> And which character was he?
>
> He was the man whom ladies helped in laundromats. He was the man who dined on frozen pies. Whose sink was full of dishes. He was the man in the raincoat who wept in late-night bars.
>
> That office, and he in it, that psychiatrist's office with its scuffed medical magazines and pieces of varnished driftwood on the waiting room's occasional tables was the stuff of comic novels, skits, the weekly fodder of stand-up comedians.
>
> In the centre of Trevore's desk sat a large, misshapen thing. The rim was squashed in four places indicating that it was probably an ashtray. On its side, Trevore's name was spelled out in spastic white slip. Peter had imagined it a grateful gift from the therapy ward of a loony bin.
>
> It presided over their conversations.
>
> *How about exercise? Are you exercising?*
>
> *No, not much.*
>
> *How about squash?*
>
> I don't know how to play.

I play myself. Squash. I play on Mondays, Wednesdays, and Fridays. In the evenings.

Following one such session he had gone home, opened the bathroom cabinet, regarded the pill bottles which had accumulated over the months. He had taken them all out and stood them on the tank above the toilet. He arranged them into four rows. In the first row he placed the Valium. In the second, the Stelazine. In the third, the Tofranil. In the fourth, the Mareline.

Uncapping the bottles, he tipped the tablets rank by rank into the toilet bowl. Red fell upon yellow, blue fell on red, tranquillizing, antidepressant psychotherapeutic agents fell, swirled and sifted onto agents for the relief of anxiety, emotional disorders, and nausea.

The results had suggested to him the droppings of a
Walt Disney rabbit.

Some nattily turned cadences there. Is this autobiography? No, as I always insist, it's art.

Though it is more or less what did happen to me.

Except that "Dr. Trevore," a pallid man who wore a tie with horseshoes on it, also tried out on me, if I recall aright, Elavil, Norpramine, Manerix, and Nardil. All of which I washed down with beer or Scotch and none of which seemed to have the slightest effect.

One day I simply stopped leaking. During this darkness I had been unable to value anything. Suddenly I was back in the world again, possibly not a ray of sunshine but able to imagine a future.

My literary life meanwhile had not been particularly productive. After *The Lady Who Sold Furniture* appeared I had moved from Clarke Irwin to what was considered *the* Canadian publisher, McClelland and Stewart, for the publication of *Going Down Slow*. The book appeared, was well reviewed, then disappeared. This was in 1972. My editor was

Anna Porter (then Anna Szigethy). I had certain expectations of a publisher. I thought that editors should keep in touch with their writers. Should be solicitous. Should be aware of intentions and of work-in-progress. Should be concerned about the shape of a writer's career. I certainly had none of this from Jack McClelland. He concerned himself only with the writers of his own age such as Mordecai Richler and Farley Mowat. As far as I can recall I had no contact with Anna Szigethy for about a year after *Going Down Slow* came out. I wanted to be in a relationship and that need for support has guided me all these years later in my conduct at the Porcupine's Quill.

There's been an effort lately to posit Jack McClelland as the conscious founder of Canadian literature. He certainly did a great deal but his taste in literature was perhaps not as keenly honed as is suggested in James King's biography *Jack*. No one could deny that Jack McClelland was an ardent nationalist, and a great publicist and impresario. I've always enjoyed the story of his publicizing Sylvia Fraser's *The Emperor's Virgin* in 1980. On a blustery day, Sylvia Fraser in a shimmering dress, two centurions carrying books, and Jack in a toga paraded down Bloor Street. An onlooker was alleged to have said: "There goes Jack McClelland—only one sheet to the wind."

No one could deny that he built the careers of Berton, Mowat, Richler, Layton, Cohen, and Margaret Laurence. But he also published a much longer list of potboilers by such worthies as Richard Rohmer and Adrienne Clarkson. And some of the reputations he built are sagging badly; the best Margaret Laurence titles seem to me to be *The Tomorrow-Tamer* and *A Jest of God*. I cannot reread *The Stone Angel* or *The Diviners*. He published far more non-fiction than fiction, popular political and sociological titles which quickly mulched down to become leafmould. His lasting legacy was the New Canadian Library series.

It was in the late sixties that the small press movement was beginning to gather steam. The House of Anansi started in

1967. Oberon Press in 1966. I was attracted by the intimacy and the energy. I thought at the time that Oberon was going to become a Canadian version of the Hogarth Press in England. I wrote to Anna Szigethy, resigning as a McClelland and Stewart author, and contracted to publish with Oberon Press. Anna was both surprised and alarmed. Alarmed, apparently, at the possibility of further defections. Matt Cohen always used to say that he owed all the fuss M&S made of him to my letter of resignation.

In 1975 Oberon published the story collection *The Teeth of My Father*. The cover was a photograph of me with Elizabeth taken by Sam Tata. This was printed in teeth-gritting yellow and lime; a second printing appeared in a more pleasing plum colour.

Nineteen seventy-five turned out to be a momentous year for reasons other than literary. I got married again. Some romances are described as whirlwind; this one was more like a tornado. In December of 1974, at a dinner party, I met Myrna Teitelbaum. Christmas intervened and I was busy with Elizabeth. I phoned Myrna after Elizabeth had gone back to New York and a mere two months later Myrna and I were married by a protonotary in St. Jean, Quebec, in a civil ceremony not much of which I remember, except that Myrna had to agree to accompany me if my work took me out of the province and I had to agree that I would refrain from beating her.

We have remained immersed in each other ever since.

INCREASINGLY BAD VIBES

I CRINGE when people describe themselves as "educators."
What pomposity it bespeaks! By 1975 I was going distinctly *off* education. The feel-good, feel-happy duo of Emmett Hall and Lloyd Dennis, authors of *Aims and Objectives for Education in Ontario*, a report tabled in 1968, together poisoned the Ontario school system and spread the taint of "child-centred" education throughout Canada. The *Hall-Dennis Report*, as it was called, almost immediately reduced English and history to elective subjects. Mix in with this short-sighted barbarism the fads and fashions rolling in from the States—drugs, brown rice, guitars, I Ching, flower power, Zen, primal screams, vibrators, identity crises, *You're Tremendous, I'm Terrific*, boring goddamn people *finding themselves* all over the damn place . . . this tidal wave of sloppy thinking and sloppy feeling left teachers facing students who rejected traditional bodies of knowledge as authoritarian intrusions on their rights and who were innocent of grammar, history, geography, literature, music, architecture, and painting, students who were, increasingly, far out.

This general morass is now dignified as "the counterculture"; I'm always surprised to see in catalogues the extremely high prices still commanded by sawdust books by such genuinely unlikeable writers as Jack Kerouac, Allen Ginsberg, and Richard Brautigan.

The sixties and early seventies were a sorry time.

My job at Loyola involved sharing an office with the new writer-in-residence, Al Purdy. Al wasn't actually in residence. He commuted from Ameliasburg. This involved him in early morning train rides during which he felt it necessary to fortify himself against the cold. By the time he arrived at Loyola he was usually fortified to the gills, cheerful but sleepy. He solved this problem by having a collapsible cot moved into our office and locking the door.

He surfaced at midday. He'd boom and bellow about in the English department office for a while, groping unfortunate secretaries and filching letterhead and then he'd phone a nearby grocery store to get a case of beer delivered. A pizza would follow and soon he'd have the place comfortable with a fug of cigar smoke. His cigars were rank, plastic tipped and dipped in port.

Al's classes in creative writing mainly involved listening to records of *Under Milk Wood* and Cyril Cusack's renderings of Gerard Manley Hopkins, recitations rather too fluttery for my taste.

On some afternoons I'd be further excluded from my office, facing a locked door while on the collapsible cot he plumbed the depths of one of the female department members.

With the advent of spring and the retreat of the snow under our office window, beer bottles began to surface, more and more every day as the sun gained strength, until they lay revealed on the playing field like corpses after a mighty battle.

I assigned during the second term an essay on Margaret Laurence's *The Diviners*. One numbed sophomore wrote a deranged screed comparing the novel with a song by Elton John. Naturally, I failed him. He complained to the English department. The Chair, in his wisdom, ordered me to justify my actions before three department members. This I declined to do.

The following academic year I found part-time work at Vanier College, Snowdon Campus. It was an unspeakable employment. The word *campus* is misleading; it suggests lawns and manicured flower beds. The college was housed in what had been an office block and fronted onto the Decarie Expressway. Immediately next door was a large A&W. With the windows closed, the heat was intolerable; with the windows open, it was impossible to make oneself heard over the traffic.

I taught two courses: creative writing and a course on the Canadian short story. Some way into this latter I was removed from the course on the grounds that I was not competent, lacking as I did an MA. The year was saved by the fact that I had one good student, now in theatre in Chicago, and by my office being adjacent to that of Barry Cameron—now a professor at UNB—who was severely shaken by what had signed up for his thoughtful courses in Canadian literature. We sustained each other by mutual bemoaning as we picked our way through the ankle-deep litter in the corridors.

The chairman of the English department had retired from the fray; he used to lock himself in his office with the head of the remedial programme and gaze at rented videotapes of dubious artistic merit.

I had become disenchanted with teaching because I couldn't find people bright enough to teach. It is impossible to teach people at more than a rudimentary level if you do not share a vocabulary. I needed to be able to say to a student, What you need to do here is shape the paragraph in the spirit of the opening paragraph of Katherine Mansfield's "Miss Brill." And have the student knowing author and story and capable of picking up the hint.

I felt the same disenchantment recently at the Humber School for Writers in Toronto, a week-long course in the summer I've been teaching for some years now. A young man brought to the class sixteen stories, none of which made the slightest sense. They were shapeless and it was impossible to divine their aim. He didn't seem to understand any questions I asked him about them. Something inspired me to ask him if he had *read* any short stories. He said he had read one but couldn't remember much about it. I wrote out a long list of titles and told him to go away and start reading. He told me that same day at lunch that he was going to live in Montreal for a couple of months to see what it was like. I said that he'd find the architecture in Montreal more pleasing than Toronto. He said, "Architecture? That's not anything *I'd* know about."

I gave up my apartment and moved in with Myrna a couple of days before we got married. She owned a house in the almost entirely Jewish enclave of Côte St. Luc. I was not entirely at ease in a community of observant or even semi-observant Jews. I wouldn't have been at ease in a community of observant anything.

I felt not at ease living in the house that Myrna had lived in with her first husband. I was feeling disenchanted with teaching, oppressed by the grind of separatist politics, constricted and confined. It was as if one cycle of my life were over and it was time to launch into new experience.

The woman who lived opposite had a pale, weedy five-year-old who sometimes played with Myrna's son, Ronald, who was the same age. When he came over his mother would screech from the middle of the road, "Don't let him near anything *treyf*."

When Pesach rolls around, the celebration of Passover, Jews are required to clean their houses and get rid of all bread and any product which is not manufactured under rabbinical supervision and designated "suitable for Passover" or *pesachdik*.

One afternoon during Pesach I was sitting on the front steps and eating a cheese sandwich. The horrid little boy drifted across and stood regarding me. In silence he broke a few twigs off a bush. He eventually said, pointing to the sandwich, "Is that pesachdik?"

"Piss off," I explained.

Côte St. Luc, I decided, was not my natural habitat.

It was to be another year before we moved.

I often daydream about my natural habitat. Bath and Clifton would serve as models. Georgian terraces clad in honey-coloured stone. Pubs with cobbled courtyards shaded by vast horse chestnut trees. Little shops filled with dubious antiques. A used-book shop where a gentle old rogue also sells fading watercolours labelled "School of Cotman 1782–1842." All a little shabby and seedy now. Once aristocratic, now déclassé, with a floating population of students, single professionals, and in the pub, the Colonel, "Call me Courtney," in his canary-yellow waistcoat drinking pink gins. There's something mildly louche about this sun-lit place, mildly raffish, Roger et Gallet savon, Eau de Cologne Jean-Marie Farina, sex in the afternoon, Spanish champagne.

At some time during this Vanier year of suffering I was invited to the University of Ottawa to give a reading. I happened to bump into the chairman of the English department, Professor Glenn Clever, who said quite casually, "Oh, by the by, would you like to be writer-in-residence here next year?"

"Yes," I said, "thank you."

"Fine," he said. "I'll send a contract."

Off he pottered.

It was agreed that I would make myself available to students (as it turned out, all one of them) two days a week. I was commuting from Montreal and sleeping over in Ottawa for one night. The department had known months in advance of my arrival. When I duly presented myself on the first day of term I was introduced to the new chairman, Professor Marcotte. He informed me that my office was at the top of the old house which served as English department offices but that unfortunately the room didn't have a desk in it. Or chair. There was, apparently, something wrong with the heating system so that the temperature in the room was stuck at over one hundred degrees.

I returned to the Lord Elgin Hotel.

It took three more weeks for the desk to appear.

The chairs took another two.

Two weeks before I left, my arrival was announced.

Deskless, chairless, studentless, I was bored out of my mind. To while away the time I decided, pinching Kent Thompson's idea, to organize a conference on the short story. I invited Clark Blaise, Hugh Hood, Kent Thompson, Alice Munro, Ray Smith, Margaret Laurence, and Audrey Thomas and they gave readings to upwards of three hundred students every evening. During the day, the critics I'd invited, W. H. New, George Bowering, Barry Cameron, Patricia Morley, Frank Davey, Doug Barbour, and Michael Dixon, gave papers on the work of writers they'd been paired with. The whole affair was introduced by Robert Weaver of CBC *Anthology*.

I had scraped together the necessary money for this conference from the Canada Council and from the University of Ottawa Student Council; the English department confined its support to insisting that papers be signed indemnifying it in case of financial shortfall. At one point, enraged and sickened by the department's *pissy* attitude, I offered in writing to make good out of my own pocket any loss that might be incurred.

As the date of the conference approached, my days were spent on the run booking hotel rooms, booking the Press Club, arranging an auditorium, checking sound systems, writing letters, confirming, soothing.

The University of Ottawa had promised to publish the papers presented at the conference but, of course, reneged. I regret to this day the loss of that volume. George Bowering gave an involving and quirky paper on Audrey Thomas. Doug Barbour was entertaining and stimulating on Ray Smith's work. Frank Davey's paper on Clark Blaise was astonishing in that he seriously advanced the view that Blaise's writing was akin to journalism—this of one of the country's most *poetic* writers.

The only unhappy writer was Margaret Laurence. I'd paired her with an academic called Patricia Morley. This woman taught at the Simone de Beauvoir Institute for Women's Studies, a name that always makes me smile because it sounds like some ghastly joint in a David Lodge novel. Compared with Patricia Morley, Margaret Atwood sounds vivacious. To say that Patricia Morley talks in a relentless monotone does not even *suggest* . . . Morley had more or less *appropriated* poor Margaret who came to me in weeping complaint and had to be bought Scotch.

I was happy escaping from Ottawa. A dismal little university. A bland, parochial little town. I was not to know then that in the future I was to spend more than twenty years there. A couple of years ago Mordecai Richler asked me how long it had been and, shaking his head sorrowfully, said, "John, John, it's a long sentence."

Back in Montreal, Elspeth Cameron, then chair of English at Loyola, offered me a job as writer-in-residence for the balance of the year. Though I religiously kept office hours, not a single student came to see me. I spent a lot of time with Harry Hill propping up the faculty club bar. Harry, though camp as a line of tents, was one of the most brilliant teachers I've ever seen in action. If Loyola had not itself been a dim little college riven by vicious academic politics, it could have built round Harry Hill a very important drama school but they predictably squandered the opportunity.

Hugh Hood published *A New Athens*, the second volume of his *roman-fleuve*, in 1977 but he'd probably written it in 1976. Myrna remembers reading the manuscript in second carbon. He phoned one day in the summer and asked us if we'd like to drive with him to look at Athens and surrounding countryside. We were much taken by the countryside and we were soon scouting houses on our own. We both had the feeling that this was the move towards something different that had been ordained for us.

We drove about the area looking at Plum Hollow, Philipsville, Forfar (which sold a five-year-old cheddar called "Old Baby"), Chantry, Elgin, and one day found an old stone house just outside Delta, a village about ten miles from Athens. I was charmed to discover that Delta was in the Township of Bastard. I was also charmed to discover that Delta was the birthplace of Lorne Pierce who had been editor-in-chief of Ryerson Press. I named my press the Bastard Press and it was under that imprint that Newlove and I published *Dreams Surround Us.*

And dreams did surround us. The house had been built in about 1840. There were exposed ceiling beams, wide-sawn plank floors, a vast garden to one side, a forty-one-acre field in the back vivid with meadow flowers, and in front of the house an ancient mulberry tree laden with plump maroon berries.

STEERING THE CRAFT

BETWEEN 1976 AND 1993 I edited and co-edited eighteen anthologies of Canadian short stories and compiled seven textbooks of Canadian stories for use in schools and universities. I did all this work with the conscious intention of changing the nature and shape of short fiction in Canada.

In 1971, David Helwig and Tom Marshall edited a story anthology for Oberon entitled *Fourteen Stories High*. This was followed in 1972 by *New Canadian Stories*, which became the title of the annuals that were to follow. David Helwig resigned from editing the series in 1975 because he had accepted a job with the CBC Drama Department which precluded outside work and through David's intervention I was offered the job as co-editor with Joan Harcourt.

The policy of the series when I took over was to publish previously unpublished work. Helwig had started the series with the intention of providing another outlet for new work and new writers. Joan Harcourt and I were receiving manuscripts by the hundred. Nearly all were atrocious. I was soon driven to begging friends for unpublished stories—and at that, I wasn't getting the cream because Oberon could not afford to match the payments offered by some of the magazines, nominal though such payments were. (An entire genre in Canadian literature was shaped by the fact that some publications paid as much as a hundred dollars for a story, others far less, or nothing.) It dawned on me slowly that we were in direct competition with the literary magazines for a very small crop of good work. There was not much point in this and I began to get restless with the whole policy and purpose of the series.

Although Joan and I got on well together, I began to hanker after the idea of a fresh co-editor, someone not quite so *nice* as Joan, someone harsher in judgement. I felt I needed to work with someone who really knew short fiction, who lived and breathed it as I did. I wanted someone who would understand style and elegance and who would be repelled by socially acceptable *themes*. I decided on Clark Blaise. Joan resigned by mutual agreement in 1977 and I persuaded Michael Macklem, Oberon's publisher, to change both the title and policy of the anthology.

The title was now to be *Best Canadian Stories* and the policy was to concentrate on republishing the best stories from the literary magazines. I *had* wanted an outright policy of republication only but Macklem argued that such a policy would be bad PR and would result in reviewers berating Oberon for closing off yet another publishing outlet. Under pressure, I agreed that we would continue to read and consider unsolicited manuscripts.

Joan Harcourt, in her farewell foreword to the 1978 book, said:

> I learned some things during my stint as co-editor of *New* (now *Best*) *Canadian Stories*, many of them small, some that I didn't want to know, but learn I did. Mostly I learned that this country is full of people shrouded in arctic light, trapped in their Canadian loneliness, sometimes writing badly about it, sometimes well, occasionally brilliantly. Probably I've read as many stories typed

on kitchen tables in efficiency apartments and in echoing old houses in small towns as has anyone in the country. Some of the writers whose stories I read cut slightly ridiculous figures, but they were fighting the battle the best way they knew. Courage is where you find it, and I do dignify them with the title "writer" even when the stories were less than good: they had a faith and that's more important than the product.

I think I learned that there is little real fiction in Canada. What we have instead are personal histories with the names changed and the facts slightly bent . . . The large run of the stories we received presented carefully crafted reliquaries, little boxes in which were enshrined little memories. Some of these reliquaries were elaborately enamelled, but mostly they were simple, sturdy constructions.

This extract from her introduction illustrates what I meant when I said that Joan was *nice*. I found the "simple, sturdy constructions" far less "carefully crafted" than she did.

(Mavis Gallant, in a letter, described them disdainfully as "pallid little 'I' stories" though *she* was talking about the ones we'd *selected*.)

It is with Joan's first paragraph that I am in violent disagreement.

". . . they had a faith and that's more important than the product."

Although Joan is saying this of *inadequate* writers, it's an attitude which has condoned and fostered the mediocrity of all Canadian writing from its beginnings to the present.

When I was a child and aunts for my birthday gave me socks, my mother used to say to my disgruntled little self, "It's the thought that counts." I considered this argument but it seemed to me that what I was left with was, inescapably, *socks*.

My desire to change the title and direction of *New Canadian Stories* was prompted by a belief that "product" was more important than "faith."

I was tired of socks.

As I grew into the job I was able to see that by presenting what I considered the best I was promoting one kind of writing and suppressing another. I was deliberately suppressing, I came to realize, Joan Harcourt's "simple, sturdy constructions." I wasn't interested in "personal histories with the names changed." I was interested in sparkling language, in play, in glorious rhetoric. I was also promoting a fiction which was looking outwards for its models and its energy. The direction of that gaze was inevitably the United States. I set out to change the concept and shape of what a story is and how it should be read.

In *Kicking Against the Pricks* (1982) I wrote:

> Where 20 years ago Canadian stories stressed content—what a story was *about*—the main emphasis now is on the story as verbal and rhetorical *performance*. Our best writers are concerned with the story as *thing to be experienced* rather than as *thing to be understood*. This more than anything else is what seems to baffle some readers—and not a few critics; it is difficult for those of us writing stories to understand why this is so since these concerns have been dominant since about 1925.

Alice Munro in a piece she wrote for me in 1982 said the same sort of thing in a different way:

> I will start out by explaining how I read stories written by other people. For one thing, I can start reading them anywhere; from beginning to end, from end to beginning, from any point in between in either direction. So obviously I don't take up a story and follow it as if it were

> a road, taking me somewhere, with views and neat diversions along the way. I go into it, and move back and forth and settle here and there, and stay in it for a while. It's more like a house. Everybody knows what a house does, how it encloses space and makes connections between one enclosed space and another and presents what is outside in a new way. This is the nearest I can come to explaining what a story does for me, and what I want my stories to do for other people.

The 1976 Oberon volume carries a foreword which said in part:

> *76: New Canadian Stories* is a transitional volume. It contains previously unpublished stories as well as stories that have appeared in the literary magazines. Starting next year, in frank emulation of Martha Foley's *Best American Short Stories*, Oberon's anthology will be entitled *77: Best Canadian Stories*. Though we will continue to consider unpublished manuscripts, our principal purpose will be to find and collect the best published stories of the year.

In 1976 I managed to work in among others, Norman Levine, Hugh Hood, Audrey Thomas, Clark Blaise, Elizabeth Spencer, and Leon Rooke.

In the foreword to the 1977 volume I wrote:

> An anthology such as this offers some slight hope. It offers to a larger audience work that otherwise might well not have been seen; it extends the life of a piece of work; it directs the attention of readers to writers who otherwise might have been consigned to the vaults on microfilm.
>
> The editorial task is not merely one of compilation; it is also critical. Frank Kermode described literary criticism as "the medium in which past work survives." We

hope that this anthology and succeeding ones will serve this function as well as offering immediate pleasure.

Into the 1978 volume, edited with Clark Blaise, went Alice Munro, Hugh Hood, Elizabeth Spencer, and Kent Thompson. In the 1979 volume we published Mavis Gallant. In 1980 Mavis Gallant *and* Alice Munro along with Guy Vanderhaeghe and a first story from Linda Svendsen which later would be a part of her brilliant collection *Marine Life*.

Clark Blaise left Canada in 1980 because his wife, Bharati Mukherjee, could no longer tolerate the racial harassment she was enduring in Toronto. The loss to Canada was considerable. Clark Blaise, one of the handful of great story writers in Canada, was always reminded that despite his having become a Canadian citizen, he wasn't a *real* Canadian. He and I were always referred to as American-born and British-born. Clark went on to a long career at Iowa and Bharati to a long career at Berkeley and the National Book Critics Circle Award for *The Middleman and Other Stories*.

To succeed Clark as co-editor, I chose Leon Rooke, another American-born. Leon, too, had an almost encyclopedic knowledge of the short story and his own exuberantly improvisational approach to the form was doubtless a liberating influence on what remained staid in my own judgement.

Leon has been and continues to be an important and shaping force in Canadian literature, so I'd like to quote from an essay I wrote about his work recently. The essay is entitled "This Here Jasper Is Gittin Ready to Talk."

> In the 1970s when I began to encounter Leon Rooke's stories in the literary magazines I recognized immediately an interesting new voice. A way of approaching the form new to Canada—though not so new in the States—was beginning to make itself heard. Or *should* have been

making itself heard for it was surprisingly difficult to get people to listen.

I remember showing some of the stories in what became *The Love Parlour*, Leon's first book in Canada, to Michael Macklem, the publisher of Oberon Press. Michael has a doctorate in literature from Princeton and taught English at Yale. He declared the stories incomprehensible but said that if I thought they were good he'd publish them on my say-so but only on condition he wouldn't have to read further.

This seeming inability to read Leon Rooke, to connect with his vitality, is puzzling because looking back at *The Love Parlour* now it doesn't strike me as wildly innovative or madly experimental. It remains a good, solid collection but it is not a stylistic trailblazer.

To get Macklem to publish Leon's second book in Canada, *Cry Evil*, I had to write little explanatory notes about each story. Macklem published the book but remained unconvinced. It was with *Cry Evil* that Leon began to move towards the sort of story that was to be his major contribution to the form. With *Cry Evil* we were treated to a display of Leon limbering up for the major work ahead. This is not to say that some of the stories in *Cry Evil* are not already masterly performances. I'm particularly fond of "The Deacon's Tale," "Adolpho Has Disappeared and We Haven't a Clue Where to Find Him," and "Biographical Notes."

Another anecdote about listening. In 1980 Leon published his first novel, *Fat Woman*. It is a book which draws with intense imagination on his Southern roots. Every line of the book is instinct with the rhythms and cadences of Southern speech yet a young Canadian fiction writer, and a good one too, reviewing the book for a major newspaper, understood it as being set in Nova Scotia.

Yet another anecdote. When Leon and I left Oberon Press I wanted to move us to ECW Press because the owners, Jack David and Robert Lecker, were friends of mine and possessed of great energy and dedication to Canadian writing. I sent some of Leon's new work to Jack David who seemed unenthusiastic. Indeed, he phoned me and asked me if I really stood behind the work, if I really considered it the genuine article. I told him very firmly that I did. A short while later, Leon was in Toronto giving a public reading and Jack David went to hear him. Jack phoned me the next day in great excitement. "*Now* I get it," he said. "Now I've *heard* him. I just wasn't getting it from the printed page."

Jack David and Robert Lecker went on to publish two major books of Leon's stories, *Death Suite* in 1981 and *The Birth Control King of the Upper Volta* in 1982.

Academic neglect of Rooke's work is easily understandable. Not many academics actually read contemporary writing and many of them were unaware of his existence. Another part of the answer, less silly than it sounds, is that Leon is playful. Not a good thing to be in any of the arts in Canada. Yet another strike against him is that he moved progressively away from normative realism into fable, fantasy, pastiche of genre writing, all in scrambled shapes of his own invention. This departure from realism did not endear him to academics whose hastily cobbled canon really had no room for his shenanigans; shenanigans, furthermore, which were suspiciously American.

But the central reason for his early neglect is that most readers were not hearing what Leon was up to. Their attention was directed elsewhere, to theme, perhaps, or form. They were in a similar situation to an earnest gallery-goer standing in front of a Rothko and asking, "What does it mean?" The answer is, "Look."

To the reader who asks, "What does it mean?" of Rooke's "Sixteen-Year-Old Susan March Confesses to the Innocent Murder of All the Devious Strangers Who Would Drag Her Down" the answer is, "Listen."

Listen.

Rooke has published four or five plays and many of the stories are essentially *scripts*—monologues or voices talking, arguing. The insistent direction in his work is theatrical. Leon himself is never happier than on a stage, the rhetoric flying high and wide and often over the top. Leon is a performer. Leon is a self-confessed ham. His stories are *performances*.

He is very prolific, having published by now some three hundred short stories in literary magazines. Most are uncollected because on further reflection he felt they simply did not work. Leon doesn't brood for months over the shape and detail of what he hopes will be a master-work; he picks up his horn and tries out a few runs, a few phrases to see if something is going to happen.

I sometimes think that Rooke's academic acceptance has been slow because academics have been slow to think of Leon as, say, a tenor sax player and the story as a jazz improvisation. If the reader *does* respond in those terms it becomes immediately obvious what Leon is up to.

Leon is leading the parade. He doesn't want a tweed-with-leather-elbow-patches response. He wants celebrants performing along with him. He wants a Second Line. At other times he wants to preach, a big Texas tenor sound, wave after wave of impossibly mounting fervour.

Leon preaching always reminds me of recordings I've heard of the Reverend Kelsey leading his Washington congregation in "Lion of the Tribe of Judah"; the preacher's voice probes at the words, repeats, hums, slides into falsetto, repeats and finds a form and then all rhythmic hell breaks loose, hands clapping, jugs grunting and booming, a trombone's urging. All rather glorious.

In the foreword to the first volume Leon and I edited together in 1981, a volume which included Blaise, Gallant, Levine, Munro, Thompson, and Svendsen, I wrote:

> Now past our tenth year, in one guise or another, and still committed to presenting each year a gathering of fine fiction, it is interesting to glance back at our tracks in the snow. Despite all the annual grumbling by reviewers, it seems clear to me that over the last ten years the general standards of story writing in Canada have been rising. The art is becoming generally more sophisticated. *Best Canadian Stories* still cannot stand comparison with *Best American Stories* but that is not, and should not be surprising; what is pleasing is that the comparison is no longer quite so devastatingly painful.

That this is not an entirely subjective judgement is attested to in remarks by W. J. Keith in his 1985 book *Canadian Literature in English*: "Thanks to Metcalf, whose numerous anthologies of short stories have been appearing regularly since the early 1970s, a whole generation of talented writers is emerging who find the short story a satisfying and infinitely varied form of expression."

Such forewords and attitudes and the demolition of the "simple, sturdy constructions" enraged the cultural nationalists who would have much preferred to remain in huddled celebration of the muddy achievement of Raymond Knister, Morley Callaghan, Hugh Garner, and Ernest Buckler.

Between 1980 and 1994 my writing was excluded from every trade anthology of national scope. I was excluded from *The Oxford Book of Canadian Short Stories in English* edited by Margaret Atwood and Robert Weaver. I was excluded from Weaver's *Canadian Short Stories: Fourth Series and Fifth Series*. I was excluded from Wayne Grady's *Penguin Book of Canadian Short Stories* and from *The Penguin Book of Mod-*

ern Canadian Stories. I was excluded from Michael Ondaatje's anthology *From Ink Lake*.

This list of names came to mind when I read in Adam Gopnik's *Paris to the Moon*, "The logic of nationalism always flows downhill, toward the gutter."

While the cultural nationalists were busily enshrining mediocrity and proclaiming it genius the academics were doing the same thing in *their* mausoleums. I have written of this extensively in *What Is a Canadian Literature?* And *Freedom from Culture: Selected Essays 1982–1992*. Academics damage the short story genre by maintaining a stolid silence on the alleged merits of writing which is deplorable. One example must suffice.

Morley Callaghan has been cemented into place as the father of the short story in Canada. Our only alleged ancestor more revered by nationalists is Duncan Campbell Scott, from whom, claims Wayne Grady, all Canadian story writers are artistically descended. Penguin Books paid Grady money for writing this know-nothing twaddle and spread the shame of it all over the world.

In the seventies John Mills was reviewing frequently in the literary magazines and Myrna became an instant fan when she read a Mills review which opened, "Coarsened as I am by years of reading for pleasure . . ." John reviewed Morley Callaghan's *Close to the Sun Again* (1977) in *Queen's Quarterly*.

> If *Close to the Sun Again* were a first novel by a young writer I would say of it that it shows some awareness of the technique of plot construction, that though the dialogue is inept and the prose generally abysmal, there are signs in the last two chapters that the author is beginning to slough the deleterious effects of high school training on his writing habits, and that he might also move on to themes of greater interest and importance if he could only empty his head of jejune notions of psychological

realism picked up God knows where. The writer is Morley Callaghan, however, who has been around a long time and is unlikely to improve; nor would he, on the evidence of what is written about him on the dust-jacket, particularly want to . . .

Hemingway is invoked twice on the dust-jacket. Callaghan worked with him on the *Toronto Star*, then lived on the periphery of his circle in Paris where, presumably, he joined the Master's declared war against rhetoric in general and the adjective in particular, while remaining well-insulated against that peculiar electricity that used to flow through Hemingway's early writing. We are also told that Edmund Wilson called him "the most unjustly neglected novelist in the English-speaking world," and that, despite this neglect, his last novel sold more than half a million copies in the Soviet Union . . . It is good to know that 60 years after the Revolution petit-bourgeois notions of what constitutes a novel are still alive and well in Mother Russia. Apart from that I don't know why Callaghan succeeds in foreign countries. Perhaps he translates well and there is some internal evidence to suggest that *Close to the Sun Again* was translated from manuscript into, let us say, Lithuanian then back into English for Macmillan by some well-intentioned, polyglot, but tone-deaf and maladroit Pole.

A passage like the following: "The scratching little hollow ping was like the beating of a heart, only not muffled like a heart: it came throbbing in the vastness of cathedral space . . ." makes a man clutch and fumble at his chest to ascertain whether his pacemaker's working properly. My own heart, and I am speaking now as a hypochondriac, does *not* make these scratching little pinging sounds, muffled or otherwise, and in any case there is, in my opinion, a contradiction between the ideas of *scratching* and *throbbing*. It is a clumsy, sloppy metaphor but at least it represents a step, or rather stagger, in the direction of colourful prose and, in contrast to such sodden, dispiriting stuff as: "She went on to say that her father had taken her to Europe, and in Paris they had gone to one of those small clubs that had fight cards. Her father had been impressed by a good-looking boy named Robert Riopelle, a middleweight, a lonely-looking boy, a kid, with all the great natural talents. The French boy had a strangely moving, noble character. The kid took a shine to her father, too . . ." it shines "like a good deed in a naughty world." So this French boy "had a strangely moving, noble character," had he? Apart from the stylistic poverty of using an auxiliary verb instead of a proper one, the sentence with its vagueness and pomposity breaks every rule in the book of narrative art (including the Jamesian ukase that the reader must be *shown*, not *told*) while creating no new rule of its own. Perhaps this is what the dust-jacket means when he says, perhaps a little too glibly, that "the novel is told in Morley Callaghan's distinctive style—so easy and flowing that it seems to be no style at all." But the style is *there*—and it is abominable.

Mills's review and my essay on Callaghan's stories "Winner Take All" will, I predict, be entirely ignored. When the next batch of Guides, Companions, and Encyclopaedias appears a Weaver clone will have been found to extol Callaghan's nonexistent virtues.

I bring this matter up not to be contentious but to illuminate the fact that we are living a critical lie. If we are blind and deaf to Callaghan's cacophonies how can we *genuinely* respond to Alice Munro's glories? How can students trust us or our works of reference if we describe as "distinguished" writing that is stumblebum?

Nearly all the editing I did between 1976 and 1993 was, as it were, *editing against the grain*. I was suppressing the "simple, sturdy constructions" and searching for sophistication, elegance, invention, language that sang. What the public, such as it is, really wanted was W. P. Kinsella and W. D. Valgardson but it wasn't going to get them from me.

In an article by Andy Lamey in the magazine *Gravitas* he quotes that sad Marxist hulk Robin Mathews, both synapses buzzing, as saying: "Metcalf has always supported the reactionary forces in Canada at the level of 'the barking dog.'" What this means I'm not entirely sure. Actually I hold no party political position; I simply find politicians embarrassing. When it comes to literary editing, however, I suspect that I've been the very reverse of reactionary.

In the foreword to *82: Best Canadian Stories* Leon Rooke wrote, "This is winsome stuff, gladdening to the heart, necessary to life and limb. The 'best' writer—our position of faith—is always the stranger, the writer not heard from yet."

I wrote an essay about Keath Fraser for *The New Quarterly* which describes the central joy of editing, the joy of finding, in Leon's words, "the writer not heard from yet."

> I first encountered Keath's writing in 1981 when I was editing Oberon's *Best Canadian Stories* with Leon Rooke. I remember I was sitting in the kitchen with a moody cup of coffee eyeing the morning's pile of manila envelopes. I ripped one open and glanced over the opening sentence. The story was entitled "Le Mal de l'Air." This is what I read:
>
> "Suppose he had a three-day-old festering on the elbow, ate pork at his mother's on Sunday and got sick: his wife would rather blame his illness on bee-stings than on worms in a good woman's meat."
>
> Huh?
>
> The second sentence:
>
> "Bees she believed just as likely to cause nausea and the shakes as they were a slowly puffed-up arm."
>
> By now I was intrigued.

By the time I'd finished the first paragraph I realized I'd found a writer of strange power and accomplishment. I read the entire story sitting there in the kitchen in a state of mounting excitement.

Here's the paragraph in full:

> Suppose he had a three-day-old festering on the elbow, ate pork at his mother's on Sunday and got sick: his wife would rather blame his illness on bee-stings than on worms in a good woman's meat. Bees she believed just as likely to cause nausea and the shakes as they were a slowly puffed-up arm. Her responses were intemperate and increasingly persistent. She had been to the doctor who could find nothing wrong inside her long, splendid body. Once she took her cello to the Gulf Islands and played on the beach for a pair of misplaced whimbrels. She wasn't happy. You had to conclude that something had infected their marriage. "Or am I just getting bitter," wondered the discomfited Miles, "as the two of us grow alike?"

What a *mysterious* paragraph this was. What could I make of it? It was alive with differing cadences, tones, and levels of diction. It was full of movement. It was busy. The first sentence changed pace at the colon, changed from a colloquial tone to something more formal. Then followed the playful buzz of "bees she believed." Then in the third sentence the diction changed again becoming Latinate, echoing perhaps the words of a doctor or psychiatrist.

But why did he use the words "a good woman's meat"? Why was she good? The word seemed to come from the unnamed wife rather than from Miles. Was it perhaps in defence of the mother whom Miles has accused of bad housewifery? In the word "good" were we hearing an incredibly compressed version of their quarrel?

The simple inversion of "Bees she believed" stressed the irrationality of her belief. The strong stresses falling one after the other prepared us for the "intemperate" responses in the next sentence. And I wonder if Keath intended us to be thinking of the phrase "bees in her bonnet."

But what on earth were "misplaced whimbrels"? According to the *Shorter Oxford*, "Applied to various small species of curlew." According to *Webster's New World Dictionary*, "any of a group of European shore birds resembling the curlew, but smaller, with a pale stripe along the crown: they breed on the islands north of England."

So did that mean the whimbrels were "misplaced"—put in the wrong place—because they're supposed to be in Europe and not on the Gulf Islands? That made no sense whatever, so I consulted W. Earl Godfrey's *Birds of Canada* and discovered that *Webster's New World Dictionary* had let me down. Whimbrels were not confined to Europe. There is a North American whimbrel also known as the Hudsonian curlew. One population of whimbrels winters in California and nests in northwest Alaska and Canada. It is a spring and autumn transient in British Columbia and common on the coast.

So a reasonable reading of "misplaced" would be that this particular pair of whimbrels hadn't migrated at the right time. But "misplace" also means "to bestow (one's love, trust, affection, etc.) on an unsuitable or undeserving object." So the whimbrels, by playful extension, are also "misplaced" because they are receiving the misplaced attention of Miles's wife.

(I was later to learn that Keath's work bulges with puns, play, complexities; it is best approached with humility and an array of dictionaries.)

The whimbrel sentence captured the wife's "intemperate" quality perfectly. The slightly sad vision of a woman on a beach playing the cello to an audience of two birds suggested about the wife hysteria, drama, theatricality of emotion. Yet at the same time the sentence was comic, of course, and the brief sentence "She wasn't happy" reinforced the comic tone.

But the comic tone also had the effect of making me wonder about Miles. What sort of husband would react in that way to his wife's distress?

And worrying at the paragraph again—*why* "whimbrels"? Did he just like the sound of it? Did he choose it for comic effect? Did he swell the sentence up with ornithological exactitude so that he could deflate it the more comically with: "She wasn't happy"?

(In 1986 at the Kingston Conference, Keath was to say: "For me pleasure is the ability to bury a reader in the story even if we don't understand it at all. Have respect for the mystery. A fiction is more than understanding; it's perception and delight." So his advice to me would probably be to relax and reread.)

Miles is "discomfited." I suspect that some readers might have read that as "discomforted" meaning essentially "made uncomfortable" but "discomfited" means something much stronger: "1. Originally, to defeat; overthrow; put to flight; hence 2. To overthrow the plans or expectations of; thwart; frustrate."

And this harsher word fits perfectly with the picture the paragraph paints of marital discord.

(In Keath's choices of words secondary meanings often seem to obliquely thicken the story's stew. The verbal noun "festering," for example, has a secondary meaning of "rankling" meaning "embittering" which accords with the word "discomfited.")

Another aspect of this busy paragraph is the sounding of the story's emotional notes: "festering," "sick," "illness," "nausea," "infected."

I read recently a book of art criticism by Robert Hughes called *Nothing If Not Critical* and was struck by the following passage on Manet. Hughes is referring to a painting from 1866 called *The Fifer*.

> Manet's sense of touch was extraordinary but its bravura passages are in the details: how the generalized bagginess of a trouser leg, for instance, rendered in flat, thin paint and firmed up with swift daubs of darker tone in the folds, contrasts with the thick creamy white directional brush strokes that model the curve of a spat. The ceaseless intelligent play of flat and round, thick and thin, "slow" and "fast" passages of paint is what gives Manet's surface its probing liveliness. There is nothing "miraculous" about it, but it was not the result of a mechanically acquired technique either. It is there because, in his best work, Manet's inquisitiveness never failed him; every inch of surface records an active desire to see and then find the proper translation of sight into mark.

Although it is always dangerous to compare painting and writing, I thought the paragraph a useful way to think about how writing works. "The ceaseless intelligent play of flat and round, thick and thin, 'slow' and 'fast' passages of paint"; those words are surely pregnant with suggestion for a way of approaching Keath Fraser's writing.

I was so impressed by Keath's work that I offered to help him get a collection published. What could I do but love the man who wrote this sentence: "His dinner lay in him like hooves."

Hooves!

There's a simile to savour.

WINNING THE WAR

IN THE ACADEMIC YEAR 1983–84 Mavis Gallant was writer-in-residence at the University of Toronto and was awarded the Canada-Australia Literary Prize, an alternating award designed to deepen the two countries' knowledge of each other's literature. The Australian High Commission in Ottawa arranged a luncheon in her honour in a private room in the National Arts Centre. Mavis had apparently requested my presence.

I strolled up to the NAC and found the room. I was alone except for a man fighting starched napery on a makeshift bar. Then Mavis arrived, escorted by a subdued suit from External Affairs. Mavis inspected the table and went around reading all the name cards. Grumbling pugnaciously about his politics, she switched the name card of a Canada Council functionary, seating him at a distance and placing me beside her.

Lunch proceeded with a litany of complaint from Mavis about the interminable line-ups at the Ontario Health Insurance office, the architectural brutality of the Robarts Library, the tardiness of Professor Solecki in providing her with a typewriter, the appalling manners of that very bearded man, you know—flapping a hand—in Alberta . . .

Until, after dessert, waiters filled the glasses again and the High Commissioner rose and made a deft and graceful little speech ending with the words:

"And now let us drink a toast to Mavis Gallant and to the day she sets foot on our shores."

In a loud Lady Bracknell voice she said, "GO to Australia! I have no intention of GOING to Australia! Why would anyone think . . . I'm writing a book. Who *in their right mind* . . ."

When the clamour died down and the High Commissioner and his entourage had departed and the man from External had simply decamped, I offered to walk Mavis back to her hotel. We strolled along Sparks Street in the sunshine and she said, "I really don't know why you keep on doing these anthologies. No one will ever thank you for them. In fact, they'll hate you. You should just get on with your own work."

Because I was rather in awe of her as a writer I said something or other bland in reply but I've often thought of that conversation and all these years later still wish I'd explained myself. I wish I'd said, "You chose to leave and at the time you did it was doubtless the smartest thing to do. You went into a kind of exile and as things turned out you live your daily life in the pleasures of Paris but your work goes first to *The New Yorker* and then, in the USA, to Random House. What I'm getting at is that you're not dependent on Paris or on France itself for your career. My case is a bit different. I chose to come here—quite possibly a mistake—but choose I did and then I reinforced that choice by becoming a citizen. I make very little money from my writing, so have to work at other things. My daily life is enmeshed in Canadian literary matters in a way that yours probably isn't in French literary matters.

"And as a writer, citizen, and teacher I feel I have responsibilities to the literature. But there's nothing particularly *virtuous* in all this. I'm just very much involved with this society, locked in mortal combat with the bloody place. I feel I have to attempt to shape taste, to encourage younger writers, to edit, to criticize—and anthologies are an expression of that."

A touch pompous but I still wish I'd said something of the kind.

In 1980 it had occurred to me to try to revive the idea of *New Canadian Writing*, that is, the idea of putting three writers together in a book, each writer being given room for a handful of stories. I decided on the title *First Impressions* because the book would, I hoped, be making a good first impression and first *impressions* are what book collectors collect, the first printing of the first edition. I took the idea to Macklem who was agreeable. I had wanted the books all to be called *First Impressions* and designated 2 and 3 and so on. But in 1981 Macklem overrode me and called the second volume *Second Impressions*. And then *Third Impressions* rendering the title meaningless. He was equally stubborn over my story collection, insisting right up to his defeat that the book should be entitled not *The Teeth of My Father* but *My Father's Teeth*. A strange deafness on his part. After I left Oberon, the series was continued as *Coming Attractions*.

Although Michael Macklem has published dozens of important books and laboured mightily on behalf of Canadian writing, no one would describe him as a fount of sweetness and light. He is one of the most abrasive men I've ever met. His idea of a conversation is to talk louder whenever his interlocutor attempts to say anything. He seems to have little grasp of social niceties. When Myrna and I first moved to Ottawa I suggested that it might be the polite thing to invite Michael and his wife, Anne, to dinner. Michael stood in the entrance hall and looked about and then said, "Well, there's some money here and I know *you* haven't got any so it must be hers."

Myrna was less than charmed.

The introduction to *Third Impressions* in 1982 is worth reproducing as I outlined a rationale for the series:

It is increasingly difficult for short story writers to make the great leap from publication in the literary magazines to publication in book form. There are the obvious primary reasons for this difficulty, which are economic, and then there are the obvious secondary reasons, which are cultural and economic—the lack of any literary infrastructure in Canada, the decay of traditional faith in the idea of investing in a literary career rather than solely in discrete books that offer the hope of immediate financial return, the deep-seated feeling in publishers and readers that short stories, while admirable, are *really*, though one wouldn't shout it, merely limbering-up exercises.

There is another, usually adverse, factor, however, which is not often discussed and that is the part played in the story writer's fortunes by chance. When I was thinking about putting this book together, I wrote to several young writers whose names were familiar to me through their work in the literary magazines. I also solicited names from such literary colleagues as Geoff Hancock of *Canadian Fiction Magazine* and Robert Weaver of CBC's *Anthology*. One of the first names on my list was Guy Vanderhaeghe, whose work over the last two years has been gaining in strength and authority and one of whose stories I had earlier selected for inclusion in *Best Canadian Stories*.

I wrote to Vanderhaeghe but I was about a week too late. A collection of his stories had just been accepted by another publisher. I was delighted for him, of course, but, given the literary climate, surprised; I found myself thinking about the vagaries of publishing. I found myself thinking how quality is sometimes only perceived by someone's directing attention to it; how such "directing" is so often at whim and attention paid to it by chance.

My own work was first published in book form simply because somebody at Clarke, Irwin had decided to take an altruistic risk on an annual volume called *New Canadian Writing*. These books, featuring the work of three writers per volume, survived for two years. *Aurora*, which published a story by Vanderhaeghe, lasted for three years before succumbing to the public's indifference. What, I wonder, might have happened to Vanderhaeghe had he been writing and publishing the *same* stories at a period when *Aurora* hadn't existed, when *Best Canadian Stories* hadn't been born. Would he have remained known only to those who read the literary magazines?

I'm afraid it's very possible.

Many people assert that if a thing is good, it will be recognized and rewarded as such, that quality, as it were, will out. The implication of this idea for us is that stuff that remains in the literary magazines *deserves* to remain there. I wish I could wholeheartedly believe that.

After more than 15 years of involvement in Canada's literary world, I don't have an exactly Panglossian view of its workings; chance seems more firmly seated in its halls of judgement than taste. I remember taking upon myself years ago the role of honorary agent for Clark Blaise; I wrote a letter of support to McClelland and Stewart urging them to publish *A North American Education*. My letter to Anna Porter, then editor-in-chief, was written in words of fire. To no avail. The manuscript was returned to Blaise pretty much by return mail; Anna Porter had thought the stories "boring." And this from the editor-in-chief of Canada's most prestigious publisher about what is, unarguably, one of the most brilliant story collections ever published in Canada.

Third Impressions itself and the earlier books in this series exist, too, by chance. They exist because I happened to be worried about diminishing opportunities for younger writers, because Michael Macklem, Oberon's publisher, happened to be prepared to listen to me that day and happened, perhaps, to have had a good breakfast. I happened to care about younger writers because I care about writing in general and because chance had so arranged things that I was *taught* to care by the great kindness shown to me when I was young by Margaret Laurence and Mordecai Richler.

The choice of writers in this book is also, to an extent, the result of chance. They are writers who have taken my eye. But I am not, God knows, without blind spots. Is there someone as brilliant as Blaise who is cursing *my* stupidity and shortsightedness? Are there brilliant stories in the literary magazines that my glazed eyes have failed to recognize?

I hope not.

But expect so.

My own beginnings were a long time ago and now I feel rather like the narrator in Norman Levine's story "We All Begin in a Little Magazine," but I can remember how wildly excited I was when I was first published in a magazine. I told everyone I met as casually as my delight allowed.

"Congratulations!" they said. "*Prism?*"

And I was forced to admit that, no, it *wasn't* available on newsstands. Or at libraries. Or anywhere really. And the years passed with my friends asking how you spelled *Wascana Review* and was *Tamarack* as in the tree—until that day arrived when five stories were published in *New Canadian Writing 1969*. The fact that the book wasn't widely available in grocery stores, nor, truth be told, in bookstores didn't bother me a bit. It was a *book*—or at least, a third of a book—and the effect on me was tonic. With that publication, I started to allow myself to think of myself as a writer; I was, in my own eyes, no longer a high-school teacher with delusions of grandeur but a published author whose book was, if you went to a hell of a lot of trouble, available.

The rewards were immediate. They were not, needless to say, financial. The most immediate reward was that I started writing even harder than before and soon had a book that was wholly mine—*The Lady Who Sold Furniture*.

Writers whose work appeared in the first two issues of *Impressions* have, apparently, been similarly galvanized. Martin Avery is publishing a novel. Ernest Hekkanen has just completed a novel. Mike Mason has published a novella and is writing with great urgency. Linda Svendsen's work has appeared again in *Atlantic Monthly* and she seems to be nearing her first collection.

The value of publication in such a book as *Impressions* is, then, for the writers, obvious. But what of readers? Are readers having foisted on them what is, if one hopes these writers are to have a long career, juvenilia? This point was fairly raised in a condescending review of *Second Impressions* written by an unhappy lady in Toronto. My heart always sinks when I glance at the foot of a review and see: *X is a freelance writer living in Y*. This tends to mean that the reviewer is either a part-time journalist in search of $75 or, worse, an unpublished writer into whose soul the iron has entered.

This reviewer of *Second Impressions* said snottily of the writing that it was "at least as competent as the writing one finds in little literary publications," which is not surprising in that most of it was *from* "little literary publications." But perhaps this reviewer is unaware that the work of Margaret Laurence, Alice Munro, Clark Blaise, Norman Levine, Jack Hodgins, Leon Rooke, Hugh Hood, and Margaret Atwood—not to mention Hemingway, Pound, Waugh—appeared or appears regularly in the little magazines.

"Little literary publications," forsooth!

Are these volumes the literary equivalent of Amateur Night with fumbling conjurors and singers excruciatingly off-key? Obviously, *I* don't believe so. Nor do the dedicated editors of the literary magazines who first published most of these stories. And obviously the editors of *Atlantic Monthly* don't think so.

On the other hand, I do believe that the writers in this book and in the earlier ones are capable of producing still better work, work that is more deeply imaginative, more complicated, more demanding. But whether they *will* go on from strength to strength depends. It depends on talent—which they obviously have—and it depends on many variables that could be lumped together under chance—money, time, tranquillity, understanding wives or husbands, health, fair winds. But perhaps more than anything else it depends on the interest and support and criticism they receive from readers.

The highlights of the three volumes were, for me, Linda Svendsen, Don Dickinson, and Isabel Huggan, who with much coaxing and prompting added to the three stories in *First Impressions* to gain international acclaim with *The Elizabeth Stories*.

Nineteen eighty-two turned out to be my last year with Oberon. There were touchy quarrels with Macklem but more serious, perhaps, was the sense that Oberon was not becoming the press we'd hoped for. Its energy was failing. The press did no advertising, organized no readings, failed to launch its new titles. Far too many of the books it was publishing were undistinguished. There were too many books of insipid poetry, too many books of merely competent stories. There were too many seasons featuring yet another volume by Raymond Souster, yet another anaemic gathering by the indefatigable Elizabeth Brewster. There was no commanding artistic vision. The books seemed random.

Oberon had published a few singular books by Hugh Hood, Leon Rooke, Norman Levine, Keath Fraser, and David Helwig but their sharpness was somehow blunted by the blandness of the company they kept. The energy and virtuosity of the writing in *Best Canadian Stories* was not reflected in Oberon's list. The press seemed to be fading.

When the breakup came with Macklem I arranged to publish with Jack David and Robert Lecker at ECW Press. I also arranged for Leon Rooke and Hugh Hood to move there. Jack and Robert were dedicated to Canadian literature but were financially unstable. In taking us on they bit off more than they could chew and Jack told me later that with the flow of books and with a coast-to-coast tour we called the ECW Roadshow we brought the press to the brink of ruin. Hugh published *None Genuine Without This Signature* and *Black and White Keys*, Leon published *Death Suite* and *The Birth Control King of the Upper Volta*, while I published *Kicking Against the Pricks*.

Leon and I were still hankering after putting our mark on the Canadian story and we persuaded Ed Carson at General Publishing to start an annual anthology which would be the flagship title for his New Press Canadian Classics series. The book was to be called *The New Press Anthology: Best Canadian Short Fiction.* I remember with pleasure the unnecessarily frequent martini-drenched planning sessions held with Ed Carson and Leon at the Courtyard Café at the Windsor Arms in Toronto.

The first volume appeared in 1984 in mass market format and from the very beginning we realized that we were dealing with a literary world that had undergone a sea change. Possibly we had ourselves effected a change. Possibly Canada was simply struggling out of its weird time warp. Alongside Alice Munro, Ray Smith, Carol Shields, Clark Blaise, Margaret Atwood, and Norman Levine, we were drawing in new names and new sensibilities which were sophisticated and innovative.

In eight short years we had moved from Joan Harcourt's "simple, sturdy constructions" and Mavis Gallant's "pallid little 'I' stories" to the joy of discovering a new writer whose opening two sentences were: "May, Minnie, Maud for God's sake, or Myrna—even worse. Names she might have worn like a crown of link sausages."

How complex, how plump, how rich.

(The opening sentences of an early Terry Griggs story called "India.")

Ed Carson had given us $1,500 to award to the best story in each volume. The prize was, of course, intended to create publicity. In that first volume we gave the prize to Mavis Gallant for "Luc and His Father." The second New Press Fiction Prize was awarded to Ray Smith for his novella "The Continental" and Rohinton Mistry achieved his first publication in book form with his story "Auspicious Occasion." After this second volume there were palace revolutions at General Publishing, defections, financial reversals, changing priorities, and the series was cancelled. Ed Carson moved to Random House.

Leon and I started talking about a new venture, an annual book which would be closer in feel to a magazine, a big magazine that featured new fiction but also included poetry, memoirs, profiles, and a review article about the year's best books. I took the idea to Macmillan and in 1988 *The Macmillan Anthology (1)* appeared with fiction by, among others, Keath Fraser, Mavis Gallant, Terry Griggs, Norman Levine, and Diane Schoemperlen. The book also featured poetry by Lorna Crozier and John Newlove. Sam Tata photographed the writers for us. Sinclair Ross wrote a memoir about life with his mother entitled "Just Wind and Horses" and John Mills wrote a comic memoir about owning a steam laundry in Montreal and his attempts to seduce Aviva Layton away from Irving. Janice Kulyk Keefer wrote a profile of Mavis Gallant and Mavis Gallant gave us "Leaving the Party," one of her comic stories about life in Paris. Michael Darling wrote "The Year in Review," a castigation of varieties of bad writing.

It was a rich book and lavishly produced.

With *The Macmillan Anthology (2)* disaster struck. Leon and I had a falling-out which we could not resolve. Leon, without much consultation, had put together a seventy-eight-page section of the book and written an introduction to it which began:

> Over the summer of 1988 and on into fall, over 80 poets, novelists, short-story writers, and dramatists were invited to contribute what I shamelessly insisted on calling Position Papers: brief documents that would lay out the writers' literary aesthetic, define major operating principles, encapsulate aims and objectives, describe the philosophical lodestone that steered the individual writer's work—and in the bargain consider, generally, the way of literature in the world. Is the humanist tradition, I asked these writers, ragged and crippled and largely defunct in these postmodernist times, or can literature still shoot, as Cynthia Ozick and others insist it must, "for a corona, subtle or otherwise, of moral grandeur"? Can it prop up humanity's flagging spirit, somehow make easier the sleep of the innocent, vanquished dead?

Leon Rooke has written some of the finest stories published in Canada yet when he edges towards his Southern-Baptist-Preacher Mode he can be capable of writing blather. Language and rhetoric grip him and the result tends to be sloppy and imprecise. Can one "prop up" spirit? What does "the innocent, vanquished dead" *mean?*

The responses Leon gathered made me cringe. Give writers a chance to be windy and pompous and they'll grab it every time. The responses made much of Love, Death, Posterity, the Human Condition, and reiterated: Only Connect.

All this was bad enough but Leon concluded this introduction with what I felt amounted to a personal attack. He wrote: "A cadre of good citizens felt kinship with the project, and gratitude for the opportunity, but refused out of firm disagreement with John Metcalf for his variety of stands on assorted issues related to art and society."

Silence would have sufficed. I felt that this was a betrayal.

I did not doubt that what Leon was reporting was accurate. As Connie Rooke said to me at about this time, "You have *no idea* how many enemies you've got out there." I was busy in 1987 and 1988 with the Tanks Campaign, Bill Hoffer's guerrilla-theatre offensive against the Canada Council. I had on all possible occasions attacked Margaret Atwood's critical book *Survival*, describing it as not only silly but dangerous; this was widely considered *lèse-majesté*. I'd also in 1987 published the pamphlet "Freedom from Culture," an attack on subsidy culture, which caused froth to appear at the corners of mouths.

One paragraph can stand for the tone of the whole.

> The purpose of the Book Purchase Programme was to give added subsidy to the publishers and to get Canadian books into the hands of Canadian readers. Year after year of purchase passed until the news leaked out that the Council had been unable to give many of the Book Kits away: even such truly captive audiences as the inmates of prisons spurned them. Kits composed of Canadian fiction were met with particular opprobrium. By 1985, in a rented warehouse on Richmond Road in Toronto, the Canada Council had accumulated 70,000 volumes of unwanted CanLit.

I'd also edited in 1987 and 1988 *The Bumper Book* and *Carry on Bumping*, volumes of squibs, jibes, vulgarities, and literary scurrility, books which drew out the enemy delightfully in their reviews: "bedevilled by spite, resentment, and jealousy," "gratuitous bitchiness," "bile," "anti-Canadian."

I was becoming a hammer of the Canadian cultural nationalists and Leon wanted to distance himself.

I edited *The Third Macmillan Anthology* with Kent Thompson. Regrettably it was to be the last. It was particularly rich with fiction by Mary Borsky, Douglas Glover, Terry Griggs, Hugh Hood, Leon Rooke, Diane Schoemperlen, and Linda Svendsen. "The Year in Review" by Kevin Connolly, Michael Darling, and Fraser Sutherland was deliciously tart. But the books were large and lavish and not selling well and Macmillan decided not to lose more money.

The coolness between Leon and me lasted for some time but Leon's a difficult man to remain angry with. So now our quarrel is water (and Scotch) under the bridge. In 1991 I republished with Porcupine's Quill some of his out-of-print stories in a volume called *The Happiness of Others* and we're soon to republish more. Myrna always proffers Scotch when Leon visits for the pleasure of hearing him say in that beguiling accent, "Well, just a touch."

In 1985 I guest edited a polemical issue of *The Literary Review*, an American quarterly published by Fairleigh Dickinson University in Rutherford, New Jersey. The title of the issue was *On the Edge: Canadian Short Stories*. Barry Cameron wrote an introduction describing for American readers the battle we were engaged in.

Try to swallow *this* academic horse pill.

> When one studies *Canadian* literature, one is not studying literature as such but the literature written in Canada or by Canadians in a nationalist context. In such a situation, a writer who has less merit on other ideological grounds—aesthetic, for instance, which is conventionally privileged by students of literature—may be more important in a social or historical sense. Thus a self-consciously

> Canadian writer like Hugh MacLennan may be given precedence on the curriculum over, say, Leon Rooke (who would, incidentally, probably be discriminated against unjustly and solely because of his post-modernist tendencies), Margaret Laurence over Mavis Gallant on the grounds of Canadian setting, or W. P. Kinsella over John Metcalf because Kinsella writes about Canadian Indians.
>
> This sort of tension between so-called nationalist (social and historical) values, on the one hand, and the apparent absence of those values despite other merits, on the other, exists of course whenever literature is situated nationally; but that tension is exacerbated when one is dealing with a nascent literature like Canada's. This is not to say that all those writers who are attractive to the nationalists lack literary merit or that the Canadian social formation and history are not inscribed in the texts of these writers collected here, but it is to say that because they do not deal overtly with acceptable ideological themes . . . most of those in this anthology have resided in or on the margins of Canadian literary discourse until very recently.

Clark Blaise, Leon Rooke, and I were editing not as scholars or academics but as writers, front-line troops in a battle to set in place the next generation of writers, hand-picked by us as gifted and as likely to stand for the positions we'd been asserting and defending. Academic critics such as David Jackel in the *Literary History of Canada, Volume Four* (1990) continue to raise their thin bleat against "rootless cosmopolitanism" but who's listening? The war is largely over. Only a few feeble pockets of resistance to clean up. A Valgardson here. A Kinsella there. Skirmishes on the lower slopes of Maude Barlow.

In 1992 I put together an anthology called *The New Story Writers*. I chose to include Don Dickinson, Keath Fraser,

Douglas Glover, Terry Griggs, Steven Heighton, Dayv James-French, Rohinton Mistry, Diane Schoemperlen, and Linda Svendsen.

Anthologizing is necessary but inexact. It is easy to recognize talent but impossible to predict the shape of careers. A couple of the writers on this list may fall away from the short story but I remain satisfied with the book.

In the fall of 2001 Kim Jernigan, Peter Hinchcliffe and I put on a short story conference as part of the Stratford Festival. It was organized by *The New Quarterly* and the Porcupine's Quill, though most of the tedious organization fell on Kim's shoulders as she was in Stratford. Kim has exquisite taste and *The New Quarterly* unerringly recognizes important new talent. Both Kim and I felt that there was a flowering going on in the story form that was extraordinary and we both felt we should examine and celebrate this efflorescence.

The conference lasted for three days and featured panel discussions, readings, and lectures. Alice Quinn, Alice Munro's editor at *The New Yorker*, came to talk about Alice's work. The central idea of the conference was that older writers would give talks on the work of younger ones. Academics were not wanted.

I found that the writers I'd celebrated in 1992 in *The New Story Writers* were suddenly not so new and mysteriously not as young as they'd been. In fact, they were now the mid-career writers lecturing on the work of writers far younger. These younger writers represent what will soon be a *third* generation.

The conference was called "Wild Writers We Have Known: A Celebration of the Canadian Short Story in English." The writers present were a roll-call: Caroline Adderson, Mike Barnes, David Bergen, Libby Creelman, Michael Crummey, Keath Fraser, Douglas Glover, Terry Griggs, Steven Heighton, Mark Anthony Jarman, Elise Levine, Annabel Lyon, K. D. Miller, Andrew Pyper, Veronica Ross, Sandra Sabatini, Robyn Sarah, Diane Schoemperlen, Russell Smith, and Michael

Winter. Leon Rooke attended as reader and godfather.

They gave us a feast of language unimaginable in 1976.

On the first evening of the conference there was a reception in a Stratford restaurant and to walk into that bar and see all those friends and acquaintances gathered, that array of very sophisticated talent, warmed the cockles and astonished me anew at what we'd done.

Kim Jernigan said to me, "Do you realize that there are twenty-one writers here and that you've edited and published sixteen of them?"

Writing about the conference in the *National Post* Jeet Heer said:

> A teacher can never fully know what impact he or she has, since students go on to have lives of their own. After many years of tireless service to Canadian literature, for which he's received little money and much abuse, Metcalf occasionally feels beleaguered and tired.
>
> Yet at the Stratford conference he will see the fruits of his pedagogical labours: an entire generation of Canadian writers committed to the deeply Metcalfian goods of cosmopolitanism and aestheticism.

ACTS OF KINDNESS AND LOVE

Myrna and I lived in Delta from 1976 to 1981. Myrna's son, Ronnie, adapted to the life astonishingly. In Côte St. Luc we could hardly pry him away from the TV. He shrank in urban nervousness even from a passing poodle. Within weeks in Delta he'd made friends with our neighbour, Wayne Woods, whose farm was half a mile away up the dirt road, and went there every day after school to help with milking and chores. He metamorphosed into a dung-stained urchin who barged his way fearlessly through herds of pressing heifers and slapped a flank with the best of them.

When Elizabeth came up for the holidays she, too, took to this country life with ease, astonishing us all one day by finding and casually picking up a black rat snake that was at least six feet long. Ronnie and she established a sideline of catching leopard frogs which they sold to American tourists who used them as live bait for bass fishing on Beverley Lake.

We were doing reasonably well financially in those years, which was just as well as this was a rocky country. Many wives had to work "out" in Hershey's chocolate factory on the line in Smith's Falls or as cleaners in Brockville's psychiatric empire. I was awarded Canada Council grants in 1976, 1978, and 1980.

Royalties were coming in from a variety of publishers. In this period I earned over $16,000 from McGraw-Hill Ryerson alone, and most of that royalties on *Sixteen by Twelve*. I wrote a large number of reports on manuscripts for the Canada Council. I was also reviewing for newspapers, reading manuscripts for Oberon Press, writing CBC commissions, and giving public readings.

The texture of our day-to-day life can best be suggested by reproducing here a memoir I wrote for Elizabeth. It is tinged a little with guilt and sadness but captures, I hope, a time and place. The memoir is entitled *Acts of Kindness and of Love* which is, of course, a quotation from Wordsworth's "Tintern Abbey."

The "beauteous forms" Wordsworth refers to are the farms, the cottages, the woods, hedges, and orchards.

> These beauteous forms,
> Through a long absence, have not been to me
> As is a landscape to a blind man's eye:
> But oft, in lonely rooms, and 'mid the din
> Of towns and cities, I have owed to them,
> In hours of weariness, sensations sweet,
> Felt in the blood and felt along the heart;
> And passing even into my purer mind,
> With tranquil restoration:—feelings too
> Of unremembered pleasure: such, perhaps,
> As have no slight or trivial influence
> On that best portion of a good man's life,
> His little, nameless, unremembered, acts
> Of kindness and of love.

In George Tetford's yard, leaning against the green-and-silver Ford pickup, sitting on the tractor, crowding at the picnic table, we're all awaiting the arrival of George's uncle Willard with his flat black box of knives. Maureen, George's wife, stays on the porch; the business of the afternoon is not for women. Down behind the barn, greasy black smoke is piling into the sky from the old tires that are heating the water in the oil drum.

Two of Maureen's kids and my daughter, Liz, are whispering with the pasty-faced and treacherous Howland kids from the next farm up the road. Their mother doses them every Saturday with molasses and sulphur but they remain chronically loathsome with sties, snot, boils, and impetigo. Nothing will purify their rotten blood. They leave Liz tied to fence posts with binder twine. They take the ladder away. They abandon her to geese.

Where the road curves we see the travelling dust of Uncle Willard's truck. One of George's dogs runs out to the gate and stands there with its bow legs quivering. Another starts yapping hysterically at the trunk of the maple tree and yaps and yaps until someone scores on its ribs with a stone. Behind Maureen on the porch, the kitchen curtains are pulled aside as George's malignant mother cranes for a better view.

Half the house and farm are hers. She has suffered from a weak heart for more than forty years. Convenient palpitations strike whenever she is crossed or thwarted. She lives to rule poor George and undermine Maureen. Her only other consolation is religion. Nominally she's a Baptist, but she watches all the TV evangelists of whatever stripe and writes away to Tennessee box numbers for strange pamphlets which she presses on visitors. Sometimes she makes doughnuts for the local children—"fried cakes" she calls them—but Liz won't eat them because she's repelled by Mrs. Tetford's upper arms, by the wobble of the sausage-mottled flab.

Uncle Willard in his truck leads the procession down to the barn. The hogs are already in the calf box in the back of George's pickup. George lowers the tailgate and fixes some old boards to form a ramp. He lifts out the battered .22 rifle that's usually kept in the barn and jiggles a single cartridge into the breech. Then reaching into the cab, he fetches out four bottles of Pepsi, a column of Styrofoam cups, and a bottle of Golden Wedding. Shots of rye are poured for all the men. Uncle Willard opens his box of knives on the hood of his truck and selects one that's been honed away over the years to a thin and wicked arc. He drinks the rye down neat and sighs.

"Well, George," he says.

George nods.

"Well, George," says Uncle Willard, "tell me this, then. Why's Labatt's Blue like making love in a rowboat?"

Uncle Willard's repertoire is inexhaustible. He's a fixture at Grinley's Feed and Seed and at White's Garage in the village. He often entertains in the back of the hardware store and is frequently to be found with his cronies at the township dump where the dump's custodian has built a crazy lean-to with scrap board and tin on which he's nailed a large sign saying: Office.

While the men are still laughing at the answer to the Labatt's riddle, George slides up the door on the calf box. The three hogs inside stare up and press back against the box's rear wall. One of Maureen's brothers hands up the .22. George shoots one of the hogs between the eyes. Maureen's brothers get a hook into its mouth and down its throat and rush the body down the ramp and onto the ground where it thrashes and works itself about. Uncle Willard sticks it in the throat and joggles the knife about in the hole so that the still-pumping heart splashes out thick blood. In the November air, steam rises from the pools of it. The hog lies on its side, its legs scoring brown tracks in the turf.

Liz takes hold of my hand and tugs at me to bend down.

I put my arm around her.

"It's OK," I say. "The pig's dead. It isn't feeling anything. That's just its nerves. There's nothing to be frightened of."

"I'm not," she says. Her eyes are alive with pleasure. "Did you hear?" she whispers. "Mr. Tetford? Say the F-word?"

George secures chains round the hocks and the carcass is hoisted up to hang head-down from the front-end loader. Maureen's brothers are trying to force another bald tire further into the fire's centre. The heat is so intense, it's difficult to get near. The tractor lurches towards the oil drum, the carcass swaying and clanking. After the hog is scalded, George and Uncle Willard select knives and start scraping off the bristles with the concentration and delicacy of barbers wielding cut-throat razors. George works with his mouth open, Uncle Willard hisses through his teeth like an ostler. Some twenty minutes later the hog hangs oddly white in the afternoon light exactly the colour of a peeled mushroom.

Uncle Willard rests against the pickup and swills Golden Wedding around his teeth.

"Well, George," he says. "There were two bulls up on a hill. An old bull and a young bull. And down below," he says, "there's a herd of heifers. So the young bull says to the old bull . . ."

Uncle Willard nods as the others laugh; he keeps his face professionally straight. He seems almost disapproving of their laughter.

"What's the difference," he says, testing the edge of a new knife on the ball of his thumb, "what's the difference between a recruit into the army and a constipated owl?"

He makes the first cut.

After excising what he now calls—because all the children have crowded back—the hog's jimmy-riddler, he knots binder twine around what he calls the waterworks to prevent leaks and dripping. Then he starts to open up the body. As he cuts, the guts start to pile and slobber out against his stomach. He braces up their weight on his fore-arm so that nothing ruptures, so that the gall bladder or matter in the intestines does not spoil the meat. He cuts the liver free and drops it into a plastic margarine pail. The dogs are watching intently. Rex whines and shuffles nearer on his behind as if he's suffering from worms. The tricky part over, Uncle Willard lets the guts slop down into the nettles where they shine and subside and spread and settle.

"What?" he says.

"Where's its speaker?" repeats the smallest Howland kid.

"It's got eyelashes," says Liz. "Look, you can touch them. Orange eyelashes."

The small Howland scowls.

"I wanna see it. I wanna see its speaker."

"*Stereos* have speakers," says Liz. "*Microphones* have speakers."

It is getting colder. The afternoon is drawing in. Liz wanders off and starts to help Maureen's brothers feed the fire. The second hog is shot and bled. George pulls the pickup closer to where they're scraping off the bris-tles and turns the radio to the country music station in Watertown, New York. Lugubrious twanging love songs fill the air, songs of confession and maudlin remorse. The level in the bottle of Golden Wedding is dropping. The carcass slips from the front-end loader and the crumbs of dirt and smudges are wiped off its stiffening white-ness with filthy rags from the milk house.

I can see that Liz is getting bored. Maureen's brothers don't want to roast corn from the crib. They don't want to cook windfalls on sticks. George has cut the first pig's head off with a chainsaw but the smallest Howland has got it and is feeding it and won't share. George's kids have gone back to the house to watch TV. The other two Howlands are playing a game with offal and a stick.

I suggest to Liz that it's getting cold and that we walk home to make hot chocolate. We wave to Maureen's brothers and say goodbyes to George and Uncle Willard who pauses in his butchering to say, "Now this here's a golden oldie, John. There was this fellah, his wife had the house painted and as he was getting into bed that night . . ."

We walked up past the corn crib and Maureen's garden and the machine shed and into the yard. George's mother rapped on the kitchen window and beckoned. She'd prepared for Liz a plastic bag of fried cakes.

"Have you got a kiss for an old woman? That's it. *Isn't* she a little angel?"

I frown at Liz who is scrubbing at her lips with the back of her hand.

"Are you good at your books? Oh, I knew it! I just knew it! What a lovely ribbon! A little scholar, is she? Well, then, here's a nice book for you to read in bed for after you've said your prayers."

And so we set off along the dirt road to walk the mile or more home.

In one hand Liz is holding the plastic bag of fried cakes and in the other she is holding a pamphlet entitled:

WHERE ARE THE DEAD?

The house towards which we were walking that November afternoon was a stone farmhouse built in the 1840s. In 1900 or thereabouts someone had built on a frame addition. The stone part of the house had a vaguely Georgian look about it though it did not aspire to the limestone elegance of the houses in Kingston. This house was cruder, dumpier, the style debased, a house for farmers, not for gentlemen. The way it sat squat into the land reminded me of stone farmhouses in Wales. Many of the stone houses in the Rideau Lakes area have this sort of look and feel and I've heard it said that they were built by masons who'd sought local employment when the building of the locks on the Rideau Canal was finished.

The locks nearest to us were at Jones Falls. We used to take the children there to watch the boats going through and to feed the fish in the fish sanctuary. The children used to sprawl on the low footbridge and plop frothy spit into the water, attracting a frenzy of minnows, and, waggling ponderously up out of the darkness into green and sunlit view, the huge catfish with a white growth on its head like a beret.

In the evenings, the locks were often deserted and silver under the green gloom of the trees. The thick scrub and bush on the far bank would be turning black in the gathering twilight and I was always moved by thinking of the immensity of effort involved in building this canal and by the grandeur of the engineering. The great dressed blocks of stone, the massiveness of the gates, the lines of defence falling back to the lockmaster's fortified house—all this classical military architecture conjured up Colonel By and his engineers and sappers and beyond them the shade of the Marquis de Vauban and Europe in its days of might and glory.

WHERE ARE THE DEAD?

Visiting the United States and Canada in 1913, writing travel pieces for the *Westminster Gazette*, Rupert Brooke said of North American landscape:

It is an empty land. A European can find nothing to satisfy the hunger of his heart. The air is too thin to breathe. He requires haunted woods, and the friendly presence of ghosts . . . The maple and the birch conceal no dryads, and Pan has never been heard amongst these reedbeds. Look as long as you like upon a cataract of the New World, you shall not see a white arm in the foam. A godless place. And the dead do not return. That is why there is nothing lurking in the heart of the shadows, and no human mystery in the colours, and neither the same joy nor the kind of peace in dawn and sunset that older lands know. It is, indeed, a new world.

Certainly the land is not as thickly haunted as the English countryside and probably never will be. Canada is too vast to become so minutely groomed and annotated. But Rupert Brooke was certainly wrong about *this* countryside. Here the dead are all around us. They are part of us and we of them. We walk a land they shaped.

Across the road from my house, up on the edge of the rocky pasture, ancient cars sit in the scrub and bush. Bees nest in the rotted upholstery. The magnificent ruin of a combine harvester seems to melt and settle with each passing year. Low juniper bushes are growing through sheets of tin rusted to the thinness of leaf. My daughter thinks of this as an archaeological site.

In my own back field she unearths from an old domestic garbage dump patent medicine bottles which must date from the eighties and nineties of the last century. These she washes and ranges on a bench in the garage along with particularly valuable stones.

In the woods there are indications even older. Foundations of cut blocks. Lilac bushes. Apple trees grown wild. This is a hard country to farm and these abandoned sites mark discouragements, debts called in, drought, the death of a wife.

The land reveals itself slowly to the newcomer. Our ghosts are in its shapes. Rocks are never far from the surface here. Fields are simply soil in pockets. This field before us is shaped in this particular way with a protruding promontory of trees making ploughing difficult because under those trees the rock has surfaced in a sheet. Over *there*, water sits well into summer because it cannot drain away. Pasture, plough, swamp, and sugar bush—these were the shapes and uses forced by soil and rock upon the settlers. I've walked the land about here for miles in all directions mapping it with my muscles. I've come to understand it. I've come to understand the fearsome effort that went into its clearing and shaping. And I've come to love it.

And this small child with whom I'm walking, this much-loved daughter, what does *she* make of this place, this people, this daughter who is only a summer and occasional visitor?

Her maps are more intense than mine. Her maps are summer maps and magical. They show the course of the stream and where the banks of wild mint grow you can walk through up to your waist and the crushed smell of it. Her maps show where the felled and rotting elms lie and where under the fungus-smelling bark the salamanders live. Her maps show the old dry manure pile at Mr. Tetford's where a pair of milk snakes live and the wooden veranda at the side of the Howland house where the great black rat snake basks in the morning sun.

Noted on her maps are ponds of leopard frogs, the platform of twigs where the red-tailed hawk is nesting, the patches in the vast cathedral sugar bush where wild garlic grows, the dead swamp trees where great blue herons sit pretending to be branches.

Her maps record the sites of panic terror.

That place along the dappled path where the partridges explode from beneath the elderberry bushes and stop your heart in your mouth.

That clearing in the birch trees where there's the footprint of a building, tumbled masonry, raspberry canes gone wild, and the shrill-ing of the cicadas building to an electric whine and then in the still heat and sudden silence the leaves on the birches turn and tremble though there's not a breath of wind.

All this, the smells and shapes of it, its textures and its lovely endless detail—this mushroom-coloured pig, those three scabbed and yellow apples high in the November branches of a roadside tree as we walk homewards on this cold afternoon—all this will haunt her. This country has possessed her. When she is grown and living in some distant city, she will walk this countryside again in dreams. These "beauteous forms," as Wordsworth calls them, will be the bedrock of her life.

When the children were on holiday we spent most of the time going for walks, catching leopard frogs, exploring surrounding villages, fishing in Upper Beverley Lake for sunfish, swimming, sitting empurpled in the tree in front of the house gobbling mulberries.

When the children were in school I was working on a book that was published by Oberon in 1978. The book contained two novellas, "Private Parts: A Memoir" and "Girl in Gingham." The book was published as *Girl in Gingham*. I had been working on the title novella in Montreal in 1975 and finished it in a rented cabin in a neighbour's sugar bush in 1976.

While I'd been working on "The Lady Who Sold Furniture" and teaching myself how to write dialogue I'd also come to revel in the *theatricality* of what I was about. In the setting-up of scenes, their juxtapositions, their starting *in medias res* with their implications emerging from dialogue and action—I was playing with all the lessons I'd absorbed from the *auteur* film directors and from Degas's paintings. The novella form fascinated me because it could be tightly controlled—page by page—as a short story could, yet at the same time was expansive enough to allow for theatrical effects. Individual scenes could be built with lyric intensity and then juxtaposed with broad comedy. Broad comedy could be tempered to become intensely moving. Writing novellas was a particularly joyful kind of playing.

Novellas, the poetic kind I was interested in, were as dense and rich as Christmas puddings. And as time went on I beat more and more candied fruits and angelica into the mix. These novellas make concentrated demands on readers but I believe the pleasures are commensurate. I used dialogue to set scenes and reveal character. The dialogue was edgy, nervous, demanding the reader's committed attention. I was not unaware of Beckett, Pinter, and the absurdist verbal pratfalls of N. F. Simpson. My dialogue was intended as pure theatre.

As an example, here's the opening of a section from "Polly Ongle."

> "*Tabourouette!*" said the waitress, depositing on their table a bowl of potato chips. "Me, I'm scared of lightning!" Turning the glass vase-thing upside down, she lighted the candle inside.
>
> "Cider?" she repeated.
>
> "No?" said Paul.
>
> "Oh, well," said Norma. "I'll have what-do-you-call-it that goes cloudy."
>
> "Pernod," said Paul. "And a Scotch, please."
>
> "Ice?"
>
> "They feel squishy," said Norma, stretching out her leg.
>
> "Umm?"
>
> "My sandals."
>
> He looked down at her foot.

What is so pleasing to me about a passage like this is that the lines of non-speech are really a continuation of the dialogue though unspoken, pleasing also that the dialogue between them while seemingly about drinks and sandals is really both character description and a silent dialogue of eroticism, seemingly entirely innocent but not. And all driving forward crisply.

As the English music-hall comedian Max Miller used to say to the audience after telling one of his more salacious jokes, "Yes, that's right. Oh, yes, it's continental stuff I'm giving you."

I ended "Polly Ongle" with its protagonist pursuing an intimate, elegiac "conversation" with a statue of General José de San Martin in a public park. It's a scene that would translate without the slightest distortion into gorgeous film. And was conceived in exactly those terms.

I have never been troubled by critics, academic or otherwise, who regard stories and novellas as a minor form. I pursued this argument with Professors Sam Solecki and W. J. Keith in our book *Volleys*. I simply cite as iron-clad refutation of their position *Death in Venice* and V. S. Naipaul's *In a Free State*, another book which flared out over my literary landscape illuminating much and filling me with delight and awe. *In a Free State* appeared in 1971 and was described as a novel but its compression and its lyrical method of movement mark it clearly, in my opinion, as a novella. V. S. Naipaul is also a wonderful story writer, a genre in which he's been undervalued. I always recommend *A Flag on the Island* and claim the story "The Nightwatchman's Occurrence Book" as one of the funniest stories in English.

"Girl in Gingham" was madly theatrical and I much enjoyed staging the scenes and pacing them effectively. It was interesting to move from fast to slow, from action to meditation, working the emotional weights of sections against each other until it all flowed into the final scene in the restaurant. The other novella, "Private Parts: A Memoir," was by its pseudo-memoir form inherently less given to dramatic scenes. I concentrated more on achieving a *tone* for the novella. I remain pleased with both pieces.

While we certainly enjoyed the peace of the country and its beauty we both found that a little peace could go a long way. It was alarming to find ourselves discussing as a topic of some fascination the passage of the snowplough and we often longed for conversation that Delta could not supply.

Paul Theroux published a novel in 1974 called *The Black House* about a recently retired man called Munday who buys an old house in a Devonshire village. He and his wife are staying at the village pub, kept by Mr. Flack, until their furniture is delivered. Here is a scene in the pub one evening.

> The men grew audible again, they coughed with force, one inhaled snuff deeply from the knuckles on the back of his hand, another smoked a rolled twisted cigarette, and the drawling was renewed: the price of apples, the cost of living, a lunatic in the next village, reckless drivers, a pair of vicious dogs Hosmer said should be put down. ("And I know how to do it.")
>
> "You could write a book about this place," said Mr. Flack, who took Munday's silence for attention.
>
> "Me?" said Munday.
>
> "Anyone who knew how," said Mr. Flack.
>
> Munday's laughter was harsh; the four men stared at him. He waited until they began another private conversation—this one about a dead badger—before he went up to his room.

I laughed out loud when I first read this. Whether Devon or Delta, it catches exactly and mordantly the scope and tenor of village conversation.

—this one about a dead badger—

To counter dead badgerdom we had throngs of visitors who came to stay for weekends, John Mills, Jack David, Ray Smith, Leon and Connie Rooke, Harry Hill, Douglas Rollins, Jim Gaite, Kent Thompson, Robert Lecker—and Hugh Hood would drop over from nearby Charleston Lake and Matt Cohen from his retreat in Verona.

Whenever Geoff Hancock, editor of *Canadian Fiction Magazine*, came to stay we spent boozy afternoons listening to the lesser Chicago luminaries. It was our own King Biscuit Time show listening to records by Magic Sam, Johnny Shines, Son House, Jimmy Rodgers, Roosevelt Sykes, Elmore James, Robert Nighthawk, Otis Rush, and Shakey Walter Horton.

On one occasion, the living room seemed to be becoming hazy with smoke.

"The ducks!" yelled Myrna.

She ran into the kitchen.

"It's not too bad," she called. "I'll baste the burned bits with orange juice. It's only Geoff Hancock."

After the fall of Saigon in 1975 we were following newspaper reports of the plight of refugees. By 1977 we were reading increasingly of boats full of refugees being attacked on the high seas by pirates and fired upon by government vessels. All this heartlessness reminded Myrna vividly of the Jews in the thirties being rejected by port after port, country after country, Canada among them, and sailing on to their deaths. She resolved that we must help.

Myrna has family connections to Naomi Bronstein who was working with orphans in Saigon in 1975. Through her we knew of Sandra Simpson, the founder of Families for Children, who was running orphanages in Vietnam and Cambodia. She also ran orphanages in Bangladesh, India, and, later, Somalia. Myrna phoned Sandra in Toronto and offered help. This was at the precise moment that Ontario was dithering about initiating the Unaccompanied Indo-Chinese Minor

Refugee Program. With Sandra's help we agreed to sponsor and became the guardians of two children who were in a Malaysian refugee camp at Pilau Bidong.

The bureaucratic foot-dragging and obfuscation were bewildering. Myrna wrote to all levels of government up to and including Flora MacDonald and Pierre Trudeau. She wrote to Employment and Immigration Canada, the Ontario Ministry of Community and Social Services, the Secretary of State for External Affairs, the Ministry of the Attorney General, the Office of the Official Guardian . . . Eventually we ended up with a brother and sister, Duong Le Binh, a girl of sixteen, and Duong Gia Phu, a boy of ten.

We had explained to Ron why we were doing this but he was difficult to win over. He said, "But I *like* being an only child." The whole situation was difficult for both him and Elizabeth.

Le Binh and Gia Phu spoke Vietnamese and Cantonese. They spoke no English. Communication was difficult. They did not seem to understand why they were with us. We decided that we needed someone who spoke English and Cantonese to explain matters to them. Fortunately we had a friend, Jack Chiang, originally from Taiwan, who was the photography editor at the Kingston *Whig-Standard.* Jack drove up from Kingston and took the two of them out in his car. They were gone for about two hours.

"Well," said Jack, "I'd get rid of them if I were you. I've never met such weird kids in my life."

He explained that they were Chinese and had lived in the Cholon sector of Saigon. The extended family had lived together in a compound almost entirely cut off from the world. Their father was a weaver. Number One Uncle was the one who "go outside," who dealt with the outside world. Jack was groping to explain exactly what we were dealing with.

"It's like they came from China two or three hundred years ago and they still think and speak like people did then. Yes, that's it. They're like, you know, those German guys that wear black suits in the States, Mennonites. They're like Amish. *That's* what they're like. Weird."

Both children were obviously unhappy and obviously missing their parents painfully. They learned English slowly. We had decided that the essence of the matter was that, for their own sakes and for their future, we had to integrate them as soon as we could. We started with names. Le Binh we decided to call Lee, Gia Phu, we changed to Jim.

We sent them to school hoping that they'd pick up some English there and we persevered at home with looking through magazines and naming objects in photographs, with endless repetitions of words and phrases. Progress was painful. Lee referred to the fridge as the *wish-wish* and after an outing to Ottawa called the Parliament Buildings the *bi how* meaning "big house."

Attempts to interest them in matters Canadian fell flat. The entire household ate with chopsticks and Myrna bought the Chinese ingredients that Lee wanted—ingredients for kou-tien, lopchong, bok choy, mustard greens, light and dark soy, fish sauce, noodles. If Myrna made a Western dish, Lee would push it around with chopsticks exclaiming in disgust, "What *this!*"

Lee and Jim gradually learned some halting English and we tried all the time to engage them in conversation. Sitting with Lee one evening looking at magazine photos and attempting to build vocabulary I came upon a photo of a model.

"Isn't she beautiful, Lee?"

"I no like it," said Lee, "round eye."

It was difficult to understand how they saw us and how they understood Canada. It was fairly obvious that they thought the Chinese way of conducting oneself was the only way. The word *ethnocentrism* only hints at how rigid they were. They behaved towards us as though they were house guests and made little attempt to join in any family activities.

They sometimes said things so revealing that they were, so to speak, a glimpse into the abyss. One day in 1979 Lee came home from school and said, "Trudeau, he gone."

"That's right, Lee."

"What happen he now?"

"Well," I said, about to launch into the idea of political parties, but she interrupted me with an expression of inquiry and drew a finger across her throat in a slitting gesture.

So much for civics.

Our neighbour gave Jim a green John Deere tractor cap. Lee snatched it from his head, saying, "Chinese boy no wear green hat." Furor developed. More floods of tears.

"Jack," I said on the phone, "what should I know about green hats?"

He listened and then explained that wearing a green hat was in ancient Chinese tradition the mark of a cuckold.

"What did I tell you?" said Jack. "Sincerely weird."

We were somewhat discouraged by the lack of progress but we took part in another campaign to bring five young men to Canada from the Southeast Asian camps. This organization was called the Rideau Committee to Save the Boat People. Five area families volunteered homes for them but we had to raise $10,000 to be held in trust to satisfy government sponsorship requirements.

In 1980 we also arranged for St. Xavier's Church in Brockville to sponsor our children's two uncles and two aunts still in Pilau Bidong Camp. Lee and Jim were much cheered to be able to spend time with them. The four of them, tiny people, lived in an apartment the church provided which they provisioned with huge sacks of rice.

Jim was of particular concern to us. He was passive and sat about the house staring into space with his mouth open. Myrna came into the kitchen one night after getting the two boys bathed and into bed and she said, "You know, that Jim . . ."

"Ummh?"

"Well, he's the first ten-year-old I've met with B.O. And," she added, "a moustache."

We grilled Lee on the matter and she confessed that everyone had lied about Jim's age because the fee to escape Vietnam was less for younger children. It was also believed in the camps that the younger children were the easier it was for them to be accepted into Canadian and American families. Jim, it turned out, was thirteen. He became something of a project for Myrna. She does tend to get the bit between her teeth. And Jim's teeth became an obsession. All his teeth were pitted with black holes and were rotten. His upper teeth were splintered into spikes and fangs. Nothing was salvable. Myrna took him to our local dentist who said he needed complete top dentures. Myrna took him at the appointed time but the dentist said she couldn't do the work that day because her assistant was off sick. Myrna, not to be baulked, said, "Show me what to do and *I'll* be your assistant." And, fearsome woman that she is, she indeed operated the water and the suction while the wreckage of Jim's teeth was removed.

During these months Myrna and I had been talking about adopting a child. Myrna was becoming increasingly interested in Families for Children and increasingly interested in Sandra Simpson. Sandra and her husband, Lloyd, were unlikely do-gooders. Sandra is a woman of great compassion and little sentimentality. She has a raucous sense of humour. Her own family is vast, being made up of all the adoption breakdowns and of children difficult to place. At one time she had well over twenty children in the house, including the crippled, the autistic, and the blind. While looking after this alarming brood Sandra was running orphanages, raising money constantly, and dealing with the bureaucracies of three and four governments at a time as she arranged international adoptions. It all seemed to an outside eye to be endless chaos—but it somehow worked.

Sandra's main aim was not international adoption but in-country care in the orphanages. It was amazing to watch this woman bend people to her will. When she opened an orphanage in Mogadishu, Myrna helped to gather supplies in Ottawa which were shipped to join everything being stored at Sandra's Montreal house. Myrna drove a forklift truck in Cohen's Demolition warehouse gathering up military cots. Sandra had secured a Canadian Forces Hercules by sweet-talking the minister of defence at a social function. When it came time to ship everything to Trenton, a truck of soldiers showed up at the house ordered there by the commander of a local army base who was enjoying the attentions of another Families for Children volunteer.

"Mrs. Simpson!" said the officer in charge of loading at Trenton, a testy man who obviously disapproved of civilian meddling, "You've subverted the Canadian Air Force to your ends and now I see you've turned your attention to the Army."

We phoned Sandra and she told us that she had two children in India that she wanted to place. The children were in the Families for Children orphanage in Coimbatore in Tamil Nadu State. The grim address was: Behind the Blind Institute on Chemical Road.

Sandra sent us photographs of a boy, Manikem, aged nine, and Rangidam, a girl aged seven.

I showed the photographs to Lee and Jim.

"What for they come?" said Jim.

Lee frowned at the photographs.

"India people same thing monkey," she said.

So in 1980 there were six children in the house. Rangi spoke Tamil. Manikem, whose name we changed to Daniel, spoke Malayalam. And then my mother and her friend arrived from England to add to this menagerie. My mother and I have had a relationship which might be described as "troubled." Now in her hundredth year, she recently told me that the happiest day of her entire life was when I was accepted into a pre-kindergarten group at the age of three.

"The relief," she said, "at getting rid of you, you can't imagine." The state between us ever since might best be described as a state of truce. I have written a version of this relationship in my novella "Private Parts." The underlying tensions reveal themselves in oblique emotional outbursts. One day in this summer visit I noticed she was getting moody and suggested we go for a walk. Tears started running down her cheeks. She burst out with a pronouncement I've been trying to think of a response to for twenty years.

"I could die happily," she said, "if only you had some decent furniture."

Rangidam stayed close to the house and close to Myrna and told us later when she had learned some English that she was frightened of the monkeys catching her. Rangi also spoke of running away from home in India and of a mother who had put her feet in the cooking fire. She had been living on the street before someone had taken her to the orphanage. Danny's situation had been more stable. His father had died in an accident and his mother had remarried. Her new husband did not accept Danny and his mother had taken him to the orphanage to protect him. Because he'd had some experience of a family he was better able to adjust than Rangi.

In 1980 ECW Press published my novel *General Ludd.* I had had a difficult time writing it and the book fell into two parts. I had intended it to be a lighthearted comedy; there was a hiatus in the writing of it and the last half became increasingly bleak. It is not a good novel. It isn't even an adequate one. I seriously considered withdrawing it before publication but then, in weakness, let it go forward. It received glowing reviews. John Moss in his *A Reader's Guide to the Canadian Novel* wrote: "*General Ludd* is probably the finest comic novel ever published in Canada. *Going Down Slow* earned Metcalf fair consideration as a writer in the tradition of Richler,

Davies, Leacock, and Haliburton. With *General Ludd*, he follows comfortably in the wake of Cervantes, or Fielding, or Trollope, or Waugh at his very best."

Such preposterous bombast over such an obviously botched attempt at a novel is why I despair of criticism in Canada. Keath Fraser got closer to the mark when he said to me that the book founders under its freight of ideas.

Lee and Jim were making it increasingly clear that they were happy only when they were with their aunts and uncles. They began to spend more time in Brockville. Myrna and I were also feeling considerable stress as Lee was falling to bits emotionally. These tensions were not Lee and Jim's fault. They were worried about their parents and wanted only to be reunited. It was probably misguided of us to expect any emotional return from them but it is difficult to live with people who refuse to connect with you.

Lee and Jim decided that they wanted to live in Brockville with their aunts and uncles. They made this move and subsequently managed to get their parents and two younger siblings out of Vietnam. The whole family was reunited and they all live in Toronto now. Both Lee and Jim are married and with children of their own.

Myrna and I and Ron, Rangi, and Dan moved to Ottawa to begin the Long Sentence.

AN EAGER EYE

PROFESSOR HENRY BEISSEL, head of the Creative Writing Department at Concordia, phoned me in 1981 inviting me to Montreal as writer-in-residence. I came to an arrangement with the department whereby I would stay in Montreal a couple of nights a week. At the time of my arrival Henry was away on tour in Germany reading his poetry. Sitting in my office one afternoon I heard his familiar accent in the corridor. I went to say hello and there he stood positively effulgent in a white linen suit and a swishy silk-lined cape.

"How went your tour?"

He considered the question and then said quite unselfconsciously, "They loved me."

I was pleased to be in Montreal, not only for the income and as a respite from my children but because I was able to spend a lot of time with Elizabeth Lang at her store on Greene Avenue in Westmount. Elizabeth let me examine and handle all her African masks and figures and made me free of her stockroom, pleased to teach me in the way Bernard Halliday had been.

Grey bun and Birkenstocks but with an almost girlish enthusiasm for art and commerce. I can see the two of us now in the intricate dance of purchase.

"Look at the lines," she'd murmur, as I ran my hands hopelessly over the horns of a *chi wara*, the antelope mask worn caplike by the Bambara tribe, the dancer's face and body hidden under cascades of raffia.

"So powerful," she'd murmur.

"Yes, *but*, Elizabeth, I've read that they were last danced—in the fields, I mean—in 1934. So there's no way . . ."

"But who's to say exactly," she'd say, "what 'genuine' means? What's genuine is what *it* says to *you*."

"But if it wasn't used for their own ritual purposes . . ."

"You've been reading books again by Americans. Rules! Rules! Who approaches Art with rules?"

"Well, that's all very well, but . . ."

"Now if we were dealing with a mask of the Guro . . ."

A tiny shrug.

The suggestion of a moue.

"But *this* . . ."

Not long afterwards, Elizabeth was tragically killed in a traffic accident. As she was stepping between two parked cars, one reversed and she was crushed to death. The Elizabeth and Justin Lang African collection, more than six hundred items, was donated to the Agnes Etherington Art Centre at Queen's, where a paltry selection is now indifferently displayed.

I had become interested in African art in the sixties and can remember the exact moment that I was drawn to it. I was walking along Sherbrooke Street and paused to look in the window of Le Petit Musée. There among Chinese bowls and flintlock pistols and a Georgian silver coffee pot stood a wooden *thing*. It had a large disc-like face with delicately suggested features and a column as a body. Tiny breasts stood out. It made me look at it harder than anything had for years. I went into the store and asked the owner, Max Klein, what that thing in the window *was*.

He explained that it was a kind of doll from the Ashanti tribe in Ghana. But not exactly a doll. Women who were pregnant or wished to become pregnant carried these "dolls" tucked in their robes at the back. The face embodied the Ashanti ideal of good looks and the doll was thought to confer these attractive features on the child-to-be-born. The object was known as an *akua ba*.

I was so moved aesthetically by this thing that I bought it on the spot, having with me, by chance, its exact price as I was on my way to pay the rent.

Over the years since then I taught myself a great deal about African carving, reading the journal *African Art* and gathering together a useful library of reference. I also read the fieldwork of ethnologists and anthropologists. I sometimes thought the inside of my head was coming to resemble the higgledy-piggledy cabinets of Oxford's Pitt-Rivers Museum. Push this button and the cabinet lights up to reveal the varied tribal concepts of the human figure: Dogon, Fanti, Luba, Fang, and Pende; push that button for cross-cultural arcana. My mind was chock-a-block with information.

There are funerary masks of the Igbo and Ibibio people of southern Nigerian—Cross River masks, too—which are decorated in white, the colour widely associated with death. The very earliest masks used a white clay as pigment but quite early on the carvers decided that a British shoe polish for white leather and sneakers called Meltonia was just the job. It amuses me to imagine scientists in the war against fake and fraud testing not for the fingerprint trace elements of Nigerian clay but for the correct formula for Meltonia Shoe Cream. Similarly, the Yoruba colour of choice was obtained from Reckitt's Blue Dye laundry bags. Beads were fashioned from the thick glass of Pond's Cold Cream jars. In Benin, they continue to cast plaques and figures of the Oba with his mudfish legs using spent cartridge cases from the Biafran war.

But information is no substitute for having handled so many pieces that the eye goes immediately to the piece that is "right." It is a fusion of knowledge, taste, and experience. The feeling is exactly like that of Jonathan Gash's Lovejoy character, an antiques "divvie," for whom bells ring when he comes across a genuine artifact.

At exactly the moment that I became near-expert, the prices skyrocketed and I had to revert to sad gazing in museums.

Le Petit Musée soon became one of my favourite shops. It carried a vast stock of antiquities and pottery and silver, glass, edged weapons, firearms, African carvings, furniture, jade, ivory, Japanese prints, Arabic bowls, calligraphy . . . This wonderful emporium was presided over by Max Klein, a tall and elegant Viennese Jew, grave of mien and manner but charged with the invigorating larcenous instincts common to all in the antiques business.

Mr. Klein's always grave demeanour and his pronouncements afforded me rich amusement. Once while gazing in abstracted manner at a vitrine, he said, "I have always understood an interest in pottery in a Canadian-born man as an infallible indicator."

On another occasion he was trying to sell me a bronze adze.

"It is," he said, "fairly obviously Celtic."

I had been boning up on the subject.

"Or possibly," I said, "Luristan."

He inclined his head.

"Or possibly," the lovely old operator conceded, "Luristan."

Over the years, I've bought many a small antiquity from Max Klein, Han jade, Luristan bronzes, amber, Greek wine cups, Kufic calligraphy from the Abbasid dynasty. I've always liked to have a few antiquities about me; apart from their beauty, they give life a context and solidity. If I can work one of these artifacts into the texture of daily life I'm doubly delighted. Rootling about one day in a coin shop in Ottawa I found two identical examples of what is known as "spade" money. These Chinese coins are rectangular in shape and bifurcate. In the upper part, the "body" as it were, there is a hole cast through. They bear a design which I've always taken to be a lotus. They date from the reign of Wang Mang (A.D. 6–23). Myrna and I use them as key rings—much to my brother's anguish—and there is a daily pleasure in touching and using something two thousand years old.

I suppose this love of ancient things dates back in part to my brother's museum in the pantry and to my almost psychotic rage and jealousy and desire at his being given by a retired missionary when he was thirteen or so a beautiful bronze Chinese bell and a pair of black figure *lekythoi*.

When young, I wanted to be a painter so intensely that the fact that I had an *anti-talent* for the activity seemed irrelevant. During my two sixth-form years I devoured Skira art books and mucked about in the art room labouring on sludgy landscapes. There was a new teacher at the school in his first year out of the Slade. We admired each other's suede shoes. Using a brush or his thumb, he'd turn an inch or two of my turgid determination into something full of life and sparkle.

"Do you think it's getting any better?" I'd ask him.

"Christ, no!" he'd say. "It's worse than shit-sausage but keep daubing away. It'll help develop your eye a bit and keep you from playing with yourself."

(Needless to say, he lasted only two terms.)

He once took me to London to visit the studio of *his* teacher, John Minton. With the brushes, the clutter, the painty smells, and the cooking sherry we drank from teacups, I felt I was at the source. There's a haunting portrait of Minton by Lucian Freud in the National Portrait Gallery in London. He committed suicide in 1967, anguished, apparently, by his homosexuality.

While I was at Bristol University I was keenly interested in the painting of William Scott and haunted the Arnolfini Gallery where he showed. At the Bristol Guild of Applied Art I used to stroke and lust after the Bernard Leach pottery.

But it was not until I came to Canada that I actually bought a painting.

I'd been one evening to Sir George Williams University, now Concordia, to listen to some wretched poet. Who it was I can't remember now but he was reading in front of an exhibition of paintings by Roy Kiyooka who was painter-in-residence that year. All next day, teaching, I saw those green egg shapes swimming before my eyes. The paintings were in the Pop-Op style but had far more *presence* than such work usually did. I phoned Kiyooka and asked him if he'd sell me the painting and let me pay for it over a period of time. He seemed perfectly agreeable and I arranged to go to his house in NDG the next evening.

He opened the door and stared at me in silence. He shuffled to one side which I took as an invitation to enter. We walked into a front room entirely bare except for a kitchen chair. Leaning against one wall was a package done up in corrugated cardboard and tape. Kiyooka still had not spoken. He stood staring intently into the empty fireplace. I had put $500 into an envelope in a vestigial notion of bourgeois manners and now handed it to him. He still just stared at me in silence. The cliché "inscrutable" flashed into my mind. Had I unknowingly breached some matter of etiquette in picture buying? Had I unknowingly flouted some intricacy of Japanese courtesy?

Feeling quite sweaty, I began to babble inanities about the weather. But something about his face . . . Slowly, very slowly, it dawned on me. He wasn't inscrutable. He was stoned. He was massively, monumentally stoned, stoned beyond even the *possibility* of speech. I picked up the painting, bade him a cheery farewell, and left him staring, rapt, into the grate.

I'm telling the story about Roy Kiyooka as a way into saying that buying a painting is essential in beginning self-education in visual art. It concentrates one's eye and aesthetic faculties as nothing else can to know that imminently you are going to part with the price of four refrigerators and a high-end dishwasher.

It's not really possible to understand a painting without living with it. Dailiness is important in revealing the painting that is flashy or meretricious, the painting where awkwardness bleeds through. Posters and reproductions of any kind are a delusion, because they always betray the original by masking texture and flattening the paint's true life. The Irish painter Jack Yeats even stipulated in his will that no reproductions of his work be made, so sure was he that reproductions betrayed.

I've been familiar for many years, through photographs, with Picasso's great painting *Night Fishing in Antibes*. I can still feel the intensity of shock at seeing the painting at MOMA in New York. No photograph had prepared me for the complexity and gorgeousness of its colour. This was a Picasso I had never known.

Lucian Freud said something simple yet profound when he said, "Learning to paint is literally learning to use paint."

Many people seem to feel intimidated by the hush of commercial galleries and the seeming disdain of their often bitchy staff but they are, after all, only *shops*. And for the most part crammed, as my painter friend Tony Calzetta says, with Stuff.

The Canadian art world should intimidate no one. It is easy to grasp. Just glance through a couple of Joyner's Canadian Art auction catalogues and you'll get the picture. What the audience, such as it is, is willing to pay for is second- and third-rate landscape paintings. Old barn, cedar rail fence, trees.

Especially trees.

Abstract work tends to cause titters of unease.

Joyner has been quoted as saying that he would not hold an auction of abstract work as the results would entirely destroy what market there is.

David Milne (1882–1953) is beginning to be recognized by the more daring.

Even in the realm of paint one cannot escape the contamination of nationalism. The Group of Seven (1920) remain Canada's pin-up boys. See "Trees" above. Canada's pin-up *girl* is Emily Carr, who trumped the deal by painting autochthonous totem poles *amidst* trees. Hugh Hood and I shared a profound loathing for her work. Hugh always claimed that it was patently obvious that these muddily coloured exercises were all versions of her vulva. I miss conversations with Hugh; they were always bracing.

Since the Group of Seven and Emily Carr, popular taste has celebrated Ken Danby, Robert Bateman, Toller Cranston, Charles Pachter, and the like. "Woodland" artists like Norval Morrisseau and Daphne Odjig blossomed. This "Woodland School" paints decorative myths and legends badly. Morrisseau first showed at the Pollock Gallery in 1962. He is often described as a shaman. I've never been sure about what it is that shamans *do* but I've rather doubted the sincerity of the man's calling since hearing Jack Pollock's comic accounts of Morrisseau's epic matings with a life-size rubber doll.

Also widely revered are the paintings of Alex Colville, weirdly frozen frames from an untold narrative, enabling the viewer to invent the implied story. What happened to the running girl? Why is she running so fast? What might she be screaming? Who is she waving at? Why should we be asking stupid questions like this?

The actual *paint* is devoid of interest.

Popular with many are Inuit carvings, dismissed by all experts in tribal sculpture as "airport art."

I like to furnish my fiction with Inuit sculpture.

"On the glass table in front of the couch lay a gigantic soapstone seal with a bulbous Eskimo trying to do something to it."

"Bulbous" was good.

("... trying to do something to it," obviously derives from Kingsley Amis. As does, "It was nice in the bathroom," from the same novella.)

Canada has had and still has superbly gifted painters but usually doesn't seem able to recognize them. *The Canadian Encyclopedia* describes painting as "an essentially reactionary form." If I were wealthy and had acres of wall space I'd chuckle to see the National Gallery silting itself up with conceptual profundities and feeble-minded videos while for absurdly low prices I'd be buying the reactionary canvases of Guido Molinari, Yves Gaucher, Charles Gagnon, William Ronald, Alexandra Luke, Ray Mead, Kazuo Nakamura, Tom Hodgson, Harold Klunder...

And Tony Calzetta.

Tony Calzetta was born in 1945 in Windsor, Ontario, to a Croatian mother and Italian father. He attended Catholic schools in Windsor and went to the University of Detroit, from which he graduated in 1968 with the degree of Bachelor of Science. Most of the courses he took were, however, in math, business studies, and accounting, and his degree might more properly be described as being in commerce.

On leaving the university, he immediately secured a job in Windsor with Price-Waterhouse, where he remained in increasing misery for two years. At the beginning of 1970, he gave notice and went to Toronto to look for work. For the next nine months he worked as a labourer for a construction company. Up in the morning dark, the crew's boss passing round brandy to numb them against the day. Following this, he drifted back to Windsor and worked in a desultory manner as a drapery installer.

During this period of drift, he somehow arrived at the idea that what he really wanted to do was to study art. Drawing and painting had always fascinated him. When a child, he had badgered his parents into buying oil paints for him, but the murky results were not wildly encouraging as he'd been unaware that turpentine was supposed to be mixed with the oil. On the slender basis of this childhood interest and in the what-the-hell climate of the time, he phoned the art department of the University of Windsor in September 1971 and was instructed to appear with his portfolio.

"You talk about embarrassment! My portfolio was a ratty piece of cardboard in which I'd got sandwiched some little drawings I'd done when I was about ten years old, a few watercolours, and a copy of a brassiere commercial from a magazine. And when I got to the interview room there were all these black portfolios open to show work that was professionally matted and I thought, Oh, my God! What have you *done* to yourself, you fool!"

He graduated with a BFA in 1975 and went to York, from which he graduated in 1977 with an MFA. His first three shows after York were at the Pollock Gallery. I first encountered the work at his third show at the Pollock Gallery in 1980. I was in Toronto on some kind of publishing business and wandered into the gallery on a whim. What hit me was one of those rare art experiences where one feels one's life suddenly illuminated, enlarged, enriched. Over the years since then Tony has become my closest friend.

It is extremely difficult to write about paintings but I will attempt to describe what I saw and first felt at that Pollock Gallery show. These were the *Cloud* paintings, the elements of landscape drawn in a cartoon-like style to make landscapes or seascapes afresh by combining the conventional "signs" for rain, clouds, waves. These paintings were at the same time very sophisticated and elegant and yet childlike. There are suggestions in them of Paterson Ewen and Philip Guston. I have one of these huge canvases in Ottawa and its charcoal-drawn centre shape has been variously referred to by visitors as a cauliflower, a mop, a brain, and an engorged sexual organ; this may say more about the visitors than about the painting.

The central problem is that the "clouds" have charcoal-drawn stems on them which attach them to the side or top of the paintings.

"*Is* it a cloud?" I say.

"Well," he says, "it *could* be. It is and it isn't."

John Newlove claims to hate all painters because, he says, at the drop of a hat they're always ready to impart to you their philosophy of life. Which derives from the one book they've ever read. Which is inevitably a work of science fiction.

One knows, rather guiltily, what he *means*, of course, but of Tony Calzetta this isn't true at all. Tony is reticent and ambiguous to the point of being shifty. He spouts no philosophy. I think he wants the paintings to remain undefined and mysterious. Talking about them makes him uncomfortable. I think he has the feeling that if we can't define the painting
then we're unable to turn it off. We'll keep looking, keep wondering, "*Is* it a cloud?"

The shocking part of the third *Cloud* exhibition at the Pollock Gallery was the energy of the line. This show broke through into what has now become the essence of his work—the combining of drawing with painting, the use of charcoal to produce a line of marvellous sensitivity. Paul Klee spoke famously of "taking a line for a walk"; Tony takes them for a hundred-metre sprint.

He said to me once, "The energy that's conveyed in a line is so exciting. The line defines the image. The line *is* the energy. Colour supplies the mood."

On another occasion, he said, "Charcoal's a sensual pleasure. There's a film on Alechinsky working and there's one part where he has a huge sheet of paper and he's putting down a line in charcoal and—oh, God!—the excitement just of the *sound*."

Tony works in series and his images—his iconography, as the art historians love to say—evolve from series to series. You couldn't possibly predict the next series but when it arrives it has an inevitability about it. Clouds move to the sides of the paintings and become curtains. Dramatic skies become pelmets. The waves turn into a stage. What were once strange floating objects in the sea now become boulders on the stage, flatirons, possibly ruined buildings. Sometimes huge slabs of rock are furnished with wheels. The paintings are somewhat surreal and nearly always cheerful if not funny.

Philip Ottenbrite, when he was working at the Mira Godard Gallery, said, "The history of Tony's work has a real logic to it and a sense of progression. He has a very personal sense of style, and elegance is the essence of that style. He makes everything he does look very easy but that ease has been *worked* for. He's bringing something new to painting. I don't want to inflate things but his work has a certain . . . majesty. He's unique. His work fits into no category and of course he's suffered because of that.

"I can tell you one important thing from personal experience. The work of many painters—it dies on the wall after two months. That never happens with Tony. Energy emanates from a Calzetta canvas and keeps on emanating. He's poured so much energy into the canvas, you see, that we keep on receiving it, the picture keeps growing and expanding for us."

Tony has always insisted on his own direction and usually, of course, to his detriment. Being funny in Canada probably isn't a good idea; being funny in Canadian painting is probably unforgivable. He gives his paintings such titles as *Jive Ass Atomic Art Queen*, *Lester's Love Wagon Leaves Late* and *The Queen Realizing the Court Was Starving Lets Out a Scream and Orders the Crew to Their Boats in Search of Herring*. And, of course, he arrived upon the scene just when the mindlessness of "conceptual" art had begun to dominate. He finds paintings with writing on them dreary beyond bearing. When he comes to stay with us he always says, "Let's go down to the National Gallery for a good read."

Tony often refers to the Theory of Stuff. The world, he says, is crammed with Stuff. Most Stuff is awful. Therefore when looking at an exhibition, hurry round and find the best painting. This saves time and effort because, the best painting found, the rest becomes Stuff. And there's no point in squandering time on Stuff. Especially when that time could be spent quaffing martinis.

It's more than possible, though, that Tony's vision and dedication to purpose will be vindicated. Who knows which of us time will treat well? I felt a sudden warning shift in the world when I went with Myrna, Tony, and his companion, Gabrielle de Montmollin, to see a Philip Guston exhibition at the National Gallery. In the first room there were examples of his work as an abstract expressionist. These were well done but there was a faded feeling about them; they were a minor part of a movement now history. When one moved on into the *Guston* Gustons—violent, crude, uncouth, almost barbaric—it was easy to see the *necessity* of his breaking out of a past which was becoming too pretty, vitiated.

I think Tony felt that warning shift in the world many, many years ago; that he did so is a measure of his originality and talent and steadfastness.

Tony's art and his day-to-day life are inseparable. His concerns are always aesthetic and he reveals himself as much in making toast as in painting. He has, typically, a professional restaurant gas stove, a Garland, and makes toast in a medieval-looking utensil, a thing exactly like a wok but with holes in it like a colander. This he sets on the gas; the toast when done is pimpled with black spots. He refuses to discuss this practice.

Not only have I had the profound pleasure of watching his work evolve over a twenty-year period but I've also had the pleasure of his friendship and learned from him so many good things: Japanese papers, Asiago cheese, tarte Tatin, the importance of Chaim Soutine, *rascasse* in bouillabaisse, the existence of the Musée Dapper in Paris, Sienna cake, martinis with a drop of fino sherry, Tio Pepe, say, instead of vermouth.

Tony's ease and charm inevitably attract a wide acquaintance, some of them quite mad. One acquaintance seriously cherishes the vision of opening a restaurant serving nothing but liver and Geneva gin. Another collects Jaguar cars. Another photographs Chinese herbal remedies. Orbiting Tony is exhausting. Days spent with him usually evolve into celebration, a key perhaps to both his life and his art. He shapes his life into ritual and ceremony. There is even a certain majesty to his hangovers. I treasure the memory of Tony, much hung over, tottering along the Danforth in search of a beef heart to roast, a sovereign cure, he claims.

A couple of years ago Tony and Gabrielle spent the winter and spring in Provence at Gabrielle's house, La Garance, in the village of Les Bouilladoires. Myrna and I visited in March and they took us to Gordes and Gabrielle showed us the tiny house Jack Pollock writes about in *Letters to M* where she had nursed him during his long decline into cocaine and AIDS. Then to Les Baux-de-Provence and a visit to the mental hospital Maison de Santé St. Paul which started as a monastery in 982. Here Vincent Van Gogh committed himself in May 1889 and stayed until May 1890. During this year he painted 150 pictures and executed 100 drawings. There was an exhibition on of sad daubs by current inmates and Tony said they exhibited better taste and attack than anything he'd seen in Toronto for a decade. Myrna went into the ancient chapel and found under the altar a mad-woman lying on the floor.

We filled Tony's *bidon* with Lubéron wine and then back to Bouilladoire for Henri Bardouin pastis and the inevitable talk: what had we been working on?

A relative of Gabrielle's who lives in Villefranche had a walled garden. In one of the walls there was a niche, perhaps constructed to house an urn or a statue of the Virgin Mary. Tony had been commissioned to make something beautiful to fill the space, something, as David Bolduc would say, to rest the eye on.

Tony had typically hurled himself into this work. He first had a pair of doors cut from steel plate. Then he welded onto the flat surface further rectangles and strips of plate to give depth and variety to the surface. Then—quintessentially Calzetta—with a grinding wheel he chased into the skin of the metal lyrical whorls, abstract arabesques.

As the garden was close to the sea Tony decided on a seascape. He fired sheets of ceramic, making shapes which fitted together to suggest a ship. He then made rows of waves for the ship to sail on. The back and sides of the niche he tiled with blue-green mosaic chips with here and there the glitter of a gold tile. I could imagine the owner opening the doors of the niche as one might open the ark of the covenant or an elaborate reliquary and gazing upon this almost Byzantine splendour.

But he wouldn't quite grasp that he was looking at the Calzetta signature, looking at a completely new expression of what Tony has been labouring on for years, the playful, elegant combination of conventional signs into new worlds of line and colour. A comparison with the conventions of Japanese prints would not be inappropriate in explaining this aspect of Tony's work.

John Bentley Mays got it about right when he said of Tony's works: "They document no recognizable reality, but simply commend *themselves*, with elegance and masculine beauty, as objects of creative work worthy of our attention."

Not long after my Kiyooka encounter, I met, through Hugh Hood, the photographer Sam Tata. Again it was happy coincidence that I'd bumped into someone eager to teach me both theoretically and by allowing me to watch him on so many occasions at work. In 1991 I edited and published with the Porcupine's Quill his *Portraits of Canadian Writers*.

Prior to meeting Sam I had not given photography much thought. In my snotty teens I probably professed to admire Man Ray but really didn't. "Art" photography seemed to be thought of as shapes that looked like breasts or buttocks but turned out to be disappointing boulders. What appreciation of photography I had was probably reserved for a nudist magazine called *Health and Efficiency* which was printed on yellowish coated stock whose smell I can recall to this day. *Health and Efficiency* featured flabby nudists whose interesting bits were hidden behind coy Ping-Pong bats or beachballs. They were about as arousing as a bulk bin of crunchy granola but in my distant youth one grasped whatever titillation was on offer, which was never, sadly, much.

Sam was born in 1911 in Shanghai. He came to Canada in 1956. He was a Parsi but brought up in Shanghai where his father managed cotton mills for the Tata industrial empire. When we first met and I found out about his background Sam was flabbergasted when I started to ask him questions about Ch'i Pai-shih, one of the painters I most admire. I don't recall now how I'd found out about the painters of the Shanghai School—most probably a scroll seen in a museum—but I had developed a passionate admiration for Ch'i Pai-shih, Ch'ên shih-tsêng, Hsü Pei-hung, and Lin Feng-mien.

In 1988 the Canadian Museum of Contemporary Photography organized a retrospective exhibition of Sam's work and Pierre Dessureault edited a catalogue entitled *The Tata Era/L'Époque Tata* to which I contributed a piece about Sam's portraits entitled "Conversations without Words." I tried to pay tribute to Sam's endless charm and humanity and tried to suggest ways of looking at the richness of his craft. What follows is culled from that tribute.

> I am neither photographer nor art critic. My only credentials for writing about Sam Tata are that we have been friends for many years and that I am a seasoned sitter;

Sam has been taking my picture regularly since about 1970, photographs that have been reproduced on the jackets of a variety of books and on posters.

The title of this very personal tribute attempts to suggest what is happening when Sam is taking someone's picture. There is between Sam and the sitter a conversation; it is a conversation without words.

This is not to suggest that Sam is taciturn or laconic. While this silent conversation is going on between photographer and subject, Sam will be talking. He rarely stops. Sam is a Vesuvius of conversation, a walking compendium of quotation and reference, a cornucopia of anecdote. His reminiscences of life on three continents flow from him unstoppably.

Sam's stories are of his childhood in Shanghai, of his eccentric expatriate British schoolmasters, of his gilded youth in Shanghai's international society, of Eurasian beauties lost and won. He tells stories of exploits and adventures in Hong King, Japan, and India and though he claims to speak nothing but a word or two of foreign languages I've heard him chatter in Shanghai dialect, Japanese, and Gujarati.

Sam's conversation on any given day might typically range over incidents in the Parsi community, the scurvy behaviour of Bombay taxi drivers, the wisdom of Akbar the Great, the novels of P. G. Wodehouse, the intricate language of Chinese courtesy and insult, the work of Atget or Cartier-Bresson, the life and paintings of Lin Feng-mien, who used to give lessons to Sam's ex-wife Rita, art forgeries in Hong Kong's Nathan Road. A newspaper headline catching his eye—the capture of a mass murderer in British Columbia—will prompt him to recall the line from a Saki story: "Waldo is one of those people who would be enormously improved by death." This in turn will lead to forthright pugnacity on the subject of capital punishment, which will in turn remind him of executions he witnessed in Shanghai before the Maoist troops rode in—a time when he wandered the dangerous streets nonchalantly taking the brilliant photographs that arrest and hold us to this day.

But however convoluted the arabesques of anecdote he always returns to his emotional centre; he always returns to stories of Toni, the daughter he so adores; to stories of his sometimes irascible Gujarati-speaking mother who in fits of exasperation used to hurl at him her tortoiseshell-backed hairbrushes; to stories of his father who by day sternly managed the Tata mills but who by night unbuttoned and sat tall in the saddle with the westerns of Zane Grey.

Sam's conversations with me are not much different from the conversations he has with the people he is photographing. He has said of portraiture: "The sitter must be willing to be photographed. The photographer must be sensitive to the sitter. And a rapport between the two has to be established."

At the beginning of a photographic session, people are wary. The task of the photographer is to get them to relax, to remove the mask. Sam works at establishing the necessary rapport through conversation. He chats with people for twenty minutes or so until they are convinced that he is not a threat. "At some point," says Sam, "both know that they're ready to go." He usually takes a full roll of twenty-four to thirty-six exposures and his experience is that the better pictures start to arrive in the middle—that is, when the sitter has moved from acquiescing in the process to actively embracing the idea of being photographed.

It's important to stress here, however, that creating that necessary rapport isn't a trick or part of some well-rehearsed schtick; Sam's conversation and the rapport it builds are an expression of his personality and nature.

If one looks at a range of Sam's portraits, most of the subjects will be found to be in eye contact or near eye contact with the photographer. Many of the photographs are intense, almost fierce. The people in these photographs are deeply involved, indeed *absorbed*, in the process of being photographed. Sam has said of the experience, "The confrontation is like a conversation—a conversation without words."

Note the words "confrontation" and "conversation"; there is no hint of self-effacement here. Sam has also said: "I cannot avoid myself in every portrait I do."

When he gathered together a selection of his portraits of artists in 1983 he chose to call the book *A Certain Identity*; he derived this title from something written by his friend and mentor Henri Cartier-Bresson: "It is true, too, that a certain identity is manifest in all the portraits taken by one photographer. The photographer is searching for the identity of his sitter, and also trying to fulfil an expression of himself."

"I have to be on my toes," says Sam. "There's a stress and tension in all this and when it's over I enjoy the relaxation; it's a pleasant kind of tiredness."

No one can be entirely unselfconscious when being photographed, of course, but paradoxically someone sitting for Sam is *least* self-conscious when most *consciously* engaged in the process of the wordless conversation.

What I've written so far with its talk of confrontation and of people fulfilling themselves and expressing themselves and attending to "inner lines of force" perhaps gives the impression that a portrait session with Sam is a deeply emotional experience akin to therapy or a group encounter. Nothing could be further from the truth. The photographer Geoffrey James got close to the nature of the experience when he wrote: "I have been photographed by Sam several times, and always experience the mild euphoria of having just discovered a painless dentist."

Because the sitter must be relaxed, Sam always prefers to work with available light and in the familiar surroundings of the subject's home; he sees the studio and the paraphernalia of tripods, flashes, and reflectors as inhibiting. Many of Sam's portraits, then, offer us the almost voyeuristic pleasure of observing domestic interiors, for there are usually *things* in Sam's pictures—ornaments, paintings, books, plants, pianos, sculpture, dogs, furniture. These furnishings and possessions further express and suggest the sitter's personality; Sam has actually called these photographs "environmental portraits."

These background details are rarely, however, merely descriptive. Sam is an artist and a considerable one. His pictures are carefully composed. He is, of course, concerned with capturing the "inner lines of force in the being of his subject" but he is equally concerned with the making of a picture, with composition, with shapes, with blackness and whiteness. In successful portraits, psychological and artistic concerns fuse.

In a word, then, Sam's concerns are painterly.

When he comes into someone's home for the first time to make a portrait, he is naturally more aware than anyone else of the quality of the light. In *this* room, the light is flat, rather dead. But *here* it's very full, very alive. And what a handsome armoire that is! From Quebec? Could he see it with the doors open? Are those chisel marks? Or an adze, perhaps? He may well be listening to the history of your armoire or telling you a story about Akbar the Great or a White Russian nightclub hostess in Shanghai—and enjoying the listening or the telling—but because he rarely crops a picture or enlarges detail, his seemingly innocent eye will be framing and composing, seeking textures as he talks.

In the long months of 1991 when Myrna's mother was in the Jewish General Hospital in Montreal dying of cancer, Myrna and I drove down every weekend from Ottawa. On those visits I'd usually walk down to Kensington Street in NDG to visit Sam and we'd pore over his prints and contact sheets. We put together a collection of one hundred photographs that Sam thought represented his best work over the years. I took the pictures away with me, promising to find a publisher. Later I wrote a biographical essay to introduce the collection.

Eleven years later that box of photographs is still sitting in my study, having been considered by publisher after publisher who delivered such verdicts as "too expensive to produce," "It's all a bit liberal-humanist, isn't it?" "Who's ever heard of him?" and "Well, they're just *pictures*—what's the hook?" Dismaying reactions to the work of a man who according to the Canadian Museum of Contemporary Photography defined an epoch.

Perhaps Sam's work will come into its own when the National Portrait Gallery opens and they're searching for exhibits. They already sound desperate for stock. An Ottawa functionary was interviewed last year by the *Ottawa Citizen* and was asked what *sort* of famous Canadians would be honoured in the proposed Gallery. He prevaricated for a while and then said, "Canadians like . . . like Northern Dancer."

Sam himself is now frail and largely lost to us. He suffered a stroke and his memory was impaired. When it happened, I went down to Montreal on the bus and went straight to the Royal Victoria Hospital. Sam saw me come into the room and said, "Why, John! What are *you* doing here?" He seemed bright and voluble and we chatted for a while and then I needed to visit a washroom. I was away a few minutes. When I went back into the room, his face lit up and he said, "John!" reaching out his hands to me. "What are *you* doing here?"

THE TANKS CAMPAIGN

I FIRST ENCOUNTERED William Hoffer through his catalogues. When I started many years ago to collect and document the short story in Canada it was inevitable I would meet Bill, though we first got to know each other through letters. He gradually became interested in what I was trying to do and helped me to narrow the focus. He was particularly helpful when I was putting together a collection of Contact Press and he eventually supervised its sale to the National Library.

"I *had* to help you sell it," he said when I again thanked him. "You owed the shop over $4,000."

We soon discovered shared convictions. Bill had very few serious customers outside the universities—he often said seventeen, worldwide—and we were both convinced that all the celebratory razzle-dazzle on the surface of things masked a deeply alarming reality. That reality was that the audience was tiny, that it had not prepared itself to be able to distinguish significant work, and that there was a blank ignorance of our literary past. We both felt there was an almost total confusion of literature with nationalism.

Literature, we both felt, had been co-opted by the state. Money, we believed, masked the truth of this reality. The large sums shovelled out through the Canada Council were cloyingly referred to as "watering the young shoots of Canadian literature" or "nurturing Canadian literature's fragile blooms."

Bill's retort: *The only plant that can't be killed by overwatering is seaweed.*

He decided that he would launch a campaign against the Canada Council and against the idea of state subsidy to protest all the toxic sludge the money had generated. His first line of attack was through his catalogues. Most dealers in antiquarian books and first editions are discreet and circumspect. It was, therefore, astonishing and liberating to read Bill's increasingly vitriolic annotations:

> Lane (Patrick) *Beware the Months of Fire.* Toronto: Anansi, 1974. Cloth in dust jacket. Of the eight "previous books by the same author," five are broadsides or leaflets. This is the CanLit equivalent of wearing elevator shoes.

or

> Davey (Frank) *Griffon.* np. (Toronto) Massasauga Editions, 1972. Small stapled wrappers. The edition limited to 200 numbered copies. A review copy, with the slip laid in. Davey produced two booklets under this imprint, both of which disfigure List 70.

or

> Davies (Robertson) *The Rebel Angels.* New York: The Viking Press, 1982. Cloth and boards in dust jacket. The first American edition of the senile civil servant's late pant around the track. When young he almost mattered, but now stands more revealed (in Charles Olson's brilliant observation of how it is in life). Catalogued in weary acceptance of the obligation, only for the money.

Bill's campaign against the idea of subsidy to the arts began in 1985. He wanted to call the campaign "Tanks Are Mighty Fine Things" after the title of a book published by the Chrysler Corporation in 1946. Permission was denied and so Bill called the campaign, simply, Tanks.

The campaign was both farcical and intensely serious. He wrote: "For more than 15 years I have used every avenue available to object to the false culture we promote in Canada, not because I have grudges, but because it is impossible for me to be a serious bookseller in a society that takes nothing seriously."

Again, he wrote: "For many years I have ridiculed the absurd spectacle of apparently grown men and women pretending to have succeeded at the very difficult tasks of art."

When questioned about what would happen when, Samson-like, he'd pulled down the pillar and the Temple of Subsidy had collapsed about him, he'd quote a Yiddish saying: *The worst truth is better than the best lie.*

What he meant by this was that even if we reduced literature to *samizdat*, to Xeroxes passed from hand to hand, that would be preferable to the lie that official CanLit had become.

Because no one would engage in debate on this topic, Bill employed a comic-book language to gain attention and to prosecute the campaign. He styled himself Commander of Tanks. Marius Kociejowski, a Canadian poet who lives in London, was given England, while I was designated Commander for Ontario and Toronto. The poet and teacher Peter Sanger was installed as District Commissioner for the Maritimes. Allies in the American book trade were also commissioned and issued titles and insignia. This small group along with a handful of delighted and appalled readers of Bill's catalogues constituted what he called his "slapstick army."

Certain writers, academics, and bureaucrats were designated "War Criminals." Bill defined as War Criminals "those who are more enthusiastic about getting grants than they are about the things they get the grants to do." He went on to say, "The fictional absolutism of the *Tanks* vocabulary . . . had the virtue of being hugely entertaining to those who were not offended by it, and incredibly offensive to those who were."

> Bowering (George), editor *Great Canadian Sports Stories*. Ottawa: Oberon Press, 1979. Cloth in dust jacket. Various tedious contributors. Offered as a scarce Bowering C item, and an out of the way anthology. Oberon Press is "owned" by Michael Macklem, one of the more ugly of the meek members of the resurrection in Canada. Macklem has attempted to be the James Laughlin of Canadian publishing, but has managed little more than strict compliance with the Official Languages Act through the publication of endless translations of bad French-Canadian novels all of which remain in print in their first printings of fewer than 200 copies in cloth. Anyone who has suffered the misfortune of actually speaking to him has discovered how offensive a man he is, how unjustified in his high opinion of himself. I take this opportunity to dispose of him; I have dispatched a war criminal indictment under separate cover.
>
> $35.00

The Tanks vocabulary began to creep even into his private correspondence. In a letter to me he wrote: "All I want to do is to roll my 11 armoured divisions into town, destroy everything without pity, burn down the unsanitary shanty towns (weird regional magazines, creative writing departments, etc., etc.) and set the Canadian people free. God, in the form of George Patton, casting man out of a Garden of Eden in which every piece of fruit is poisoned . . ."

Bill's opening shot of the campaign was by way of pamphlet. He wrote: "In London, Marius Kociejowski, a Canadian poet in exile, showed me his essay *The Machine Minders*. It was so perfectly suitable to what I was trying to do with *Tanks* that I brought it back and made it the first *Tanks* imprint, using it as an example of criticism, and as a way of walking point with my metaphorical army of ideas against subsidies to the arts."

The second shot fired was my own pamphlet "Freedom from Culture." This appeared in 1987 and over the following year was printed in four editions. One of these editions was printed in large numbers by the Fraser Institute, a "strange bedfellows" deal that Bill had struck.

The pamphlet's intention was to be funny about Subsidy, Government, Bureaucracy, and the Administration of Culture but utterly serious in pointing out that:

> It is not only individual writers who are softened and subverted by grants; the method by which grants are awarded has further emasculated our literary world. The Canada Council prides itself on its jury system. Grants are given to writers by juries of their peers. Officers of the Council do not interfere or attempt to influence decisions. Everyone prides themselves on this exemplary arm's length relationship with government. But this very jury system which protects writers from direct government influence is responsible for a totally servile literary climate in the country.
>
> Canadian writers do not brawl in the country's newspaper columns. We lack the pleasures of literary brouhaha and imbroglio. We don't have honest reviewing, we don't have pungent criticism, we don't have open faction. Reviews written by Canadian writers are usually ecstatic—or cautious, circumspect, tepid. Spades tend to get described not as spades but as agricultural implements. CanLit suffers from terminal politeness.
>
> Very few writers in Canada care to express publicly their honest opinions about the work of other writers

and of the literature in general. Every writer in Canada knows that the writer he criticizes today may be sitting on a jury tomorrow and handing out grants—or not, as the case might be. Self-interest dictates lies. Or, at best, silence.

Even the academic critics are in a similar situation since their commentaries on and discussion of the texts are similarly juried by the Canada Council. Fatuous flatulence or costive noodling, it all gets the professorial nod. Backs are scratched and logs are rolled. There are conferences to attend. Readings to deliver. Subsidized seminars in Tahiti.

We're all in this together.

...

And what of audience?

From 1957 onwards, million upon million has been spent in Canada to provide us with a literature. We have, in effect, tried to buy a literature much as a parvenu might hire a decorator to create for him instant antiquity—and with much the same embarrassing results.

The policies and activities of the Council and other granting agencies have flooded the country with unwanted and unreadable books; alienated readers in public libraries offer up silent thanks for the maple leaf stickers on spines which identify books as Canadian. Worse than this flood of inadequacy, the Council has put into place a parody of the entire machinery of a literary culture; for the benefit of no readership, subsidized books are reviewed in subsidized journals by subsidized writers. It all fills one with the slightly uneasy amusement one feels in watching a chimpanzees' tea party.

Nor can we rely on our academics to comment on the Emperor's New Clothes and destroy this machinery gone mad because they themselves are a paid part of it; they are subsidized to inflate, conflate, huff and puff. We can't expect the monkey to berate the organ-grinder.

It's fairly obvious by now that the Canada Council has failed. In failing to build an audience it has failed entirely. Indeed, the Council's existence absolves any possible audience from responsibility. "Art and suchlike," we might imagine people saying, "it's nothing to do with me. The State takes care of that sort of thing."

The perpetuation of its own bureaucratic routines and the expansion of its "programmes" have become the Council's *raison d'être*.

Writing in Canada became CanLit.

CanLit is fast petrifying into Culture.

The values of artists are necessarily elitist. The values of a bureaucracy are necessarily bureaucratic. The Canada Council in its administration of Culture is quite understandably concerned with regional representation, with aboriginal representation, with proportional language representation, and with equality of sexual representation on juries and in awards. Such a concern with "fairness" is laudable in a political context; in artistic terms it is risible.

What the Council *really* wants—though it would claim otherwise—is to use its funding as an equivalent of the federal equalization payments to the provinces. Fund more women in Saskatchewan. More painters needed in New Brunswick. Too many anglophone writers in Toronto. A dearth of francophone drama in Manitoba.

And if applicants with vaguely artistic aspirations couldn't qualify as any conceivable variety of artist, they could always apply for the popularist Explorations Grant—the type of programme described by Charles Osborne [of the Arts Council of Great Britain] as "that perversion of the aesthetic urge invented by bored arts administrators yearning to become social workers."

What has all this to do with art?
With literature?

These and other such observations brought down on my head more vituperation and seething hatred than I could have imagined. The go-back-to-where-you-came-from brigade frothed and spluttered in apoplectic rage tossing about words like *traitor*, *fascist*, and *Brit*. Even today, sixteen years later, these dumbores are still hooting their outrage like chimps who've had their peanuts pinched.

The Canada Council itself was sufficiently worried by "Freedom from Culture" that it hired Professor Tom Henighan of Carleton University to write an article refuting it. This he sat himself down to do but found halfway through that I'd converted him.

The Tanks campaign's main offensive was the publication of six volumes Bill intended to be exemplary—exemplary both as literature and as book design. He was setting out to prove that exceptional literature, beautifully designed, could be produced without subsidy and could make a profit.

The books were *Eight Poems*, by Norm Sibum; *The Voyeur and the Countess Wielpolska*, by George McWhirter; *The Topography of Typography* by El Lissitzky; *Five Stories*, by W. P. Kinsella; *Corpses, Brats and Cricket Music*, by George Faludy, translated from the Hungarian by Robin Skelton; and *Autobiographies*, by Elizabeth Smart (edited by Christina Burridge).

What to say of these books?

Norm Sibum's poems are, as always, interesting and involving. George McWhirter's two-page poem is competent; laid into the folder are two lithographs of trees by Diane Ostoich, lithographs which stand in no relation whatsoever to the poem.

Marius Kociejowski's essay *The Machine Minders* is disfigured by Maureen Sugrue's awful illustrations.

I'm not able to say how well Robin Skelton translated George Faludy's poetry as I cannot read Hungarian. The verse *sounds* as if he's got it right but I must admit that Skelton makes me uneasy. His own poetry is correct and competent but somehow bloodless. His claims to have been a "witch" must surely give any sane person pause. My ex-wife worked for years for a New York publisher of books concerning the occult—a natural, if not inevitable, place for her to end up. She once phoned me to ask if I knew a Robin Skelton because they'd just received from him the typescript of a book of "spells." One spell, she said, caused levitation.

The Topography of Typography is four sheets printed beautifully by Glenn Goluska at his Imprimerie Dromadaire. It is, like all such exercises, precious.

I have profound problems with Elizabeth Smart. I *loathe* her writing and consider *By Grand Central Station I Sat Down and Wept* an abomination, a foul gush of emotional incontinence. I considered her relationship with George Barker sad and shabby; when I met her in Toronto she had become an utterly hopeless drunk. George Barker sticks in my mind less for his poetry than for his remark in a London pub to the young Norman Levine: "Sorry chum, nothing personal. But coming from Canada, you haven't got a chance."

I begged Bill not to publish W. P. Kinsella's crudities. Back came contempt, condescension, accusation, paranoia—to all of which I paid little attention. Bill's hostilities were reflex.

The Tanks books were frankly a hodge-podge. They weren't beautiful. The artwork did not marry the texts and in some cases was simply inept. The format of the books (eleven by about seven inches) seemed to emphasize their awkwardness.

Although the books were the campaign's loudest salvo, there was a constant chatter of small arms fire which never seemed to quiet—letters, conversations in the shop and on the phone, harangues at book fairs, reissues of "Freedom from Culture," and, of course, the increasingly vituperative catalogues.

Even though Bill was positively bleeding money on the project and was deeply depressed about the failure of the books to sell, he soon managed to turn defeat into victory. In the sometimes strange way his mind worked he now started to propose that the fact that he had produced the books with his own money and not with "funny money" was a victorious protest in itself against the system and a standing rebuke to it. The failure of the books to sell he put down to media hostility or indifference, apathetic bookstore owners, and a Canadian literary sensibility numbed by thirty years of subsidized inanity.

Had his books been good books, I could have agreed with him more wholeheartedly.

During the National Book Festival in April 1987, there was a debate in Vancouver between the forces of Tanks and the forces of the Canada Council: Bill and I defending our objections, and Andreas Schroeder and David Godfrey defending subsidy. The debate was chaired by Eleanor Wachtel. The question was, Have government subsidies benefited Canadian literature?

Bill had commissioned a striking poster from Carol Moiseiwitsch and these were widely displayed in Vancouver. The debate took place on a Monday evening and on the preceding Saturday in the *Globe and Mail* William French announced that there was no point in going since all the tickets were sold out. There were no tickets as the event was free of charge. Despite this confusion, about 150 people turned up and the evening was filmed by the local community TV channel.

Everyone seemed mildly hysterical and paranoid. More heat than light was shed; books were brandished; statistics bandied about. A local crazy had to be escorted out in full rant denouncing logging, the persecution of beluga whales, and harmful rays emitted by the CBC. Other hecklers took his place.

There are over 350 wonderful presses in this country! shouted one.

Shame! cried another. *Shame!*

Eleanor Wachtel tried to impose order.

The level of debate was infantile. David Godfrey held up a book of poems by Dorothy Livesay and demanded to know whether she was a worthy poet. It was conceded that she had *some* value. Then, declared Godfrey, the argument was won as the book in question, this very book, had been published by a subsidized small press. *His* press. And so on. Bill Hoffer said suddenly that Dave Godfrey had no moral right to be speaking in this debate as he owned a company that wrote software for the Chinese military. Dave Godfrey threatened to sue Bill Hoffer if Hoffer ever repeated that remark. Hoffer repeated it.

It was a ridiculous evening. According to subsequent newspaper accounts the pro-subsidy forces were victorious; to us it seemed simply a cacophony.

Dave Godfrey behaved with concentrated viciousness and after the debate jostled his way out without speaking to anyone. I insisted on stopping him and shaking his hand; he snarled at me about the company I kept. I had not gone to Vancouver for a fight; I had gone there for what was to me an important intellectual discussion. The discussion didn't really take place; it's essential for Canada's future that it does.

It seems to me now, looking back, that the Great Vancouver Debate marked the beginning of an emotional disintegration in Bill. He wrote of that night: "I didn't do well at the debate, and John had to carry most of the weight. Everything had simply become too terrible to endure."

But he was later to write—and I think with some justice: "It was a peculiar event in many ways. But it happened, and that was the victory. For the first time the dreaded language of objection achieved enough legitimacy to require response."

Much of Bill's life was lived in a mess and an uproar. He was tall and almost emaciated and moved with awkward vigour. He looked rabbinical and not Reform either. His suits and flapping jackets were far from clean and his body odour was sometimes so fearsome that after his visits Myrna threw wide every window and bundled his sheets into the washing machine with dispatch. His control of his diabetes was intermittent and he was often soaked in diabetic and alcoholic sweats. He drank too much at home and was profligate in bars. He became infatuated easily, amours which always seemed to involve theatrical scenes with husbands or boyfriends and sudden international travel.

And Bill talked. Words poured out of him. His energy was exhausting. He was a complex and cranky man and essentially contentious by nature. Enemies abounded; plots against him were always afoot. His rhetoric could easily spiral into incoherence. Even his friends and those who agreed with his basic ideas could sometimes be left wondering if they were in the company of a genius or a madman.

I remember him sitting in our kitchen launching some complicated flight, words tumbling out of him, when Myrna suddenly interrupted. She said, "But that doesn't follow. That doesn't make sense."

He turned upon her and snapped, "There is nothing wrong with the transmission. Check the set."

When he was drinking in the afternoons he often conducted his business from a strip joint near his Gastown shop called, I seem to remember, No. 5. It was loud and smelled like a lion's cage that had been hastily sluiced out with Old Dutch. I remember once listening to Bill's explication of whatever he was explicating that day while alleged sisters on the stage inside a glass-sided shower soaped each other with interminable suds. He seemed known to most of the customers and was addressed by waiters and bouncers as "Professor."

All was not earnest lecture or exhortation, however. Bill was often bubbling with wit and stratagems, provocations he found amusing. An event. A Party. A Black-Tie Party. A Social Event. *The* Black-Tie Social Event of the Vancouver Season. On and on it swelled in his mind.

He'd hold a Book Burning!

In the parking lot beside his store he'd have waiters circulating with champagne while from the stock in the warehouse he'd burn . . . whatever was that day's rage and contempt, all the bill bissett books, all grOnk pamphlets, all bpNichol's endless verbiage, all productions of blewointment press, crates of Fred Cogswell's Fiddlehead Poetry Books . . .

> Nichol (B.P.) *Still*. Vancouver: Pulp Press, 1983. Original wrappers. Author's signed presentation to Bill Bissett, who has scrawled a number of notes relating to grant opportunities on the first and last leaves. Winner of the Three-Day Novel-Writing Contest. Steve Osborne and I made this contest up as a joke in 1976, never thinking that literature could fall so low as to take it seriously.

But this sketch of Bill leaves out of the picture that flamboyant, eccentric, slightly crazy as he may have been, he was at the same time probably the most gifted bookman Canada has ever seen. He had a bloodhound nose for books. From other bookstores, from Goodwills, from junk furniture stores, from dumpsters, Bill would conjure rarities.

I remember walking along Wellington Street in Ottawa with him and his sudden wheeling into a junk furniture store and unearthing from under a wind-up gramophone a July 1956 *Esquire* containing a Mavis Gallant story and two copies of *Chatelaine* dated March 1956 and July 1956 carrying two Alice Munro stories: "How Could I Do That?" (uncollected) and "Good-by Myra." Bill bought these for pennies and said to me outside, "I *could* give you these but I'm going to charge you $20 to teach you a lesson."

Bill's catalogues, or lists, as he modestly insisted on calling them, were an education in themselves but visits to the store and to the warehouse entirely rearranged one's understanding of such words as *scarce* or *rare* as one gazed, pop-eyed, on a dozen copies of John Newlove's *Grave Sirs* or on a stack of Gwendolyn MacEwen's *The Drunken Clock*. Or looked at the boxes in the basement which contained the entire remaindering of Mavis Gallant's *The Pegnitz Junction*.

In the early days of Oberon Press, Michael Macklem had a marketing arrangement with a small London publisher called Dobson. Oberon books in England were distributed under Dobson's imprint. Bill had the idea of going to see Dobson and cornering Oberon books whose print runs would have been tiny. This scheme fell through because Dobson was too lethargic to locate boxes and open them but it illustrates Bill's piratical gusto.

And then in the catalogues came the great discoveries . . . When Frederick Philip Grove was revealed as Felix Paul Greve, it was Bill who unearthed all the work in German, helped in this, in part, by Professor Dr. Walter Pache, then at Trier and subsequently at the University of Augsberg. It was Bill who was instrumental in revealing, through research in the University of Calgary archives, that Brian Moore had written four paperback thrillers under the names Michael Brian and Bernard Mara, all of them preceding his "first" book, *The Lonely Passion of Judith Hearne*.

Peter Howard of Serendipity Books in California has written of these and similar feats: "These acts no other Canadian bookseller could emulate."

When I was looking through the collection of papers and documents Bill and I had intended publishing as "The Tanks Diary" I came across a letter to Bill from John Newlove. It concerned buying a set of the Tanks books and the last few lines seem prescient now.

"I did see you at the Antiquarian Book Fair. I said hello to you. But you were fulminating and sailed on by like some rusty, derelict freighter careering madly towards the rocks."

Not long after the failure of the Tanks campaign Bill told me that as W. H. Auden had said of Yeats that Ireland had "hurt him into poetry" so he felt that Canada had hurt him into redefining himself. He said he felt Canada was too primitive to allow him to be the person he wanted to be. He closed the shop, shipped his books to Peter Howard in California, and moved to live in Moscow, where he learned Russian every day from a tutor and had visions of opening a store which would deal not in modern first editions but in the antiquarian books of Europe. In 1997 he developed cancer of the brain and returned to Victoria to die in his father's care.

Let me, sadly and affectionately, give him the last word.

Ringwood (Gwen Pharis) *The Courting of Marie Jenvrin.* Toronto: Samuel French (Canada) Limited, 1951. On the copyright page appears a brief plug by the publisher that ought to warm the hearts of our new nationalists.

"Printed in Canada on Canadian paper by Monetary Times Printing Co. of Canada, Ltd., Toronto, Canada."

Original printed wrappers. A bright copy, but the text is occasionally marked in pen.

LEGO

DOUBT should always nag the anthologist. It is a necessary anxiety. Surely posterity . . . This is one of my horrors. One of the 4 a.m. rehearsals when sleep won't come. Is it possible—surely not?—that posterity might view me much as I view such silly old buggers as Sir Arthur Quiller-Couch, A. L. Rowse, and Arthur Bryant?

It is entirely possible.

But, for me, the die is cast.

How, then, do I set about making choices?

In the year I was born, 1938, Cyril Connolly published a book about literary style called *Enemies of Promise*. When I read this book years later it changed and deepened my understanding of literature to such an extent that I can say absolutely seriously that the book changed my life. Connolly's career as writer, reviewer, editor, publisher, book collector, cultural impresario, and *arbiter elegantiae* also suggested to me the possibility of a literary life lived passionately. Here from the book's opening chapter is the passage which had such a profound impact on me so many years ago:

What kills a literary reputation is inflation. The advertising, publicity and enthusiasm which a book generates—in a word its success—imply a reaction against it. The element of inflation in a writer's success, the extent to which it has been forced, is something that has to be written off. One can fool the public about a book but the public will store up resentment in proportion to its folly. The public can be fooled deliberately by advertising and publicity or it can be fooled by accident, by the writer fooling himself. If we look at the boom pages of the Sunday papers we can see the fooling of the public going on, inflation at work. A word like genius is used so many times that eventually the sentence "Jenkins has genius. *Cauliflower Ear* is immense!" becomes true because he has as much genius and is as immense as are the other writers who have been praised there. It is the words that suffer for in the inflation they have lost their meaning. The public at first suffers too but in the end it ceases to care and so new words have to be dragged out of retirement and forced to suggest merit. Often the public is taken in by a book because, although bad, it is topical, its up-to-dateness passes as originality, its ideas seem important because they are "in the air." *The Bridge of San Luis Rey*, *Dusty Answer*, *Decline and Fall*, *Brave New World*, *The Postman Always Rings Twice*, *The Fountain*, *Good-bye Mr. Chips* are examples of books which had a success quite out of proportion to their undoubted merit and which now reacts unfavourably on their authors, because the overexcitable public who read those books have been fooled. None of the authors expected their books to become best-sellers but, without knowing it, they had hit upon the contemporary chemical combination of illusion with disillusion which makes books sell.

But it is also possible to write a good book and for it to be imitated and for those imitations to have more success than the original so that when the vogue which they have created and surfeited is past, they drag the good book down with them. This is what happened to Hemingway who made certain pointillist discoveries in style which have led almost to his undoing. So much depends on style, this factor of which we are growing more and more suspicious, that although the tendency of criticism is to explain a writer either in terms of his sexual experience or his economic background, I still believe his technique remains the soundest base for a diagnosis, that it should be possible to learn as much about an author's income and sex-life from one paragraph of his writing as from his cheque stubs and his love-letters and that one should also be able to learn how well he writes, and who are his influences. Critics who ignore style are liable to lump good and bad writers together in support of pre-conceived theories.

An expert should be able to tell a carpet by one skein of it; a vintage by rinsing a glassful round his mouth. Applied to prose there is one advantage attached to this method—a passage taken from its context is isolated from the rest of a book, and cannot depend on the goodwill which the author has cleverly established with his reader. This is important, for in all the books which become best-sellers and then flop, this salesmanship exists. The author has fooled the reader by winning him over at the beginning, and so establishing a favourable atmosphere for putting across his inferior article—for making him accept false sentiment, bad writing, or unreal situations. To write a best-seller is to set oneself a problem in seduction. A book of this kind is a confidence trick. The reader is given a cigar and a glass of brandy and asked to put his feet up and listen. The author then tells him the tale. The most favourable atmosphere is a stall at a theatre, and consequently of all things which enjoy contemporary success that which obtains it with least merit is the average play.

One sentence from these paragraphs was the Damascus Road experience for me.

"An expert should be able to tell a carpet by one skein of it; a vintage by rinsing a glassful round his mouth."

This sentence changed the way I thought and felt about prose. As the sentence grew in my mind, the implications and ramifications continued to amaze me. The sentence forced me first of all to stop thinking about plot or context. It forced me to think about verbs and nouns, adjectives and adverbs, the nature and level of diction, the placement of words, the rhythms of sentences, the functions of punctuation. In brief, it forced me to consider writing as *technical performance*, as rhetoric organized to achieve certain emotional effects.

The sentence also implies, of course, that the entire story, the entire book, must be written with an intensity that will live up to and survive the sort of scrutiny given to the one paragraph. Connolly is implying a prose written with the deliberation usually given to poetry.

The sentence further implies that form and content are indivisible, that the *way* something is being said *is* what is being said.

The sentence also suggests that a piece of writing should be a refined pleasure—as is wine, as are the old Persian carpets made before the introduction of aniline dyes. This in turn implies that good prose is not something we read through for comprehension, for information, as a medium for getting us from A to B. Connolly suggests we *taste* the prose, fondle it, explore and experience it. What a radical way of looking at prose this is! For when we have explored it, we have not finished with it; we cannot then dismiss it as "understood." We can come back to it again and again as we do with paintings or music. "Understanding" in the utilitarian high-school or university sense is a barrier to understanding. If we have read properly, we have not "understood" the prose—an intellectual activity—rather, we have *experienced* the prose by entering into a relationship with it. Prose which is brilliantly performed offers inexhaustible pleasures.

So much conventional writing is close to being automatic writing. Without formal innovation—which is a breaking through crusted convention to emotion and significance—writing becomes portly and arteriosclerotic. It is salutary for a young writer to watch the comfortably middlebrow, authors once internationally acclaimed, parading to oblivion . . .

When I look back down the vista of books that have come and gone, when I idly pick up this one or that to read a paragraph or two—as I happened to glance last week at John Buchan's *The House of the Four Winds* and at J. B. Priestley's
The Good Companions—I'm always struck now by the flabby, imprecise language, by the sheer padding and hackery, by the use of words and phrases as mere verbal counters which, shuffled together, clack out conventional sentences.

Here, for example, is the first paragraph of the first chapter of *The House of the Four Winds*. I have italicized the clichés, the verbal counters, and the deliberately archaic usages which stand for "rusticity."

> The inn at Kremisch, the Stag with the Two Heads, has an upper room *so bowed with age* that it *leans drunkenly* over the village street. It is a bare place, which must be chilly in winter, for the old *casement* has many chinks in it, and the china stove does not look efficient, and the *rough beechen table*, marked by many beer mugs, and the seats of beechwood and hide *are scarcely luxurious*. But on this summer night to one who had been tramping all day on roads deep in white dust under *a merciless sun*, it seemed a *haven of ease*. Jaikie had eaten *an admirable supper* on a corner of the table, a supper of cold ham, an

> omelet, hot toasted rye-cakes and *a seductive cheese.* He had drunk wine tapped from a barrel and *cold as water from a mountain spring*, and had concluded with coffee and cream in a blue cup as large as a basin. Now he could light his pipe and watch the green dusk deepen behind the onion spire of the village church.

This was never writing; it is the equivalent with words of joining together bits of Lego.

Innovative shapes must be forged in language which is precise and quick to the touch. Touching that language must be like touching skin or an animal's pelt. Nothing else will do; nothing else will last. This is not to say that the writing must be "poetic" or fancy in any way; rather, it must be precise, concentrated, and above all, appropriate.

Let us look at a more contentious example.

Rohinton Mistry's first book of stories, *Tales from Firozsha Baag*, was reviewed by Michael Darling in *The Macmillan Anthology (1)*. He wrote in part:

> Mistry is not deceived that story-writing is an academic game of narrative hide-and-seek; he has a moral vision and a desire to impart it through carefully structured language. The fact that the language often fails him does not negate the sincerity of the attempt . . .
>
> Mistry's weakness is his diction, which occasionally seems to evoke the legacy of the Raj; phrases like "high dudgeon," "unbeknownst to," and "cherubic features" don't really fit the contexts into which they're placed. Also, the Indian words are often strung together in what seems like an unnecessary striving for "local colour": "*Bawaji* got *paan pichkari* right on his white *dugli* . . ." A little of this goes a long way, which Mistry seems to be aware of, as by the end of the book the non-English words are few and far between.

Darling has, as usual, put his finger exactly on the problem. Consider the following quotations:

> The first light of morning barely illumined the sky as Gustad Noble faced eastward to offer his orisons to Ahura Mazda. The hour was approaching six, and up in the compound's solitary tree the sparrows began to call.

and

> Erie had been listening all that week to thaw, a trickle of melt tickling her inner ear, the sound of water dripping off the eaves, *drip* into that handful of bare stones by the corner of the barn, *drop* off the branches of the forsythia out front.

The first quotation is the opening sentences of Rohinton Mistry's *Such a Long Journey*, the second the opening of Terry Griggs's "Man with the Axe."

It is immediately obvious that the writers approach language in an entirely different spirit. Terry Griggs is specific, concentrated, *wired*, one might say, alive to every nuance. Listen to the pretty run of *i*-sounds in "a trickle of melt tickling her inner ear." One can hear the sounds and see the nest of gleaming pebbles the drips have excavated.

The problem with Mistry's opening sentences is more complicated than the use of such almost archaic words as *illumined* and *orisons*. The very rhythms of the sentences are flat and conventional and such constructions as "the first light of morning" and "barely illumined the sky" are little more than formulas, counters shuffled into place.

The use of the word *orisons* is injudicious. *Orisons* is not as neutral as *prayers* because it suggests prayers within the Christian tradition, suggests Catholic Europe. The only uses of the word I can remember in literature are in Wilfred Owen's

"Dulce et Decorum Est" and Hamlet to Ophelia: "Nymph, in thy orisons/Be all my sins remembered." The scene is traditionally played with Ophelia reading from a missal.

The use of the word *call* is inappropriate, *call* being associated with the distinctive cry of larger birds, rooks, say, or loons. Sparrows chirp. Or at least do something with an *i* in it.

Consider now the following paragraph from *Such a Long Journey*:

> Besides, Crawford Market was a place he despised at the best of times. Unlike his father before him, who used to relish the trip and looked on it as a challenge: to venture boldly into the den of scoundrels, as he called it; then to badger and bargain with the shopkeepers, tease and mock them, their produce, their habits, but always preserving the correct tone that trod the narrow line between badinage and belligerence; and finally, to emerge unscathed and triumphant, banner held high, having got the better of the rogues. Unlike his father, who enjoyed this game, Gustad felt intimidated by Crawford Market.

While there is probably an intention to suggest something of the father's zest and vocabulary in this paragraph, we should not overlook the formulaic writing. Here now is the same paragraph with phrases and clauses which are formulas or close to it italicized and with the particularly British stylistic tic of pairing words indicated with brackets.

> Besides, Crawford Market was a place he despised *at the best of times*. Unlike *his father before him*, who used to relish the trip and *looked on it as a challenge*: *to venture boldly* into the *den of scoundrels*, as he called it: then to (badger and bargain) with the shopkeepers, (tease and mock) them, their produce, their habits, *but always preserving the correct tone that trod the narrow line* between

> (badinage and belligerence); and finally, *to emerge (unscathed* and triumphant), *banner held high, having got the better of the rogues*. Unlike his father, who enjoyed this game, Gustad felt intimidated by Crawford Market.

I wish that this were a caricature of the father, deliberately employing a string of formulas and deliberately employing a faded diction to capture him, but what I suspect is Lego.

Choosing stories, then, and editing.

I am likely to enter a story in an arbitrary manner. I might read the first sentence first but am just as likely to read a paragraph at random. All that concerns me is to get a feel for the quality of the language—the Connolly prescription. When I start reading, I'm waiting for the writing to plug me into its current. I am more excited by a single spark of language than I am by reams of solid competence. A hash of a story, a veritable dog's dinner, can interest me more than quires of competence if it's touched by the fire of language.

I was reading a story the other day by a beginning writer, perhaps the second story she has published. Within four sentences I knew she was a writer I wanted to read and keep an eye on.

> They call it a state of emergency. White dervishes scour Stephen-ville, the blue arm of the plough impotently slashes through the snow. In St. John's where my mother is, the wires are frozen with sleet and the electricity is out. She's in the plaid chair, I know, one emergency candle and a flashing drink of rye.

The spark?

Well, yes, of course—*flashing*.

A LONG SENTENCE: THE OTTAWA YEARS

WHILE TRUDGING along Bank Street in December one year in solidly frozen snow that would be there until April I heard rapping on a window and glanced up to see Richard Simmins sitting at a café table. I joined him for a coffee and we sat talking about books and writing. Richard, now dead too early, was important in what cultural life Ottawa affords.

His first career was as a curator and he was responsible, among much else, for mounting the Regina Five exhibition at the National Gallery of Canada in 1961 and then sending the show on its travels, giving many Canadians their first glimpse of abstract painting. One of the Regina Five was Ronald Bloore, a painter of great elegance and austerity. I regret to this day not buying a painting of Bloore's called *Byzantine Doors*, a white-on-white painting from his *Byzantine Light* series, a painting I still sometimes see as I'm drifting off to sleep.

Richard's success in his curatorial career was accompanied, however, by increasingly self-destructive drinking which caused him to crash, losing his job and his marriage. Later he joined Alcoholics Anonymous and reconstituted himself as a bookseller. His shops, first on Bank, subsequently on

Sparks, and finally on Dalhousie, were social centres for young writers, painters, and musicians. Richard had a great interest in my collecting and took pleasure in finding for me stubborn volumes.

The teaching aspect of bookselling, the fathering and fostering, has been to an extent destroyed by the sale of books on the Internet. As Janet Inksetter of Annex Books in Toronto said to me recently, "I didn't enter into this way of life to spend my days sitting in front of a screen."

I greatly enjoyed Richard and always dropped into his store to chat, to buy books, to listen to his elegant anecdotes. If he'd accumulated a clutch of my books, he'd say, "Would you mind signing these for stock?" And I used to write in all of them *For Al Stock—with best wishes* . . .

Richard, perhaps because of his curatorial past, was keenly interested in archives and urged me to start keeping a diary. He used to say, "Although you can't think this yet, can't see yourself in that way, you're already a figure of historical importance. I can see that. Others can already see that. So what you must do is archive yourself."

I pass on this advice to writers younger than myself with whom I work. Most feel the attitude pretentious or immodest. I counter with an anecdote about sitting on a session of the National Archival Appraisal Board under the chairmanship of David Russell, ex-archivist for the Province of Ontario. We were evaluating that day the papers of John McCrae, author of "In Flanders Fields."

David, a man of vast erudition and geniality, said of the papers that there was a diary McCrae had kept (probably illegally) in the trenches and eight hundred letters, starting with letters McCrae had written at the age of seven and ending with letters written from the front in 1915. David said that in his many years of experience the mere existence of eight hundred letters was such a rare occurrence that he had few other instances against which to compare and measure.

My younger writer friends—especially those editing magazines—must be accumulating correspondence which would put the McCrae numbers in the shade. It's a pity to think that false modesty on the part of some is squandering the wholeness of our literary past.

I was persuaded by Richard's arguments and started keeping a diary; currently I'm writing in volume 33.

One of Richard's typically wry anecdotes was about receiving a phone call from a woman with books to sell. She lived some way out in the country and Richard probed a bit in order to decide if the trip was worth his while.

What *sort* of books were they? Textbooks? *National Geographic* magazines? *Readers' Digest* Condensed Books? No, no, none of them. No, just books. All kinds. Then the clinching question.

"How many," asked Richard, "would you say there are?"

A long considering silence.

"Oh," said the woman, "about a cord."

When we'd finished talking books that December morning we sat in companionable silence watching the plodpast of the scabbed and skanky panhandlers and derelicts making their way from Big Buds (Where Your Dollar Makes More Cents) to Tim Hortons Donuts. I was fidgeting with packets of Sweet'n'Low. It was too cold to snow. The coloured lights in the window of Radio Shack looked almost alluring.

"Ottawa, John," suddenly intoned Richard. "Ottawa lacks magic."

Trips to hospitals, dentists, grocery shopping, the cinema in Kingston, the ferrying of visitors to and from Brockville railway station—after five years Myrna felt she was turning into a chauffeur. She wanted to move back to a city where the children could walk to activities or take buses. She was also becoming bored with Delta. I, of course, retreated every day to write and edit, leaving her long days to fill after the children had clambered into the school bus.

I had never learned to drive. In England for years after the war cars were not readily available. My father as a clergyman was allowed to own one for his pastoral visiting but the thought of letting a boy near it would never have entered his mind. A girlfriend at Bristol tried to teach me. There was but one lesson. The whole business I knew to be utterly beyond me. I drove into the back of a parked car. Myrna *claims* that I am so oblivious to cars that when someone asked what make of car we had I said, "It's grey."

We decided that we were pretty much forced to remain in Ontario. Montreal would have been our first choice. Myrna was born there and spoke French from an early age. I had lived there for many years and thought it Canada's most civilized city. But we did not want to place Danny and Rangidam in a situation where they would have to learn yet another language when their grip on English was uncertain. And Myrna was simmering with rage that the Parti Québécois had defined her as an allophone. PQ linguistic mumbo jumbo meaning that she wasn't *pure laine* and wasn't welcome.

Toronto was impossible for both of us. Myrna has that old Montreal contempt for the place which stems from the days when Toronto was white-sliced and irredeemably hick. For me Toronto was impossible because it offered too many distractions, jazz, other writers, painters, bookstores. I had a need to be out of the swim.

We pondered Kingston. I liked Sydenham Ward with its stylish limestone houses, felt refreshed by their age. But the rest of Kingston was slummy and then degenerated further into strips and malls. We also felt dubious about a city which lived on institutions—a university, the army, hospitals, prisons.

"Imagine the parties!" said Myrna.

And so we began to think about Ottawa. I had been to Ottawa in the winter of 1962 and found it frozenly hideous; it put me in mind of John Betjeman's aesthetic plea, "Come, friendly bombs, and rain on Slough!"

We made several forays in 1981 and on one of these found ourselves driving along the edge of a small park. I saw a For Sale sign outside a reasonably elegant three-storey Victorian house and said, "That's the one for us!" We secured an appointment to look inside and the inside was very elegant indeed, having been refurbished by its owner whose profession was building and restoration.

Myrna said that one couldn't just . . . and forced us to look at a dreary succession of doomed structures. We returned to that first house and bought it, though Myrna was aghast at the price and predicted a future, not distant either, of ruin and penury. We sold the farm and fields in Delta, Myrna's mother, Annie Mendelson, contributed generously, and I sold my manuscripts and correspondence to the Special Collections at the University of Calgary and contributed my mite.

With three children in the house we had to decide how we were to live. I've found that most memoirs skate rather airily over such matters:

> . . . so we gathered the children and took ship the next week for Istanbul . . .

Only people like actors and painters who live desperately seem to remember early struggles. Montreal lives for me in memories of Brunswick sardines and day-old kaiser rolls marked down at Cantor's Bakery. Annabel Lyon told me recently that she does like real food but eats tofu "for economic reasons."

I was brought up to believe that in marriages men supported women. I felt that any other arrangement was unmanly. How, then, Myrna wanted to know, was I going to proceed?

We could scarcely rely on grants. We could scarcely uproot three children every year as I travelled to take up writer-in-residence posts in the Yukon or Winnipeg. Royalties on fiction would barely buy the children shoes. Getting a job teaching would stop me from writing.

Myrna proposed that I carried on doing what I did best, contributing where I could, while she would get a job to support us. After much angst and travail we fell into the pattern she proposed. Myrna proposed this because it was a practical solution to a problem but she also believes passionately in the importance of literature and has a luminous spirit. Everything I've been able to achieve in literary life is her gift to me—and to writing in Canada in general—and I am grateful to her daily.

John Mills, in biblical mode, describes such an arrangement as living "in the sweat of one's frau," referring to God's words to Adam on expelling him from Eden, "In the sweat of thy face shalt thou eat bread."

The Ottawa years stretched ahead. How right Richard Simmins was when he said Ottawa lacked magic. It is clean. It is green. It is the country's capital and contains such national institutions as the Archives, the hideous, ever-leaking National Library, and the National Gallery, yet it remains little more than a small Victorian town, the integrity of its architecture desecrated by brutal highrises and apartment buildings. The residents seem blind to this vandalism and to the telephone poles that line the streets and the wires festooned above; I almost reeled one day when Councillor Diane Holmes said to me that she thought Elgin Street one of the most beautiful streets in the world. Elgin Street! One of Ottawa's few virtues for me is that while I'm locked away for hours every day I know I'm not missing a thing. I regard the place as a backwater backdrop.

It is difficult for an autobiographer to make writing sound interesting. There is only so much any reader can take of "so the next day he again got up at 6 a.m., shovelled in the cornflakes, and then sat at his desk for another seven hours writing with his Pilot Fineliner on yellow pads of ruled paper." I'm going to let the reader assume that this is precisely what happened most days and I'll talk of other things.

Dull as Ottawa was our personal lives were far from dull and we were soon to be placed under almost unbearable stress. Rangidam, free of the fear of attack by monkeys, began to behave with increasing abandon. She wandered off and offered herself up to strangers for adoption. She stole bicycles. She shoplifted. She stole other children's lunches. She stole and sold her older brother's clothes. She stole money from the parents of playmates, on one occasion plundering a single father's considerable savings towards Christmas. She turned into an implacable liar and showed no remorse.

Myrna and I were endlessly worried about her but all the lies and larceny were but the hors d'oeuvres. As puberty set in she started claiming that men had exposed themselves or attacked her in parking lots, in a cinema, in a public park. The police were a little puzzled because the people she described were so vividly distinguished—red hair and massive facial scars, for example—that they'd have been found or identified quickly. But weren't.

Then came a call from the police. Rangi had told other children at school that her brothers had raped her. Myrna and I knew that this was arrant nonsense, such nonsense, indeed, that before the arrival of the police Myrna laughed it off, saying that it was nice to think of *something* the three of them did together.

The police team arrived at the house with their carrying-case of articulated sex dolls and began an interrogation of the children—a decidedly uncomical evening. They concluded eventually that the story was not true.

These troubles did not end and we became adept at dealing with social workers and Children's Aid, though Myrna learned the language far more quickly than I did. I would argue and remonstrate and achieve nothing; Myrna, smarter than I, simply adopted a dopey expression and said, "I don't think I'm comfortable with that."

"Comfortable!"

Rangidam remained incorrigible and was eventually sent by Children's Aid to a group home which attempted to treat her. The two rather strange ladies who ran the home tried to inculcate discipline, restraint, and affection by making each child responsible for the care of a pet. In Rangi's case no results were discernible. Long before this—utterly desperate—I had had her examined by a psychologist who had concluded that she had been so badly damaged in her years in India that she was simply not capable of many ordinary human emotions.

All this was grindingly sad and the grief did not subside for years. One night three or four years after these events we received a call from the Major Crimes Squad in Vancouver asking if we had a daughter of East Indian descent. Could we fax a photo? They had a corpse.

The corpse turned out not to be Rangidam and she continued to wander lost in a world of petty crime, prostitution, drug-dealing and addiction, a world she inhabits still.

But life had to go on. Otherwise we'd all have been driven broodingly mad. Between 1981 and 1990 I wrote and edited more than twenty books. The first book I wrote in the new house was *Kicking Against the Pricks*, a collection of essays about literary life in Canada. This book was important not for its sales or popularity but because it cemented my reputation amongst media hacks as being a "curmudgeon" or a "gadfly," epithets bestowed on anyone who disagrees with ignorant, tasteless mainstream opinions about literature in Canada. The book also seemed to render me *persona non grata* with universities coast to coast.

I felt increasingly isolated in a critical sense. The adulation of Robertson Davies can serve as a good example. I reviewed his relentlessly bad novel *The Rebel Angels* in 1981, pointing out that *all* the characters, young, old, male, and female, spoke in exactly the same voice. No one else seemed to consider this a flaw. A bleating chorus sounded Davies's genius. Poor benighted Beverley Slopen, then a book columnist for the *Toronto Star*, chided my review for being "churlish," a comment which suggests the gooey depths of media sycophancy. Much was made by the Canadian media of the fact that Anthony Burgess admired Davies; not one among them ever considered the possibility that Burgess as a novelist was possibly worse than Davies.

(Though I remain an admirer of Burgess's *Inside Mr. Enderby*, one of his few books not hobbled by intellect.)

Years later I wrote of Davies: "Like the yokels at a medicine show the audience was awed by the gravity of mien, the silver splendour of the beard, the Edwardian knickerbockers.

"This *had* to be art."

Of course, to describe someone as a curmudgeon or a gadfly is dismissive and a way of rejecting the criticism without addressing it. I felt driven to writing and editing critical work because Canadian literary judgements are usually fatuous. *The Bumper Book, Carry On Bumping, What Is a Canadian Literature?* and *Volleys* all appeared during the eighties, unleashed into a world where David Staines, the buffoonish dean of arts at the University of Ottawa and general editor of the New Canadian Library series, could state in print that Morley Callaghan was a better writer than Ernest Hemingway, a world which institutes its awards and prizes in the names of mediocre writers like Marian Engel and Matt Cohen, a world where increasingly only the winners of prizes are read.

In 1986 Macmillan published *Adult Entertainment*. It contains two novellas, "Polly Ongle" and "Travelling Northward," and three short stories. I felt that I had been writing at full stretch and remain pleased with this book. Reviews were generally good. The book was shortlisted for the Governor General's Award, though only because Norman Levine who was on the jury made himself awkward on its behalf; the other jurors were, he said, entirely dismissive.

I had at this time acquired David Colbert as an agent. David was aggressive, abrasive, rude, and arrogant which as long as I wasn't on the receiving end I considered excellent traits in an agent. He managed to place *Adult Entertainment* with St. Martin's Press in New York. The book was well received in the *Los Angeles Times* and the *Washington Post* and was selected by the *New York Times Book Review* as one of the Notable Books of the Year.

However, the editor I was dealing with at St. Martin's left to join another press about three weeks after the book came out. It was explained to me that in large houses in the States books are sponsored and nurtured by their editors. Without an editor to promote it a book simply withers on the vine. This is precisely what happened to *Adult Entertainment*. Despite being selected as a Notable Book it was remaindered within a year.

The novella "Travelling Northward" will, I hope, be the title novella in a new book of pieces about its protagonist Robert Forde. Forde is a novelist and quite a few people have assumed he's an alter ego. There's a germ of truth in that but these Forde stories are not autobiographical in the usual sense. I've been thinking about the shape of this book for years now and feel pleasantly alarmed that its constituent pieces are so untraditional. Several are concerned with the nature of the rupture that took place in our civilization after about 1950. Forde is puzzled. Something happened and he doesn't know what it was. But it's decidedly nothing good. The stories are composed through archipelagoes, as it were, of brooding imagery. The piece I'm working on now, "Ceazer Salad," is a meditation recording a walk up Elgin Street to the Parliament Buildings. *Travelling Northward* is a book which is both daunting and alluring, daunting because it is unlike anything I've ever attempted before and alluring for exactly the same reason.

During these years that I was writing and editing books I was also collecting them. I was working on press collections—Contact, Oberon, and Anansi—and on the idea that had come to me in Bernard Halliday's musty house in Leicester so many years earlier. Building a collection as opposed to simply haphazardly acquiring books is time-consuming; it is rather like conducting a ceaseless conversation. One is incessantly looking at books in stores, writing letters, talking to dealers, reading catalogues, attending book fairs, learning points and prices, overseeing standing orders, reading reviews, making the rounds—a buzz as of bees hangs over the whole enterprise.

I was buying books locally from Rhys Knott, Patrick McGahern, and David Dorken and from the Toronto dealers Janet Inksetter, David Mason, Steven Temple, Richard Shuh and Linda Woolley, Nelson Ball, and Nicky Drumbolis. I was also buying books from Ken Lopez in Massachusetts and from dealers in New Jersey and Boston. In England I was buying books from Dalian Books, Ulysses Book Store, David Rees, and Ian McKelvie, among others.

I bought Alice Munro translations from Germany, Finland, Sweden, France, Holland, Spain, and Denmark and chased down her advance proofs and editions in England and the States. When you increase this sort of effort to twelve authors it becomes something of a chore.

Last year Myrna and I and my daughter-in-law Kate Fildes and her mother, Isabel, finished a mammoth cataloguing of all this material which we entitled rather grandiosely, *The Short Story in Canada: Books from the Library of John and Myrna Metcalf*. We catalogued 5,192 items. The Rare Books and Special Collections Division of McGill University Libraries has expressed interest in acquiring the collection.

It was also during the early eighties that live jazz came back into my life. The Château Laurier had a "pub" in its inner depths called the Cock and Lion and some entirely misguided manager decided on a jazz policy for the hotel. This policy held for two years or more. I shudder to think how much money they must have lost. On some nights there were as few as six people in the bar, on other nights the room bulged with noisy mobs from conventions. Every week a new band took the stage, playing louder and louder to drown out the braying of conventioneering proctologists.

I remember an ancient Bud Freeman steadying himself against the side of the piano, giving a slight bow, and introducing himself by saying, "I'm very glad to be here tonight. At my age I'm glad to be anywhere." I remember taking Laurel Massé out for lunch, a brilliant bouncy singer from Chicago who used to sing with the Manhattan Transfer before jazz claimed her utterly. Mose Allison singing "Parchman Farm." Scott Hamilton and Warren Vaché, Chet Baker, Canadian friends P. J. Perry from Winnipeg and Dave Turner from Montreal. Zoot Sims sitting on a kitchen chair playing with a breathy, lyric intensity; we didn't know then that he was dying of cancer. The list of great musicians went on and on and late nights again took their toll.

Zoot Sims—and this anecdote catches the flavour of the man—was once on a CBC show with Oscar Peterson and Oscar pompously said, "Tell me, Zoot. What is the future of the saxophone?" Zoot studied his battered old horn and said, "Well, I'm thinking of having it replated."

After the first set one night I bought a drink for and was chatting with Robert Rodney Chudnick, better known as Red Rodney, Charlie Parker's trumpet player. He joined Parker in 1949 and stayed with the band until 1952; he told me that when they were travelling he was always ordered to carry Parker's suitcase. He also talked about his heroin addiction, an addiction he'd sought so that he too by "crossing over the line" might play with Parker's endless invention.

I remember thinking at the time: I am talking to a man who played with Bird. As with many things in my life I couldn't get over how strange it was, strange that a little boy who'd grown up using the Elizabethan *thee* and *thou* in a stronghold of clog-wearing primitive Methodists in Yorkshire should be drinking Scotch in what my scholarly brother still refers to as the "New World" with a pioneer bop trumpet player.

Quite unlike life in the manse.

The writing life is necessarily solitary and needs a firm discipline. The occasional day spent working with other people or simply in conversation comes as a treat in itself. I always look forward to days at the Archives evaluating literary material for tax credit. There is something pleasantly collegial about working with David Russell and, say, Peter Harcourt and John Moldenhaur.

There is also the coarse, snoopy pleasure of reading people's letters and diaries. It is a condition of this kind of work, though, that one's lips have to remain sealed, which is a pity because some of the gossip is of high grade. The huge archive of the Colbert Agency was an eye-popper as we studied the royalty statements of about half the writers in Canada. We were all fascinated by the chatty archive of John "Buffy" Glassco, author of *Memoirs of Montparnasse*, and author also of *Contes en Crinoline*, *Fetish Girl*, *The English Governess*, and *The Temple of Pederasty*. His remarks concerning Margaret Atwood were of peculiar interest.

Any appraisal is, in fact, something of a fiction. We collude in saying that ten boxes of paper are "worth," say, $40,000. William Hoffer wrote in his essay "Cheap Sons of Bitches: Memoirs of the Book Trade":

> As is the case in so many areas of Canadian cultural life, there is no genuine market for most Canadian literature. As a member of the National Archival Appraisal Board, I

> am constantly forced to consider the "technical" value of collections of manuscripts, while at the same time fully aware that were the material to be auctioned, it would bring nothing. Similarly, the pricing of Canadian first editions has been somewhat technical. Both booksellers and book buyers have eventually "assigned" value to particular books.

It was this hollowness at the centre, this central lie, that drove us to the Tanks campaign.

By 1993 Myrna had had enough of the civil service. The lively people she had worked for earlier, like Pierre de Blois, had left, and people with little, correct minds had risen to positions of power. Poor John Newlove whom they'd earlier been able to protect was now nagged and threatened by a senior manager, exquisitely dim in the manner of CNN's Connie Chung, for such infractions—despite John's explanation of its etymology—as permitting the use of the word *niggardly*. Such was the atmosphere Myrna fled.

Our son Ron had finished high school and had turned his hand to a variety of jobs, settling on the restaurant business and becoming the general manager of Dunn's Famous Smoked Meat restaurant in the Ottawa market. After some time, the owner, Stanley Devine, sent him to Toronto to open a branch of Dunn's on Adelaide Street. He oversaw this with great success and we were very proud of him. After a period of illness in Toronto he returned to Ottawa intent on opening his own restaurant. Myrna and he went into partnership and on November 11, 1993, opened the Elgin Street Diner. Our younger son, Dan, works there as well.

Myrna said that selling hamburgers was *intellectually* more interesting than working in the public service.

The restaurant is open twenty-four hours a day, 365 days a year. Breakfast is served twenty-four hours a day. The restaurant employs thirty-five staff. The food is simple "diner food," club sandwiches, burgers, fries, milkshakes, but is of high quality. The poutine has been voted the best in Ottawa and has been discussed by poutine lovers on the CBC; I have *seen* this dish on numerous occasions, but nothing could tempt me.

During the daytime the Elgin Street Diner, under Myrna's control, or under Ron's wife, Kate Fildes, is a family and neighbourhood hangout. Small children demand Myrna's presence and tell her long tales of their daily doings; she gives her most favoured ones dollops of ice cream. Old people, too, who are lonely and bored confide in her and she makes them feel valued and at home. Even the mildly crazed are cared for; one old lady asked daily for a table for six, the other five, her nonexistent family, being on their way. Myrna solved this by seating her at a table for one and saying, "They always take a little while to get here so I'll put you here for now and move you when they arrive." Myrna at work is a display of natural goodness.

The overnight shift is an entirely different scene and my son Ron rides herd on it. When the bars close, the Diner fills to capacity and pulsates with noisy, inebriated energy and stays that way for hours. People congregate there from all over the city. Over the years, the Diner has become an Ottawa institution.

The Diner's business has increased every year and some part of this is owing to the cheerful service of the staff and the patient talents of Jason Hughes, the Diner's chef.

Myrna, Ron, and Kate are kind enough to let me use the Diner as an unofficial "office" to entertain visiting authors. It is an office distinguished by walls hung with blow-ups of Sam Tata photographs, sadly the only permanent exhibition of his work in Canada.

On the rare days when driblets of money arrived in the mail I'd be tempted to go out for lunch and nearly always went to Chez Jean-Pierre on Somerset Street. The restaurant was owned and run by Jean-Pierre Muller from Strasbourg who had been the chef at the American embassy but had quit, saying he didn't want to spend the rest of his life making hamburgers. I knew whenever I went that Charles Ritchie would likely be there.

I'd read and enjoyed his diaries, particularly *Storm Signals*, which covers the war years in London. I'd first met him when having breakfast and a brood in a café on Elgin Street. I'd finished reading the *Globe and Mail* and as I passed his table said, "Mr. Ritchie. Would you care for the *Globe and Mail*?" He looked up in patrician horror and said, "Good *God*, no!"

We got to know each other quite well and he would sit drinking cognac in Chez Jean-Pierre spinning out anecdotes about Vincent and Alice Massey, Mike Pearson, Elizabeth Bowen, Mackenzie King whom he loathed, and John Diefenbaker, whom he'd loathed even more. He described Diefenbaker as "a congenital liar" and King as "neurasthenic." This increasingly gaunt and frail man who'd been ambassador to Washington and high commissioner to the United Kingdom told me that for twenty years he'd tried to write fiction but couldn't and that that failure had induced in him a permanent melancholy. Aesthetic standards, he used to say, are the only standards worth upholding. Life's most rewarding activities, he claimed, were gossip and sexual intercourse. Family life, he said, made him long for the brothel.

By about 3 p.m. he'd be close to legless, though faultlessly weaving stories still, and Jean-Pierre, who was fond of him, would drive him the short distance home to his apartment.

If I bumped into him on the street I'd always stop to chat and ask whether he was working on a new diary.

"Oh," he'd say, "one needs to scribble away at *something* if only to stop oneself getting into the sherry at 10 a.m."

He stopped me on Elgin Street one January morning in 1987 and told me that someone had given him a copy of *Adult Entertainment* for Christmas.

"What a long, bleak day I'd been expecting," he said, "the insufferable dreariness of festivity, but you saved Christmas for me. What *lovely* writing! I *chortled*."

Another of the pleasures of Ottawa was escaping from the place and during the eighties I travelled on Canada's behalf and on behalf of PEN International to academic conferences in Germany, France, Italy, and Yugoslavia.

I was sitting at my desk one morning when the phone rang. The caller identified himself as Guy Gervais of the cultural section of External Affairs.

"Would you," he said, "be prepared to go to teach about Canadian literature for two months in Milan?"

I said that I'd be very interested indeed but before I could give him a firm answer I'd have to consult my wife. I said I'd call him back. I called Myrna at Official Languages and she was agreeable and thought she could wangle some time off to join me for part of the stint.

"Mr. Gervais?"

"Yes."

"This is John Metcalf."

There was a silence.

"I'm returning your call of this morning. About Milan."

"Milan?"

"The teaching job. I spoke to my wife and she's agreeable."

The silence stretched and became uncomfortable.

"*Who* did you say that you are?"

"John Metcalf. We spoke earlier. This morning."

Another silence.

"*Oh, my God!*" he said. "I thought you were W. O. Mitchell."

This is how I ended up in Bologna, sent there as a consolation prize.

Mark Twain was once asked on his return from Europe what he had thought of Rome.

"Rome . . ." he said to his wife. "Was that the place we saw the yellow dog?"

I'm afraid I'm a very Twainish tourist and much of what follows is quirky, idiosyncratic, and unreliable. I do make efforts to see the Cathedral, the Gallery, and the Castle but my attention is more usually on the doorlatch than the door.

The first of these travels was in 1984 when I went to Munich and Grainau in Bavaria to give a paper entitled "The Curate's Egg." It was principally an illustration of Morley Callaghan's manifold ineptitudes and a celebration of Hemingway's felicities. As I left the lecture hall I heard a little martinet from Vienna, his Polish-sounding surname a concatenation of consonants, sputtering to his cronies, "He was lecturing us! He *dared* to lecture us!"

Following the lecture I was sitting having a drink with Professor Dr. Walter Pache of the University of Trier when we were approached by my Ottawa neighbour Richard Tait. He asked if he might join us and I said with a cold rage of which I hadn't thought myself capable, "I can't physically prevent you but I'd rather you didn't."

Richard lived four doors away from us. He was an anglophile diplomat very much in the Charles Ritchie mould. He had been Canada's ambassador to the European Union in Brussels and on his return to Ottawa had been placed in charge of cultural matters in External Affairs. He was bitter about this as Culture was a resounding demotion. He claimed the department was simply a dumping ground for the eccentric and mentally ill. He said one of his male employees came to work every day on a tricycle dressed in pieces of what looked like eighteenth-century French military uniform and put in eight solid hours of knitting.

Richard administered a fund used to buy paintings and prints for External Affairs and for Canadian embassies around the world. I interested him in Tony Calzetta's work. Richard had a good eye and owned some lovely bowls (hmmm!) which I always admired when visiting. Tony had left the Pollock Gallery and now was exhibiting at Mira Godard's, probably the most prestigious gallery in Toronto at that time.

I arranged to meet Richard in Toronto and I took him to meet Tony and look at the studio. He was enormously enthusiastic and told Tony that he'd buy some drawings and quite probably three canvases. He also promised Tony, *guaranteed* Tony, a show at the Canadian gallery in New York, the 49th Parallel, a state-owned gallery designed to spotlight Canadian art and artists.

Richard and I arranged to meet the next morning at Mira Godard's and look at Tony's new exhibition together. The canvases were large, vibrant, gorgeous in their colours. Myrna and I recently donated one of the paintings from this series, *Advance Machine Romance*, to the University of Toronto Art Centre.

While Richard and I were looking, I was chatting to him about the difficulties of Tony's life as an artist, the struggle to make ends meet, the wasting of his time in having to do drywall and construction work. I told him about an exhibition at Mira Godard's, a first exhibition for a young painter from New York, where the canvases were priced at $12,000, when a Canadian painter *at mid-career* would be charging $5,000 or less. I told him that Tony, because so original, found it difficult to get support, that he'd just been turned down *again* for a Canada Council grant.

"Turned down!" said Richard. "I wasn't told this. I can't..."

He waved his hand about the gallery.

"This is a professional judgement."

He shook his head.

"I'm sorry," he said, "I'm sorry but he's forfeited official credibility."

On the floor above Tony's show there was an exhibition on of watercolour landscapes by Dorothy Knowles of Saskatchewan. The paintings were competent, inoffensive, irrelevant. Richard, I learned subsequently, returned to the gallery and bought the entire show.

In Grainau I was still angry with this paltry man and over the years the incident has not receded. It has become emblematic for me of the danger of the state and its bureaucracy. Its relationship with art is usually capricious and always contagious.

Another German expedition took in Trier, Bonn, and Siegen in Westphalia. In Siegen I was teaching for Professor Dr. Christian Thomson, a most unlikely academic, jovial and with a vast appetite for visual arts. He decided that he would make a film of me to exercise his students and for fun resolved to shoot it in the large house, now a gallery and museum, where Sir Peter Paul Rubens was born in 1577. The "Sir" was conferred by Charles I of England in return for a decorated ceiling. The film is in my archives at the University of Calgary.

Christian took a party of us to the house when it was officially closed and proceeded to set up lights and tripods and all the paraphernalia of film-making. One of his students knocked over a heavy light stand which crashed into the wall near a painting. There were no audible alarms or sounds of sirens but within two minutes the grounds filled with uniformed police in jeeplike vehicles and armed with machine guns. Shouting from a window, Christian negotiated our surrender.

The following year Christian was guest editing an issue of a Swiss magazine which was to explore the scope of Canadian painting and sculpture. He came over to stay with us and I took him to Toronto to meet various painters and look round the galleries. He was quickly drawn to the work of Medrie McPhee. I had also arranged a lunch with John Bentley Mays who was then the *Globe and Mail* art critic. Mays was aggressive and awkward. The first thing he said was, "Why would anyone want to write about Canadian art? There is no Canadian art worth writing about."

He went on to say that he had never owned a painting, that he couldn't understand why anyone would want to. He was rude to the waiter. He was dismissive towards Christian. He was wearing a shiny grey suit, possibly silk, and on his lapel he sported a diamanté brooch which was a portrait of a crowned Queen Elizabeth II. I was faintly embarrassed.

In 1987 I represented Canada, along with Michael Ignatieff, at the PEN International Conference which was held at Lake Bled. In a novella entitled "Forde Abroad" I used this Slovenian excursion as a backdrop but instead of Bled called *my* resort Splad. In the real Bled is the summer palace of ex-King Peter; Cecil Parrott, who translated *The Good Soldier Svejk* for Penguin, was as a young man tutor to the two Crown Princes there. I often think of Svejk explaining to the Lieutenant that the cat died "after inadvertently eating a tin of shoe polish."

The conference was steamy with politics and there were endless hintings about separation and an independent Slovenian state. Wild Macedonians orated. Montenegrins emoted. Han Suyin drifted about conferring. Every word was freighted. There was much talk of the Role of the Artist. I didn't really grasp much of what was going on.

Subsequently I gave lectures in Belgrade, Novi Sad, Sarajevo, and Skopje in Macedonia. Belgrade was hideous with Soviet concrete. I remember thinking during the recent war that if anywhere *had* to be bombed Belgrade wasn't much of a loss.

The Hotel Moskva, in which I stayed, was vast and almost completely empty. The menu in the dining room offered a dish called Butter Tart with Chicken Pluck. I *was* curious but settled for a salad and some Kashkaval cheese, a favourite of Myrna's grandfather. A notice in my room offered to launder my "nightshirst."

In Belgrade I saw a gang of middle-aged women working on road repair with picks and shovels, a sight that made me peculiarly uncomfortable. I dabbled my hand in the Danube. I was filmed by a TV crew walking along the bank of the Sava

River and discoursing. There is nothing like a TV camera for transforming even a sage into an immediate horse's ass.

In Sarajevo I of course went to see the footprint painted on the pavement where the assassin had stood to shoot the Archduke Francis Ferdinand and his wife on June 28, 1914. More interesting than the rather bland architecture of the Austro-Hungarian nineteenth century were the Muslim alleys, markets, and mosques. Visiting dignitaries always bring the gift of a carpet to the main mosque and the carpets are spread on top of each other so that to kneel on them one has to mount the pile on a stepladder.

I stayed at the Holiday Inn in Sarajevo, which was shelled into ruins in the recent war. The university professors of English, all trained in the USA, nearly all seemed to have second jobs to make ends meet. Journals and books were too expensive for them to buy and the university library lagged behind by years. The Holiday Inn had been built for the Winter Olympics some years earlier. Patches of wasteland had been turned into little flower gardens while the Olympics were on but as soon as anything flowered it was picked and was on sale in the market the next morning; the authorities were forced to station soldiers overnight at every garden plot. Nearly everything about Bosnia and Herzegovina struck me as wilted and run-down, an imitation of a Western country, their Westernness merely an inheritance from the Austro-Hungarian imperium and all of it marking time until it relapsed into a more vital Muslim chaos.

Chaos increased the farther south one went. In Skopje in Macedonia my hotel room door had had a hole in it repaired by hammering over the hole a piece of tin. This crude repair seemed to suggest much about the social fabric.

These junkets to foreign countries continued with Greek temples in Agrigento, crusader castles, Roman amphitheatres in Syracuse and Taormina where Leon Rooke and I took to the stage and orated to throat-pulsing lizards warming themselves on the ancient stone.

Rome I remember not for a yellow dog but for a toilet. In a ramshackle hotel near the end of the Via della Croce, a hotel warmly commended by Leon and Connie Rooke, the toilet stood in a tiled room which sloped to a central drain. When flushed, the water circulated in an unsteady oval and, against the laws of nature, rose terrifyingly up the toilet bowl until it reached the rim and hurled turds onto the floor.

Strasbourg I remember chiefly because Carol Shields launched into a feminist harangue claiming that I was a misogynist and deliberately excluded female writers from anthologies and from the list of the Porcupine's Quill. What provoked this harpy act I have no idea; I had to struggle to hold on to the fact that she had written *Various Miracles*. Ray Smith was so appalled that he later wrote her a strong letter of protest.

Ray and Myrna and I months before the conference had made a reservation at Le Crocodil. Ray, I remember, ordered *canard pressé*. I consulted the Jeeves-like sommelier about Alsatian wines and he said in a snooty manner, "What a pleasure it is, monsieur, not to be serving Coca-Cola to Japanese businessmen."

But of all these junkets Bologna was the best. I had initially agreed to go for two months but then decided that that was too long and cut the time to one month. Guy Gervais, bless him, again mismanaged and the cheque I received in Bologna, sent from Rome, was not for four weeks but for eight. I had so much money I literally could not spend it. Cashing the cheque was a vastly comic performance which started with one teller but swelled to a shouting, gesticulating mob of about twenty employees casting doubt on the cheque's authenticity because it had been issued in Rome by, as the manager described them, "southern monkeys."

The department of foreign literary studies was housed in a large and beautiful *palazzo*. One approached along arcaded streets with barrel-vaulted ceilings which were so beautiful that the simple act of walking under them made one feel positively regal.

The department di Lingue e Letterature Straniere itself was another matter. Its Canadian operations doubtless owed their existence to large sums of Canadian government money. I am not saying that its activities were fraudulent but I would say that the department seemed to accept theses in large numbers from students I would have thought not quite prepared for the task at hand.

On my first day there I gave a lecture about Canadian literature to roughly thirty-five students, a lecture which lasted about one and a half hours. Afterwards I asked why the entire class was female. I was told that literature wasn't important enough to lead to a well-paying job and that therefore it was not a suitable subject for men. I also asked why there had been no questions. The answer to that was twofold; they didn't ask questions, said Professor Giovanna Capone, firstly, because they'd been taught not to and, secondly, because they were probably embarrassed to attempt English in public.

After this first heroic lecture everyone seemed to think I'd performed sterling service and should take the rest of the month to recover; I was urged to travel to Rome, Florence, Milan, and Venice to take in the sights.

Myrna came to join me halfway through and I was achingly lonely for her by then and met her at the railway station with roses and took her back to the Albergo Centrale where our shutters opened onto a sea of waving red roof tiles.

We went to Florence where we did all the touristy things. But more than the Uffizi and the Pitti Palace I remember a twenty-year-old Meursault we were served in the Enoteca Restaurant preceding the *menu dégustation.*

In Venice we ate on the terrace of the Hotel Danieli overlooking the Grand Canal and at its far side the great Palladian church of S. Giorgio Maggiore, a building so perfect, so elegant it moved me nearly to tears. Our waiter at the Danieli was a memorable disgrace, goosing the busboy, and preening intolerably. When I asked him for pepper he brought a mill which ground white pepper. I asked him if he had black and he said, "Oh, eat it up merry christmas!"

My other vivid memory of Venice was of the pavements and squares fouled with spittle, phlegm, and mucus.

Although I loved roaming the streets of the old city of Bologna and visiting its many churches and although I spent time seeking out paintings and prints by the Bolognese painter Giorgio Morandi, our driving interest was in food. The Italians call Bologna "Fat City" because of the wonderful restaurants and because of the rich produce of Emilia Romagna. Myrna and I, gastronomic rubes, were eager to taste everything and we started eating three full meals a day, something we do not ordinarily do.

We had to try genuine mortadella, the original bologna. And the sweet prosciutto from Palma and the salty prosciutto from the Chianti wine region and the acorn-fed prosciutto of San Daniele. We nibbled on Parmigiano-Reggiano. I discovered mâche. Myrna became a devotee of olive oil.

We applied ourselves to *melanzane al forno*. We put to the test *risotto alla milanese*. We tackled *fagioli in stufa* and *torta di funghi*. We made inroads on *insalata di gamberi alla menta* and *pollo al limoni*. We attacked the *ossobuca alle cipolle*. We gorged on the richness of *polenta con mascarpone e tartufi*.

One evening towards the end of our stay we were sitting in yet another serious restaurant. We were the only customers. The waiter was attentive and charming. We discovered that he had until recently been working in a family restaurant in England. We chatted about Soho and life in London. He ardently supported Tottenham Hotspurs. He brought us an apéritif of Campari and suggested that we start with a very fine, very delicate *quadrucci in brodo*.

We studied the menu. I tried to decide between *quaglie con uva* and *coniglio ripieno*, quail and rabbit. Myrna decided on a shrimp salad with diced cold potatoes and mayonnaise.

The soup was delicious. But filling. The broth, the waiter told us, was made from the dark meat of an entire turkey. It took us some time to finish. My apéritif sat in front of me. I sipped some mineral water. When our waiter returned and set before us rabbit and shrimps I knew that it was the end.

"I can't," I said. "I can't eat this."

"I've been taking senna pods," said Myrna. "It's been five days."

"I'm sorry," I said, "but I just *can't*."

"But we'll hurt his feelings," Myrna said, "and he's been so kind."

"Even a mouthful," I said, "and I know I'd be sick."

We sat for a few minutes and when the waiter went through the bat doors into the kitchen Myrna took the rabbit and the red peppers and the shrimps and potatoes and radicchio and mayonnaise and scraped them into her handbag which she closed with a click.

AN AESTHETIC UNDERGROUND

IN NOVEMBER 1988, Professor J. R. (Tim) Struthers staged a conference at the University of Guelph to celebrate my fiftieth birthday. To my considerable embarrassment he called the conference "Coming of Age: John Metcalf and the Canadian Short Story." Papers were presented. Lectures were delivered. And in the evenings writers read. Among the writers present were Leon Rooke, Keath Fraser, Hugh Hood, Alice Munro, Clark Blaise, Kent Thompson, Ray Smith, Jane Urquhart, Doug Glover, and Dayv James-French.

On the final day of the conference, Myrna and Alice Munro, restive in this academic environment, retreated to the faculty club to absorb dry martinis. Connie Rooke was to drive us out later to her house in Eden Mills for a final party. She had a list of errands to run before we headed to Eden Mills and among them was to pick up some boxes of *empañadas* she was going to serve at the party—*empañadas* being Latin American pasties or turnovers stuffed with ground meats or vegetables and spiced with hot peppers. Connie was rather flustered with all she had to do and kept remarking that whatever we did we mustn't forget to pick up the *empañadas*. She stopped in a shopping mall and walked off out of sight.

Into the silence in the car Alice said in a puzzled and slightly querulous voice, "Who *are* the Empañadas?"

But it was not at that splendid party that I first drifted into contact with the Porcupine's Quill. That had happened two evenings earlier at a conference dinner at the Bookshelf Café in Guelph. I found myself seated at the same table as Tim and Elke Inkster, the Porcupine's Quill owners. We were soon discussing the idea of reprinting important Canadian books. What prestigious publishing this would be! As the wine bottles emptied, the vision took on greater clarity. It rose before us, shining. I would select and edit these volumes with John Newlove, whom I would recruit as soon as I returned to Ottawa, and they would sell not only to the General Reader in bookstores but to students in universities and colleges all over Canada, thereby preserving our literary heritage and bringing into the Porcupine's Quill coffers vast sums of money.

It seemed to us foolproof.

We decided to call these reprints the Sherbrooke Street Series.

In the fall of 1993, I wrote for the PQ catalogue:

> Sherbrooke Street in Montreal has many memories for Tim Inkster, John Newlove, and for me. Tim went to high school at Loyola of Montreal on Sherbrooke Street and I taught at the college for several years. John Newlove and I have both been writers-in-residence there. We all have a vision of Sherbrooke Street as it used to be, the elegant and dignified grey stone houses, the stately trees ... It was at one time the Champs-Elysées, as it were, of Montreal.
>
> Now the street has fallen prey to developers and has been vandalized by urban planners, the Van Horne mansion wrecked illegally, the heritage streetscape desecrated with brutal concrete, the trees all felled.
>
> Something of the same thing has been happening to our literature. The past is being forgotten; books are slip-

ping out-of-print and out of mind. The outlines of our literary history seem to be blurring; careers seem to be sliding into general oblivion.

The Sherbrooke Street series is our way of attempting to save the vision. We are reprinting and keeping in print important books from our literary past. We cannot have a literature unless the books are available to readers and are being read; we cannot have a future unless we are securely anchored in a past. We are, St. Augustine reminded us, what we remember. Sherbrooke Street asserts the importance of what we have achieved and is our small gesture of faith in the excellence of what will evolve.

On my return to Ottawa from Guelph in 1988, I talked John Newlove into co-editing the series but he grew bored with the idea and withdrew entirely after about six weeks. We continued to put his name on the books and in the catalogue because I thought it looked more impressive to have two of us, but one day in 1993 I bumped into John in the street and he said that if we didn't stop using his name he'd sue. I didn't really think that he would—but with John you can never be *quite* sure.

I wanted each Sherbrooke Street volume to have an introduction by the author, setting the book in a literary and historical context. In cases where this wasn't possible, I intended commissioning an expert to do the job for me. We thought that these introductions or afterwords would also make the books bibliographically significant to libraries and institutions.

In this, we were mistaken.

I attended three annual meeting of the Learned Societies at great expense, manning a Porcupine's Quill booth, attempting to sell Sherbrooke Street books and other PQ titles to Canada's assembled academics. In the three years we sold a total of something like thirteen books.

I recall one shambling scholar at our booth picking up Ray Smith's *Cape Breton Is the Thought-Control Centre of Canada.*

"Is there anything about sailing in this book?"

"Not that I recall, no."

"Ah, well then, it wouldn't interest me *because*, you see," he said triumphantly, "it's *sailing* I'm interested in."

Thinking about the meetings of the Learned Societies reminds me of one attended by ECW Press in Winnipeg. Jack David and Robert Lecker always used to put on wine-and-cheese receptions. They bought wine locally and hired locals to dispense it. An academic surveyed the jumble of bottles on the table and asked of the local, "Where is the Côtes-du-Rhône?"

"Down the corridor," replied the local, "and on your left."

When we started Sherbrooke Street I assumed that we'd keep adding to the series until we arrived at something like the New Canadian Library or the New Press Canadian Classics. This was not to be. When I was setting up a reading tour for Norman Levine to promote and celebrate the 1993 republication of *From a Seaside Town* and *Canada Made Me* I was shocked that McGill, his own university, had no interest whatsoever in hosting a reading. "Nobody teaches him," I was told. My contact in Calgary told me that a few older people might turn out but there wouldn't be any students there because they wouldn't have heard of him as he wasn't on any courses. We were forced to face the brute fact that there really wasn't much of an academic market at all and that the general readership was indifferent. Quietly we let the series lapse.

The reprint books were *Cape Breton Is the Thought-Control Centre of Canada* by Ray Smith (1989); *Lunar Attractions* by Clark Blaise (1990); *The Improved Binoculars* by Irving Layton (1991); *Europe* by Louis Dudek (1991); *The Happiness of Others* by Leon Rooke (1991); *Dance with Desire* by Irving Layton (1992); *From a Seaside Town* and *Canada Made Me* by Norman Levine (1993).

Of these titles perhaps only *Europe* was a mistake. It certainly doesn't stand up as poetry but it's interesting for its ambition. Louis was important more as a teacher and an enthusiast and he is warmly remembered by those he taught such as Michael Darling, David Solway, and Michael Gnarowski.

The Happiness of Others preserves the best of Leon Rooke's stories from *The Love Parlour* and *Cry Evil*, volumes long out of print with Oberon Press. Ray Smith wrote a lengthy and important introduction to *Cape Breton*, essential reading for anyone interested in the short story in Canada.

By the end of 1992 I was beginning to see the shape of the Press in an editorial sense. Between 1974, when they founded the Porcupine's Quill in Erin Village northwest of Toronto, and 1989 when I started working with them, Tim and Elke had published a great deal of poetry but little fiction. I wanted to publish fewer poetry titles and place considerable emphasis on short fiction.

In 1989 I thought that the Press was too slight. Tim and Elke had published some good books but not enough of them. We had to gain mass and weight. Nor was Tim really thinking in national terms. I remember him saying to me in the early days, "Oh, Porcupine's Quill books don't get reviewed."

What I had in mind was building a better press than Contact Press or the House of Anansi had been. I wanted, quite simply, the best literary press in Canada.

This is how I put it in an essay in *The New Quarterly*:

> I wanted to counter apathy and blandness. I wanted to shock homogenized minds with the experience of writing at high voltage. I wanted the press to assert relentlessly literature's importance. I wanted the press to be a national press and of national importance. I wanted nothing "small" about this small press. I wanted the press to become something of a "movement." Not a movement

committed to a particular "ism," but a gathering together of writers with an aesthetic approach to literature and with a lust for excellence. I wanted our writers to draw strength from community. I wanted each to embolden the next. I wanted writers who loved language and who would swagger and flaunt. I wanted elegance. I wanted sophistication. I wanted a press crackling with energy. I wanted to draw together into one place so many talented writers that we would achieve critical mass and explode upon Canadian society in a dazzling coruscation showering it with unquenchable brilliance.

There was, of course, no money. I was willing to do this job without a salary—which Tim certainly couldn't have afforded—because I was attracted by the extreme romanticism of the task, by the vision of what could be wrought. I was bringing to the Press years of literary experience and a host of literary contacts, contacts not really available to Tim and Elke isolated in Erin Village. I was also bringing to the Press a readiness to talk to people, to listen, to soothe, to cajole.

Tim is very much not a "people person." He is paranoid, belligerent, bloody-minded, and extremely intelligent, all qualities which are probably essential to survival in small press publishing. I sometimes get phone calls from the more emotionally frail among my writers complaining that he has yelled at them or been astonishingly rude. I explain to these ruffled feathers that he has too much on his plate and that he's snarly because harassed.

Hostile and gloomy as he sometimes can be, he is at the same time something of a hero to me. I admire his energy, his devotion to what he does, his obstinate use of Zephyr Antique laid paper, the beautiful end-products of his passion. The fact that Tim still binds his books in the traditional manner and that he binds them with a Smythe book-sewing machine made in 1907 might suggest why I like and admire him and why we've worked together for fifteen years without homicidal incident.

Although I wanted to change the emphasis of the press I certainly wanted to continue publishing poetry but I wanted Selected Poems and Collected Poems rather than slim volumes by tyros. We started in 1990 with George Johnston's collected poems *Endeared by Dark*. Mark Abley wrote about the book and the Press in the Montreal *Gazette*:

> "The way I look at it," Tim Inkster told me the other day, "the printing excellence we're known for is a very sophisticated and understated marketing tool. The authors we publish are important, and we want to make sure their works last."
>
> But there's more to it than that. Just think of the magnificent cover that graces George Johnston's collected poems, *Endeared by Dark*. Since Johnston is a noted translator from Old Norse, Inkster decided that a Viking motif would be appropriate for the book. His unofficial editor-in-chief, John Metcalf, found a photograph of the celebrated Oseberg Ship in Norway but the photo was not good enough to reproduce directly. So Inkster passed it to an artist, Virgil Burnett; and from Burnett's pen-and-ink drawing, Inkster had a magnesium die made. Onto each cover, the die was then foil-stamped by hand.
>
> A complicated process—but the result is a joy to behold. "It's about as nice a production as I've ever had," Johnston says wryly. Against a pale, gray-blue background, the ship's embossed prow soars in gold. "Visually, it's something of a ghost ship," Inkster explains. "The way you perceive the image changes according to your angle of view. It's designed to sail through your imagination."
>
> And one way or another, that's what a lot of Porcupine's Quill books have been doing of late.

Tim printed five hundred copies of *Endeared by Dark*; total advance trade sales in Canada were forty-five copies.

As the years passed we published Irving Layton, Gael Turnbull, Don Coles, Richard Outram, John Newlove, P. K. Page, and Christopher Wiseman.

Gael Turnbull is an anomaly in this list, being far more "experimental" than any of the others.

Some years ago I became interested in a small literary press called Contact Press which was run in the fifties and sixties by Louis Dudek, Irving Layton, Raymond Souster, and Peter Miller. Myrna and I formed the first complete collection of the books of the press, a collection now in the National Library of Canada.

The Contact Press was perhaps the most centrally important press in the history of Canadian poetry, publisher of the first or very early work of Doug Jones, Alden Nowlen, Eli Mandel, Phyllis Webb, Louis Dudek, Irving Layton, Raymond Souster, Leonard Cohen, W. W. E. Ross, F. R. Scott, Milton Acorn, Gwendolyn MacEwen, John Newlove, Al Purdy, George Bowering, and Margaret Atwood.

One of the early books of the press was entitled *Trio* and it contained the first poems published in book form of three young writers—Eli Mandel, Phyllis Webb, and Gael Turnbull.

Also distributed by the Contact Press were four mimeographed pamphlets of French-Canadian poets translated by Turnbull in 1955—an early effort at crossing borders and cultures. Gael was living at the time in Iroquois Falls, Ontario, where he practised as a doctor and anaesthetist. He was assisted in the translations by Jean Beaupré, a French teacher in the local high school. Together they presented samples of the work of Paul-Marie Lapointe, Gilles Hénault, Roland Giguère, and Saint-Denys Garneau.

Gael Turnbull was much influenced by Raymond Souster and the Contact Press movement and by Cid Corman and the Black Mountain poets in the States. When he returned to

England in 1957, he founded Migrant Press, one of the pioneer small presses for modern poetry in Britain.

I enjoyed the poetry and made efforts to find out about the man. I located him in Edinburgh and went there to see him, bearing with me an offer to publish a Selected Poems in Canada. I spent a couple of nights in my hotel room sitting up into the small hours reading new material and rereading until I was bleary-eyed. The eventual result was *While Breath Persist* which was published by the Porcupine's Quill in 1992.

Whenever I think about Gael Turnbull, I think of his reciting the final lines of "Twenty Words, Twenty Days."

> . . . and I remember an Edinburgh room
> and one saying, when I asked what he'd done that day,
> how much—
> "I tore it up . . . I wisnae pure enough
> when I wrote . . . I wisnae pure enough . . ."

In 1993 we published Don Coles's *Forests of the Medieval World*. It was the winner of the 1993 Governor General's Award for Poetry. Tim was ecstatic. Then it turned out that Don thought public readings and any sort of public appearance were little short of hucksterism and deeply detrimental to poetry's dignity. He refused to perform. Tim was apoplectic and coarse descriptive invective issued from the telephone for days. There was a gala evening for the winners at the National Library where I had to read in Don Coles's place. Among other of his poems, I read "My Son at the Seashore, Age Two," a pretty little thing.

> He laughs and a breeze
> lifts his hair. His face tilts up
> towards what has happened
> to his hair, that it should lift,
> and his laugh goes. Why
> is this happening, his suddenly

serious face wants to know, and
what is happening. But
all it is is a little breeze
lifting his hair for a few seconds,
a little breeze passing by
on its way to oblivion—
as this day is on its way there too,
and as that day, twenty years ago,
was, too.

When I read the last, soft words I heard someone catch their breath. For some reason I was certain it was a woman.

We have also had the honour of publishing the glittering poetry of Richard Outram. Four of his collections are still in print with us: *Man in Love*, *Hiram and Jenny*, *Mogul Recollected*, and *Dove Legend*. Alberto Manguel wrote an essay on Richard Outram in a recent book, *Into the Looking-Glass Wood*. He wrote: "I discovered, in fact, that Outram's entire career had been one of absences. He has never received a national, let alone international award, nor a Canada Council grant; he has never been included in any major anthology of Canadian poetry, rarely been acknowledged in reviews . . ."

Manguel then goes on to claim that Richard Outram is "one of the finest poets in the English language."

Who could resist exploring such a resounding judgement? The answer to *that* rhetorical question is, Nearly every Canadian.

The easiest way into Richard's work is through *Hiram and Jenny*. Hiram and Jenny are two quirky maritime characters and the poems celebrate in playful and gorgeous language their comings and goings, their maunderings and heroics.

Here are just a few lines from "Techne."

Hiram is washing his socks in the creek.
Not far offshore, unseen,

crammed with warheads and comic books
a nuclear submarine

noses about with her cornfed crew,
bored, but ready to cope
at the drop of a ciphered word. . . .

Who could resist reading on? But you will.

By 1991 I had also fully realized what had been nebulous before, that ink and paper were only a part of a literary press. Literary presses which *were* mainly ink and boards and paper—presses like Black Moss, say, or Mosaic—are largely inert. I would never underestimate the importance of Tim's printing and design. He has won awards from the Leipzig Book Fair, the Art Directors' Club of New York, the Alcuin Society and the Society of Graphic Designers of Canada, yet at the same time I believe that a press lives fully only when it creates a personality and mythology.

Faber and Faber had that mythology under T. S. Eliot and continued having it under Charles Monteith; Macmillan in England had it in the late nineteenth and twentieth centuries; Boni and Liveright had it under the hand of Ezra Pound. It comes about, I think, when a certain group of authors, a generation perhaps, come to be associated with a press. In their commingling, the by-product is a glamour, a glitter of talent. The mythology is nurtured by launches, by lunches, by burgeoning friendships and mild rivalries. It grows through editorial soothing and encouragement which is not some insincere schtick but is a genuine interest in the work and its creator. It comes about through a sense of community and shared purpose. It comes about through a shared aesthetic interest in literature. It brings people into a more than commercial association.

The mythology of the press is built by the commingling of the reputations of such brilliant and disparate writers as

Caroline Adderson, Michael Winter, Steven Heighton, Libby Creelman, Russell Smith, Andrew Pyper, Mike Barnes, Annabel Lyon, Terry Griggs . . . It is also built by application to endless detail. By phone calls to alert writers to reviews. By letters to celebrate or commiserate. By conversations about books, writing, ideas, reviewing. By the press's ever-expanding Web site.

A good example of that attention to detail is the bookmarks Tim makes, each featuring an author photographed at his or her local bookstore. A simple enough thing to do, but when these bookmarks are distributed all over the country they're just one more reminder of the press's specialness.

The press also builds mythology by turning its principals into a cast of characters. When *The New Quarterly* was about to publish a special issue on my editing work, the editor, Kim Jernigan, wrote in a letter, "You have, as you must know, a reputation for being FORMIDABLE." I have no idea how this slander got abroad but Steve Heighton amplified it in his *New Quarterly* contribution.

> How do I know what John is like with the others? I know because whenever I happen to meet other writers he's edited, we always end up huddled together and asking, in hushed tones, "So, what kind of thing does he write on *your* stories?"
>
> I usually answer with a few choice samples of Metcalfian marginalia: "Another EXCREMENTAL metaphor." "Oh Christ, Heighton, are you KIDDING?" And my personal favourite, which appeared, in large caps, between the lines of an unmedicably ailing story, later put down: "YOU CAN ONLY SAY THAT ABOUT HORSES, YOU DINK."

Thus in the play that is the Porcupine's Quill I have been cast as the Formidable Editor. I have myself cast Tim as Don Quixote, writing of him ". . . if one is going to tilt at windmills, who better to ride with than that gloomy aesthete Tim Inkster with his antique Zephyr laid?"

And Elke? Elke is the *éminence grise*, the Power Behind the Throne.

Such imaginary characters are as real and vital to the living press as the cold steel of the Heidelberg Kord 64 in the workshop's basement.

Beginning in 1991 the pace of the press was picking up so fast that we were under considerable pressure. Of the five titles shortlisted for the 1991 Governor General's Award for Fiction two were Porcupine's Quill books of short stories, *Blue Husbands* by Don Dickinson and *Quickening* by Terry Griggs. And the pressure never let up. To give the reader some idea of the pace, the House of Anansi over a period of twenty-three years and under five or six editors published about 160 books. Over a period of fifteen years, alone, I will have acquired and edited more than 100 books. By the year 2000 I was feeling tired and overworked.

I had a phone call one day in 2000 from Carmine Starnino in Montreal wanting to come up to Ottawa to chat. Was it all right to bring a friend? This meeting was momentous. The friend turned out to be the poet Eric Ormsby, whose work I was already familiar with. We felt immediately at ease with each other and fell into delightful conversation in which, mutually, nothing needed to be explained. It's most unusual to feel such immediate mutual attraction.

This lovely meeting was an event I think of almost religiously as the Advent of Ormsby.

Eric studied librarianship at Rutgers University and took a Ph.D. degree from Princeton in Near Eastern studies and Classical Arabic. He has worked as a curator in Near Eastern studies at Princeton. He has been a director of libraries at two research institutions: the Catholic University of America and, for ten years, until 1996, at McGill University where he is currently a professor of Islamic studies.

He has published four collections of poetry and a recent book of essays, *Facsimiles of Time: Essays on Poetry and Translation.*

John Updike wrote about Eric's poems: "He is a most excellent poet, resonant and delicately exact with words and objects. Ormsby's reverent attention to things as they are lights up his every page with a glow."

I soon persuaded Eric to turn his reverent attention onto the Porcupine's Quill and he now functions as poetry editor for the Press, taking some of the pressure off me. His first book for the Press was David Solway's *The Lover's Progress*, followed by Norm Sibum's *Girls and Handsome Dogs*. Norm and Eric celebrated the publication of this handsome book vigorously; Norm flaked out on Eric's couch. In the morning Eric's wife, Irena, came downstairs and Norm sat up and said brightly: "Good morning! May I give you a lift home?"

Starting in 1990 the short story collections started to flow: *Victims of Gravity* by Dayv James-French; *Quickening* by Terry Griggs; *Blue Husbands* by Don Dickinson; *Flight Paths of the Emperor* by Steven Heighton; *Man and His World* by Clark Blaise; *Bad Imaginings* by Caroline Adderson; *City of Orphans* by Patricia Robertson; *A Litany in Time of Plague* by K. D. Miller; *Lives of the Mind Slaves* by Matt Cohen . . . the list flows on and on and all the work is of very high quality, all marked by an intensity and originality in the use of language.

When I started out in the sixties Hugh Garner was considered a heavyweight; Morley Callaghan reigned. The prose was bangers-and-mash. *My* story writers are mercurial, their prose an extremely delicate instrument indeed.

I feel rash enough to claim that most of what I've chosen stands above the ruck. I am ever more certain that a writer's use of language is the key to that choosing. I wolf through manuscripts and become immediately impatient if I do not feel the urgency of the writer's language, the compression, the precision, the suggestion. I receive endless letters of inquiry which explain to me that the proposed stories are about autistic children, child abuse, gay mores in Vancouver, the problems of female artists, hospital stories from a doctor's perspective, and as I sigh and groan and curse I think of Paul Fussell's comment on Evelyn Waugh: "Waugh is indispensable today because, for one thing, he is that rarity, a writer who cares about language. He knows that writing is an affair of words rather than soul, impulse, 'sincerity,' or an instinct for the significant. If the words aren't there, nothing happens."

But the delight when the words *are* there. When I open the manila envelope and read:

> One side of Aunt Ella's face was purple. One arm and one leg were, too. The purple skin looked rougher than the rest, and I wondered if it would feel hot if I touched it. She and her brother George, who was not purple anywhere, sipped their soup exactly together. First they raised their spoons to their lips, then they took the same shivery sip, then they lowered their spoons back down to their bowls. As if they'd practiced.
>
> K. D. MILLER

Or this:

> My parents were married in a high wind that was conceived in the tropics and born in a jet stream. As it crawled up the coast, playing with flags and sailboats, teething on cliffs and peninsulas, it matured into a lusty and vigorous gale. A product of incompatible air currents—polar and equatorial, with a trace of African Simoon ancestry—it blew like a bastard, sweeping suddenly into the orchard where the wedding ceremony was proceeding at a lazy mid-August sun-sodden pace.
>
> TERRY GRIGGS

Or this:

> His most vivid childhood memory was of sickness, which he loved. He loved staying in bed all day, reading books, eating Jell-O, flesh broth, globs of honey and aspirin crushed between two spoons. He loved the natural disorders of his body—vomiting, diarrhea, infections, swellings, pale sleeps and altered appetites. Because his parents did not believe in TV and because he had a window, Morris watched weather. He saw blushing sunrises, curtains of rain holding in the night, snow in the blue afternoons. Morris missed prodigious amounts of school, was top of his class, and never wore a hat, in the hopes of catching something special.
>
> ANNABEL LYON

We went on to publish *On earth as it is* by Steven Heighton; *Driving Men Mad* by Elise Levine; *Influence of the Moon* by Mary Borsky; *Help Me, Jacques Cousteau* by Gil Adamson; *Lovers and Other Strangers* by Carol Malyon; *Telling My Love Lies* by Keath Fraser; *The Garden of Earthly Delights* by Meeka Walsh; *Kiss Me* by Andrew Pyper; *Buying on Time* by Antanas Sileika; *If I Were Me* by Clark Blaise; *Small Change* by Elizabeth Hay; *Promise of Shelter* by Robyn Sarah; *Learning to Live Indoors* by Alison Acheson; *Love in a Warm Climate* by Kelley Aitken; *The King of Siam* by Murray Logan; *Aquarium* by Mike Barnes; *Devil's Darning Needle* by Linda Holeman; *Give Me Your Answer* by K. D. Miller; *One Last Good Look* by Michael Winter; *Walking in Paradise* by Libby Creelman; *How Did You Sleep?* by Paul Glennon; *Oxygen* by Annabel Lyon; *The One with the News* by Sandra Sabatini; and *Gambler's Fallacy* by Judith Cowan.

People often ask where and how I find the manuscripts we publish. Very few indeed get chosen from what arrives in the mail. I've only accepted six unsolicited MSS since 1989.

This is simply because most are awful in horrible ways. I look at so much material that it should be obvious I can't read it all. Connolly's paragraph plus two more for good measure are enough to do the trick. Covering letters are also a good short cut; if the salutation is "Hi!" or "Hello, Porcupine's Quill" I read no further.

I laughed in delighted recognition a few years ago when I was reading Humphrey Carpenter's biography of Ezra Pound, a life entitled *A Serious Character*. The sentences that made me laugh concerned the writer and editor Ford Madox Ford.

> Pound delighted in Ford's brisk off-the-cuff literary judgements, which were nearly always right, and in his ability as an editor to detect the quality of a manuscript almost by its smell.
>
> ("I don't read manuscripts," Ford would say, "I know what's in 'em.")

I find manuscripts by glancing at what arrives in the mail, by reading the literary magazines, and by following up the recommendations of Porcupine's Quill writers. The writers obviously have a sense of what's going to appeal to me. Steve Heighton, Elise Levine, Caroline Adderson, Leon Rooke, and Diane Schoemperlen all pass along suggestions. I trust their eyes and ears and I welcome their help; it works towards making the press a shared venture, an aesthetic underground. I was going to use the word *network* but I think the word *web* is more precise. The filaments of the web stretch from coast to coast and sometimes, nearly invisibly, stretch far back into the past.

An example of that would be Mary Swan from Guelph. She sent me a letter of inquiry. Her track record in the magazines looked good. She sent me stories and an extraordinary novella entitled "The Deep." I accepted immediately. Some weeks later she heard that "The Deep" had won first prize in the *O Henry Award Stories* in the States. All this might seem completely random but wasn't. A filament was jiggling the web. Years before, Mary had been taught in Toronto by Alice Munro. They had kept in touch. Years later when Mary had a collection ready Alice had recommended me as an editor; "Tough but fair," Mary said Alice had said.

Another example of the way the web works. In 1980 Clark Blaise and I edited *Best Canadian Stories 80* for Oberon. We were both charmed by a story named "Esso" by a new young writer called Linda Svendsen. Years later she published the magnificent collection *Marine Life*. Fast-forward again and she is teaching writing at UBC, head of the Creative Writing Department. I got a letter from her a couple of years ago saying she had a student whose work she thought might interest me. I wrote to the student and in return was sent a wad of stories. They were astonishing, exciting, odd, entrancing. We published the stories in 2000. The book was *Oxygen*, the author Annabel Lyon.

Sometimes I receive collections of stories or novels which I don't consider publishable in their submitted form but there may be in the MS a spark of language, a tension, that suggests that the writer is capable of a better book. In that sort of case I have to take a gamble. Will I be able to tease from this writer a different book, a better book? Will the writer accept a new direction? Have I the energy to enter into this manuscript? Is this going to work between us emotionally? Or should I simply reject the manuscript? Temperamentally, I incline to the gamble; I want to bet on what the writer *will* do rather than has done.

Gil Adamson's *Help Me, Jacques Cousteau* is an example of a book that evolved. Gil came to me as a result of a recommendation by Steve Heighton. She sent in a collection of stories that seemed to me disparate in style and subject matter, too much a grab bag. I wrote to her suggesting that the funniest and the most moving of the stories concerned families and that she should group these stories together and write some new ones, thereby creating a linked collection. I sensed that at some level these particular stories had an autobiographical impulse and were intensely felt. Gil at first resisted the book I could sense but gradually relaxed into writing it.

She wrote in the book's acknowledgements: "Any resemblance to persons living or dead is not only coincidental, but is also a damned lie, according to my mother."

For the last few years I've been teaching every summer at the Humber School for Writers at Humber College in Toronto. The course is usually in the last week of July. This is developing into another source of manuscripts. I have published from Humber, Sharon English (*Uncomfortably Numb*) and Mary-Lou Zeitoun (*13*).

One of the pleasures of that week at Humber is the company of Mark Leyner, Bruce Jay Friedman, Tim O'Brien, and D. M. Thomas. In 1999 Mordecai Richler taught there and was rather badly behaved. On the opening morning of classes Joe Kertes, the director of the course, dropped into Mordecai's room to see that all was well. Mordecai was sitting on the edge of the desk smoking a cheroot and staring out of the window. The class was sitting in strained silence. Nothing seemed to be happening. Joe said brightly, "So! Shall we make a start?" Mordecai shuffled himself around and said, "What would be the point?"

For the record, however, since the first time I met him in 1970, Richler treated me with great courtesy, kindness, and generosity. I still remember with acute embarrassment interviewing him in the early seventies in his study in his Westmount house to discover halfway through that I'd pressed the wrong buttons on my tape recorder. He confined himself to a sigh.

Last year Humber was enlivened by the presence of Roddy Doyle. Mary-Lou Zeitoun read the opening chapter of her novel *13* as class work; *13* is a story as told by a thirteen-year-old punk rocker. When she'd finished, Roddy Doyle said,

"Fuckin' great!" I thought that would make an excellent blurb for the back of the book. He did write one for her but it was more decorous.

In 1993 in addition to the Sherbrooke Street setback the Press suffered another. I had wanted to link the Porcupine's Quill with a similar literary press in the States or England. Literary presses have always tended to be internationalist and my hope was that we could select half a dozen American authors, say, and promote them in Canada while the other press promoted some of our authors in the States. I hoped that we could have launches and reading tours for the Americans and that all this would lead to our literary worlds drawing closer together.

Tim and I got in touch with the publisher and editorial director of Gray Wolf Press, Scott Walker. The press is based in Minneapolis. We exchanged books and catalogues and discussed on the phone the idea of some kind of co-operation. Scott and a couple of his editors were to be in New York for a book fair and we agreed to meet there. As it was a warm, pleasant day we met in Central Park and spent a few hours discussing the price of paper, unit costs, and the non-viability of short story collections in the US market. It slowly became clear that they considered our list *too* literary. I thought theirs too commercial. And their unit costs were about a quarter of ours.

This venture cost Tim a lot of money in plane fares and hotels and restaurants and I've never heard the end of it. The taxi to La Guardia drove at such demented speed that when we reached the airport, a very shaken Tim had to have a little lie-down. And the most vivid memory for both of us is the small printed posters tacked to the trees in Central Park. They said: Please Do Not Feed the Rats.

Since this attempt and after probes at Carcanet Press in England I've come to the conclusion that small presses are *necessarily* individualist. I very much value my own freedom at Porcupine's Quill and I certainly wouldn't welcome an advisory board. I find the products of boards and committees generally *lumpy*—like the annual *Journey Prize Anthology*. Though I do still sometimes hanker after an American or British component I know the deal would founder on the rock of Tim's dedication to Zephyr Antique laid.

"Sure their books are cheaper," said Tim about Gray Wolf. "Nastier, too. Nasty paper. Perfect bound."

End of subject.

He was right.

In 1994, the books were brilliant but sales were not and Tim was on the verge of bankruptcy. He phoned me in deep despond and asked me to start dismantling the list by placing our writers with other publishers. Tim needed $14,000 to survive and couldn't raise it anywhere his pride would allow him to. I called Anna Porter at Key Porter Books and we talked around the problem for a while and then I baulked. Our list was building in 1994 in exactly the way I'd dreamed. We positively glittered. *Quickening* by Terry Griggs, *Blue Husbands* by Don Dickinson, *Flight Paths of the Emperor* by Steven Heighton, *Dance with Desire* by Irving Layton, *A Night at the Opera*, by Ray Smith, *Forests of the Medieval World* by Don Coles, *Bad Imaginings* by Caroline Adderson—I *could not* cast these pearls away.

And then a dream of salvation came to me.

Sometime earlier in Ottawa on my ceaseless rounds I'd dropped in at a used book store called Benjamin Books. The owner of the store, whose interests run more in Marxist-Leninist directions than in literary ones, said he had a box of books that might interest me. The books came from the libraries of Archibald Lampman, his wife, Maud (Playter) Lampman, his father-in-law, Edward Playter, his sister Isabelle who married Ernest Voorhis, and his daughter Natalie who married Loftus MacInnes, son of the poet Tom MacInnes.

The books had belonged to a member of the Lampman–MacInnes family.

It was a treasure trove of Canadian material. It included the dedication copy of Lampman's first book, *Among the Millet and Other Poems*; he had copied out the dedicatory poem "To My Wife" and inscribed the book "To My Beloved Maud." The highlight of the collection was a holograph book of Lampman's sonnets written a year before *Among the Millet* was published. There are 101 differences between the holograph versions and the printed versions. There was also a clutch of signed presentation books to Lampman by William Wilfred Campbell, Bliss Carman, Charles G. D. Roberts, and John Henry Brown. Masses of Duncan Campbell Scott all inscribed to Lampman's daughter, Natalie. There were completely unrecorded leaflets, poems, and pamphlets. There was even a signed photograph of Duncan Campbell Scott and Rupert Brooke dated August 1913 taken in the garden of Scott's house, now destroyed, on Lisgar Street in Ottawa.

The store's owner, Mordy Bubis, really wasn't paying sufficient attention and sold the books to me for $7,000. I added to this collection a lot of Duncan Campbell Scott material I'd collected over the years down to and including his Christmas cards which all carried poems, some of them unrecorded. It seemed obvious that all this material ought to be in the National Library. I offered it but they declined, saying they already had a lot of Lampman. I thought this was rather like the British Museum saying they already had lots of Shakespeare but the National Library is something of an intellectual morgue at the best of times. Eventually I sold the entire collection to Michael Gnarowski for $20,000 which was a figure absurdly low but I needed money to save the press.

The next problem was Tim's pride. I doubted he would simply accept $14,000 as a gift. I proposed, therefore, that he sell me the archives of the Press from 1989 onwards. The University of Guelph had been buying them previously but had informed Tim and Elke that although they were still interested in acquiring them they would no longer pay. Tim agreed to my proposal and I sent him a cheque. It amused me to think that Archibald Lampman and Duncan Campbell Scott were reaching out from the grave in continued support of Canadian literature. I bought from Tim a second batch of archives when I sold my Anansi collection to the National Library. I'm hoping that this rather vast archive, along with all the edited manuscripts and correspondence, will end up in McGill's Rare Book Room.

I felt from the beginning that the books we were publishing would not survive unless they existed in a critical context, unless they were discussed and compared and evaluated. Canadian history—and that includes its literature—is a sorry, insubstantial thing like the wake of a ship, churned foam continually flattening out and disappearing, leaving no track or trace. The books can only survive if people are reading them and that is why I wanted criticism addressed to the Common Reader even if the Common Reader is in short supply. The universities seemingly have little interest in contemporary writing and their professors have chosen to look inward and talk to each other in constipated jargon. I felt that what we needed was passionate and intelligent criticism from people for whom literature was part of life, from people who lived books, from people who wanted to share their passions. I also felt that it was not essential for me, editorially, to agree with all their opinions and arguments. The important thing, it seemed to me, was the current of passion itself, a current that would engage, introduce, reevaluate, provoke, disparage, praise.

We began the critical series in 1990 with *Volleys*, a debate amongst W. J. Keith, Sam Solecki, and me about the importance of the short story as a genre. In 1991 we published *An Independent Stance* by W. J. Keith and in 1993 *How Stories Mean*, a compendium of comment by writers on the genre.

These books appeared under the series title Critical Directions under the editorship of J. R. (Tim) Struthers. The books are lively but sales were bleak. Again we let the series lapse.

Conscience nagged, however, and I knew we had a duty here and so I re-started the critical series with *Ripostes* by Philip Marchand in 1998. Phil had won my early enthusiasm and support for the intelligence and vigour of his reviewing in the *Toronto Star*. The book caused a mild uproar; he had called into question the reputations of Margaret Atwood, Timothy Findley, and Michael Ondaatje. He was irreverent about the Writers' Union of Canada, saying memorably of Lenore Keeshig-Tobias, then chair of the Racial Minority Writers' Committee, that she was "famous for her ability to weep in public." The book was, amazingly, soon sold out.

We continued in 2000 with T. F. Rigelhof's *This Is Our Writing*. In 2001, Eric Ormsby's *Facsimiles of Time*. In 2002, Stephen Henighan's *When Words Deny the World*, a book which sold out entirely in about a month. I have in the works major essay collections from David Solway, Carmine Starnino, and Michael Darling.

What accounts for the success of this critical series, I believe, is its thoughtful opposition to much academic and media opinion, opposition usually backed by devastating quotation. These books are a sustained attack on what Philip Marchand in one of his essays calls "our dogged Canadian willingness to be bored."

Terry Rigelhof on Robertson Davies suggests the tone:

> If Davies hadn't added two more volumes to turn *Fifth Business* into the first volume of the Deptford Trilogy and demonstrated that he was incapable of writing in anything other than a stilted style or inventing any voice, male or female, that wasn't Dunstan Ramsay's, I'd be more tempted to celebrate his achievement here.

I'm pleased with the impact of the critical series. It is impinging on the awareness even of those not much given to reading.

The lacklustre *Globe and Mail* columnist James Adams launched a counterattack recently in his *Weekend Diary*. He quotes the travel writer Pico Iyer:

> When a Canuck reads a sentence such as "Toronto is by official UN statistics the single most multicultural city in the world; it is also statistically the safest city in North American and, by the reckoning of many, the one with the richest literary culture," he or she automatically tenses up and gets ready for the follow-through put-down.
>
> Which had that sentence been written by John Metcalf, Stephen Henighan, Philip Marchand or another member of the Porcupine's Quill group, would have occurred.

Notice the pathetic implication—*as always*—that to criticize a Canadian book is to criticize Canada. Where does the newspaper *find* these stand-on-guard dorks?

In 1997 Tim Inkster acquired from Douglas Fetherling the journal *Canadian Notes and Queries*. Fetherling had shifted the journal away from academic concerns and towards being "a periodical of Canadian literary and cultural history." I took over the editorship with Number 51.1. We regard *CNQ* as a part of the critical component of the Porcupine's Quill. With our reviews, profiles, interviews, and essays we wish to intrude rudely on the bland mindlessness of Canadian literary life. Michael Darling is the book review editor. Carmine Starnino is the poetry editor.

In 2001 we published a brilliant essay by David Solway entitled "Standard Average Canadian or The Influence of Al Purdy." In essence, the essay described Purdy as the Stompin' Tom Connors of Canadian poetry and deplored his influence on younger poets.

Tim had been receiving a grant of $3,000 a year towards the magazine's expenses from the Ontario Arts Council. After the David Solway essay appeared, Lorraine Filyer, the Ontario Arts Council Literary Supremo, phoned Tim and informed him that she and her henchthingies, as Frank magazine would say, had decided to reduce his grant to zero. The reason she gave was the journal's "lack of editorial vision." Tim promptly secured financing for the magazine from the Upper Canada Brewing Company, a better class of people.

The most recent issue of the journal was a special issue on Norman Levine. Cynthia Flood contributed a definitive essay on Norman's style which is the very model of what literary criticism should be.

Norman wrote in the journal: "*Canada Made Me* was published by Putnam in November 1958. A long review by Paul West in the Christmas issue of the *New Statesman and Nation* was read by Honor Balfour of the London office of *Time*. She interviewed me. When her piece appeared, the 500 copies that McClelland had went quickly. He wouldn't take any more. Nor would any other Canadian publisher. I had to accept that Canadian publishing was closed to my work."

Norman told me that when he was writer-in-residence at UNB in Fredericton he gave a reading at the Saint John campus and afterwards a professor came up to him and said, "Are you the Levine that wrote *Canada Made Me*?" Norman said that he was and the scholar spat at his feet and walked away.

Yet I've long held that *Canada Made Me* sits at the centre of Canadian literature. It is concerned with the essence of Canada: immigration, the lives of immigrants. How deeply that spitting scholar would loathe such an opinion! Not many readers have discovered the book yet but we have reprinted it and it is available. It sells three or four copies in a year. It will not go away. We do somewhat better with the reprint of *From a Seaside Town* but only because the Tate St. Ives buys copies regularly.

Norman is of singular importance to me. He is the very figure of the artist. He has worked quietly for decades forging a radical style. He has survived. He has survived the indifference of audience and he has produced stories which are at the centre of achievement in Canadian literature, "A Small Piece of Blue," "We All Begin in a Little Magazine," "Champagne Barn," "Something Happened Here" . . .

He has also had to endure the crassness of the Canadian literary world. I have already mentioned that Cynthia Good of Penguin Books Canada, who published *Champagne Barn* and, later, *Something Happened Here*, was quoted in the *Ottawa Citizen* as saying: "At the time, we considered Norman to be on a par with Alice Munro or Mavis Gallant. We weren't alone. That's how many people viewed him at the time."

At the time?

She is quoted later as saying that sales of *Something Happened Here* were "modest." Aha! Norman's fall from grace was linked to numbers, was it? She is equating sales with achievement. And in this she's not alone.

Jenny Jackson, the *Ottawa Citizen* books columnist, wrote in review of Clark Blaise: "The book is put out by Porcupine's Quill, the press of the unjustly forgotten, those with the PR epitaph 'a writer's writer' . . ." Her words attempt to be patronizing. She goes on to gloat that Clark never "broke through" to a "mass audience." Could one suggest that if writers are "unjustly forgotten" then it just might be the duty of a books columnist to *seek* justice for them. "A writer's writer" means that the writer is so good other writers are influenced by him or her. Isn't Jackson's job to connect that excellence with a readership? But it isn't really literature that is her subject matter. What she's really interested in is *exactly* PR. Recently she wrote in a review of Stephen Henighan: "His first four books of fiction have earned respectful reviews, if little money."

Sales.

Numbers.

What a squalid little mind she has! I despise her pat acceptance of the status quo. People who employ numbers arguments are usually coarse souled. I had thought of sending her a poker-work plaque, elegantly executed, of the old graffito: Eat Shit! Fifty Billion Flies Can't Be Wrong!

Sarah Hampson, continuing this trend of Levine-bashing, wrote a slighting and obtuse profile of Norman which was published in the *Globe and Mail* in July 2002. She concentrated on what she perceived as his eccentricity and his penury.

"Levine unlocks the door to his apartment; pushes it forward and gestures for me to enter first. The smell of time rises up from a soiled mauve carpet, a sagging floral-print sofa . . ."

She managed not to see his grandeur.

Inspired by Norman's anecdotes over the years about St. Ives and about the painters who were his friends—Peter Lanyon, Terry Frost, Patrick Heron, and Francis Bacon—Myrna and I decided to go there for a holiday to see the Alfred Wallis paintings in the Tate St. Ives. Wallis was a primitive painter so powerful that after you've seen the paintings you can only see St. Ives itself through his eyes. He died in 1942 and is buried in the cemetery above Porthmeor Beach in a grave covered with Bernard Leach tiles.

Holidays with Myrna are usually boot-camp affairs as she insists on climbing mountains, hacking across moors in knee-deep heather, squelching through bogs. On this occasion she wheedled me into walking the cliff path from St. Ives to Zennor, an expedition I now think of as the Zennor Death March. The distance is only about ten miles but the path follows the ups and downs of the headlands and the "walk" often becomes a vertiginous scrabble, the sea surging and sloshing hundreds of feet below; later, I read that that walk was rated as "severe." We did this without water or proper shoes and many hours later collapsed in Zennor into the one-roomed Tinners' Arms, a pub once frequented by Katherine

Mansfield and D. H Lawrence, where we rehydrated with many pints of meditative ale and caught the Land's End bus back to St. Ives.

Between 1989 and 2002 the Porcupine's Quill has published about twenty novels. I said earlier that I felt that most of what I'd chosen to publish stands above the ruck. I feel this more strongly about the story collections than I do about the novels. There are a few story collections, too, that I have reservations about but novels present real problems. They do everywhere. I wonder sometimes if Canada has ever produced a great novel. Possibly Mordecai Richler's *St. Urbain's Horseman*. I'm still not sure.

There are twentieth-century names against which we have to weigh all novels before we can talk lightly of "greatness" or "significance." Conrad, Joyce, Beckett, Naipaul, Waugh, Nabokov...

The recent Toronto media uproar about Dennis Bock's ill-written *The Ash Garden* is a perfect illustration of judgements passed without the felt weight of tradition. A perfect line for a critic is Spender's "I think continually of those who were truly great." What I am getting at is that there are thousands of novels but very few like, say, Graham Swift's *Waterland*. We ought to *know* the fate of most of "The New Face of Fiction." Most novels are fated to become literature's leafmould.

Leafmould. Concurrent with the writing of this book I've been editing for the Press, of course, and putting together an issue of *Canadian Notes and Queries* containing an essay on the House of Anansi and a bibliography of the press which runs from the founding in 1967 to 1989 when the press was bought by Jack Stoddart. Noting what was published year after year and trying to decide now what was worthy and what was a mistake has inevitably left me considering the value of what I am doing with the Porcupine's Quill. How much of the work is likely *not* to become leafmould? Anansi published forty-eight poetry titles; I'd say that seven are still of interest. Of the fifty-five fiction titles there are thirteen I can reread and commend.

It is not a criticism of the House of Anansi that so many of its books have become leafmould. The books of any literary press—of all presses—are of a time and place and it is inevitable that many will not be of lasting significance. But cherished by posterity or forgotten entirely, all these books are essential in the growth of a nation's literature. What is important is, in Dennis Lee's words, that we "wrestle with the mind and passion of our own time and place." What is important is that ambitious books are written and read, that new writers are launched, new readers won over, that the delight of reading and writing is handed on. The shape and significance of a literature take a very long time to reveal themselves.

There were reasons why the House of Anansi published so much that was fated to disappear. Anansi was a strident nationalist wake-up call to an almost comatose industry. The very act of publishing a Canadian book was for Anansi a political act. The press was also under enormous pressure to publish from the generation it was addressing. And publish it did—poets, hippies, ravers, practitioners of experimental prose, American draft evaders, cosmic weed smokers . . . Anansi was perhaps too much a part of the sixties ferment to be objective about its choices.

I have some hopes that the publications of the Porcupine's Quill will fare better. I haven't had to suffer the heated expectation of an entire generation as Anansi did; during the years I've been editing almost the reverse has been true. Literature has lost its sixties and seventies glamour, nationalism has languished, cultural ferment has subsided into apathy and indifference. Ideal conditions for making cool—and purely aesthetic—choices. Another factor in favour of the survival of Porcupine's Quill books is that I am much older than Dennis Lee was when he was making those choices, older and less driven. I like to think that age gives me a certain distance; I'm less likely than Dennis was to get involved in the moment.

All of which brings me circling back to the subject of novels. Most "mainstream" novels are fated to become leafmould and this is why I try to keep away from them. A nasty part of me rubs its hands with glee whenever I read in a review that a novel records the doings of two or three generations of whoever . . . *there's* one I won't have to bother with.

As I put this in "Travelling Northward":

> Six figure sums were routinely advanced to *artistes* who penned swollen sagas of powerful industrial families, of immigrant families rising from poverty to become powerful industrialists, of landowning families who diversified into powerful new industries and became more powerful than they'd been before but at the same time becoming riven by incest, insanity, possession by the devil, litigation and Alzheimer's, homosexual and lesbian inversion, poltergeists and hysterectomy, losing that guiding vision of their founder old Grandfather Ebenezer who used to kneel on the good earth running soil through his wise old fingers saying wise dawn things to little barefoot Mattie who never forgot a single utterance . . . and who went on to found an empire in oil, microchips, and laser-beam technology before renouncing the world and establishing an Ecological Foundation and Nature Reserve in memory of Grandfather Ebenezer where she cleaned up oil-fouled seabirds and imparted gentle wisdom to little barefoot Bobbie who three hundred pages later would corner the world market in extruded protein.

Working with Tim and Elke I'm able to publish novels which are eccentric and quirky, novels no commercial house would ever touch. I cannot write about them all but I delight in having published Alexander Scala's *Dr. Swarthmore*, Keath

Fraser's *Popular Anatomy*, Susan Perly's *Love Street*, Leo Simpson's *Sailor Man*, Terry Griggs's *The Lusty Man*, Ray Smith's *A Night at the Opera*, and Harold Rhenisch's *Carnival*.

I don't claim that these are "great" novels but they're lovely performances and they all gave me great pleasure. Alexander Scala's *Dr. Swarthmore*, a darkly comic tale of divine revelation and capitalism, has a curious history. Scala wrote it after leaving Harvard when he was twenty-two. He submitted it to Penguin Books which rejected it on the quaint grounds of blasphemy. Scala was so insulted that he put the MS in a drawer for thirty years. Steven Heighton in Kingston, a friend of Scala's, read the MS and phoned me to commend it. I loved the book from its opening page.

A review said of it: "Assuredly the first novel of the new millennium in which the Second Person of the Trinity has a walk-on part in a cheap suit."

All of these novels received far less than their due because they are all unusual and demanding and we do not have enough money to publicize them in the way the commercial houses do. Brenda Sharpe, who created the Porcupine's Quill Web site, claims that Leo Simpson's *Sailor Man* is one of the best books the Press has ever published. It received, to the best of my knowledge, one review, and sold 368 copies.

Of all our novels *How Insensitive* and *Noise* by Russell Smith have provided me with the most fun. I received from Russell a letter of the utmost snottiness and a sample chapter of *How Insensitive*. The letter, as I recall it, described Canadian literature as being concerned with angst on farms. Canadian literature was written by boring middle-aged people for other boring middle-aged people. *His* book, in contrast, was by a young urban person and reflected Canada's *real* urban concerns and blah, blah. He concluded the letter by saying more or less that I probably wouldn't like the book because I was myself a boring middle-aged establishment fart. I was charmed by the sheer aggression of this letter and even more charmed by the writing itself. Russell has written scenes more brilliantly funny than any other Canadian writer. He is a master of dialogue. Comparison with Kingsley Amis would not be inappropriate. *How Insensitive* sold an astonishing number of copies—well into the thousands. *Noise*, a better book, sold far fewer copies. Inexplicable. Although *How Insensitive* was short-listed for the Governor General's Award, reviews of both books have been mixed and there is in general a grudging reaction to Russell's work. Part of this can be explained by the fact that Canadians tend to resist humour. They are made uneasy by sophistication and Russell is *very* sophisticated indeed. He is also an intellectual and his questing intelligence is displayed in the construction of his prose and in the narrative devices he invents.

I fell into his work with immediate relish because I recognized how supremely gifted he is and I also recognized—and deeply approved of—his influences—Waugh and Kingsley Amis. There is about Russell a very British quality which comes from his South African background and that too might explain Canadian unease with his sprightly writing.

Here's a snippet of two punks in a Swiss Chalet, from *Noise*; his work is crammed with such vignettes.

> There were two punks with mohawks at the cash counter, waiting for someone to materialize behind it. James waited behind them for a minute. There didn't seem to be anybody working in the whole place. He shivered in the air conditioning. The Muzak breezed along. The punks were looking about, too. They had a glazed look. One of them had a T-shirt which read, "WHERE'S THE FUCKING MONEY YOU OWE ME?"
>
> "What's with all these pictures of like Heidi houses?" said one.
>
> The other one squinted at the blown-up posters on the walls.

"Switzerland," he announced.

"Why Switzerland?"

"It's a Swiss Chalet, right."

James glimpsed movement through a hatch into the kitchen, and waved his arm at whatever it was.

"I don't get Switzerland," said the first punk, as slowly as if in a dream. "I mean it's never really turned me on, you know?"

"Yeah. It's not sexy."

"Exactly. Switzerland's not sexy. Fuck Switzerland."

"Fucking Swiss bastards. Fuck 'em."

The novels I choose for the Press are always fun but the main focus for me remains short fiction. The Press is already *the* press for the short story, so in 2002 I turned my attention to a related form, the novella. I suggested to Tim that we start publishing stand-alone novellas. The form is an awkward one for publishers; conventional wisdom is that novellas are too long for magazines and too short for books and if they're published at all they're published in collections of stories.

I wanted to take novellas out of their surrounding clutter and shine the spotlight on them in much the same way that museum curators have abandoned display cabinets crammed with jumbled objects and have highlighted a few exquisite artifacts in austere cases.

A single novella can live in one's mind and imagination as vividly as can a novel. There is no need to defend the idea. I simply look back at the years of pleasure given me by such novellas as Thomas Mann's "Death in Venice," Nathanael West's "Miss Lonelyhearts," Philip Roth's "Goodbye, Columbus," Evelyn Waugh's "Scott-King's Modern Europe" . . . We started our programme with two intense and sophisticated novellas by David Helwig ("The Stand-In") and Mary Swan ("The Deep").

Some people are curious about the process of editing. I have always felt editing to be mildly impertinent and arrogant and I only feel that I can do it because I am a writer myself and know that most of the writers I work with have read my fiction and have some regard for it.

Major editing involves rearranging the building blocks of a story, cutting passages, finding a more effective starting place, giving greater weight to pertinent images. This is emotional and intuitive work.

Minor editing, though vastly important, is line-by-line testing and probing. An aspect of this kind of editing more common than readers might suppose is forcing writers to be logical and precise. I edited two books for the Honourable Heward Grafftey, science minister in Joe Clark's brief government, because he was a neighbour and because I like him. I remember handing him a chapter scored with red ink marking lapses in logic.

"But, well," he sputtered, "I am by training a lawyer."

"Then I'm glad," I replied, "you're not representing *me*."

I once wrote jokingly that the essence of editing was to go through each typescript finding the word *careen* and crossing it out. Writers refuse to accept that the word means "to cause a ship to lean or lie on one side for calking, barnacle removal, or repair." It can (only just) have an extended meaning of leaning sideways but such a meaning is compromised by its "ship" connotations. The word derives from the Latin *carina*, the keel of a ship. Writers believe the word to mean "rapid motion" or "reckless motion" possibly confusing it with *career*, from the Latin *currere*, to run, with connotations of war chariots. Driving this through writerly skulls is difficult.

The ideal editor must accept the uniqueness of each text and deal with it on its own terms. I try not to impose anything of my own style but rather seek to understand a book's rhetoric and then work to ensure that the writer performs that rhetoric to the top of his bent. I also feel quite strongly that an editor can only *suggest* changes; the writer must be ultimately responsible for the work.

The level and depth of editorial meddling is dictated not by some abstract theory but by the typescript itself. Sometimes good editing is the ability to see when little or none is needed. There are some writers who are so painstaking and meticulous and who have so burnished their manuscripts that editing is more or less a formality. I'm thinking here of such writers as Keath Fraser, Caroline Adderson, Annabel Lyon, and Mary Borsky.

Editorial meddling also has national characteristics. The British generally tend to feel that getting a book *right* is the writer's problem; they are less likely than other nationalities to accept a flawed book and work on it. American editors, because they *are* editors and editors *edit*, are more likely to regard finished books as interesting *seeds* of possible books. Consider the editing career of Gordon Lish at Knopf and *Esquire*; his work on Raymond Carver was so extensive that some American critics have said that Lish's name should be on the books as co-author. When I came to Canada in the sixties there were editors but at the Ryerson Press they were usually ex-salesmen who had done well on the road and had been rewarded with a comfortable berth in Toronto; they seemed to favour books on antique cars. I also had an impression that many editors in Canada were from the UK just as trade union activists seemed to be exclusively Scottish.

Some writers operate in what I think of as "closed systems." You can't go inside them except in superficial ways. This is because they've perfected a style and vocabulary that is so idiosyncratic or mannered that an outsider, an editor, cannot really contribute. Terry Griggs would be a good Canadian example. Ronald Firbank springs to mind. How did Robert Bridges edit Gerard Manley Hopkins? All that an editor can usefully do with a closed-system writer is say, These stories are stronger than these, so let's drop the weaker ones. This was exactly the process with Terry Griggs's extraordinary collection *Quickening*.

At the opposite end of the scale are writers whose work cries out for intercession. This is not to be negatively critical. A writer's style is the outcome of, among other things, temperament. Some writers write in a passionate outpouring of words and that approach seems to them necessary and natural. Steven Heighton writes in this way and in my editing of his work I always attempt to prune his lushness, concentrate, suggest the dryness of *fino* rather than the sugar of *oloroso*, the marksman's rifle rather than the shotgun blast. He is always good-natured about my plaintive nagging. In the *New Quarterly* special issue on my editing work Steve reproduced a letter I'd sent him about a story which appeared in his collection *On earth as it is*. The story was "Townsmen of a Stiller Town" which takes place in a morgue, an important detail given my first quoted note.

I wrote in part . . . "P. 22. If Basil had been drinking rye his breath wouldn't be 'briny.' What about 'a breath as foul and harsh as formaldehyde'?

"P. 20, middle of page. 'Joliffe's pipe on its side, sifting ash over papers.'

"You *cannot* say this. 'To sift' is a precise action of riddling material over a grill—metaphorically, I suppose you could 'sift through archives.' But a *pipe* can't *sift*.

"*Please* please an old man and change this.

"Sorry to fuss so much but getting things *right* will mean that your work will live. Get them *wrong* and wild dogs will gnaw at your corpse."

Possibly the loving combat I'm always locked in with Steve comes from my own temperament, from my own neurotic writing methods. I write an initial sentence usually many times over until it strikes me as perfect in diction and rhythm. Then I do the same thing with the second sentence. But joining the second sentence to the first changes both and so I rewrite both. This slightly mad process goes on, sentence by sentence, for weeks.

Sometimes manuscripts beg to be reshaped or rewritten. It often happens that the energy level in a story drops in one or more places. A good editor can feel these lapses or collapses as easily as an electrician can check current with a voltmeter. Conversely the voltmeter can pick up an energy surge; sometimes a paragraph or a couple of pages will stand out from surrounding competence and proclaim themselves and it often turns out that that paragraph or those pages are the emotional core of the story demanding to be taken out and reshaped.

To return to the image of a voltmeter checking current. This is as real to me as sewing on buttons might be for someone else. And, for me, as commonplace. I remember performing tricks once at the Humber School for Writers. A student submitted a story to the class and I rather astonished her by saying, "This story you've totally invented just as you've invented the characters. It's all rather plodding, I'm afraid. The only place in the story where you've connected to any real emotion is in the description of the inside of the sheds in the garden. And those sheds are drawn from your own life and childhood." She agreed that this was true, so I sent her off to think more about sheds.

I am not saying here that the current surges because material is autobiographical or "sincere," or that the "real" is more real than the imagined. It is simply that the real, the sheds, came alive in her story because *nouns* were coming into play. She was looking at *things* rather than playing with Lego. Sometimes the voltmeter picks up a sentence or paragraph because the writer is not concentrating sufficiently on the imagined world. When writers wander from the concrete, the particular, the current always drops. As I work on this book, I'm working with an ex-Humber student, Judith McCormack, on a short story collection. One of the stories is called "The Cardinal Humours." Here is its opening sentence:

> When Eduardo de Majia left Barcelona on an overcast, grey-yellow day in the fall of 1873, he left behind his wife

> and his two sons, and he took with him trunks and barrels of medicaments, bitter syrups, dried herbs, astringent tonics, white powders of various kinds, and sixty-three vials of tinctures.

I noticed that I wrote to her . . . "Page 1 'white powders of various kinds' is very weak after the more specific things which precede. Try one of: nostrums, infusions, lenitives, paregorics, carminatives, balsams—all words fitting to the tradition and period.

"'Bitter syrups' also sounds a bit dodgy. 'Syrup' is defined as 'any *sweet* thick liquid.' Rethink this one.

"And come to think of it, 'astringent tonics' sounds a touch unlikely."

Well, I admit.

It possibly *is* a strange way to spend one's days.

Of recent years, Tim and I have had to revise our vision of the Press. Our earlier conventional assumptions about nurturing careers crumbled under the increasing commercialization of the industry in Canada and the advent of agents. Our writers were being offered advances we couldn't come anywhere near meeting and they defected to Doubleday, Anansi, Key Porter, HarperCollins, McClelland and Stewart, Random House, and Knopf. I suggested to Tim that under his logo he print: *Purveyors to the Trade.* Tim, reviewing the list of publishers and authors, said rather grimly, "Well, I suppose we must be doing *something* right."

We sulked for a while but soon came around to realize that we couldn't expect young writers to turn down the chance of a reasonable income when all we can offer is an advance of $500. We understood that we'd have to see the function and purpose of the Porcupine's Quill differently. We had become, willy-nilly, a launching pad for careers, so we needed to stop thinking "defection" and to embrace the new reality. We needed to see ourselves as talent scouts and expansive impresarios.

Tim, with his always wily business sense, recouped some of his expenses by selling authors' first books to the larger publishers of their second books for republication and then, with considerable chutzpah, advertising the fact on his Web site, thereby using the major publishers to aggrandize the Porcupine's Quill's reputation.

I want to end this section on the Porcupine's Quill on a celebratory note because I feel we have much to celebrate. The Press has achieved all that I'd wanted at the beginning. Our writers are elegant and sophisticated. They love language and flaunt it. Joan Harcourt's "carefully crafted reliquaries, little boxes in which are enshrined little memories" have been firmly suppressed. And the Press does indeed crackle with energy. There's little question we're the best literary press in Canada. Perhaps in North America.

Along with acquiring manuscripts and editing where necessary and with printing and binding, a press has to *sell* books. Launchings are an effective way of selling books and are necessary to an author's sense of occasion. We launched books in Toronto and Ottawa and I'll conclude with an account of the Magnum Reading Series and the celebration of Irving Layton's eightieth birthday.

That one evening can stand for the entire spirit of the Porcupine's Quill adventure.

In 1990 I was in Toronto visiting Tony Calzetta. Tony had an exhibition on at the Lake Gallery and we went together to look at the paintings. I was introduced to Fran Hill, the gallery's director. Chatting with Fran was a friend from university days, Lise Giroux. Fran and Lise had both studied art history at York University. Lise told me that she, too, was from Ottawa and was opening a bookstore there. I promised to drop in. The Magnum Readings and Exhibitions Series evolved from this chance encounter.

Lise Giroux and Yoni Freeman together ran side-by-side establishments, the Magnum Book Store and Opus Bistro.

The bookstore was managed by Paula Black while Opus was managed by Lise. Yoni, originally from Israel, was the presiding culinary genius. Prior to opening Opus he had worked under Jamie Kennedy and Michael Stadtlander, two of Toronto's most acclaimed chefs, at the Scaramouche restaurant. When I reported to Myrna that Yoni was from Israel, she, as an ex-kibbutznik, claimed that the words *Israeli chef* constituted a perfect oxymoron but she was won over after the first mouthful.

The Opus Bistro quickly built a reputation as being one of the best restaurants in Ottawa. It was always packed with noisy and happy diners and reservations were necessary days in advance. *Where to Eat in Canada (1993)* raved about Yoni's cooking:

> His cooking may look simple and straight-forward, but actually it's about as simple as an ode by Horace. Try his black-bean soup with smoked pork, his blue-cheese salad with pears, his baked salmon with horseradish and sour cream—which we much prefer to his blackened sole. The menu is constantly changing and dishes like liver with calvados, cellentani with fresh squid and mussels, salmon with pink peppercorns and roast duckling with sour cherries are now little but a memory . . .

It seemed obvious to all of us that good food and drink were the natural partners of good books and paintings. Our conversations circled around ways and means and motives. Lise had a vision of the Magnum Book Store becoming a cultural centre and a cultural force in Ottawa. Sitting at the commodious Opus bar we consumed many a meditative Gibson (two ounces of Bombay Sapphire gin, three drops of vermouth, two cocktail onions).

We were setting out, we realized, to build a community. We were tired of cultural events being ghettoized in universities and auditoria, tired of institutional battery-acid coffee in Styrofoam cups, tired of littered floors, tired of dragooned student audiences wearing reversed baseball caps. We wanted something more intimate and gracious. We wanted the audience involved in the whole venture, able to meet and mingle with the writers and painters and—which is just as important—with each other. We wanted everyone to share in a coffee, a beer, a glass of wine, and enjoy paintings and conversation in a relaxed atmosphere.

This idea of building a community was also pursued in the generous hosting of writers and painters at Opus Bistro for dinner on the Saturday preceding the reading on Sunday evening. But—central question in the arts—who was going to pay the bills? We had visions of corporate sponsors and of sponsorship by publishers but these visions remained visions. No corporate entity showed the slightest interest in what we were attempting. Inevitably, Lise and Yoni shouldered the burden; Fran Hill and I helped by donating our time and energies.

I suggested to Lise a mechanism that would allow us to pay the readers and give us at the same time a faint chance to recoup some of our costs. We would ask each reader to give us a piece of previously unpublished work. For this work we would give the reader $200—the same sum paid by the Canada Council for a reading. I would then make thirty Xerox copies of the piece and staple them into card covers. Each would carry the following statement of limitation:

> *Here first published in an edition of thirty copies*
> *of which*
> *four are* hors de commerce *and*
> *twenty-six are numbered and signed.*

This we did for every reading. We charged $25 for these limited editions. They cost about $100 to make, so adding that to the fee paid the reader brought the cost to $300. To break even we had to sell twelve. This never happened. Nor in nine years of operation at Magnum and at other venues did we attract a single student or professor from either of Ottawa's universities.

I stapled the Xeroxed sheets into blue card covers and gradually these expensive editions became known as "Blue Things." Some Toronto dealers had standing orders for multiple copies but the audience in general was unable to see the significance of the severity of the limitation. I saw one of the early "Blue Things," Leon Rooke's story "Daddy Stump," quoted in a rare book dealers' catalogue recently at $225.

To help in building the community and to publicize the readings and exhibitions we sent out a Xeroxed newsletter to a mailing list we were always building. Lise also listed the readings and exhibitions on the daily menus. We did this not merely as advertising but because we wanted to integrate literature and painting into daily life.

The newsletters typically had notes on the writers by me, comments on the exhibitions by the painters themselves, Paula Black's list of new and recommended books, and a recipe by Yoni—Fall Fruit Chutney, Barbecue Flank Steak Sandwich, Shrimp with Feta Cheese and Harissa . . . that last the beginnings of Yoni's obsession with extremely hot peppers.

The design and organization of the newsletter was taken over by Brenda Sharpe who, like all of us, donated her time and expertise to the enterprise.

The Magnum Readings and Exhibitions Series started in April 1991 with a reading by me and an exhibition by Tony Calzetta. Since then we have heard Leon Rooke, Hugh Hood, Ray Smith, Dayv James-French, Terry Griggs, Diane Schoemperlen, Rohinton Mistry, Joan MacLeod, Douglas Glover, Irving Layton, Jane Urquhart, Mark Frutkin, Don Dickinson, Clark Blaise, Norman Levine, Carol Shields, Steven Heighton, Gael Turnbull, George Elliott Clarke, Matt Cohen, Audrey Thomas, Yann Martel, Isabel Huggan, John

Mills, John Newlove, and the adorable Caroline Adderson.

We hung exhibitions by Tony Calzetta, Andrea Bolley, David Bolduc, Alex Cameron, Richard Gorman, Gordon Rayner, Tony Urquhart, Peter Templeman, Blair Sharpe, Dieter Grund, Catherine Beaudette, and Clive D'Oliviera with a summer show of photographs of the readings by our "official" photographer, Micheline Rochette.

Right from the start there seemed to be something magical about the series. The first audience was about a hundred strong and we never dipped lower than thirty-five. Magnum Book Store had a small café area at the rear where Yoni served lunch four days a week. Those walls as well as space in the bookstore proper were hung with paintings. And the *kind* of interaction that I'd dreamed of actually happened. While the first show was up—works on paper by Tony Calzetta—two women were having lunch in the Magnum café. When finished, they asked the waiter for the bill and one of them, pointing at the pictures, said, "And I'd like that one and she'll take the pale pink one over there."

Perfect.

Exactly the way pictures should be bought.

Burt Heward, the *Ottawa Citizen* books editor, covered our activities faithfully in his Saturday column and Nancy Baele, the *Citizen* art critic, covered most of the shows. The CBC began to record the readings and interview the writers. Gradually we began to recognize the same faces in the audience and in the Opus Bistro afterwards. We began to put names to faces. We were beginning to grow into a community.

Because we developed a core of regulars and because those regulars came to trust my taste I was able to present at Magnum writers who were not well-known—in some cases Porcupine's Quill writers launching a first book—and give them the experience of a large and enthusiastic audience. I even dared to present five poets—Carol Shields, Irving Layton, Gael Turnbull, George Elliott Clarke, and John Newlove.

There were some wonderful moments at the Magnum Readings but the most moving of the weekends was that on which we staged a party for Irving Layton's eightieth birthday. The Porcupine's Quill had just released *Dance with Desire: The Love Poems of Irving Layton*. The first copies arrived at Magnum the day before the party. I had commissioned Richard Gorman to do drawings for the book and Rick had come down from Toronto to celebrate the occasion.

(While the book was in production I'd gone to Rick's house to pick up the drawings. It was a surreal morning. Rick had been up all night drinking brandy and painting. He showed me around. Kitchen. A living room draped in sheet plastic used as a studio. Bedroom. Then he opened a door onto a room entirely bare. He made no comment. Lying on the floorboards were three very dead Christmas trees.)

Lise had set up a big table in the bookstore café area and had festively set the table with a centrepiece of mimosa. Present were Rick Gorman, Fran Hill and friend, Doris Cowan, Ken Rockburn, Micheline Rochette, Randall Ware, Myrna and I, and, of course, Irving and his wife Anna.

Ken Rockburn ran a CBC radio show called *Medium Rare* which featured music and interviews with writers and musicians. He asked if he might discreetly record the dinner conversation. He later broadcast an edited version on his program.

I bought some hand-made paper and Myrna designed and printed special menus. We also contributed a couple of bottles of Veuve Clicquot to toast Irving and wish him many happy returns. What a splendid evening it was! What bits of it I remember. I've never dared listen to the tape.

IN HONOUR OF IRVING LAYTON
On the occasion of
Irving Layton's
eightieth birthday

and on the launching of
Dance with Desire: The Love Poems of Irving Layton
Saturday, March 7, 1993

Split Pea Soup with Smoked Pork
or
Avocado Salad with Salmon Caviar
(Konocti Fumé Blanc, Lake County, California 1989)
Baked Lamb Rack with Rosemary Sauce
or
Gulf Shrimps with Roasted Red Peppers and Garlic
(Vina Santa Rita Reserva, Maipo Valley, Chile 1988)

Chocolate Terrine with Fresh Strawberries

Ken Rockburn not only recorded conversation at the dinner but subsequently wrote a memoir. Here's a brief excerpt from his 1995 book *Medium Rare: Jamming with Culture*:

> The evening began with a round of toasts to Layton, who, in turn raised his glass to his wife, Anna, for her "love, compassion and inspiration." He then proposed a challenge to the table that would be responsible for the progress of the remainder of the evening; he asked each of us to recall some strange and wonderful story, something which had happened to us personally that we could not explain, some odd occurrence or, better still, some eerie event or coincidence which illustrated the mystery of life.
>
> "Because this is an unusual evening," he said, "where writers and painters and sculptors are getting together. You know, what the hell is literature all about, what the hell is poetry all about if it isn't about a defiance of reality? Reality smells, it stinks, unless it's gotten ahold of by the artists who transmute it into something strange and wonderful. So I want strange stories that show the

remarkable and the magical in all our lives. Those of us who are lucky enough to have a line to our childhood know it's there."

As Layton spoke, his wife Anna, sitting beside him, would watch him carefully, picking up his napkin from the floor when it slid unnoticed from his lap, providing an appropriate word when one failed to come to him, or repeating in his ear the words of one of the other guests if Layton failed to hear. Her attention was unobtrusive and not in the least patronizing, which could easily have been the case for any other couple whose age difference was nearly fifty years . . .

"I will soon be eighty . . ."

"You are." From Anna.

"Anna is . . ."

Anna smiled. 'Thirty-two."

"Thirty-two. I am Jewish—listen carefully, take it in—Anna is an Acadian, a Catholic. In other words, her cultural background is quite different from mine. The disparity in age is quite clear."

All eyes tried not to be on Anna.

"I mean, eighty," Layton shook his head. "A guy of eighty doesn't even dream of an erection anymore, you know."

"Oh, Irving," chided Metcalf, "stop telling these awful lies."

"Surely you dream?" I asked hopefully.

"Irving," offered Richard Gorman, "you won't be eighty until you're 110."

"God bless you for saying that," said Layton. "But you would say, if you were a sociologist, that the chances of the two of us having a happy and successful and wonderful marriage that has endured for nearly ten years, would be very slim. Very few would be willing to bank their savings on anything like this.

"Yet here are Anna and I, after ten years, as much in love, if not more, than we were at the beginning. And that's what life is all about, that's what poetry is all about, that's what the poets are always talking about. They're always trying to make people aware that there is magic about, the unpredictable, there's chance and there's beauty and there's love."

More food came, more wine was consumed and more stories were told. Myrna Metcalf told of a strange encounter at the neolithic stone ring at Avebury, the dishevelled Richard Gorman told a wonderful tale about giving the Rideau River offerings of tobacco, in the Indian fashion, for allowing itself to be the subject of a mural he was painting, and how the ritual had attracted all manner of wildlife to the spot; the brooding boyfriend of Fran Hill told a story that *seemed* to involve drug use and that weird state of consciousness between sleep and wakefulness, though everyone was too drunk by that time to understand whatever it was he was trying to say.

On Sunday, the scene at Magnum Books was pure Hollywood. People were lined up for a full block an hour before the reading was supposed to start. We had engaged the services of an off-duty policeman to handle the door and as the time ticked by we began to fear for public safety. The bookstore was jammed with bodies. Every chair was taken, people were sitting on the floor and standing three deep around the walls. Fervent Layton fans had come from as far away as Montreal and London.

We estimated that we crowded in about 190 people and we turned away another 130 or so at the door, many of whom gathered outside singing very loudly: *Happy birthday, dear Irving! Happy birthday to you!* After the reading we sold more than one hundred books.

I'd segregated Irving in the Opus Bistro so that he could sit down and rest himself and so that, at the appointed time, he could make a suitable entrance. Irving and Anna and Lise and I sat at the bar waiting. Irving sipped at a snifter of cognac. I numbered the Blue Things, passing them over one by one for Irving to sign. That finished, I glanced at my watch yet again. We all seemed to be feeling a little nervous, unnerved almost by the numbers. At eight o'clock we walked through the connecting passage into Magnum Books to face the heat and expectation of the crowd.

I climbed onto the makeshift stage to introduce the evening.

Phil Jenkins, Ottawa author and columnist for the *Ottawa Citizen* wrote about the reading as follows:

> "Give me a moment while I let the rum and Coke descend to my toes," Irving Layton said, and the crowd at the poet's informal eightieth birthday party at Magnum Books gave him the moment.
>
> And what a crowd it was. A sea of respect jammed into a space the size of a backyard swimming pool, with Layton down at the front on the springboard, waiting to dive into the poems of the new edition of *Dance with Desire*. (The original edition appeared in 1986. This one, a classy volume with swirling charcoal drawings of bodies in love by ex-Ottawa resident Richard Gorman, includes some extra poems chosen by John Metcalf.)
>
> ". . . I like to think I have joined the ranks of the great amorous poets; Ovid, Robbie Burns, John Donne," Layton pronounced as the rum and Coke reached his toes. Then he began to read, and the room filled with poems tapped out on hip bones, saintly wantons, breast strokes, taxi horns honking for Marilyn, sonnets scribbled in taverns, religious nudges, favoured erogenous zones and civilized seductions—and laughter, our laughter, at the

thrust of his wit and the rolling of his rhythms.

He read for an hour, an act of stamina and gratitude that proved his love of performance and wish to please. He finished with a poem to his wife, *I Take My Anna Everywhere*, crossing the stage to stand before her and recite it like a suitor, The last two lines read:

All the men who see her
want to live their wrecked lives forever.

There were flowers and a standing ovation for our hero of the horizontal. "I'm grateful for the moment," Layton told us. Then, like a pub entertainer who is sure that the crowd is in love and ready for more, he took requests from the audience, six in all, that included a Bishop, an ode to his mother from whose speech cadence he claimed to get his "impeccable sense of rhythm," and a long, throat-tiring account of his first trip to Paris.

After the sixth there was a silence in which you could have heard a simile drop. "Perhaps we should stop here and move into the bar," John Metcalf wondered. Layton agreed with that, looked out over the sea of respect and gave us this entirely suitable closing remark.

"At 80, I'm in the prime of senility. All I worry about now is whether there will be anyone left to come to my funeral; whether my fly is up or down. And how the hell the world is going to get along without me."

L'ENVOI

I CROSSED THE BRIDGE and started up the steep little hill to Leon Rooke's house when I felt a deep stab of pain in my chest. I stood still looking back to the stream where a heron posed in the shallows. The pain stopped immediately and I went on my way to get of a couple of beers from Leon's fridge for Tim and me. Indigestion? Two rather greasy pakoras I'd eaten earlier?

It was September 1997, the Eden Mills Writers' Festival, the village dense with thousands of visitors. Every year Tim and Elke man a booth selling books and I always attend because the day is my annual "office day" with writers and publishers dropping by the booth to chat.

The next day I took the bus from Guelph to Toronto and arrived early at Union Station. To pass some time I thought I'd walk to Nicholas Hoare's bookstore on Front Street. Just outside the station that same pain, but agonizing, clamped me motionless. I could scarcely breathe. I managed to lean against the low wall, conscious only of legs and feet passing by.

It was, of course, angina. I was sent to the hospital for a stress test and in December had an angiogram which revealed a ninety-five per cent blockage in one artery. The surgeon said that normally they'd have carried on and performed the required angioplasty then and there, but that budget restraints under the Harris government meant that I'd have to join a waiting list. I waited until April of the next year for the angioplasty. They inserted into the artery a piece of tubing called a stent. Learning this new word was the only pleasing aspect of the whole terrifying business. The peculiar horror of the operation is that one is conscious while it is going on. When the operation is over, the patient has to lie still in bed with a sack of sand compressing the incision into the femoral artery in the groin up which they have fed the surgical equivalent of a plumber's snake.

"If you feel anything wet or hot," said the nurse, "press the alarm button. We'll only have seconds."

All this struck me as not far removed from having your arm sawn off in the cockpit of a ship of the line and the stump cauterized in boiling pitch.

For a while after the operation I felt tired and diminished. The anxiety of the eight months of waiting for the operation cost me sorely. Since then, life has been ruled by pills in the morning and pills in the evening. The sight of the Nitroglycerin Sublingual Spray is a daily reminder of mortality. My real priorities were being nudged aside by electrocardiograms and fasting blood tests.

Gradually, however, the world stopped contracting. The Press needed my attention. *Canadian Notes and Queries* needed stropping to a keener edge. Where in Canada, Michael Darling aside, could I find reviewers like Florence King whose review of *Parachutes and Kisses* by Erica Jong contained the sentence "Jong's sow-in-heat prose style is impossible to quote in a newspaper . . ." Two new novellas seemed to be ripening in my mind. One of them involving the ancient mistress of a G. D. Roberts–like poet whose ashes she brings back to Fredericton for interment in the cathedral and who ends up winning a parcel of moose steaks at a darts shoot-out in the Legion Hall. A new book of critical essays was also bobbing about.

But during this period of restricted action I was able to step back a pace or two from the daily onrush and hullabaloo of the Press and consider the profound changes in the literary scene since 1989 when I'd joined up with Tim and Elke. Rampant commercialization was making so much din that quieter voices were ignored or drowned out in the uproar. An aesthetic underground was never more necessary.

Steven Heighton said to me recently, "Literature used to be about literature. Now it's about money."

Money, and Prizes. Prizes proliferating. And along with them the manufacturing of celebrity by the manipulation of publicity budgets. Literature metamorphosing into Show Biz.

Writers were once validated by what they wrote; now they seek validation from journalists and TV personalities. Who would *wish* to be sandwiched between a poodle trainer and a lighthouse keeper, enduring the unctuosities of a Peter Gzowski, a Pamela Wallin or a Peter Mansbridge? Who would *wish* to discuss *le mot juste* with Jan Wong, a journalist who in her youth embraced the aesthetic subtleties of Mao's Cultural Revolution? Who would *wish* to be interviewed on Evan Solomon's TV show *Hot Type*, an experience I would imagine like being slobbered on by an enthusiastic Labrador? How could writers be lured by siren songs so *crummy*? It is the shallowness that appals. Yet the celebrity manufactured by these nonentities is what many writers seem to crave; for many this mindless exposure is a component of "success."

Under these conditions and with an unsophisticated readership, books turn into commodity, into "product," and they are packaged and sold as such. The ludicrous frenzy created over and around Ondaatje's *The English Patient* can serve as an example. Philip Marchand in the *Toronto Star* was the only critic to say publicly that the book was ill-written and tedious.

Prizes, too, have become a problem. There is something anti-literary about prizes. Literature is not a competition. Prizes deform a literature by focusing attention on a small clutch of books. The awards do not confer *literary* status; they are transparently marketing schemes. Media interest is less in theme and style than it is in the sum of money awarded. In Canada, prizes are celebrated in nationalistic rather than literary terms; *we won* is the national and media attitude rather than we read and experienced and enjoyed.

When the short list for the Booker Prize was announced in 2002 the *Globe and Mail* published two fascinating letters to the editor on the subject on the same day. One was an upswelling of smarmy Babbittry from Douglas Gibson, president and publisher of McClelland and Stewart Ltd. The other was an indignant outburst from Stephen Henighan, author most recently of a book of literary essays, *When Words Deny the World*.

Gibson wrote:

> The news that three Canadian authors have been nominated for the Booker Prize must bring pride and pleasure to all of us. James Adams is correct to dwell on the remarkable international success of our authors in recent years.
>
> In the past few months, we have read many pessimistic stories about Canadian publishing, centring on the financial failure of the General Publishing group. By happy contrast, now is a time to celebrate Canadian accomplishment and to recognize the farsighted role played by our government agencies—specifically, the Department of Canadian Heritage and the Canada Council—in supporting our authors and nurturing the publishers that launch them.
>
> If there were a writing Olympics, our men and women would be on the podium all the time, and our national anthem would be played so often that even non-Canadians would know the words.

Henighan wrote:

> James Adams's claim of a "golden age" in Canadian literature (Some Day, They'll Call This the Golden Age—Sept. 25) overlooks the uncomfortable fact that the appearance of three Canadians on the Booker shortlist coincides with the judges' decision to shortlist more "fun" and "popular" books. This is a commercial, not a literary, triumph. The Booker shortlist confirms that the Canadian publishing industry has perfected a strain of easily exportable, no-name entertainment.
>
> Mr. Adams himself underlines the commercial roots of his bias when he defines each book he mentions in terms of the prize money it has earned. "Golden age" is a gross misnomer. The metaphor Mr. Adams should have used comes from the history of American robber-baron capitalism. This is our Gilded Age. The difference is that, during the U.S. Gilded Age, writers stood outside the commercial glare and criticized it.

Journalistic engagement with our culture has sunk now to columns in the *Globe and Mail* with smartass titles like "Arts Ink," which on this day of writing informs us that Michael Jackson suffered minuscule burns while setting off fireworks at a charity concert.

Rarely do we hear sane voices rising above "hype" and "buzz." Rarely do we find people taking the long view, patiently comparing books from the present with books from the past. Rarely do we hear reference to the "crafte so longe to lerne." The universities, once a countervailing influence, seem to have abandoned any public role and teachers of literature either echo media endorsement or simply play with themselves.

Bloated bogus novels trumpeted.

Florid verbiage.

And an audience that can't seem to tell the difference.

We are in a mess.

But so, I am cheered to find, is Australia.

I read recently *Snakecharmers in Texas: Essays 1980–1987* by Clive James. In a review of Robert Hughes's *The Fatal Shore* written for *The New Yorker*, James looked back over Australian literature's recent past and I was astonished to find that what he had to say about Australia was almost identical to what I had said about Canada in *Freedom from Culture: Selected Essays 1982–1992*.

Clive James, author of a delicious three-volume autobiography which begins with *Unreliable Memoirs*, wrote of Australia:

> Ardent republicans would like Australia to be self-sufficient in the arts the way it is in minerals. The idea that any one country can be culturally self-sufficient is inherently fallacious, but in the forward rush of Australian confidence during Gough Whitlam's period of government, when grants were handed out to anybody with enough creative imagination to ask for one, reason was thrown into the back seat. For the last fifteen years, Australian artists in all fields, supposedly free at last from the imposition of being judged by alien—i.e. British—standards, have been judged by their own standards, and almost invariably found to be the authors of significant works. The glut of self-approval has been most evident in literature, which in normal circumstances customarily produces a strong critical movement to accompany any period of sustained creativity but in Australia's case has largely failed to do so. The undoubted fact that some very good things have been written can't stave off the consideration that many less good things have been given the same welcome . . . In Australia, while literature is rapidly becoming a cash crop, a literary community

> has been slower to emerge. Criticism is too often, in the strict sense, tendentious. Scale is duly hailed, ambition lauded, but the direction of the book—does it point the way? does it give us purpose?—is usually the basis of assessment. There are not many critics detached enough to quibble over detail, and ask why so many great writers have produced so little good writing.

The relatively recent arrival of literary agents in Canada has accelerated the commercialization of the literary world. Agents want to make money and therefore take on as clients only writers whose books have commercial potential. Agents demand big advances for their writers. In most cases, the Canadian reading public is not large enough to buy a sufficient number of books to earn back the advance. If foreign sales are not made, the publisher is bound to lose. This situation will be tolerated while publishers are in competition to build lists but cannot be sustained indefinitely.

One possible effect of all this might be that books will be tailored with an international audience in mind. This, in turn, will probably tilt the work towards genre writing. The large publishers will become less and less interested in books likely to appeal only to Canadian experience; publishing power resides in New York and London and those arbiters are more familiar with martinis than they are with moose and Mounties.

If the large houses, as they are rumoured to be doing, start the practice of refusing to read un-agented manuscripts, then another layer of commercialization will have been put in place. Authors will have to be approved by agents whose *raison d'être* is to sell work with commercial potential.

In my 1987 Tanks Campaign pamphlet against the idea of subsidy I concluded with these words:

> Publishing and all other aspects of the literary life in Canada need to be put on a commercial footing. I think

that is the only way we can regain dignity and perspective.

Free from government aid and approval, our writing can better work its magic on readers. In *Required Reading*, Philip Larkin wrote: "I think we got much better poetry when it was all regarded as sinful or subversive, and you had to hide it under the cushion when somebody came in. What I don't like about subsidies and support is that they destroy the essential nexus between the writer and the reader. If the writer is being paid to write and the reader is being paid to read, the element of compulsive contact vanishes."

Despite the fact that sound commercial practice would leave us with a smaller—and much different—literary world, it would at least be *ours*, the possession of individuals. We would be free from Culture, free from nationalism, free from CanLit, and free for the first time in many years to begin the building of a literature in Canada, a literature, in Philip Larkin's words, of compulsive contact.

Having actually watched the process of commercialization over the fifteen years since I wrote those words, I have to admit that I was wrong. Commercial publishing in Canada has no place for the poetry of George Johnston or Eric Ormsby, no place for the essays of W. J. Keith, no place for the delicacies of Mary Borsky, Clark Blaise, or Libby Creelman. I still believe, passionately, in Larkin's "compulsive contact," still believe our literature needs to separate itself from the state. I have no idea how that can be effected. I have no answers other than the willing co-operation of individuals.

Reviewing in 1964 *Kipling's Mind and Art* edited by Andrew Rutherford, Evelyn Waugh wrote of Kipling's priorities—and politics—a few sentences which aptly describe mine too.

> He believed civilization to be something laboriously achieved which was only precariously defended. He wanted to see the defences fully manned and he hated the liberals because he thought them gullible and feeble, believing in the easy perfectibility of man and ready to abandon the work of centuries for sentimental qualms.

I thought often during the writing of this book of the House of Anansi. The press was sold to Jack Stoddart of General Publishing in 1989, the same year I started working with the Porcupine's Quill. It was as if the Porcupine's Quill was assuming the task which must be taken up by new people every twenty years or so.

Dennis Lee said in an interview in the *Montreal Star* in 1969:

> Literature is a whole dimension of being a citizen of a country, which we've generally been deprived of. Without it, you have something less than an adequate society. You don't have enough nourishment. It's an underdeveloped situation.
>
> We give a hoot. It's a civilized act to wrestle with the mind and passions of our own time and place.
>
> And if we don't do that, we're less than civilized.

Exactly so, Dennis.

And that is why, lofty tree or future leafmould, the wrestling must go on.

BIBLIOGRAPHY

Books by John Metcalf

New Canadian Writing 1969. Clarke, Irwin. Toronto, 1969.
The Lady Who Sold Furniture. Clarke, Irwin. Toronto, 1970.
Going Down Slow. McClelland and Stewart. Toronto, 1972.
The Teeth of My Father. Oberon Press. Ottawa, 1975.
Girl in Gingham. Oberon Press. Ottawa, 1978.
General Ludd. ECW Press. Toronto, 1980.
Selected Stories. McClelland and Stewart. Toronto, 1982.
Kicking Against the Pricks. ECW Press. Toronto, 1982.
Adult Entertainment. Macmillan. Toronto, 1986.
Adult Entertainment. St. Martin's Press. New York, 1990.
Adult Entertainment. Random House of Canada, 1990. Paperback release.
What Is a Canadian Literature? Red Kite Press. Guelph, 1988.
Volleys (with Sam Solecki & W. J. Keith). Porcupine's Quill. Erin, 1990.
Shooting the Stars. Porcupine's Quill. Erin, 1993.
Freedom from Culture. ECW Press. Toronto, 1994.
Acts of Kindness and of Love (with Tony Calzetta). Presswerk Editions, 1995.

An Aesthetic Underground. Thomas Allen Publishers. Toronto, 2003.
Forde Abroad. Porcupine's Quill. Erin, 2003.
Standing Stones: The Best Stories of John Metcalf. Thomas Allen Publishers. Toronto, 2004.
Shut Up He Explained. Biblioasis. Windsor, 2007.
Going Down Slow. Biblioasis. Windsor, 2007. (Reprint)
The Canadian Short Story. Oberon Press, Ottawa, 2014.

Books Edited by John Metcalf

TRADE BOOKS

Best Canadian Stories 1976 (with Joan Harcourt). Oberon Press. Ottawa.
Best Canadian Stories 1977 (with Joan Harcourt). Oberon Press. Ottawa.
Best Canadian Stories 1978 (with Clark Blaise). Oberon Press. Ottawa.
Best Canadian Stories 1979 (with Clark Blaise). Oberon Press. Ottawa.
Best Canadian Stories 1980 (with Clark Blaise). Oberon Press. Ottawa.
Best Canadian Stories 1981 (with Leon Rooke). Oberon Press. Ottawa.
Best Canadian Stories 1982 (with Leon Rooke). Oberon Press. Ottawa.
Here and Now: Canadian Stories (with Clark Blaise). Oberon Press. Ottawa, 1977.
First Impressions. Oberon Press. Ottawa, 1980.
Second Impressions. Oberon Press. Ottawa, 1981.
Third Impressions. Oberon Press. Ottawa, 1982.
Making It New. Methuen Publishing. Toronto, 1982.
The New Press Anthology: Best Canadian Stories (Vol. I) (with Leon Rooke). General Publishing. Toronto, 1984.

The New Press Anthology: Best Canadian Stories (Vol. II) (with Leon Rooke). General Publishing. Toronto, 1985.

The Bumper Book. ECW Press. Toronto, 1987.

Carry on Bumping. ECW Press. Toronto, 1988.

Writers in Aspic. Véhicule Press. Montreal, 1988.

The Macmillan Anthology 1 (with Leon Rooke). Macmillan. Toronto, 1988.

The Macmillan Anthology 2 (with Leon Rooke). Macmillan. Toronto, 1989.

The Macmillan Anthology 3 (with Kent Thompson). Macmillan. Toronto, 1990.

How Stories Mean (with J. R. [Tim] Struthers). Porcupine's Quill. Erin, 1993.

The New Story Writers. Quarry Press. Kingston, 1992.

Cuento canadiense contemporáneo. John Metcalf (compilador), traducción: Juan Carlos Rodriguez. Universidad Nacional Autonoma de México. Mexico, 1996.

Hugh Hood. Light Shining Out of Darkness and Other Stories. McClelland and Stewart. Toronto, 2001.

Best Canadian Stories 2007. Oberon Press. Ottawa.

Best Canadian Stories 2008. Oberon Press. Ottawa.

Best Canadian Stories 2009. Oberon Press. Ottawa.

Best Canadian Stories 2010. Oberon Press. Ottawa.

Best Canadian Stories 2011. Oberon Press. Ottawa.

Best Canadian Stories 2012. Oberon Press. Ottawa.

Best Canadian Stories 2013. Oberon Press. Ottawa.

Best Canadian Stories 2014. Oberon Press. Ottawa.

TEXTBOOKS

Wordcraft (Books 1–5). J. M. Dent and Sons. Toronto, 1967–77. (Vocabulary and comprehension books, Grades 7–11.)

Rhyme and Reason. Ryerson Press. Toronto, 1969. (Poetry textbook, Grades 8–10.)

Salutation. Ryerson Press. Toronto, 1970. (Anthology of world poetry. Grades 10–12.)

Sixteen by Twelve. McGraw-Hill. Toronto, 1971. (Canadian short stories. Grades 10–12.)
The Narrative Voice. McGraw-Hill. Toronto, 1971. (Canadian short stories. University text.)
Kaleidoscope. Van Nostrand Reinhold. Toronto, 1972. (Canadian short stories. Junior high school.)
The Speaking Earth. Van Nostrand Reinhold. Toronto, 1972. (Canadian poetry. Grades 9–11.)
Stories Plus. McGraw-Hill. Toronto, 1979. (Canadian stories. Grades 10–12.)
New Worlds. McGraw-Hill. Toronto, 1980. (Canadian stories. Grades 8–9.)
Making It New. Methuen. Toronto, 1982. (Trade and university text.)
Canadian Classics. McGraw-Hill Ryerson. Toronto, 1993.

For Oberon Press

At Peace. Ann Copeland. 1978.
Taking Cover. Keath Fraser. 1982.
The Elizabeth Stories. Isabel Huggan. 1984.
The Love Parlour. Leon Rooke. 1977
Cry Evil. Leon Rooke. 1980.

For Quarry Press, Macmillan and ECW Press

Hockey Night in Canada and Other Stories. Diane Schoemperlen. 1991.
The Man of My Dreams. Diane Schoemperlen. 1990.
Death Suite. Leon Rooke. 1981.

For the Porcupine's Quill Press

Cape Breton Is the Thought-Control Centre of Canada. Ray Smith. 1989.
The Improved Binoculars. Irving Layton. 1991.
Lunar Attractions. Clark Blaise. 1990.
Europe. Louis Dudek. 1991.
Endeared by Dark: The Collected Poems of George Johnston. 1990.
Victims of Gravity. Dayv James-French. 1990.
Volleys. Solecki, Metcalf, Keith. 1990.
Quickening. Terry Griggs. 1991.
Blue Husbands. Don Dickinson. 1991.
The Happiness of Others. Leon Rooke. 1991.
Portraits of Canadian Writers. Sam Tata. 1991.
An Independent Stance. W. J. Keith. 1991.
Flight Paths of the Emperor. Steven Heighton. 1992.
Dance with Desire. Irving Layton. 1992.
While Breath Persist. Gael Turnbull. 1992.
A Night at the Opera. Ray Smith. 1992.
Thank Your Mother for the Rabbits. John Mills. 1992.
Man and His World. Clark Blaise. 1992.
Forests of the Medieval World. Don Coles. 1993.
Bad Imaginings. Caroline Adderson. 1993.
How Stories Mean. John Metcalf and J. R. (Tim) Struthers. 1993.
Apology for Absence. John Newlove. 1993.
Mogul Recollected. Richard Outram. 1993.
Shooting the Stars. John Metcalf. 1993.
From a Seaside Town. Norman Levine. 1993.
Canada Made Me. Norman Levine. 1993.
Onlyville. Cynthia Holz. 1994.
City of Orphans. Patricia Robertson. 1994.
Thrand of Gotu. George Johnston. 1994.
How Insensitive. Russell Smith. 1994.
A Litany in Time of Plague. K. D. Miller. 1994.
Lives of the Mind Slaves. Matt Cohen. 1994.

Popular Anatomy. Keath Fraser. 1995.
On earth as it is. Steven Heighton. 1995.
Driving Men Mad. Elise Levine. 1995.
The Lusty Man. Terry Griggs. 1995.
Influence of the Moon. Mary Borsky. 1995.
Help Me, Jacques Cousteau. Gil Adamson. 1995.
Lovers and Other Strangers. Carol Malyon. 1996.
Sailor Man. Leo Simpson. 1996.
Telling My Love Lies. Keath Fraser. 1996.
The Garden of Earthly Delights. Meeka Walsh. 1996.
Kiss Me. Andrew Pyper. 1996.
The Porcupine's Quill Reader. Eds. Tim Inkster and John Metcalf. 1996.
Dancer. Shelley Peterson. 1996.
Buying on Time. Antanas Sileika. 1997.
If I Were Me. Clark Blaise. 1997.
Small Change. Elizabeth Hay. 1997.
Sleeping Weather. Cary Fagan. 1997.
Jacob's Ladder. Joel Yanofsky. 1997.
Promise of Shelter. Robyn Sarah. 1997
Collected Poems (Vol. 1). P. K. Page. 1997.
Collected Poems (Vol. 2). P. K. Page. 1997.
The Schemers and Viga Glum. George Johnston. 1997.
Learning to Live Indoors. Alison Acheson. 1998.
Love in a Warm Climate. Kelley Aitken. 1998.
The Bubble Star. Lesley-Anne Bourne. 1998.
Belle of the Bayou. Joanne Goodman. 1998.
The King of Siam. Murray Logan. 1998.
Mixed-Up Grandmas. Carol Malyon. 1998.
Ripostes. Philip Marchand. 1998.
Noise. Russell Smith. 1998.
Aquarium. Mike Barnes. 1999.
Devil's Darning Needle. Linda Holeman. 1999.
Give Me Your Answer. K. D. Miller. 1999.
Old Flames. Kim Moritsugu. 1999.

Abby Malone. Shelley Peterson. 1999.
The Man Who Loved Jane Austen. Ray Smith. 1999.
One Last Good Look. Michael Winter. 1999.
Crossing the Salt Flats. Christopher Wiseman. 1999.
Southern Stories. Clark Blaise. 2000.
Kurgan. Don Coles. 2000.
Walking in Paradise. Libby Creelman. 2000.
How Did You Sleep? Paul Glennon. 2000.
Oxygen. Annabel Lyon. 2000.
Carnival. Harold Rhenisch. 2000.
This Is Our Writing. T. F. Rigelhof. 2000.
Great Expectations. Grant Robinson. 2000.
The One with the News. Sandra Sabatini. 2000.
Love Street. Susan Perly. 2001.
Facsimiles of Time. Eric Ormsby. 2001.
Gambler's Fallacy. Judith Cowan. 2001.
Dr. Swarthmore. Alexander Scala. 2001.
Pittsburgh Stories. Clark Blaise. 2001.
A Kind of Fiction. P. K. Page. 2001.
Dove Legend. Richard Outram. 2001.
Holy Writ. K. D. Miller. 2001.
The Lover's Progress. David Solway. 2001.
13. Mary-Lou Zeitoun. 2002
When Words Deny the World. Stephen Henighan. 2002.
Seasoning Fever. Susan Kerslake. 2002.
A Tourist's Guide to Glengarry. Ian McGillis. 2002.
The Understanding. Jane Barker Wright. 2002.
The Stand-In. David Helwig. 2002.
The Deep. Mary Swan. 2002.
Uncomfortably Numb. Sharon English. 2002.
The Syllabus. Mike Barnes. 2002.

For Biblioasis

Catalogue Raisonne. Mike Barnes. 2005.
Bright Objects of Desire. Michele Adams. 2005.
Airstream. Patricia Young. 2006.
Hitting the Charts. Leon Rooke. 2006.
Saltsea. David Helwig. 2006.
Time's Covenant: Selected Poems. Eric Ormsby. 2007.
Little Eurekas. Robyn Sarah. 2007.
The Flush of Victory. Ray Smith. 2007.
Boys. Kathleen Winter. 2007.
The Goldfish Dancer. Patricia Robertson. 2007.
Cold-Cocked. Lorna Jackson. 2007.
Once. Rebecca Rosenblum. 2008.
Dragonflies. Grant Buday. 2008.
Selected Essays. Clark Blaise. 2008. (with J.R. Struthers).
The Lily Pond. Mike Barnes. 2008.
Three Balconies. Bruce Jay Friedman. 2008.
Flirt: The Interviews. Lorna Jackson. 2008.
Thought You Were Dead. Terry Griggs. 2009.
The English Stories. Cynthia Flood. 2009.
What Boys Like. Any Jones. 2009.
Brown Dwarf. K.D. Miller. 2010.
The End of the Ice Age. Terence Young. 2010.
Combat Camera. A.J. Somerset. 2010.
The Meagre Tarmac. Clark Blaise. 2011.
Suitable Precautions. Laura Boudreau. 2011.
The Big Dream. Rebecca Rosenblum. 2011.
Something about the Animal. Cathy Stonehouse. 2011.
Lucky Bruce. Bruce Jay Friedman. 2011.
In the Field. Claire Tacon. 2011.
All the Voices Cry. Alice Petersen. 2012.
Malarky. Anakana Schofield. 2012.
Blood Secrets. Nadine McInnis. 2012.
Canary. Nancy Jo Cullen. 2013.

Keeping the Peace. Colette Maitland. 2013.
The Monkey Puzzle Tree. Sonia Tilson. 2013.
The Pope's Bookbinder. David Mason. 2013.
The Strength of Bone. Lucie Wilk. 2013.
Red Girl Rat Boy. Cynthia Flood. 2013.
Paradise & Elsewhere. Kathy Page. 2014.
The Freedom in American Songs. Kathleen Winter. 2014.
The Video Watcher. Shawn Stibbards. 2015.
Backspring. Judith McCormack. 2015.

Biblioasis Short Fiction Series

Balduchi's Who's Who. Leon Rooke. 2005.
Saturday Night Function. Annabel Lyon. 2005.
The Sociology of Love. Clark Blaise. 2005.
Mr. Justice. Caroline Adderson. 2005.
A Theory of Probablility. Judith McCormack. 2005.
Bigmouth. Terry Griggs. 2005.
Reynolds and the Theory of Dream. Russell Smith. 2006.
Graves of the Heroes. Patricia Robertson. 2006.
The Flying Woman. Sharon English. 2006.
1957 Chevy BelAir. Guy Vanderhaeghe. 2007.
Speck's Idea. Mavis Gallant. 2008.

Reading Series Publications

THE MAGNUM BOOK STORE READINGS

Acts of Kindness and of Love. John Metcalf.
Daddy Stump. Leon Rooke.
Sixty Billion Humans. Hugh Hood.
A Night at the Opera. Ray Smith.
Contacts. Dayv James-French.
Tag. Terry Griggs.

Trouble. Diane Schoemperlen.
Passages. Rohinton Mistry.
Extracts from Works-in-Progress. Joan MacLeod.
An Excerpt from the Redeemer. Doug Glover.
A Selection of Poems. Irving Layton.
Fragment of a Novel-in-Progress. Jane Urquhart.
An Excerpt from In the Time of the Angry Queen. Mark Frutkin.
An Excerpt from a Novel-in-Progress. Don Dickinson.
I Had a Father. Clark Blaise.
For Gods and Fathers. Steven Heighton.
From a Family Album. Norman Levine.
Keys. Carol Shields.
Dusters. Gael Turnbull.
Provençal Songs. George Elliott Clarke.
Waiting for Angel. Matt Cohen.
An Extract from Graven Images. Audrey Thomas.
Seven Stories. Yann Martel.
How I Got Started and Why I Can't Stop. Isabel Huggan.
Extract from Black Nightingale. John Mills.
Poems. John Newlove.

THE FOOD FOR THOUGHT READING SERIES

The Lady and the Servant. Norman Levine.
Landscape with Poisoner. Caroline Adderson.
The Boy from Moogradi. Leon Rooke.
Lieutenant Lukac's Cat. John Metcalf.
Hiram and Jenny. Richard Outram.
Provence and Mystery Stories. David Helwig.
Delirium. Cynthia Holz.
Our People. Carol Shields.
Berry Season. Patricia Robertson.

ACKNOWLEDGEMENTS

My thanks are due to the many Canadian writers who have granted me permission to quote from their work. Especial thanks to Patrick Toner (*If I Could Turn and Meet Myself*), Ray Smith ("Ontological Arseholes: Life with Montreal Story Teller"), and Robert Giddings (*You Should See Me in Pyjamas*), who granted me also ghastly flashes of my younger self.

I have kindly been given permission to reprint from the following: P.J. O'Rourke, *Age and Guile Beat Youth, Innocence, and a Bad Haircut*, copyright 1995, reprinted by permission of Random House Canada; John Mills, review of Morley Callaghan's *Close to the Sun Again*, from *Queen's Quarterly*; Keath Fraser, *Le Mal de l'air*; Leon Rooke, introduction to *Macmillan Anthology (2)*; Barry Cameron, introduction to *On the Edge: Canadian Short Stories* for *The Literary Review* (Fairleigh Dickinson University); the Tanks Campaign, from William Hoffer's catalogues; Michael Darling's review of Rohinton Mistry's *Tales from Firozsha Baag*, in *Macmillan Anthology (1)*; Mistry, *Such a Long Journey*; Lisa Moore, quoted in *Quarry Magazine*, 1992; Hoffer, "Cheap Sons of Bitches: Memoirs of the Book Trade," written for *Carry On Bumping*; Mark Abley's review of George Johnston's *Endeared by Dark*; Don Coles, "My Son at the Seashore, Age Two"; Richard

Outram, "Techne"; Steven Heighton, *The New Quarterly*; the Porcupine's Quill Press and K.D. Miller; Terry Griggs; Annabel Lyon; Russell Smith, *Noise*; Judith McCormack, "The Cardinal Humours"; Ken Rockburn, *Medium Rare*.